MEMORIZE SAT VOCABULARY THE QUANTUM WAY

Xuhua Chen

MEMORIZE SAT VOCABULARY THE QUANTUM WAY

ISBN-13: 978-0955575150
First Published January 2010
by Xuhua Chen
xuhuachen123@gmail.com,
Printed in Great Britain for Xuhua Chen

Introduction

With this book, you will learn a highly effective technique that uses the link of individual letter to help you in memorizing the meaning of a word.

There are nearly 5,000 SAT entries in the book. The definitions are extracted from WordNet.

#Entry of this book

*precarious 08-51-29 (a.) 1. fraught with danger 2. affording no ease or reassurance 3. dangerously insecure 4. not secure; beset with difficulties [parlous perilous premise problematic provisional reassure recovery risky ease easy equivocal carious chancy critical across afford ambiguous assumption indefensible infirm insecure open uncertain undersea uneasy unjustified unpredictable unsafe unsteady unsure unwarranted safety sea security sensitive shaky shifty stormy surgery /ace race racer/] "a precarious truce"

1) *precarious: SAT word entry.

2) 08-51-29: 08 is a range of the entry's frequency rank; 51 is an AB index; 29 is a frequency of the entry. Further down the line, there will be more explanations of what these numbers mean.

3) (a.): Parts of speech. Abbreviation of this book: a. - Adjective ad. - Adverb n.- Noun v.- Verb.

4) 1. fraught with danger 2. affording no ease or reassurance 3. dangerously insecure 4. not secure; beset with difficulties: Definitions of the word which are extracted from WordNet.

5) [parlous perilous premise problematic provisional reassure recovery risky ease easy equivocal carious chancy critical across afford ambiguous assumption indefensible infirm insecure open uncertain undersea uneasy unjustified unpredictable unsafe unsteady unsure unwarranted safety sea security sensitive shaky shifty stormy surgery: Cue words.

6) /ace race racer/]: Back words and/or partial back words.

7) "a precarious truce" : Example.

#Explanation of word Frequency in this book

abound **07-40-35 (v.) 1. be abundant or plentiful; exist in large quantities 2. be in a state of movement or action [abundant amount bound brim bristle burst overflow] "The room abounded with screaming children"*

The first two numbers is a frequency within a range, e.g. **07** indicates that 'abound' ranks within 6,001 to 7,000. The number ranges in this book are between 01 to 20 which show the ranks from 1 to 20,000. The smaller the number, the higher the frequency it is.

The calculation of frequency in this book is based on Per Article Per Count (PAPC) method, i.e. a word is counted only once regardless how many times it appears on an article. The corpus used in this book is a collection of newspaper articles from the internet.

It seems that Per Article Per Count (PAPC) not only can retain the characteristic of traditional True Count method but also avoid the problem that, when using True Count method, 'pylori' has higher frequency than 'prizes' on BNC (British National Corpus).

The following example can show why PAPC reflects the realty better:
Word A appears 1 time on all 100 articles; Word B appears 100 times on one of the 100 articles. While the tradition True Count method gives count of 100 for both words, the PAPC gives counts of 100 for Word A and ONLY 1 for word B.

#AB index – American and British English comparison index

abound 07-40**-35 (v.) 1. be abundant or plentiful; exist in large quantities 2. be in a state of movement or action [abundant amount bound brim bristle burst overflow] "The room abounded with screaming children"*

The second two number is an AB index which indicates the tendency of American and British people use a word, i.e. who use the word more. An AB index is derived form word frequency.

An AB index can be 00 to 100. A number that is greater than 50 means the entry is more likely to be used by the British. If it is less than 50 it means that the entry is more common amongst the American. Entry 'absolutely' has an AB index of 64 which is greater than 50 therefore it is used more often by the British. Entry 'guess' has an AB index of 47 which is slightly less than 50 hence it is used by the American a little bit more.

To be consistent with the two digits number, a 00 AB index is converted to AA (100% American) and a 100 to BB (100% British).

The formula of AB index is as follow:
AB index = 100 x Word Frequency of British / (Word Frequency of British + Word Frequency of American).

If an entry is the head word of a lemmatised word group then its AB index calculation is based on the group total. For instance 'appraise' is the head word of the following word group (each number is the AB index of the individuals):

appraise	32
appraised	22
appraiser	03
appraisers	02
appraises	18
appraising	31
appraisingly	40

For 'appraise', 21 is the average of the above.

The following are examples that explain AB index:

guess 47 – (<50) the American use it a little bit more than the British
flat 72 – (>50) the British use it more than the American

percent 01 – (<50) the American use it much more than the British. '%' and 'per cent' are more common in the UK
per 81 – (>50) The figure may be a result of that the British use 'per cent' much more than the American
oversight 24 – (<50) the American use it more than the British
labored AA – used by the American
labour BB – used by the British

#Frequency

abound 07-40-35** (v.) 1. be abundant or plentiful; exist in large quantities 2. be in a state of movement or action [abundant amount bound brim bristle burst overflow] "The room abounded with screaming children"*

The last numbers **35** is a frequency of the entry. It indicates that, for every 10,000 articles of which 5,000 are from American and the other 5,000 are from British, the word likely appears on 35 of the articles.

If an entry is the head word of a lemmatised word group then its frequency calculation is based on the group total. For instance the frequency calculation of 'appraise' is the total of the following word group:

appraise
appraised
appraiser
appraisers
appraises
appraising
appraisingly

From below examples you can see "abate" has a much higher frequency than "abase":

abase 23-54-1** (v.) 1. cause to fee shame; hurt the pride of [abash base belittle bruise bump bust self shame sink smash spite subjugate embarrassment] "They both abase themselves before the same master"*

abate 09-32-23** (v.) 1. make less active or intense 2. become less in amount or intensity [abstract alleviate allowance alter amount attrition bate become benumb blunt breakage takeoff tame tare tax temper terminate thin tree ease end erode eviscerate exhaustion extract /tab/] "The storm abated"*

Memorize SAT vocabulary the quantum way

The book tries to introduce a new technique which uses the link of individual letters to allow you to memorize the meaning of a target word. See the following for how the links are established:

imp **i**nfant eg**o** **o**neself noti**o**n **i**dea cere**b**ral **b**rain

The first word is the one you want to memorize and the second one is a 'cue' word which gives you a clue of what the meaning of the first word is. While the individual letters of the target word can be at any place within the word, the letter for cue word will always be the first one. This book provides collections of cue word for nearly 5,000 SAT words. The following examples show how to choose a cue word:

*metaphor 05-43-68 (n.) 1. a figure of speech in which an expression is used to refer to something that it does not literally denote in order to suggest a similarity *[makeshift mannered match mean meaty meet mimic modality effect emblematic equal exchange exploit expression extension token transfer trope tropology agent allegory allusive alternative association peculiar pointed produce proportion proxy* ***hide*** *hypallage hyperbole occur once opposition ornament oxymoron readable real refer referential relation represent reserve /pat pate/]*

For 'metaphor', it can be separated as 'me + tap + h + or'. 'h' is the letter that we are after. From the cue word list within the square brackets we can choose 'hide' which has close meaning to 'metaphor'.

metap**h**or **h**ide

*meander 10-49-20 (n.) 1. a curve in a stream (v.) 1. to move or cause to move in a sinuous, spiral, or circular course *[maunder maze mean meandrous mesh mess migratory motion move earth elaborate entangle entire err erratic affluent aimless amble ancient anfractuosity architecture art natural nomadic deflection depart design devious direction divagate double drift duct range reflection relaxed* ***river*** *roam round route rove run]*
For 'meander', we simply choose 'river' as a cue word to help us remembering the meaning of 'meander'.

meande**r** **r**iver
Here are some examples:

hive – HIVE - Honey Is Very Expensive
rouge – ROUGE - Red Onions Usually Get Eaten
paucity – PAUCITY - Poor And Ugly CITY
paramour – paraMour - Mistress
imp - IMP - Infants Must Play
mountebank - mountEbank - Entertainer

Surely you can use this technique to learn foreign languages:

poisson – n. French word fish.
POISSON - Purchasing One Interesting Salmon; SON

onda – n. Spanish word wave
ONDA – Oceans Never Die away

Cue words can also be used to memorize words that are easily confused. See the following for examples:

*apprise 21-16-2 (v.) 1. give information or notice to 2. increase the value of, as of a currency 3. gain in value, as of a currency 4. make aware of *[acquaint advise affair amount anew announce aware point post prise proclaim publish rent report revalue reveal impart increase* ***inform*** *instruct send speak student enlighten essential]*

*appraise 12-21-13 (v.) 1. place a value on; judge the worth of something 2. consider in a comprehensive way *[accord agree analyze appreciate* ***assess*** *audit pace pass performance political praise price prize professional rank rate reassess reckon reevaluate religious renew revise identify inspect score set situation sound standard step study survey employee estimate evaluate evaluation examine express]* "I will have the family jewels appraised by a professional"

The first different letters are 'i' for 'apprise' and 'a' for 'appraise'. The best match on the cue word list are 'inform' for 'i' and 'assess' for 'a'.

appr**i**se **i**nform appr**a**ise **a**ssess

Here are some more examples:

principAL - A Leader
principLE - Law Education

stationAry - Abiding
stationEry - Envelope

preLude - Leading
preClude - Close

loatH - Hesitate
loatHE - Hate Enemy

demuR - Refuse
demurE - Elegant

deCry - Criticise
deScry - See

If you want to see a comprehensive collection of cue words, please have a look on the book of *Memorize English Vocabulary the Quantum Way.*

 # Use back words and partial back words to memorize vocabulary
Back words are words that when read backwards spell another, entirely different word. There are not many back words but plenty of partial back words. 'animal' and 'lamina' are back words; 'precarious' and 'racer' are partial back words. Any words that are enclosed in back slashes in this book are back words or partial back words of the entry. See the following for examples:

*precarious 08-51-29 (a.) 1. fraught with danger 2. affording no ease or reassurance 3. dangerously insecure 4. not secure; beset with difficulties [parlous perilous premise problematic provisional reassure recovery risky ease easy equivocal carious chancy critical across afford ambiguous assumption indefensible infirm insecure open uncertain undersea uneasy unjustified unpredictable unsafe unsteady unsure unwarranted safety sea security sensitive shaky shifty stormy surgery ***/ace race racer/***] "a precarious truce"

/ace race racer/ are back words of 'precarious'. It is easier to remember the meaning of 'precarious' by thinking that a backward 'racer' runs – it is risky. Here are some more examples:
(pivotal) PIVotal <= VIP ; (sloop) SLOOP <= POOLS; (pariah) paRIAH <= HAIR;
(pliable) pLIABle <= BAIL

A

*abase 23-54-1 (v.) 1. cause to fee shame; hurt the pride of [abash base belittle bruise bump bust self shame sink smash spite subjugate embarrassment] "They both abase themselves before the same master"
*abate 09-32-23 (v.) 1. make less active or intense 2. become less in amount or intensity [abstract alleviate allowance alter amount attrition bate become benumb blunt breakage takeoff tame tare tax temper terminate thin tree ease end erode eviscerate exhaustion extract /tab/] "The storm abated"
*abbess 23-58-1 (n.) 1. the superior of a group of nuns [bess bridget sister superior /ebb/]
*abbey 05-89-63 (n.) 1. a church associated with a monastery or convent 2. a convent ruled by an abbess 3. a monastery ruled by an abbot [abb abbot building /ebb/]
*abbot 12-88-12 (n.) 1. the superior of an abbey of monks [abb abbey ascetic beadsman bot brother]
*abdicate 13-53-10 (v.) 1. give up, such as power, as of monarchs and emperors, or duties and obligations [abandon abjure damage demit depose divorcee document down drop duty intention cast cate cease cede cession claim throne /acid/] "The King abdicated when he married a divorcee"
*abdication 18-58-4 (n.) 1. a formal resignation and renunciation of powers 2. the act of abdicating [abandon document down intention claim office notice]
*abdomen 12-48-12 (n.) 1. the region of the body of a vertebrate between the thorax and the pelvis [abomasum alimentary animal anus appendix artery arthropod bay beer behind belly below blood bowel brain branch descend diaphragm dome duodenum omasum major mammal maw middle midriff muscle elongate embonpoint endocardium entrails natural navel neck /mod nemo/]
*abdominal 11-60-14 (a.) 1. of or relating to or near the abdomen [anal arrange belly body diagonal duodenal mina move ileac intestinal lateral /mod/] "abdominal muscles"
*abduction 11-59-16 (n.) 1. the criminal act of capturing and carrying away by force a family member; if a man's wife is abducted it is a crime against the family relationship and against the wife 2. (physiology) moving of a body part away from the central axis of the body [axis biological body deal capture carry central criminal organism]
*abed 20-48-2 (ad.) 1. in bed [abe bed]
*aberration 12-45-13 (n.) 1. a state or condition markedly different from the norm 2. a disorder in one's mental state 3. an optical phenomenon resulting from the failure of a lens or mirror to produce a good image [abet alienate anomaly apparent astronomy bend bias eccentricity edge emotion error excursus raise rambling rarity ration trick turning twist illness illusion image indirect inferiority irregularity obliquity oddity oddness optics neutral nonconformity normal]
*abet 12-43-12 (v.) 1. assist or encourage, usually in some wrongdoing [advance advocate aid angel assistant attach backer bailout befriend benefit bet bettor buff ease egg embellish encourage endorse energize extra tempter trim]
*abeyance 20-45-2 (n.) 1. temporary cessation or suspension [abandon abe alert apathy break business end entropy estate non caesura catatonia cessation condition /aye nay/]
*abhor 14-50-8 (v.) 1. find repugnant [abominate antipathy aversion hate reject repugnant revolt]
*abhorrence 20-51-2 (n.) 1. hate coupled with disgust [abhor abomination aversion hate hatred odium repugnance revulsion emotion execration couple]
*abhorrent 18-59-4 (a.) 1. offensive to the mind [abominable antipathetic arouse base beastly behavior hate heinous horrent horrid objectionable obnoxious obscene offensive recent repellent repulsive revulsive execrable nasty nauseating nearly novel noxious] "an abhorrent deed"
*abide 06-52-54 (v.) 1. put up with something or somebody unpleasant 2. dwell (archaic) [accept accommodate accord address adhere aged allow antique archaism area attached attitude await bear belief benchmark berth bide billet bite brave brook build ignore immobile impermanent indefatigable inhabit intact delay dig digest district dome domicile down dragon durable dwell emplacement endure equip establishment expense expression extend]
*abject 11-75-14 (a.) 1. most unfortunate or miserable 2. of the most contemptible kind 3. showing humiliation or submissiveness 4. showing utter resignation or hopelessness [abandon bad beggarly join excessive execrable extremely comply consent contemptible corrupt cowardice crawl cruelty timeserver treatment trick truckle turpitude] "abject cowardice"
*abjure 23-53-1 (v.) 1. formally reject or disavow a formerly held belief, usually under pressure [abandon abdicate abnegate abstain annul avoid backwater unsay rebuff recant refrain reject release religion repudiate resignation retract early except exclude]
*ablution 23-74-1 (n.) 1. the act of washing yourself (or another person) [bath body lather lavation liquid upright turkish ion irrigation nozzle]
*abnegate 23-47-1 (v.) 1. deny oneself (something); restrain, esp. from indulging in some pleasure 2. deny or renounce 3. surrender [abandon abjure abstain abstinence avoidance believe negate negative neutrality nonviolence even gentle give god temper temperate title tranquillity turndown /age tag/]
*abnormal 10-50-20 (a.) 1. not normal; not typical or usual or regular or conforming to a norm 2. (psychology) departing from the normal in e.g. intelligence and development 3. much greater than the

normal [aberrant absurd anomalous anxiety atrocious atypical normal nutty odd oddball off mad malformed manic maze mental loco lunatic] "abnormal powers of concentration"
*abominable 18-56-4 (a.) 1. unequivocally detestable 2. exceptionally bad or displeasing [abject able abnormal atrocious awful bad base black burke obscene odious odor offensive outrageous manner mean miserable monstrous illegal improper incorrect nasty naughty negative notorious little loathsome lousy lovable low edmund egregious enormous evil evoke exceptional execrable experience extremely /ban bani mob/] "abominable treatment of prisoners"
*abomination 18-57-4 (n.) 1. a person who is loathsome or disgusting 2. hate coupled with disgust 3. an action that is vicious or vile; an action that arouses disgust or abhorence [abhorrence allergy annoyance arouse atrocity bad blight bogey obliquity odium outrage malevolent mischief misogyny moral mortal ill infection injury intense nation nausea toward toxin transgression treatment trial /mob/] "his treatment of the children is an abomination"
*aboriginal 14-67-8 (a.) 1. being or composed of people inhabiting a region from the beginning 2. having existed from the beginning; in an earliest or original stage or state (n.) 1. a dark-skinned member of a race of people living in Australia when Europeans arrived [aborigine ancestral area arrive atavistic australian autochthonous basic begin bud original race radical region rudimentary inaugural indigenous inhabit inventive genetic germinal gestation group nascent natal native near late life live local /giro rob/]
*abound 07-40-35 (v.) 1. be abundant or plentiful; exist in large quantities 2. be in a state of movement or action [abundant amount bound brim bristle burst overflow] "The room abounded with screaming children"
*abrasion 20-35-2 (n.) 1. an abraded area where the skin is torn or worn off 2. erosion by friction 3. the wearing down of rock particles by friction due to water or wind or ice [abra abrasive abstraction area attrition beat bedrock body break buff burn removal rent resistance rock rope rub run sand scratch scuff skin smooth superficial surface surgical ice incision injury organ]
*abridge 16-44-6 (v.) 1. reduce in scope while retaining essential elements [abate abbreviate abstract alleviate assemble bereave bleed bob bowdlerize bridge brief brusque reap reduce reduction relaxation relieve reserved restrict retain ridge right indelicate damp decrease deduction deprive digest dock gnomic edit element elide elliptic epigrammatic epitomize erase essential expurgate extent]
*abrogate 18-27-4 (v.) 1. revoke formally [abate abolish annul refute repeal rescind retract reverse revoke rid ruin obliterate overrule gainsay gate extinguish /ago tag/]
*abrupt 05-39-67 (a.) 1. exceedingly sudden and unexpected 2. marked by sudden changes in subject and sharp transitions 3. surprisingly and unceremoniously brusque in manner 4. extremely steep [aggressive arduous bang bluff blunt bold brief brisk brusque rapid rash ready reply river rude rush unawares unceremonious unexpected unforeseen unplanned upper painting part pass plump plunge pointless pop precipitous prose terse topic transition truculent] "abrupt prose"
*abscess 20-62-2 (n.) 1. symptom consisting of a localized collection of pus surrounded by inflamed tissue [accumulate asphyxiate asthma atrophy bacterial bleed blister bodily boil seizure sensation shock sore surround swell symptom carbuncle cavity cess chill convulsion cough edema emaciate eruption eschar]
*abscond 18-77-4 (v.) 1. run away; usually includes taking something or somebody along [abandon absent absquatulate avoid away bolt break bunk scape secret skedaddle subtract con omit nonexistent debt decamp delete departed desert detention disappear]
*absence 03-61-205 (n.) 1. failure to be present 2. the state of being absent 3. the time interval during which something or somebody is away 4. epilepsy characterized by paroxysmal attacks of brief clouding of consciousness (a possible other abnormalities) [abnormality brief scarcity seizure sen shortfall show spike surprise empty epilepsy escape exigency need negative non note class cortical cut] "he was surprised by the absence of any explanation"
*absolution 20-51-2 (n.) 1. the condition of being formally forgiven by a priest in the sacrament of penance 2. the act of absolving or remitting; formal redemption as pronounced by a priest in the sacrament of penance [acquittance amnesty bless sacrament salvation satisfaction saving shrift sin solution sparing status still liberty temporal immunity indemnity]
*absolve 14-51-8 (v.) 1. grant remission of a sin to 2. let off the hook [acquit amnesty blame sacrament say service shrive sin solve spare stop obligation obliterate official let liberate vindicate except excuse exemption exonerate] "The priest absolved him and told him to say ten Hail Mary's"
*absorb 04-44-105 (v.) 1. suck or take up or in 2. engross (oneself) fully 3. cause to become one with 4. take in, also metaphorically 5. take up, as of debts or payments 6. take up, as of knowledge or beliefs 7. become imbued; of liquids, light, or gases, in chemistry 8. engage or engross wholly [abstract accept acquire adapt admit adsorption affect amount appropriate arrest assimilate attention attract become belief bemuse black blend blot sale savvy science sense shock skill soak solution sop sorb spellbound spend sponge star stargaze study suck oblivious obsess occupy osmose rapt read realize receive recognize rivet /bros/] "absorb the costs for something"
*absorption 12-49-13 (n.) 1. (chemistry) a process in

which one substance permeates another; a fluid permeates or is dissolved by a liquid or solid 2. (physics) the process in which incident radiated energy is retained without reflection or transmission on passing through a medium 3. the process of absorbing nutrients into the body after digestion 4. the social process of absorbing one cultural group into harmony with another 5. complete attention; intense mental effort 6. the mental state of being preoccupied by something [abstraction application assimilation attrition bemuse bile science spend squander state study obsession osmosis relation reverie pensive percolate preoccupation process trance implication inclusion involve ion /pros/] "the absorption of photons by atoms or molecules"
*abstain 11-50-16 (v.) 1. choose to refrain 2. refrain from voting [abandon abnegate abstinence alcoholic anchorite ascetic avoid beverage save serve shun spare stain stay teetotal trim ingest neutral] "I abstain from alcohol"
*abstemious 23-65-1 (a.) 1. sparing in consumption of especially food and drink 2. marked by temperance in indulgence [abstinence ascetic austere behavior self slight slim small smoker sober spartan stem supper table teetotal temperate thin eat excessive exiguous extreme mark meager meal mean miserly moderate much impoverish indulge /met/] "the pleasures of the table, never of much consequence to one naturally abstemious"
*abstinence 14-53-8 (n.) 1. the trait of abstaining (especially from alcohol) 2. act or practice of refraining from indulging an appetite [abstention alcohol asceticism austerity avoidance beverage self sensuous serenity sexual sober sobriety soul stability sunset suppression teetotal temperate tine totally trait tranquillity impartial impulse intoxicate non nonviolence eremite eschew exclusion calm chastity control cool]
*abstruse 19-50-3 (a.) 1. difficult to penetrate; incomprehensible to one of ordinary understanding or knowledge [abstract arcane arduous blind bury sea secret severe steep student tend theory thorny tough tricky turtle rarefy recondite rigorous rough rugged ruse unknown uphill eclipse educate esoteric exoteric] "the professor's lectures were so abstruse that students tended to avoid them"
*absurd 05-62-66 (a.) 1. completely devoid of wisdom or good sense 2. inconsistent with reason or logic or common sense [abnormal amusing anomalous argue bizarre scream seeming silly strange surd unbelievable unpleasant unreasonable unthinkable ridiculous rubbish daft derisory desirable devoid disproportionate doubtful dull] "the absurd predicament of seeming to argue that virtue is highly desirable but intensely unpleasant"
*abundant 08-38-31 (a.) 1. present in great quantity [abound affluent ample ant blooming bottomless bountiful bumper natural numerous deficient demand diffusive teem thick thrive torrential /nub/] "an abundant supply of water"
*abusive 08-53-29 (a.) 1. expressing offensive reproach 2. characterized by physical or psychological maltreatment [anger annoyance atrocious blameful brutal bully bus unmannerly unspeakable sadistic scandalous scoff scornful scurrilous secure sexual slander illegal imminent improper incorrect inoffensive insulting intend vicious vile vilify violent vulgar epithet excommunicate execrate express] "abusive punishment"
*abut 16-21-6 (v.) 1. lie adjacent to another or share a boundary [adjacent adjoin appose bestride border boundary but butt touch /tub tuba/]
*abysmal 13-63-10 (a.) 1. very great; limitless 2. so deep as to be unmeasurable; unfathomable [aby appalling astronomic awful backward bad bottomless yawn sea severe shallow soundless spatial stupid surface measure mighty misery monstrous monumental lateral limitless] "abysmal misery"
*abyss 13-55-10 (n.) 1. a bottomless gulf or pit [aby apparently arroyo awful below benthos bottomless break sea seam situation slot space split surface]
*academic 03-53-200 (a.) 1. marked by a narrow focus on or display of learning especially its trivial aspects 2. hypothetical or theoretical and not expected to produce an immediate or practical result 3. associated with academia or an academy (n.) 1. an educator who works at a college or university [art aspect cade classroom closet college conduct conventional course curriculum design diligent discussion display domain donnish educator emphasize erudite expect extramural mandarin mark member moot idealistic imaginary immediate impractical institution intend irrelevant] "the academic curriculum"
*academician 19-42-3 (n.) 1. someone elected to honorary membership in an academy 2. an educator who works at a college or university 3. a scholar who is skilled in academic disputation [academic accomplishment advance art classicist clerk college concern discipline disputation educator elect mastery membership institution noteworthy]
*academy 03-52-216 (n.) 1. an institution for the advancement of art or science or literature 2. a secondary school (usually private) 3. a learned establishment for the advancement of knowledge 4. a school for special training [achievement advance american ancient annual architecture art award cade charter civil college conservatory create cultivate educational elect elementary english equipment establishment membership middle military motion]
*accede 14-41-8 (v.) 1. submit or yield to another's wish or opinion 2. be compatible or in accordance with 3. to agree or express agreement [accept acclaim accordance acquiesce adhere agreement allow ascend assent assume attain cede check cheer come comply condition connive consent cooperate correspond criminal endorse enter

express defer deign duty]
*accelerate 04-49-100 (v.) 1. cause to move faster 2. move faster [activate add aggravate atomize car concentrate constituent crowd enhance exacerbate exaggerate lose race rate reduce reinforce retard rev rush triple /tare/] "The car accelerated"
*accept 01-51-693 (v.) 1. react favorably to; consider right and proper 2. give an affirmative reply to; respond favorably to 3. tolerate or accommodate oneself to 4. receive willingly something given or offered 5. take on as one's own the expenses or debts of another person 6. admit into a group or community 7. consider or hold as true 8. be sexually responsive to, used of a female domesticated mammal 9. of a deliberative body: receive (a report) officially, as from a committee 10. be designed to hold or take 11. make use of or accept for some purpose [abide acknowledge admit adopt agreement allow approve assent attack attempt carry catch cause cep chance charge credit current embrace endorse espouse establish experience pass permit pick pocket popular practice pulldown tackle textual tolerate traditionalism trust] "I cannot accept the dogma of this church"
*access 02-55-387 (n.) 1. the right to obtain or make use of or take advantage of something (as services or membership) 2. a way of entering or leaving 3. the right to enter 4. the act of approaching or entering 5. (computer science) the operation of reading or writing stored information (v.) 1. obtain or retrieve from a storage device; as of information on a computer 2. reach or gain access to [addition admittance arrest avenue cess channel connection court entryway exit expansion extension sally scene spell] "How does one access the attic in this house?"
*accessible 04-46-88 (a.) 1. capable of being reached 2. easily obtained 3. easy to get along with or talk to; friendly 4. capable of being read with comprehension [access adapt aloof announce approachable attendant available candid challenge circulate clear come comfort computer converse current easily easy employ enter expansive extrovert secure seem service simple specialist spread statement straightforward suit susceptible immediate influence inherent broadcast business likely] "a town accessible by rail"
*accession 12-84-12 (n.) 1. agreeing with 2. the act of entering upon or attaining to a position or right 3. something added to what you have already 4. the act of attaining a new office or right (v.) 1. make a record of additions to a collection, such as a library [accord acquisition admittance advance agreement appointment assent attainment cession compliance concurrent consent continuation earnings election enter expansion imminent inauguration inflation obtain offshoot near]
*accessory 06-53-55 (a.) 1. relating to something that is added but is not essential (n.) 1. a supplementary component 2. clothing that is worn or carried, but not part of your main clothing 3. someone who helps another person commit a crime [abet access another appointment associate colleague combined couple engaged extension extrapolate serve share spare offshoot other reinforcement]
*acclaim 05-61-76 (n.) 1. enthusiastic approval (v.) 1. praise vociferously 2. clap one's hands or shout after performances to indicate approval [accept acknowledge admit applause approval approve assent candidate celebrity character cheer claim clap commendation compliment comply crowd lack legendary indicate magnify marked meet message modest move mythical] "the book met with modest acclaim"
*accolade 10-73-19 (n.) 1. a tangible symbol signifying approval or distinction [adulation apotheosis award championship citation cola compliment congratulation laurel letter lionize decoration degree deify distinction encomium eulogy exaltation /dal/]
*accommodate 04-41-105 (v.) 1. have room for; hold without crowding 2. provide with something desired or needed 3. make fit for, or change to suit a new purpose 4. be agreeable or acceptable to 5. make compatible with 6. provide housing for 7. provide a service or favor for someone [accept accord adapt adjust advance afford allow alter amiable available change civil condition contribute cooperative country crowd cultivation obedient obliging observe offer maintain measure meek meet modify date decent deferential delicate discipline disposition donate tactful tailor tame tender theater theory thoughtful tolerant entertain equip establish /ado tad/]
*accompaniment 08-38-28 (n.) 1. a subordinate musical part; provides background for more important parts 2. an event or situation that happens at the same time as or in connection with another 3. the act of accompanying someone or something in order to protect them [accessory add adjunct agreement alliance anime association auxiliary carry closely coincidence composition concomitant connection conspiracy convoy cooperation crash occurrence offshoot melody musical part pendant perfect place plainsong polyphonic protection provide natural important improvise increment item escort extension extrapolate tailpiece tenor thunder torrential transit treble trim /mina/]
*accompanist 16-28-6 (n.) 1. a person who provides musical accompaniment (usually on a piano) [comp musician piano play profession provide instrumentalist soloist]
*accompany 02-46-277 (v.) 1. be a companion to somebody 2. perform an accompaniment to 3. go or travel along with 4. be associated with [affinity agree associate assort attached attend attending circumstance coincide collocate combine come company complement construe convoy couple current occasional occur old ongoing orchestra match meeting move musical mutual pair part passing perform pitch play prevalent proceed

provide nurse]
*accomplice 10-52-19 (n.) 1. a person who joins with another in carrying out some plan (especially an unethical or illegal plan) [abet accessory ally assistant associate carry coco collaborate colleague commit companion complice comrade confederate conspirator contribute crime misdeed partner party plan plot purpose lead illegal effort]
*accomplish 07-14-39 (v.) 1. to gain with effort 2. bring to execution [achieve act approach attain average carry cause certain come comp complete conclusion cut makeup manage marriage mature mean method pay performance point produce progress pull pursue least letter implement indicate industrialize inflict issue score set setback strike successful surgery swing hack handle high hit home]
*accordion 13-42-10 (a.) 1. arranged in parallel folds (n.) 1. a portable box-shaped free-reed instrument; the reeds are made to vibrate by air from the bellows controlled by the player [accord arrange celesta clavichord concertina control organ reed double driven instrument]
*accost 16-47-6 (v.) 1. speak to someone 2. approach with an offer of sexual favors [accessible address advance aggressive approach approximate available catch come confront conversation cost curtsy offer salute sexual solicit speak stop suggestive talk toward trap travel]
*account 01-50-842 (n.) 1. a record or narrative description of past events 2. a statement of money owed for goods or services 3. the quality of taking advantage 4. the act of informing by verbal report 5. a statement that makes something comprehensible by describing the relevant structure or operation or circumstances etc. 6. a statement of recent transactions and the resulting balance 7. importance or value 8. a short account of the news 9. grounds 10. a formal contractual relationship established to provide for regular banking or brokerage or business services (v.) 1. be the sole or primary factor in the existence, acquisition, supply, or disposal of something 2. furnish a justifying analysis or explanation 3. keep an account of 4. to give an account or representation of in words [advantage amount annual arrange cast consideration count credit use narrative note number tab table tale total] "Passing grades account for half of the grades given in this exam"
*accredit 10-55-20 (v.) 1. grant credentials to 2. provide or send with official credentials; as of envoys 3. give credit for [academic accept acknowledge ambassador appoint approve ascribe assign attribute authorize certify charter commit confirm consulate country credit criterion ratify recognize recommend repute responsibility educate embassy empower enable endorse envoy degree delegate deputize detail duty immigration impute initial institution intelligence introduce transfer /tide/]
*accretion 19-49-3 (n.) 1. an increase by natural growth or addition 2. (astronomy) the formation of a celestial object by the effect of gravity pulling together surrounding objects and gases 3. (biology) growth by addition as by the adhesion of parts or particles 4. (geology) an increase in land resulting from alluvial deposits or water-borne sediment 5. (law) an increase in a beneficiary's share in an estate (as when a co-beneficiary dies or fails to meet some condition or rejects the inheritance) 6. something contributing to growth or increase [accumulation agglomerate amass astronomy ion /iter/] "he scraped away the accretions of paint"
*accrue 10-57-18 (v.) 1. grow by addition, as of capital 2. come into the possession of [account accumulate add advance amass amount appreciate area assignment capital claim come consequence crescendo refer return right rise rue enforce enlarge ensue] "The interest accrues"
*accumulate 05-41-66 (v.) 1. collect or gather 2. get or gather together [accrue add advance amass appreciate aside associate attached catch chain collect come compile conglomerate couple cover create cumulate current unfaithfulnes unify unite magazine mass match mount layby league liability lie link lot lump tape thesis tie embrace encompass evidence /alum/]
*accuracy 06-54-52 (n.) 1. (mathematics) the number of significant figures given in a number 2. the quality of nearness to the truth or the true value [account arrange atomic attribute avoid clock compass conscientious correct critical curacy reproduce right rigid rigorous] "he was beginning to doubt the accuracy of his compass"
*accurate 03-51-144 (a.) 1. exact in performance or amount; strictly correct 2. conforming exactly or almost exactly to fact or to a standard or performing with total accuracy [absolute accept accounting almost amount attentive authentic capable careful close complete conformity conscientious correct critical curate unerring religious reproduction right rightly rigorous tactful target total trueful typist entirely error exactly exigent expression exquisite] "an accurate reproduction"
*accursed 23-63-1 (a.) 1. under a curse [appalling awful cursed curst effect enduring damned dated deserve detestable doom]
*accusation 04-44-128 (n.) 1. a formal charge of wrongdoing brought against a person; the act of imputing blame or guilt 2. an assertion that someone is guilty of a fault or offence [admission allegation asseverate attribute aver charge claim complaint connection court criminal sati slander statement support illegal implication imprecation impute incriminate inculpate indictment intimate offense]
*accusatory 20-39-2 (a.) 1. containing or expressing accusation [claim sato telltale trouser /rota/]
*accuse 01-50-564 (v.) 1. bring an accusation against;

level a charge against 2. blame for, make a claim of wrongdoing or misbehavior against [abuse allege arraign article attack attribute calumniate case censure charge cite claim commit condemn confront correspondent court criminate criticism criticize undesirable upbraid use shakeup shoe slander smear smirch spousal sue suggest sully suspect engage express]
*acerbic 14-54-9 (a.) 1. sour or bitter in taste 2. harsh or corrosive in tone [acerb acid acidulous acrid acrimonious assassination astringent caustic coarse comment corrosive criticism cut embitter enemy ethics rankle remark resent rough barbed barrage biting bitter blistering burn incisive irritate] "an acerbic tone piercing otherwise flowery prose"
*acetate 23-34-1 (n.) 1. a salt or ester of acetic acid 2. a fabric made from cellulose acetate fibers [acid cellulose chemistry compound cotton enamel tate /tec/]
*ache 07-61-39 (n.) 1. a dull persistent (usually moderately intense) pain (v.) 1. be the source of pain 2. have a yen for 3. feel physical pain [abdominal abnormal accident afflict ail angina anguish artery aware cerebral chilling comprehend constant contraction crave creep cut hanker head hone hunger hurt ear eat]
*acid 05-51-66 (a.) 1. harsh or corrosive in tone 2. (chemistry) containing acid (n.) 1. any of various water-soluble compounds having a sour taste and capable of turning litmus red and reacting with a base to form a salt 2. a powerful hallucinogenic drug [acerbic acrid adhesive agent angry atom caustic cid compound content corrosive criticism cut imperative impressive ingredient inorganic irritate dilute discontented dissolve donate driving dry]
*acknowledge 02-34-401 (v.) 1. express obligation, thanks, or gratitude for 2. express recognition of the presence or existence of, or acquaintance with 3. report the receipt of 4. declare to be true or admit the existence or reality or truth of 5. accept as legally binding and valid 6. accept (smeone) to be what is claimed or accept his power and authority [accept across admit allow announce concede confess consider conventional correct knowledge oral orthodox own warrant witness worshipful legendary echo endorse establish decent declare decorous deed deem disclose grant /won wonk/]
*acknowledgment 08-48-26 (n.) 1. the state or quality of being recognized or acknowledged 2. a statement acknowledging something or someone 3. a short note recognizing a source of information or of a quoted passage [acceptance admission answer comeback communication concession know note warrant leaf letter line echo epistle excuse declaration dispatch due grace makeup matter message missive tail text tribute /won wonk/]
*acme 19-30-3 (n.) 1. the highest level or degree attainable 2. the highest point (of something) [achievement all ambition apex apogee artist attain authorization career championship command continuum control cover crown culmination management mirror most edge effective elevation end] "his landscapes were deemed the acme of beauty"
*acoustic 08-53-30 (a.) 1. of or relating to the science of acoustics (n.) 1. a remedy for hearing loss or deafness [absorb amplify auditory aural auricular carry control curative cure otic otology oust ultrasonic science sonic sound study subsonic supersonic therapy instrument] "acoustic properties of a hall"
*acquaint 19-40-3 (v.) 1. make familiar or acquainted 2. cause to come to know personally 3. inform [accustom actor advise affair anew apprise aware clue colleague come community computer country quaint impart inform instruct introduce neighbor notify tell] "permit me to acquaint you with my son"
*acquaintance 07-47-39 (n.) 1. a relationship less intimate than friendship 2. a person with whom you are acquainted 3. personal knowledge or information about someone or something [account acquaint association aware camp casual classmate colleague companion connected consciousness consociate contact conversant country quarter understand influential information instruction intelligence intimate introduction neighborhood nod notify technique transmission trouble enlightenment evidence experience expertise] "I have trouble remembering the names of all my acquaintances"
*acquiesce 12-37-12 (v.) 1. to agree or express agreement [accept adapt adjustment agreement approve assent assured authority carry certainty challenge cheer coincide collaborate command comply concession concur condition connive consent contract cooperative create criminal quick quietism ungrudging uniformity illegal incline instruction eager encourage endorse enthusiastic express sanction signify soul statement stock store submit subservient succumb supine support]
*acquiescence 18-35-4 (n.) 1. agreement with a statement or proposal to do something 2. acceptance without protest [accept agreement assent compliance concession consent contract create quiescent eager signify statement submission]
*acquire 02-37-431 (v.) 1. come to have or undergo a change of (physical features and attributes) 2. take on a certain form, attribute, or aspect 3. come into the possession of something concrete or abstract [absorb accept accidental add admit adopt animal assimilate assume attain capture certain claim come concrete contract quire uncle undergo upon incur ingest inheritable innate invite reach realize reassume receive recover recuperate regain rent retrieve run earn elaborate embrace engage environmental explicate express]
*acquisition 02-35-392 (n.) 1. the act of contracting or assuming or acquiring possession of something 2. something acquired 3. the cognitive process of acquiring skill or knowledge 4. an ability that has been acquired

by training [accomplishment achievement acquire asset claim craftsman illumination increment inheritance instruction ion skill sophistication theft object obtain /itis/] "the acquisition of wealth"
*acquit 07-43-39 (v.) 1. pronounce not guilty of criminal charges 2. behave in a certain manner [absolve accusation affected amnesty assert assoil cancel carry charge clear comport conduct confused criminal quit unnatural impress indulge innocent insist investigate toward]
*acquittal 12-37-13 (n.) 1. a judgment of not guilty [accordance acquit acquittance adhere appeal authority care case charge clearing collection compliance condemn court criminal quittance impose law liquidate]
*acreage 14-25-8 (n.) 1. an area of ground used for some particular purpose (such as building or farming) [acre area continuum enclose estate expanse expansion extent ground] "he wanted some acreage to build on"
*acrid 18-45-4 (a.) 1. strong and sharp 2. harsh or corrosive in tone [acerbic acid acrimony acute assassination astringent austere caustic character choke clash comment conflicting corrosive criticism cut rancorous remark rid rigorous roughness rubber incisive irritate denunciation] "the acrid smell of burning rubber"
*acrimonious 11-75-14 (a.) 1. marked by strong resentment or cynicism [acerbic acrid anger astringent contentious cross cutting cynicism rancorous resentment rigorous rough ill incisive indignant ireful mad mark mon mordant unfriendly severe sharp sore spiteful strong] "an acrimonious dispute"
*acrimony 15-60-7 (n.) 1. a sharp and bitter manner [acerbity acridity antipathy astringent attitude caustic choler corrosive rancor rankle resentment roughness ill incisive malevolent malignity manner mony mordant offensive]
*actionable 23-55-1 (a.) 1. affording grounds for legal action [action anarchist applicable authorize chargeable consultant criminal tortuous triable illegitimate illicit implement irregular offense outlaw basis bootleg lawmaker legal legitimate effective /ban/] "slander is an actionable offense"
*actuality 19-35-3 (n.) 1. the state of actually existing objectively [achievement actual attainment authenticity certainty conformity true truthful life incarnation indisputable intend irrefutable] "a hope that progressed from possibility to actuality"
*actuary 13-75-11 (n.) 1. someone versed in the collection and interpretation of numerical data (especially someone who uses statistics to calculate insurance premiums) [act annuity apply arithmetic assurance auditor calculator clerk collection computer concern conduct controller theory underwriter rate reckon reckoner recorder registrar risk]
*actuate 23-40-1 (v.) 1. put in motion or move to act 2. give an incentive for action [act activate activity affect animation arouse career circuit circulate cognitive compassion compel thrust touch trigger trip unrest emotional energize excite /taut/]
*acumen 13-62-10 (n.) 1. a tapering point 2. shrewdness shown by keen insight [accurate acuity acute astute clever cogency cum manifest mind natural /emu/]
*acute 05-59-79 (a.) 1. (medicine) having or experiencing a rapid onset and short but severe course 2. having or demonstrating ability to recognize or draw fine distinctions 3. extremely sharp or intense 4. ending in a sharp point 5. of an angle; less than 90 degrees 6. of critical importance and consequence (n.) 1. a mark (') placed above a vowel to indicate pronunciation [accent active actuate aggressive amazing angle annoyance appendicitis astonish astute aware awesome century chronic classical comment consequence conspicuous copious course crisis critical crucial cute cutting unconscionable understand unusual urgent thin threatening tough edge emergency end enthusiastic exceptional experience exquisite extreme eyesight] "acute appendicitis"
*adamant 07-64-40 (a.) 1. not capable of being swayed or diverted from a course; unsusceptible to persuasion (n.) 1. very hard native crystalline carbon valued as a gem [abundant adam allotropic amorphous appeal atomic dark decision determined diamond diffusion divert dour drill mind native non tendency tetravalent transmit /mad/] "he is adamant in his refusal to change his mind"
*addendum 08-02-30 (n.) 1. textual matter that is added onto a publication; usually at the end [accessory accidental add afterthought appendix epilogue extend extension extrapolate nonessential unessential magazine main material matter /mud/]
*addle 16-60-6 (v.) 1. mix up or confuse 2. become rotten; of eggs [absorb add age amaze amuse assemble astound dazzle decay deteriorate disorient disturb divert dizzy drench drunken leaked lick long edible egg embarrass engage engross entangle entertain]
*adduce 23-52-1 (v.) 1. advance evidence for [ad arise denote describe discovry drag duce cite evidence]
*adhere 06-47-49 (v.) 1. come or be in close contact with; stick or hold together and resist separation 2. follow through or carry out a plan without deviation 3. be compatible or in accordance with 4. be a devoted follower or supporter 5. stick to firmly 6. be loyal to [abide accede acceptance account adjoin admiration adopt agglomerate agglutinate agree aid approval attach attached deviation devoted devotion different direct discharge disobedience dress heed here homage hug husband ecclesiastical embrace endorsement espouse esteem excessive execution extreme red religious remain resist respect rice rule] "You must adhere to the rules"
*adherence 13-39-10 (n.) 1. faithful support for a religion or cause or political party 2. the property of sticking together (as of glue and wood) or the joining of

surfaces of different composition [aid attach devotion different disobedience ecclesiastical excessive extreme religious cabalism composition concept cultural]
*adherent 14-38-9 (a.) 1. sticking fast (n.) 1. someone who believes and helps to spread the doctrine of another [absolutism accept adhere adhesive advocate aficionado animism antinomian applaud aristotle attendant dangle dependent devotee disciple distinction divinity doctrine dualism dummy hedonist help henchman humanist eclectic enthusiast esoteric existentialism extol realist reform reject religious retainer root naturalist nominalism tail teach tend testament theology thug tout trinity]
*adhesion 23-56-1 (n.) 1. abnormal union of bodily tissues; most common in the abdomen 2. a fibrous band of scar tissue that binds together normally separate anatomical structures 3. the property of sticking together (as of glue and wood) or the joining of surfaces of different composition 4. faithful support for a religion or cause or political party [abdomen absence aid anatomical attraction deviation different healthy hold ecclesiastical excessive extreme eye scar separate slip stick structure substance support surface surgery ion old normal /noise/]
*adieu 19-53-3 (n.) 1. a farewell remark [acknowledgment adios aloha arrivederci auf day die expression]
*adjacent 06-32-52 (a.) 1. near or close to but not necessarily touching 2. having a common boundary or edge; touching 3. nearest in space or position; immediately adjoining without intervening space [abut adjoining attached degree describe door join cent circumstance city close connect consecutive edge element endwise near necessarily neighboring next touch] "had adjacent rooms"
*adjudge 16-91-5 (v.) 1. declare to be [accomplish achieve admit dead decide declared decree deem defendant determine down judge judgment judicial umpire existence]
*adjunct 12-19-12 (a.) 1. relating to something that is added but is not essential 2. of or relating to a person who is subordinate to another (n.) 1. something added to another thing but not an essential part of it 2. a construction that is part of a sentence but not essential to its meaning and can be omitted without making the sentence ungrammatical 3. a person who is an assistant or subordinate to another [accessory accord add affair aide ancillary appendage appurtenance assistant associate association attachment auxiliary deal detail discipline division dominant join jun junction juxtaposition ungrammatical union unite near non nonessential close colleague connection construction temporary tie trimming]
*adjutant 19-79-3 (n.) 1. an officer who acts as military assistant to a more senior officer 2. large Indian stork with a military gait [administrative agent aid ant armed assistant authority deputy]
*administrator 04-29-130 (n.) 1. the party appointed by a probate court to distribute the estate of someone who dies without a will or without naming an executor 2. someone who administers a business 3. someone who manages a government agency or department [administration agent deputy director dog manager master mini impresario intendant supercargo raffle rector official /rota tart/]
*admissible 18-47-4 (a.) 1. deserving to be admitted [accept adequate admission allow allowable apply appropriate decent decisive deserve document material membership miss moderate inclusive incorporate inviting involve irresistible sensible significant sound sufficiency suitable sure belonging legality legitimize logical eligible enter evidence excuse exempt] "admissible evidence"
*admittance 19-57-3 (n.) 1. the right to enter 2. the act of admitting someone to enter [abstract accession admit due matriculate mean measure idea impedance ingress tradition nature clinic college current eleanor electrical enter entry escape]
*admonish 13-36-11 (v.) 1. admonish or counsel in terms of someone's behavior 2. take to task 3. warn strongly; put on guard [advise alert apart assumption danger daunt discourage dissuade mild mon monish move objurgate notify incite induce intimidate scold spank strong harm]
*admonition 16-19-6 (n.) 1. cautionary advice 2. a firm rebuke [advice advisory advocacy alarm appropriate approve danger deter deterrent direction dissuasive down dressing mild monition monitory moral objurgate opinion notify idea imminent instructive intend intimidate ion talk telling thought threat ticking]
*ado 16-52-6 (n.) 1. a rapid bustling commotion [agitation annoyance anxiety din disadvantage disturbance dustup]
*adoration 15-63-7 (n.) 1. a feeling of profound love and admiration 2. the act of admiring strongly 3. worship given to God alone [admiring adulation affection alone appreciation devotion oration regard respect reverence idolize]
*adorn 07-48-39 (v.) 1. make more attractive by adding ornament, colour, etc. 2. be beautiful to look at 3. furnish with power or authority; of kings or emperors [add adjunct ado already alter apartment applique arm array attractive authority day deck decoration design diagonal different dignify distinguish drawing dress ornament ornate outfit overload redecorate redo refurbish ribbon room needlework /rod/]
*adroit 14-53-9 (a.) 1. skillful (or showing skill) in adapting means to ends 2. quick or skillful or adept in action or thought [accomplished achieve adapt adept agent apt artful artistic artless deft desire dexterous dextrous diplomatic display distinguish droit ready reply resourceful ingenious intelligent tactful talented

technician] "cool prudence and sensitive selfishness along with quick perception of what is possible--these distinguish an adroit politician"
*adulterate 20-46-2 (a.) 1. mixed with impurities (v.) 1. corrupt, debase, or make impure by adding a foreign or inferior substance; often by replacing valuable ingredients with inferior ones [adult airy alloy alter attenuate damage debase deceive deficient devalue dilute distort doctor down ulcerate uneven unfinished unsound unsuitable lace lacking less liquor literary load taint tarnish tenuous thin twist element erroneous etherealize expand extend extraneous rarefied ravage reduce replace rig ruin /tare/] "adulterate liquor"
*advent 08-54-27 (n.) 1. arrival that has been awaited (especially of something momentous) 2. the season including the four Sundays preceding Christmas 3. (Christian theology) the reappearance of Jesus as judge for the Last Judgment [accomplishment achievement advance appearance arrival await date dawn vent ecclesiastical near teach theology] "the advent of the computer"
*adversary 08-35-29 (n.) 1. someone who offers opposition [adverse alien antagonist antichrist armed assailant devil dissentient duel versa enemy recalcitrant relation repugnant resist resolution rival rule second soul]
*adverse 06-54-52 (a.) 1. contrary to your interests or welfare 2. in an opposing direction [alien antagonistic antithetic approve argumentative describe desire detrimental difficult direction discrepant verse encourage enemy reverse rigorous rival sinister stem stressful] "adverse circumstances"
*adversity 09-61-21 (n.) 1. a state of misfortune or affliction 2. a stroke of ill fortune; a calamitous event [affliction danger difficulty distress due victim experience extremity ruin sit stroke struggle suffering ill irremediable tough trouble] "debt-ridden farmers struggling with adversity"
*advert 07-BB-36 (n.) 1. a public promotion of some product or service (v.) 1. give heed (to) 2. make a more or less disguised reference to 3. make reference to [admire allude arouse assume attention audience authority devil directly drag dredge drop vert via ear editorial entry exclusive radio raise recital reference relate relevant remember report resort television throwaway top touch trailer]
*advertiser 13-34-10 (n.) 1. someone whose business is advertising [adman advocate tout seller supporter]
*advisory 04-37-98 (a.) 1. giving advice [admonitory advance advisor data deliberative didactic directive impending implication inform informative instructive sententious severe synodic recommend report review] "an advisory memorandum"
*advocacy 06-15-45 (n.) 1. active support; especially the act of pleading or arguing for something [activism advise aegis aid argue auspice direction drumbeat vehement vociferous voucher opinion care championship charity]
*advocate 03-27-214 (n.) 1. a person who pleads for a cause or propounds an idea 2. a lawyer who pleads cases in court (v.) 1. speak, plead, or argue in favour of 2. push for something [abortion answer arm attorney defender deputy direct vicegerent vindicate votary cate champion coach counter tout encourage endorse espouse /taco/]
*aerial 08-58-31 (a.) 1. in or belonging to the air or operating (for or by means of aircraft or elevated cables) in the air 2. (botany) growing in air 3. characterized by lightness and insubstantiality; as impalpable or intangible as air (n.) 1. a pass to a receiver downfield from the passer 2. an electrical device that sends or receives radio or television signals [acrobatics airborne aircraftman airy angle antenna apparition aspire atmospheric electricity elevated eminent equally ethereal expose radio raise receive reek reflector rial rod roomy root run immaterial impalpable imperceptible imponderable insubstantial intangible involve lack land light line literary live lofty long /aire lair/] "aerial particles"
*aeronautics 11-09-15 (n.) 1. the theory and practice of navigation through air or space [aeronautic aircraft airline airship art astronautics aviation electronic energy equilibrium external ratio reduce rigid rotate operate natural navigation unyielding technology theory travel interplanetary centrifugal cruise science shaft shape soar space stiff structure support]
*affable 10-58-17 (a.) 1. diffusing warmth and friendliness [agreeable amiable approachable attentive fable familiar fine friendly befitting benevolent blissful bonhomie light likable loose loquacious easygoing enjoyable /baff/] "an affable smile"
*affect 02-50-237 (n.) 1. the conscious subjective aspect of feeling or emotion (v.) 1. act physically on; have an effect upon 2. make believe 3. connect closely and often incriminatingly 4. have an effect upon 5. have an emotional or cognitive impact upon [act actuate adopt alter arouse assume attack fake fictitious flourish forge energize evidence experience express carry change concern tell tense tinge tone treatment trouble] "Will the new rules affect me?"
*affectation 16-50-5 (n.) 1. a deliberate pretense or exaggerated display [act affect air appearance artificial assume attitude face false fashionable feign front effect euphuism exaggerate characteristic cheat chic conduct create custom tactics theatrical tone trait trick imposture impress inflation insincerity intend orotund]
*affiliate 04-18-92 (n.) 1. a subordinate or subsidiary associate; a person who is affiliated with another or with an organization 2. a subsidiary or subordinate organization that is affiliated with another organization (v.) 1. join in an affiliation 2. join in an affiliation 3. keep company with; hang out with [accept accompany

accord admit agreement ally anew arm assort attachment fall family father federation fellow filiate filiation financial form formal foster fuse ilia implicate incident inclusion incorporate insider interact intimacy involved large league liaison link local lodge team tie toward treaty twin embrace enate enroll enter /tail/] "They affiliated themselves with the organization"
*affinity 10-45-19 (n.) 1. (immunology) the attraction between an antigen and an antibody 2. the force attracting atoms to each other and binding them together in a molecule 3. a natural attraction or feeling of kinship 4. inherent resemblance between persons or things 5. a close connection marked by community of interests or similarity in nature or character 6. kinship by marriage or adoption; not a blood relationship 7. (biology) state of relationship between organisms or groups of organisms resulting in resemblance in structure or structural parts [abstraction adoption affair agreement anatomical anthropology antigen appearance arouse association atom attract family fancy favor feeling fini force friendly identification identity immigrant immunology inclination influence inherent interest intersection nature near thing trust turn type /niff/] "basic dyes have an affinity for wool and silk"
*affirmative 09-16-22 (a.) 1. affirming or giving assent 2. supporting a policy or attitude etc 3. expecting the best (n.) 1. a reply of affirmation [absolute acceptance affirm agreement answer approve argument assertion attitude avouch avowal favor indicate inharmony interest ratify ready reconcile refusal reply mammal true vote eager emphatic encourage endorse equivalent existence expect express extension /riff vita/] "an affirmative decision"
*affix 14-17-8 (n.) 1. a linguistic element added to a word to produce an inflected or derived form (v.) 1. add to the very end 2. attach to 3. attach or become attached to a stem word; of grammatical morphemes [add anchor append ascribe attachment attribute fasten fix form formative front identify infix inflection inserted inside interpolate invent] "affix the seal here"
*affluence 14-47-9 (n.) 1. abundant wealth [abundant financial freedom full fund unlimited ease currency comfortable]
*affront 12-56-12 (n.) 1. a deliberately offensive act or something producing the effect of an affront (v.) 1. treat, mention, or speak to rudely [abuse aggrieve aspersion atrocity failure flout front remark rude offensive openly outrage taunt treat]
*afire 19-04-3 (a.) 1. lighted up by or as by fire or flame [abandon ablaze aflame alight ardent avid faithful fiery fire firework flaming ignite impassioned inspired interested ire reek resolute eager earnest enthusiastic excite excited] "forests set ablaze (or afire) by lightning"
*afoot 14-57-9 (a.) 1. traveling by foot 2. currently in progress (ad.) 1. on foot; walking [accidental accompany afloat foot occasional occur ongoing talk tour town travel trial] "she was afoot when I saw her this morning"
*afresh 16-80-6 (ad.) 1. again but in a new or different way [again anew fresh freshly recent resh encore story /serf/] "start afresh"
*afterthought 14-37-9 (n.) 1. thinking again about a choice previously made 2. an addition that was not included in the original plan [addendum appendix flip tag think thought turnaround early envoi epilogue extra reconsider reflection rethink reverse review halt hindrance holdup obstruction origin garage]
*agglomerate 23-42-1 (a.) 1. clustered together but not coherent (v.) 1. form into one cluster [accumulation addition aggregate aggregation agreement assemble association gather gathering geology glob glom gob grouping league link lump marriage mass meeting ecumenism embodiment encompass eruption rock round tie trove /mol tare/] "an agglomerated flower head"
*aggrandize 19-03-3 (v.) 1. add details to [accelerate accomplishment actually add advance amplify augment awesome glamorize glorify graduate grand grandiloquence great grow raise rarefy reinforce deepen deify deliberate detail develop dilate disproportionate distinguish dramatize immortalize improve increase influence intensify embellish embroider enhance enlarge erect exaggerate expand extend extreme]
*aggravate 07-40-38 (v.) 1. exasperate or irritate 2. make worse [abnormal accelerate alter anger animal annoy assault attack augment galling get grade grate gripe reduce reinforce rent resistance ride rile rise ruffle rupture vex tear tease torment transform triple trivial trouble eat enhance enlarge exacerbate exaggerate exasperate excite exercise extreme] "This drug aggravates the pain"
*aggravation 16-50-5 (n.) 1. an exasperated feeling of annoyance 2. action that makes a problem or a disease (or its symptoms) worse 3. unfriendly behavior that causes anger or resentment [acceleration already anger animation annoying arouse augment galvanize recover redouble resentment rigor vexation vexatious vicissitude taunt tighten tiresome trial trivial trouble twit incite infuriate intensify ion irritation nature nuisance] "the aggravation of her condition resulted from lack of care"
*aggregate 08-70-30 (a.) 1. gathered or tending to gather into a mass or whole 2. (botany) formed of separate units in a cluster (n.) 1. the whole amount 2. a sum total of many heterogenous things taken together (v.) 1. amount in the aggregate to 2. gather in a mass, sum, or whole [account add agreement all amalgamate amass amount animal assemblage assemble association gain game gate gather gathering geology gob gravel great gross group raise rally range resemble reserve road rock roundup ruck earn ecumenism embodiment encompass entity everything exhaustive tale tally team tend tie totality trove /age tag/] "the aggregate amount of indebtedness"

*aggression 06-61-49 (n.) 1. a feeling of hostility that arouses thoughts of attack 2. violent action that is hostile and usually unprovoked 3. a disposition to behave aggressively 4. deliberately unfriendly behavior 5. the act of initiating hostilities [aggress ambitious anger antagonism armed arouse assault assertion attack attitude getup grinder gumption raid raise remark resentment resist rush encroach enemy engagement enmity sally say spirit spiteful steal strike infiltrate initiate injury intimidate invasion irritation offensive onset onslaught oppose]
*aggrieve 11-74-14 (v.) 1. infringe on the rights of; in law 2. break the heart of; cause to feel sorrow [abuse afflict angry annoy authority great grieve right rule ill impair impose infect inflict infringe injury injustice irritate embitter envenom victimize violate]
*aghast 14-70-9 (a.) 1. struck with fear, dread, or consternation [afraid agha amaze anxious appal apprehension astound gape gaze ghost hast head horrify hypnotize shock snake struck stun surprise tail terrify thunderstruck]
*agile 09-52-25 (a.) 1. moving quickly and lightly 2. mentally quick [active acute alert alive animal attentive galloping gil graceful gymnast intelligent lightly lightness limber lithe lively energetic expeditious express] "sleek and agile as a gymnast"

*agitate 10-51-20 (v.) 1. cause to be agitated, excited, or roused 2. try to stir up public opinion 3. change the arrangement or position of 4. exert oneself continuously, vigorously, or obtrusively to gain an end or engage in a crusade for a certain cause or person; be an advocate for 5. move or cause to move quickly back and forth 6. move very slightly [abstract advertise advocate afflict agita air anxious apprehensive argue arouse arrange attack attempt gain gas impatient incense incite inflammatory interest introduce involuntarily irritate tense thrash thresh throb thrown tickle toss tranquillize tremor tremulous trouble try turbid turbulent turn electrify embarrassed embroil emotional engage exasperate excited exert /tig/]
*agog 20-74-2 (a.) 1. highly excited [agape ago alert arouse avid await aware galvanize gaze gossipy observe optimistic overwhelm]
*agrarian 18-24-4 (a.) 1. "an agrarian (or agricultural) society" [agricultural agronomic amount arable aria geoponic redistributio reformer rich rural rustic interest native natural] "an agrarian (or agricultural) society"
*ail 19-41-3 (n.) 1. aromatic bulb used as seasoning (v.) 1. be unwell, ill, or ill disposed 2. cause bodily suffering to [ache add affect afflict anguish aromatic axis ill impart inconvenience irk irritate lacerate large literary]
*ailment 08-28-28 (n.) 1. an often persistent bodily disorder or disease; a cause for complaining [abnormality affection ail allergy ill infirmity injury malaise mild minor move nauseate non normal travel turmoil]
*airtight 16-45-5 (a.) 1. having no weak points 2. not allowing air or gas to pass in or out [alibi allow argument attack immune impermeable impregnable invulnerable resistant rustproof tight gas gastight hermetic /git tri/] "an airtight defense"
*airy 08-48-26 (a.) 1. open to or abounding in fresh air 2. characterized by lightness and insubstantiality; as impalpable or intangible as air 3. having little or no perceptible weight; so light as to resemble air 4. not practical or realizable; speculative [abound aerie air animate apparition appearance ascent aspire atmospheric attenuate idealize idle imaginary impalpable improve indifferent insubstantial intangible rare rarity realize reckless regardless resemble resilient rich roomy yeasty] "airy rooms"
*akin 08-54-33 (a.) 1. similar or related in quality or character 2. related by blood [accord affiliate agree allied amateur analogous ancient kin kindred kinship] "a feeling akin to terror"
*alabaster 20-52-2 (a.) 1. of or resembling alabaster (n.) 1. a compact fine-textured usually white gypsum used for carving 2. a very light white 3. a hard compact kind of calcite [achromatic arsenic asbestos asphalt lava least level lightness lily limestone basalt baster bauxite bitumen black brimstone sandstone schist semi shale sheet silver skin slate smooth soapstone statue talc tellurium transparent emery epidote realgar resemble rhodonite rock] "alabaster statue"
*alacrity 18-65-4 (n.) 1. liveliness and eagerness [abrupt accept animation anxious appetite life lively compliance consent cooperative crit rapidity rash ready immediate impatient impulsive tractable] "he accepted with alacrity"
*albino 20-65-2 (n.) 1. a person with albinism: white hair and pink eyes and milky skin [albin albinism animal anomaly lack lactescent last leukoderma lightness blond iris]
*album 03-67-206 (n.) 1. a book of blank pages with pockets or envelopes; for organizing photographs or stamp collections etc 2. one or more recordings issued together; originally released on 12-inch phonograph records (usually with attractive record covers) and later on cassette audio tape and compact disc [alb ana annual anthology attractive audio autograph later ledger literary log logbook lyric baby beauty binder blank blotter book bound bum unify mean memento miscellany musical]
*alchemy 13-69-10 (n.) 1. a pseudoscientific forerunner of chemistry in medieval times 2. the way two individuals relate to each other [alkahest assimilation assumption lapse life living change charm claim conversion cure hate hem hoodoo early elixir enchantment experiment magic maintain medieval metal mysterious]
*alcohol 04-59-132 (n.) 1. any of a series of volatile hydroxyl compounds that are made from hydrocarbons

by distillation 2. a liquor or brew containing alcohol as the active agent [abuse additive agave agent ammonia analgesic animal anodyne antiseptic appetizer aromatic asia atom australasia lactate light liquor lotus central charcoal cider class clear coal coho coke colorless compound obtain oil opium organic origin oxide half hard heroin highly home hooch hop horse hydroxyl] "alcohol (or drink) ruined him"
*alcoholism 10-47-19 (n.) 1. Habitual intoxication; prolonged and excessive intake of alcoholic drinks leading to a breakdown in health and an addiction to alcohol such that abrupt deprivation leads to severe withdrawal symptoms 2. an intense persistent desire to drink alcoholic beverages to excess [abrupt addiction adverse affect alcohol lead consumption crash craving habitual habituate health heavy inebriate intake intense intoxicate irrational irresistible severe social stop symptom mania motive /silo/]
*alcove 16-44-6 (n.) 1. a small recess opening off a larger room [arbor area large library carrel conservatory corner cove cover cubicle opening oriel enclosure external]
*alder 16-67-6 (n.) 1. wood of any of various alder trees; resistant to underwater rot; used for bridges etc 2. north temperate shrubs or trees having toothed leaves and conelike fruit; bark is used in tanning and dyeing and the rot-resistant wood [acacia american angiosperm area ash aspen laburnum last leaf light lignify lime deciduous distinct dye eastern elevated elm european red resistant rhombi rot rowan rust]
*alderman 14-50-8 (n.) 1. a member of a municipal legislative body (as a city council) [alder archon assemblyman last lawgiver lawmaker legislative legislator local elder reeve reorganization represent representative magistrate mayor member municipal]
*ale 10-71-17 (n.) 1. fermented alcoholic beverage similar to but heavier than beer [add alcoholic amber law lighter effervescent english]
*alias 13-51-10 (ad.) 1. as known or named at another time or place (n.) 1. a name that has been assumed temporarily [assign assume language lias locate identify /sail/] "Mr. Smith, alias Mr. Lafayette"
*alien 05-47-74 (a.) 1. being or from or characteristic of another place or part of the world 2. not contained in or deriving from the essential nature of something (n.) 1. a person who comes from a foreign country; someone who does not owe allegiance to your country 2. a form of life assumed to exist outside the Earth or its atmosphere 3. anyone who does not belong in the environment in which they are found (v.) 1. arouse hostility or indifference in where there had formerly been love, affection, or friendliness [adverse affection alter apart assign lien immigrant independent isolation enemy exclusive exile narrow natural negative] "an economic theory alien to the spirit of capitalism"
*alienate 05-49-62 (v.) 1. arouse hostility or indifference in where there had formerly been love, affection, or friendliness [abrupt absolute abstraction affection age alien alone aloof alter apart arouse assignment attitude law leave lethargy live lonesome lose lunacy impose indifference infuriate ingredient insular irrationality irreconcilable irritate isolate elation essential estrange estranged exacerbate exclude expel negativism negotiate tear title toward trade transform transmittal turn turnover twitch]
*alienation 11-43-14 (n.) 1. the feeling of being alienated from other people 2. (law) the voluntary and absolute transfer of title and possession of real property from one person to another 3. the action of alienating; the action of causing to become unfriendly 4. separation resulting from hostility [absolute alone antipathy authority aversion law impose ingredient isolation essential title transfer oppose ownership] "the power of alienation is an essential ingredient of ownership"
*allay 11-52-15 (v.) 1. lessen the intensity of; calm; as of anxieties and fears 2. satisfy (thirst) [abate all alleviate anger anxiety appease assuage lessen lie lull]
*allege 03-77-196 (v.) 1. report or maintain [abuse accuse affirm all announce answer apparent appointment argue article asseverate assign assume attribute aver later legal lie enunciate excuse expert explicable express give given grant /gell/] "He alleged that he was the victim of a crime"
*allegiance 08-51-29 (n.) 1. the act of binding yourself (intellectually or emotionally) to a course of action 2. the loyalty that citizens owe to their country (or subjects to their sovereign) [acquiesce adhere adhesion all attachment liege life long lord lose loyalty emotional ethics ethnic game goal group imperative interest charge cherish citizen commitment constant country course /gell/]
*allegory 13-44-10 (n.) 1. a short moral story (often with animal characters) 2. an expressive style that uses fictional characters and events to describe some subject by suggestive resemblances; an extended metaphor 3. a visible symbol representing an abstract idea [allusion analogy apologue assumption legend liken logotype emblem extended gory opposition overtone relation romance /gell/]
*alleviate 08-51-29 (v.) 1. make easier 2. provide physical relief, as from pain [abate aid allay ameliorate amend anesthetic appease assistance assuage lessen levi lie lighten lightening loosen lower lull ease easement easy emollient extenuate improve tame temper tranquilizer /vell/]
*alley 07-39-39 (n.) 1. a narrow street with walls on both sides 2. a lane down which a bowling ball is rolled toward pins [access across aisle all avenue lane last left ley line exit expressway /yell/]
*alliance 03-47-172 (n.) 1. the state of being allied or confederated 2. a formal agreement establishing an association or alliance between nations or other groups

to achieve a particular aim 3. a connection based on kinship or marriage or common interest 4. an organization of people (or countries) involved in a pact or treaty 5. the act of forming an alliance or confederation [accord affair agreement aim alignment all association austria axis link include nation case central charter close club coalition combine community confederation cooperation cordial corporation enemy entente establish /nail/] "the shifting alliances within a large family"
*allocate 06-56-56 (v.) 1. distribute according to a plan or set apart for a special purpose [accord align allow anew apart army array aside assign award lineup locate lot ordain camp collocate compose tag task team triangulate trip earmark emplace /colla olla taco/]
*allot 11-40-16 (v.) 1. allow to have 2. administer or bestow, as in small portions 3. give out [abstract accord administer allo allow apart apply apportion appropriate aside assign available award lavish legal lineup lot offer ordain tag task ten tender transfer /olla toll/]
*allotment 13-58-10 (n.) 1. the act of distributing by allotting or apportioning 2. a share set aside for a specific purpose [accord again aid allot amount apportionment array aside asset assignment assistance lot order tag tract tucker marshal meal measure earmark end /olla toll/]
*alloy 13-64-11 (n.) 1. a mixture containing two or more metallic elements or metallic and nonmetallic elements usually fused together or dissolving into each other when molten 2. the state of impairing the quality or reducing the value of something (v.) 1. lower in value by increasing the base-metal content; of metals 2. make an alloy of (metals) [add additive admixture adulterant aggregate allay allo alter aluminum amalgam amount antimony arsenic artificial atom lead lighter line low /olla/] "brass is an alloy of zinc and copper"
*allude 08-28-28 (v.) 1. make a more or less disguised reference to [advert alleged less lude discrepancy disguise drop explicit /dull/] "He alluded to the problem but did not mention it"
*allusion 10-34-18 (n.) 1. passing reference or indirect mention [all allegory assumption attention undertone suggestion supposition symbolism import indirect innuendo insinuation intimate overtone nuance /sull/]
*ally 03-42-198 (n.) 1. an associate who provides assistance 2. a friendly nation (v.) 1. become an ally or associate, as by a treaty or marriage [affiliate alignment all apply assistant associate assort land likeness lily link] "he's a good ally in fight"
*almanac 18-31-4 (n.) 1. an annual publication including weather forecasts and other miscellaneous information arranged according to the calendar of a given year 2. an annual publication containing tabular information in a particular field or fields arranged according to the calendar of a given year [accord alma anniversary annual arrange astronomical manual miscellaneous calendar /can/]
*aloof 11-51-15 (a.) 1. remote in manner (ad.) 1. in an aloof manner [accept alone apart away languid lethargic listless local lofty loo loof off open overhead forbidding formal freeze frosty /fool/] "stood apart with aloof dignity"
*altar 09-47-23 (n.) 1. the table in Christian churches where communion is given 2. a raised structure on which gifts or sacrifices to a god are made [alt area leg lord table tar raise religious]
*alter 03-45-158 (v.) 1. make an alteration to 2. make or become different in some particular way, without permanently losing one's or its former characteristics or essence 3. cause to change; make different; cause a transformation 4. remove the ovaries of 5. insert words into texts, often falsifying it thereby [abate accommodate adapt adjustment affect again alt amplitude animalize land leaven limit tack temper transform emasculate reduce reform revive revolutionize] "The advent of the automobile may have altered the growth pattern of the city"
*alteration 09-50-21 (n.) 1. the act of making something different (as e.g. the size of a garment) 2. an event that occurs when something passes from one state or phase to another 3. the act of revising or altering (involving reconsideration and modification) [accommodation adjustment analysis lessen transition turnabout ease ration renewal restructure revolution improvement individuation overthrow nativity /tare/]
*alternate 06-25-55 (a.) 1. occurring by turns; first one and then the other 2. allowing a choice 3. every second one of a series 4. (botany) of leaves and branches etc; first on one side and then on the other in two ranks along an axis; not paired (n.) 1. someone who takes the place of another person (v.) 1. go back and forth; swing back and forth between two states or conditions 2. exchange people temporarily to fulfill certain jobs and functions 3. do something in turns 4. reverse, as of direction, attitude, or course of action 5. be an understudy or alternate for a role [agent allow alternative approximate arrange attitude attorney axis cyclic lady leaf learn level lieutenant logroll lose love tack temporary ternate title trade turn elation entire equal essence even exchange exchangeable receive recurring regular reliever repeat replace replacement respond reverse role rotate night non] "the cleaning lady comes on alternate Wednesdays"
*alternative 02-59-394 (a.) 1. necessitating a choice between mutually exclusive possibilities 2. allowing a choice 3. pertaining to unconventional choices (n.) 1. an alternative action [additional agent allow another automatic available less life loophole temporary tend tentative theory token true easy economical equal establishment exchangeable exclusive reach refuse replace representative reserve right native natural necessitate non nothing imitation immediate impossible

institutionalize interchange value variant vicarious voluntary /vita/] "an alternative plan"
*altitude 08-51-29 (n.) 1. elevation especially above sea level or above the earth's surface 2. the perpendicular distance from the base of a geometric figure to opposite vertex (or side if parallel) 3. angular distance above the horizon (especially of a celestial object) [abscissa alt angle angular apex astronomy azimuth latitude layer length level lofty longitude low tall toplofty declination distance earth elevation eminence establish exaltation] "the altitude gave her a headache"
*alto 09-17-24 (a.) 1. of or being the lowest female voice 2. (of a musical instrument) second highest member of a group 3. of or being the highest male voice; having a range above that of tenor (n.) 1. a singer whose voice lies in the alto clef 2. the pitch range of the lowest female voice 3. the lowest female singing voice 4. the highest adult male singing voice [accompaniment achieve adagio adult allegro alt andante arpeggio artistic auditory last line low lying tenor tone treble] "alto clarinet or recorder"
*altruism 16-57-5 (n.) 1. the quality of unselfish concern for the welfare of others [agape attempt attitude truism recognition right unacceptable unselfish utilitarianism sacrifice selfless mark mean modesty money]
*amalgam 14-39-9 (n.) 1. an alloy of mercury with another metal (usually silver) used by dentists to fill cavities in teeth; except for iron and platinum all metals dissolve in mercury and chemists refer to the resulting mercury mixtures as amalgams 2. a combination or blend of diverse things [admixture alga alloy assemblage magma material mercury metal mixture molten liberal /glam mag/] "his theory is an amalgam of earlier ideas"
*amalgamate 15-61-7 (a.) 1. joined together into a whole (v.) 1. to bring or combine together or with something else [add aggregate alloy ally alter amalgam associate mass mercury merge metal mingle mix modify music gather transform embody emulsify encompass entity /glam mag/]
*amass 07-54-38 (v.) 1. collect or gather 2. get or gather together [accrue accumulate accumulation aggregate amount aside assemble associate attached marshal mass match meeting salt score scrape secrete span splice stack stacked stash stockpile store]
*amateur 04-58-117 (a.) 1. engaged in as a pastime 2. lacking professional skill or expertise (n.) 1. someone who pursues a study or sport as a pastime 2. does not play for pay [admire apprentice athlete authority mate matter maven mediocre mental mortal talented technician theatrical tinker train trifle effort engage enjoy enthusiast epicurean expert expertise extra unpaid unprofessional unskillful recreational root /rue/] "an amateur painter"
*ambiguous 08-39-28 (a.) 1. (psychology) having no intrinsic or objective meaning; not organized in conventional patterns 2. having more than one possible meaning 3. open to two or more interpretations; or of uncertain nature or significance; or (often) intended to mislead [abstruse agnostic amalgamate ambi ambivalent assemble mario message mislead misleading mixed multi mysterious behavior blend impenetrable increase indeterminate indistinct inkblot interpretation intrinsic ironic uncertainty unclear uneasy unequivocal unreliable unsure obscure opaque oracular organize science scramble significance situation skeptical statement suspect /gib/]
*ambitious 03-55-156 (a.) 1. requiring full use of your abilities or resources 2. having a strong desire for success or achievement [accomplish achievement aggressive ambit anxious aspire magnificent manqu market mental mind mistake motivate bold imagination impressive increase indefatigable initiative task tony ostentatious undertake utopian schedule set share single sounding standard striving strong successful] "ambitious schedule"
*ambivalent 10-44-17 (a.) 1. characterized by a mixture of opposite feelings or attitudes 2. uncertain or unable to decide about what course to follow [amalgamate amphibious antinomy assurance attitude medley mingle mislead mix bivalent blend indecisive indicate indiscriminate interpretation intricate ironic varied lack eclectic equivocal nature] "she felt ambivalent about his proposal"
*ambulance 06-62-51 (n.) 1. a vehicle that takes people to and from hospitals [articulate automobile machine mental minicab motorcar bus lance locomotive lorry cable car carry coach combustion engine equip]
*ambush 07-57-34 (n.) 1. the act of concealing yourself and lying in wait to attack by surprise (v.) 1. hunt (quarry) by stalking and ambushing 2. wait in hiding to attack [animal anticipate assault astonish attack main mug blind blitz bush bushwhack unexpected scupper shadow sport stalk stay still strike surprise harry hide hideout hit hunt]
*ameliorate 18-34-4 (v.) 1. to make better 2. get better [accommodation adjustment advance alter amendment around meliorate mend mitigate modify modulate educate enhance enrich eugenics lard lift light lighten improvement overthrow raise recover refine reform relieve repair revive revolution right rise tack takeoff transition turnabout /oil roil taro/]
*amenable 15-48-7 (a.) 1. disposed or willing to comply 2. responsible to a higher authority [accessible accountable acquiesce adjust advance affect agreeable answerable authority available matthew meek mend minded eager elevate enable enquiry enthusiastic behavior better biddable law liable lift likely /ban bane/] "someone amenable to persuasion"
*americanism 15-53-7 (n.) 1. loyalty to the USA and its institutions 2. a custom that is peculiar to the United States or its citizens 3. an expression that is

characteristic of English as spoken by Americans [accept american english expression institution chauvinism citizen country custom nationalism nationality sacrifice speak style /cire/]
*amicable 12-61-13 (a.) 1. characterized by friendship and good will [affection agree agreeable akin amiable anger attract mellow ill inharmony cable cheerful civil cooperative bad befitting benevolent blissful brotherly likable lovable loveable empathetic enjoyable enmity]
*amity 20-30-2 (n.) 1. a cordial disposition 2. a state of friendship and cordiality [absence accordance agreement amiable amit mutuality identity tranquil]
*amorous 15-60-7 (a.) 1. inclined toward or displaying love 2. expressive of or exciting sexual love or romance [adventure affair affectionate amatory amor aphrodisiac ardent attraction moonlight oversexed ride romantic undersexed unloving sentimental sex show straight] "feeling amorous"
*amorphous 16-31-5 (a.) 1. having no definite form or distinct shape 2. without real or apparent crystalline form 3. lacking the system or structure characteristic of living bodies [adrift afloat aggregate alternate apparent mass meaningless mineral moody morpho muddy obscure obvious opaque organism rambling random real restless particle promiscuous property protoplasm haphazard hazy heteromorphic uncertain unpredictable unsettled stray structure sweeping system /prom/] "amorphous clouds of insects"
*amortize 16-01-5 (v.) 1. liquidate gradually [account acquittance alienate amor asset assignment makeover money obligation redeem reduce reduction regular remittance remunerate remuneration repay retirement trade transfer transmittal turnover installment ecclesiastical eliminate enfeoff exchange /zit/]
*amour 14-50-9 (n.) 1. a usually secretive or illicit sexual relationship [adultery affaire amorous our relationship]
*amphibious 16-46-5 (a.) 1. relating to military forces prepared for operations launched from the sea against an enemy shore 2. operating or living on land and in water 3. relating to or characteristic of animals of the class Amphibia [adaptable adjust adult ambivalent animal aquatic assault medley military mingle mix patchy place pluralism prepare promiscuous heterogeneous indiscriminate intricate ironic bio blend operation scramble sea shore supple syncretism] "amphibious troops"
*amphitheater 16-AA-5 (n.) 1. a sloping gallery with seats for spectators (as in an operating room or theater) 2. an oval large stadium with tiers of seats; an arena in which contests and spectacles are held [agora ancient area arena arrange art auditorium mark marketplace mat milieu pit place platform play produce public hall head hippodrome hold house interior terrain theater theatre tier tiltyard enclosure entertainment entrance range recess ring rome roof room round]
*amplitude 23-25-1 (n.) 1. (physics) the maximum displacement of a periodic wave 2. greatness of magnitude 3. the property of copious abundance [abundance adequate affluent amount area attain magnitude mass mathematics matter maximum pendulum philosophy phone pipe plenty positive power profusion large level light lip lit lot immense infinity interference talkative tirade trough depth diameter dimension displacement electronics energy expansive extent exuberant]
*amply 14-46-8 (ad.) 1. to an ample degree or in an ample manner 2. sufficiently; more than adequately [abundant adequate amazing appropriate magical magnificent manner meager minimal particularly plentiful ply prominent properly largely lavish liberal] "these voices were amply represented"
*amputate 12-59-13 (v.) 1. remove surgically; of limbs [abscission abstract annihilation appendage mutilate pare part peel prune pushing takeout tate tearing transplant truncate eliminate except exclude /tup/]
*amusement 07-32-40 (n.) 1. an activity that entertains 2. a feeling of delight at being entertained [amuse arcade attention attraction merry military satisfaction spectacular sport stage stimulate ease educational edutainment enjoy enjoyment entertainment extreme theme titillate /sum uma/]
*anachronism 14-48-8 (n.) 1. an artifact that belongs to another time 2. something located at a time when it could not have existed or occurred 3. a person who seems to be displaced in time; who belongs to another age [age ana anomaly antedate anticipation archaism artifact custom history holdover relic occur idea invention seem set slip solecism survival manmade misapply misdate mistime modern /can/]
*anagram 19-77-3 (n.) 1. a word or phrase spelled by rearranging the letters of another word or phrase (v.) 1. read letters out of order to discover a hidden meaning [acrostic amphiboly native gram read rearrange rebus riddle malapropism mean]
*analogous 16-26-5 (a.) 1. similar or correspondent in some respects though otherwise dissimilar 2. (biology) corresponding in function but not in evolutionary origin [akin alike allow analog animal answer appear living organism origin uniform science serve similar structure study] "brains and computers are often considered analogous"
*analogy 09-49-22 (n.) 1. drawing a comparison in order to show a similarity in some respect 2. an inference that if things agree in some respects they probably agree in others [agent agree agreement already alternative analog animal appear near language liken likeness linguistics logical observation operation opposition organ ghostwriter god great] "the operation of a computer presents and interesting analogy to the working of the brain"
*analyst 01-41-632 (n.) 1. someone who is skilled at

analyzing data 2. an expert who studies financial data (on credit or securities or sales or financial patterns etc.) and recommends appropriate business actions 3. a licensed practitioner of psychoanalysis [advocate affecting anal analyze applicant assay assessment austria neurology license live sale security separate sexual shrink sigmund skillful specialize stock study test]
*analyze 06-01-59 (v.) 1. make a mathematical, chemical, or grammatical analysis of; break down into components or essential features 2. consider in detail and subject to an analysis in order to discover essential features or meaning 3. break down into components or essential features 4. subject to psychoanalytic treatment [account accuracy air anal analyst apart appraise appreciation arrange ascertain assay assessment assign nature note list look essential evaluate evidence examine experiment explore express] "analyze a sonnet by Shakespeare"
*anarchy 11-56-16 (n.) 1. a state of lawlessness and disorder (usually resulting from a failure of government) [absence aloof amorphous anarch anomie authority nihilism rebellion revolution riot chaotic complete confusion control hassle hazy /cran rana/]

*anathema 13-54-10 (n.) 1. a detested person 2. a formal ecclesiastical curse accompanied by excommunication [abhorrence abomination accompany agreeable antipathy appeal arraign authority aversion thema thundering hate hex ecclesiastical evil excommunicate excoriate execration malediction malison /tana/] "he is an anathema to me"
*anatomy 10-51-19 (n.) 1. a detailed analysis 2. alternative names for the body of a human being 3. the branch of morphology that deals with the structure of animals [analyze architecture arrangement atom texture tissue trunk organology ornithology osteology makeup making manufacture mortal /tana/]
*ancestry 12-44-12 (n.) 1. the descendants of one individual 2. inherited properties shared with others of your bloodline [acquire affiliate agnate alliance animal attribute nobility noble clansman connection consanguinity enation entire extraction sept share sibling side source special stemma stock strain successive tree tribesman try race rank relative rumor]
*anchor 05-34-75 (n.) 1. a central cohesive source of support and stability 2. a mechanical device that prevents a vessel from moving 3. a television reporter who coordinates a broadcast to which several correspondents contribute (v.) 1. secure a vessel with an anchor 2. fix firmly and stably [affix aground ancho annex arm assistance attach narrow nautical nest newsman camp cast catch central chain channel climb coast cohesive connect correspondent craft hamper handcuff head hold hook race rear relay relocate remain report responsible restrain rivet rock rope] "anchor the lamppost in concrete"
*anecdote 07-51-36 (n.) 1. short account of an incident (especially a biographical one) [account narrative dote tale /tod/]
*anemia 18-01-4 (n.) 1. a deficiency of red blood cells 2. a lack of vitality 3. genus of terrestrial or lithophytic ferns having pinnatifid fronds; chiefly of tropical America [abnormality absorption ally america amniocentesis asphyxiate asthma atrophy average nausea necrosis neoplasm newborn eat edema emaciate enzyme etiolated malignant malnutrition marasmus marrow maternal mean mostly mother muddy impotent include incompatible increase indy inflammation inherit intrinsic iron ischemia itch /aim/]
*anemic 16-AA-6 (a.) 1. lacking vigor or energy 2. relating to anemia or suffering from anemia [allergic arthritic ashen attempt nerveless neuritis neutral effete encephalitis energy epileptic malaria mat medicine muddy imbecile impotent insipid cancer chicken colorless cowardly] "an anemic attempt to hit the baseball"
*anesthetic 19-03-3 (a.) 1. characterized by insensibility (n.) 1. a drug that causes temporary loss of bodily sensations [agent alleviate anodyne area assuage narcotic nightcap numb numbing ease emollient entire esthetic ether sedate sensitivity soften soothe spine stunning substance temporary topical tranquilizer hard hypnotic impassible impervious incapable inject insensible insensitive cathartic cause circulatory cleanse cocaine consciousness /cite/] "the young girls are in a state of possession--blind and deaf and anesthetic"
*anew 11-22-15 (ad.) 1. again but in a new or different way [afresh again new newly encore way write /wen/]
*angelic 16-56-6 (a.) 1. marked by utter benignity; resembling or befitting an angel or saint 2. of or relating to angels 3. having a sweet nature befitting an angel or cherub [admirable adorable affection angel annoy appealing attract nature glorify godly good evil likable lovable loveable incorrupt innocent care charming cherubic childlike clear concern /leg/] "angelic benificence"
*anguish 08-51-28 (n.) 1. extreme distress of body or mind 2. extreme mental distress (v.) 1. suffer great pains or distress 2. cause anguish or make miserable [ache adversity affliction agony angst anxiety nausea give great grief grieve grim uneasy unhappy upset infelicity inquietude inundate sad shoot sorrow suffering hurt]
*angular 13-46-11 (a.) 1. having angles or an angular shape 2. measured by an angle or by the rate of change of an angle [akimbo angle asteroid awkward gaunt gawky gula undress unfinished ungainly lanky lot rangy rate raw rawboned right round rude /lug/] "angular momentum"
*animate 06-46-58 (a.) 1. (linguistics) belonging to the class of nouns that denote living beings 2. endowed with animal life as distinguished from plant life 3. relating to

animal life as distinct from plant life 4. endowed with feeling and unstructured consciousness (v.) 1. heighten or intensify 2. give new life or energy to 3. give life-like qualities to 4. make lively [activism aggressive alert alive alter anima appear arouse nerve neuter non imagination impatient incline inert infect inform infuse inject insentient inspire interest invigorate masculine minded modify motivate move technique thrust tolerance transform treatment trenchant eager encourage energy enliven enthusiastic exalt excite excited exhilarate /mina/] "the word `dog' is animate"
*animosity 11-43-15 (n.) 1. a feeling of ill will arousing active hostility [acrimony ani antagonism antipathy arouse ill malevolent malice sore sour spirit spleen /mina/]
*annals 14-46-9 (n.) 1. reports of the work of a society or learned body etc 2. a chronological account of events in successive years [account achievement adventure anna annual archive arrange autobiography narrative nation necrology learn legend letter list scroll secure society story successive]
*annex 09-28-22 (n.) 1. an addition that extends a main building (v.) 1. take illegally, as of territory 2. attach to 3. take by conquest; as of territory [accessory add addendum additional affix and angle anne appendix appropriate arm arrogate assistant assume attached attachment authority auxiliary nationalize new nip edifice ell embezzle entity epilogue everybody execution extension extort]
*annihilate 15-53-7 (v.) 1. kill in large numbers [abate abolish amputate antiparticle army negative nip nuclear nullify immolate intentional invalidate isolate hila liquidate lop lynch takeout ten thrash truncate easy eliminate end entire eradicate except exist exterminate extinguish /inn tali/]
*annotate 16-31-6 (v.) 1. add explanatory notes to or supply with critical comments"The scholar annotated the early edition of a famous novel" 2. provide interlinear explanations for words or phrases [add notate note novel observe teacher early edition explanatory /ton/] "The scholar annotated the early edition of a famous novel"
*annual 01-49-670 (a.) 1. (botany) completing its life cycle within a year 2. occurring or payable every year (n.) 1. a plant that completes its entire life cycle within the space of a year 2. a reference book that is published regularly once every year [accord accumulate album amphibian angiosperm ann arrange astronomical authoritative notebook lack lasting ledger life living locomotion log logbook] "an annual trip to Paris"
*annuity 10-67-18 (n.) 1. income from capital investment paid in a series of regular payments [advance aid allowance amount ann assistance assurance unable underwriter until income interval investor tontine year] "his retirement fund was set up to be paid as an annuity"
*annunciation 20-41-2 (n.) 1. a festival commemorating the announcement of the Incarnation by the angel Gabriel to the Virgin Mary; a quarter day in England, Wales, and Ireland 2. a formal public statement 3. (Christian religion) the announcement to the Virgin Mary by the angel Gabriel of the incarnation of Christ [affirmation allegation angel ann announcement april authoritative notify ukase utterance certain chosen christianity circular communicate conclusion creed incarnation independence ireland teach testament official old ordinance]
*anonymous 05-53-75 (a.) 1. not known or lacking marked individuality 2. having no known name or identity or known source [allow author nameless obscure onymous ordinary maker mall mark mysterious undistinguished unexceptional unidentified unknown unmemorable unnamed unnoticed unsigned unspecified unsuited secluded secret sequester shadowy shop source /nona/] "anonymous authors"
*antagonism 14-42-9 (n.) 1. a state of deep-seated ill-will 2. (biochemistry) interference in or inhibition of the physiological action of a chemical substance by another having a similar structure 3. an actively expressed feeling of dislike and hostility 4. the relation between opposing principles or forces or factors [aggression agon allergy animosity antipathy antithesis apply attribute aversion nausea negative neutralize nullification tension truculent good obstruct official opposition organism ill impede inconsistency individually inequality inherent inhibition international showdown shudder socialism strife structure substance suspect main malevolent manifest martial militarism muscle /nog/] "the inherent antagonism of capitalism and socialism"
*antarctic 13-69-10 (a.) 1. of or relating to Antarctica 2. at or near the south pole (n.) 1. the region around the south pole: Antarctica and surrounding waters [arctic aren near north region cap circle cold continent cover ice]
*ante 11-63-15 (n.) 1. (in poker) the initial contribution that each player makes to the pot (v.) 1. place one's stake, in a poker game [ahead amount ant ere]
*antecedent 16-43-5 (a.) 1. preceding in time or order (n.) 1. a preceding occurrence or cause or event 2. someone from whom you are descended (but usually more remote that a grandparent) 3. the referent of an anaphor; a phrase or clause that is referred to by an anaphoric pronoun 4. anything that precedes something similar in time [agency anaphoric ancestor announcer antecede anticipatory ascendant neuroscience trailblazer early elder element exist express call chief circumstance clause come component conditional consider deal descend determinative direct] "phrenology was an antecedent of modern neuroscience"
*antediluvian 23-66-1 (a.) 1. of or relating to the period before the Biblical flood 2. so extremely old as seeming

to belong to an earlier period (n.) 1. any of the early patriarchs who lived prior to the Deluge 2. a very old (or old fashioned) person [aged ancient ante antiquated antique tenement timeworn traditionalism troglodyte early elderly extremely dad deluge diluvium dodo duration idea law live long longhair venerable /lid/]
*antenatal 21-98-2 (a.) 1. occurring or existing before birth [natal exist]
*anterior 17-47-5 (a.) 1. (zoology) of or near the head end or toward the front plane of the body 2. earlier in time (n.) 1. a tooth situated at the front of the mouth [album ana anatomy animal ante antecedent attack near tooth treasury early elder exist exordium inaugural initiatory old omnibus] "his malocclusion was caused by malposed anteriors"
*anteroom 21-45-2 (n.) 1. a large entrance or reception room or area [alliance ante area atrium narthex nave edifice enclose entry reception roof room open /moo moor/]
*anthology 10-39-18 (n.) 1. a collection of selected literary passages [album ana aquarium arabic artist author treasure hold ology omnibus library literary garden garland glean]
*anthropology 07-29-34 (n.) 1. the social science that studies the origins and social relationships of human beings [affine analysis anatomy anthropometry approach archeology asia aspect nature taxidermy taxonomy technique theory traditional tribe helminthology herbal herpetology historical humankind race racial relationship observable observer ology origin ornithology outside paleontology part people pertain phenomena prehistoric protozoology provide psychology limit genesis group]
*antic 08-63-31 (a.) 1. ludicrously odd (n.) 1. a ludicrous or grotesque act done for fun and amusement (v.) 1. act as or like a clown [actor adventure aggressive amuse amusing animate anti appear around artifice assume tease tomfoolery trick trip impossible inconceivable incredible intend caper casual cavort clown comic comical conduct costume] "Hamlet's assumed antic disposition"
*antichrist 21-61-2 (n.) 1. the adversary of Christ (or Christianity) mentioned in the New Testament; the Antichrist will rule the world until overthrown by the Second Coming of Christ [adversary antagonist teach testament christ christianity come religion resist role rule second]
*anticlimax 17-75-5 (n.) 1. a disappointing decline after ad previous rise 2. a change from a serious subject to a disappointing one [narrate tone trivial importance increase career chain climax close comedown comic communicate compel conclusion last letdown lower matter] "the anticlimax of a brilliant career"
*antidote 09-59-21 (n.) 1. a remedy that stops or controls the effects of a poison [administer agent alkaloid amount answer antacid anti antivenin nerve neutralize nightshade nullify therapy toxin insecticide dilate disease drug offset organophosphate effect extract eye /dit tod/]
*antipathy 13-63-10 (n.) 1. a feeling of intense dislike 2. the object of a feeling of intense aversion; something to be avoided [allergy anger antagonism anti aversion avoid avoidance nausea negative noncooperation toward ill inconsistency indisposition intense interference perfunctory perversity phobia hate hatred horror hostility /pit/] "cats were his greatest antipathy"
*antipodes 23-81-1 (n.) 1. any two places or regions on diametrically opposite sides of the Earth [antipode antithesis antonym nowhere indefinite inverse perspective place pole offset opposite outskirt diametrical earth setoff side surface /pit/] "the North Pole and the South Pole are antipodes"
*antiquary 21-91-2 (n.) 1. an expert or collector of antiquities [anti interested]
*antiquate 13-41-11 (v.) 1. make obsolete or old-fashioned 2. give an antique appearance to [abandon ago alter ancient anti appearance tenement transform idea irrecoverable quaint update early elapse expire extinct extremely]
*antique 04-41-94 (a.) 1. out of fashion 2. made in or typical of earlier times and valued for its age 3. belonging to or lasting from times long ago (n.) 1. an elderly man 2. any piece of furniture or decorative object or the like produced in a former period and valuable because of its beauty or rarity (v.) 1. shop for antiques 2. give an antique appearance to [abandon accord age ago alter ancient anti appearance art artifact attire necessarily neolith timeworn tough tradition traditionalism transform treat idea immemorial immutable interest inveterate item quality unfashionable early elderly enduring expire] "the beautiful antique French furniture"
*antiseptic 17-54-5 (a.) 1. clean and honest 2. thoroughly clean and free of or destructive to disease-causing organisms 3. (extended sense) of exceptionally clean language 4. freeing from error or corruption 5. made free from live bacteria or other microorganisms (n.) 1. a substance that destroys micro-organisms that carry disease without harming body tissues [agent alcohol alleviate antibiotic aseptic nitrogen noxious tame thimerosal thymol tissue toxin treat infection instrument intestinal iodine sanitary septic sterilize surgical symptom pathogenic penetrating peroxide pesticide poison powder practice prevent calomel camphor chlorine cleanse colorless compound corruption cresol /pes/] "doctors in antiseptic green coats"
*antithetical 19-21-3 (a.) 1. sharply contrasted in character or purpose [already nature early entirely exact express character complete constitute contrast country] "practices entirely antithetical to her professed beliefs"
*anxious 04-65-111 (a.) 1. (colloquial) eagerly desirous

2. mentally upset over possible misfortune or danger etc; worried 3. causing or fraught with or showing anxiety [affliction afford afraid agitation alarm animate annoy apprehensive avid nauseous nervous night imitate impatient impetuous indicative interest intolerant irk itch uneasy unhappy unquiet untroubled upset urgent sad scary security seek show solicitous speak spirited] "anxious parents"
*apartheid 08-42-32 (n.) 1. the former official policy of racial segregation in South Africa [africa alien apart parochialism people political privilege race racial racism retirement retreat tight early economic ethnocentrism exclusion exclusive insulation isolation isolationism issue deal detachment different discrimination division /die trap/]
*apathy 12-62-13 (n.) 1. an absence of emotion or enthusiasm 2. the trait of lacking enthusiasm for or interest in things generally [absence abstraction affective alienate aloof passive passivity path phlegm pococurante preoccupation tic torpor trait twitch heartless heavy hopeless human /tapa/]
*aperture 19-36-3 (n.) 1. a device that controls amount of light admitted 2. an opening in something 3. an opening; usually small [access adjust admit alley amount avenue part pass pert photograph piece player pollen pore pressure prick puncture embouchure enter epidermis equipment exit eye eyehole regulate rupture temperature tube tunnel uncork underpass unobstructed unstop]
*apex 14-57-8 (n.) 1. the highest point (of something) 2. the point on the celestial sphere toward which the sun and solar system appear to be moving relative to the fixed stars [achievement acme angle ape apparent appear attainment part peak pitch point prime pyramid edge elbow elevation empyrean]
*aphorism 17-43-5 (n.) 1. a short pithy instructive saying [abridgment accept adage ana apophthegm apothegm axiom phrase pithy place pleasantry precept opinion oracle oris retort riposte rule instructive sally say see short statement succinct maxim merit moral motto music]
*aplomb 13-64-11 (n.) 1. great coolness and composure under strain [assured perpendicular poise possession orthogonal mind /mol/]
*apocalyptic 11-56-15 (a.) 1. prophetic of devastation or ultimate doom 2. of or relating to an apocalypse [apostolic augur portentous predict prefigure prophetic ominous oracular outcome cal calamity canonical catastrophe lower talkative textuary threatening tragedy ill inauspicious inspired intervention /cop/]
*apogee 19-63-3 (n.) 1. a final climactic stage 2. apoapsis in Earth orbit; the point in its orbit where a satellite is at the greatest distance from the Earth [achievement acme all apex astronomical peak period phase pitch point ogee orbit great earth edge end extremity /ego/]
*apology 05-63-65 (n.) 1. an expression of regret at having caused trouble for someone 2. a formal written defense of something you believe in strongly 3. a poor example [acknowledgment admission automobile pathetic penance poor pretense pretext protestation office ology letter litigation logomachy gloss grief guise] "he wrote a letter of apology to the hostess"
*apostasy 23-56-1 (n.) 1. the state of having rejected your religious beliefs or your political party or a cause (often in favor of opposing beliefs or causes) 2. the act of abandoning a party or cause [abandon accommodation adaptation adjustment allegiance party perfidy political post oppose opposition overthrow schism shift smash success switch tergiversate traitor transition treachery treason triumph turncoat /sat/]
*apostate 21-59-2 (a.) 1. not faithful to religion or party or cause (n.) 1. a disloyal person who betrays or deserts his cause or religion or political party or friend etc. [allegiance atheistic party political profane promise proselyte protest object obligation sacrilege secessionist separatist state tergiversate traitorous treasonable true turncoat easily]
*apostle 14-43-9 (n.) 1. an ardent early supporter of a cause or reform 2. (New Testament) one of the original 12 disciples chosen by Christ to preach his gospel 3. any important early teacher of Christianity or a Christian missionary to a people [adherent patriarch post priest propagandist saint teacher elder epistle evangelist] "an apostle of revolution"
*apothecary 21-66-2 (n.) 1. a health professional trained in the art of preparing and dispensing drugs [art pharmacology pharmacy pill prepare prevent professional provider pusher occupation theca train treat haberdashery health help effect caregiver chemist commerce composition confectionery roller /ace race top/]
*apotheosis 17-55-5 (n.) 1. model of excellence or perfection of a kind; one having no equal 2. the elevation of a person (as to the status of a god) [admiration approval assumption paragon peak perfection point pot power praise prestige transform translation tribute height high homage honor human elevation equal escalate esteem exaltation excellent saint sanctify show status stylish summit suppose ideal idolize imitation immortalize importance impressive /top/]
*apparel 06-05-53 (n.) 1. covering designed to be worn on a person's body (v.) 1. provide with clothes or put clothes on [appoint array article attire pare position prim protection provide rag raiment robe ecclesiastical element equipment excessive linen]
*apparent 03-50-197 (a.) 1. readily apparent to the eye 2. appearing as such but not necessarily so 3. clearly apparent or obvious to the mind or senses [account advantage affecting airy allow appear attribute autistic parch parent patent pay penetrating perceptible perhap

physics plain pottery profound prominent public reactionary ready reason reasonable recognize rent reveal easy effect emotional evident explicit express eye naked necessarily neglect noticeable tangible theory tinsel truth] "the effects of the drought are apparent to anyone who sees the parched fields"
*apparition 17-46-5 (n.) 1. a ghostly appearing figure 2. an act of appearing or becoming visible unexpectedly 3. the appearance of a ghostlike figure 4. something existing in perception only [amaze appear arise audible avatar perception phantom phenomenon presentation public realize recall rise imagine incorporeal invention ion issue theophany trip occurrence opening origin nature near] "we were unprepared for the apparition that confronted us"
*appease 10-61-20 (v.) 1. make peace with 2. overcome or allay 3. cause to be more favorably inclined; gain the good will of [abate aggressive allay alleviate angry assuage attenuate pacify pad pamper patch peace physical placate propitiate ease extenuate satisfy say settle soothe stay steady still]
*appellate 10-06-20 (a.) 1. of or relating to or taking account of appeals (usually legal appeals) [account authority proceeding ella empower law legal lower /tall/] "appellate court"
*appellation 17-43-5 (n.) 1. identifying word or words by which someone or something is called and classified or distinguished from others [alternative appellative ella epithet eponym label language tag term title identify inner name namesake neighborhood nickname nobility /tall/]
*append 18-42-4 (v.) 1. add to the very end 2. state or say further 3. fix to; attach [add affix agreement annex attached authorize part pend plus postfix prefix principal process encumber end express extra necklace novel decorate document] "He appended a glossary to his novel where he used an invented language"
*apposite 18-90-4 (a.) 1. being of striking appropriateness and pertinence [adapt apply appropriate apropos apt pat pertinent posit opportune seasonable sort striking successful suit suiting image involve tailored timely evocative] "the successful copywriter is a master of apposite and evocative verbal images"
*appraise 12-21-13 (v.) 1. place a value on; judge the worth of something 2. consider in a comprehensive way [accord agree analyze appreciate assess audit pace pass performance political praise price prize professional rank rate reassess reckon reevaluate religious renew revise identify inspect score set situation sound standard step study survey employee estimate evaluate evaluation examine express] "I will have the family jewels appraised by a professional"
*appreciable 14-47-8 (a.) 1. enough to be estimated or measured [able amount apparent ascertain assess palpable partly perceptible plain ponderable purely real recognize relatively enough estimate evident extent clear compute concrete considerable important incomplete leastwise] "appreciable amounts of noxious wastes are dumped into the harbor"
*apprehend 13-39-10 (v.) 1. take into custody, as of suspected criminals, by the police 2. get the meaning of something 3. anticipate with dread or anxiety [accept anticipate anxious appreciate arrange arrest aware perceive pick picture pinch police possess pretend read realize recognize end excited experience hear hold nab nail nature net detain difficulty dig digest dread /her/]
*apprehensive 13-51-11 (a.) 1. quick to understand 2. mentally upset over possible misfortune or danger etc; worried 3. in fear or dread of possible evil or harm [afford afraid alive angst anxious aware panic parent perceptive perspicacious perturb possible reassure ride ease easy edgy evil excitable happen harm hawthorne hen hesitant nathaniel nervous nervy non security sensible shrewd strained implication insightful intelligent irritable /her/] "a kind and apprehensive friend"
*apprise 21-16-2 (v.) 1. give information or notice to 2. increase the value of, as of a currency 3. gain in value, as of a currency 4. make aware of [acquaint advise affair amount anew announce aware point post prise proclaim publish rent report revalue reveal impart increase inform instruct send speak student enlighten essential]
*approbation 21-60-2 (n.) 1. official approval 2. official recognition or approval [acclamation account admiration admiring agreement approval authorize permission pleasure praise pro probation prompt raving ready recognition regard respect official okay opinion benediction blessing idolize imprimatur nod notarize /tab tabor/]
*appropriate 02-49-270 (a.) 1. suitable and fitting 2. meant or adapted for an occasion or use 3. appropriate for achieving a particular end; implies a lack of concern for fairness 4. suitable for a particular person or place or condition etc 5. being of striking appropriateness and pertinence (v.) 1. take possession of without permission or take with force, as after a conquest or invasion 2. give or assign a share of money or time to a particular person or cause [adapt adopt advantage aid allow and applicable apply apposite appro apt arrogate aside assistance pat portion practical press propriety raid recommend relevant reserve right occupy ordain order overrun inspired invade involve earmark eligible employ entitle expediency] "a book not appropriate for children"
*apropos 19-47-3 (a.) 1. of an appropriate or pertinent nature (ad.) 1. by the way 2. at an opportune time [about against apply apposite appropriate apt arrive pat pertinent place preposition prop proper regarding relevant right opportune seasonable seemly situation sort specific suitable suiting] "apropos, can you lend me some money for the weekend?"

*apt 06-44-47 (a.) 1. at risk of or subject to experiencing something usually unpleasant 2. being of striking appropriateness and pertinence 3. mentally quick and resourceful 4. (usually followed by 'to') naturally disposed toward [alert angry answer apposite appropriate apropos artistic pertinent plastic preference prompt proper propriety pupil talented teachable telling tend toward turn] "he is apt to lose"
*aqueduct 12-10-12 (n.) 1. a conduit that resembles a bridge but carries water over a valley [across anatomy arch arroyo electric entrench dike distance ditch duct canal carry channel conduit construction course culvert curve cut tailrace trench trough tunnel]
*arabesque 18-28-4 (n.) 1. position in which the dancer has one leg raised behind and arms outstretched in a conventional pose 2. an ornament that interlaces simulated foliage in an intricate design [acciaccatura animal appoggiatura arab arm raise rich riddle run ballet basketwork beautify behind body elaborate elegance embellish screening shape sieve simulate solo stand stretch symmetrical /bar/]
*arbiter 13-47-11 (n.) 1. someone with the power to settle matters at will 2. someone chosen to judge and decide a disputed issue [amateur arbitrator authority referee role bencher biter indicator influential intermediate issue think transaction trendsetter epicurean expert /bra/] "she was the final arbiter on all matters of fashion"
*arbitrary 08-36-30 (a.) 1. based on or subject to individual discretion or preference or sometimes impulse or caprice [absolute accord accountable arb aristocratic arrest arrogant authoritarian authoritative random rash reason repressive responsibility rule base bossy illogical impulsive inconsistent independent irrational irresponsible temperamental thoughtless trait tyranny /bra/] "an arbitrary decision"
*arbitrate 21-38-2 (v.) 1. act between parties with a view to reconciling differences [adjudicate appease arrange ask assess rate reconcile referee represent bargain intermediate intervene talk third try /bra tart/]
*arbor 12-05-13 (n.) 1. tree (as opposed to shrub) 2. a framework that supports climbing plants 3. any of various rotating shafts that serve as axes for larger rotating parts [alcove angiosperm arb axis radiant read rest retreat revolving rod rotate rowlock belvedere bower branch oarlock oppose /bra rob/] "the arbor provided a shady resting place in the park"
*arboreal 23-60-1 (a.) 1. of or relating to or formed by trees 2. resembling a tree in form and branching structure 3. inhabiting or frequenting trees [ape ramous roof bifurcate boreal branch bushy evergreen ligneous live /aero bra rob/]
*arboretum 16-33-6 (n.) 1. a facility where trees and shrubs are cultivated for exhibition [afforest arbor area rainforest reforest bed boondocks border botanical building exhibition timberland tree /bra mut mute rob/]
*arcade 10-48-19 (n.) 1. a covered passageway; often between streets with shops or stalls 2. a structure composed of a series of arches supported by columns [access alley amusement arca arch area avenue roof room cade channel cloister colonnade column computer connection construction cover curve defile device dome enclose entertainment entity exit]
*archaeology 08-67-27 (n.) 1. the branch of anthropology that studies prehistoric people and their cultures [evidence ology]
*archaic 12-48-12 (a.) 1. so extremely old as seeming to belong to an earlier period 2. little evolved from or characteristic of an earlier ancestral type [abandon ancestral ancient antediluvian antiquated antique arch ramshackle relinquish resigned retired classical cousin idea]
*archangel 19-50-3 (n.) 1. an angel ranked above the highest rank in the Celestial Hierarchy 2. a biennial cultivated herb; its stems are candied and eaten and its roots are used medicinally [angel attendant rank root candy celestial change cherub chief compound cultivate hebrew herb hierarchy high nine gabriel garden genus god green guardian eat leaf /leg/]
*archbishop 06-67-50 (n.) 1. a bishop of highest rank [abuna anselm antipope archpriest rector canon cardinal chaplain curate hierarch becket bishop suffragan patriarch pope prelate primate]
*archdeacon 19-88-3 (n.) 1. (Anglican Church) an ecclesiastical dignitary usually ranking just below a bishop [administrative anglican assist ranking reverend canterbury ceremonial christian church cloth communion country deacon dignitary ecclesiastical england national]
*archetype 09-58-22 (n.) 1. an original model on which something is patterned [antitype arch art recur refined repeat representative ripen rule cast characteristic classic classical collective consummate criterion cut habitual epitome example exemplary expert turn paragon pattern perfect period polished precedent predictable prototype psychology]
*archipelago 13-60-10 (n.) 1. a group of many islands in a large body of water [ait archi atoll reef cay holm indie insular islet /epi gal gale/]
*ardent 08-37-28 (a.) 1. characterized by intense emotion 2. glowing or shining like fire 3. characterized by strong enthusiasm [abandon admire affair alexander amount and anxious appeal arden ready reflect relentless resolute responsive revolutionary dart dedicated deep dent desire devoted disposed drunk dull eager ember emit emotion enthusiastic excitement exciting express extreme eye tireless toast torrid] "ardent love"
*ardor 18-01-4 (n.) 1. a feeling of strong eagerness (usually in favor of a person or cause) 2. intense feeling of love 3. feelings of great warmth and intensity [accomplish activity affection ahead anger application attempt avid ready regard religious resolution

revolutionary dampen dedication desire devotion dor drive /rod/] "they were imbued with a revolutionary ardor"
*arduous 11-49-16 (a.) 1. characterized by toilsome effort to the point of exhaustion; especially physical effort 2. difficult to accomplish; demanding considerable mental effort and skill 3. taxing to the utmost; testing powers of endurance [abrupt abstruse accomplish remain require rigorous rough rugged day delicate demanding dictionary difficult duo uphill utmost onerous operose oppressive overcome severe sheer six skill speed steep strain strenuous /oud/] "worked their arduous way up the mining valley"
*argot 21-43-2 (n.) 1. a characteristic language of a particular group (as among thieves) [applesauce arg rubbish garble gibberish gobbledygook talk tommyrot tripe trumpery twaddle /tog/]
*arid 13-49-11 (a.) 1. lacking sufficient water or rainfall 2. lacking vitality or spirit; lifeless [academic anhydrous animation annual athirst rainfall region rid romance impotent infertile interest issue dead deplete describe desert desiccate dry dull] "an arid climate"
*aristocracy 13-65-11 (n.) 1. the most powerful members of a society 2. a privileged class holding hereditary titles [ancestry archiepiscopate aristo autonomy rank realm republic royalty run intellectual isabella second sheriff society spain status superior suzerain temporal theocracy title triumvirate tyranny occupy ochlocracy oligarchy overlap chancellor consider country county cream crust /arco cot/]
*aristocrat 10-64-19 (n.) 1. a member of the aristocracy [address archduke aristo rajah royal rule indiana inspire seignior social son sovereign squire superior support swell thoroughbred title old class country cultural /arco cot/]
*armada 16-62-6 (n.) 1. a large fleet [ada argosy army marine division /dam/]
*armful 23-61-1 (n.) 1. the quantity that can be contained in the arms [arm]
*armory 14-02-9 (n.) 1. a collection of resources 2. a place where arms are manufactured 3. a military structure where arms and ammunition and other military equipment are stored and training is given in the use of arms 4. all the weapons and equipment that a country has [achievement answer arm armor array arsenal available range resource rick ring rose machine magazine manufacture medal metal metalwork military missile munition opponent ordinary ordnance orle yard] "he dipped into his intellectual armory to find an answer"
*aroma 10-41-17 (n.) 1. any property detected by the olfactory system 2. a distinctive odor that is pleasant [atmosphere attribute aura rank receptor redolent reek roma odor olfactory mannerism marking member mold /amora mora/]
*arraign 10-06-20 (v.) 1. accuse of a wrong or an inadequacy 2. call before a court to answer an indictment [accuse allege anathema answer article report reprobation impeach imply inadequate incriminate indictment information]
*arrange 02-47-244 (v.) 1. arrange attractively 2. set into a specific format; of printed matter 3. plan, organize, and carry out (an event) 4. make arrangements for 5. put into a proper or systematic order 6. adapt for performance in a different way 7. arrange thoughts, ideas, temporal events, etc. [abstract accord adapt adjust agreement align alphabetize appearance array artistic assemble attractive auditory range rank rate regulate represent right ring rubric nature neaten necessary next normalize give grade groom group engaged essence external] "arrange the books on the shelves in chronological order"
*arrangement 03-50-228 (n.) 1. a piece of music that has been adapted for performance by a particular set of voices or instruments 2. the spatial property of the way in which something is placed 3. an orderly grouping (of things or persons) considered as a unit; the result of arranging 4. an organized structure for arranging or classifying 5. the thing arranged or agreed to 6. the act of arranging a piece of music [accord agreement approach arrange assembly attack range ready regularity nocturne notation game grade grouping guideline enterprise equipment exercise manufacture marshal model tactics technique term] "they made arrangements to meet in Chicago"
*arrival 03-66-211 (n.) 1. someone who arrives (or has arrived) 2. the act of arriving at a certain place 3. accomplishment of an objective [accomplishment achieve advent aircraft airport anchor appear appearance approach await recent report return rival rope immigrant important influx ingress intruder issue vehicle vessel view visitor voyage landing late location] "they awaited her arrival"
*arrogance 07-65-36 (n.) 1. overbearing pride evidenced by a superior manner toward inferiors [overconfident conceit condescension consider egotism evidence /ago nag orra/]
*arrogant 05-63-73 (a.) 1. having or showing feelings of unwarranted importance out of overbearing pride [affected air ant artificial assured audacity reason reassure repressive ridicule obtrusive official oppressive overconfident overweening gall grinding nerve toplofty tyranny /ago nag orra/] "an arrogant official"
*artful 09-42-23 (a.) 1. not straightforward or candid; giving a false appearance of frankness 2. marked by skill in achieving a desired end especially with cunning or craft [ability achieve acute address adept adroit ambitious appearance arch arrange art artless astute ready resourceful tactical taste technique time trait treacherous tricky twist facility false foxy frank fraudulent furtive underhanded unnatural untruthful lack]

*arthurian 19-81-3 (a.) 1. of or relating to King Arthur and the Knights of the Round Table [round table]
*articulate 06-49-55 (a.) 1. expressing yourself easily or characterized by clear expressive language 2. consisting of segments held together by joints (v.) 1. put into words or an expression 2. speak, pronounce, or utter in a certain way 3. provide with a joint, as of two pieces of wood 4. express or state clearly [adjust assemble associate raise regulate relate render talk tell tie trustee impart include intelligible chain child communicate concern couple cover understandable unite utter labialize language late league link lock easily embrace encompass enunciate expressive] "articulate speech"
*artifice 14-41-8 (n.) 1. a deceptive maneuver (especially to avoid capture) [action answer art artful avoid racket ready rig tactical trick tricky trump improvise insincere intrigue inventive false feint fetch fice capture catch clever coup craft cunning effort engineering expedient /fit/]
*artless 19-58-3 (a.) 1. characterized by an inability to mask your feelings; not devious 2. showing lack of art 3. simple and natural; without cunning or deceit 4. (of persons) lacking art or knowledge [aboveboard accordance achieve admission adroit advantage art artful arty authenticity awkward real refined relaxed require responsibility round thoughtless totally translation transparent trusting lack legitimate less literal elegance experience explicit show simplicity sincere sincerity skill sophistication special straightforward]
*ascend 12-44-12 (v.) 1. travel up, "We ascended the mountain" 2. become king or queen 3. go along towards (a river's) source 4. go back in order of genealogical succession 5. slope upwards 6. come up, of celestial bodies [accede advance angle arise aspire scale scend see shift slope slow soar sound source stairway status steep study succession sun surface surge career celestial certain circle climb climber come course crest early ebb end enter escalate necessarily night date death decline dip downward drop dusk duty] "We ascended the mountain"
*ascendant 18-58-4 (a.) 1. tending or directed upward 2. most powerful or important or influential (n.) 1. position or state of being dominant or in control 2. someone from whom you are descended (but usually more remote that a grandparent) [above absolute ahead ancestor antecedent ascend astrology senior sign sire specific strength successful superior supreme chief chosen class climb consider control east eclipse ecliptic economically empower excel exercise exist defeat descend direct distinguished domination dominion tend topping transcend triumphant] "rooted and ascendant strength like that of foliage"
*ascending 16-46-6 (a.) 1. moving or going or growing upward (n.) 1. the act of changing location in an upward direction [aerial airy ascend aspire sink soar steep climb colossal elevated eminent ethereal dominate downward drift gyrate] "the ascending plane"
*ascension 16-34-6 (n.) 1. (Christianity) celebration of the Ascension of Christ into heaven; observed on the 40th day after Easter 2. (astronomy) the rising of a star above the horizon 3. (New Testament) the rising of the body of Jesus into heaven on the 40th day after his resurrection 4. the act of changing location in an upward direction 5. a movement upward [airborne apostle apotheosis ascent assumption soar spring surge clamber climb effort elevation epistle escalade increase ion]
*ascent 10-59-20 (n.) 1. an upward slope or grade (as in a road) 2. the act of changing location in an upward direction 3. a movement upward [acclivity addition airborne airplane altitude amendment angle assumption scale scent set side slope space spiritualism spread successful surge car career change cheer climb course current effort elevation enhance expansion extension temperature tender travel trend tumescent]
*ascertain 12-61-13 (v.) 1. be careful or certain to do something; make certain of something 2. after a calculation, investigation, experiment, survey, or study 3. learn or discover with certainty 4. find out, learn, or determine with certainty, usually by making an inquiry or other effort [actual appraise ask assured attest see set settle show site study survey calculation capacity certain certainty certify clinch conceive confirmed consider contemplate effectual ensure establish experiment realize reassure recognize resolve test truthful try tumble inquire inspect insure investigation numerate]
*ascetic 17-52-5 (a.) 1. pertaining to or characteristic of an ascetic 2. practicing great self-denial (n.) 1. practices self denial as spiritual discipline [abbot abstinence adhere apologetic austerity school self sensual severe slight small spartan spiritual strict candid choose christian comfort commonplace consumption continent early eremite exiguous existence expiate thin tic top train impoverish invalid isolationist /cite tec/] "ascetic practices"
*ascribe 12-48-13 (v.) 1. make undue claims to having 2. attribute or credit to [advance alleged anthropomorphize apply arrogate assign attribute author saddle say scribe sensualist surmise canalize cat chalk charge cite claim clever contentment credit refer repute responsibility impute incorporate internalize believe belong blame error explicable externalize]
*asexual 21-57-2 (a.) 1. not having or involving sex [androgynous apparent sex sexless sexual somatic spore lack link /aux/] "an asexual spore"
*ashen 19-61-3 (a.) 1. ash-colored or anemic looking from illness or emotion 2. made of wood of the ash tree [aghast anemic appal appearance ash ashe ashy awed woody sad shelley shock slaty speak stun haggard hen horrify hue emotion etiolated extremely neutral non] "a face turned ashen"
*askance 19-48-3 (a.) 1. (used especially of glances) directed to one side with or as if with doubt or suspicion

or envy (ad.) 1. with suspicion or disapproval 2. with a side or oblique glance [aside ask askew awry side sidle skeptical spatial squint straight suspicious course critical crook cynical edgewise elizabeth envy eye] "he looked askance at the offer"
*aspersion 21-55-2 (n.) 1. a disparaging remark 2. an abusive attack on a person's character or good name 3. the act of sprinkling water in baptism (rare) [abusive accusation allegation asper atrocity attack sacrament say scandal signify slam slander slight slur smear spiritual sprinkling statement strong suggestion pax pester pick prig enormity ethnic exception race rap rebirth reflection remark reputation incense injury insult integrity obloquy offense outrage nagging niggling ninny nit]
*aspirant 14-42-8 (a.) 1. seeking advancement or recognition 2. desiring or striving for recognition or advancement (n.) 1. an ambitious and aspiring young person [achievement addict admission advance ambitious apply aspire assistance attain audience seek solicitor spirant striving strong success suitor perfectionist petition postulant inspire iran recognition request /rip/] "a lofty aspirant"
*aspiration 06-62-56 (n.) 1. a will to succeed 2. a cherished desire 3. a manner of articulation involving an audible release of breath 4. the act of inhaling; the drawing in of air (or other gases) as in breathing [aim ambitious assimilation score security stop plan point project pull ideal inspiration intention ration reason reliance resolve respiration target objective occlusive nasal /rip/]
*aspire 05-56-67 (v.) 1. have an ambitious plan or a lofty goal [aerial aim ambitious assured attain seek shoot soar spire steep sublime plan project prominent propose public purpose intention resolve expect /rip/]
*assail 08-15-27 (v.) 1. attack someone physically or emotionally 2. launch an attack or assault on; begin hostilities with, as in warfare 3. attack verbally, in speech or writing [aggressive ambush apart artillery assai assault attack sacred sail search set shout side slash snipe speech start storm strategic strike strong struggle sudden surprise surround implicate incriminate indecent initiative involve language lash launch lean left lie low lying /ass lias/]
*assailant 10-36-18 (n.) 1. someone who attacks [accost adversary aggressor ambush assail attack savage search secret sexual shedder slash south spill stab stone injury intercourse intimidate invade launch law nightrider tough transgresse /alias ass lias/]
*assassin 09-59-23 (n.) 1. a murderer (especially one who kills a prominent political figure) who kills by a treacherous surprise attack and often is hired to do the deed [actor alarmist animal apache attack sass science secret slaughter slay strangle study surprise /ass sass/] "his assassins were hunted down like animals"
*assassinate 08-45-31 (v.) 1. murder; esp. of socially prominent persons 2. destroy or damage seriously, as of someone's reputation [asperse assassin attack seriously shoot slander slay smear smirch snuff social sudden sully intentional treacherous eliminate enemy /ass sass/] "Anwar Sadat was assassinated because many people did not like his peace politics with Israel"
*assassination 05-37-69 (n.) 1. an attack intended to ruin someone's reputation 2. murder of a public figure by surprise attack [assassin attack attempt shoot slay sudden surprise intend tradesman treacherous obloquy /ass sass/]
*assay 21-29-2 (n.) 1. an appraisal of the state of affairs (v.) 1. analyze (chemical substances) 2. make an effort or attempt [adventure affair agent agree amount analyze antigen appraisal approach ass assess assessment attempt sample say score scrutinize search seek ser shake shot show space specific standard step stop stress strive study substance /ass/] "they made an assay of the contents"
*assent 15-52-7 (n.) 1. agreement with a statement or proposal to do something (v.) 1. to agree or express agreement [acceptance accepting acclaim acquiesce affirm agreement applaud approval approve sanction sent signify statement submit subservient succumb supine eager encourage endorse equivalence expression never nod tally time tory /ness/] "he gave his assent eagerly"
*assess 03-57-156 (v.) 1. place a value on; judge the worth of something 2. charge (a person or a property) with a payment, such as a tax or a fine 3. estimate the value of (property) for taxation 4. set or determine the amount of (a payment such as a fine) [accord account adjuster amount appreciate approximate ask assign authoritative score sess set sound standardize step survey enough establish estimate evaluate evaluation exact examine express /sess/]
*assessor 15-56-7 (n.) 1. an official who evaluates property for the purpose of taxing it [amount appraise assay assess assistant specialize surveyor estimate evaluate exciseman expertise oceanography official ombudsman ordinary recorder revenuer /sess/]

*assiduous 13-59-11 (a.) 1. marked by care and persistent effort [alert ardent ass attentive aware sedulous show stable steady stubborn indefatigable industrious insistent invincible diligent dogged undaunted unflinching uninterrupted observe obstinate operose /diss oud/] "her assiduous attempts to learn French"
*assimilate 12-43-12 (v.) 1. make similar 2. become similar to one's environment 3. take up, as of knowledge or beliefs 4. become similar in sound; in phonetics 5. take into solution, as of gas, light, or heat [absorb accord add admit adopt amalgamate articulate sense set shape stop stress strong impoverish include incorporated indoctrinate ingest integrate master match meet merge mid mixed late learn leaven level light liquid low tense

thick transform eat eclectic embrace even /miss missa tali/] "Immigrants often want to assimilate quickly"
*assuage 13-54-11 (v.) 1. cause to be more favorably inclined; gain the good will of 2. satisfy (thirst) 3. provide physical relief, as from pain [abate age allay alleviate alter ameliorate amend anesthetic angry satisfy season slake soften soothe still subdue underplay gain gentle good gratify ease emollient extenuate /gauss/]
*asterisk 14-16-9 (n.) 1. a star-shaped character * used in printing (v.) 1. mark with an asterisk [aster attention sentence sign sound speech star structure symbol exist reference represent item /sire/]
*astringent 18-39-4 (a.) 1. sour or bitter in taste 2. tending to draw together or constrict soft organic tissue (n.) 1. a drug that causes contraction of body tissues and canals [acerbic acidic acrimony alleviate aluminum austerity authoritarian severe sharp soft sour speak stern stringent styptic substance sulphate sweet symptom tart taste teeth tend tone toughness treat trenchant reduction rigorous roughness rugged incisive inclement irritate isthmus neck grim grip edge exacting exigent] "astringent cosmetic lotions"
*astute 08-67-28 (a.) 1. marked by practical hardheaded intelligence [acute alert arch sharp show shrewd smart smooth strategic stu tactical tenant trenchant tricky understanding]
*asylum 06-69-55 (n.) 1. a shelter from danger or hardship 2. a hospital for mentally incompetent or unbalanced person [almshouse attack safety sanatorium sanctuary security shelter snake structure lair loony lum unbalance madhouse member mental]
*atheism 18-61-4 (n.) 1. the doctrine or belief that there is no God 2. a lack of belief in the existence of God or gods [agnosticism apostasy attitude theism toward heresy humanism existence incredulity infidelity irreverent secularism skepticism misbelief]
*atone 14-68-8 (v.) 1. make amends for 2. turn away from sin or do penitence [abbey accord amend answer apologize appease tone turn expiate]
*atonement 18-59-4 (n.) 1. compensation for a wrong 2. the act of atoning for sin or wrongdoing (especially appeasing a deity) [amend amends apology appease atone offset expiation meed mistake money /meno/]
*atrocious 14-70-8 (a.) 1. shockingly brutal or cruel 2. exceptionally bad or displeasing 3. provoking horror [abominable accident acute alarming animal appalling appearance arrant awful awfully terrible terribly torment tragic truculent rack rank roc ruthless obnoxious obscene odor offense outrageous commit contemptible crime criminal cruel cry illegal improper incorrect infamous inhuman uncivilized unclean undesirable undue unspeakable savage shabby sharp shock shoot sweep] "murder is an atrocious crime"
*atrocity 07-60-35 (n.) 1. the quality of being shockingly cruel and inhumane 2. an act of atrocious cruelty [abuse acute awful taunt terrorism treatment trip repellent rigor roughness offense omission outrage city compassion consideration corruption crime cruelty cut ill infection inflict intensity]
*attache 17-09-5 (n.) 1. a specialist assigned to the staff of a diplomatic mission 2. a shallow and rectangular briefcase [adept ambassador artist assign attach authority technician carry case chancellor charge civil consultant cultural handle handyman emissary envoy expert /cat/]
*attenuate 19-27-3 (a.) 1. reduced in strength (v.) 1. weaken the consistency of (a chemical substance) 2. become weaker, in strength, value, or magnitude [abate adulterate airy alleviate amount amplitude assuage tabetic tail temper tenuous thinner thread tone twiggy ease eat effect elongate emaciate emission erode ethereal exhaust expand expose narrow natural undernourished unman unnerve unsubstantial /nett/]
*attest 10-36-20 (v.) 1. authenticate, affirm to be true, genuine, or correct, as in an official capacity 2. provide evidence for; stand as proof of; show by one's behavior, attitude, or external attributes 3. establish or verify the usage of 4. give testimony in a court of law [actual admission affirm alleged announce approve architectural argue assert assurance attitude attribute authority aver avow tell test testimony ticket trueful try effectual emphatic ensure enunciate establish evidence exist express external secure set settle show signature solemn sophistication stand statement strengthen substantiate suggest support swan swear /set/] "His high fever attested to his illness"
*attune 13-37-11 (v.) 1. adjust or accustom to; bring into harmony with [acclimatize accommodate accord accustom achieve adapt adjust agree akin alter tailor together tune understanding united empathetic enable equalize equip /nut/]
*auburn 11-17-15 (a.) 1. (of hair) "auburn hair" [uncolored bay brazen bronze brown burn red redhead roan russet rusty /rub/] "auburn hair"
*auctioneer 10-74-18 (n.) 1. an agent who conducts an auction (v.) 1. sell at an auction [agent auction charge commodity conduct transaction objective equivalent exchange]
*audacious 09-70-21 (a.) 1. invulnerable to fear or intimidation 2. unrestrained by convention or propriety 3. disposed to venture or take risks [adventurous arrogant undaunted uninhibited unrestrained daring dauntless defiant defy cold confident cool independent insulting intrepid obtrusive overweening saucy selfish shameless /cad/] "audacious explorers"
*audible 10-54-17 (a.) 1. heard or perceptible by the ear [acoustic articulate aural unbearable definite distinct distinctive imperceptible impossible intensity line loud ear enough /bid/] "he spoke in an audible whisper"
*audition 07-51-41 (n.) 1. the ability to hear; the auditory faculty 2. a test of the suitability of a performer (v.) 1. perform in order to get a role [absolute actor

actress apply art attention audience audit auscultate identify impaired interview testing tone trial try tryout originate outperform outside] "She auditioned for a role on Broadway"
*auditory 21-44-2 (a.) 1. of or relating to the process of hearing [acoustic auditor aural organ /roti/] "auditory processing"
*augment 10-39-20 (v.) 1. grow or intensify 2. enlarge or increase [add aggravate amplify annoy aug upsurge gain grammar great grow magnify major mount multiply musical enhance enlarge expand extend tension thicken] "The recent speech of the PLO chairman augmented tensions in the Near East"
*augur 15-67-7 (n.) 1. (in ancient Rome) a religious official who interpreted omens to guide public policy (v.) 1. indicate by signs 2. predict from an omen [adumbrate advance age ancient anticipate argue astrology aug auspicate authoritative geomancy guide religious republic ring roman rome /rug/]
*augury 23-57-1 (n.) 1. an event that is experienced as indicating important things to come [anticipation apprehend art astrology augur auspice /rug/] "he hoped it was an augury"
*august 02-60-497 (a.) 1. of or befitting a lord 2. profoundly honored (n.) 1. the month following July and preceding September [adopt aggregation american aristocracy aristocratic assumption autumnal awesome awful general glorious grand grandiose grave great gregory gust season september show soar solar solemn solstice splendor stately striking style summertime superb suppress towering]
*aura 08-43-32 (n.) 1. a sensation (as of a cold breeze or bright light) that precedes the onset of certain disorders such as a migraine attack or epileptic seizure 2. a distinctive but intangible quality surrounding a person or thing 3. an indication of radiant light drawn around the head of a saint [air appearance aspect atmosphere attack attribute aureole undertone unusual radiant rainbow ring romance]
*aural 14-50-8 (a.) 1. of or pertaining to hearing or the ear 2. relating to or characterized by an aura [acoustic animal apparatus atmosphere auditory aura receptor response] "an animal with a very sensitive aural apparatus"
*aurora 13-43-10 (n.) 1. the first light of day 2. an atmospheric phenomenon consisting of bands of light caused by charged solar particles following the earth's magnetic lines of force 3. goddess of the dawn; counterpart of Greek Eos [alpenglow ancient arch atmospheric australia until roman]
*auspice 11-35-15 (n.) 1. a favorable omen [administration aegis ancient approval augury authority umbrella second sign spice sponsor support pastor patronage policy portent prediction presage prodigy prognosticate promising protector public indication influence interpret care championship city control council encouragement endorse eye]
*auspicious 14-59-8 (a.) 1. attended by favorable circumstances 2. tending to favor or bring good luck [accident advantageous appropriate ask attend unfortunate useful sign sort sound spic star success suitable pleasant present profitable promising propitious prosperous providential ill inspirit campaign capital cheer circumstance convenient omen opportune] "an auspicious beginning for the campaign"
*austere 09-48-24 (a.) 1. severely simple 2. practicing great self-denial 3. of a stern or strict bearing or demeanor; forbidding in aspect [abstemious abstinence ascetic aspect authoritarian uncluttered undecorated unembellished uniform unimaginative unsmiling self serious severe simple single small somber stark stere stern strict style suggest thin tough earnest elaborate elementary essential existence expression reason rigid rough rugged rustic]
*authentic 06-51-58 (a.) 1. not counterfeit or copied 2. conforming to fact and therefore worthy of belief [accept account accurate antique approve unassuming unique unquestionable untrustworthy upward telling textual then traditionalism true trusty hearsay historical honest evangelical evidentiary eyewitness naturalistic necessary new note novel imaginative implicit instrument irresistible certain chant christianity church composition conform copy correct counterfeit creative current] "an authentic account by an eyewitness"
*authenticity 08-51-29 (n.) 1. undisputed credibility [actuality artless attribute authentic authoritative undisputed unique usage traditionalism trustworthy truthful historicity honesty natural newness novelty innovation inventive invincible calculable canonicity correct creativity credible]
*authoritarian 09-44-23 (a.) 1. characteristic of an absolute ruler or absolute rule; having absolute sovereignty 2. likened to a dictator in severity 3. expecting unquestioning obedience (n.) 1. a person behaves in an tyrannical manner [absolute accord agreement arbitrary arrogant author authorize autocratic undemocratic undue unquestioning unsparing unyielding tend timid totalitarian tough toward tyrannical tyranny harsh heteronomous hidebound obedience official oppressive overtime ranking regime republican rule ideal imperious important incline influential invade narrow nearsighted /tiro/] "an authoritarian regime"
*autobiography 05-63-63 (n.) 1. a biography of yourself [account adventure annals author obituary biography record resume profile hagiology history yourself /bot/]
*autocracy 21-51-2 (n.) 1. a political system governed by a single individual 2. a political theory favoring unlimited authority by a single individual [absolutism autarchy authority auto unlimited unscrupulous theory think totalitarian tyranny one opposition organization orientation characterize citizen commonwealth

constitution country create represent restricted ruler /arco cot/]
*autocrat 19-45-3 (n.) 1. a dictator or dictatorial person [answerable arrogate authority auto unconstrained unlimited usurp tyrant oligarch oppress oppressive caesar commissar cruel czar ruler /arco cot/]
*automaton 19-52-3 (n.) 1. someone who acts or responds in a mechanical or apathetic way 2. a mechanism that can move automatically [android anomaly apathetic unusual tomato obey machinery mechanism move notice] "only an automaton wouldn't have noticed"
*autonomous 10-40-18 (a.) 1. of political bodies 2. existing as an independent entity 3. of persons; free from external control and constraint in e.g. action and judgment [absolute agent arbitrary authoritarian auto unbidden unforced unfreeze uninvited theocracy totalitarian offer official optional neutral nonaligned nonpartisan monarchic monocracy moral self separate sovereign spontaneous /mono/] "an autonomous judiciary"
*autonomy 08-41-32 (n.) 1. immunity from arbitrary exercise of authority: political independence 2. personal independence [aesthetic agent arbitrary aristocracy autarky authority auto theocracy triumvirate tyranny ochlocracy oligarchy neocolonialism meritocracy mobocracy monarchy moral /mono/]
*autopsy 10-21-18 (n.) 1. an examination and dissection of a dead body to determine cause of death or the changes produced by disease (v.) 1. perform an autopsy; do a post-mortem [analysis auto technique observe organ overlook perform peruse postmortem produce scan science scrutiny see specialty study survey /pot spot/]
*autumnal 15-68-7 (a.) 1. of or characteristic of or occurring in autumn 2. characteristic of late maturity verging on decline [autumn maturity mood late /mut/] "the autumnal equinox"
*auxiliary 12-47-13 (a.) 1. functioning in a subsidiary or supporting capacity 2. relating to something that is added but is not essential (n.) 1. someone who acts as assistant [accessory add adjuvant agent aid aide ally ancillary another appurtenance army assistant available ulterior unessential uphold ilia immediate importance incidental inessential instrumental large library lieutenant little replace require reserve role /rail/] "the main library and its auxiliary branches"
*avalanche 10-43-20 (n.) 1. a slide of large masses of snow and ice and mud down a mountain 2. a sudden appearance of an overwhelming number of things (v.) 1. of snow masses in the mountains [abundance affluent alan amplitude appearance apply arrive volcano lavish lot lower luxuriant natural necessarily numerous coast collision copious crystal happen earth electron enough extravagance exuberant /lava/] "the program brought an avalanche of mail"
*avarice 19-61-3 (n.) 1. reprehensible acquisitiveness; insatiable desire for wealth (personified as one of the deadly sins) 2. extreme greed for material wealth [acquisitive anger avid avidity voracity rapacity ravenous reprehensible rice incontinent insatiable intemperate ira cheap close covet cupidity entail envy excessive extreme]
*aver 21-69-2 (v.) 1. report or maintain 2. to declare or affirm solemnly and formally as true [acknowledge affirm allege announce answer argue asseverate attest authoritative ave avow verify victim vouch emphatic enunciate express recite registrar relate report]
*averse 11-71-15 (a.) 1. (usually followed by 'to') strongly opposed [abhorrent afraid allergic antagonistic anti antipathetic axis verse recoil reluctant request resistant risk short shrink stem strong sulky sullen]
*aversion 12-57-12 (n.) 1. a feeling of intense dislike 2. the act of turning yourself (or your gaze) away [abhorrence allergy angry animosity antipathy averse avoid version enmity execration racism refusal repulsion resistance shudder shuning slow strong stubborn indisposition indocile intense obstinate odium opposition nausea]
*avert 06-42-45 (v.) 1. turn away or aside 2. prevent the occurrence of; prevent from happening [abstract anticipate arise aside aver avoid veer effect enter estop exclude eye remove repel thwart transfer turn]
*aviary 21-50-2 (n.) 1. a building where birds are kept [via roof]
*avid 08-41-27 (a.) 1. (often followed by 'for') ardently or excessively desirous 2. marked by active interest and enthusiasm [adventure affection ambition animate anxious ardent avaricious vital vivacious vivid voracious impatient importunate insistent interest desirous devour /diva/] "avid for adventure"
*avocation 21-03-2 (n.) 1. an auxiliary activity [amuse auxiliary vocation occupy call career cave interest /ova taco/]
*avow 14-48-9 (v.) 1. to declare or affirm solemnly and formally as true 2. admit openly and bluntly; make no bones about [accept acknowledge admit affirm allow announce assert association attest authoritative aver avo validate verify vindicate vouch vow official openly ostensible own warrant window witness /ova/]
*awaken 10-24-19 (v.) 1. make aware 2. stop sleeping 3. cause to become awake or conscious [affect again alarm alert alive alter annoy arouse asleep awake aware wake waken whet workup kindle emotional enrage excite expose]
*awry 11-44-14 (a.) 1. turned or twisted toward one side 2. not functioning properly (ad.) 1. away from the correct or expected course 2. turned or twisted to one side [abroad adrift align amiss angle aside askew aslant astray went wide wig wonky wrong wry red regular roily] "something has gone awry in our plans"
*azalea 16-30-6 (n.) 1. any of numerous ornamental

shrubs grown for their showy flowers of various colors [ale laurel lavender leaf leathery lilac low elder evergreen]
*azure 18-67-4 (a.) 1. of a deep somewhat purplish blue color similar to that of a clear October sky (n.) 1. a light shade of blue (v.) 1. color azure [achievement achromatic add air arm unicorn rose royal eagle electric empyrean ether eye] "Morning azured the village"

B

*babble 14-63-9 (n.) 1. gibberish resembling the sounds of a baby (v.) 1. to talk foolishly 2. utter meaningless sounds, like a baby, or utter in an incoherent way 3. flow in an irregular current with a bubbling noise, as of water 4. divulge information or secrets; spill the beans [baby backward baffle bag bean blabber blather blether blither blurt bombast break bring brook bubble burble buzz abb absurdity amphigory argot arrest attention lap

leak let lightheaded loud low excite expose express]
*bacterium 17-50-5 (n.) 1. single-celled or noncellular spherical or spiral or rod-shaped organisms lacking chlorophyll that reproduce by fission; important as pathogens and for biochemical properties; taxonomy is difficult; often considered plants [act reaction]
*badger 10-65-17 (n.) 1. sturdy carnivorous burrowing mammal with strong claws widely distributed in the northern hemisphere (v.) 1. annoy persistently 2. persuade through constant efforts [badge bait beat bedevil beleaguer belief beset black bother boy bug burrow adopt aggravate animal annoy arm asian devil distribute disturb dog dun get gripe effort exact exasperate exercise rag ride rip ruffle /dab/]
*baffle 06-65-50 (n.) 1. a flat plate that controls or directs the flow of fluid or energy (v.) 1. be a mystery or bewildering to 2. check the emission of (sound) 3. hinder or prevent (the efforts, plans, or desires) of [baff bamboozle beat bedevil bemuse betray bewildering bilk blast blow bother bound brave breakfast buffet accomplish addle amazing answer face failure fix floor flummox foil forestall fox frustration fuddle letdown lick limit elude embarrassment enigma /fab/]
*bailiff 16-84-6 (n.) 1. an officer of the court who is employed to execute writs and processes and make arrests etc. [bail beadle beagle butler agent arrest attorney include inspector invest landowner last law legal librarian lictor lieutenant factor federal feed forcible functionary /ilia/]
*baize 23-88-1 (n.) 1. a bright green fabric napped to resemble felt; used to cover gaming tables [bright brocade alpaca artifact astrakhan]
*bale 10-75-19 (n.) 1. a large bundle bound for storage or transport 2. a city in northwestern Switzerland (v.) 1. make into a bale [bale bas basel bitter block bound budget bundle burden accumulate administrative ale amass anguish area lade landlocked last loading encumbrance europe extremity] "bale hay"
*baleful 18-70-4 (a.) 1. deadly or sinister 2. threatening or foreshadowing evil or tragic developments [bad bale baneful behavior beneficent black boding alarming apocalyptic largely lethal literary look lower eagle effect evil fateful fear fierce forbidding foreboding foreshadow unfavorable unfortunate unlucky] "the Florida eagles have a fierce baleful look"
*balk 08-32-30 (n.) 1. the area on a billiard table behind the balkline 2. an illegal pitching motion while runners are on base 3. something immaterial that interferes with or delays action or progress 4. one of several parallel sloping beams that support a roof (v.) 1. refuse to comply [baffle ball baseball batter baulk beam beat betray billiard bind blight blow bond bottom boundary brave achieve act actually agriculture architecture area ask aversion land last left letdown lion long knee] "a player with ball in hand must play from the balk"
*ballad 07-46-42 (n.) 1. a narrative poem of popular origin 2. a narrative song with a recurrent refrain [ball barcarole brindisi bucolic anacreontic anthem aubade late lie linseed lyric date dirge distinct dithyramb ditty /dal/]
*balsam 13-37-11 (n.) 1. any seed plant yielding balsam 2. a fragrant ointment containing a balsam resin 3. any of various fragrant oleoresins used in medicines and perfumes [balm balsa benzoic brilliantine brown acid aid ambrosia apply aromatic assistance lanolin last liniment lotion salve scent seed semisolid simple soothe substance syrup mean medicine mixture musk /slab/]
*banal 09-58-22 (a.) 1. obvious and dull 2. repeated too often; overfamiliar through overuse [belief bewhiskered bland boring bromidic anal answer asinine average axiom nail normal lack]
*barbaric 14-58-8 (a.) 1. without civilizing influences 2. unrestrained and crudely rich [barba blatant bloody brutal brutish aesthetic aggressive alien animal rich rough rude ruthless improper incorrect influence intrusive invade civilize clumsy color compare consider crude cruel culture /abra bra/]
*baritone 08-33-27 (a.) 1. lower in range than tenor and higher than bass (n.) 1. a male singer 2. the second lowest brass wind instrument 3. the second lowest adult male singing voice [blow brass bravura accompaniment adagio adult allegro alpenhorn alphorn alto andante arpeggio range rebec instrument tenor tone trombone tuba tube oboe operatic ophicleide euphonium] "a baritone voice"
*barometer 10-49-17 (n.) 1. an instrument that measures atmospheric pressure [amount aneroid atmospheric automatic radiosonde readout record rule opinion measure mercury meter model mood extent test touchstone type /mora rete/]
*barrage 08-48-29 (n.) 1. the heavy fire of artillery to saturate an area rather than hit a specific target 2. the rapid and continuous delivery of linguistic communication (spoken or written) (v.) 1. attack with a barrage [bank bar battery beat bombard burst advance angry area arm artillery assault attack audience rage rake rapid roll round ruffle gate groin gunfire earthwork embankment enemy eruption] "The speaker was barraged by an angry audience"
*barren 09-49-22 (a.) 1. not fertile or productive 2. without offspring 3. providing no shelter or sustenance 4. incapable of sustaining life 5. not bearing offspring (n.) 1. an uninhabited wilderness that is worthless for cultivation [bare barre bear blank bleak brush bush abortive area arid austere real reject reproduce rocky early effect effete empty energy exert exhaust nugatory null] "the barrens of central Africa"
*barring 07-33-36 (n.) 1. the act of excluding someone by a negative vote or veto [banish bar blackball blockade afternoon apart arrive relegate riddance impede interdict negative]
*bask 09-58-25 (v.) 1. be exposed 2. derive or receive

pleasure from; get enjoyment from; take pleasure in [adore appreciate ask avid satisfaction savor seal soak spread stretch sun sunbathe] "She relished her fame and basked in her glory"
*bass 04-39-92 (a.) 1. having or denoting a low vocal or instrumental range (n.) 1. the lowest part in polyphonic music 2. the lowest part of the musical range 3. nontechnical name for any of numerous edible marine and freshwater spiny-finned fishes 4. the member with the lowest range of a family of musical instruments 5. the lowest adult male singing voice 6. an adult male singer with the lowest voice 7. any of various North American freshwater fish with lean flesh (especially of the genus Micropterus) 8. the lean flesh of a saltwater fish of the family Serranidae [baritone below body bow brass bridge bull burden accompany adult alto american amplifier ass atlantic audio sacred saltwater sea short sing six soprano sound sousaphone spiny sport string striper]
*baste 17-37-5 (n.) 1. loose temporary stitches (v.) 1. cover with liquid before cooking 2. sew together loosely, with large stitches 3. strike violently and repeatedly [bash bast batter beat belt brown add aggression align application attack saturate seam sew simmer slight sow steam stitch strike switch tack temporary thrash thread thump toast try] "baste a roast"
*baton 08-52-28 (n.) 1. a thin tapered rod used by a conductor to direct an orchestra 2. an implement passed from runner to runner in a relay race [bar bat brand achievement arm armory taint taper tarnish team thick thin tie ton twirl official onus orchestra ordinary orle narrow next nightstick /tab/]
*battalion 07-62-35 (n.) 1. an army unit usually consisting of a headquarters and three or more companies 2. a large indefinite number [band body bunch amount ant antenna army attal average team throng train troop legion organize outfit /oil tab/] "a battalion of ants"
*batten 16-58-6 (n.) 1. a strip fixed to something to hold it firm (v.) 1. furnish with battens; of ships 2. secure with battens [bar batt beef boat boom border branch anchor articulate tack tarpaulin theater thin thrive tie edge engorge nail narrow nautical /nett tab/] "batten down a ship's hatches"
*batter 04-41-131 (n.) 1. a ballplayer who is batting 2. a flour mixture thin enough to pour or drop from a spoon (v.) 1. strike against forcefully 2. strike violently and repeatedly 3. make a dent or impression in [ballplayer bang baseball baste bat batsman batt beat blow break bruise buffet bunt burn butchery butter abuse aggression assault assume athlete attack tackle team tent terrorize thin third thump try turn end enough rape regular repeat right riot rob ruin run /tab/]
*bauble 16-67-6 (n.) 1. a mock scepter carried by a court jester 2. cheap showy jewelry or ornament or clothing [ball bangle bite block add agate little emblematic]
*bawl 18-78-4 (v.) 1. shout loudly and without restraint 2. cry loudly 3. make a raucous noise [bay bellow blubber boom buy buzz aggressive awl wail water weep whisper whoop wind lament lilt loud low] "Don't bawl in public!"
*beatify 19-61-3 (v.) 1. fill with sublime emotion; tickle pink (exhilarate is obsolete in this usage) 2. declare (a dead person) to be blessed; the first step of achieving sainthood 3. make blessedly happy [beam beat bewitch big blessed blessing blissful elate elevated eminent emotion ennoble enshrine escalate exalt excellent exhilarate extremely exuberant achieve adjudge aggrandize angelic apotheosize archaism ascent assumption awesome thrill throne tickle toward transport immortalize inebriate intoxicate felicity fill first /fit/]
*beau 12-68-13 (n.) 1. a man who is the lover of a girl or young woman 2. a man who is much concerned with his dress and appearance [bea beloved blood boyfriend british english esquire exquisite accomplishment admire adult affect amoroso appearance ask]
*becalm 19-76-3 (v.) 1. make steady [become bring calm lack move /ace lace/]
*beck 08-57-30 (n.) 1. a beckoning gesture [bear branch brook burn evocation carriage channel communicate creek kinesics]
*bedeck 17-48-5 (v.) 1. decorate [bead beautify bedizen bejewel blazon embellish embroider endue enrich deck decorate disguise drape dress dud cap clad clothe color costume /cede/]
*bedlam 18-65-4 (n.) 1. a state of extreme confusion and disorder 2. pejorative terms for an insane asylum [bed bin blast booby borrow brawl brouhaha extreme din disarray discord disorder donnybrook loan loony anarchy asylum madhouse mayhem mental modern]
*befriend 10-56-19 (v.) 1. become friends with [bailout become benefit bind bond ease emotional environment favor friend rally rescue restore doctor]
*beget 18-42-4 (v.) 1. make children [bear become beg biological birth blood bring engender establish evolve generate gestate get teem tense /teg/]
*begrudge 14-70-8 (v.) 1. be envious of; set one's heart on 2. wish ill or allow unwillingly [envy express give grudge grudging refuse resent unselfish unwilling deny desire dime /urge/]
*belabor 23-09-1 (v.) 1. attack verbally with harsh criticism 2. to work at or to absurd length 3. beat soundly [batter beat belt bludgeon effort emphasize exert express labor labour lace lash length literary absurd accentuate aggression alliterate apart assonant attack obvious overstate rawhide real repeat rhyme /bale rob/] "belabor the obvious"
*belie 10-56-20 (v.) 1. be in contradiction with 2. represent falsely [bel blowup burlesque evidence exaggerate explode expose express lie line look

impression impugn intention invalidate]
*believe 01-59-2046 (v.) 1. follow a credo; have a religious faith; be a believer 2. credit with veracity 3. be confident about something 4. judge or regard; look upon; judge 5. accept as true; take to be true [band bank behavior belie boyfriend buy effective esteem exist expect expression let likely look imagine impressive incredible inferior inquire ist valid veracity view votary /veil/] "I believed his report"
*belittle 13-53-11 (v.) 1. belittle 2. lessen the authority, dignity, or reputation of 3. express a negative opinion of [bate bitchy effort erode express lessen lesser libelous little lower importance indignity influence talk totally trash trivialize /tile/] "Don't belittle his influence"
*belle 08-54-29 (n.) 1. a young woman who is the most charming and beautiful of several rivals [ball beautiful bell bunny enchantress lady last live looker] "she was the belle of the ball"
*bellicose 17-47-5 (a.) 1. having or showing a ready disposition to fight [battle bell bicker bloody enemy energetic eristic litigious impulse incline inimical irascible irritable chauvinist combative confrontation contentious offensive officer savage scrappy show soldierly /cill/] "bellicose young officers"
*belligerent 13-57-11 (a.) 1. characteristic of an enemy or one eager to fight 2. engaged in war (n.) 1. someone who fights (or is fighting) [battle battler bitter bloody boxing brawl butter eager enemy enforcer engage enmity entertain eristic eye law learn liger litigious loudmouthed ill individual invade irascible irritable gamecock gladiator goon gorilla gouge grappler ground ready recognize riot rival rome rough nation tempered throw thug tone tough train try /gill/]
*bemoan 10-65-20 (v.) 1. regret strongly [bewail elegize express moan mourn]
*bemuse 08-80-28 (v.) 1. cause to be confused emotionally [baffle beery befuddle besot bewilder ecstatic elsewhere emotional engross exhibit maze meditation merry mixed muddle muse mystify unconscious underplay upset school situation sodden stargaze statement stun /sum/]
*benediction 18-66-4 (n.) 1. the act of praying for divine protection 2. a ceremonial prayer invoking divine protection [benedict benefit benison blessing boon expression deity divine invoke ceremonial christianity cognizance communicate contrition credit thanksgiving /cide den/]
*benefactor 10-50-17 (n.) 1. a person who helps people or institutions [backer blood bondsman encouragement factor favor acceptance advice aid angel captivity champion tissue trouble obligor offer organ reform refrain rejection release rescue /cafe fen/]

*beneficent 19-48-3 (a.) 1. doing or producing good 2. generous in assistance to the poor 3. doing or producing good [benefice benevolent benignity brightness effect eleemosynary evil neighborly favorable fortunate friendly full intent charitable charity cheery contributor cooperative /fen/] "the most beneficent regime in history"
*beneficial 07-56-41 (a.) 1. tending to promote physical well-being; beneficial to health 2. promoting or enhancing well-being [balance bene benign body bonny bracing effect effective employ enhance entitle excellent exercise experience nice night noble fair famous favorable fine influence invigorate capital conducive constructive country advantageous agreement appropriate arm auspicious laudable limitation /fen laic/] "an arms limitation agreement beneficial to all countries"
*beneficiary 06-48-52 (a.) 1. having or arising from a benefice (n.) 1. the recipient of funds or other benefits 2. the semantic role of the intended recipient who benefits from the happening denoted by the verb in the clause [baron bene bequeath ecclesiastical entity feoffee feudatory fund incumbent insurance intend clause clergy allottee annuitant arise assignee realty receiver recipient rentier residentiary role /fen/] "a beneficiary baron"
*benefit 01-51-796 (n.) 1. a performance to raise money for a charitable cause 2. something that aids or promotes well-being 3. financial assistance in time of need (v.) 1. be beneficial for 2. derive benefit from [bene better bill build business effect employment enlarge entertainment equity estate eventually exchange extra net non financial fit forward fundraiser further idea ill improve incidental increase injection insurance interest title trust turn type /fen/]
*benevolence 19-56-3 (n.) 1. disposition to do good 2. an inclination to do kind or charitable acts 3. an act intending or showing kindness and good will [emotion evil lenient love charity compassion considerate]
*benevolent 09-47-22 (a.) 1. doing or producing good 2. generous in assistance to the poor 3. intending or showing kindness 4. generous in providing aid to others 5. having or showing or arising from a desire to promote the welfare or happiness of others [behavior bene beneficial benignity big blessing bonny boon brightness eleemosynary elegant emotion evil excellent expedient nature neighborly nice noble valid value virtuous obliging office openhearted overlook largesse laudable lenient liberal lofty love lucky tender tenderhearted thoughtful tolerant /love oven/] "a benevolent society"
*benign 07-57-42 (a.) 1. (pathology) not dangerous to health; not recurrent or progressive (especially of a tumor) 2. of disposition or manner 3. pleasant and beneficial in nature or influence [behavior ben benevolent bland bracing branch bright effect nature neighborly neutral nice non indulgent influence innocuous intention invigorate generous genial gentle golden good growth /gin/] "a benign smile"
*bequeath 13-61-11 (v.) 1. leave or give by will after one's death [barter behind bequest bestow birthright eat

enfeoff entail entire estate exchange ultimogeniture alienate amortize appreciation assignment aunt tell testament trade transfer transmittal turnover hand handover heir hereditament] "My aunt bequeathed me all her jewelry"
*bequest 16-52-6 (n.) 1. (law) a gift of personal property by will [bequeath birthright endowment entail estate quest ultimogeniture settlement succession testament title]
*berate 11-66-16 (v.) 1. censure severely or angrily [bawl blacken blame bring enter excoriate execration express rag rate real rebuke remonstrate reproof revile abuse angrily apart assault attack tell tirade trounce /tare/]
*bereave 10-81-19 (v.) 1. deprive through death [bad beef beggarly beloved bleed empty experience express reave relieve remove rob robbery ruin abridgment]
*bereft 12-67-12 (a.) 1. unhappy in love; suffering from unrequited love 2. sorrowful through loss or deprivation [bad beef empty experience express remove feel] "bereft of hope"
*berth 07-47-38 (n.) 1. a job in an organization 2. a bed on a ship or train; usually in tiers 3. a place where a craft can be made fast (v.) 1. provide with a berth 2. secure in or as if in a berth or dock 3. come into or dock at a wharf [basin bed bert big bishop boat build bunk business editor elder embankment emirate employment engagement religious remain render reside room tenant tenure tie tier train treasury haven head high honorary hook hot house]
*beseech 19-42-3 (v.) 1. ask for or request earnestly [beg bid earnest entreat see seek supplication conjure crave /cee/]
*beset 09-55-22 (v.) 1. to assail or attack on all sides:"The lioness..beset by men and hounds." Pope 2. annoy continually or chronically 3. decorate or cover lavishly with gems [backbreaking beat beautify beget bother bound embarrassed embellish emotional enclose encompass encrust epidemic set side stable staff standard stereotype strike surround task tease torment treat trouble trying]
*bestial 21-60-2 (a.) 1. resembling a beast; showing lack of human sensibility [base best bloody bodily boor brutish earthy sadistic satanic savage sensibility sex show sordid treatment troglodyte truculent infernal inhumane instinct intellect animalist anthropophagus atrocious lack lapse /lait/]
*bestride 19-84-3 (v.) 1. get on the back of [back board bridge entranceway side sit span stand straddle stride top toward twist ride imbricate dictate dominate /dirt/]
*betide 21-93-2 (v.) 1. become of; happen to [bechance become befall break eventuate tide transpire trust turnup ill develop /dit edit/]
*betrothal 23-59-1 (n.) 1. a mutual promise to marry 2. the act of becoming betrothed or engaged [becoming betroth engagement espousal token troth ring rite ritual observance agree /tort torte/]
*bevel 21-34-2 (a.) 1. having the slant of a bevel (n.) 1. two surfaces meeting at an angle different from 90 degrees 2. a hand tool consisting of two rules that are hinged together so you can draw or measure angles of any size (v.) 1. cut a bevel on; shape to a bevel [back bank biased body buttress edge eve various vertical large last lean leg letter ligature listing logotype] "bevel the surface"
*bewilder 08-62-30 (v.) 1. cause to be confused emotionally 2. be a mystery or bewildering to [baffle bamboozle beat bedevil befuddle bemuse bother breathless bug elude embarrassed emotional enchant entangle entrance escape wilder wonder incomprehensible lose daze dazzle difficult disconcert dismay disorient disoriented disturbed dumbfound rattle riddle ruffle /web/]
*bibliography 17-36-5 (n.) 1. a list of writings with time and place of publication (such as the writings of a single author or the works referred to in preparing a document etc.) [belletrist book bookworm index introduction issue item itinerary leaf listing literature lore ordered ghostwriter graphy guidebook read recto refer review annalist appendix array article author page place poet preliminary prepare printer publisher head history humorist /oil/]
*bibliophile 21-50-2 (n.) 1. someone who loves (and usually collects) books [book bookworm learn long love person phile printer publisher humanity editor /oil poi/]
*bibulous 23-65-1 (a.) 1. given to or marked by the consumption of alcohol [behavior bib binge blot boozy incontinent indulgent inebriate inordinate intoxicate unbridled unlimited unrestrained osmotic overindulge scottish sing soak sober stupefy substance swill swinish] "a bibulous fellow"
*bid 01-62-646 (n.) 1. an attempt to get something 2. an authoritative direction or instruction to do something 3. (bridge) the number of tricks a bridge player is willing to contract to make 4. a formal proposal to buy at a specified price (v.) 1. make a serious effort to attain something 2. make a demand in card games, as for a card or a suit or a show of hands 3. ask someone in a friendly way to do something 4. ask for or request earnestly 5. invoke upon 6. propose a payment; as at sales or auctions [baba base become behalf behest beseech bridge buy imperative implore incline injunction instruction intend invite invoke issue dealer decide declared demand desperate dictation direction dispose]
*bide 10-60-17 (v.) 1. dwell (archaic) [bad bear beseech bespeak betoken bid bite brave bridge brook instruction invite invoke day dealer delay demand dig direction divine dwell earnest effort endeavor endure exist expression extend]
*biennial 13-44-10 (a.) 1. occurring every second year

2. (botany) having a life cycle lasting two seasons (n.) 1. a plant having a life cycle that normally takes two seasons from germination to death to complete; flowering biennials usually bloom and fruit in the second season [bicentennial bimonthly biology birthday biyearly bloom branch ephemeral evergreen exotic amphibian angiosperm anniversary annual lack lasting life live locomotion /inn lain/] "they met at biennial conventions"
*bier 21-45-2 (n.) 1. a coffin along with its stand 2. a stand to support a corpse or a coffin prior to burial [base box bury rest] "we followed the bier to the graveyard"
*bigamist 23-62-1 (n.) 1. someone who marries one person while already legally married to another [better adultery already marry mate mist spouse timer /gib mag/]
*bigamy 23-65-1 (n.) 1. having more than one spouse at a time 2. the offense of having two or more wives or husbands living at the same time [impose gamy adultery authority marry matrimony monandry monogyny /gib mag/]
*bigot 09-51-23 (n.) 1. a prejudiced person who is intolerant of any opinions differing from his own [balky bear believe biased big blind bug illiberal inisist inordinate insular intolerant intransigent irrational get obdurate obstinate open opinion opinionated oracular outrageous tenacity tolerate toward /gib tog/]
*bilateral 11-43-14 (a.) 1. having identical parts on each side of an axis 2. having two sides or parts [bifurcate bipartite bivalent identical lateral affecting ambidextrous asymmetric axis talk twain two twofold reciprocal representative return /tali/]

*bilge 21-68-2 (n.) 1. water accumulated in the bilge of a ship 2. where the sides of the vessel curve in to form the bottom (v.) 1. cause to leak; as of vessels 2. take in water at the bilge; of vessels [balderdash barrel base below beneath binary boat boil boss bottom bow bowel bunch bunkum ice idea inflict inside interior inward leak light lip liquid load loop low lump gall garbage gas ear effluent enclose enter /glib/]
*bilingual 13-27-11 (a.) 1. using or knowing two languages (n.) 1. a person who speaks two languages fluently [language lingual linguist naturally] "bilingual education"
*biography 04-53-126 (n.) 1. an account of the series of events making up a person's life [biograph book idealize idolize obituary general greek record resume roman account adventure annals past people play produce profile program hagiography hagiology history yourself]
*biology 06-39-55 (n.) 1. the science that studies living organisms 2. characteristic life processes and phenomena of living organisms 3. all the plant and animal life of a particular region [bacteriology basic behavior biochemist biophysics biota body botany ichthyology idea identity imitation include independent inheritance interaction isomorphic ology ophiology organ origin ornithology outer lack less life live low gelatin genetics geographic group growth] "the biology of viruses"
*birthright 17-49-5 (n.) 1. a right or privilege that you are entitled to at birth 2. personal characteristics that are inherited at birth 3. an inheritance coming by right of birth (especially by primogeniture) [basic belong bequest birth immaterial inherit interest reversion right title heir hereditament heritage /rib tri/] "free public education is the birthright of every American child"
*bitterness 08-46-30 (n.) 1. a sharp and bitter manner 2. a feeling of deep and bitter anger and ill-will 3. the taste experience when quinine or coffee is taken into the mouth 4. the property of having a harsh unpleasant taste [bud ill indignation intense tart taste throat tongue enmity enough envy experience extreme rancor resentment score sensation sharp soluble sour stimulus strong sulky sullen]
*blandness 18-53-4 (n.) 1. the trait of exhibiting no personal embarrassment or concern 2. lacking any distinctive or interesting taste property 3. smooth and gracious in manner [banality lack absence appetite distinctive dull embarrassment enrage excellence exhibit smooth social spoil suavity] "the blandness of his confession enraged the judge"
*blase 21-06-2 (a.) 1. very sophisticated especially because of surfeit; versed in the ways of the world 2. nonchalantly unconcerned 3. uninterested because of frequent exposure or indulgence [ban benefit benumb blah bore lack lase lay leaden lifeless listless aloof apathetic appealing ataractic attitude savoir season show slow sophisticated star successful superior surfeit easygoing enlighten experience exposure] "the blase traveler refers to the ocean he has crossed as `the pond'"
*blaspheme 23-54-1 (v.) 1. utter obscenities or profanities 2. speak of in an irrevent or impious manner [belittle blast loud abuse anathematize articulate asp sacred shout speak street swear profanity putdown hex excommunicate execrate express malign man manner mention]
*blasphemous 19-56-3 (a.) 1. grossly irreverent toward what is held to be sacred 2. characterized by profanity or cursing [backslide behavior blue lack language lapse abusive apostate asp atheistic sacrilegious scurrilous shoe show sinful profanity hold enter epithet evil excommunicate express malediction obscenity offensive undutiful ungodly utterance] "blasphemous rites of a witches' Sabbath"
*blatant 08-56-32 (a.) 1. conspicuously and offensively loud; given to vehement outcry 2. without any attempt at concealment; completely obvious [barefaced bitter blat blazing bluster bold brash brawl brazen musical lamentable law light literary loud loudness low lurid

abominable agonizing appeal arrant attempt awfully tawdry terribly transparent tumultuous turbulent noisy non notably noticeable notorious]
*blaze 05-58-66 (n.) 1. noisy and unrestrained mischief 2. a cause of difficulty and suffering 3. a strong flame that burns brightly 4. a light-colored marking 5. great brightness (v.) 1. shoot rapidly and repeatedly 2. shine brightly and intensively 3. burn brightly and intensely 4. indicate by marking trees with blazes 5. move rapidly and as if blazing [bark beam behavior black blast blistering brand brightness brilliance burn last law laze lead leave light line lit live location log across add affect alight alone amount annoyance appear ardent arrow atmosphere attempt attention attract earmark emit emotion emphasis eruption experience explosion eye] "the blaze spread rapidly"
*bleak 05-61-71 (a.) 1. providing no shelter or sustenance 2. offering little or no hope 3. unpleasantly cold and damp [bare barren black blow lamentable landscape leak life little lonely look low expectation expose affecting afflict arctic austere keen]

*blemish 13-59-11 (n.) 1. a mark or flaw that spoils the appearance of something (especially on a person's body) (v.) 1. mar or spoil the appearance of 2. mar or impair with a flaw 3. add a flaw or blemish to; make imperfect or defective [bag beat bemire bloated blot blotch bowleg brand break lacerate lacking lesion line earmark engrave error mar mark maul mediocre mess mis mixed imperfection imprint inaccurate inadequate incomplete injury scar score scratch sight skin slur smear smirch smudge soil split spoil spot stain harm hole homely hurt] "a facial blemish"
*blithe 11-49-14 (a.) 1. carefree and happy and lighthearted 2. lacking or showing a lack of due concern [beam blissful boon bright lack laughing lightsome lithe love ignorance indifferent insouciance interest irrepressible true happy heart high hopeful easygoing elated exalted exhilarate] "spoke with blithe ignorance of the true situation"
*blockade 11-38-16 (n.) 1. a war measure that isolates some area of importance to the enemy 2. prevents access or progress (v.) 1. hinder or prevent the progress or accomplishment of 2. render unsuitable for passage 3. obstruct access to 4. impose a blockade on [bank bar barrier battle besiege block check contain cover arm arrest attack embarrass /dak/]
*bodice 17-45-5 (n.) 1. part of a dress above the waist [basque blouse body boob one ornamental dice dress cardigan close costume cover crew extend]
*bodily 10-67-18 (a.) 1. of or relating to or belonging to the body 2. having or relating to a physical material body 3. affecting or characteristic of the body as opposed to the mind or spirit (ad.) 1. in bodily form [bear beastly belonging benjamin biological bod body brutish oppose organic orgiastic defect distinguished illness incorporeal indigenous inherit instinct lapse last /lid lido/] "a bodily organ"
*bogus 09-62-22 (a.) 1. fraudulent; having a misleading appearance [bad bastard bog brummagem garble good unnatural unreal useless sham simulate spurious superior synthetic /gob/]
*boisterous 11-45-15 (a.) 1. noisy and lacking in restraint or discipline 2. violently agitated and turbulent 3. full of rough and exuberant animal spirits [bluster bois brawl bully obstreperous orderly ordinary overexcite social spirit stormy strident surface swaggering sympathy teenager tempestuous thunder tumultuous turbulent energy enthusiasm exuberant ezra rage rambunctious rant restraint roar rough undisciplined unruly uproarious] "a boisterous crowd"
*bole 21-70-2 (n.) 1. a soft oily clay used as a pigment (especially a reddish brown pigment) 2. a Chadic language spoken in northern Nigeria and closely related to Hausa 3. the main stem of a tree; usually covered with bark; the bole is usually the part that is commercially useful for lumber [bark barrel brown oily ole organ language last leafstalk liquid lumber earth elevated elongate /lob/]
*bolero 18-37-4 (n.) 1. music written in the rhythm of the bolero dance 2. a short jacket; worn mostly by women 3. a Spanish dance in triple time accompanied by guitar and castanets [ballroom basque blouse bodice bole boob open orchestra rhythm /lob/]
*boll 21-32-2 (n.) 1. the rounded seed-bearing capsule of a cotton or flax plant [balloon bladder bubble orb orbit last /lob/]
*bolster 04-43-89 (n.) 1. a pillow that is often put across a bed underneath the regular pillows (v.) 1. support; of morale, theories, etc. 2. prop up with a pillow or bolster 3. add padding to [backup beam bed boost buttress last litter load long seat short sleeping solid spread spring stay strengthen strong support sustain theory timber top embolden encourage engineering raise ratify reassure regular reinforce rigid /lob slob/]
*bomb 02-49-432 (n.) 1. strong sealed vessel for measuring heat of combustion 2. an explosive device fused to denote under specific conditions 3. an event that fails badly or is totally ineffectual (v.) 1. throw bombs at or attack with bombs 2. fail to get a passing grade [badly ballet balloon batter beam begin bill blast blitz booby bottle break briefcase building burst offensive onset onslaught open opera massive material measure mechanism medicine metal midair mine missile mission monologue mortar mount munition /mob/] "The Americans bombed Dresden"
*bombard 08-57-33 (n.) 1. a large shawm; the bass member of the shawm family (v.) 1. cast, hurl, or throw repeatedly with some missile 2. throw bombs at or attack with bombs [bard barrage bass battery begin blast blitz body bomb breed bullet burst oboe offensive onslaught outward overwhelm medieval member mine

missile mortar musical accelerate airplane approach area arm artillery assault atomize attack radiation rake range ray release repeatedly request run delayed destroy direct dissociation dive down drop drumfire /drab mob/]
*bombardier 18-61-4 (n.) 1. a noncommissioned officer in the British artillery 2. the member of a bomber crew responsible for using the bombsight and releasing the bombs on the target [bombard british officer member meteorology military aircrew appointed artilleryman releasing responsible rifleman enlist /drab mob/]
*bombast 17-51-5 (n.) 1. pompous or pretentious talk or writing [bast blah bluster boast brag ornamentation orotund magniloquent absurdity affectation amphigory show side style swagger talk trash turgidity twaddle /mob/]
*boon 09-45-21 (a.) 1. very close and convivial (n.) 1. a desirable state [behalf benefit benevolent bless blessing bonus boo breeze outcome] "boon companions"
*boorish 17-65-5 (a.) 1. ill-mannered and coarse and contemptible in behavior or appearance [base behavior bully oafish refined rough rude ignorant ill impolite insensitive stupid swinish husband] "was boorish and insensitive"
*bore 03-65-194 (n.) 1. a person who evokes boredom 2. (mining terms) a hole or passage made by a drill; usually made for exploratory purposes 3. diameter of a tube or gun barrel 4. a high wave (often dangerous) caused by tidal flow (as by colliding tidal currents or in a narrow estuary) (v.) 1. drill a hole into 2. cause to be bored [barrel bear benumb bigmouth birth blase board boring bring broach brook burke office oil onsite operation opposite ore realize red regardless remark remove repetitive resemblance responsibility rest revolt ribbon right ring routine eager earn earth endure enervate engage estuary evoke excavation excessive excite expense explosive exposure extract /rob/]
*borough 04-38-105 (n.) 1. one of the administrative divisions of a large city 2. an English town that forms the constituency of a member of Parliament [bailiwick bishopric bronx buckingham burgh oblast once outskirt own region responsible ride rough royal run govern government grant great greenwich hamlet house hundred /rob/]
*bosom 13-71-10 (a.) 1. very close in friendship or affection (n.) 1. (archaic) the chest considered as the place where secret thoughts are kept 2. a person's breast or chest 3. cloth that covers the chest or breasts 4. a close affectionate and protective acceptance 5. either of two soft fleshy milk-secreting glandular organs on the chest of a woman 6. the locus of feelings and intuitions (v.) 1. hide in one's bosom 2. hug, usually with fondness [bear become being best bite blood body breast buddy burst organ seat secret security see soft som soul source special spirit squeeze story suspicion mama mammary melt midst might /sob/] "a bosom buddy"
*botanical 10-33-19 (a.) 1. of or relating to plants or botany [biology botanic botanica bulbous tuberous cereal leguminous] "botanical garden"
*botany 18-48-4 (n.) 1. the branch of biology that studies plants [bark basal base basis biology bladder blister branch bud open orchid organism outer outgrowth ovary taxonomy thicken tissue tooth toward trumpet tube absorb amnion anatomy any apex arise arrange astrobiology axis narrow naturalist node young]
*bountiful 15-35-7 (a.) 1. given or giving freely 2. producing in abundance [backer beneficent big bighearted blooming bottomless boun openhanded openhearted opulent overflow unselfish unsparing unstinting numerous teem thrive tipper inexhaustible fat flourish fond freely fruitful full lavish liberal love lush /fit/]
*bowdlerize 23-50-1 (v.) 1. edit by omitting or modifying parts considered indelicate [bleach bow omit whiten work delete delouse depurate literature lustrate edit element erase essential expurgate reduce reform remove rescind retain indelicate] "bowdlerize a novel"
*bowler 04-96-89 (n.) 1. delivers the ball to the batsman in cricket 2. rolls balls down an alley at pins 3. a hat that is round and black and hard with a narrow brim; worn by some British businessmen [bad ball batsman black bowl brim british business weather worn last lawn lid roll round]
*boycott 05-45-65 (n.) 1. a group's refusal to have commercial dealings with some organization in protest against its policies (v.) 1. refuse to sponsor; refuse to do business with [ban bar beef boy business buy objection omission organize ostracize cease challenge circumscription client commercial company compunction customer taboo turnout /yob/]
*brace 05-60-81 (n.) 1. a support that steadies or strengthens something else 2. a rope on a square-rigged ship that is used to swing a yard about and secure it 3. either of two punctuation marks ({ or }) used to enclose textual material 4. the stock of a tool used for turning a drilling bit 5. an appliance that corrects dental irregularities 6. a structural member used to stiffen a framework 7. elastic straps that hold trousers up (usually used in the plural) 8. two items of the same kind 9. a set of two similar things considered as a unit (v.) 1. support by bracing 2. support or hold steady and make steadfast, with or as if with a brace 3. prepare (oneself) for something unpleasant or difficult 4. cause to be alert and energetic [bag bar bear beef belt bolster both building burden race ready reanimate recreate refreshing renew resist revive revivify rope rousing activate additional affect alert analeptic appeal application arm arouse cable carry cast cheer cold column constitutional couplet cross energy enliven entreat exhilarate /carb/] "brace your elbows while working on the potter's wheel"
*brae 21-74-2 (n.) 1. (Scotland) a slope or hillside [bagpipe bra britain /ear/]
*braggart 23-59-1 (a.) 1. exhibiting self-importance (n.)

1. a very boastful and talkative person [big bigmouth blowhard bluff boast brag bragg ranter raver reason roister gasbag talkative /garb rag/]
*brandish 10-61-18 (n.) 1. the act of waving (v.) 1. exhibit aggressively 2. move or swing back and forth [betoken brand breathe represent reveal rollout abstract accord advertise affect aggressive air apparent demonstrate develop disclose display illuminate incarnate indicate send shake show signal sport swing handle highlight holdup]
*brash 08-55-28 (a.) 1. offensively bold 2. presumptuously daring [backward behavior bluff blunt bold brazen rash realistic reckless restraint right rough rude rule abrupt admission age aggressive arrogant ash say self severe sharp short stuff harsh hasty hubris] "a brash newcomer disputed the age-old rules for admission to the club"
*brass 05-46-64 (n.) 1. the persons (or committees or departments etc.) who make up a body for the purpose of administering something 2. impudent aggressiveness 3. an ornament or utensil made of brass 4. a wind instrument that consists of a brass tube (usually of variable length) blown by means of a cup-shaped or funnel-shaped mouthpiece 5. an alloy of copper and zinc 6. a memorial made of brass [band blunt board body bread ribbon rock rude aide arch aristocracy ass something stone string structure]
*bravado 11-57-15 (n.) 1. a swaggering show of courage [balls bluster boast bold rant real rodomontade ado adventurous arrogant audacity vanity vaunt daring defy despite display ostentation outward]
*bravo 10-59-18 (n.) 1. a murderer (especially one who kills a prominent political figure) who kills by a treacherous surprise attack and often is hired to do the deed 2. a cry of approval as from an audience at the end of great performance (v.) 1. applaud with shouts of"bravo" or"brava" [booth acclaim actor animal applaud approval assassinate attack audience avo oswald /ova/] "bravo"
*bray 11-80-14 (n.) 1. the cry of an ass (v.) 1. braying characteristic of donkeys 2. laugh loudly and harshly 3. reduce to small pieces or particles by pounding or abrading [bay beat boom bra break rasp ray reduce roar rumble abrade animal ass atomize audible yap yell yelp]
*brazen 10-55-19 (a.) 1. unrestrained by convention or propriety 2. made of or resembling brass (as in color or hardness) (v.) 1. face with defiance or impudence [bald bay behavior belief bertrand blatant bodacious bold boundless brassy brave braze bronzy rash resonant rough rude russell alloy angeles arrogant ashamed auburn audacious exhibitionist express extravagant noisy notorious] "brazen it out"
*brazier 19-80-3 (n.) 1. large metal container in which coal or charcoal is burned; warms people who must stay outside for long times [barbecue bra brassy burn room /izar/]
*breach 03-80-144 (n.) 1. a failure to perform some promised act or obligation 2. an opening (especially a gap in a dike or fortification) 3. a personal or social separation (as between opposing factions) (v.) 1. make an opening or gap in 2. act in disregard of laws and rules [basic become betray beyond boob bore breakthrough budget reach refer relation rent require respect rift rip rule run rupture each empty enter error estrange evil excavation abyss afoul alienate allow apart atrocity avoid care check civilization come commit conflict contravene crack cut hiatus hole hope humanity]
*breadth 08-59-28 (n.) 1. the extent of something from side to side 2. an ability to understand a broad range of topics [bigness body bread broad radius range reach room ecumenism expansion experience extent acreage amidship amount area degree detail direction distance teacher thickness tolerant topic tract height] "a teacher must have a breadth of knowledge of the subject"
*breaker 09-48-26 (n.) 1. a quarry worker who splits off blocks of stone 2. a device that trips like a switch and opens the circuit when overloaded 3. waves breaking on the shore [begin billow block body bore break breeder radio ride ridge ripple rise rock roller eagre engineering equerry across analyze]
*breech 23-53-1 (n.) 1. opening in the rear of the barrel of a gun where bullets can be loaded [barrel bed behind belly block body buttock rear rearward ree replace reverse rifle rope rump engineering cable cartridge cask chain closer container cylindrical hardpan heel hold /cee/]
*brethren 14-53-9 (n.) 1. the members of a male religious order [betray blood bret brother bud buddy religious engage title humorous nephew niece nuncle]
*brevity 15-62-7 (n.) 1. the attribute of being brief or fleeting 2. the use of brief expressions [brachylogy brief brusque reserve rev economical expressive taciturnity terse transient /verb/]
*bridle 14-65-9 (n.) 1. headgear for a horse; includes a headstall and bit and reins to give the rider or driver control 2. the act of restraining power or action or limiting excess (v.) 1. put a bridle on 2. respond to the reins, as of horses [band bite bond break react rear rein reply respond restraint restriction ride rider rope rule idle include incorporate indignation inhibit iron decelerate draft drench driver lash lead leash leather limiting line litter long enchain encumber enjoin excess exercise express] "bridle horses"
*brigade 06-74-59 (n.) 1. army unit smaller than a division (v.) 1. form or unite into a brigade [background band battalion body brig bunch rank regiment gang garrison general goal group achieve appearance army attitude detail division /dag/]
*brigadier 10-86-18 (n.) 1. a general officer ranking below a major general [below brig bureaucrat ranking representative general aide army detective /dag/]
*brigand 23-68-1 (n.) 1. an armed thief who is (usually)

a member of a band [bandit belonging brig robber roving intention isolated gangster armed /nag/]
*brimstone 19-67-3 (n.) 1. an old name for sulfur [best mineral multivalent stone sulfur sulphur tasteless odorless old native non element]
*brine 16-60-6 (n.) 1. water containing salts 2. a strong solution of salt and water used for pickling (v.) 1. soak in brine [below binary boil brin bromine brown burn rapid react rock room ice iodine nature necessarily non element evaporation]
*bristle 08-51-29 (n.) 1. a stiff hair 2. a stiff fiber (coarse hair or filament); natural or synthetic (v.) 1. rise up; of animals fur or hair; as in fear 2. be in a state of movement or action [battleship beat bite bother bristly brush burst rage ramp react response ride rife rise rist room imperial implement incense indignant irritate scream set short show sight slender solid spike spine stand stiff sting stubble stud substance suggestion swarm synthetic tease teem thick thistle throng toddler torment lavish look elongate embitter exasperate exercise]
*brittle 10-59-19 (a.) 1. having little elasticity; hence easily cracked or fractured or snapped 2. lacking warmth and generosity of spirit 3. (of metal or glass) not annealed and consequently easily cracked or fractured (n.) 1. caramelized sugar cooled in thin sheets [bone breakable bring britt broken rich impetuous impulsive inelastic insecure irritable tacky temper temporary tense thin toffee transitory lack last lightweight likely little easy elasticity emaciate ephemeral evanescent] "brittle bones"
*broach 14-46-8 (n.) 1. a decorative pin worn by women (v.) 1. bring up a topic for discussion [below bite blue boat bore breastpin bring brooch raise recommend refer rent risk roach roast ope open address advance air artistic auger awkward capsize cask clip completely container cover crack cut handle heavy hole honeycomb]
*broadcast 02-51-395 (a.) 1. made widely known especially by radio or television 2. sown by casting over a wide area especially by hand (ad.) 1. so as to scatter or be distributed widely or in all directions (n.) 1. message that is transmitted by radio or television 2. a radio or television show (v.) 1. broadcast over the airwaves, as in radio or television 2. sow over a wide area, esp. by hand 3. cause to become widely known [bandy bare beam bed book broad radiation reforest render report reset response retail open overspread accessible air airwave announcement attenuate declared dilution display distribution drill communicate convey current seed set strew telecast transmit transplant] "the broadcast news"
*brogan 21-76-2 (n.) 1. a thick and heavy shoe [boot ankle /ago nag/]
*brogue 17-76-5 (n.) 1. a thick and heavy shoe [ballet bootee regional rogue rubber galoshes gum upper espadrille]
*brokerage 05-13-62 (n.) 1. a stock broker's business; charges a fee to act as intermediary between buyer and seller 2. the business of a broker; charges a fee to arrange a contract between two parties 3. place where a broker conducts his business [barter bond broker business buy buyer retail organization overly enterprise exchange agent aggressive anchorage arrange /gare/]
*bronchitis 17-63-5 (n.) 1. inflammation of the membranes lining the bronchial tubes [breathing bronc bronchopneumonia bunion bursitis respiratory rhinitis obstruction ophthalmia osteomyelitis otitis nephritis neuritis noisy chronic cold colitis cough cystitis hepatitis illness infection inflammation influenza irritation thrombophlebitis torticollis tube severe siderosis silicosis sinusitis spasm sputum]
*brooch 17-61-5 (n.) 1. a decorative pin worn by women (v.) 1. fasten with or as if with a brooch [badge bead bracelet breastpin broach rhinestone ring roo ornament catch chain circle clasp clothe crown hinge /coo/]
*brook 04-35-131 (n.) 1. a natural stream of water smaller than a river (and often a tributary of a river) (v.) 1. put up with something or somebody unpleasant [bear beck body branch brave burn race recompense remark river rivulet rook run overlook kill]
*brotherhood 10-35-19 (n.) 1. the feeling that men should treat one another like brothers 2. people engaged in a particular occupation 3. the kinship relation between a male offspring and the siblings 4. an organization of employees formed to bargain with the employer [bargain benignity blood brother radical relationship religion restricted occupation offspring order organize overthrow trade treat humanity economic employer enation engage enjoyment decline dedicated]
*browbeat 19-59-3 (v.) 1. be bossy towards 2. discourage or frighten with threats or a domineering manner; intimidate [badger beat big blarney bossy bounce break brother bullyrag repress rule oppress override walkover wheedle enslave exercise around autocratic terrorize threat threaten timid toward tyrannize]
*brusque 13-60-10 (a.) 1. marked by rude or peremptory shortness [blunt brief brisk broad reply reserved rough round rude unchecked unequivocal unguarded salesgirl severe sharp short show silent speech quiet elliptic epigrammatic explicit] "try to cultivate a less brusque manner"
*buffet 07-43-36 (n.) 1. a piece of furniture that stands at the side of a dining room; has shelves and drawers 2. a meal set out on a buffet at which guests help themselves 3. usually inexpensive bar (v.) 1. strike against forcefully 2. strike, beat repeatedly [bang bar batter battle beat blow board bottle box bread buff bump butter failure film finally fist flight foil food forceful frustration furniture eat eatery eel egg escritoire tableware tavern tease tent trouble /teff/] "Winds

buffeted the tent"

*buffoon 17-62-5 (n.) 1. a rude or vulgar fool 2. a person who amuses others by ridiculous behavior [behavior booger buffo bugger bumbling butt unite face fool old nobleman /off/]
*buffoonery 23-51-1 (n.) 1. acting like a clown or buffoon [banter batty behavior buffoon business folly foolish frivolity frivolous overact nutty eccentricity representation /off/]
*bulbous 18-45-4 (a.) 1. like a bulb 2. curving outward [belly botanic bulb bulgy bunchy leguminous look orb orbiculate outward shape spherical spheroid square swell swollen /blub/]
*bullock 12-68-13 (n.) 1. young bull 2. castrated bull [bible bovine bull lamb last leveret owlet calf castrate cattle chick colt cow cub cygnet kid]
*bulwark 16-47-6 (n.) 1. an embankment built around a space for defensive purposes 2. a protective structure of stone or concrete; extends from shore into the water to prevent a beach from washing away 3. a fence-like structure around a deck (v.) 1. defend with a bulwark [bailey bank bar barrier battlement beach blow boom britain buffer build buttress umbrella levee logjam long loophole wall wash water weir width work abatis abutment across aegis alliance ark arrow artificial attack average rampart redoubt region regular road roadblock roman keep /awl/]
*bumper 07-62-38 (a.) 1. extraordinarily abundant (n.) 1. a mechanical device consisting of bars at either end of vehicle absorb shock and prevent damage [bar barrier beverage big break brim broadcast bump umbrella unusual machine mammoth mask mat mechanism mega motorcar mouthful music panel piece pilot plentiful present prevent principle profuse program project propel protect pull engine extraordinary radio rim] "a bumper crop"
*bumptious 21-66-2 (a.) 1. offensively self-assertive [backward behavior biggety brash brassy brazen bump uppity modesty perky presumptuous pride pushy temperament impertinent impudent insulting obtrusive offensive opinion saucy self smug state]
*bungle 11-61-15 (n.) 1. an embarrassing mistake (v.) 1. make a mess of, destroy or ruin 2. spoil by behaving clumsily or foolishly [bad ball behavior blooper blow blunder blundering bobble boggle boner boob boor botch bull bumble bung butcher ungainly unintentional unsuccessful untidy unwieldy negligent normal gaffe gaucherie gawky glaring goldbrick gowk graceless lapse line looby look louse loutish lubberly ludicrous lumber effect embarrass err error /nub/] "I bungled it!"
*buoyancy 16-61-6 (n.) 1. cheerfulness that bubbles to the surface 2. the property of something weightless and insubstantial 3. irrepressible liveliness and good spirit [bouncy breezy bubble buoy optimism yeasty adaptable admire airy animation ascent cheerful chirpy compare /nay you/]
*buoyant 07-72-34 (a.) 1. characterized by liveliness and light-heartedness 2. tending to float on a liquid or rise in air or gas [balloon balsa blithe boat breezy bright buoy upbeat upward optimistic afloat airy animate tend /nay you/] "buoyant balloons"
*bureau 03-18-155 (n.) 1. furniture with drawers for keeping clothes 2. an administrative unit of government [bailiwick body united urea escritoire agency authority /rub/]
*bureaucracy 06-44-57 (n.) 1. nonelective government officials [basis bureau bureaucrat unite red regulation rigid round routine rule run elect examination administrative apply appointed authority carry category chinoiserie civil collective complex /rub/]
*burgeon 08-72-28 (v.) 1. grow and flourish [become big blow brew bud build burg rapid riot root runner gain gather gemmule germinate great growth effloresce enlarge escalate expand offshoot outgrow nascent /grub rub/] "The burgeoning administration"
*burgess 09-80-21 (n.) 1. a citizen of an English borough [borough burg english satirical story /grub rub/]
*burgher 21-62-2 (n.) 1. a citizen of an English borough 2. a member of the middle class [borough bourgeoisie burgess burgh university upper urbanite reform representative resident hold humorous english exurb /grub rub/]
*burnish 12-37-12 (n.) 1. the property of being smooth and shiny (v.) 1. polish and make shiny [black bowl bright brown buff burn until radiance ray reflect refulgent repeat roughness rub improve instrument send shellac shiny shoe silver sleek smooth surface hair /rub/]
*bursar 19-94-3 (n.) 1. the treasurer at a college or university [banker bookkeeping bursa university ratepayer receive remunerate school steward accountant assistant auditor /rub/]
*bustle 07-47-41 (n.) 1. a rapid bustling commotion 2. a framework worn at the back below the waist for giving fullness to a woman's skirt (v.) 1. move or cause to move energetically or busily [beat below boast brisk burst busily bust busy unquiet unrest unsettled upset urge scramble showy side skirt stir stirring structure support surround take tumult turbulent turmoil last leap lively eddy energetic exciting expedite] "The cheerleaders bustled about excitingly before their performance"
*butt 06-70-54 (n.) 1. thick end of the handle 2. a large cask (especially one holding a volume equivalent to 2 hogsheads or 126 gallons) 3. a joint made by fastening ends together without overlapping 4. a victim of ridicule or pranks 5. the small unused part of something (especially the end of a cigarette that is left after smoking) 6. the fleshy part of the human body that you sit on 7. finely ground tobacco wrapped in paper; for smoking 8. sports equipment consisting of an object set

up for a marksman or archer to aim at (v.) 1. place end to end without overlapping 2. to strike, thrust or shove against, often with head or horns 3. lie adjacent to another or share a boundary [backside balance barrel base beam behind bite blow body border bottom boundary bum bump bun bunt but union unused tail target thick thrust thus tip tobacco tool touch trapshooting trick trunk tub /tub/]
*buttress 13-32-11 (n.) 1. a support usually of stone or brick; supports the wall of a building (v.) 1. reinforce with a buttress 2. make stronger or defensible [backup bank beam beef brick build uphold upkeep temper thesis toughen tress ratify rear refresh reinforcement rig right rock embankment scripture solid source staff stand stay stone strengthen strong structure support supporter /tub/]
*byway 18-48-4 (n.) 1. a side road little traveled (as in the countryside) [beltway boulevard bypath byroad way wynd alleyway artery aspect avenue /yaw/]

C

*cabal 17-65-5 (n.) 1. a clique that seeks power usually through intrigue 2. a plot to carry out some harmful or illegal act (especially a political plot) (v.) 1. engage in plotting or enter into a conspiracy, swear together [cab camarilla camp carry cast catholic caucus cell circle clique club collusion complot connivance conspire coterie crowd addition agreement artifice association avenge bal band blend blow body last lead league]
*cabinet 03-58-199 (a.) 1. relating to or used in making cabinets 2. relating to or being a member of a governmental cabinet (n.) 1. a cupboard-like repository or piece of furniture with doors and shelves and

drawers; for storage or display 2. persons appointed by a head of state to head executive departments of government and act as official advisers 3. housing for electronic instruments, as radio or television 4. a storage compartment for clothes and valuables; usually it has a lock [cabin chief china closet commode component conference congress constitution corresponding court cover advisory appointed area armoire assembly association assume bench board boat bookcase breakfront british bunker bureau infrastructure instrument electronic escritoire executive tallboy television temporary toiletry tribunal] "cabinet wood"
*cacophony 13-53-11 (n.) 1. a loud harsh or strident noise 2. loud confusing disagreeable sounds [chaos clamor clumsy combination confuse conversation croaky crude agitation atonality passion phony pierce plain pleasant pompous harsh heavy hell hen husky noise noisy non]
*cadaverous 23-64-1 (a.) 1. very thin especially from disease or hunger or cold [cadaver cavernous cold colorless concentration corpse anemic ashen attenuate deathly dim disease dull eerie emaciate etiolated excess extremely resemble uncanny undernourished unearthly shrivel sickly skeleton suggest]
*cadence 14-32-9 (n.) 1. (prosody) the accent in a metrical foot of verse 2. a recurrent rhythmical series [chord chorus church close coda composition counterpoint absence accent accentuate aden amen analysis anapest arabesque art dance decline development division drop duration embellish emphasis end exposition note number]
*cadenza 19-45-3 (n.) 1. a brilliant solo passage occuring near the end of a piece of music [cadence coloratura composition acciaccatura aden appoggiatura arabesque division elaborate embellish extempore near]
*cadet 10-53-18 (n.) 1. a military trainee (as at a military academy) [cade academy age armed attend dated temporary theme training]
*cadge 21-61-2 (v.) 1. ask for and get free; be a parasite 2. obtain or seek to obtain by cadging or wheedling [cad chapman come costermonger ask drone generosity grub]
*cajole 12-57-13 (v.) 1. influence or urge by gentle urging, caressing, or flattering [caress certain coax compliment conjure course adopt adulate advocate allure argument arm jawbone juggle ole outreach outwit overreach letdown lobby lure ensnare entice excessive exhort]
*calculus 16-22-6 (n.) 1. a hard lump produced by the concretion of mineral salts; found in hollow organs or ducts of the body 2. the branch of mathematics that is concerned with limits and with the differentiation and integration of functions 3. an incrustation that forms on the teeth and gums [cal algebra arithmetic statistics stone]
*caliber 09-01-22 (n.) 1. diameter of a tube or gun barrel 2. a degree or grade of excellence or worth [candidate capacity center character circumference class competence connect cut cylinder ability ali amount area arm large length level line low ideation inferiority instinct internal interval barrel bigness body bore bulk bullet equipment excellence executive expansion external range reach rise round]
*callow 14-74-8 (a.) 1. lacking experience of life [adolescent adult allow arrest awkward lack lacking last life original wanting /olla/] "a callow youth of seventeen"
*calorie 07-61-39 (n.) 1. unit of heat defined as the quantity of heat required to raise the temperature of 1 gram of water by 1 degree centigrade at atmospheric pressure 2. a unit of heat equal to the amount of heat required to raise the temperature of one kilogram of water by one degree at one atmosphere pressure; used by nutritionists to characterize the energy-producing potential in food [calor centigrade characterize convert amount atmospheric large origin raise require energy equal erg]
*calumny 23-57-1 (n.) 1. a malicious attack 2. an abusive attack on a person's character or good name [calling calumniate catty character communicate contumely criticism crude abuse abusive accusation alum animadversion argument aspersion assassination attack libel lie living lying malicious misrepresent]
*calvary 19-21-3 (n.) 1. a hill near Jerusalem where Jesus was crucified 2. any experience that causes intense suffering [capital cause christian city crucify accord ancient land large local]
*calvinism 19-58-3 (n.) 1. the theological system of John Calvin and his followers emphasizing omnipotence of God and salvation by grace alone [catholic christendom church alone separate]
*came 01-53-1669 (v.) 1. develop into 2. be received, as of news on the radio or television 3. come to one's mind; suggest itself 4. add up in number or quantity 5. be found or available 6. come to pass; arrive, as in due course 7. happen as a result 8. come under, be classified or included 9. enter or assume a condition, relation, use, or position 10. reach a destination; arrive by movement or by making progress 11. cover a certain distance 12. exist or occur in a certain point in a series 13. come from; be connected by a relationship of blood, for example 14. to be the product or result 15. reach a state, relation, or condition 16. extend or reach 17. be a native of 18. come forth 19. move toward, travel toward something or somebody or approach something or somebody 20. experience orgasm 21. have a certain priority 22. proceed or get along [cam category certain classify closet college color come condition connect contact course add amount anger appear approach arise arrive assume available massacre mean midnight mind mouth move early emanate ensue enter exist experience extend /mac/] "He came singing down the road"

*cameo 08-70-28 (n.) 1. engraving or carving in low relief on a stone (as in a brooch or ring) [carve character color come actor anaglyph appearance mask medallion movie emboss engrave evocation ocean /mac/]
*campaign 01-51-966 (n.) 1. several related operations aimed at achieving a particular goal (usually within geographical and temporal constraints) 2. a series of actions advancing a principle or tending toward a particular end 3. a race between candidates for elective office 4. an overland journey by hunters (especially in Africa) (v.) 1. exert oneself continuously, vigorously, or obtrusively to gain an end or engage in a crusade for a certain cause or person; be an advocate for 2. run, stand, or compete for an office or a position 3. go on a campaign; go off to war [camp cause competition course activity advertise advocate aware military movement party people persuade politics press principle program progress promotion push interest issue /mac/] "he supported populist campaigns"
*canard 18-50-4 (n.) 1. a deliberately misleading fabrication [chicken concoction create cry account aircraft artifice attached nard near nose report romance rumble rumor deliberate dodge duckling /rana/]
*canary 08-83-30 (a.) 1. having the color of a canary; a light to moderate yellow (n.) 1. someone acting as an informer or decoy for the police 2. (informal) a female singer 3. a moderate yellow with a greenish tinge 4. any of several small Old World finches [cage camp cantor cardinal chaffinch chickadee chromatic cockatoo colloquialism color communicate confidential creamy croon crush cuckoo adapt adjacent alto aureate auric azores nark nary native nightingale noted numerous nuthatch rat return reveal ringdove ripe robber robin yellow yodel /rana/]
*candid 08-47-31 (a.) 1. characterized by disconcerting directness in manner or speech; without subtlety or evasion 2. informal or natural; especially caught off guard or unprepared 3. starkly realistic 4. openly straightforward and direct without reserve or secretiveness [catch chatty childlike conversational critic accessible accusation admission and approach artifice artless austere authentic native nature neat neutral never design devious direct disconcert distasteful documentary dry dull impartial impromptu inability indirect informal ingenuous innocent interview]
*candor 13-01-10 (n.) 1. ability to make judgments free from discrimination or dishonesty 2. the quality of being honest and straightforward in attitude and speech [candidness communicative conspicuous cricket accessible and andor approachable attitude austerity naivety natural non direct discrimination dishonesty distasteful open openly opinion outgoing outspoken refresh round /rod/]
*canine 13-54-10 (a.) 1. of or relating to a pointed conical tooth 2. (zoology) of or relating to or characteristic of members of the family Canidae (n.) 1. one of the four pointed conical teeth (two in each jaw) located between the incisors and the premolars 2. any of various fissiped mammals with nonretractile claws and typically long muzzles [cannibal carnivorous carrion chew chiefly claw closely conic crown cuspid cutter africa alert america amphibian animal aquatic asia attack nine nocturnal non north incisor insectivore invertebrate ear eurasia eye eyetooth]
*canon 07-65-37 (n.) 1. a rule or especially body of rules or principles generally established as valid and fundamental in a field or art or philosophy 2. a collection of books accepted as holy scripture especially the books of the Bible recognized by any Christian church as genuine and inspired 3. a complete list of saints that have been recognized by the Roman Catholic Church 4. a contrapuntal piece of music in which a melody in one part is imitated exactly in other parts 5. a priest who is a member of a cathedral chapter 6. (North America) a ravine formed by a river in an area with little rainfall [canyon catch catholic century chapter check christianity church cipher clergyman collection composition conduct connected consecrate contrapuntal convention counterpoint create cryptography accept act album anon anthology array art artistic authority narrow neoclassical norma north note omnibus opus ordinance ordonnance /nona/] "the neoclassical canon"
*cant 18-59-4 (a.) 1. having the slant of a bevel (n.) 1. stock phrases that have become nonsense through endless repetition 2. a slope in the turn of a road or track; the outside is higher than the inside in order to reduce the effects of centrifugal force 3. two surfaces meeting at an angle different from 90 degrees 4. a characteristic language of a particular group (as among thieves) 5. insincere talk about religion or morals (v.) 1. heel over [camber capacity chat climb code corner accent affected alert angle ant applesauce noise nook talk taradiddle tilt tip tommyrot tosh tripe trumpery twaddle]
*cantankerous 17-53-5 (a.) 1. (British) stubbornly obstructive and unwilling to cooperate 2. having a difficult and contrary disposition [confrontation contrary cooperate cross crotchety crusty aggressive anger argumentative awkward tanker tenacious testy tetchy touchy kingdom excitable obstructive occupy old ornery ugly unite unpleasant unwilling sayer scotland shipbuilder sour spectator stroppy stubborn stuffy sullen]
*cantata 14-39-8 (n.) 1. a musical composition for voices and orchestra based on a religious text [calypso canticle capric chamber chorus coloratura comic composition con concerto conform country crescendo critical adagio allegro alto andante anta anthem appealing aria arpeggio nocturne taste theme tone traditional twelve]
*canto 18-37-4 (n.) 1. the highest part (usually the

melody) in a piece of choral music 2. a major division of a long poem [cant choral chorus composition contralto couplet air alto aria note tenor treble tune octave octet]
*canvass 10-66-17 (n.) 1. the setting for a narrative or fictional or dramatic account 2. a tent made of canvas 3. an oil painting on canvas 4. heavy closely woven fabric (used for clothing or chairs or sails or tents) 5. the mat that forms the floor of the ring in which boxers or professional wrestlers compete 6. an inquiry into public opinion conducted by interviewing a random sample of people 7. a large piece of fabric (as canvas) by means of which wind is used to propel a sailing vessel (v.) 1. get the opinions of people, for example 2. consider in detail and subject to an analysis in order to discover essential features or meaning 3. solicit votes from potential voters in an electoral campaign [campaign canvas case clothe combination court crusade address air analyze appeal argue nay ventilate vet vote sail say seek set ship solicit study stump survey]
*capacious 18-53-4 (a.) 1. large in capacity [capa carry commodious comprehensive copious abundant ample average plentiful infinite sizable size spacious spreading /cap capa/] "she carried a capacious bag"
*capillary 21-55-2 (a.) 1. relating to or involving capillarity 2. (anatomy) "a capillary network" 3. long and slender with a very small internal diameter (n.) 1. a tube of small internal diameter; holds liquid by capillary action 2. any of the minute blood vessels connecting arterioles with venules [carotid cerebra circulate conduit connect cortex cross cylindrical anatomy aorta arteriole artery attraction physics pillar instrument intertwine ligament liquid long resemble ropy /lip lipa ralli/] "capillary action"
*capitulate 14-64-8 (v.) 1. surrender under agreed conditions [cave cede concede condition consent abandon acquiesce agree argument possession power pressure unavoidable late /tip/]
*caprice 15-62-7 (n.) 1. a sudden desire [capri capricious characteristic conceit accompany arbitrary peculiarity petulant popularity potpourri price impulsive inconsistency]
*capricious 13-53-11 (a.) 1. changeable 2. determined by chance or impulse or whim rather than by necessity or reason [capri casual change changeable corruptible adrift alternate arbitrary passing patchy persecution pluralism preference random reason refusal restless rough ruler impossible impulsive indiscriminate irresponsible unaccountable uncertain undetermined unexpected unreliable skeptical staggering sudden summer system] "a capricious summer breeze"
*caption 08-25-29 (n.) 1. translation of foreign dialogue of a movie or TV program; usually displayed at the bottom of the screen 2. brief description accompanying an illustration (v.) 1. provide with a caption, as of a photograph or a drawing [circumstance clear communicate continuous criticism accompany adverse apt argument article artwork attach attractive authority photograph picture precede print production program provide publish television title translation identify illustration image]
*captivate 09-56-26 (v.) 1. attract; cause to be enamored [catch charm charming coax con confounded convince aghast alluring amaze appeal appetizing apt attention attractive awe awed paper persuade piquant pleasing pleasure popeyed prepossessing psychological puzzle take taking tease terror thrilling thunderstruck trance transport incantation induce infatuated influence interesting intrigue inviting irresistible vamp voluptuous enamor enchant endear enthral entrance]
*carcass 12-57-12 (n.) 1. the dead body of an animal especially one slaughtered and dressed for food [cadaver carrion clay corpse almost anatomy animal arca ash rattletrap remain remains ruin shell skeleton slaughter soma stiff structure /sacra/]
*cardiac 10-46-17 (a.) 1. of or relating to the heart [cardia circulatory colic colonic connect coronary abdominal affect anal arrest rectal duodenal ileac internal intestinal /caid/] "cardiac arrest"
*cardinal 05-29-84 (a.) 1. serving as an essential component 2. being or denoting a numerical quantity but not order (n.) 1. (Roman Catholic Church) one of a group of more than 100 prominent bishops in the Sacred College who advise the Pope and elect new Popes 2. the number of elements in a mathematical set; denotes a quantity but not the order 3. crested thick-billed North American finch having bright red plumage in the male 4. a variable color averaging a vivid red [cardi catholicchief central chief christian christianity church control absolute abuna administrative advise algorithm appointed archpriest authority average radical red roman ruling dean digital dominant impossible inflame integral necessary negative numeric leading logarithmic lurid] "a cardinal rule"
*caricature 08-55-33 (n.) 1. a representation of a person that is exaggerated for comic effect (v.) 1. represent in or produce a caricature of [car cartoon charade color comedy comic composition create aggrandize amplify anamorphosis ape art attempt represent ridiculous imitation impersonate inappropriate incongruity inflation ingenuity irony takeoff tout travesty twist understate unsuccessful effect enhance evoke exaggerate expansion extreme /ruta/] "The drawing caricatured the President"
*carnage 10-63-18 (n.) 1. the savage and excessive killing of many people [casualty cavalry cheyenne command consumption custer accident american anna antonio arna ravage rebel river ruination native near genocide great group excessive execution]
*carnal 17-53-5 (a.) 1. of the appetites and passions of the body 2. of or relating to or belonging to the body 3. of or relating to the body or flesh [chassis coarse cold concupiscence contrast corporeal criminality amorous

anatomy animal animality appetite arna randy recidivism remain nuptial nymphomaniac lapse lascivious lewd libido lust]
*carnivorous 19-57-3 (a.) 1. relating to or characteristic of carnivores 2. (used of plants as well as animals) feeding on animals [cannibalistic capable carn catch commensal animal nourishing nutritious insectivore invertebrate vegetarian omnivorous organism scavenge /vin/] "the lion and other carnivorous animals"
*carouse 18-56-4 (n.) 1. revelry in drinking; a merry drinking party (v.) 1. engage in boisterous, drunken merry-making [carousal celebrate arouse racket randy revel revelry riot roil roister rouse orgy unrestrained uproarious skylark spree symposium engage escapade]
*carrion 21-54-2 (n.) 1. dead and rotting flesh; unfit for human food 2. the dead and rotting body of an animal [carcass carr clay corruption animal ash rank raw refuse remains rot obscenity offal ordure necrosis /noir/]
*cartilage 13-54-10 (n.) 1. tough elastic tissue; mostly converted to bone in adults [cart cell change collagen compose connective convert cushion adam adult animal apple arytenoid attached respiratory tendon throat thyroid tissue tough translucent infancy intercellular large larynx gelatin give gristle growth ear elastic embed /gal/]
*cartridge 14-34-8 (n.) 1. ammunition consisting of a cylindrical casing containing an explosive charge and a bullet; fired from a rifle or handgun 2. a module designed to be inserted into a larger piece of equipment 3. an electro-acoustic transducer that is the part of the arm of a record player that holds the needle and that is removable 4. a light-tight supply chamber holding the film and supplying it for exposure as required [cartouche case cassette change container ammo ridge roll tone turntable disc dope dummy gun emulsion /dirt/] "he loaded a cartridge of fresh tape into the tape deck"
*caste 14-48-8 (n.) 1. social status or position conferred by a system based on class 2. (Hindu) a hereditary social class stratified according to ritual purity 3. a social class separated from others by distinctions of hereditary rank or profession or wealth [cast class colony community condition confer criterion cultural accord ant area ashram aspect separate sept set since specialize stage stand status still stratify supreme theory thousand title totem truth earthly echelon economic estate eternal exclusive] "lose caste by doing work beneath one's station"
*castigate 13-60-11 (v.) 1. censure severely 2. inflict severe punishment on [call carpet cast censure chastise chew chide correct criticize angrily assail attack scold scolding scorch scourge severe slash strong tell thrash ticking trounce impose inflict insensitive excoriate /git tag/]
*casual 04-48-113 (a.) 1. occurring or appearing or singled out by chance 2. hasty and without attention to detail; not thorough 3. without or seeming to be without plan or method; offhand 4. suited for everyday use 5. marked by blithe unconcern 6. not showing effort or strain 7. employed in a specified capacity from time to time 8. characterized by a feeling of irresponsibility 9. natural and unstudied [calm careless cavalier chance clear cool accidental additional automatic seasonal side slapdash smooth spontaneous system unassuming uncertain unconventional unexpected unintentional unplanned unpremeditated lay light loose] "an ability to interest casual students"
*casualty 04-55-100 (n.) 1. someone injured or killed or captured or missing in a military engagement 2. a decrease of military personnel or equipment 3. someone injured or killed in an accident 4. an accident that causes someone to die [capture casual cause circumstance civilian collision combat course crash accident adventure armed serious service shipwreck shock soldier statistic suffer underdog unfortunate lessen loss target tragedy]
*cataclysm 19-35-3 (n.) 1. a sudden violent change in the earth's surface 2. an event resulting in great loss and misfortune [calamity casualty cata cave city cold composition cosmic crash crop accident affect alluvium apocalypse apoplexy atmosphere terrible torrent tragedy trouble tsunami layer loss luck scale severe shipwreck shock shortage smoke starvation stroke structure sudden sun surface major meltdown misadventure misfortune mishap /cat cata/]
*catalyst 08-56-32 (n.) 1. (chemistry) a substance that initiates or accelerates a chemical reaction without itself being affected 2. something that causes an important event to happen [cata cause cell chemistry compound country creator accelerator act activate affect agent agitprop author thermolysis troublemaker leaven yeast science spark specific split spur stimulant stimulus substance] "the invasion acted as a catalyst to unite the country"
*cataract 16-58-6 (n.) 1. clouding of the natural lens of the eye 2. a large waterfall; violent rush of water over a precipice [capsule cascade chute cloud collapse condition cover crash affect amaurosis artificial atar torrent total trachoma treat rain rapid replace river rush /carat rata/]
*catastrophe 07-53-37 (n.) 1. a state of extreme (usually irremediable) ruin and misfortune 2. an event resulting in great loss and misfortune 3. a sudden violent change in the earth's surface [calamity casualty color conclusion crash accident action argument theme tone topic tragedy scheme story strophe subject recognition resolution revulsion ruinous omega overturn payoff plan plot effect end ending /port sat/]
*catharsis 17-43-5 (n.) 1. (psychoanalysis) purging of emotional tensions 2. purging the body by the use of a cathartic to stimulate evacuation of the bowels [cleanse complex crap abreaction accord analysis athar audience technique tension theory tragic treat trot release relieve

remove repress respite rid run sediment set sigmund spiritual stimulate stool surcease surface suspension identify intense intermission]
*cathode 21-47-2 (n.) 1. a negatively charged electrode that is the source of electrons in an electrical device 2. the positively charged terminal of a voltaic cell or storage battery that supplies current [cat cause cell charge chemical circuit conductor contact conversion current accumulator anode apply arrange terminus transport tube hydrogen depot device electron emit energy evacuate]
*catholicism 12-53-13 (n.) 1. the beliefs and practices of a Catholic Church [catholic christianity church alexandria antioch teach testament old savior monotheism moscow]
*caucus 08-11-27 (n.) 1. a closed political meeting (v.) 1. meet to select a candidate or promote a policy [camp candidate close collect committee conclave conference convention council alliance arrange assembly assignation union unite select session side sit special]
*causal 18-59-4 (a.) 1. involving or constituting a cause; causing [causa connect constitute contributory scarcity] "a causal relationship between scarcity and higher prices"
*caustic 13-50-11 (a.) 1. harsh or corrosive in tone 2. of a substance, especially a strong acid; capable of destroying or eating away by chemical action (n.) 1. any chemical substance that burns or destroys living tissue [circle compound cool corrosive critical cutting acerbic acidic acrid acute angry arc astringent unkind sarcastic scathing severe sharp sour sulphurous tart terse tic trenchant incisive ironic irritate]
*cede 10-41-19 (v.) 1. give over; surrender or relinquish to the physical control of another 2. relinquish possession or control over [cease concrete confer control convey country enfeoff exchange deliver drop dump]
*censor 09-48-23 (n.) 1. a person who is authorized to read publications or correspondence or to watch theatrical performances and suppress in whole or in part anything considered obscene or politically unacceptable (v.) 1. forbid the public distribution of; as of movies or newspapers 2. subject to political, religious, or moral censorship [cancel classified close communication conceal control crush cut edit enigmatic erase esoteric evaluate excise expurgate extinguish narrow nitpick screen secret silence smother stifle suppress occult omit outlaw remove repress rescind restricted review] "This magazine is censored by the government"
*censorious 21-70-2 (a.) 1. harshly critical or expressing censure [call censor condemn conscientious contemptuous convey criticize eager error exacting execrate express narrow selective sensitive severe stern strict strong objurgate overcritical reprobative revile ridicule incline inveigh uncritical] "was censorious of petty failings"
*censure 10-50-18 (n.) 1. harsh criticism or disapproval 2. the state of being excommunicated (v.) 1. rebuke formally [catholic certain christian church comment condemn contempt conviction criminate criticize culpable ecclesiastical ensure exclusion excommunicate excoriate expression notice sacrament scorn sentence severe sinful soil spot statement strong unholy real rebuke reject remark report reprehensible reprimand review roman]
*census 07-23-36 (n.) 1. a period count of the population (v.) 1. conduct a census [carry code combination conduct content count element enumerate number numeration user scroll set statement survey] "They censused the deer in the forest"
*centenary 09-81-21 (a.) 1. of or relating to or completing a period of 100 years (n.) 1. the 100th anniversary [celebrate cent complete anniversary remembrance year]
*centimeter 15-65-7 (n.) 1. a metric unit of length equal to one hundredth of a meter [centime equal tenth term thousandth meter metric /emit rete/]
*centurion 15-88-7 (n.) 1. (in ancient Rome) the leader of 100 soldiers [capital catholic century charge church city corporal empire engage eternal europe experience tercentenary tiber turion republic roman rome italy officer /noir/]
*cereal 09-56-26 (a.) 1. made of grain or relating to grain or the plants that produce it (n.) 1. grass whose starchy grains are used as food: wheat; rice; rye; oats; maize; buckwheat; millet 2. a breakfast food prepared from grain 3. cereal grain suitable as food for human beings [cane cattail central cere chiefly cook corn cornflakes cracked crop crush cultivate cut ear eat erect europe radicular real reed rhizoid rhizome rice rye africa animal annual aquatic asia lawn leguminous light loblolly] "a cereal beverage"
*ceremonial 09-40-23 (a.) 1. marked by pomp or ceremony or formality (n.) 1. a formal event performed on a special occasion [celebrate cere ceremony courtly enterprise eucharist exercise rigid mannered mummery mystery observance occasion office ordinance imposing inauguration initiation institution affair august liturgy lofty /lain mere nome/] "a ceremonial occasion"
*ceremonious 23-36-1 (a.) 1. rigidly formal or bound by convention [careful cere civil convention correct establish eucharist excessive regal regardful reply require respectful rigid ritualistic majestic moving observe imperious imposing impressive seem solemn stiff striking /mere nome/] "their ceremonious greetings did not seem heartfelt"
*cessation 16-47-6 (n.) 1. a stopping [cease cess close cohabit conclusion court effect end separation standstill stop subsidence surcease suspension abandon abeyance agreement apodosis termination terminus thunder interruption interval omega /ass tass tasse/] "a cessation of the thunder"

*chafe 14-29-8 (n.) 1. soreness and warmth caused by friction 2. anger produced by some annoying irritation (v.) 1. become or make sore by or as if by rubbing 2. cause annoyance in; disturb, esp. by minor irritations 3. feel extreme irritation or anger 4. warm by rubbing, as with the hands 5. tear or wear off the skin or make sore by abrading 6. cause friction [cha check chevy chivy choler chronic close condition continually cook cut hand harass harry hassle hasten hinder home hostility hot hurt abnormal afflict aggravate anger annoying antagonize area arouse felt file fracture fray fret friction ear eat emotional erode exasperate excite excoriate exercise experience extreme] "he had a nasty chafe on his knee"
*chagrin 13-40-10 (n.) 1. strong feelings of embarrassment (v.) 1. cause to fee shame; hurt the pride of [character child completely composure confusion crestfallen crush hangdog humble humiliation hurt abase abash afflict agitate anger annoyance ashamed grin guilt reduce reluctant reserved restrained inadequate injure irritation]
*chameleon 15-55-7 (n.) 1. a faint constellation in the polar region of the southern hemisphere near Apus and Mensa 2. lizard of Africa and Madagascar able to change skin color and having a projectile tongue [cayman changeable cheetah classification color configuration constellation crocodile harlequin hemisphere human africa agama alligator amel anole madagascar mercury monitor moon mortal earth leatherback leg leopard lizard long ocelot old opal ophite nacre near]
*chancery 14-65-8 (n.) 1. a court with jurisdiction in equity 2. an office of archives for public or ecclesiastic records; a court of public records [cabinet chamber chancer closet conduct court headquarters historical archive assembly assize ecclesiastic embassy equity record registry relation]
*chaos 04-57-96 (n.) 1. a state of extreme confusion and disorder 2. (Greek mythology) the most ancient of gods; the personification of the infinity of space preceding creation of the universe 3. the formless and disordered state of matter before the creation of the cosmos [cacophony cha cloud commotion complete condition confusion cosmos creation hassle haze hazy hebrew agitation aloof anarchy ancient apparently obscurity ochlocracy science sensitivity separate space suppose sweat]
*characteristic 04-51-98 (a.) 1. typical or distinctive (n.) 1. a distinguishing quality 2. a prominent aspect of something 3. the integer part (positive or negative) of the representation of a logarithm; in the expression log 643 = 2.808 the characteristic is 2 4. (electronics) any measurable property of a device measured under closely specified conditions [cast character constitutional cut habitude hallmark heal hue appropriate aroma aspect attribute realistic regular representative taint tang taste trademark earmark emotional exemplary image impression index safety shape sort style system /sire/] "heard my friend's characteristic laugh"
*characterize 06-01-59 (v.) 1. be characteristic of 2. describe or portray the character or the qualities or peculiarities of [certain character chart clearly connote consideration highlight hint adumbrate argue attention attribute register remember representative reveal testify think trait typify earmark egotist evoke exemplify express identify illustrate individuate involve] "You can characterize his behavior as that of an egotist"
*charlatan 17-69-5 (n.) 1. a flamboyant deceiver; one who attracts customers with tricks or jokes [char cheat claim con counterfeit craniology customer humbug advice artist attract read ringer lead trickster true]
*chary 23-45-1 (a.) 1. characterized by great cautious and wariness [cagey cagy calculate canny careful cautious char concern hesitant answer avoidance reluctant restrained risk]
*chasm 13-60-10 (n.) 1. a deep opening in the earth's surface [cavity cha check cleft continuity crack crater crevasse cut hiatus hole hollow abyss aperture apparently arroyo slot space split surface mine moat]
*chasten 14-65-9 (v.) 1. censure severely 2. restrain or temper 3. correct by punishment or discipline [call carpet castigate censure chaste chew chide confession constrained control correct criticize curb harsh hasten housebreak humble humiliate hush abate admonish allay alleviate alter angrily scold self severe shame show slowdown soften stable subdued subjugate suppress tame temper tempered transform trounce embarrass extenuate]
*chastise 13-38-11 (v.) 1. censure severely [call cane carpet castigate censure chew chide correct correction criticize harsh hast admonish angrily scold scolding scourge severe spank tell thrash trounce insensitive expression] "She chastised him for his insensitive remarks"
*chastisement 23-81-1 (n.) 1. verbal punishment 2. a rebuke for making a mistake [castigate censure correction criticism scolding telling expression mistake]
*chastity 18-56-4 (n.) 1. abstaining from sexual relations 2. morality with respect to sexual relations [clarity cleanliness clear concern conduct control correct hast honor human abstinence appetite appropriate avoidance sex simplicity sin smooth spotless strong style supernatural tasteful teetotal terse transparency impeccable indulge infallible innocence]
*chateau 10-43-20 (n.) 1. an impressive country house (or castle) in France [castle chat citadel country house attached turret estate]
*chattel 21-62-2 (n.) 1. personal as opposed to real property; any tangible movable property (furniture or domestic animals or a car etc) [captive car chat churl combustion concubine helot hereditament hold animal area automobile tangible thing thrall effect engine estate land lease]

*chauvinist 16-54-6 (n.) 1. a person with a prejudiced belief in the superiority of his or her own kind 2. an extreme bellicose nationalist [center cha civic colored country hardhat hawk homo hundred aggressive unreason illiberal influence interested intolerant nationalist nationalistic nonobjective sexist superiority sway twist]
*check 02-51-458 (n.) 1. the state of inactivity following an interruption 2. the act of inspecting or verifying 3. additional proof that something that was believed (some fact or hypothesis or theory) is correct 4. the bill in a restaurant 5. an appraisal of the state of affairs 6. a written order directing a bank to pay money 7. the act of restraining power or action or limiting excess 8. (chess) a direct attack on an opponent's king 9. a textile pattern of squares or crossed lines (resembling a checkerboard) 10. obstructing an opponent in ice hockey 11. a mark indicating that something has been noted or completed etc. 12. a mark left after a small piece has been chopped or broken off of something 13. something immaterial that interferes with or delays action or progress (v.) 1. stop for a moment, as if out of uncertainty or caution 2. put a check mark on or next to 3. slow the growth or development of 4. lessen the intensity of; temper; hold in restraint; hold or keep within limits 5. be careful or certain to do something; make certain of something 6. make an examination or investigation 7. examine so as to determine accuracy, quality, or condition 8. abandon the intended prey, turn, and pursue an inferior prey, of falcons 9. arrest the motion (of something) abruptly 10. block or impede (a player from the opposing team) in ice hockey 11. consign for shipment on a vehicle, as of luggage 12. decline to initiate betting, in poker 13. hand over something to somebody as for temporary safekeeping 14. place into check in a game of chess 15. stop in a chase esp. when scent is lost 16. verify by consulting a source or authority 17. write out a check on a bank account 18. be verified or confirmed; pass inspection 19. mark into squares or draw squares on; draw crossed lines on 20. make cracks or chinks in 21. hold back, as of a danger or an enemy; check the expansion or influence of 22. become fractured; break or crack on the surface only 23. find out, learn, or determine with certainty, usually by making an inquiry or other effort 24. train by instruction and practice; esp. to teach self-control 25. be compatible, similar or consistent; coincide in their characteristics [charge cheque compare control correspond heck hold ensure equal exchange] "check the brakes"
*chicanery 19-51-3 (n.) 1. the use of tricks to deceive someone (usually to extract money from them) [catch cheat chicane clever coup craft hairsplitting hedge hoax hot humbug intend intrigue achieve advantage art artful artifice non equivocation evasion expedient extract racket read rob roguish ruse]
*chiffon 13-55-11 (a.) 1. as thin and soft as chiffon 2. of pastry; having a light delicate texture achieved by whipping or adding whipped egg whites (n.) 1. a sheer fabric of silk or rayon [calico camel canvas cashmere chenille chi chintz cloth cook corduroy cotton create crepe crochet cross hair heavy horsehair fabric felting fiber fine flannelette fleece fluffy food fur opposite organdy natural nylon /off/] "chiffon taffeta"
*chisel 12-48-13 (n.) 1. an edge tool with a flat steel blade with a cutting edge (v.) 1. engage in deceitful behavior; practice trickery or fraud 2. deprive somebody of something by deceit 3. carve with a chisel [calculate character cheat chi clearly clever con conman crafty create cunning cut harvest hatch have hew hoodwink hook incise indirect inscription insidious insubstantial scam score scratch set shape sharp skill surcharge swindle engrave etching euchre exceptional extract layout lead light line lithography] "Who's chiseling on the side?"
*chivalry 18-71-4 (n.) 1. courtesy towards women 2. the medieval principles of knighthood [chiv chivalrous civility collective combination concept consider courtly custom heroism honor ideal idealism impartial intrepid valiant valor virtuous aristocracy arm armed attentive liberal life lofty loyalty religious righteous royalty rule]
*cholera 17-49-5 (n.) 1. an acute intestinal infection caused by ingestion of contaminated water or food [chickenpox choler contaminate cowpox hepatitis hookworm hydrophobia ornithosis osteomyelitis leprosy leptospirosis lockjaw elephantiasis epidemic erysipelas rabies ringworm rubeola acute ague anthrax asiatic]
*choral 09-45-22 (a.) 1. related to or written for or performed by a chorus or choir (n.) 1. a stately Protestant (especially Lutheran) hymn tune [choir choric coloratura composition concern harmonic heroic hora hymn hymnal operatic oral organization alto anthem arrange liturgical lutheran lyric] "choral composition"
*christ 05-58-73 (n.) 1. a prophet of the first century; to Christians he was both God and man--the Messiah sent to save the human race from the sin it inherited through the Fall of Man (circa 8 BC - 29 AD) 2. any expected deliverer [century child chosen chris claim connected convert cultural harm hebrew highly human race redeemer redemption religious rescue inherit inspiration interpreter israelite salvation save savior second sent sermon shepherd sin son speak surprise taboo teacher tie trinity]
*christen 13-67-11 (v.) 1. administer baptism to [call ceremony child christ coffeepot raise identify inaugurate include institute introduce sanctify ship specify sprinkle style tag term title entitle establish name nickname nominate]
*christendom 21-71-2 (n.) 1. the collective body of Christians throughout the world and history [church collective history thousand tie entity europe occupation]
*chromatic 18-21-4 (a.) 1. able to refract light without

spectral color separation 2. (music) based on a scale consisting of 12 semitones 3. being or having or characterized by hue [chroma cold colored coloring cool harmonious rainbow ocular ophthalmic optical match medley motley tonal tone] "chromatic lens"
*chronic 05-49-67 (a.) 1. (medicine) being long-lasting and recurrent or characterized by long suffering 2. having a habit of long standing [compulsive conditional confirmed constant continue course habitual habituate hardy rapid recurrent remain repeat ron rooted routine onset non illness implant indigestion ingrained instil invalid inveterate irreversible] "chronic indigestion"
*chronology 14-27-9 (n.) 1. arrangement of events in time 2. a record of events in the order of their occurrence 3. the determination of the actual temporal sequence of past events [calendar confession continuity hagiology history humanity record registry relation resume obituary occurrence ology narrative necrology language lasting legend liberal list log long general]
*cipher 17-48-5 (n.) 1. a message written in a secret code 2. a secret method of writing 3. a person of no influence 4. a quantity of no importance 5. a mathematical element that when added to another number yields the same number (v.) 1. convert ordinary language into code 2. make a mathematical calculation or computation [calculate cast compute cross ideogram initial integer punk puppet pushover hand her emblem endorsement estimate reckon resolve runt]
*circulate 05-41-65 (v.) 1. move through a space, circuit or system, returning to the starting point, as of air or liquids 2. cause to be distributed 3. cause to become widely known 4. become widely known and passed on 5. move in circles 6. cause to move in a circuit or system 7. move around freely 8. cause to move around [cater compass concrete content convection course cycle include introduce issue reach report return revolve room route royalty rumor run unhurried utter lap late letter liquid location loop abstract advertise air announce area around talk taste transfer travel twist encircle enclose encompass environment]
*circumference 18-52-4 (n.) 1. the size of something as given by the distance around it 2. the length of the closed curve of a circle [close covering crown cum curve cycle integument radius rim ring roughly round magnitude march margin facade fixed fringe front edge envelope equal extent external noose]
*circumlocution 23-53-1 (n.) 1. a style that involves indirect ways of expressing things 2. an indirect way of expressing something [circumvolution clever convoluted convolution crinkle indirect involve redundancy round roundabout undulation unpleasant meander literally locution oblique orbit tortuous truth turning twist necessary /olm/]
*circumnavigate 16-76-6 (v.) 1. travel around, either by plane or ship [coast compass cross cycle island round row run motorboat navigate around voyage gyre travel traverse earth encircle encompass /tag van/]
*circumscribe 17-32-5 (v.) 1. restrict or confine, "I limit you to two visits to the pub a day" 2. draw a line around 3. to draw a geometric figure around another figure so that the two are in contact but do not intersect [commodity concentrate condition confine consumption content contract corner curb curtail curve cut independent intersect reduce restriction mark mathematics minify mitigate moderate modify satisfy scarce scribe season separate set shape side small surface surround bar boundary box enclose extent]
*circumspect 13-58-10 (a.) 1. heedful of potential consequences [cagey careful cautious chary consider curious idle indolent investor recommend reflective relaxed reluctant uncommunicative unhurried mark meticulous mindful moderate safe sensible shuffling small sound spec staggering poke possible potential provident prudent prudential easy enlighten tender tentative thorough] "circumspect actions"
*citadel 14-46-8 (n.) 1. a stronghold into which people could go for shelter during a battle [castle city institution town acropolis ade ancient defensive donjon life /led/]
*cite 02-27-373 (v.) 1. repeat a passage from 2. refer to 3. commend 4. make reference to 5. advance evidence for 6. refer to for illustration or proof 7. call in an official matter, such as to attend court [call case catalogue charge come commend complain composition connection consideration count court create illustrate imply impress incorrect indite ingeminate instance interlocutor invention iterate task tax tell testify think title try entry evidence evoke example exemplify existence explain express]
*claimant 09-81-21 (n.) 1. someone who claims a benefit or right or title [candidate claim compensation complainant libelant accuse admission appellant apply aspirant assistance impeach impute indict informer inheritance throne title] "claimants of unemployment compensation"
*clamor 11-01-14 (n.) 1. a loud harsh or strident noise 2. loud and persistent outcry from many people (v.) 1. utter or proclaim insistently and noisily 2. make loud demands 3. compel someone to do something by insistent clamoring [cacophony call claim commotion compel complain crowd cry lot loud adjure agitate amor angry appeal articulate mayor murmur mutter oblige opposition outcry racket rattle request roar row] "he clamored for justice and tolerance"
*clamorous 19-39-3 (a.) 1. conspicuously and offensively loud; given to vehement outcry [compel conspicuous critical crucial loud loudmouthed acute amorous angry articulate attention mob multivocal obstreperous offensive outcry rackety radio raucous riotous rowdy uproar uproarious urgent scream shout sound strident]
*clan 08-55-32 (n.) 1. group of people related by blood

or marriage [chief children circle class clique close community coterie crowd label level live lot aim ancestor ancient ashram nation nature network number]
*clandestine 10-42-20 (a.) 1. conducted with or marked by hidden aims or methods [conceal conduct covert line agent aim arm avow dagger destine enemy engage sale secret show slinky sly sneaky stealthy troop illegal intelligence intrigue investigate] "clandestine intelligence operations"
*clangor 23-27-1 (n.) 1. a loud resonant repeating noise (v.) 1. make a loud resonant noise 2. make a loud noise, as if striking metal [certain chime clash cling loud noise repeat resonant ringing]
*clarify 05-52-65 (v.) 1. make clear by removing impurities or solids, as by heating 2. make clear and (more) comprehensible [clear comprehensible confusion cooking cracking crystallize lar leach learn less light liquid lucubration account add allegorize alter ambiguity analyze application rationale ravel reason rectify refine refinement remove idea illuminate illustration impurity facilitation fat filter filtration flesh food formulate free /fir/] "clarify the mystery surrounding her death"
*clarion 17-40-5 (a.) 1. loud and clear (n.) 1. a medieval brass instrument with a clear shrill tone (v.) 1. blow the clarion 2. proclaim on, or as if on, a clarion [call cello clarinet clear cup length levy lip loud alpenhorn alphorn althorn rain recruit register reproduction instrument intensity ion oboe octave ophicleide organ /noir/] "a clarion call"
*classify 12-37-12 (v.) 1. arrange or order by classes or categories 2. declare unavailable, as for security reasons 3. assign to a class or kind [catalog catalogue category certain class conceal count lift limit list access accord alga analyze anew argue arrange assess assign attribute authorize available scheme screen security sensitive separate shard size sort stamp stereotype subsume identify index factor from] "How would you classify these pottery shards--are they prehistoric?"
*cleanse 09-55-26 (v.) 1. clean one's body or parts thereof, as by washing 2. purge of an ideology, bad thoughts, or sins [canonize care cathartic cavity clarify clean cleaning compensatory consecrate contamination corrupt lather lave licking lustrate ease emollient enshrine entire exalt expiate external allegiance alleviate animal apologetic appearance assuage nazi neaten numbing saint scrub sin soap society soften spray square suppose suspension]
*clearance 06-72-46 (n.) 1. the distance by which one thing clears another; the space between them 2. permission to proceed 3. vertical space available to allow easy passage under something [certificate cheap clear commercial consent countenance cultivate land leap leave length license limit live easy eliminate entitle extent allowance approval area authorization available await range reach reduce release remove room] "the plane was given clearance to land"
*clemency 16-31-6 (n.) 1. good weather with comfortable temperatures 2. leniency and compassion shown toward offenders by a person or agency charged with administering justice [charge charity chore clem comfortable commutation compassion condolence court law laxness leniency liberate lightening easy endurance equitable excuse mercy mild moderation youth]
*clement 09-69-25 (a.) 1. (of weather or climate) physically mild 2. (used of persons or behavior) inclined to show mercy [charitable clem climate compassionate condition condolence last lax lenient easygoing experience extreme melt mercy mild moderate temperate tenderhearted tolerant] "clement weather"
*clientele 09-46-23 (n.) 1. customers collectively [children class client collective consumer customer trade] "they have an upper class clientele"
*clinch 06-54-56 (n.) 1. (in boxing) the act of one boxer holding onto the other to avoid being hit and to rest momentarily 2. a small slip noose made with seizing 3. a tight embrace (v.) 1. secure by clinching 2. hold in a tight grasp 3. flatten the ends (of nails and rivets) [clasp clench close clutch come complete conclude conclusive connection construction cord craft create cuddle last line link loop lover inch inside insure interface nail nautical neck nip noose nut half hammer hand head hip hit hitch hold hole hug] "The boxer clinched his opponent"
*cling 05-58-68 (n.) 1. fruit (especially peach) whose flesh adheres strongly to the pit (v.) 1. hold on tightly or tenaciously 2. to remain emotionally or intellectually attached 3. come or be in close contact with; stick or hold together and resist separation [call cell certain child clash cleave clink clip close clump clustering clutch cohere cohesive come conglutinate contact contour cry custom label latch ling linger loud love lung idea inseparable intellectual nip noise note glue grain grapple grasp grasping grind grip gripping groan grow] "The dress clings to her body"
*clot 10-53-19 (n.) 1. a lump of material formed from the content of a liquid (v.) 1. change from a liquid to a thickened or solid state 2. coalesce or unite in a mass 3. cause to change from a liquid to a solid or thickened state 4. turn into curds,as of dairy products [cake circulate clabber clod cluster coagulum coalesce compact congeal content couple cream crowd curd curdle league link liquid lot lump lumpy oaf obscure origin tenacious thicken thrombus throng tough traffic transform turn]
*clothier 21-26-2 (n.) 1. a merchant who sells men's clothing [chemist cloth confectionery costumier last trade haberdasher haberdashery hosier ironmongery engage retail]
*clumsy 08-63-32 (a.) 1. not elegant or graceful in expression 2. lacking grace in movement or posture 3. difficult to handle or manage especially because of shape 4. showing lack of skill or aptitude [careless carry

casual cello chair clunky coarse contrary coordinate creature crude cumbersome lack lad leg load long low lum lumber lumpy ungainly unguarded unhappy unseemly unwary unwieldy maladroit manage manner messy move say shape shelf shoe show size skill slapdash sloppy slut special stiff style]
*coagulate 21-51-2 (a.) 1. transformed from a liquid into a soft semisolid or solid mass (v.) 1. change from a liquid to a thickened or solid state 2. cause to change from a liquid to a solid or thickened state [cake change coagula coalesce colloid concrete congeal consistency cream curdle current adhere agglomerate alter gel gelatinize glob gob grasp group grumous undergo large liquid lump thicken thrombus tissue transform turn egg embolus embrace /lug/] "coagulated blood"
*coalesce 15-32-7 (v.) 1. fuse or cause to grow together 2. mix together different elements [chemical cleave clog clot clutter coal college color combine come commingle compound comprise conflate conjugate connect organ original outline add admix alloy ally amalgamate amalgamation associate link lose easily element embody emulsify encompass entity school scramble separation shape shuffle single specific stick syncretize]
*coalition 03-39-167 (n.) 1. an organization of people (or countries) involved in a pact or treaty 2. the union of diverse things into one body or form or group; the growing together of parts 3. the state of being combined into one body [central charter coal combine composition concretion conjugation control cordial corporation corps country organize achieve addition afghanistan agreement alignment ally antisocial association austria axis league link inclusion incorporate integration treaty nation]
*coax 09-49-24 (n.) 1. a transmission line for high-frequency signals (v.) 1. influence or urge by gentle urging, caressing, or flattering [cablet cajole caress certain charm con conductor course obtain open optical adopt advocate allure arm]
*coda 15-41-7 (n.) 1. the closing section of a musical composition [cease chorus close cod communicate composition conclusion create curtain offshoot omega opus ornament death development division dramatic accessory add addendum additional adjunct afterthought appendix attachment /ado doc/]
*coddle 17-21-5 (v.) 1. treat with excessive indulgence 2. cook in nearly boiling water [certain child cocker cocoon cod consumption cooking cosset cotton curry oblige overprotectiv dandle devil egg excessive /doc/]
*codicil 23-58-1 (n.) 1. a supplement to a will; a testamentary instrument intended to alter an already executed will [chorus cod collection conclusion consequence declare devise die disposal document impose infix inheritance instrument intend interpolate law legal /doc/]
*coerce 12-36-12 (v.) 1. to cause to do through pressure or necessity, by physical, moral or intellectual means :"She forced him to take a job in the city" [castrate certain city club coe compel cow crude oblige oppress overwhelming enslave exert railroad relentless repress]
*coercion 14-33-8 (n.) 1. the act of compelling by force of authority 2. using force to cause something [calculate cion civilian compulsion constraint obedience observance occupancy enforce enjoy evict expulsion religious rendering rugby ideologic instill insure intimidate nature]
*coercive 18-26-4 (a.) 1. serving or intended to coerce [coe effect instead intend intimidate] "authority is directional instead of coercive"
*coffer 10-59-19 (n.) 1. an ornamental sunken panel in a ceiling or dome 2. a chest especially for storing valuables [cache caisson casket ceiling chest component construction offer organization ornamental file fisc flat form fund exchequer repository reservoir]
*cogent 15-51-7 (a.) 1. having the power to influence or convince 2. powerfully persuasive [capital clear coherent compel convince operative gent goodly grand effective elegant excellent exercise necessarily nice noble tell trenchant /ego/] "a cogent analysis of the problem"
*cogitate 23-52-1 (v.) 1. consider carefully and deeply; reflect upon; turn over in one's mind 2. use or exercise the mind or one's power of reason in order to make inferences, decisions, or arrive at a solution or judgments [careful causal centre cerebrate chew colligate come conceptualize conclusion connection consider contemplate content offer opinion give ideate inference intent tate think tie try turn arrive attention attentive employ exercise /tig/]
*cognizant 21-02-2 (a.) 1. (usually followed by 'of') having knowledge or understanding [comprehend conscious credit oblige omniscient onto grateful impressive insightful intelligent acknowledge acquainted ant aware thankful /zing/] "our youth are cognizant of the law"
*cohere 21-31-2 (v.) 1. come or be in close contact with; stick or hold together and resist separation 2. cause to form a united, orderly, and aethestically consistent whole 3. have internal elements or parts logically connected so that aesthetic consistency results [cell cleave cling close clump combine come communicate conform conglutinate connect connected consistent contour correspond credible orderly overlap hang harmonious harmonize here hit hold hug easy element embrace red resist]
*coherent 07-50-38 (a.) 1. capable of thinking and expressing yourself in a clear and consistent manner 2. marked by an orderly, logical, and aesthetically consistent relation of parts 3. sticking together [capable chorus clear clearly cohere coincide comprehensible confused connection constant correct credible crisp oneness orderly organize overlap harmonious harmony

hold electromagnetic equivalent explicit express rapport rational reasonable reasoning reconcile reflect relation non tenacious tend think] "a coherent argument"
*cohesion 12-67-12 (n.) 1. the state of cohering or sticking together 2. (botany) the process in some plants of parts growing together that are usually separate (such as petals) 3. (physics) the intermolecular force that holds together the molecules in a solid or liquid [change complex condition connection consistency ontogeny organization hold energy science separate simple solidity stick study influence interrelate ion natural /noise/]
*cohesive 12-42-12 (a.) 1. causing cohesion 2. cohering or tending to cohere; well integrated [cleave cling cohere consistent organize hardy hold entity single solid stick strong impartible infusible inseparable interrelated vigorous viscid /vise/] "a cohesive agent"
*coincide 05-65-75 (v.) 1. be the same 2. happen simultaneously 3. go with, fall together [check cide coherent combine come compatible concur consistent cooperative correspond overlap inharmony intersect ditto dovetail echo equal exactly exist] "The two events coincided"
*coincidence 06-62-52 (n.) 1. an event that might have been arranged although it was really accidental 2. the quality of occupying the same position or area in space 3. the temporal property of two things happening at the same time [chance chorus concurrent condition conjunction connection conspiracy contemporaneous correspondence cross oneness overlap identical identity incidence indistinguishable interval determined equality equivalence exist] "he waited for the coincidence of the target and the cross hairs"
*coincident 23-23-1 (a.) 1. occurring or operating at the same time 2. matching point for point [circle coextensive coincide combine comparable concurrent congruent conterminous corporate correspond coterminous couple operate incident inclusive inharmony equal exactly exist twin] "a series of coincident events"
*colander 19-57-3 (n.) 1. bowl-shaped strainer; used to wash or drain foods [clarify cook cradle lander large liquid net dish drain ender refinery retain riddle rocker]
*collaborate 04-40-89 (v.) 1. work together on a common enterprise of project 2. cooperate as a traitor [coincide columnist combine convert cooperate critic occupy lean accord achieve agree annalist apostate author backslide betray bibliography bolter borate reciprocate recreant research review team tergiversate traitor editorialize enemy enterprise exert /allo ball rob taro/]
*collage 09-24-26 (n.) 1. a paste-up made by sticking together pieces of paper or photographs [cloth colla combination composition consider copy cyclorama likeness abstraction accumulation aggregation altarpiece art artistic assemblage assortment group engrave /allo gal gall/]
*collapse 02-58-337 (n.) 1. the act of throwing yourself down 2. a mishap caused by something suddenly falling down or caving in 3. an abrupt failure of function or health 4. a sudden large decline of business or the prices of stocks (especially one that causes additional failures) (v.) 1. collapse due to fatigue, an illness, or a sudden attack 2. break down, literally or metaphorically 3. fold or close up, as of an umbrella or a music stand 4. lose significance, effectiveness, or value 5. cause to burst 6. suffer a nervous breakdown 7. fall apart; also used metaphorically [capable changeable colla contract crack crash crisis crumple overturn lack lag loss attack part pine pitch plunge portable sink slight slump stack sustain ebb erupt evaporate] "The wall collapsed"
*collapsible 21-52-2 (a.) 1. capable of collapsing or being collapsed [capable colla part portable stack inflatable bent boat] "a collapsible boat"
*colleague 02-61-378 (n.) 1. a person who is member of your class or profession 2. an associate you work with [chum class classmate comrade confrere consult coworker league aide assistant associate girlfriend gossip] "the surgeon consulted his colleagues"
*collective 04-50-124 (a.) 1. done by or characteristic of individuals acting together 2. forming a whole or aggregate 3. set up on the principle of collectivism or ownership and production by the workers involved usually under the supervision of a government (n.) 1. members of a cooperative enterprise [capitalistic cluster collect combine combined communal control cooperative coordinate corporate create officer operate organization ownership ecumenic element ensemble enterprise entity tend together total totally train indeterminate integrate vague venture /cell cello/]
*collector 04-40-89 (n.) 1. a crater that has collected cosmic material hitting the earth 2. a person who is employed to collect payments (as for rent or taxes) 3. a person who collects things 4. the electrode in a transistor through which a primary flow of carriers leaves the region between the electrodes [candidate capable careful carrier catalog charge check circuit citizen coin collect conductor container conveyance cosmic covet crater critic open owe owner leaf lover earth electrode employ endorse enhance enthusiast epicurean expert tax taxation ticket title toward transistor region rent rhapsodist root /cell cello/]
*collegian 21-04-2 (n.) 1. a student (or former student) at a college or university [continue learner educational enrol graduation ian institution /gell/]
*collide 07-47-37 (v.) 1. crash together with violent impact 2. be incompatible; be or come into conflict 3. cause to collide [car clash close color come conflict contact corridor crash cross object oppose oppugn lid impact impinge incompatible damage destruction disagree dissent duel encounter /dill/] "The cars collided"

*collier 12-61-12 (n.) 1. someone who works in a coal mine [coalmine collie laborer last]
*collision 06-51-54 (n.) 1. (physics) an brief event in which two or more bodies come together 2. a conflict of opposed ideas or attitudes or goals 3. an accident resulting from violent impact of a moving object [clash close come competition confrontation contact cover crash obstinate oil onslaught opinion oppose overlap idea impact important inconsistency injury insure interest interference ion science serious ship shipwreck shock showdown smash spill striking negative noncooperation /sill/] "the collision of the particles resulted in an exchange of energy and a change of direction"
*colloquial 17-52-5 (a.) 1. characteristic of informal spoken language or conversation [casual chatty conversational cozy create language letter uneducated unstudied idiomatic informal interlocutory appropriate] "wrote her letters in a colloquial style"
*colloquialism 23-57-1 (n.) 1. a colloquial expression; characteristic of spoken or written communication that seeks to imitate informal speech [colloquial crave]
*colloquy 23-10-1 (n.) 1. a conversation especially a formal one 2. formal conversation [chat communion conference conversation converse literary]
*collusion 13-57-11 (n.) 1. secret agreement 2. agreement on a secret plot [coincidence community complicity connivance conspiracy cooperation octet underhand underplot union secret simultaneous solidarity synergy illegal intrigue involve ion /sull/]
*colossus 14-66-8 (n.) 1. someone or something that is abnormally large and powerful 2. a person of exceptional importance and reputation [campanile column contemporary course cupola obelisk opinion lantern large leviathan life lighthouse loss shaft size skyscraper stalwart statue strong unusual /solo suss/]
*combustion 14-40-9 (n.) 1. a process in which a substance reacts with oxygen to give heat and light 2. the act of burning something 3. a state of violent disturbance and excitement [campfire chemical combust commotion compound confusion crematory cylinder ordinance oxidize oxygen malicious material backfire blazing blistering burn uproar sear singe smelt smoke substance thermogenesis ignition incendiarism incinerate inflammation ingle inside internal noise] "combustion grew until revolt was unavoidable"
*comely 19-55-3 (a.) 1. according with custom or propriety 2. very pleasing to the eye [clarity clear come conform constant correct custom maiden mark modesty money ease elegance emotional exciting eye lass likely limpid literary look lovely lucidity]
*comestible 23-69-1 (a.) 1. suitable for use as food (n.) 1. any substance that can be used as food [canal capable cheer chew chow come condition convert cook cuisine cut organism meat metabolize mind easy eat eatable edible energy spread substance suitable sustenance sweet table taste tender tissue tucker ingesta board build /bit/]
*comical 09-61-22 (a.) 1. arousing or provoking laughter [comic courtroom mirthful much impish absurd amusing antic arouse laughter look ludicrous]
*commemorate 06-48-53 (v.) 1. call to remembrance; keep alive the memory of someone or something, as in a ceremony 2. mark by some ceremony or observation 3. be or provide a memorial to a person or an event [call camp celebrate ceremony concentration consecrate observe occasion orate mark memory mind monumental remembrance remind reverence rite alive anniversary /taro/]
*commentary 05-57-77 (n.) 1. a written explanation or criticism or illustration that is added to a book or other textual material [clarify coda codicil comment criticism critique observation marginalia material message editorial epilogue essay exegesis explanatory extend notation note notice tail textual thesis treatise add affix analysis appendix record remark report review]
*commingle 21-09-2 (v.) 1. mix or blend 2. mix together different elements [chemical clutter coalesce color combine compound conflate conglomerate conjugate organ original outline makeup meld melt merge mingle mix immix intermix interweave narrative gradual grow literary lose easily element emulsify] "His book commingles sarcasm and sadness"
*commission 01-48-641 (n.) 1. a fee for services rendered based on a percentage of an amount received or collected or agreed to be paid (as distinguished from a salary) 2. the act of granting authority to undertake certain functions 3. a special group delegated to consider some matter 4. the state of being in good working order and ready for operation 5. a formal statement of a command or injunction to do something 6. an official document issued by a government and conferring on the recipient the rank of an officer in the armed forces 7. a group of representatives or delegates 8. a task that has been assigned to a person or group 9. the act of committing a crime (v.) 1. put into commission; equip for service; of ships 2. charge with a task 3. place an order for [candidate charge court credit cut ordain output overhaul make management meeting mission income instruction interest service share stock name net nominate]
*commitment 02-53-291 (n.) 1. an engagement by contract involving financial obligation 2. the act of binding yourself (intellectually or emotionally) to a course of action 3. the trait of sincere and steadfast fixity of purpose 4. the official act of consigning a person to confinement (as in a prison or mental hospital) 5. a message that makes a pledge [campaign cause charge cherish commit confine consignment contract court crime oath objectionable obligation official operation ought matter mental message minority mission movement must imperative institution interest involve

issue task team tell tenacity trait true earnest effort emotional energy engagement enterprise ethical ethnic need] "a man of energy and commitment"
*committal 19-97-3 (n.) 1. the official act of consigning a person to confinement (as in a prison or mental hospital) 2. the act of committing a crime [commit confine consignment crime official mental law lawbreaker liberty]
*commodious 23-25-1 (a.) 1. large and roomy [capacious contented convention cozy odious deep inconvenient infinite uncomfortable useful utilitarian sizeable soft spacious spreading suitable] "a commodious harbor"
*commodity 04-32-109 (n.) 1. articles of commerce [chiefly clothe coarse competition consumption country obligation offer ornamental manmade material merchandise mixed modi damage date delivery demand destruction direct import intermediate item textile trade]
*commotion 14-36-9 (n.) 1. the act of making a noisy disturbance 2. a disorderly outburst or tumult 3. confused movement [catch centre chaos charivari confusion convulsion outburst outcry malaise motion move mutiny mutual tempest tension todo trouble tumultuousnes turmoil incident inquietude insurrection involve irritation natural nervous noisy /tom/]
*commute 06-46-59 (v.) 1. exchange a penalty for a less severe one 2. travel back and forth regularly, as between one's place of work and home 3. change the order or arrangement of 4. transpose and remain equal in value; of variables or operators, in mathematics 5. exchange or replace with another, usually of the same kind or category [capital category centimeter change compensate contrary convert cooperate course criminal current obtain one operator original map math metamorphose modify money mute undergo trade transpose travel trip trust turn electricity element equal essence establish exchange expect /tum/] "These operators commute with each other"
*commuter 05-41-70 (n.) 1. someone who travels regularly from home in a suburb to work in a city 2. a passenger train that is ridden primarily by commuters [camper car carry city climber commute cruiser customer operate major mariner mountaineer user tourist train transport travel traveler excursionist explorer rail regular ride rider rubbernecker /tum/]
*comparable 05-31-84 (a.) 1. conforming in every respect 2. able to be compared or worthy of comparison [capable closely comparative conform corresponding match meal measure parable parallel period pertinent precede proportionate akin alike analogous refer relative respect restaurant lack like link eat enough equal everywhere /bar/]
*comparative 06-59-52 (a.) 1. having significance only in relation to something else 2. relating to or based on or involving comparison (n.) 1. the comparative form of an adjective [calm change class commensurate comp comparable condition congenial consider cost count match modest parallel partly pertinent proportionate amount analogous apposite approximate associative attribute reasonable refer relation relevant inferior investigate visible ease effective equivalent expect express extent /vita/] "comparative linguistics"
*comparison 03-57-168 (n.) 1. relation based on similarities and differences 2. examining resemblances or differences 3. qualities that are comparable [close community contrast outlay match mental metaphor mimic parallel paris parity part people personnel point potential process profit proxy affinity agent agreement allegory alternative analogy appearance appraisal assessment association relation relationship representative reserve respect identity imitation initial same scrutiny semblance show sign similitude spare nature near note] "no comparison between the two books"
*compassionate 09-51-22 (a.) 1. showing merciful compassion 2. showing or having compassion 3. showing recognition of unusually distressful circumstances (v.) 1. share the suffering of [care charitable child circumstance clement compassion concern condole condolence considerate out mark melt mercy mild moderate mother motivate patient pity accepting ache affectionate alleviate shakespeare share show soft sorry suffering sympathize sympathy inhumane interest nice nurture tenderhearted tolerant toward easygoing eat empathetic express /sap/] "sparing the child's mother was a compassionate act"
*compensate 05-51-79 (v.) 1. make amends for; pay compensation for 2. make up for, make good 3. make payment to; compensate 4. make up for shortcomings or a feeling of inferiority by exaggerating good qualities 5. do or give something to somebody in return 6. make reparations or amends for [clash comp confront contrast correction counterweigh cover obverse offset outweigh money partner pay performance perverse poise profitable proportion protect psychology effort emphasize equate error exchange expiate negative neutralize nullify salary satisfy service settlement shortcoming suffer switch accident adjust alter alternate amend antagonistic antithetic arm atone tender trade trait transform transpose]
*competence 09-57-25 (n.) 1. the quality of being adequately or well qualified physically and intellectually [capability capacity cell compete condition control court outside maturity measure might minimum moment parole party perform permit physical power proficiency prowess efficiency embryonic enable enough expertise talent teacher technique time tissue train]
*competent 07-52-40 (a.) 1. adequate for the purpose 2. properly or sufficiently qualified or capable or efficient [capacity clever comfortable compete control court cunning office official okay masterful medicine meeting mighty minimum momentous party performance

position powerful prepared printer proficient prominent properly purpose effective efficient effort empower enough excellent expert task test totalitarian training typist neat nimble] "a competent typist"
*competitive 02-57-285 (a.) 1. showing a fighting disposition without self-seeking 2. subscribing to capitalistic competition 3. involving competition or competitiveness [capitalistic cheap combative compete contend counter cross cutthroat obstinate manner match militant modest perverse petit position practice price pursuit economically emulous enemy energy enterprise toward try improve incline inexpensive inimical involve value viable vying] "competitive games"
*competitor 03-46-171 (n.) 1. the contestant you hope to defeat [center challenger champion coach commercial competition contestant opponent opposition outfielder method militant participate personal petit place player position preeminent promising pugilist eliminate end enemy enforcer engage entrant tackle thug tie tilt titleholder tough tournament infielder reach remain respect riot rival rough /roti/]
*complacent 10-69-19 (a.) 1. contented to a fault [consequential contented contentment overweening manner place please possible life live absolutely anxious eager excessive teacher] "he had become complacent after years of success"
*complement 06-49-51 (n.) 1. a complete number or quantity 2. something added to complete or make perfect 3. number needed to make up whole force 4. a word or phrase used to complete a grammatical construction 5. either of two parts that mutually complete each other 6. one of a series of enzymes in the blood serum that are part of the immune response (v.) 1. make complete or perfect; supply what is wanting or form the complement to [cast catalyst cell charge clause comp construction counterpart crew crowd object octave officer oiler opposite organ outfit man mate meal mob movement music mutual pair parallel part party people perfect personnel picture predicate produce protein level likeness load eight element enzyme equal everything expression extra navigator nine note tailpiece tally team total touch] "a full complement"
*complex 02-44-353 (a.) 1. complicated in structure; consisting of interconnected parts (n.) 1. a compound described in terms of the central atom to which other atoms are bound or coordinated 2. a conceptual whole made up of complicated and related parts 3. a whole structure (as a building) made up of interconnected or related structures 4. (psychoanalysis) a combination of emotions and impulses that have been rejected from awareness but still influence a person's behavior [combined comp confusing convoluted critical obfuscate obscure oneness maze mesh mingle perplex possession puzzling laborious labyrinthine eclectic elaborate ethos] "a complex set of variations based on a simple folk melody"
*compliant 14-71-9 (a.) 1. disposed or willing to comply 2. willing to carry out the orders or wishes of another without protest 3. easily influenced or imposed on 4. evidencing little spirit or courage; overly submissive or compliant [comply constant content obedient obliging observant manipulate meticulous mold plastic pliant prompt prone limber lithe loyal impressionable incline indulgent acquiesce active agree amenable approve tractile /nail/] "children compliant with the parental will"
*complicate 03-42-183 (v.) 1. make more complex, intricate, or richer 2. make more complicated [compound confused convoluted cramp obfuscate obscure ornate magnify matter meander modify muddle muddy multifarious mystify perplexplus politics prefix labyrinthine implicate interrelated intricate involve abstruse alter analyze arduous attach tag tangle theme thorny thwart tough transform triple twist easy elaborate enhance enough entangle exacerbate exaggerate explain extent] "There was a new development that complicated the matter"
*complication 06-42-54 (n.) 1. a situation or condition that is complex or confused 2. the act or process of complicating 3. puzzling complexity 4. any disease or disorder that occurs during the course of (or because of) another disease 5. a development that complicates a situation [case character circumstance color combination come complex condition confused court obstruct obstruction onerous operation medical mix mood movement paralysis pass plication plot present problem process puzzling laborious line illness impair impede incident initial interrelated introduction involve abnormal action affair architecture argument arise tangle technicality theme] "her coming was a serious complication"
*complicity 12-41-12 (n.) 1. guilt as an accomplice in a crime or offense [collusion commit community complicit connivance conspiracy cooperative crime octet offense onus manipulate morale mutuality participation partnership peccant plot illegal implication intrigue involve teamwork trick trio]
*compliment 07-60-38 (n.) 1. a remark (or act) expressing praise and admiration (v.) 1. express respect or esteem for 2. say something to someone that expresses praise [cajolery charm commendation comp conceit congratulation offer oil orchid paper physics posy praise present largesse last icon incense encomium esteem eulogy excessive expression eyewash takeoff trade tribute] "He complimented her on her last physics paper"
*component 04-36-108 (a.) 1. forming or functioning as part of a whole (n.) 1. something determined in relation to something that includes it 2. an artifact that is one of the individual parts of which a composite entity is made up; especially a part that can be separated from or attached to a system 3. an abstract part of something

[capability circumstance clock compo composition constituent content oscillator magnetic making matter mechanical molecule part percentage plate nature earth effector electronic element transmitter] "component parts"
*comport 23-25-1 (v.) 1. behave well or properly 2. behave in a certain manner [carry certain check child compo conduct confused consistent opinion manner move perform pose posture property recover right tally toward]
*composer 03-38-152 (n.) 1. composes music as a profession [cage collaborate columnist compose critic orchestrate madrigal maker monograph musicology pamphleteer poet scorer songwriter storyteller encyclopedist essayist ethnomusicology review]
*composure 09-76-25 (n.) 1. steadiness of mind under stress [calm comfort compo control cool mind mood perturb philosophy placid poise possession problem sangfroid self serenity silence sleep steady still strain stress usual reconciliation repose resignation restraint ease equanimity euphoria expectation] "he accepted their problems with composure and she with equanimity"
*comprehensible 17-50-5 (a.) 1. (of meaning) capable of being penetrated or comprehended 2. readily comprehended or understood 3. capable of being understood or interpreted [capable clear clearly cognizable coherent comp conceivable meaningless mind pellucid penetrate perceive perceptible perspicuous plain ready recognize einstein enough enunciate exoteric experience explicate explicit expressly hear scrutable seize simply idea interpret limpid logical loud lucid luminous /her/] "an idea comprehensible to the average mind"
*comprehension 14-49-8 (n.) 1. an ability to understand the meaning or importance of something (or the knowledge acquired as a result) 2. the act of comprising something 3. the relation of comprising something [capacity cognitive command comp conception condition connection containment coverage open mastery membership participation precognition prehension rationality reception relation education eligible embrace encompass exercise sanity savvy sense set short student idea ideation importance inability inclusion inclusive incorporate intellectual /her/] "how you can do that is beyond my comprehension"
*comprehensive 04-55-119 (a.) 1. including all or everything 2. being the most comprehensive of its class 3. broad in scope [clear comp complete corporate one outright overall main maximum mighty perfect plain powerful radical regular encompass entire extensive heavy holistic serious straight strong inclusive intensive irresistible veritable voluminous /her/] "comprehensive coverage"
*compress 09-36-22 (n.) 1. a cloth pad or dressing (with or without medication) applied firmly to some part of the body (to relieve discomfort or reduce fever) (v.) 1. squeeze or press together 2. make more compact by or as if by pressing [close constrict contract crowded cut material medicine moisten mow packed pad part pinch pointed poll poultice press pressure process push reap reduce relieve reserved resist retrench rub easy elide elliptic ensphere epigrammatic epitomize save scrag short shrink small soft sore space spasm squeeze storage strangle stunt substance substantial summary] "compress the data"
*compression 14-41-8 (n.) 1. an increase in the density of something 2. encoding information while reducing the bandwidth or bits required 3. applying pressure 4. the process or result of becoming smaller or pressed together [clustering coarctate compress crush curtail pinch pressure purse recapitulation reduction retrench elision ellipsis epitome solidify squeeze stricture isthmus neck nip]
*comprise 05-71-72 (v.) 1. form or compose 2. include or contain; have as a component 3. be composed of [chorus conquer constitute contain couple cover occupy marshal mass mix money pair part predicate present presuppose prise province range receive record require idea imply included incorporate introduce involve serve song span stone straddle substance sum supplement surround syndicate embody embrace encompass entire essence extend] "The land he conquered comprised several provinces"
*compulsion 12-61-12 (n.) 1. using force to cause something 2. an irrational motive for performing trivial or repetitive actions against your will 3. an urge to do or say something that might be better left undone or unsaid [clout coercion comp compulsory consciousness constraint craving obligation obligement obsession occupancy mania mighty momentum motive perform premises pressure process pull push undone unfit unsaid unwilling urge urgency landlord leave legal lethargy logic spontaneous steam stress strong superpower incentive inconsistent indifference influence intrude irrational irresistible need] "though pressed into rugby under compulsion I began to enjoy the game"
*compulsory 07-86-39 (a.) 1. required by rule [comp compulsive conclusive constrain obligatory mandatory moral must participant peremptory perform physical pressing ultimate unavoidable urgent law lecture legal school skating sport read require restrain routine rule] "in most schools physical education are compulsory"
*compunction 21-58-2 (n.) 1. a feeling of deep regret (usually for some misdeed) [challenge complaint conduct conscience conscientious objection offence march misdeed misgiving modesty past pause penance penitent picket unction unwilling throe trip]
*compute 08-35-29 (v.) 1. make a mathematical calculation or computation [cache calculate calculator capitalize cast certain cipher classify collate combine comp correct cpu cypher obtain off operation out

machine magnitude mainframe map math measure meter multiply pace perform physical plot possible present prize probe processor program proportional prorate tally tentative theory think tot total triangulate entity estimate evaluate extrapolate /tup/]
*conceal 05-54-82 (v.) 1. hold back; keep from being perceived by others, as of emotions or expressions of emotions 2. prevent from being seen or discovered [cache camouflage careful cave censor classified cloak close cloud congeal corner cover covert create curtain obfuscate obscure obstruct occult once niche nonappearance nook earth eclipse emotion enigmatic ensconce envelop esoteric evasive evidence existence expression abstruse agent ambush anger apply arcane asylum attempt avoid lair latent launder less lie look lurk]
*concede 02-60-242 (v.) 1. give over; surrender or relinquish to the physical control of another 2. be willing to concede 3. make a clean breast of 4. acknowledge defeat [candidate cede clean compromise confess control country oppose own election enough existence debate declare defeat discount disregard]
*conceit 12-50-13 (n.) 1. feelings of excessive pride 2. the trait of being vain and conceited [comparison conclusion consideration crack create observation obtrusive once opinion outspoken narcissism notion ethos exaggerate excessive expect expression extreme eye idea imaginative immodest importance impression independence inventive theme theory thought tolerate toy trait /tie/]
*conceive 05-45-78 (v.) 1. judge or regard; look upon; judge 2. become pregnant; undergo conception 3. have the idea for [cause certain child coin commit comprehend consider construct create observe occasion once opinion originate note notice elaborate emotion envision establish esteem estimate experience express idea imagine inferior institute invention view vision visualize vivify /vie/] "He conceived of a robot that would help paralyzed patients"
*concerto 06-42-51 (n.) 1. a composition for orchestra and a soloist [calypso canticle capric chamber classical coloratura comic concert conform continuo crescendo critical operetta oratorio orchestra organ overture nocturne early establish rap reggae requiem rock romantic rondo round tone traditional twelve]
*concession 04-41-99 (n.) 1. the act of conceding or yielding 2. a contract granting the right to operate a subsidiary business 3. a point conceded or yielded [calm cession contribution cut offer endowment establishment exception shop store supply surrender impart indulgence intervene investiture] "he got the beer concession at the ball park"
*conciliate 08-31-28 (v.) 1. cause to be more favorably inclined; gain the good will of 2. make compatible with 3. come to terms [calm charming ciliate civilian come compatible compromise conduct consonance cool cooperation oppose overcome negotiation noncombatant nonviolence impartial incite incline irenic lenity lie lull absence accord agreement allay anger animosity appease arbitration arouse assuage tear theory tolerant tone tranquillize exist /tail/]
*conciliatory 11-34-15 (a.) 1. making or willing to make concessions 2. overcoming animosity or hostility [compromise conciliator overcome animosity antagonize appease arouse assuage tear tone yield /rota tail/]
*conclave 19-57-3 (n.) 1. a confidential or secret meeting [cardinal caucus chapter christianity clave college committee confidential congress council negotiation levee arrange assembly assignation audience vestry eisteddfod elect /eval/]
*conclusive 10-51-20 (a.) 1. final and deciding 2. forming an end or termination; especially putting an end to doubt or question 3. expressing finality with no implication of possible change [categorical certain con conclude convince obligatory outcome outright overwhelming nation necessary nuncupative last lead limiting ultimate unambiguous univocal unlimited utter significant straight sure implication impose impressive indecisive inevitable interpretation irrefutable valid entire equivocal evidence express extreme] "conclusive proof"
*concomitant 21-46-2 (a.) 1. following as a consequence (n.) 1. an event or situation that happens at the same time as or in connection with another [changeover closely coexist combine connection consequence contemporaneous coordinate couple occurrence offshoot omit natural manage mate meeting mutual incidental inconspicuous increment isochronous tailpiece tie twin accompany affiliate agree associate attendant attending]
*concord 11-23-15 (n.) 1. capital of the state of New Hampshire; located in south central New Hampshire on the Merrimack river 2. the determination of grammatical inflection on the basis of word relations 3. town in eastern Massachusetts near Boston where the first battle of the American Revolution was fought 4. a harmonious state of things in general and of their properties (as of colors and sounds); congruity of parts with one another and with the whole 5. agreement of opinions 6. the first battle of the American Revolution (April 19, 1775) (v.) 1. go together 2. be in accord; be in agreement 3. arrange by concord or agreement 4. arrange the words of a text so as to create a concordance [calm charity compatible convention cord opinion order organization overlap rapprochement reconcile regularity resolve respect revolutionary routine deliberation deploy disposition duet]
*concur 09-46-21 (v.) 1. happen simultaneously 2. be in accord; be in agreement [cant check coexist coincide combine come con correspond opinion overlap reach reciprocate reconcile resolve]
*concurrence 21-14-2 (n.) 1. acting together as of agents

or circumstances or events 2. agreement of results or opinions 3. the temporal property of two things happening at the same time 4. a state of cooperation [character circumstance coincidence concur conflict conjunction connection consensus contemporaneous correspondence operation opinion exist]
*concurrent 13-34-11 (a.) 1. occurring or operating at the same time [character coincide collective combine community conflict congress connection contemporary cooperative corporate couple current octet operate operation opinion unanimous understanding union unison unite unopposed radius reciprocal rodeo roundup ecumenism engagement equal equidistant even exist tangential together twin]
*concussion 11-33-14 (n.) 1. any violent blow 2. injury to the brain caused by a blow; usually resulting in loss of consciousness [check collision concuss consciousness crash cut onslaught organ scratch shaking shock sudden impact impinge injury]
*condensation 18-47-4 (n.) 1. (psychoanalysis) an unconscious process whereby two ideas or images combine into a single symbol; especially in dreams 2. the process of changing from a gaseous to a liquid or solid state 3. the process or result of becoming smaller or pressed together 4. a shortened version of a written work 5. atmospheric moisture that has condensed because of cold 6. the act of increasing the density of something [cling clustering coarctate compression conde conglomeration contraction outline overview neck decrease draft drop enhance exaggerate explosion set stick survey abbreviation abridgment abstract acceleration inseparable intensify isthmus]
*condense 12-46-12 (v.) 1. make more concise 2. undergo condensation; change from a gaseous to a liquid state and fall in drops 3. become more compact or concentrated 4. cause a gas or vapor to change into a liquid 5. develop due to condensation 6. remove water from 7. compress or concentrate [capsulize chemistry close cold compress concrete conde consolidate contract cook crowded cut outline narrow nip nutshell decrease deepen dense develop different digest distill dock double down drop due edit element elide elliptic encapsulate enhance epigrammatic essential exacerbate exaggerate express scope set short shrink six small specific squeeze steam strengthen substantial sum summary] "water condenses"
*condescend 21-30-2 (v.) 1. behave in a patronizing and condescending manner 2. do something that one considers to be below one's dignity 3. debase oneself morally, act in an undignified, unworthy, or dishonorable way 4. treat condescendingly [concession consider okay nod debase deign demean descend dignity disdain dishonorable endorse sanction social stoop superior]
*condolence 13-58-11 (n.) 1. an expression of sympathy with another's grief [card comfort commiseration compassion concern condole consolation death leniency easement encouragement expression] "they sent their condolences"
*condone 10-49-19 (v.) 1. excuse, overlook, or make allowances for; be lenient with [cancel condon consider countenance criticize obey occasional overlook disregard endure excuse exonerate /nod/]
*conducive 13-53-11 (a.) 1. tending to bring about; being partly responsible for [causative city con constructive contributory useful instrumental intend intermediary effect employ encourage] "working conditions are not conducive to productivity"
*conduit 12-43-12 (n.) 1. a passage (a pipe or tunnel) through which water or electric wires can pass [cable canal carry channel computer con connect connection control convey course cover current cylindrical obstruction opening outlet overpass dam defile discharge ditch drainage duct underpass ingress inlet intersection trench tube tubing tunnel turn] "the computers were connected through a system of conduits"
*confectioner 18-45-4 (n.) 1. someone who makes candies and other sweets [confection create orphan found town industrial]
*confectionery 15-85-7 (n.) 1. a food rich in sugar 2. a confectioner's shop [candy caramelize central chemist cherry chew chicle chocolate choice collective colored combine commerce compote confectioner consider cooky cover nut nuts flavor florist food frosting fruit eat enclose establishment taffy technique toffee topping treat true tuck ice imitation ironmongery retail rich]
*confederacy 19-27-3 (n.) 1. a union of political organizations 2. the 11 southern states that seceded from the United States in 1861 3. a group of conspirators banded together to achieve some harmful or illegal purpose 4. a secret agreement between two or more people to perform an unlawful act [coalition composition corps opportunity federation fellowship fusion embodiment encompass engineering dixieland racy region rig ring addition agreement area association /care def rede/]
*confederate 13-22-10 (a.) 1. of or having to do with the southern Confederacy during the Civil War 2. united in a confederacy or league (n.) 1. a supporter of the Confederate States of America 2. a person who joins with another in carrying out some plan (especially an unethical or illegal plan) 3. someone who assists in a plot (v.) 1. form a group or unite 2. form a confederation with; of nations [carry champion civil collaborate combine commit concert contribute cooperate corporate crimea organize nation northern federate form friend fulfill furtherance fuse effort entity danger divide reciprocate region accessory affiliate ally american army assist attend team /def rede tare/]
*confer 07-38-34 (ad.) 1. compare (used in texts to point the reader to another location in the text) (v.) 1. have a

conference in order to talk something over 2. present [certain coach compare con consult control converse convey counsel offer opinion negotiate never famous favor former enfeoff extend rain reader recommend render resistance reward right] "We conferred about a plan of action"
*conferee 18-AA-4 (n.) 1. a person on whom something is bestowed 2. a member of a conference [communicate confer consultation favor formal exchange receiver recipient] "six honorary were conferred; the conferees were..."
*confessor 21-65-2 (n.) 1. a priest who hears confession and gives absolution 2. someone who confesses (discloses information damaging to themselves) [christianity church communicate confess faith spiritual religious rite]
*confidant 12-47-12 (n.) 1. someone to whom private matters are confided [consultant counselor neighbor familiar favor female friend instructor intimate discuss acquaintance adviser advocate affection alter amigo ant teacher tell trust]
*confide 09-55-24 (v.) 1. To confer a trust upon 2. reveal in private; tell confidentially [candid care charge childlike commit con consign credulous custody obligation openhearted outspoken naive nor few foolish frank fulfill full impart important incline ingenuous innocent insinuate intimate intrust delegate depend desire direct discover distrustful divulge enfeoff enough entrust expect expose]
*confidence 02-66-411 (n.) 1. a state of confident hopefulness that events will be favorable 2. a feeling of trust (in someone or something) 3. freedom from doubt; belief in yourself and your abilities 4. a secret that is confided or entrusted to another 5. a trustful relationship [certainty classified confide conviction cool courage own nerve never face failure faith favorable fear fearless freedom friendship full imminent impudent intimacy intimate dauntless dependence desire diffident economy enigma entrust equilibrium expectation]
*confident 02-67-280 (a.) 1. having or marked by confidence or assurance 2. not liable to error in judgment or action 3. persuaded of; very sure [capacity certain cocksure confide convince cool optimistic overweening nature fact faithful fearless follow fond forward fulfill intrepid day deal decided definite depression determined doubt doubtless eager equanimous error excessive expand expect talent together] "a confident speaker"
*confinement 11-40-14 (n.) 1. the act of restraining of a person's liberty by confining them 2. concluding state of pregnancy; from the onset of labor to the birth of a child 3. the state of being confined [canal captivity carry cervix childbed close commitment conclude confine constrained control crowd custody obliquity official onset narrow nativity near fetus force immure imprison incarcerate inclusion intern isolation enclosure envelop martyr mental moderation musculature thining tighten torment torture toward travail]
*confiscate 08-44-31 (a.) 1. surrendered as a penalty 2. taken without permission or consent especially by public authority (v.) 1. take temporary possession of as a security, by legal authority [cate child cloverleaf collectivize commandeer communize consent nationalize forcible forfeiture illegal impound impress security seize sequester sequestrate shipment socialize steal stop support surrender agent annex appropriate artwork attach authority takeaway temporary treasury effort enemy expropriate]
*conflagration 18-46-4 (n.) 1. a very intense and uncontrolled fire [campfire combustion crematory fire flame forest foxfire great rage rapid ration ignition inferno ingle intense /gal/]
*confluence 15-25-7 (n.) 1. a place where two things come together 2. a coming together of people 3. a flowing together (as of rivers) [combine come coming component concourse congress convergence convergent course creek current onrush outflow natural flow flue fluency focus form liaison link locate undertow unification union earth] "Pittsburgh is located at the confluence of the Allegheny and Monongahela rivers"
*conformity 14-45-8 (n.) 1. orthodoxy in thoughts and belief 2. acting according to certain accepted standards 3. correspondence in form or appearance 4. concurrence of opinion 5. hardened conventionality [care certain character close community compliance concurrent conform consistency conventionality correspondence custom obedience observation oneness opinion orientation orthodoxy ossification overlap near nicety norm faithful fashion finish fixed formality regularity regulation religious require respect right rule manner metaphor mimic identity imitation intersection tally think time traditionalism]
*confront 03-46-168 (v.) 1. deal with (something unpleasant) head on 2. be face to face with 3. present somebody with something, usually to accuse or criticize 4. oppose, as in hostility or a competition [certain challenge challenging child circumvent clash clear competition consequence contradictory contrast costume criticize cross object obstacle obverse opposition orient overcome overhang near nonplus facing fact finally foil force front frustrate reference relate repugnant resist respect reverse ring rivalry ruin tackle terrible threaten thwart] "You must confront your opponent"
*congeal 19-50-3 (v.) 1. become gelatinous [cake clot coagulate concrete conge cool curdle opposition nip gel gelatinous gelid glacial gob grasp embrace enzyme add adhere agglomerate liquid lopper lumpy]
*congenial 13-38-10 (a.) 1. suitable to your needs or similar to your nature 2. used of plants; capable of cross-fertilization or of being grafted [capable charity cheerful chorus civil coincide combination compatible confidence cooperation oneness outgoing overlap nature

neighborly nice genial gracious graft gratify empathy enjoyable equivalent exist express identity inharmony interest intersection intimacy accordance affable agreement akin allied amiable atmosphere attitude likable link love /lain/] "a congenial atmosphere to work in"
*congest 10-46-18 (v.) 1. become or cause to become obstructed [capacity charge chock choke clog close conge cover crowd obstruct occlude organ overfill overweight gluey glut gorge gum excessive silt slow soak solid squeeze stay stick street stuff substantial thickset /segno/]
*congregate 12-50-13 (a.) 1. brought together into a group or crowd (v.) 1. move together [come concentrate congress couple crowd office gate gathering group raise rendezvous accumulate amass animal assemble teem throng /age tag/]
*conjecture 13-49-10 (n.) 1. a hypothesis that has been formed by speculating or conjecturing (usually with little hard evidence) 2. reasoning that involves the formation of conclusions from incomplete evidence 3. a message expressing an opinion based on incomplete evidence (v.) 1. to believe especially on uncertain or tentative grounds [certain cognitive coherent con conclusion confidence confute construct controvert opinion origin outcome natural notional judgment elaborate election estimate estimation evidence expect explicate expression tentative theory thesis thinking true unusual reassemble refute repute retrace ritual]
*conjoin 21-64-2 (v.) 1. make contact or come together 2. take in marriage [carpentry ceremony chain combination come concert connect contact couple covalent create open join ingraft inosculate]
*conjugal 21-53-2 (a.) 1. of or relating to marriage or to the relationship between a wife and husband [connubial nuptial jugal union uxorious adore affectionate languish loving /lag/]
*conjugate 17-93-5 (a.) 1. joined together especially in a pair or pairs 2. of a pinnate leaflet; having only one pair of leaflets 3. (chemistry) formed by the union of two compounds 4. (chemistry) of an organic compound; containing two or more double bonds each separated from the other by a single bond (n.) 1. a mixture of two partially miscible liquids A and B produces two conjugate solutions: one of A in B and another of B in A (v.) 1. unite chemically so that the product is easily broken down into the original compounds 2. add inflections showing person, number, gender, tense, aspect, etc. 3. undergo conjugation, in biology [chain chemistry coalesce combine commingle compound conflate corporate couple cover one onomatopoeic organism original nature necessarily join joint undergo unify union unity gain gate gather gender genetic glue grammatical accord add affiliate alternation angle aspect assemble associate tape tense tie triple easy eclectic element embrace encompass entity equilibrium essence exist /tag/] "conjugate the verb"
*conjunction 07-50-35 (n.) 1. an uninflected function word that serves to conjoin words or phrases or clauses or sentences 2. the state of being joined together 3. the temporal property of two things happening at the same time 4. the grammatical relation between linguistic units (words or phrases or clauses) that are connected by a conjunction 5. (astronomy) apparent meeting or passing of two or more celestial bodies in the same degree of the zodiac 6. something that joins or connects [coalition coincidence colligate conjunct connection conspiracy junction junta juxtaposition unification union tie inclusion incorporate interlink]
*conjure 06-61-49 (v.) 1. evoke or call forth, with or as if by magic 2. ask for or request earnestly 3. engage in plotting or enter into a conspiracy, swear together [cabal call calling charm circumvent cite command complot con conspire crave create curse outreach outwit overthrow juggle unemployment raise recall recite require requisition earnest engage entertain entreat evil evoke]
*connive 17-50-5 (v.) 1. encourage or assent to illegally; in criminal behavior 2. form intrigues (for) in an underhand manner [calculation cockatrice coincide combined community conn conspire cook cooperative criminal openly operator opportunist overt nothing ignore illegal informer intrigue encourage engineer exploit express /inn vin/]
*connoisseur 10-44-18 (n.) 1. an expert able to appreciate a field; especially in the fine arts [cognoscenti collector conn consultant craftsman oenophile nature nut sensitivity sharp specialty statesman editor enthusiast epicurean esthete exciseman expert review /ion rue/]
*connotation 13-49-11 (n.) 1. an idea that is implied or suggested 2. what you must know in order to determine the reference of an expression [coloring consequence overtone name nature negative notation nuance tenor thus tinge touch transfer typical additional allegory allusion apart apply association assumption idea identify impact imply import individual inference inherent intension interpret /ton/]
*connote 19-12-3 (v.) 1. express or state indirectly 2. involve as a necessary condition of consequence; as in logic [characterize condition conn consequence cowardice cozy necessary note tell testify evidence evince exhibit expression /ton/]
*conquer 06-61-49 (v.) 1. take possession of without permission or take with force, as after a conquest or invasion 2. overcome by conquest 3. to put down by force or authority [capture castle character check choke climb completely con conceal confound control country crime crush curb obtain occupy overthrow overwhelm nascent quell quench quieten unman uprise usurp enslave expression reduce repress requisition restraint rid right]

*conscience 06-52-56 (n.) 1. a feeling of shame when you do something immoral 2. conformity to one's own sense of right conduct 3. motivation deriving logically from ethical or moral principles that govern a person's thoughts and actions [censor compunction concern conduct conformity cruelty obedience science scruple self shame share social standard superego idea ignore immoral inadequate inner integrity issue ego emotion ethics evil] "a person of unflagging conscience"
*conscientious 10-53-17 (a.) 1. characterized by extreme care and great effort 2. guided by or in accordance with conscience or sense of right and wrong [careful carry caution close critical obedient observant narrow nice scient scrupulous sensitive serious show speak strict incorruptible industriousne injustice effort ethical exacting exercise exquisite extreme task thorough upright upstanding] "conscientious application to the work at hand"
*conscious 04-55-122 (a.) 1. knowing and perceiving; having awareness of surroundings and sensations and thoughts 2. intentionally conceived 3. showing realization or recognition or something; followed by"of" [calculate capacity careful choose cognizant combination completely con concern consider critical observe omniscient operation nice niggling notice sensory sentient serious show shrewd shroud shy sleepless slow speak still stimulus studious succeed surround impressive inarticulate injure insightful insomnia intentional understanding unintended] "a conscious effort to speak more slowly"
*conscript 15-60-7 (n.) 1. someone who is drafted into military service (v.) 1. enroll into service compulsorily [commandeer compulsory nation novice script service summon raise rally recruit rookie impress induct personnel press tenderfoot trainee] "The men were conscripted"
*consecrate 17-55-5 (a.) 1. solemnly dedicated to or set apart for a high purpose (v.) 1. appoint to a clerical posts 2. render holy by means of religious rites 3. give entirely to a specific person, activity, or cause 4. dedicate to a deity by a vow [commit crate ordain sanctify set employ anew] "a life consecrated to science"
*consecutive 03-35-168 (a.) 1. in regular succession without gaps 2. one after the other 3. successive (without a break) (ad.) 1. in a consecutive manner [chronological come con concert connected consistent continuous orderly ordinal next sequential serial show space subsequent successive element enlarge ensue uninterrupted tight trailing increase interruption] "we numbered the papers consecutively"
*consensus 04-45-99 (n.) 1. agreement of the majority in sentiment or belief [character chorus compromise con concept concurrent conflict opinion see sentiment society equilibrium unanimous understanding unison]
*consequential 19-44-3 (a.) 1. having important issues or results [charming circuit classical comprehensive consequent control cost official opinion outstanding overweening name senior serious significant strong substantial eminent empower ensue eventful exaggerate quality telling totalitarian important include indirect influential insurance intense issue absolute after arise authorize autocratic leading legislation loss /lait/] "the year's only really consequential legislation"
*conservatism 09-47-21 (n.) 1. a political orientation advocating the preservation of the best in society and opposing radical changes [calm characterize con contrast control cool obscurantist opposition orientation nation neutrality nonviolence school serenity society stability steady supporter even extreme radical reaction repose represent restraint return rightist view abnegate abstinence advocate approach temperate theory think traditionalism tranquillity impartial matter mild]
*conservative 02-53-416 (a.) 1. avoiding excess 2. opposed to liberal reforms 3. resistant to change 4. conforming to the standards and conventions of the middle class 5. unimaginatively conventional (n.) 1. a person who has conservative ideas or opinions [careful compromise con control off orthodoxy neutral saving square stable stalwart elder reasonable regular restrained antediluvian antique authoritarian temperate tory traditionalism imperialist /vita/] "a conservative estimate"
*conservatory 08-54-29 (n.) 1. the faculty and students of a school specializing in one of the fine arts 2. a schoolhouse with special facilities for fine arts 3. a greenhouse in which plants are arranged in a pleasing manner [cellar chest closet common condition conservator control cultivation orangery nursery schoolhouse shelf side specialize standard storeroom study summerhouse educational exchequer exhibition rack receive retreat rick roof room vat vault advance archive arrange arsenal art attic tank teach treasury young /rota/]
*consign 09-70-21 (v.) 1. give over to another for care or safekeeping 2. commit forever; commit irrevocably 3. send to an address [care charge charter check child clerk commit communicate condemn confide convey obtain official nanny negotiate newsagent safekeeping sale secretary sell send ship shipment sign soak spectator spread steward switch impart implement import instrument intrust irrevocable getter give good guarantee] "consign your baggage"
*consistency 06-62-48 (n.) 1. a harmonious uniformity or agreement among things or parts 2. the property of holding together and retaining its shape 3. (logic) an attribute of a logical system that is so constituted that none of the propositions deducible from the axioms contradict one another 4. logical coherence and accordance with the facts [class clear close cohesive consist contradict correct cream crowd orderly orthodoxy overlap non scale scratch shape share sheer smooth solid stability standard steady stick structure

impermeable important inconsistent inference intersection tally task texture thickness tight time easily enough equanimity essential even explicit] "when the dough has enough consistency it is ready to bake"
*console 07-62-39 (n.) 1. a small table fixed to a wall or designed to stand against a wall 2. housing for electronic instruments, as radio or television 3. a scientific instrument consisting of displays and an input device that an operator can use to monitor and control a system (especially a computer system) 4. an ornamental scroll-shaped bracket (especially one used to support a wall fixture) (v.) 1. give moral or emotional strength to [cabinet calculation calm cheer comfort compute control cover operator ornamental scientist set shelf smooth solace sole solo soothe source stand still strength support swell leg lessen lull ease echo electronic emotional encourage] "the bust of Napoleon stood on a console"
*consolidate 05-34-81 (v.) 1. make firm or secure; strengthen 2. unite into one 3. bring together into a single whole or system 4. form into a solid mass or whole 5. make or form into a solid or hardened mass [close combine company confirm contract crowded one overnight narrow nip scatter school secure separate set single solid solidify squeeze stability strengthen substantial lead impermeable include incorporated increase interfuse deepen dense depth double add ally amalgamate assimilate associate thickset town triple eclectic embody encompass enhance establish /tad/] "The companies consolidated"
*consonance 23-15-1 (n.) 1. the repetition of consonants (or consonant patterns) especially at the ends of words 2. the property of sounding harmonious [calm chorus close combination constant correspondence oneness overlap note similarity simultaneousl sonance sound stability steady symphony accordance affinity agreement assonance echo equanimity equivalence even excel /nano/]
*consonant 18-50-4 (a.) 1. involving or characterized by harmony 2. in keeping (n.) 1. a letter of the alphabet standing for a spoken consonant 2. a speech sound that is not a vowel [central character chord close composite concordant conformable constant continuant conventional cord occlusive open orderly narrow nasalize near show sibilant sound speak stop stress strong accord accordant affricate agreement alphabetic alveolar ant articulation aspiration automatic tense thick throat tip tongue trend tune /nano/]
*consort 12-63-12 (n.) 1. the husband or wife of a reigning monarch 2. a family of similar musical instrument playing together (v.) 1. keep company with; hang out with 2. go together 3. keep company; of male animals [check choir chorus coincide colleague color compatible concord cooperation correspond criminal oneness orchestra overlap secret see ship sort sovereign specialize spend spouse square steady strange symphony rapport regular reign relationship roommate run tally teammate time toward travel treaty tune]
*conspicuous 07-54-41 (a.) 1. obvious to the eye or mind 2. without any attempt at concealment; completely obvious 3. noticeable in an unpleasant way 4. inclined to flaunt [celebrated clearly conceal consequential copious crying obtrusive obvious ostentatious outstand necktie noble notable notably noticeable notorious salient show significantly since special spectacular spic strike surprise particularly patent plain pointed preen pretentious prominent important impressive incredible indiscretion injudicious intense invisible uncommon unconcealed unmistakable unpleasant unusual] "a tower conspicuous at a great distance"
*conspiracy 04-47-99 (n.) 1. a group of conspirators banded together to achieve some harmful or illegal purpose 2. a plot to carry out some harmful or illegal act (especially a political plot) 3. a secret agreement between two or more people to perform an unlawful act [cabal circle coalition coco collusion commit confederacy coup craft scheme science secret sedition shift silence simultaneous situation strategy study subversive persecution piracy plan plot plotter ploy politics practice promise purpose illegal inclusion incorporate intrigue racket rig ruse agreement art association avenge /rip/]
*conspirator 12-40-12 (n.) 1. a member of a conspiracy [claim cockatrice collaborate commit con connive convict crime crook oate operator opportunist outlaw scheme secret serpent snake subversive parliament people plan plotter purpose illegal informer intrigue rat role accessory accomplice achieve agree assassinate titus traitor trimmer turncoat /rip rota/]
*conspire 07-43-43 (v.) 1. act in unison or agreement and in secret towards a deceitful or illegal purpose 2. engage in plotting or enter into a conspiracy, swear together [cabal careful combine commit complot conjure connive consolidate contrive couple court operate organize overthrow scheme secret smudge spire stock subversive swear synchronize partner plan plot purpose illegal inconvenience interact intrigue reciprocate rig engage engineer enter /rip/] "They conspired to overthrow the government"
*constable 07-91-37 (n.) 1. a lawman with less authority and jurisdiction than a sheriff 2. English landscape painter (1776-1837) 3. (British) a police officer of the lowest rank [captain castle chief commissioner cop occupy official narc northwestern scotland sergeant sheriff stable superintendent tipstaff township trooper administrative artist authority beagle below bobby british bull landscape last law lawman less lictor lieutenant low english europe /bats/]
*constellation 13-40-10 (n.) 1. an arrangement of parts or elements 2. a configuration of stars as seen from the earth [celebrity centaur cup cynosure name notable somebody star stella superstar end lion lot luminary

astrology idol immortal inevitable /tall/]
*consternation 12-60-12 (n.) 1. fear resulting from the awareness of danger [confusion cowardice nation scare shock specific stampede stock terror trepidation emotion exchange experience accompany affright alarm anticipation anxiety aware awe]
*constituency 05-66-68 (n.) 1. the body of voters who elect a representative for their area [citizen citizenry community con constituent country couple customer occupation official orbit organization outlook outside nation serve site society support territory tie turf inhabitant usual elector electorate enfranchise entity young]
*constituent 07-37-43 (a.) 1. constitutional in the structure of something (especially your physical makeup) 2. forming or functioning as part of a whole (n.) 1. a member of a constituency; a citizen who is represented in a government by officials for whom he or she votes 2. an artifact that is one of the individual parts of which a composite entity is made up; especially a part that can be separated from or attached to a system 3. an abstract part of something 4. (grammar) a word or phrase or clause forming part of a larger grammatical construction [capability circumstance composition con content original nature selective specialty stuff index inside integral item underlie earth electronic element essential]
*constrain 17-54-5 (v.) 1. hold back 2. restrict [chain check circumstance clog coerce compel confine control crowd cumber curb oblige obtund necessitate setback shortage skill soften squeeze stiffen strain tame temper throttle tie tighten trammel refrain regulation restrict retrench rule abate access alleviate arrest impede incarcerate industry inhibit injure intern]
*constrict 15-39-7 (v.) 1. squeeze or press together 2. become tight or as if tight [catch childbirth choke close compress control cover crowded obstruct occlude organ narrow nearsighted neck nip scrag secure shrink shut slam slender slow small snake spasm squeeze stop strangulate strict suffocate taper throat tight reduce restrict restricted rub illiberal incommodious inhibit insular involuntarily]
*consul 10-50-20 (n.) 1. a diplomat appointed by a government to protect its commercial interests and help its citizens in a foreign country [chancellor charge chief citizen city commercial con country official negotiation nuncio legate live]
*consulate 11-39-15 (n.) 1. diplomatic building that serves as the residence or workplace of a consul [cabinet chamber closet consul official nobility scope serve shop structure study leadership legation live lodge lordship administer ancient archiepiscopate aristocracy townhouse tribunate edifice embassy emirate /talus/]
*consume 04-49-123 (v.) 1. destroy completely 2. spend extravagantly 3. serve oneself to, or consume regularly 4. eat immoderately 5. engage fully 6. use up, as of resources or materials [contract corky corrode curtail obsessive occupy overwhelming nihilism sample sap sate saving shift short small spellbind spend spent spoon strong subversive suicidal surround unbearable uncontrollable upheave utilize macerate magnetic material meal meat mesmerize miniaturize misspend molder monopolize munch eat employ engross erode exhaust expend /emu/]
*consumer 02-47-521 (n.) 1. a person who uses goods or services [cannibal carnivore carnivorous chain chew client community consume country customer omnivore organism non nourishment service shopper smoke snuff squander user market material mouth music eat eater ecology employ employer enjoy excess extravagant reckless respective /emu/]
*consummate 10-54-20 (a.) 1. having or revealing supreme mastery or skill 2. without qualification; used informally as (often pejorative) intensifiers 3. perfect and complete in every respect; having all necessary qualities (v.) 1. make perfect; bring to perfection 2. of marriages [capital chief chronic clear omnipresent outright skillful stark straight succeed summate supreme ubiquitous ultimate universal unskilled utter make manage model able absolute accomplished achieve talented thoroughgoing top total train end errant everlasting excellent execute expert] "a consummate artist"
*consumption 05-55-79 (n.) 1. the process of taking food into the body through the mouth (as by eating) 2. (economics) the utilization of economic goods to satisfy needs or in manufacturing 3. the act of consuming something 4. involving the lungs with progressive wasting of the body [cannibal cause chew crop nibble nutrition savor science sear service slaughter sumption undo usage usance use mess misuse munch pasture peck perdition taste thin impoverish ingest intake] "the consumption of energy has increased steadily"
*consumptive 23-63-1 (a.) 1. tending to consume or use often wastefully 2. afflicted with or associated with pulmonary tuberculosis (n.) 1. a person with pulmonary tuberculosis [cancer case chronic collapsible connect cough originate outpatient nephritic neuritis nihilism sick subversive suffering suicidal suitable sump malaria malignant material measly mental paralytic patient person physical podagra productive pulmonary tabetic tend tuberculosis tumor ill incurable internecine invalid valetudinarian vandalism edema encephalitis energy engage epileptic exploit] "water suitable for beneficial consumptive uses"
*contagion 19-41-3 (n.) 1. any disease easily transmitted by contact 2. the communication of an attitude or emotional state among a number of people 3. an incident is which an infectious disease is transmitted [children clothe communicate cor corrupt cupid curse taint tendency throat toxicity tract transmit acute agio angina attitude genital grippe group illness impurity incident

infectious influenza intercourse itch] "a contagion of mirth"
*contagious 13-41-11 (a.) 1. easily diffused or spread as from one person to another 2. (of disease) capable of being transmitted by infection [capable carry catching clothe communicable consign convey noxious taking transmit transpose affect agio assign grin indirect infectious infective inoculate interchange sporadic spreadable spreading] "a contagious grin"
*contaminate 07-37-41 (v.) 1. make radioactive by adding radioactive material 2. make impure [cankered charge colly combine cont corrupt cut organism nasty noisome noxious taint tarnish transform tref twist abandon activate adulterate alloy alter antiseptic association material microorganism misuse mix modify mortify impurity industry infect infest injure irradiate element environment evidence exploitation /anima mat/]
*contemplate 04-57-100 (v.) 1. reflect deeply on a subject 2. think intently and at length, as for spiritual purposes 3. consider as a possibility 4. look at thoughtfully; observe deep in thought [calm careful certainty cogitate con conduct confidence consideration obsession open overview nature navel nirvana template engagement entertain examine exercise expectation eye matter mean meditation mind monomania muse past peaceful plan policy ponder practice predict premeditate process profound lengthy litany long look lucubration abstruse aim anticipation appeal application attentive /met/] "contemplate one's navel"
*contemporaneous 19-41-3 (a.) 1. occurring in the same period of time 2. of the same period [coetaneous coeval coexist collateral composer concurrent current new tempora topical exist extant modern period phase present rate rise running actual agree asis simultaneous synchronous /met/] "a rise in interest rates is often contemporaneous with an increase in inflation"
*contemporary 02-49-257 (a.) 1. occurring in the same period of time 2. belonging to the present time 3. characteristic of the present (n.) 1. a person of nearly the same age as another [chronicle coeval collateral computer connected current ongoing nearly new nice novel now table temporary tie topical trend trendy equal era exist extant match medicine middle mod modern modernize modish parallel peer period phase present problem progressive rate related rise role room running accompany age agree approximate associate asynchronous /met/] "contemporary trends in design"
*contemptible 21-55-2 (a.) 1. deserving of contempt or scorn 2. worthy only of being despised and rejected [character cheap common completely contempt courage creature crude obscene offensive oliver outrageous nasty nobility noble nothing notorious noxious terrible trashy treat twopenny earth egregious enormous estimable execrable majesty mean mere merit miserable monstrous pathetic petty pitiful poor purpose ignominious infamous inferior bad base blame lack little loathsome lousy low lowdown /bit met/] "a contemptible lack of courage"
*contemptuous 13-57-10 (a.) 1. expressing extreme contempt [cavalier challenging condescending contempt objurgate nervy toplofty exclusive execrate exhibit express extreme malapert minimize pejorative pert prig utter scornful show smart sneer snobby strong supercilious /met out/]
*contender 04-60-108 (n.) 1. the contestant you hope to defeat [candidate challenger champion chance combatant competitor contend contestant nominee thug tie tilt titleholder tough tournament eliminate emulator enemy enforcer engage entrant defeat disputant duelist reach remain respect riot rival rough runner]
*contentious 07-46-40 (a.) 1. inclined or showing an inclination to dispute or disagree, even to engage in law suits 2. having or showing a ready disposition to fight 3. involving or likely to cause controversy [capable central chauvinist combative content controversial create critical offensive officer nature naysay tim touchy truculent element enemy energetic engage enjoy eristic impulse incline inimical interested irritate uncontroversi unfriendly savage scrappy seeming show soldierly spirit statement style suit] "a style described as abrasive and contentious"
*contiguous 18-14-4 (a.) 1. very close or connected in space or time 2. having a common boundary or edge; touching 3. connecting without a break; within a common boundary [city close connect coterminous near nearby neighboring next touching immediate unbroken unconnected uninterrupted sequence share short side situate space /git/] "contiguous events"
*contingency 09-52-23 (n.) 1. a possible event or occurrence or result 2. the state of being contingent on something [chance circumstance clause condition crisis occasion occurrence opportunity other natural nonessential incident incidental independence inessential interrelate introduce gamble grammar guess emergency eventuality exigency expense extra]
*contingent 07-41-40 (a.) 1. possible but not certain to occur 2. uncertain because of uncontrollable circumstances 3. determined by conditions or circumstances not yet established (n.) 1. a gathering of persons representative of some larger group 2. a temporary military unit [capable case cause certain chance circumstance commission condition confession congress country cut odd open organization other nation nonessential nudge team temporary thinkable troop true impossible include indirect inevitable installment interest gang gathering george glancing grazing group eliot end establish exist expense extra] "each nation sent a contingent of athletes to the Olympics"
*continuance 21-39-2 (n.) 1. the act of continuing an activity without interruption 2. the period of time during which something continues 3. the property of enduring or continuing in time [chorus completion conclusion

constant course note nuance tag timeless traverse incessant indestructible infinity interruption unbroken until abiding addendum adjourn again age amount antiquity arrange art endless enduring eternity experience extension /unit/]
*continuation 09-37-23 (n.) 1. the act of continuing an activity without interruption 2. the consequence of being lengthened in duration 3. a part added to a book or play that continues and extends it [carry chorus completion consequence offshoot organization table tag tailpiece tendency textual identify increment innate installment interruption abiding accessory add addendum additional again already attachment /unit/]
*continuity 08-55-31 (n.) 1. uninterrupted connection or union 2. a detailed script used in making a film in order to avoid discontinuities from shot to shot 3. the property of a continuous and connected period of time [calm camera cohesive color commentary comprehensive connection consistent costume oscillation narrative next television term theme tone traditional important incessant incident include interrupt item unchanging uniformity union unity /unit/]
*continuous 05-46-60 (a.) 1. (mathematics) of a function or curve; extending without break or irregularity 2. continuing in time or space without interruption [ceaseless change chemical constant continue continuo correspondent curve orderly near neverending non nonstop thematic tight timeless toward illness incessant infinite inspire interval irregularity ubiquitous unbroken unceasing unending uniform uninterrupted unremitting science sequence shape shin six solar space stay stick stop straight stream strive sufficient sustain /unit/] "a continuous rearrangement of electrons in the solar atoms results in the emission of light"
*contort 17-55-5 (v.) 1. twist and press out of shape [computer cont crooked crumple curve natural torture tree truth twine twirl twist /trot/]
*contour 11-44-15 (n.) 1. any spatial attributes (especially as defined by outline) 2. a line drawn on a map connecting points of equal height (v.) 1. form the contours of [characteristic complex concavity configuration conformation connect cont convexness crook curve cut occupy operate outline narrow nature thin trace relation relief round]
*contraband 17-38-5 (a.) 1. distributed or sold illicitly (n.) 1. goods whose importation or exportation or possession is prohibited by law [chargeable cigarette commodity contra country criminal offer official outlaw neutral taboo tax territory trade triable refusal rejection rule run accept actionable anarchist anomic ban bar behind bootleg buy dealer denial disapprove dishonest distribute drug duty /bar/]
*contradiction 07-47-41 (n.) 1. (logic) a statement that is necessarily false 2. opposition between two conflicting forces or ideas 3. the speech act of contradicting someone [challenge claim clash conflicting contradict controversy opposition necessarily negation nullification reasonable refute relation ambiguity analyze answer antagonism antithesis aspect decline denial determine difference disagree dismissal disputation idea ignore illogicality immune inconsistency inconsistent inference interaction interference /dart/] "the statement `he is brave and he is not brave' is a contradiction"
*contradictory 08-41-27 (a.) 1. of words so related that both cannot be true and both cannot be false 2. in disagreement 3. that confounds or contradicts or confuses 4. unable to be both true at the same time (n.) 1. two propositions are contradictories if both cannot be true (or both cannot be false) at the same time [clash compatible competitive confuse contradict contrast cross obstinate obverse odd opposite noncooperation nullify tend true relation alien ambiguous ambivalent antagonistic antonym argumentative assistance attribute deny differ disagreement discrepant display inconsistent invalid irrational /dart/] "`perfect' and `imperfect' are contradictory terms"
*contravene 12-87-12 (v.) 1. go against, as of rules and laws 2. deny the truth of [combat come committee conflict contra contradict cross observance offend opinion oppose opposition overstep negate negative transgress traverse trespass truth regulation reject repudiate resist rule run abjure afoul violate violation encroach equipment exclude]
*contribution 02-53-293 (n.) 1. an amount of money contributed 2. act of giving in common with others for a common purpose especially to a charity 3. a voluntary gift (as of money or service or ideas) made to some worthwhile cause 4. any one of a number of individual efforts in a common endeavor 5. a writing for publication especially one of a collection of writings as an article or story [charity claim college compensation conscientious cont offertory order organization notice tax team tip toll toward tribute try recognize regular religious repay requisition retirement role idea impact impart influence input interest investiture involve beneficent bestow blackmail broadcast business ultimatum /tub/] "I am proud of my contribution to the team's success"
*contributor 05-54-69 (n.) 1. a writer whose work is published in a newspaper or magazine or as part of a book 2. someone who contributes (or promises to contribute) a sum of money [cont newspaper backer book /tub/]
*contrite 18-58-4 (a.) 1. feeling or expressing pain or sorrow for sins or offenses 2. feeling regret for a fault or offence [offering trite regret remorseful repentant rueful ruthful excusatory express]
*contrivance 18-41-4 (n.) 1. the faculty of contriving; inventive skill 2. a device that very useful for a particular job 3. an artificial or unnatural or obviously contrived arrangement of details or parts etc. 4. an elaborate or deceitful scheme contrived to deceive or

evade 5. the act of devising something 6. any improvised arrangement for temporary use [color conception coup craft organization originate theme tone tool racket recognition resource idea incident innovation instrument vance vehicle action apparatus appliance art attack effort enterprise episode] "his skillful contrivance of answers to every problem"
*contrive 08-68-29 (v.) 1. come up with (an idea, plan, explanation, theory, or priciple) after a mental effort 2. make or work out a plan for; devise 3. put or send forth [calculate carry cast clever coin come computer cont cook corner create creative obtain organize originate natural negotiate novel teacher theory throw tree try turnout rationalize reality rig idea impression ingenious intense intrigue invent view effective effort elaborate engineer excogitate explanation] "They contrived to murder their boss"
*control 01-45-1333 (n.) 1. the economic policy of controlling or limiting or curbing prices or wages etc. 2. a mechanism that controls the operation of a machine 3. a relation of constraint of one entity (thing or person or group) by another 4. great skillfulness and knowledge of some subject or activity 5. discipline in personal and social activities 6. the state that exists when one person or group has power over another 7. the activity of managing or exerting control over something 8. a standard against which other conditions can be compared in a scientific experiment 9. (physiology) regulation or maintenance of a function or action or reflex etc 10. power to direct or determine 11. a spiritual agency that is assumed to assist the medium during a seance (v.) 1. control (others or oneself) or influence skillfully, usually to one's advantage 2. lessen the intensity of; temper; hold in restraint; hold or keep within limits 3. handle and cause to function 4. exercise authoritative control or power over 5. verify by using a duplicate register for comparison 6. verify or regulate by conducting a parallel experiment or comparing with another standard, of scientific experiments 7. have a firm understanding or knowledge of; be on top of 8. be careful or certain to do something; make certain of something [capital careful championship checked chief conduct constrained cont cool coordinate credit official order orderly oversight neutrality nonviolence numen tame test topmost totalitarian try ranking ready record regulate rein ruling leading lessen leverage lie] "control the budget"
*controller 06-50-44 (n.) 1. someone who maintains and audits business accounts 2. a mechanism that controls the operation of a machine 3. a person who directs and restrains [careful checked chief clerk control order overseer taskmaster test treasurer trustee try receiver recorder regulator rein liquidator]
*contusion 23-15-1 (n.) 1. an injury that doesn't break the skin but results in some discoloration 2. the action of bruising [cont tiny tissue trauma typhoid shiner skin spot striking surface injury] "the bruise resulted from a contusion"
*conundrum 11-71-15 (n.) 1. a difficult problem [challenge confuse consideration difficult drum raise riddle mystery]
*convalesce 21-67-2 (v.) 1. get over an illness or shock [vale vigor ameliorate effect energy shock spend]
*convalescence 21-58-2 (n.) 1. gradual healing (through rest) after sickness or injury [natural acute sickness spirit strength subside symptom]
*convalescent 18-49-4 (a.) 1. of or for or relating to convalescence or convalescents 2. returning to health after illness or debility (n.) 1. a person who is recovering from illness [child convalesce natural acute effect sick spirit strength suffering symptom treatment] "convalescent home"
*convene 07-29-39 (v.) 1. meet formally 2. call together [call cite collect come con convoke council court open organize evoke] "The council convened last week"
*convenience 06-49-52 (n.) 1. the quality of being useful and convenient 2. the state of being suitable or opportune 3. a device that very useful for a particular job 4. a toilet that is available to the public [can circumstance close closet collective comfort compass con contrivance cook cozy offer opportune outfit outhouse near necessary value ease easy engine equip equipment expediency impedimenta inject installation interest invent] "chairs arranged for his own convenience"
*converge 09-42-23 (v.) 1. be adjacent or come together 2. come together so as to form a single product 3. in mathematics: approach a limit as the number of terms increases without limit 4. move or draw together at a certain location [center certain city collect come concentrate condition congregate contact couple crowd near nigh nip verge embrace environmental eventually extend rapid reach rendezvous resemble response road gather gradual group] "The lines converge at this point"
*convergent 23-41-1 (a.) 1. tending to come together from different directions [come confluence converge course oblique right tend]
*conversant 21-47-2 (a.) 1. (usually followed by 'with') well informed about or knowing thoroughly [career coach colleague complex confrere conscious contact custom versant education experience relation road sensible sentient skill stranger study accomplished acquainted acquire alive association awake aware technical train trend] "conversant with business trends"
*conversion 04-65-107 (n.) 1. a spiritual enlightenment causing a person to lead a new life 2. a successful free throw or try for point after a touchdown 3. a change in the units or form of an expression: "conversion from Fahrenheit to Centigrade" 4. an event that results in a transformation 5. (psychiatry) a defense mechanism represses emotional conflicts which are then converted into physical symptoms that have no organic basis 6. a

change of religion 7. act of exchanging one type of money or security for another 8. interchange of subject and predicate of a proposition 9. the act of changing from one use or function or purpose to another [calculation cast composition creation overthrow novelty variety version elaborate embezzle extremism raise reaction rebirth renewal renovate revolution shape shift switch improvement innovation] "conversion from Fahrenheit to Centigrade"
*convertible 07-41-37 (a.) 1. capable of being exchanged for or replaced by something of equal value 2. designed to be changed from one use or form to another 3. capable of being changed in substance as if by alchemy (n.) 1. a car that has top that can be folded or removed 2. a corporate security (usually bonds or preferred stock) that can be exchanged for another form of security (usually common stock) 3. a sofa that can be converted into a bed [capable car cash change changeable combustion commute convert coordinate corporate corresponding couch coupe currency ordinary negotiable value vehicle equal even exchange really receive red redeemable relevant remove replace resolve retaliate returnable right roof tantamount top trade transmute transpose identical interchange becoming bed bond legal liquid lounge /bit/] "convertible securities"
*convex 21-30-2 (a.) 1. curving or bulging outward [con concave curve optics outwardly oxbow vault ellipsoid embowed exterior]
*conveyance 17-77-5 (n.) 1. document effecting a property transfer 2. act of transferring property title from one person to another 3. the transmission of information 4. something that serves as a means of transportation 5. the act of transporting something from one location to another [cable camera car carry chair change charter claim collection colony communicate confer connection contractual convey country official overland ownership notify vehicle vessel vesting voluntary effect embezzle end enfeoff exchange aboard access accomplish aircraft animal announcement artifact assignment attached authority /aye nay/]
*conviction 03-49-171 (n.) 1. (criminal law) a final judgment of guilty in a criminal case and the punishment that is imposed 2. an unshakable belief in something without need for proof or evidence [case censure certitude cognitive complete condemn confidence content convict court criminal opinion verdict view impose imprison instance tenet true trust] "the conviction came as no surprise"
*convivial 14-63-9 (a.) 1. occupied with or fond of the pleasures of good company [celebrate club company conducive cordial cordiality occupy nature noisy vial vivacious incline associate atmosphere lively] "a convivial atmosphere at the reunion"
*conviviality 21-59-2 (n.) 1. a jovial nature 2. a boisterous celebration; a merry festivity [celebrate companionable cordiality nature noisy associate tendency]
*convoluted 13-47-11 (a.) 1. rolled or coiled together 2. highly involved or intricate [coil complicate concentric convolute curl needlework negotiation vague labyrinthine language lasting legal long understand tangle tax tortuous turn twist elaborate extremely deceive deform denote difficult draw] "a convoluted shell"
*convolution 23-31-1 (n.) 1. the shape of something rotating rapidly 2. the action of coiling or twisting or winding together 3. a convex fold or elevation in the surface of the brain [central coil complication con crabbed crooked curve occipital orotund outer vaulting ventricle vermis vortex lobe lofty lurid tangle technicality temporal tortuous twist inflation intricacy intricate involve involved]
*convoy 08-56-31 (n.) 1. a procession of land vehicles traveling together 2. a collection of merchant ships with an escort of warships 3. the act of escorting while in transit (v.) 1. escort in transit [caravan carry cavalcade collection company con conductor consider vehicle yeoman]
*convulse 18-49-4 (v.) 1. be overcome with laughter 2. make someone convulse with laughter 3. cause to contract, as of muscles 4. of muscles 5. move or stir about violently [chafe claw comedian compress con constrict contract crowd cut output overcome nip violent unco unsettle until upset lacerate laughter savage shake shudder spasm squeeze stab start sting stir strong economy emotion entertain excite exhilarate express extreme] "The comedian convulsed the crowd"
*convulsion 17-48-5 (n.) 1. violent uncontrollable contractions of muscles [catastrophe chill climax clonus con condition consciousness contraction occurrence orgasm outburst outcry overturn nausea necrosis vertigo violent visitation vomit uncontrollable upheaval upturn laughter limb literary lockjaw lumbago seizure shake shaking shock spasm stir stroke sudden symptom ictus impaired inflammation insanity itch]
*copious 12-59-12 (a.) 1. large in number or quantity (especially of discourse) 2. affording an abundant supply [comprehensive countless coverage creative opulent overflow party pious plentiful plenty pregnant press produce productive profuse inexhaustible seminal spacious supply swarm] "she took copious notes"
*coquette 19-56-3 (n.) 1. a seductive woman who uses her sex appeal to exploit men (v.) 1. talk or behave amorously, without serious intentions [captive catching changeable charming chat coquet oppose quicksilver unpredictable unreliable enchantress engage entice entrance exchange exciting exotic exploit taking talk tease temptress try]
*cordial 12-43-13 (a.) 1. diffusing warmth and friendliness 2. sincerely or intensely felt 3. showing warm and heartfelt friendliness (n.) 1. strong highly flavored sweet liquor usually drunk after a meal [casual

cheer cord courteous offhand openhearted recreation relaxed renewal delirious desirable drunk inebriant informal intense irregular affable agreeable amiable ardent liberal lively loose /laid/]
*cordon 10-65-18 (n.) 1. cord or ribbon worn as an insignia of honor or rank 2. adornment consisting of an ornamental ribbon or cord [catch chain chamber close color control cord objection obstruction official order ornamental outpost relieve ribbon riddle rub decoration deterrent difficulty divide /nod/]
*cornice 15-59-7 (n.) 1. a decorative framework to conceal curtain fixtures at the top of a window casing 2. a molding at the corner between the ceiling and the top of a wall 3. the topmost projecting part of an entablature (v.) 1. furnish with a cornice, as in architecture [capital case ceiling central classical climb column conceal construction corn curtain ornamentation overhang render roof room rose ice edge entablature]
*cornucopia 17-37-5 (n.) 1. the property of being extremely abundant [collection commissary container copious cornu cumulate ornament overflow repertory resource rich rick painting pile plenty produce profusion property prosperity provision inventory abundant accumulation adequate amass art]
*corollary 18-42-4 (n.) 1. a practical consequence that follows naturally 2. (logic) an inference that follows directly from the proof of another proposition [circumstantial complement conclusion consequence consequent continuation corolla observation obvious offspring outcome outgrowth reasoning reinforcement repercussion resultant legacy little logical love accessory accompaniment add addendum aftermath already analyze append attendant /allo/] "blind jealousy is a frequent corollary of passionate love"
*coronation 09-85-24 (n.) 1. the ceremony of installing a new monarch [ceremony consecration corona crown office organization appointment assignment assumption inauguration induction initiation instal investiture]
*coronet 19-70-3 (n.) 1. a small crown; usually indicates a high rank but below that of sovereign 2. margin between the skin of the pastern and the horn of the hoof [chain chief circular cor crown orb orbit ordinary ornamental reign ring rod rose necklace noose eagle earring escutcheon tiara tincture tissue top torque /tenor/]
*corporal 11-73-16 (a.) 1. affecting or characteristic of the body as opposed to the mind or spirit 2. possessing or existing in bodily form (n.) 1. a noncommissioned officer in the army or airforce or marines [carnal centurion corpora corporeal officer oppose reredos paten personnel physical piscina possess affecting animal appointed army lascivious]
*corporate 02-44-401 (a.) 1. possessing or existing in bodily form 2. of or belonging to a corporation 3. done by or characteristic of individuals acting together 4. organized and maintained as a legal corporation [coherent collective combine combined community company comprehensive concern corpora couple organize rate pair people physical possess affiliate agency allied associate team town trade embody employee exist /taro/] "corporate rates"
*corporeal 23-51-1 (a.) 1. having material or physical form or substance 2. affecting or characteristic of the body as opposed to the mind or spirit [carnal combination concern corporal create objective oppose reincarnate phenomenal physical pore earthly embody erotic affecting animal lascivious /aero/] "that which is created is of necessity corporeal and visible and tangible"
*corps 05-33-81 (n.) 1. a body of people associated together 2. an army unit usually consisting of two or more divisions [college combat commission cor council crowd occupation officer organization outfit rank regiment regular ring rot pack part party people permanent platoon prepare press program section service set society soldier specialize stater support sustain] "diplomatic corps"
*corpse 07-64-36 (n.) 1. the dead body of a human being [cadaver carcass clay corps cremation reliquiae remain remains shadow slim stiff earth end]
*corpulent 21-66-2 (a.) 1. excessively fat [chubby chunky coarse crass obese obesity overweight rotund plump podgy portly property pudgy puffy lent lusty excessive thickset thin tubby]
*correlate 15-41-7 (a.) 1. mutually related (n.) 1. either of two correlated variables (v.) 1. to bear a reciprocal or mutual relation 2. bring into a mutual, complementary, or reciprocal relation [check coincide collateral colligate complementary connection consistent correspondent counterpart couple obverse range reciprocal reciprocate relate relation relativize report effect equate equivalent likeness linear link logical affiliate agree allied ally apply associate assume tally tie twin /tale taler/] "Do these facts correlate?"
*corroborate 12-39-12 (v.) 1. give evidence for 2. establish or strengthen as with new evidence or facts 3. support with evidence or authority : make more certain or confirm [certain certify check circumstantiate claim coincide collateral compatible confirm confirmed consistent ratify reassert reference reinforce represent backup bear bolster borate buttress account affirm affirmation agree assistance attest authority tally truth establish evidence experiment explanation /rob taro/]
*corroboration 21-44-2 (n.) 1. confirmation that some fact or statement is true [confirm affirmation authentication true]
*corrode 16-42-6 (v.) 1. cause to deteriorate due to the action of water, air, or an acid 2. become destroyed by water, air, or an etching chemical such as an acid [candidate canker chemical constant criticism crumble oxidize rode ruin rust damage decay decline decompose decrease destroy deteriorate dilapidate disintegrate dive

drip due eat ebb erode etching /dorr/] "The acid corroded the metal"
*corrosion 17-44-5 (n.) 1. a state of deterioration in metals caused by oxidation or chemical action 2. erosion by chemical action [chemistry composition condition consequence consumption cor corruption crumble oxidize reddish reduce resolution roughness rust shrinkage spoilage steady strength structure substance surface symptom impair incoherent indentation iron]
*corrosive 14-51-8 (a.) 1. of a substance, especially a strong acid; capable of destroying or eating away by chemical action (n.) 1. a substance having the tendency to cause corrosion (such a strong acids or alkali) [capable caustic chemistry compound constructive cor counterproductive cut ominous radium ravage review ruinous sarcastic scar sharp striking strong substance imperative impressive incisive ingredient vicious vigorous vital vitriolic eat effective element erode erosive /visor/]
*corruption 04-44-118 (n.) 1. lack of integrity or honesty (especially susceptibility to bribery); use of a position of trust for dishonest gain 2. decay of matter (as by rot or oxidation) 3. moral perversion; impairment of virtue and moral principles 4. destroying someone's (or some group's) honesty or loyalty; undermining moral integrity 5. in a state of progressive putrefaction [contamination corrupt cutting obfuscate obscure outrage resolution rot rotten rust perversion poison pollution prostitution putrid torture toxin tricky ill immoral impropriety induce injury /purr/] "the luxury and corruption among the upper classes"
*cosmetic 06-51-52 (a.) 1. serving an esthetic rather than a useful purpose 2. serving an aesthetic purpose in beautifying the body (n.) 1. a toiletry designed to beautify the body [car code color compact concerning conduct cos cover ornamental seem serve shiny since skin stick substance sundries superficial surface surgery makeup mascara enamel esthetical eye taste temporary thin toiletry improve intend /cite item/] "cosmetic fenders on cars"
*cosmic 10-41-17 (a.) 1. of or from or pertaining to or characteristic of the cosmos or universe 2. inconceivably extended in space or time [catastrophe celestial colossal creation osmic outer outsize overgrown significance sizable size space spacious stupendous macrocosm magnitude mammoth monstrous monumental immense inconceivable infinite interstellar] "cosmic laws"
*cosmology 17-37-5 (n.) 1. the metaphysical study of the origin and nature of the universe 2. the branch of astrophysics that studies the origins and structure of the universe [casuistry cataclysmic celestial chemical closure collide concern constant cool cosmography observer occur ology ontology originate scientific shortly solar sophistry speed structure study sufficient mark mass matter metaphysics microwave light logic galaxy gaseous gravitation year]
*cosmopolitan 09-54-24 (a.) 1. (ecology) growing or occurring in many parts of the world 2. composed of people from or at home in many parts of the world; especially not provincial in attitudes or interests 3. of worldwide scope or applicability (n.) 1. a sophisticated person who has travelled in many countries [catholic chic city civil cos country crowd culture old season society state subject mature people plant posh practice public immigrant international total travel trim national neat nifty /pom/] "a cosmopolitan herb"
*cosmos 12-38-13 (n.) 1. the whole collection of existing things 2. everything that exists anywhere 3. any of various mostly Mexican herbs of the genus Cosmos having radiate heads of variously colored flowers and pinnate leaves; popular fall-blooming annuals [celestial closure collection colorful consider cos creation cultivate orderly outside sky space star study sufficient supernatural system macrocosm mane matter metagalaxy mexico mostly]
*coterie 16-54-6 (n.) 1. an exclusive circle of people with a common purpose [cabal cabinet camarilla camp cast century circle clique core cote country crowd officer outfit team tight tribe troop trust early exclusive reagan regiment ring rogue rule inner interest intrigue]
*counsel 03-28-201 (n.) 1. a lawyer who pleads cases in court 2. direction or advice as to a decision or course of action (v.) 1. give advice to [career case caution children coach collection communicate conduct consultation context council court official opinion opportunity urge negotiate seek set speak speculation standard steer study substance suggestion support effect est exhort exhortation expert explanation law lawsuit lawyer lead legal likelihood literary lucubration]
*countenance 12-73-12 (n.) 1. the human face ('kisser' and 'smiler' and 'mug' are informal terms for 'face'; 'phiz' is British) 2. formal and explicit approval 3. the appearance conveyed by a person's face (v.) 1. give permission [care cast championship clearance count obey okay oke overlook uphold upon nod nourish nurture tolerate trait turn endorsement endure entitle abide admit advocate air allow authorize] "a pleasant countenance"
*counteract 13-50-10 (v.) 1. oppose and mitigate the effects of by contrary actions 2. oppose or check by a counteraction 3. act in opposition to 4. destroy property or hinder normal operations [cancel challenge check colleague complaint control correct counter crossing curb objection obstinate offset operation opposition oppugn undermine upset negativism neutralize noncooperation normal nullify temper thwart track traverse effect elude equiponderate expiation railroad reaction reduce refuse resistance respond restraint right ruin run amends antagonize atonement automatic /care/] "This will counteract the foolish actions of my colleagues"
*counterbalance 15-52-7 (n.) 1. an equivalent

counterbalancing weight 2. equality of distribution 3. a compensating equivalent (v.) 1. make up for, make good 2. oppose and mitigate the effects of by contrary actions 3. place in opposition: can also be used in an abstract sense [clash consideration correct counter obverse offset outweigh undercurrent undo negative neutralize nullify thwart transfix equate equivalent redeem retain reverse balance ballast buffer accommodate adjust amend level /bret/]
*counterfeit 10-47-18 (a.) 1. not genuine; imitating something superior (n.) 1. a copy that is represented as the original (v.) 1. make a copy of with the intent to deceive [card coin comparison copy corresponding counter create criterion cuckoo onomatopoeia ostensive unauthentic unreal nature teaser emulate equal exchange reality reflect repetition represent reserve fact fake false favor feel fictive forgery fraudulent icon image imitate impersonate impostor impression inauthentic insincere intent invent /fret tie/] "counterfeit emotion"
*counterpart 04-56-120 (n.) 1. a duplicate copy 2. a person or thing having the same function or characteristics as another [colleague complete contract coordinate copy correspond correspondent counter obverse opposite original tally transaction triplicate twin effect equal exactly repetition reproduction rival parallel party peer picture play actor ally analogue associate /trap/]
*countervail 21-25-2 (v.) 1. compensate for or counterbalance 2. oppose and mitigate the effects of by contrary actions [cancel clash colleague compensate contrary correct counter cross offset operation oppose overcome neutralize normal thwart traverse effect equate equiponderate exert rectify redeem resist accommodate adjust amend automatic idea influence level]
*countryman 09-58-26 (n.) 1. a man from your own country 2. a man who lives in the country and has country ways [citizen clown compatriot country countrywoman offer unsophisticated native test raise resident reveal rural rustic muzhik mythology adoption]

*courageous 09-54-26 (a.) 1. possessing or displaying courage; able to face and deal with danger or fear without flinching [calm cowardly oblivious unafraid undaunted undertake resolute adventurous audacious gallant gamey gamy gritty gutsy enemy enterprise safe seek spirited spunky stalwart stouthearted]
*course 01-59-1278 (ad.) 1. as might be expected (n.) 1. facility consisting of a circumscribed area of land or water laid out for a sport 2. a connected series of events or actions or developments 3. part of a meal served at one time 4. general line of orientation 5. a line or route along which something travels or moves 6. a mode of action 7. education imparted in a series of lessons or class meetings 8. (construction) a layer of masonry (v.) 1. move along, of liquids 2. hunt (game) with hounds [capture career cave certainly chase court obviously order ours outing raceway rank revolution run scent sight sport execution exit expedition] "he took a course in basket weaving"
*courtesy 06-68-55 (n.) 1. a courteous or respectful or considerate act 2. a courteous or respectful or considerate remark 3. a courteous manner [call ceremony certainly charge civility comment conduct congenial considerate consideration court obligation offer office opinion urbanity usage regard remark respect rude toward turn elegance esteem etiquette excellence express sake seat service show sit social sociality statement /set/]
*covenant 11-58-15 (n.) 1. a signed written agreement between two or more parties (nations) to perform some action 2. (Bible) an agreement between God and his people in which God makes certain promises and requires certain behavior from them in return (v.) 1. agree to a covenant 2. enter into a covenant [catholic ceremony certain christian church city clause communion compact concordat confirmation consortium contract convention coven owner vatican vow engage enter exchange express accord administer agreement arrangement transaction treaty]
*covert 08-47-27 (a.) 1. secret or hidden; not openly practiced or engaged in or shown or avowed 2. (law) of a wife; under the protection of her husband (n.) 1. a flock of coots 2. a covering that serves to conceal or shelter something [camouflage case clandestine cloak closet cloth collusive conceal connive coot corner cover crouch obfuscate obscure observable occult openly overt veiled vestment virtual earth eclipse engage envelop express eye rebel refuge retreat rice rule run tail tented textile thicket thief translucent tree trench tunnel twill] "covert actions by the CIA"
*covetous 21-71-2 (a.) 1. showing extreme cupidity; painfully desirous of another's advantages 2. immoderately desirous of acquiring e.g. wealth [collection commercialism cupidity old eager employer envy express extreme eye show stingy success] "he was never covetous before he met her"
*covey 21-22-2 (n.) 1. a small collection of people 2. a small flock of grouse or partridge [cast clutch collection colony cove crew crowd old outfit]
*cower 14-66-8 (v.) 1. crouch or curl up 2. show submission or fear [cow crawl creep cringe crouch curl curve waist wallow welter wince recoil]
*coxswain 23-44-1 (n.) 1. the helmsman of a ship's boat or a racing crew [charge cicerone cock courier cox crew oversee shepherd ship speed steersman swain wheelman navigate navigator]
*coy 10-59-19 (a.) 1. affectedly modest or shy especially in a playful or provocative way 2. modestly or warily rejecting approaches or overtures 3. showing marked and often playful or irritating evasiveness or reluctance to make a definite or committing statement

[cajole capricious clearly colt commit conduct confidence confused conscious coquette offensive overture young] "a politician coy about his intentions"
*crag 18-75-4 (n.) 1. a steep rugged rock or cliff [cliff comb conglomerate rag rake ratchet rocky rough rugged gneiss granite]
*cranium 23-50-1 (n.) 1. the part of the skull that encloses the brain [carpus cavity clavicle coccyx connective continuation cord coronal cover cran radius rib rigid acoustic age nasal ilium infant inner ulna unite upper magnum meatus membranous /narc/]

*crass 11-69-15 (a.) 1. (of persons) so unrefined as to be lacking in discrimination and sensibility [classical complete crude rank refinement regular rough arrant asinine ass sensibility shock stark stupid]
*cravat 21-80-2 (n.) 1. neckwear worn in a slipknot with long ends overlapping vertically in front [clothe cummerbund article ascot vat veil vertical tie]
*crave 07-65-43 (v.) 1. have a craving, appetite, or great desire for 2. plead or ask for earnestly [call choose conjure covet crash rave raving require requisition accompany ache addiction adjure alcoholism appetite ask athirst earnest entreat]
*craven 10-80-18 (a.) 1. lacking even the rudiments of courage; abjectly fearful (n.) 1. an abject coward [caitiff chicken contempt courage coward crave raise raven recreant rudiment run] "the craven fellow turned and ran"
*craving 11-59-16 (n.) 1. an intense desire for some particular thing [raving abnormal accompany appetite ask implore intense granville great]
*creak 11-73-14 (n.) 1. a squeaking sound (v.) 1. make a high-pitched, screeching noise, as of a door [caterwaul chirrup crick rasp resound emit keen kind] "the creak of the floorboards gave him away"
*creamery 23-48-1 (n.) 1. a workplace where dairy products (butter and cheese etc.) are produced or sold [cheese creamer milk]
*creamy 07-48-35 (a.) 1. of the color of cream 2. thick like cream [canary chromatic citron color consistency cream rich ecru eggshell emulsion albescent amount aureate auric mellow milky yellow] "creamy translucent pebbles"
*crease 09-69-24 (n.) 1. an angular or rounded shape made by folding 2. a slight depression in the smoothness of a surface (v.) 1. make wrinkles or creases into a smooth surface 2. make wrinkled or creased 3. scrape gently 4. become wrinkled or crumpled or creased [character cockle creese crinkle crinkly crisp crush cut rake ridge ripple ruck ruffle rumple rut ease enchase enfold engrave angle score scratch scrunch sculpture seam shape show skin suit surface]
*credence 13-55-11 (n.) 1. the mental attitude that something is believable and should be accepted as true 2. a kind of sideboard or buffet [certain certainty christianity church claim complex confidence container counter cred credulity reception room degree dependence dine disposition drawer] "he gave credence to the gossip"
*credible 06-52-59 (a.) 1. a common but incorrect usage where 'credulous' would be appropriate 2. capable of being believed 3. appearing to merit belief or acceptance [capable conceive conclusive confidence convince rational realistic reasonable recognition reliable easy edible effective evidence expect dependable determinative disposed distinction imagine incorrect inspire believe beyond legitimate likely little logical /bid bide/] "completely credible testimony"
*credulity 19-58-3 (n.) 1. tendency to believe readily [cred ready reliable imprudent innocence tendency trait trusting /lude/]
*credulous 19-65-3 (a.) 1. disposed to believe on little evidence 2. showing a lack of judgment or experience [capable childlike confide confiding convince crazy cred ready reliant rely easy evidence experience depend disposed dizzy dumb unaffected unbelieving uncritical unquestion unsophisticated unsuspected unwary lack little loony show silly simplicity sophisticated stupid /lude/] "the gimmick would convince none but the most credulous"
*creed 12-59-13 (n.) 1. the body of teachings of a religious group that are generally accepted by that group 2. any system of principles or beliefs [catholic century church connection cooperation course credo real reed reformation religious roman ecumenism enunciate eucharist expanded declaration denomination different doctrine document dogma /deer/]
*crevasse 21-73-2 (n.) 1. a deep fissure [check cleft crack cut rent rift rupture excavation valley void abyss arroyo ass seam slot split /ave aver save saver/]
*crevice 17-47-5 (n.) 1. a long narrow depression in a surface 2. a long narrow opening [chap check chink cleft concavity crack cranny crater crust cut rent respect rift rock rupture earth empty excavation valley vent vice void volcano imprint incision]
*criterion 05-56-73 (n.) 1. the ideal in terms of which something can be judged 2. a basis for comparison; a reference point against which other things can be evaluated [calculate canon check code college community comparison condition control country crit receive reference region regulation representative rule ideal imaginary indicator instance table total touchstone trial try epitome essay evaluate exchange experiment ordered orient original norm norma /noir/]
*critique 09-37-26 (n.) 1. an essay or article that gives a critical evaluation (as of a book or play) 2. a serious examination and judgment of something (v.) 1. appraise critically [careful censure colleague comment copy creative crit criticism rave recent referee remark report review roast iteration quality editorial elaborate enthusiastic essay evaluation examination extravagant]

*crockery 17-81-5 (n.) 1. tableware (eating and serving dishes) collectively [cement china collective container cook crock crocker cup refractory rockery open earthenware egg eggcup enamelware]
*crucible 12-73-13 (n.) 1. a vessel made of material that does not melt easily; used for high temperature chemical reactions [cauldron chemical churn circumstance collect container criterion cross reaction receptacle retort beaker beater blender bottom burden lathe liquid easy emulsifier endure engine essay]
*crusade 07-49-35 (n.) 1. any of the more or less continuous military expeditions in the 11-13th centuries when Christian powers of Europe tried to recapture the Holy Land from the Muslims 2. a series of actions advancing a principle or tending toward a particular end (v.) 1. exert oneself continuously, vigorously, or obtrusively to gain an end or engage in a crusade for a certain cause or person; be an advocate for 2. go on a crusade; fight a holy war [campaign candidate cause commitment crus struggle activity advertise drive effort electioneer expedition]
*crush 04-51-132 (n.) 1. leather that has had its grain pattern accentuated 2. the act of crushing 3. a dense crowd of people 4. temporary love of an adolescent (v.) 1. break into small pieces 2. come out better in a competition, race, or conflict 3. to compress with violence, out of natural shape or condition 4. come down on or keep down by unjust use of one's authority 5. make ineffective 6. become injured, broken, or distorted by pressure 7. humiliate or depress completely 8. crush or bruise [case chagrin charge chasten cheat chouse circumvent clincher clobber conquer crestfallen crinkly cross crowd crunch crus race regretful relish repress repressed roller rout ruin rumple undone unnerve uphill upset scoop settler shaft shake silence sour squash steamroller stopper strained strenuous subdue subjugate suppress surpass hangdog heavy hefty host humble humiliate]
*crustacean 19-49-3 (n.) 1. any mainly aquatic arthropod usually having a segmented body and chitinous exoskeleton [class claw cover crayfish crust shellfish shrimp animal antenna appendage aquatic arthropod enclose /cat/]
*cryptic 13-47-11 (a.) 1. of an obscure nature 2. having a secret or hidden meaning 3. having a puzzling terseness [cabalistic camouflage carson circle classified close clue code coloring conceal concise confined crossword crypt rache recondite restricted riddle past perplex policy possible potential prolix protective puzzling technique tenebrous terse totally incapable incomprehensible indirect inexplicable inner inscrutable insurance] "the new insurance policy is written without cryptic or mysterious terms"
*crystallize 17-01-5 (v.) 1. make free from confusion or ambiguity; make clear 2. assume crystalline form; become crystallized 3. cause to form crystals or assume crystalline form 4. cause to take on a definite and clear shape [cake calcify callous candy clarify coated come comprehensible concrete confusion cook crusty crystal reinforce remark resolve science set shape shed solidify sort steel straighten strengthen sugar thicken toughen try ambiguity assume light lithify idea illuminate impregnate incrust indurate interaction effloresce elucidate energy /zilla/] "He tried to crystallize his thoughts"
*cudgel 21-60-2 (n.) 1. a club that is used as a weapon (v.) 1. strike with a cudgel [club clue cud cut deal drub give lace large lash /leg/]
*culinary 08-41-30 (a.) 1. of or relating to or used in cooking [cooking cuisine nary art /rani/]
*cull 08-64-27 (n.) 1. the person or thing rejected or set aside as inferior in quality (v.) 1. remove something that has been rejected 2. look for and gather [case castoff cognitive collect crop cul cut unwanted last look lop] "cull the sick members of the herd"
*culpable 11-71-16 (a.) 1. deserving blame or censure as being wrong or evil or injurious [censure chargeable complicity criminal criminality unholy liable peccant punishment able amiss behavior blame burden evil]
*culprit 08-58-27 (n.) 1. someone who perpetrates wrongdoing [charge civil connection criminal cul law lawbreaker perpetrate problem prove responsible transgresse trial]
*culvert 23-28-1 (n.) 1. a transverse and totally enclosed drain under a road or railway [cable canal carry channel conduit cover underground liquid vert embankment enclose race railway road runnel tailrace totally transverse tunnel]
*cumbersome 11-41-15 (a.) 1. difficult to handle or use especially because of size or weight 2. not elegant or graceful in expression [careless carry clothe clumsy complicate contrary cumber ungainly unmanageable unwieldy machinery maladroit manage blundering bulky bungling burdensome elegant elephantine encumber expression repeat rumor shape size sloppy stiff style superincumbent oafish onerous oppressive] "a cumbersome piece of machinery"
*cumulative 08-31-27 (a.) 1. increasing by successive addition [claim collective commit consecutive create criminal cum magnify material measure multiply large law less absolute accumulate add additive advance aggregate amass arrear telling total impose include increase interest irresistible valid value variable effective entitle error eventual evidentiary exchange /alum vita vital/] "the benefits are cumulative"
*curable 21-42-2 (a.) 1. being such that curing or healing is possible [capable condition correct cure recoverable remedy repair resilient restore able additive agent ameliorate amend /bar/] "curable diseases"
*curator 05-29-72 (n.) 1. the custodian of a collection (as a museum or library) [catalog chamberlain charge choose collection controller cur custodian ranger

receiver accountant administrative animal attendant attorney treasurer trustee organize overseer /rota/]
*curio 18-59-4 (n.) 1. erhaps worthy of collecting [cast cent collection consider cur unusual rap rarity resistance rush improbable interest item oddity oddment outstand]
*curmudgeon 16-60-6 (n.) 1. a crusty irascible cantankerous old person full of stubborn ideas [cantankerous citizen consider crusty cur disagreeable golden elderly old oldster]
*curriculum 06-46-55 (n.) 1. a course of academic studies [course crash cul undertake university rapid read receive research institution intense lead lecture literacy major message minor]
*cursive 23-22-1 (a.) 1. having successive letter joined together (n.) 1. rapid handwriting in which letters are set down in full and cursively connected within words without lifting the writing implement from the paper [calligraphy century chirography clearly connected copperplate cur curve uncial rapid round run screenplay script scriptural set shorthand slant smooth speak style successive implement inscribe italicize various effortless engrave engross] "cursive script"
*cursory 14-57-9 (a.) 1. hasty and without attention to detail; not thorough [careless casual consideration courtesy cursor uncritical unwilling urgent random rapid regardless reveal rough short slight small structural superficial oblivious offhand oppose] "a casual (or cursory) inspection failed to reveal the house's structural flaws"
*curt 11-31-16 (a.) 1. marked by rude or peremptory shortness 2. brief and to the point; effectively cut short [cavalier concise contract courtesy crisp crusty cultivate cur cut unceremonious understand reply reserved response retort roughness rude taciturnity terse tight transient]
*curtail 07-36-43 (v.) 1. place restrictions on 2. terminate or abbreviate before its intended or proper end or its full extent [check circumscribe confine consume control country crop curb curt cut unable ration reap reduce rein relieve remove restriction retrench tap telescope terminate trim truncate abate abbreviate abridgment abstract arrest attrition immobilize impair inhibit inhibition injunction intend leach length lesser limit lower] "curtail drinking in school"
*curtsy 21-62-2 (n.) 1. bending at the knees; a gesture of respect made by women (v.) 1. a gesture of respectful greeting, for women 2. make a curtsy; usually done only by girls and women; as a sign of respect [curt uncover upper recognize respectful reverence royalty salute scrape shake shame sign situation stage stoop submission]
*cygnet 23-78-1 (n.) 1. a young swan [calf chick colt cub young gosling neck nestle net eaglet]
*cynical 05-64-62 (a.) 1. believing the worst of human nature and motives; having a sneering disbelief in e.g. selflessness of others [carping caustic contemptuous critical cynic nagging nature negative niggling nihilism ironic antisocial]
*cynicism 08-57-27 (n.) 1. a cynical feeling of distrust [caustic contempt cynic negativism nihilism innuendo invective irony sarcasm scorn skepticism suspicion misanthropy]

D

*dabble 11-62-15 (v.) 1. dip a foot or hand briefly into a liquid 2. play in or as if in water, as of small children 3. work with in a non-serious manner [dally dampen dash daub dilettante dip douse duck dunce dunk abb abecedarian amateur amuse around astronomy bedew besprinkle bill bottom brief busy liquid local loiter lowbrow engage experiment /bad/] "She dabbles in astronomy"
*dainty 14-57-9 (a.) 1. of delicate composition and artistry 2. affectedly dainty or refined 3. excessively fastidious and easily disgusted 4. especially pleasing to the taste (n.) 1. something considered choice to eat [dai deft delicious delightful dessert detail diminutive dinner discrimination disgust dish doe drink acute affected agreeable airy alimentation ambrosia aromatic artistry ascent asepsis attention immaculate immortal indecisive injury insignificant irresolute neat nectar nice nicety nim nourishment nutritious tasty teacup tender thin tidbit tidy tiny tissue titbit toilet touch treat tweer yummy] "a dainty teacup"

*dally 18-68-4 (v.) 1. behave carelessly or indifferently 2. talk or behave amorously, without serious intentions 3. waste time 4. consider not very seriously [dabble dawdle deal delay drag abide affection ally amorous await lag last lazy leave lightly linger loiter look lounging young /lad/]
*daring 06-56-57 (a.) 1. disposed to venture or take risks 2. radically new or original (n.) 1. the trait of being willing to undertake things that involve risk or danger 2. a challenge to do something dangerous or foolhardy [dangerous daredevilry dashing dauntless defiance defy disregard dodgy doughty drama dress adventurous assault attempt audacious audacity avantgarde radical rash reckless refuse require resolute ring risky intrepid investor involve nest never gallant game glitter great]
*darwinism 18-66-4 (n.) 1. a theory of organic evolution claiming that new species arise and are perpetuated by natural selection [darwin arise natural scientific selection species modern mutation]
*daunt 06-60-57 (v.) 1. cause to lose courage [dash deter discourage dishearten dismay disquiet dissuade divide dog admonish affright afraid alarm anxious aunt awe unman unnerve upset task terrorize threat threaten thwart timid timorous]
*dauntless 21-56-2 (a.) 1. invulnerable to fear or intimidation [daring daunt determined discourage admiration audacious unable unaccustomed undaunted unflinching unlikely lionhearted explorer spunky stalwart stouthearted]
*dearth 11-55-15 (n.) 1. a severe shortage (especially a shortage of food) 2. an insufficient quantity or number [default defect deficiency drought dryness earth exiguous absent acute amount arid rare rarity]
*debacle 08-64-31 (n.) 1. a sudden and violent collapse 2. flooding caused by a tumultuous breakup of ice in a river during the spring or summer 3. a sound defeat [defeat deluge disaster down drop drub dry end beat body bouleversement breakup acle alluvion calamity catastrophe cave chaotic collapse crash lambaste land lather licking /abed bed/]
*debase 15-61-7 (v.) 1. corrupt morally or by intemperance or sensuality 2. corrupt, debase, or make impure by adding a foreign or inferior substance; often by replacing valuable ingredients with inferior ones 3. lower in value by increasing the base-metal content; of metals [damage defile degrade degree demean demoralize deprave depressed deteriorate dilute diminish dirty disgrace dishonor divert dollar element embezzle enfeeble execrable extraneous base beggarly belittle besmirch bump bust abandon abject abuse accuse adulterate alloy alter amount astray atrocious school sensualize shabby shame short sink slight small soil stretch substance sully /abed bed/]
*debatable 12-70-13 (a.) 1. open to doubt or debate 2. open to argument or debate 3. capable of being disproved [deniable dispute doubtful dubious extremely actually argument arouse table liable /abed bata bed tab/]
*debauchery 18-72-4 (n.) 1. a wild gathering involving excessive drinking and promiscuity [debauch decadence dissolute drink drunken excessive bacchanalia behavior unrestrained carouse rakish revelry riot /abed bed/]
*debonair 18-52-4 (a.) 1. having a sophisticated charm 2. having a cheerful, lively, and self-confident air [dapper dash dashing ease elegant behavior bona breezy brisk buoyant obliging optimist nonchalant affable airy insouciance refined resilient /bed/] "a debonair gentleman"
*debut 02-68-287 (n.) 1. the act of beginning something new (v.) 1. appear for the first time in public 2. present for the first time to the public 3. make one's debut [early embark engage entertainment entry environment exhibition ballet begin benefit bill bring but unveiling tryout /bed tub tube/] "The and debuts a new song or two each month"
*decadence 13-63-10 (n.) 1. the state of being degenerate in mental or moral qualities [debauchery decline degeneration degradation depravity dissolution downcast drop dying ebb effete excess cadence civilization comedown condition corrupt abandon abject /ace dace/]
*decamp 14-80-9 (v.) 1. leave a camp 2. run away; usually includes taking something or somebody along 3. leave suddenly (very informal usage) [dawn debt depart desert elude escape exit camp abrupt abscond absquatulate avoid pack pay persuade place powder /ace mac mace/] "The hikers decamped before dawn"
*decapitate 13-70-11 (v.) 1. cut the head of [death decimate defenestrate demolish die electrocute execute capita capitate crucify cut amputate intentional truncate /ace pace tip/]
*decay 06-51-44 (n.) 1. the organic phenomenon of rotting 2. a gradual decrease; as of stored charge or current 3. the process of gradually becoming inferior 4. an inferior state resulting from the process of decaying 5. the spontaneous disintegration of a radioactive substance along with the emission of ionizing radiation (v.) 1. fall into decay or ruin 2. lose a stored charge, magnetic flux, or current; as of particles in nuclear fission 3. undergo decay or decomposition [deca decline decrease degeneration deteriorate disrepair dwindle ebb erode erosion collapse consume corrosion corruption ablation apart atomize atrophy /ace/] "The unoccupied house started to decay"
*deceit 12-64-12 (n.) 1. the quality of being fraudulent 2. the act of deceiving 3. a misleading falsehood [dec deliberate delusion design device dishonesty dissimulate dodge dressing duplicity elaborate entertain evasion exaggerate expedient card cheat chicanery clever communicate conceal conspiracy coup illusory impersonate imposture indirection influence insidious

intention intrigue issn tactic trap treachery trick true /tie/]
*deceitful 18-62-4 (a.) 1. intended to deceive 2. marked by deliberate deceptiveness especially by pretending one set of feelings and acting under the influence of another [deceit deep defraud deliberate designing devious diplomatic dishonorable disposed duplicity escape cheat clever cunning cute ice indirect infernal influence ingenious intentional inventive israel tactical tax testimony thin tongue traitor treacherous tricky twofaced faithless fallacious feline fraudulent furtive underhanded untrustworthy untruthful little lying /tie/] "deceitful advertising"
*deceive 08-62-33 (v.) 1. cause someone to believe an untruth 2. be false to; be dishonest with [deceptive defile defraud delude despoil devious dishonest dodge double dubious dupe elaborate elude enemy engage entrap evade evildoer exaggerate cheat chisel circumvent con conceal conjure convict convince cover cozen criminal crook cross cuckold illiterate illusion illusory impersonate insincere insurance intention inveigle victimize villain violate /vie/] "The insurance company deceived me when they told me they were covering my house"
*decency 09-59-22 (n.) 1. the quality of being polite and respectable 2. the quality of conforming to standards of propriety and morality [dec decorum desirable dignity elegance erect etiquette character civility clean common conform convention correct courtesy nice nobility normative]
*decent 03-77-177 (a.) 1. according with custom or propriety 2. socially or conventionally correct; refined or virtuous 3. enough to meet a purpose 4. (informal) decently clothed 5. conforming to conventions of sexual behavior 6. observing conventional sexual mores in speech or behavior or dress (ad.) 1. in the right manner [decorous delicate demure desirable dignity dress due elegant element enough ethical expression carry cent circle civil civilize clad clean clothe colloquialism comely common communicate conduct conform correct courteous naked neckline never nice noble normative taste thoughtful timely traditional] "from a decent family"
*deciduous 18-65-4 (a.) 1. (of plants and shrubs) shedding foliage at the end of the growing season 2. (of teeth, antlers, etc.) being shed at the end of a period of growth [deci describe development downward drop dying early easy ephemeral evanescent evergreen caducous changeable collapse compose corruptible impetuous impulsive insubstantial interval unstable organism sag scale season set shed shrub sink stage /dice oud/] "deciduous teeth"
*decimal 19-56-3 (a.) 1. numbered or proceeding by tens; based on ten 2. divided by tens or hundreds (n.) 1. a proper fraction whose denominator is a power of 10 2. a number in the decimal system [decasyllabic deci denary denominator derive differential digit digital divided even exponential express cardinal coinage concept count impossible indefinitely infinite integral measurement algorithm aliquot logarithmic /mice/] "the decimal system"
*decimate 13-46-11 (v.) 1. kill one in every ten of, as of mutineers in Roman armies 2. kill in large numbers [damage death deci demolish destroy devastate die dissolve down effective eliminate engorge entire eradicate exterminate extinguish carry condemn confound consume cut incinerate industry inflict intentional massacre much mutinous almost animal annihilate army ten /mice/]
*decipher 11-53-16 (v.) 1. convert code into ordinary language 2. read with difficulty [decode demonstrate determinable difficulty divine doable enlighten establish exemplify explicable expound cipher clarify code convert crack illustrate impossible interpret paraphrase piece plumb popularize print puzzle hieroglyph read readable resolve rewrite riddle /pice/] "Can you decipher this letter?"
*decisive 04-61-102 (a.) 1. unmistakable 2. determining or having the power to determine an outcome 3. forming or having the nature of a turning point or crisis 4. characterized by decision and firmness [death debate deci decided definitive determine document doubt earnest entire evidence explicit express extreme campaign certain certainty character clearly commit conclusive confidence controversy convince crisis critical crucial immediate important impose indefinite inevitable influential irresolute serious set settle show significant strong sure valid victory vital vote /sice/] "cast the decisive vote"
*declamation 21-48-2 (n.) 1. vehement oratory 2. recitation of a speech from memory with studied gestures and intonation as an exercise in elocution or rhetoric [dramatic elocution emotion exercise express clam long loud address art audience matter memory theatrical tirade intonation opera oratory narrative]
*declamatory 21-56-2 (a.) 1. ostentatiously lofty in style [dramatic effect elevated elocution eloquent concern content convoluted labyrinthine lofty loud lurid affected amatory arresting aureate magniloquent meaningful meretricious talk tall theatrical tortuous tumid turgid oratorical orotund ostentatious ostentatiousl overwrought rhetorical /rota/]
*declarative 23-25-1 (a.) 1. relating to the use of or having the nature of a declaration 2. (grammar) relating to the mood of verbs that is used simple declarative statements (n.) 1. a mood (grammatically unmarked) that represents the act or state as an objective fact [decided declaratory emphatic enunciate express clara conceive linguistic absolute assert assertive represent indicative inflection interrogatory /vita/]
*decode 13-52-10 (v.) 1. convert code into ordinary language [decipher decrypt demonstration

determination difficulty direct discover disentangle divine edit electronic elucidate encrypt end exemplify explain channel cipher clarify code convert crack cracking cryptic cypher ordinary outcome /doc/]
*decorate 04-48-109 (v.) 1. make more attractive by adding ornament, colour, etc. 2. be beautiful to look at 3. award a mark of honor, as a medal, to 4. provide with decoration [dandify deck decor elaborate embellish embroider encrust engild enhance enrich equip caparison cite coat colored complicate ornament ornate overload refurbish renovate restore add adorn appoint array tag titivate trim /taro/]
*decorous 16-52-6 (a.) 1. characterized by propriety and dignity and good taste in manners and conduct 2. according with custom or propriety [decent decor demure dignity done dress due earnest elegant expect extreme comely conduct conform constant conventional correct custom customary orthodox receive recognize respectable restrained right understated unsmiling urbane sedate seemly serious set solemn staid stiff suitable] "the tete-a-tete was decorous in the extreme"
*decorum 14-54-9 (n.) 1. propriety in manners and conduct [decency decor delicacy demure dignity element etiquette character civility compatible conduct correct custom occasion orderly respectable restraint right urbanity usage manner modesty mores]
*decoy 14-38-8 (n.) 1. a beguiler who leads someone into danger (usually as part of a plot) 2. something used to lure victims into danger (v.) 1. lure or entrap with or as if with a decoy [danger deathtrap deceive deception deco delude device distracter divert driven dummy easy enclose entangle enthusiastic entice entrap establishment exaggerate cajole capture carry catch charm cheat coax confederate coy customer]
*decree 07-42-42 (n.) 1. a legally binding command or decision entered on the court record (as if issued by a court or judge) (v.) 1. issue or demand by decree 2. decide with authority [dec decision demand desire diktat edict enactment enjoin establish charge commission condemn reach report require rescript rule]
*decrepit 14-50-9 (a.) 1. worn and broken down by hard use 2. lacking physical strength or vitality [damage debile dec decay deteriorate dilapidate disable down effect elderly enervate enfeeble childlike condition creaky crumble ragged ramshackle rickety robust rundown rusty physical poor impaired incapacitate infirm injure tacky tape tired totter /tip/]
*decry 12-47-13 (v.) 1. express strong disapproval of [denounce deprecate diminish disapproval disgrace disparage down education excoriate express censure complain condemn criticize cry racism rail reprobate run rundown]
*dedication 07-58-43 (n.) 1. complete and wholehearted fidelity 2. the act of binding yourself (intellectually or emotionally) to a course of action 3. a message that makes a pledge 4. a ceremony in which something (as a building) is dedicated to some goal or purpose 5. a short message (as in a book or musical work or on a photograph) dedicating it to someone or something [decisive determined duty earnest enshrine ethics index intent introduction canonize cation ceremony charge constant abandon address allegiance ardor assignment tail text true obligation occasion ordination ought /acid cide/]
*deduce 14-68-8 (v.) 1. conclude by reasoning; in logic 2. reason by deduction; establish by deduction [decide deem derive determine draw dream duce educe establish evidence evoke experience extract extrapolate understand unused capable collect come comprehend conclusion consider construe credit]
*deface 16-46-6 (v.) 1. mar or spoil the appearance of 2. deface a building facade, for example [damage deflower destroy disfigure distort facade face flaw appearance check cheek crack craze cut /cafe/] "scars defaced her cheeks"
*defamation 12-37-12 (n.) 1. a malicious attack 2. an abusive attack on a person's character or good name [damage denigrate depreciation disparage false abusive argument aspersion assassination attack malicious tort traduce insult intend obloquy offense]

*defame 10-40-19 (v.) 1. charge falsely or with malicious intent; attack the good name and reputation of someone [damage denigrate deprecate depreciation derisory derogatory destroy disapprove discredit disparage disparaging drag false fame abusive accuse argument article asperse assassinate attack attaint malign minimize misbehavior misrepresent muckrake mud mudslinging] "The journalists have defamed me!"
*default 06-44-54 (n.) 1. loss due to not showing up 2. an option that is selected automatically unless an alternative is specified 3. act of failing to meet a financial obligation 4. loss resulting from failure of a debt to be paid (v.) 1. fail to pay up [debt decline decrease departure device discharge drop due escape evasion failure fault file financial flee absence absent alternative ante appearance arrears automatic avoidance undone unless user lack law leave loose loss] "he lost the game by default"
*defendant 04-28-125 (n.) 1. a person or institution against whom an action is brought in a court of law; the person being sued or accused [defend diehard disputant dissident naysayer negativism accessory accuse answer authority]
*defensible 18-39-4 (a.) 1. capable of being defended [def defend deserve due equitable excuse exempt explain fit forgive secure sound square strong immune impregnable inoffensive invulnerable balance legal legitimate level]
*defensive 03-41-167 (a.) 1. attempting to justify or defend in speech or writing 2. intended or appropriate for defending against or deterring aggression or attack 3.

serving as or appropriate for defending or protecting (n.) 1. an attitude of defense; especially in the phrase"on the defensive" [def defend deflect design deter dike disposition distrustful excusatory expect express favor flood fortify foster safeguard score screening self serve shelter shield speech stance strategy immunize indicate intend value vigilant] "defensive weapons"

*defer 06-38-54 (v.) 1. submit or yield to another's wish or opinion 2. hold back to a later time [deal def delay detain exam execution extend fawn force recess reluctant remit require reschedule reserve respite]

*deference 12-45-13 (n.) 1. a courteous expression (by word or deed) of esteem or regard 2. a disposition or tendency to yield to the will of others 3. courteous regard for people's feelings [dean dedication deed defer devotion die disposition duty esteem estimation ethics expression favor fealty first flatter regard respect reverence charge commitment compliancy consideration courtesy] "his deference to her wishes was very flattering"

*deferential 17-48-5 (a.) 1. showing deference [dear deferent disarming duteous dutiful ethical exhibit express fair full regardful respectful reverent tactful thoughtful insinuate admiring affable agreeable attentive /lait/]

*defiance 07-58-37 (n.) 1. a hostile challenge 2. intentionally contemptuous behavior or attitude 3. a defiant act [dare despite disobedience dispute effrontery engage estimate factious fiance fight fractious indomitable influence insolent insubordinate insurgency intentional irrepressible attitude audacity authority negativism noisy non noncooperation call challenge cheeky complaint /naif/]

*defiant 07-61-41 (a.) 1. boldly resisting authority or an opposing force [daring defy deliberate difficult disdain disobedient disposed force fractious incline indomitable insolent insubordinate intractable irrepressible aggressive ant arrogant attitude audacious authority non tend toward tractable /naif/] "brought up to be aggressive and defiant"

*deficiency 06-30-49 (n.) 1. lack of an adequate quantity or number 2. the state of needing something that is absent or unavailable [dearth def default defect deficit demand desert drought eliot erroneous essential exiguity expect failing failure fall famine fault fewness flaw imperfection impoverish inadequate incomplete insight insufficiency interval callow catch clean complete condition crack credit critical nail necessary need neglect normal nutrition]

*deficient 14-45-9 (a.) 1. inadequate in amount or degree 2. falling short of some prescribed norm 3. of a quantity not able to fulfill a need or requirement [damage def defective degree deplete education element embryonic enough erroneous expect extent failing fall faulty flaw follow fulfill fund imperfect inadequate incomplete infant ingredient injure insufficient callow clumsy need non norm tact task trivial] "a deficient education"

*defile 21-49-2 (n.) 1. a narrow pass (especially one between mountains) (v.) 1. place under suspicion or cast doubt upon 2. spot, stain, or pollute 3. make dirty or spotty, as by exposure to air, of metals; also used metaphorically [damage destroy dirty disgrace dishonor doubt draw embezzle empty enough excavation exit exposure fault file fleck force ford formation foul impair imperfect infect injure intersection lane leak location long lower /life/]

*definite 08-56-31 (a.) 1. precise; explicit and clearly defined 2. known for certain [date decisive delimit describe determined develop different direct distinct doubt down drop easy entire establish exact explicit express final finite fixed flat flower form full implication individual inevitable inner narrow necessary noteworthy nothing tenacious total tree turn] "I want a definite answer"

*deflate 10-53-20 (v.) 1. collapse by releasing contained air or gas 2. become deflated or flaccid, as by losing air 3. produce deflation in 4. reduce or cut back the amount or availability of, creating a decline in value or prices 5. release contained air or gas from 6. reduce or lessen the size or importance of [decline decrease deny depress destroy devalue different diminish disappointed dispute dive down drop economy embarrass empty erode expanded explode expose extent fall fatigue fill flaccid flat flatten fold lessen lesser let letdown lose lower abate ablate abridge affect alter amount argument attenuate available theory throttle transform trim turn] "deflate a balloon"

*deflect 06-62-46 (v.) 1. prevent the occurrence of; prevent from happening 2. turn from a straight course , fixed direction, or line of interest 3. turn aside 4. draw someone's attention away from something 5. impede the movement of (an opponent or a ball), as in sports or fights [debar def deter deviate direction disconcert discourage distracted divert draw effect embarrassment estop exclude feel fence fend fight fixed flex flurry forbid force forestall line loop change come competitor confuse contact cool course criticism curve thief turn turnoff twist]

*deforest 17-36-5 (v.) 1. remove the trees from [denude desolate devastate enemy entire forest remove stripe tree] "The landscape was deforested by the enemy attacks"

*deform 16-43-6 (v.) 1. make formless 2. cause to assume a crooked or angular form 3. assume a different shape or form 4. twist and press out of shape 5. become misshapen 6. alter the shape of (something) by stress [damage defective dent depression different disfigure disorder distort distorted diversify dough dwarf earthquake essence extend extract faulty fit flatter flaw flex form formless freakish full obfuscate obscure office original outward overthrow rachitis rebuild reform

revive rickety rococo rod rolling mar misshapen modify monstrous muddle mutilate] "the heat deformed the plastic sculpture"
*deformity 18-54-4 (n.) 1. an affliction in which some part of the body is misshapen or malformed 2. an appearance that has been spoiled or is misshapen [damage deform disease disfigure disorder distress due extend facial fantastic far fault flaw foot form fourth frequently oblique oddity offensive outward repulsive retardation ricket rift rocky main malaise mark mental misshapen mole monstrous mountain ill incapable injury irregularity talipes terrible third toe track tree twist]
*defraud 09-39-22 (v.) 1. deprive of by deceit [deceive delude deprive diddle dishonest dupe embezzle enough euchre extort fleece foil fool fraud fudge return rip rob rook rustle abstract and appropriate]
*defray 18-19-4 (v.) 1. bear the expenses of [discharge exchange expense finance fray fund redeem reimburse acknowledge]
*degenerate 12-55-13 (a.) 1. unrestrained by convention or morality (n.) 1. a person whose behavior deviates from what is acceptable especially in sexual behavior (v.) 1. grow worse [debauched decadent decline degraded desert desire deteriorate deviate devolve dissolute drop ebb effete err generate nefarious rebuild return revive riotous rot abandon alloy alter taint tired trip turn /renege tare/]
*degradation 14-43-9 (n.) 1. changing to a lower state (a less respected state) 2. a low or downcast state [decadency decline demoralize dilapidate disgrace drop dying exclusion exile expatriate gradation gross rank reduction routine ruin abandon abase abject atrocious ignominy incoherent infamy obloquy obnoxious odious opprobrium nefarious /tad/]
*degrade 10-48-18 (v.) 1. reduce the level of land, as by erosion 2. lower the grade of something; reduce its worth 3. reduce in worth, character, etc.; disgrace; dishonour [grade]
*dehydrate 15-65-7 (v.) 1. preserve by removing all water and liquids from 2. remove water from 3. lose water or moisture [deprive describe desert desiccate drain dry egg embalm evaporate exercise experience healthy hydrate hydrogen refrigerate remove rot rub add arid atom thirsty tissue torrefy towel trip /tardy/] "carry dehydrated food on your camping trip"
*deify 21-50-2 (v.) 1. consider as a god or god-like 2. exalt to the position of a God [deference divine duty elevation embodiment emperor escalate esteem exalt exaltation extol idealize idolize immortalize incarnation familiar favor fetishize financial flattery young /fie/] "These young men deify financial success"
*deign 19-65-3 (v.) 1. do something that one considers to be below one's dignity [demean descend dignity down endorse invitation grant great nod]
*deity 13-48-10 (n.) 1. any supernatural being worshipped as controlling some part of the world or some aspect of life or who is the personification of a force [daemon declared deep demigod demigoddess destiny die disharmony divinity dream egyptian enmity idol immortal incorporeal indy inspiration tension terrify teuton treat /tie/]
*dejection 23-61-1 (n.) 1. a state of melancholy depression 2. solid excretory product evacuated from the bowels [dark defecate deject depression despondent detachment dirt disappointment discharge discourage dog doggy drop dung eject euphoria evacuate evacuation excrete catharsis child compulsion crap tarry thick tic trot turd twitch inadequate indifference insensible obscene obsession oppress ordure newborn]
*delectable 14-38-9 (a.) 1. extremely pleasing to the sense of taste 2. capable of arousing desire [dainty darling delightful desire dish electable enjoyable exquisite extremely likable lovely luscious lush capable charming choice tasty toothsome absolutely achieve adorable agreeable ambrosial appetizing arouse attractive /led/] "the delectable Miss Haynes"
*delectation 23-62-1 (n.) 1. a feeling of extreme pleasure or satisfaction 2. act of receiving pleasure from something [define delight desire elect enjoyment entertain experience extreme amuse appreciation obvious /led/]
*delete 09-50-24 (v.) 1. remove or make invisible 2. edit, delete, or revise; of books, etc. 3. wipe out magnetically recorded information [dead decided dele demagnetize depart device disappear disk divide divorce edit efface eliminate end erase excise exclude expel expunge extinct lacking leave lift list terminate transcription /led/] "Please delete my name from your list"
*deleterious 21-41-2 (a.) 1. harmful to living things [damage deadly delete destructive detrimental effect lethal live toxic ruinous injurious ominous unfavorable unprofitable useless /led rete/] "deleterious chemical additives"
*delicacy 09-45-25 (n.) 1. something considered choice to eat 2. the quality of being beautiful and delicate in appearance 3. lightness in movement or manner 4. subtly skillful handling of a situation 5. refined taste; tact 6. smallness of stature 7. lack of physical strength [deli delicate detail difficulty easy exact excellence choice concern culture accuracy adroit airy ascent /led/]
*delineate 14-28-9 (a.) 1. represented accurately or precisely (v.) 1. delineate the form or outline of 2. describe in vivid detail 3. trace the shape of 4. determine the essential quality of 5. make a mark or lines on a surface [definition deli demarcate depict describe description design detail determine diagrammatica different down draw elevation engage essential etch evocation evoke exemplify explain explanation express leave letter life light limn line lipstick long illustration image impression indicate instrument intersect narrative notation noticeable account accurate allocate allocation

alphabet appearance art author table tint touch trace tree /led/]
*delirious 13-57-10 (a.) 1. experiencing delirium 2. marked by uncontrolled excitement or emotion [deli delighted disturbed drunk ecstatic elated emotional enthusiastic excited experience extremely exuberant lack lightheaded lively lunatic ill injury insane intense irrational rage rambling rant restraint roaring off orgasm orgiastic uncontrollable uncontrolled unhinge unrestrained unsettled sick steamy storm /led rile/] "a crowd of delirious baseball fans"
*delude 11-71-14 (v.) 1. be false to; be dishonest with [deceive deliver diddle dishonest dodger dupe easy elude enchant enemy engage entrap exploit last lead leg letdown unfaithful unreal unsophisticated untrue /led/]
*deluge 10-54-18 (n.) 1. an overwhelming number or amount 2. a heavy rain 3. the rising of a body of water and its overflowing onto normally dry land (v.) 1. fill quickly beyond capacity; as with a liquid 2. fill or cover completely, usually with water 3. charge someone with too many tasks [deal dip downpour drop drown dry duck duration earth engulf enough extent extravagance land landslide lavish legion liquid little local lot luge galaxy great /led/]
*delusion 09-62-26 (n.) 1. (psychology) an erroneous belief that is held in the face of evidence to the contrary 2. a mistaken or unfounded opinion or idea 3. the act of deluding; deception by creating illusory ideas [deception defective disguise disorder dissemble distortion dream drug dynamic elusion embarrass entangle entrap erroneous error evidence exist life look unfounded unorthodox unreal science seeming self severe show sin state strong suffering symptom idea illusion illusory imagine imposture include incorrect induce influential opinion ostentation outwit overreach nihilism notion /led/] "he has delusions of competence"
*demagogue 17-28-5 (n.) 1. an orator who appeals to the passions and prejudices of his audience [dangerous debate declamation deliver dictator elicit elocution eloquence emotive engage exciter manipulate mouth agitator agitprop agog ancient appeal audience gain orator oratory ordinary urge /game/]
*demeanor 08-54-27 (n.) 1. (behavioral attributes) the way a person behaves toward other people [demean deportment distinguishing doing expression manner method mien move act address air appearance appropriate attitude attribute outward reckless reflect]

*demented 13-69-10 (a.) 1. affected with madness or insanity [daft dement derange disoriented disturbed entirely mad madness manic maze mental tetched touched]
*demerit 21-75-2 (n.) 1. a mark against a person for misconduct or failure; usually given in school or armed forces 2. the quality of being inadequate or falling short of perfection [deficiency desirable disadvantage discuss disgrace drawback mark merit misconduct much render imperfection inadequate infamy /tire/] "ten demerits and he loses his privileges"
*demise 06-56-46 (n.) 1. the time when something ends [death decease defunct demi departure descent die downfall drop end exchange exist expiry martyr inanimate sainted sale settle sleeping slow stillborn]
*demobilize 21-01-2 (v.) 1. release from military service or remove from the active list of military service 2. retire from military service [disarmament disband discharge dismiss dismissal dissolve duty military mobilize muster breakup list]
*demolish 06-53-50 (v.) 1. destroy completely 2. humiliate or depress completely 3. defeat soundly [damage debate defeat demo deny depress destroy destruction devour dismantle disprove eat end enemy engulf evil mince mortify opponent overthrow overwhelm level invitation irreparable scoff settle severe shame silence smash sound split sport structure hand harmful home humble humiliate hurt /silo/] "the wrecking ball demolished the building"
*demonstrable 14-59-8 (a.) 1. necessarily or demonstrably true 2. capable of being demonstrated or proved [definite demon demonstrate discernible dispute easy evident evince exhibit exist man manifest obvious necessarily noticeable service show supportable sure sustainable test true rail ready real recognize absolute actual apparent bag lack lying /bar nome/] "demonstrable truths"
*demonstrate 02-49-299 (v.) 1. march in protest; take part in a demonstration 2. provide evidence for; stand as proof of; show by one's behavior, attitude, or external attributes 3. establish the validity of something, as by an example, explanation or experiment 4. show or demonstrate something to an interested audience [demon describe determine direct display dispute establish evidence example exhibit expound express march mark mean object operate overhaul name school set show solve substantiate support testify rally reflect represent reveal air approve argue attitude /nome tart/]
*demonstrative 19-54-3 (a.) 1. given to or marked by the open expression of emotion 2. serving to demonstrate (n.) 1. a pronoun that points out an intended referent [demon describe designate devoted display editorial effusive emotional enlighten evidence expansive expressive mark meaningful melt metaphor obvious open outgoing outspoken name newsy sentimental serve show showing soft specify toward referent representative reticent revelation romantic adore affectionate annotate appear identify idiosyncrasy individual informative instructive intend /nome tart vita/] "an affectionate and demonstrative family"
*demonstrator 07-35-38 (n.) 1. a teacher or teacher's assistant who demonstrates the principles that are being taught 2. someone who participates in a public display of group feeling 3. someone who demonstrates an article

to a prospective buyer [decoder define demon device disputant dragoman editor employ explain explicate expound march mel member merchandise metaphrast occupation opposition organization outside sale scholiast sell show store supporter teach trainer translator tutor reformist activist advocate annotate article assistant /nome rota tart/]
*demote 12-45-13 (v.) 1. assign to a lower position; reduce in rank [delegate depute designate devalue discharge dismiss down downgrade elevate emote expel mote move task turnout /tom tome/] "She was demoted because she always speaks up"
*demur 15-43-7 (n.) 1. (law) a formal objection to an opponent's pleadings (v.) 1. take exception to 2. enter a demurrer [debate delay deliberate deny dispute dissent doubt emu enter exception expostulate express march mild modesty unwilling rage raise rally reaction refuse reluctance reservation retreat rule /rum/]
*demure 14-54-9 (a.) 1. affectedly modest or shy especially in a playful or provocative way [decent decorous demur earnest elegant manner modest more mure unsmiling reserved /rum/]
*denigrate 13-47-10 (v.) 1. belittle 2. charge falsely or with malicious intent; attack the good name and reputation of someone [damage darken defame degrade depreciate derogate despise destroy disdain disparage down drag ebonize express negative influence ink insult intent good grate reputation revile ridicule abuse accuse article asperse assassinate attack talk tarnish teardown traduce /gin/]
*denizen 14-40-8 (n.) 1. a person who inhabits a particular place 2. a plant or animal naturalized in a region [deep den develop district dwell earth eastern england epithet europe native naturalize nazareth north incumbent independent inhabit inmate island zealand /zine/] "denizens of field and forest"
*denominate 14-35-9 (v.) 1. assign a name or title to [define description designation express nominate indication assign title /one/]
*denomination 12-32-13 (n.) 1. a group of religious congregations having its own organization and a distinctive faith 2. identifying word or words by which someone or something is called and classified or distinguished from others 3. a class of one kind of unit in a system of numbers or measures or weights or money [definition description designation distinguished division epithet eponym expression name nature neighborhood nickname nobility nomination non number offshoot order organization make mark meaning measure money moniker identify ilk inner ism adhere affiliate allocation alternative appellative assignment attend attribute term title type /one/] "he flashed a fistful of bills of large denominations"
*denominator 15-44-7 (n.) 1. the divisor of a fraction [degree divisor mina multiple indicate integer average taste /one rota/]
*denote 10-50-19 (v.) 1. make known; make an announcement 2. have as a meaning 3. be a sign or indication of [deceive define demonstrate designate diagnostic disclose disparaging display early emblematic euphemize evidence exhibit express expressive extension name note number tell termination testify title transfer treaty trump twist typify /one ton tone/] "Her smile denoted that she agreed"
*denouement 13-67-10 (n.) 1. the outcome of a complex sequence of events 2. the final resolution of the main complication of a literary or dramatic work [death den design development dramatic effect end explain omega outcome unscramble untangle upshot main mood motif movement termination theme tone twist /one/]
*denounce 05-34-88 (v.) 1. announce the termination of, as of treaties 2. to accuse or condemn or openly or formally or brand as disgraceful 3. speak out against 4. give away information about somebody [damn decry deplore deprecate describe designate disapproval disgraceful disloyalty doom enounce exam excoriate express objurgate openly censure charge cheat cite classmate compromise condemn criticize /one/] "He denounced the Nazis"
*denude 19-61-3 (v.) 1. lay bare [defoliate deprive destroy discard divest drain dry erosion exhaust expose naked nude uncover uncovered undress unveil /dun dune/] "denude a forest"
*denunciation 13-33-11 (n.) 1. a public act of denouncing [damning decry den denounce doom enunciate evil excoriate execration censure charge complaint condemn count criticism imminent indictment inflict information accuse act admonition anathematize appeal arraign attack taxing thunderous tirade]
*deplete 08-46-33 (v.) 1. use up, as of resources or materials [decrease depreciation diarrhea digest diminish dip down drain drop eat eliminate empty energy enjoy entirely excess exhaust expend expenditure pay perspiration profuse purge leakage lessen let limited loss lot luxuriate temporary thus tire truncate]
*deplorable 15-48-7 (a.) 1. bad; unfortunate 2. bringing or deserving severe rebuke or censure 3. of very poor quality or condition [decision deserve difficult disastrous disgraceful distress disturb dreadful egregious enormous error execrable extremely painful pathetic pitiful poignant poor poverty lamentable law loathsome lousy low offensive outrageous overwhelming rank rebuke regrettable reprehensible right rotten able accuse affair affecting appalling awful bad base blame bring /bar baro/] "my finances were in a deplorable state"
*deplore 09-31-23 (v.) 1. express strong disapproval of 2. regret strongly [declare deprecate dirge disapprove discontent displeasure divine elegize evil execrate express extremely perceive pick plain point political prisoner punishment lament lore real regret repent rue] "We deplore the government's treatment of political

prisoners"
*depopulate 21-59-2 (v.) 1. reduce in population [desolate disease enforce epidemic evacuate physical populate population area /pope/] "The epidemic depopulated the countryside"
*deport 06-50-55 (v.) 1. behave in a certain manner 2. expel from a country 3. hand over to the authorities of another country [deal deliver demean difficult dignity disseminate eliminate exile expel export extradite perform perfuse port pose posture property proscribe purge push opinion ostracize oust outlaw recognize refugee relay relegate remove repatriate right throw toward transport transpose turnover /rope trope/]
*deportment 21-63-2 (n.) 1. (behavioral attributes) the way a person behaves toward other people [demeanor deport distinguishing doing pattern people personal posture practice presence propriety reckless tactics tone toward manner method move /rope trope/]
*deposition 13-14-11 (n.) 1. the natural process of laying down a deposit of something 2. the act of putting something somewhere 3. (law) a pretrial interrogation of a witness; usually done in a lawyer's office 4. the act of deposing someone; removing a powerful person from a position or office [declaration deploy deposit dismissal down eject ember examination excommunicate expulsion pigment place plant position powerful pretrial process profession put oath office oust overthrow sediment silt situation statement station storage stratum substance suspension impeach impose increase installation interrogatory testimony ticket true natural nonsuit note /itis/]
*depositor 14-18-9 (n.) 1. a person who has deposited money in a bank or similar institution [deposit previous saver institution investor return /roti/]
*depository 14-17-8 (n.) 1. a facility where things can be deposited for safekeeping [depositor display document edge embankment entrepot exchequer panel pick pile place pool precious provide public owner safe shelf shore side space sperm stack stockpile store industry installation tank tier till transact treasury rack read reclaim record repertory repository reservoir rick room row /roti/]
*deprave 18-53-4 (v.) 1. corrupt morally or by intemperance or sensuality [damage debauch decadent decline degenerate degrade demoralize destroy different dirty disgusting distress drop dying ebb effete envenom evil execrable passive pervert petty poison pollute poor prejudice profane profligate prostitute ravage rave ravish regression reprobate reptile retrogression rotten ruin abandon abject abuse accuse afflict alter aristocrat astray atrocious value vice vicious vile villainous vitiate vulgarize]
*depravity 18-62-4 (n.) 1. a corrupt or depraved or degenerate act or practice 2. moral perversion; impairment of virtue and moral principles [debauchery decadence decadency degeneration degradation demoralize dissolute duty enormity evil execrable parlor perversion petty poor practice principle profligate rank right rotten abandon abject accord atrocious various vice vile violation virtue immoral impair intellectual transgression turpitude]
*deprecate 11-67-15 (v.) 1. express strong disapproval of; deplore 2. belittle [declare decry deem deflate denigrate deplore despise diminish disapprove disdain disparage effort express pejorative pick puncture putdown reduce reject remark ridicule cate censure comment computer condemn criticize apology teacher tend /ace/] "The teacher should not deprecate his student's efforts"
*depreciate 17-45-5 (v.) 1. belittle 2. lower the value of something 3. lose in value [decline decrease deflate denigrate devalue diminish dis disparaging dive dollar downgrade drain eat effort erode extent extract pare plummet plunge puncture range reduce refund remove run calculation consider consume criticize curtail cut impair income abstract abuse allow apprize takeoff tax teacher treat trim]
*depreciation 10-54-18 (n.) 1. decrease in value of an asset due to obsolescence or use 2. a decrease in price or value over time 3. a communication that belittles somebody or something [decline defame devalue dip disdain downgrade drop ebb effeminate erosion expenditure percentage plunge premium recipient reduction respect concession cut impair impoverish indignity ion abate alleviate allowance traduce nosedive] "depreciation of the dollar against the yen"
*depress 13-43-10 (v.) 1. lower (prices or markets) 2. lower someone's spirits; make downhearted 3. lessen the activity or force of 4. cause to drop or sink 5. press down [dampen decrease deject demoralize devaluate different dig discourage dishearten dismay displace dive down drop dull economy enervate engrave excavate pare pick pit pockmark position press price push rain recess reduce reservoir retrench rise sad setback sink slow space spirit stamp strength] "These news depressed her"
*depression 04-46-111 (n.) 1. sad feelings of gloom and inadequacy 2. a long-term economic state characterized by unemployment and low prices and low levels of trade and investment 3. a sunken or depressed geological formation 4. a mental state characterized by a pessimistic sense of inadequacy and a despondent lack of activity 5. angular distance below the horizon (especially of a celestial object) 6. pushing down 7. a concavity in a surface produced by pressing 8. a time period during the 1930s when there was a worldwide economic depression and mass unemployment 9. a state of depression and anhedonia so severe as to require clinical intervention 10. an air mass of lower pressure; often brings precipitation [decline dig dip disorder disturbance drill euphoria excavation expansion painful peak pocket pression recession recovery reduction

impression incision indifference obsession oppress nick nock notch]
*depth 03-57-147 (n.) 1. (usually plural) the deepest and most remote part 2. degree of psychological or intellectual depth 3. extent downward or backward or inward 4. the intellectual ability to penetrate deeply into ideas 5. (usually plural) a low moral state [dark debase deep degree denote dept despair distance downward draft draught drop epidermis erudition expansion experience extent part penetration perception petty physical pitch place point position possibly power profundity projectile proportion psychological target tedious thin thorough tiny tone top trivial tune height hit hole hollow] "the depth of the water"
*derelict 10-73-19 (a.) 1. deserted or abandoned as by an owner 2. failing in what duty requires (n.) 1. a person unable to support himself 2. a ship abandoned on the high seas [delinquent desert devil dilapidate diligent discard duty employment entirely evict exile expel refuse reject relaxed relict remiss require ruin rundown lack law lax left live long loose inadvertent inattentive irresponsible caitiff careless carry castoff concern condition tramp trash truant] "a derelict ship"
*dereliction 17-66-5 (n.) 1. willful negligence 2. a tendency to be negligent and uncaring [default defect delinquency derelict desertion dilapidate disregard enormity error evil rat reckless recreant relinquish lapse laxness loose impropriety infidelity injustice carelessness conduct tort trespass trip offense outrage oversight negligence nonconformity nonobservance]
*deride 09-54-25 (v.) 1. treat or speak of with contempt [dare diminish disdain disparage rally ride ridicule roast insult /dire/] "He derided his student's attempt to solve the biggest problem in mathematics"
*derision 13-72-11 (n.) 1. contemptuous laughter 2. the act of deriding or treating with contempt [discourtesy disdain disparage disrespect expression raillery rash reckless remark respect ridicule ridiculous imprudent inconsistent ion irrational satire scoff scorn show silly smock sport squelch stultify stupid offensive /sire/]
*derivation 21-41-2 (n.) 1. a line of reasoning that shows how a conclusion follows logically from accepted propositions 2. (historical linguistics) an explanation of the historical origins of a word or phrase 3. the source from which something derives (i.e. comes or issues) 4. inherited properties shared with others of your bloodline 5. (descriptive linguistics) the process whereby new words are formed from existing words or bases by affixation: 'singer' from 'sing'; 'undo' from 'do' 6. drawing of fluid or inflammation away from a diseased part of the body 7. drawing off water from its main channel as for irrigation [deduction derive development effect eponymy extraction race rise rootage imitation infringe ion issue acceptance acquisition ancestry assumption taking taproot theme offspring origin originate outcome] "he prefers shoes of Italian derivation"
*derivative 08-59-29 (a.) 1. resulting from or employing derivation (n.) 1. the result of mathematical differentiation; the instantaneous change of one quantity relative to another; df(x)/dx 2. (linguistics) a word that is derived from another word 3. a financial instrument whose value is based on another security [date depend derive development dewey differentiation document due echoic ensue explicable rate ratio reckoning relationship respect result rule imitative impose impute inflection instrument involve value variable vat acquire agreement alleged amount angle approach asset attribute authority tangent traceable /vita/] "a derivative process"
*derive 05-45-83 (v.) 1. come from; be connected by a relationship of blood, for example 2. obtain 3. develop or evolve, esp. from a latent or potential state 4. come from 5. reason by deduction; establish by deduction [decide deduce deduct descend development differentiation draw earn educe elaborate establish etymology evidence evolve experience extrapolate reach reap reasoning receive relationship rive incomplete induce infer] "derive pleasure from one's garden"
*dermatology 13-51-11 (n.) 1. the branch of medicine dealing with the skin and its diseases [deal derma disease doctor medicine affect technique /lot lota/]
*derogatory 15-52-7 (a.) 1. expressive of low opinion [deprecate detract diminish discreditable disdain disparaging expressive remark ridicule offensive opinion gator abase abusive tend /ago rota tag/] "derogatory comments"
*derrick 10-20-17 (n.) 1. a framework erected over an oil well to allow drill tubes to be raised and lowered 2. a simple crane having lifting tackle slung from a boom [dome drill elevator equipment erect erector raise rick rig rotate cargo column crab crane]
*descendant 07-41-37 (a.) 1. going or coming down (n.) 1. a person considered as descended from some ancestor or race [daughter denote descend descent design downward dynasty early effect seed son sound successor child children clan come concept conclusion confuse consider aftermath animal antecedent ascending treasure tribe]
*descendent 23-60-1 (a.) 1. going or coming down (n.) 1. a person considered as descended from some ancestor or race [descend downward sink sliding clan come consider tribe]
*descent 07-49-43 (n.) 1. the act of changing your location in a downward direction 2. properties attributable to your ancestry 3. a movement downward 4. a downward slope or bend 5. the kinship relation between an individual and the individual's progenitors 6. the descendants of one individual [declivity degeneration depreciation describe deteriorate dive downward drop dying embarrassment exemplify extension scale scent seed sept slope stock career children climb collapse course crash narrate nexus tree

tumble]
*desecrate 14-48-8 (v.) 1. violate the sacred character of a place or language 2. remove the consecration from a person or an object [damage dear debase deconsecrate defile devastate disgrace distort divert embezzle emotional sack sacred sanctity scandal set shame cemetery character church confound consecration contrary convert corrupt crate ravage ravish religious remove render reverse rite abomination abuse adulterate alloy assault atrocity attack taint turn twist] "desecrate a cemetary"
*desert 03-61-171 (a.) 1. located in a dismal or remote area; desolate (n.) 1. an arid region with little or no vegetation (v.) 1. desert (a cause, a country or an army), often in order to join the opposing cause, country, or army 2. leave someone who needs or counts on you; leave in the lurch [defect demand demarcate deposit dereliction des deserve desolate disapproval discipline dismal ditch dominant dry due duty earth eastern egypt empty escapee excellence exhaust sacrilege sahara sandy scourge sea secessionist semiarid separatist shot sinai slight solitary strand stretch rat rate recompense red region reject remote reprisal rescue retired return revenge reward tenant tergiversate territory thirsty traitor treachery /tres/] "a desert island"
*desiccated 19-63-3 (a.) 1. thoroughly dried out 2. lacking vitality or spirit; lifeless 3. preserved by removing natural moisture [decay dehydrate deplete describe desert dry dull egg emotionless energy exercise settle shrink shrivel snobbery sonata spirit split spoil sweat camp cigar coconut creature animation arid technical trip] "old boxes of desiccated Cuban cigars"
*designate 04-28-100 (a.) 1. appointed but not yet installed in office (v.) 1. give an assignment to (a person) to a post, or assign a task to (a person) 2. assign a name or title to 3. decree or designate beforehand 4. design or destine [define delegate demote design determine duty earmark elect elevate entitle set state style identify indicate intend nickname nominate advance aim allot appointed appropriate assign assignment tap term title /tang/]
*desist 17-49-5 (v.) 1. choose to refrain [des discontinue disuse eat end stay stop surrender teetotal terminate]
*despair 05-61-70 (n.) 1. the feeling that everything is wrong and nothing will turn out well 2. a state in which everything seems wrong and will turn out badly (v.) 1. abandon hope; give up hope; lose heart [dejection depression desire desolate discourage dishearten dismay drop emotional exasperate experience extremity sad seem sloth soccer status success surrender pair pessimism profound prostrate abandon acceptance affective anguish apathy infelicity relinquish renounce rescue resignation /apse/] "Don't despair--help is on the way!"
*desperado 21-56-2 (n.) 1. a bold outlaw (especially on the American frontier) [deceive devil early eradicate executioner exterminator settlement slaughter state strangle swindle pacific pesticide plus poison racketeer reckless renegade republic rough rowdy achieve ado alaska american apache assassinate ocean outlaw /dare/]
*desperate 02-69-273 (a.) 1. (of persons) dangerously reckless or violent as from urgency or despair 2. showing extreme courage; especially of actions courageously undertaken in desperation as a last resort 3. desperately determined 4. arising from or marked by despair or loss of hope 5. showing extreme urgency or intensity especially because of great need or desire 6. fraught with extreme danger; nearly hopeless (n.) 1. a person who is frightened and in need of help [dangerous demonic deplorable determined dire dismal drastic dreadful eager exquisite extremely scandalous serious severe shock slapdash perilous pinch precipitous pressing rage rare rash rate reckless risky acute amok anxious atrocious tenuous terrible thwart /tare/] "they prey on the hopes of the desperate"
*despicable 15-59-7 (a.) 1. worthy only of being despised and rejected 2. morally reprehensible [deserve develop dire dirty disgraceful dreadful earth egregious enormous evil execrable sad shameful slavery small sorry pathetic petty poor purpose ignoble ignominious infamous cable character cheap common completely courage creature crime crude abject appalling atrocious awful bad base blame brutal lack little loathsome lousy low]
*despite 01-60-1048 (n.) 1. lack of respect accompanied by a feeling of intense dislike 2. contemptuous disregard [deeply defy disdain dislike disregard dump enormity slap slight spite stubborn pert preposition prevent ignore indicate injury insult intense taunt today toplofty /tip/]
*despond 23-82-1 (v.) 1. lose confidence or hope; become dejected [dejected depressed discourage droop drop early election extreme sad sag slough supporter pond] "The supporters of the Presidential candidate desponded when they learned the early results of the election"
*despondent 16-57-6 (a.) 1. without or almost without hope [dejected depressed despond discourage dismal downhearted extremely sad seem subdued suicidal pessimistic pine] "despondent about his failure"
*despot 17-61-5 (n.) 1. a dictator or dictatorial person [dictatorial disciplinarian driver emperor empire spot stickler strongman people pharaoh power prince oligarch oppress toward tyrant /top/]
*despotism 21-42-2 (n.) 1. dominance through threat of punishment and violence 2. a form of government in which the ruler is an absolute dictator (not restricted by a constitution or laws or opposition etc.) [despot dictatorship dominance domineering exist secret shogunate single stalin suppression paternalism people political power punishment one opposition oppress terrorism threat totalitarian tyrant maintain mean

monarchy monocracy /top/]
*destitute 14-50-8 (a.) 1. poor enough to need help from others [deficient deplete deprive des drain empty enough exhaust strip subsistence idea impoverish indigent innocent insolvent]
*desultory 17-50-5 (a.) 1. marked by lack of definite plan or regularity or purpose; jumping from one thing to another [dance dangerous definite depart disorganize eccentric enemy episodic erratic evidence soldier staggering stray system uncertain uneven unfocused unmethodical unpredictable labyrinthine lack loose lurch temporary tory turning twist random regularity risky rough /use/] "desultory thoughts"
*detect 04-45-105 (v.) 1. discover or determine the existence, presence, or fact of [determine discovery distinguish drink electronics encounter entity error espy evident existence eye tangible tec trace trap catch circumstance crime] "She detected high levels of lead in her drinking water"
*deter 05-58-66 (v.) 1. try to prevent; show opposition to 2. turn away from by persuasion [daunt deem deflect disapprove discourage dissuade divert estop exclude try turn turnoff reject repel restrain /rete/]
*deteriorate 04-45-94 (v.) 1. grow worse 2. become worse or disintegrate [damage decay decline degenerate del depreciate descend deter devolve difference disintegrate dog drop enhance enlarge erode exacerbate exasperate tack thin tired transition turnabout recover recuperate relapse renewal revive revolution rot ruin illness improvement increase injure intensify overthrow accommodation adaptation adjustment alter annoy augment /rete taro/] "His mind deteriorated"
*determination 04-59-122 (n.) 1. a position or opinion or judgment reached after consideration 2. the quality of being determined to do or achieve something 3. the act of determining the properties of something 4. the act of making up your mind about something [decision decisive definition designation desire diligence dogged effect effort end tenacity termination refute resolve meaning measure idea indefatigable interpretation issue name action answer appointment award option /rete/] "his determination showed in his every movement"
*deterrent 08-46-32 (a.) 1. tending to deter (n.) 1. something immaterial that interferes with or delays action or progress [defend delay destroy deter difficulty dismay doubt effect encourage enemy exemplary expostulatory expression tend trouble try reasoning restrictive rub negative notify nuclear /rete/] "the deterrent effects of high prices"
*detest 13-61-10 (v.) 1. dislike intensely; feel antipathy or aversion towards [despise disdain distaste down execrate test toward scorn /set/]
*detract 11-60-16 (v.) 1. take away a part from; diminish [decrease diminish down drain erode extract tract trim reduction refine remove abate abrade abstract away character curtail cut /cart carte/] "His bad manners detract from his good character"
*detriment 13-57-11 (n.) 1. a damage or loss [damage denial destruction disadvantage encroach evil expense toxin rime robbery ill impair infection injury mayhem mischief mutilate /emir/]
*deviance 23-59-1 (n.) 1. a state or condition markedly different from the norm 2. deviate behavior [different disorder eccentricity etiquette ian accept anomaly non normal condition customary /naive/]
*deviate 14-47-8 (n.) 1. a person whose behavior deviates from what is acceptable especially in sexual behavior (v.) 1. turn aside; turn away from 2. be at variance with; be out of line with 3. turn aside 4. cause to turn away from a previous or expected course [deflect degenerate depart desire deteriorate detour different digress direction disagree distinguished disturb divert drift eat electron engage enjoy err erratic excursive variance various vary veer via improve impulsive inconstant inflict interpose irregular aberration abnormal abstract acceptable adult alter ameliorate anal aside assorted atom attract theoretical travel trend trip turn twist] "The river was deviated to prevent flooding"
*devious 14-60-9 (a.) 1. indirect in departing from the accepted or proper way; misleading 2. deviating from a straight course 3. characterized by insincerity or deceit; evasive [dark deceitful depart design destination dimension direction dubious elaborate erratic erring evasive extend eye vagrant veer vulpine indirect insincerity intention intricate involved oblique orbital unconscionable underhand unethical unfair unscrupulous usual scenic scheming secretive shifty sincere sly smooth sneaky spatial standard subtle success suspicious] "used devious means to achieve success"
*devise 04-47-100 (n.) 1. a will disposing of real property 2. (law) a gift of real property by will (v.) 1. arrange by systematic planning and united effort 2. come up with (an idea, plan, explanation, theory, or priciple) after a mental effort 3. give by will, esp. real property [death declare design development die director discover dispose document eat effort elaborate enable equipment erection estate evolve excogitate execution explanation extraction venture vise idea impose improvise inherit initiative intend intrigue invention item scheme set shape smelt spatchcock spawn speed state strike supply]
*devout 10-63-19 (a.) 1. devoutly religious 2. earnest [dear deceitful dedicated deeply deity devo devotional doubtless earnest vehement observant open theism]
*dexterity 15-61-7 (n.) 1. adroitness in using the hands [deft dexter difficulty diplomacy ease efficiency effortless expertise talent technique touch resourceful right ingenuity /tire/]
*dexterous 21-38-2 (a.) 1. skillful in physical movements; especially of the hands [deft dexter

dextrous diplomatic ease easy efficient excellent expert tactful talented ready resourceful sharp skillful smart some]
*diabolic 15-56-7 (a.) 1. showing the cunning or ingenuity or wickedness typical of a devil 2. extremely evil or cruel; expressive of cruelty or befitting hell [damnable demonic depraved despot devil devilish dreadful ill infernal influence ingenuity inhumane instrument abo animal anthropophagus appalling art atrocious awful bad base beastly befitting bloody brutish odious ogre lit calculation cannibalistic cold connect corrupt cruelty cuning cursed /lob/]
*diagnose 05-61-69 (v.) 1. subject to an analysis; usually used in a medical context 2. determine or distinguish the nature of a problem or an illness through a diagnostic analysis [describe detail determine devoted discover disease distinguish doctor identify illness injury interview alleviate analyze graduate name nature nose nurse school splint spot strap study essential establish examine /son song/]
*diagnosis 07-57-41 (n.) 1. identifying the nature or cause of some phenomenon [decision definition description designation determine disease disorder identify illness interpretation action analysis award nature opinion order sentence serology smear study /son song/]
*dialect 11-47-14 (n.) 1. the usage or vocabulary that is characteristic of a specific group of people [diction differ identify idiom idiomatic immigrant isogloss accept adult alec argot language langue leap localism locution easily expression cant class colloquial community composition consider talk tongue toward /laid/] "the immigrants spoke an odd dialect of English"
*dialogue 04-43-110 (n.) 1. a literary composition in the form of a conversation between two people 2. the lines spoken by characters in drama or fiction 3. a conversation between two persons 4. a discussion intended to produce an agreement [day debate deliberation dialog difference diplomatic disagree discussion dramatic duologue idea imaginative impartial interview investigation accompany actor agreement airing analysis antimasque last limited line literature open opera oppose original gasser giveaway union employer enemy examination exchange extravaganza /laid/]
*diaphanous 21-44-2 (a.) 1. so thin as to transmit light [dandelion delicate dilute down insect insubstantial airy attenuate papery peekaboo pellucid hat nous opposite section see seethrough sheer silk slight small stock subtle surface /paid/] "a hat with a diaphanous veil"
*diatribe 16-46-6 (n.) 1. thunderous verbal attack [debate declamation denunciation discourse invective abuse address attack talkathon thunderous tirade tribe rant rating read revile berate bitter blacken eulogy execration exhortation]
*dictum 16-54-6 (n.) 1. an authoritative declaration 2. an opinion voiced by a judge on a point of law not directly bearing on the case in question and therefore not binding [decision declaration determination dictate directly document imperative impose interjection case code collection comment conclusion teach thought truism truth tum ukase utterance manifesto maxim mention moral motto /mut/]
*didactic 14-36-8 (a.) 1. instructive especially excessively [dictate direction disciplinary dramatic idyllic illumination improve informative instructive absence act admonitory advise advisory attitude authoritative canonical catechize cautionary coach cultural teach tend tendency theater tuition tutor /cad cadi/]
*difference 01-51-546 (n.) 1. a significant change 2. a variation that deviates from the standard or norm 3. a disagreement or argument about something important 4. the quality of being unlike or dissimilar 5. the number that remains after subtraction; the number that when added to the subtrahend gives the minuend [departure deviation differ difficulty disagreement dispute dissimilar diversity division drift dustup flexion eagle eccentricity epact row runin charge chief controversy credit /fid/] "there are many differences between jazz and rock"
*differential 12-53-13 (a.) 1. relating to or showing a difference 2. (mathematics) involving or containing one or more derivatives (n.) 1. the result of mathematical differentiation; the instantaneous change of one quantity relative to another; df(x)/dx 2. a quality that differentiates between similar things 3. a bevel gear that permits rotation of two shafts at different speeds; used on the rear axle of automobiles to allow wheels to rotate at different speeds on curves [deal derive different digital discrepancy discriminative disparity dissimilar distinction division impression index infinitesimal instantaneous involve feature figure first flavor function earmark equation even exact radical rate real rear reckoning respect reverse rotation nature negative neutral tangent taste accurate angle attribute axle line lineament logarithmic logic low /fid lait/] "differential treatment"
*differentiate 09-54-21 (v.) 1. be a distinctive feature, attribute, or trait; sometimes in a very positive sense 2. mark as different 3. become different during development; of cells 4. become distinct and acquire a different character 5. calculate a derivative; take the derivative; in mathematics 6. evolve so as to lead to a new species or develop in a way most suited to the environment, of populations of plants and animals [describe difference different discriminate display distinguished identify increase involve figure earmark entail express reckon regular relieve reveal note tell testify transmute adjust alter apart argue arrangement attribute /fid/]
*diffidence 21-63-2 (n.) 1. lack of self-confidence

[decision fear emotional characterize complex]
*diffident 14-65-8 (a.) 1. lacking self-confidence 2. showing modest reserve [decision demur dent deprecatory doorway doubtful dubious insecure falter fearsome emotional nervous tentative timid tremulous /diff fid/] "she was diffident when offering a comment on the professor's lecture"
*diffusion 19-49-3 (n.) 1. (physics) the process of diffusing; the intermingling of molecules in gases and liquids as a result of random thermal agitation 2. the spread of social institutions (and myths and skills) from one society to another 3. the property of being diffused or dispersed 4. the act of dispersing or diffusing something [direction dispersion distribution infuse insecticide intermingle feature fertilizer flow fluid fungicide fusion uneven until scattering science scope space spatial spray spread story substance suffuse surface /fid suff/]
*dignitary 12-48-13 (n.) 1. an important or influential (and often overbearing) person [dig dignity important influential interest nabob name notable tycoon /gid rating ting/]
*dignity 05-53-63 (n.) 1. formality in bearing and appearance 2. the quality of being worthy of esteem or respect 3. high office or rank or station [decorum dig direct discrimination distinction due impersonality impressivenes interest glory goodness grand grandeur gravity great name natural neat nobility noble tasteful terse trait true tycoon /gid ting/] "it was beneath his dignity to cheat"
*digress 21-54-2 (v.) 1. lose clarity or turn aside esp. from the main subject of attention or course of argument in writing, thinking, or speaking 2. wander from a direct or straight course [detour deviate dig direct divagate divert drift give ramble road roam sheer shift sidetrack speaking story stray /gid/] "She always digresses when telling a story"
*dilapidated 11-51-16 (a.) 1. in deplorable condition [damage decay decrepit deplorable derelict destruct disrepair injure partly pier tatterdemalion tenement tumbledown]
*dilate 19-57-3 (v.) 1. become wider 2. add details, as to an account or idea; clarify the meaning of and discourse in a learned way, usually in writing [describe detail discourse discuss dissertation distend dwell idea increase inflate instance large late learn length lengthen lucubration account add aggrandize amplify augment talk tumefy elaborate elucidate enlarge evolve exemplify expatiate expound extensive /lid tali/] "His pupils were dilated"
*dilatory 23-58-1 (a.) 1. inclined to waste time and lag behind 2. wasting time 3. using cautious slow strategy to wear down opposition; avoiding direct confrontation [dawdle delay deliberate dilator direct down drag incautious incline indifferent indolent intend lag lagging lax lazy linger long apathetic appointed avoid tardy tarry tend opposition reluctant remiss restive /lid rota tali/]
*dilemma 05-73-74 (n.) 1. state of uncertainty or perplexity especially as requiring a choice between equally unfavorable options [deadlock difficulty disturbance impasse lead lemma logic embarrassment emma enigma enthymeme equally message mode mood mystify alternative argument /lid/]
*dilettante 18-54-4 (a.) 1. showing frivolous or superficial interest; amateurish (n.) 1. an amateur who engages in an activity without serious intentions and who pretends to have knowledge [dabble dated deep desultory devotee idolize ignoramus interested lover lowbrow effort emotional engage epicurean expert technician trifle tyro admire affecting amateurish ante art authority nut /lid/]
*diligence 10-74-18 (n.) 1. conscientiousness in paying proper attention to a task; giving the degree of care required in a given situation 2. a diligent effort 3. persevering determination to perform a task [degree determined industry insistency intent laborious law legal loyalty gen give great ear earnest effort energy exertion expect note notice careful concentration constant contract /lid/] "his diligence won him quick promotions"
*dilute 06-47-45 (a.) 1. reduced in strength or concentration or quality or purity (v.) 1. lessen the strength or flavor of a solution or mixture 2. corrupt, debase, or make impure by adding a foreign or inferior substance; often by replacing valuable ingredients with inferior ones [dead debase deceive decrease delicate diminish dissolve doctor down impaired impoverish impure inane increase indifferent inferior ingredient insipid intention irrigate issue lace lacy lessen light liquor lute unsavory unsubstantial tasteless temper tenuous thicken thinner thread ease effect ethereal evaporate exchange expand extend /lid/] "diluted alcohol"
*diminution 19-41-3 (n.) 1. change toward something smaller or lower 2. the act of decreasing or reducing something 3. the statement of a theme in notes of lesser duration (usually half the length of the original) [decline depression dim dip duck impair mitigate modulate mollify numbing temper truncate /tun/]
*dimly 14-43-9 (ad.) 1. in a dim indistinct manner 2. in a manner lacking interest or vitality [diffuse dim indistinct interest manner muted lack] "we perceived the change only dimly"
*dint 18-64-4 (n.) 1. interchangeable with 'means' in the expression 'by dint of' [dent depression dig din drive drum imprint indentation indenture influence interchange notch tamp tattoo thump]
*diplomacy 06-43-46 (n.) 1. subtly skillful handling of a situation 2. negotiation between nations 3. wisdom in the management of public affairs [deft delicacy deterrent diploma discretion imperialism ingenuity international intrigue politics proficiency prowess machination maneuver mastery ability address adept

agreement capacity command control /camo mol/]
*diplomat 03-33-151 (n.) 1. an official engaged in international negotiations 2. a person who deals tactfully with others [delicacy diploma international internuncio politician pro proficient legate marksman address adept agreement artist authority tactics technician treaty /mol/]
*diplomatic 04-47-125 (a.) 1. skilled in dealing with sensitive matters or people 2. relating to or characteristic of diplomacy 3. able to take a broad view of negotiations between states [deal deep deft delicate dialogue diplomat discreet document immunity ingenious insidious international inventive people perceptive political print prudent old original magisterial mark masterly matter ministerial accurate acute ambassador artful artistic tactful tactical talk thoughtful tricky cautious civic clean clever concern consul copy /mol/] "diplomatic immunity"
*directory 08-53-27 (n.) 1. an alphabetical list of names and addresses 2. (computer science) a listing of the files stored in memory (usually on a hard disk) [database diet different director disk dispatch index information instruction item rectory reference register release report room rule encyclopedia engineering enlightenment evidence calendar catalog compute conference congress contact court table telephone tenant transmission tribunal ordered organization yearbook /rid/]
*disagree 04-38-116 (v.) 1. be of different opinions 2. be different from one another [debate deny depart deviate different disallow discord dispute dissent distinguished distress diverge diversify down indisposed involuntary irreconcilable issue secede separate several show squabble strike strong sullen accordance affect agree agreement alienate argue assent assorted averse gibe grating recalcitrant reject repugnant resistant row effect /gas/]
*disallow 10-77-18 (v.) 1. command against [debar declare default deny dispute impugn inhibit injunction interdict issue sallow shutout social suppress accept late legal let levant oppose ostracize outlaw overrule welsh withhold /olla/]
*disappear 02-54-266 (v.) 1. become invisible or unnoticeable 2. get lost, esp. without warning or explanation 3. cease to exist [day decamp default dematerialize depart departure desertion die dissolve immaterial immersion imperceptible intense invisible scram secret skedaddle slow spatial stop subsequent succumb sudden abandon abscond absent appear arrest pass people perish political prior public ebb eclipse effect elope end entire escape evanesce evaporate existence exit expire explanation recede regime remove retreat /pas/] "He disappeared without a trace"
*disappoint 09-69-22 (v.) 1. fail to meet the hopes or expectations of [dash desire discontent disenchant disgruntle dishearten disillusion dissatisfy down sadden satisfactory scotch short spoil standup abandon appoint attractive awaken plan prevent prove putout tantalize tease thwart /pas/]
*disapprove 09-51-22 (v.) 1. refuse to approve 2. consider bad or wrong [decline deny deplore deprecate discount dismiss dissent ignore scout soil spurn stain statement abjure approve attaint petition pillory practice prevent protest putdown rebel rebuff refuse reject renounce opposition ostracize vilify except exclude expostulate /pas/] "I disapprove of her child rearing methods"
*disarm 09-49-22 (v.) 1. remove offensive capability from 2. make less hostile; win over 3. take away the weapons from; render harmless [deactivate deflate defuse demilitarize deprive disable disband divest immobilize incapable incapacitate incline safe silence strangle strength strip supply suspicious agree allure appease arm armed attract realize reduce remove render manacle military mollify muzzle] "Her charm disarmed the prosecution lawyer completely"
*disavow 14-15-8 (v.) 1. refuse to acknowledge; disclaim knowledge of; responsibility for, or association with [declare deny disallow disclaim disown dispute impugn six swallow abjure abrogate acknowledge admit annul assertion association avouch avow avowal openly oppose withdrawal /ova/] "Her husband disavowed her after 30 years of marriage and six children"
*disavowal 23-30-1 (n.) 1. denial of any connection with or knowledge of [denial abjure assertion avowal]
*disburse 15-18-7 (v.) 1. pay out [deposit discharge dispose distribute distribution invest issue schedule service settlement spend squander binder budget burse remittance retirement exchange expend /rub/]
*discard 05-46-66 (n.) 1. anything that is cast aside or discarded 2. the act of throwing out a useless card or to failing to follow suit 3. getting rid something that is regarded as useless or undesirable (v.) 1. throw or cast away [decline deep deny discount dismiss dispose dispute down dump ignore impugn invalidate scout scrap sell shadow shed shoot six spurn stage suit surrender suspension card cashier cast castaway chuck clearance close clothe confute contradiction abandon abdicate aside attempt away rebuff reclaim refuse reject remove renounce require retire rid right rocket rubbish]
*discern 08-45-28 (v.) 1. detect with the senses [determine differentiate discover distinguish divine drawing identify indisputable insight intellect see seize sense separate showing sky skyline spot capable clearly comprehensible conceptualize conspicuous convict easy espy essay evident explicit express extricate realize recognize remark report reveal naked note notice]
*discernible 12-53-13 (a.) 1. capable of being perceived clearly 2. perceptible by the senses or intellect 3. capable of being seen or noticed [difficult discern distinct drawing imperceptible impossible intellect see sky skyline capable clearly earth easy erasure essay evident report negotiation newspaper notice behavior /bin/] "things happen in the earth and sky with no

discernible cause"
*disciple 10-48-17 (n.) 1. someone who believes and helps to spread the doctrine of another [dangle dependent disc dummy shadow student supporter castigate convert correction courtier creature partisan penalize public pupil lackey learner enthusiast evangelist]
*disciplinary 06-74-56 (a.) 1. relating to discipline in behavior 2. designed to promote discipline 3. relating to a specific field of academic study [design didactic disc domain illuminate indulgent inflict informative instruction scholarly scientific specific stern study castigate classroom corrective cultural cut penal penalize preaching problem promote punitive punitory lecture lesson academic across area autodidact retribution rule /rani/] "disciplinary problems in the classroom"
*discipline 03-56-172 (n.) 1. training to improve strength or self-control 2. a system of rules of conduct or method of practice 3. the trait of being well behaved 4. a branch of knowledge 5. the act of punishing (v.) 1. train by instruction and practice; esp. to teach self-control 2. punish in order to gain control or enforce obedience [desert development direction disc improvement independence indulgent instruction stoic straiten castigate coach concern confined control copyright correction cramped patent pay payment penalize philosophical prescribe lead lenient limited narrow neat nurse educate empire enduring exercise] "in what discipline is his doctorate?"
*disclaim 21-29-2 (v.) 1. renounce a legal claim or title to 2. make a disclaimer about [declare deny dismiss disown dispute idea ignore impugn scout spurn strong swallow challenge claim connection contradict criticize cross legal lie abjure accept affirm assert authority minimize] "He disclaimed any responsibility"
*discolor 18-13-4 (v.) 1. lose color or turn colorless 2. cause to lose or change color 3. change color, often in an undesired manner [dapple darken define desire detergent different dim dirty dot drain dull dye imprint inky insect sallow scorch score scratch shame shirt sickly silver smoky spot stain sun sunburn cadaverous checkoff cicatrize color colorize colorless course crimson cut original overexpose lackluster launder lightening line lose lurid luster red remove riddle] "The painting discolored"
*discomfit 19-60-3 (v.) 1. cause to lose one's composure [defeat destroy disco dish disturb disturbed down incapable irk scattered self settle silence spike spoil stump call chagrin challenge cloud composure confused control convulse cross outdo outwit overwhelming maze miserable misplace mist mortify muddle fail fall faze fire fixed floor fluster foil forth frustrate fuss throw thwart trim trounce trump turbulent]
*discomfort 07-56-36 (n.) 1. the state of being tense and feeling pain 2. an uncomfortable feeling in some part of the body [depression difficulty disagreeable distress disturb drug inconvenient inquietude irritation sad sharp sickness sore status suffering cheerless comfort comfortless malaise mental mild misery mournful flatness formal relaxed tasteless tedium tender tense trouble]
*disconcert 10-61-19 (v.) 1. cause to feel embarrassment 2. cause to lose one's composure [defeat deflect destroy deter dish dismay disoriented displeasure disturb draw dumb ill intricate scary self shake shock shuffle slight speaker startling stir stranger stump call calm chagrin challenge chaotic charming chilling cloud composure concert confuse constant control cross crush off overawe nervous nonplus ease elicit elude embarrassment emotional enervate enigmatic enkindle entangle evoke experience raise rattle response rock roily ruffle ruin throw thwart trouble turbulent]
*disconnect 15-32-7 (v.) 1. make disconnected, disjoin or unfasten 2. of electrical appliances [decouple depart detached difference disengage disinterest disjoin disparity disunite divide divorce isolate separate sever shut source speaker spiritual split supply cancel concern connect connection cut cutout effect eject electricity emotional estrange expel telephone tie]
*disconsolate 18-69-4 (a.) 1. sad beyond comforting; incapable of being consoled 2. causing dejection [dark day dejection depressing desolate despondent die disappointed disco dismal dispiriting incapable inconsolable sad somber son strike suicidal cheerless cold comforting console crush lack landscape low apathetic extremely]
*discontinuance 23-08-1 (n.) 1. the act of discontinuing or breaking off; an interruption (temporary or permanent) [disfranchise dismount donor inherit interruption conclusion continue termination end]
*discord 13-35-10 (n.) 1. lack of agreement or harmony 2. strife resulting from a lack of agreement 3. disagreement among those expected to cooperate 4. a harsh mixture of sounds (v.) 1. be different from one another [different disagreement disco disharmony dispute dissonance disturbance division dryness idea incompatible inequality inharmonious inharmony interval scratchy shivaree situation sound speech split strife cacophony chord clash combination conflict controversy conventionall cooperate opinion opposition outcry require resolution roughness row rub]
*discourse 10-36-19 (n.) 1. extended verbal expression in speech or writing 2. an extended communication (often interactive) dealing with some particular topic 3. an address of a religious nature (usually delivered during a church service) (v.) 1. to consider or examine in speech or writing 2. carry on a conversation 3. talk or hold forth formally about a topic [debate descant dialogist discussion dispute impersonate instruction investigate sermonize chin consider converse course criticize orate outline rap reader review essayist examine

exercise explain expound]
*discover 01-59-536 (v.) 1. see for the first time; make a discovery 2. make a discovery 3. make a discovery, make a new finding 4. get to know or become aware of, usually accidentally 5. make known to the public information that was previously known only to a few people or that was meant to be kept a secret 6. find unexpectedly 7. discover or determine the existence, presence, or fact of 8. identify as in botany or biology, for example [design determine develop dig disclose distinguish identify impart improvise investigation see sight spot survey calculation closet coin come concoct contrive cover observe originate view encounter evolve existence experiment expose realize recognize reveal rundown]
*discredit 08-50-32 (n.) 1. the state of being held in low esteem (v.) 1. cause to be distrusted or disbelieved 2. reject as false; refuse to accept 3. damage the reputation of [damage demean deny disgrace dishonor dismiss dispute disrepute distrust doubt ignore impugn infidelity insult invalidate scandal school seem shame shoot slight slur smear story suspect suspicion calumniate canal cast commentary confute contest credit reduce reflection refuse refute reject reputation ruin esteem evil explode expose express taint tarnish theory true /tide/] "The paper discredited the politician with its nasty commentary"
*discreet 08-67-29 (a.) 1. marked by prudence or modesty and wise self-restraint 2. heedful of potential consequences 3. unobtrusively perceptive and sympathetic [dark deal deliberate diplomatic dry icy impersonal imprudent inaccessible inconspicuous injudicious investor safe scree secret self sensible shrink simple subtle sympathetic careful cautious circumspect cold confidential considerate cool reasonable recommend removed reserved restrained enlighten ensure evasive expressionless tasteful tentative thorough thoughtful trust /tee/] "his trusted discreet aide"
*discrete 17-37-5 (a.) 1. constituting a separate entity or part [depart describe detached disagree distribute division independent individual isolated separate several spread suspend choppy completely constitute contrast crete removed element entity episodic exotic extraneous teeth tenuous] "a government with three discrete divisions"
*discriminate 07-43-40 (a.) 1. marked by the ability to see or make fine distinctions 2. noting distinctions with nicety (v.) 1. treat differently on the basis of sex or race 2. recognize or perceive the difference 3. distinguish [delicate diagnostic distinguish divide idiosyncrasy incisive individuate secern selective separate severalize sharp sophisticated specialize strict categorize change characterize classify compare contrast criminate critical cultivate refined reflective remark meticulous modify acute adoptive analyze anatomize apart appreciative atomize tactful extricate] "discriminate judgments"
*discursive 19-43-3 (a.) 1. (philosophy) proceeding to a conclusion by reason or argument rather than intuition 2. (of e.g. speech and writing) tending to depart from the main point or cover a wide range of subjects [deductive depart drift indirect inference intelligent sensible shift spiral categorical conceptual conditional conversational cursive understanding undirected rambling range rational reasonable roundabout vagabond vagrant veer episodic erratic excursive expansive]
*discussion 02-43-329 (n.) 1. an exchange of views on some topic 2. an extended communication (often interactive) dealing with some particular topic [deal debate decision deliberation detailed dialogue discourse discuss idea interest interview investigation side sit speak study survey chat communication conclusion conference congress consider conversation convey occur open oral outline negotiation next note] "the book contains an excellent discussion of modal logic"
*disdain 07-47-35 (n.) 1. lack of respect accompanied by a feeling of intense dislike 2. a communication that indicates lack of respect by patronizing the recipient (v.) 1. reject with contempt 2. look down on with disdain [dai daring decline defiant defy deny depreciation derision derisive despite detest discourtesy disgust disparage disregard disrespectful down ignore immediately impertinent impudent indicate insulting intense scorn scouting self show sneer snobby snub social spurn student superior accept accompany advance air aloof antipathy aristocrat arrogant audacious aversion]
*disenfranchise 14-44-9 (v.) 1. deprive of voting rights [deprive disfranchise disqualify dominate immunity subjugate subordinate enfranchise enslave enthrall exclude right alienate]
*disengage 15-56-7 (v.) 1. release from something that holds fast. connects, or entangles 2. become free; as of gears, for example 3. free or remove obstruction from [depart detach detached difficulty dig disconnected divided divorce idle influence isolated scattered segregated separate set sever situation snow split stop sword earth easygoing eject engage entangle escape estranged expel extricate gear grip abrupt abstract alienate attack available] "I want to disengage myself from his influence"
*disentangle 19-59-3 (v.) 1. extricate from entanglement 2. release from entanglement of difficulty 3. smoothen and neaten with or as with a comb 4. free from involvement or entanglement 5. separate the tangles of [decipher determination discharge dislodge divine down dredge drill interpretation involve scalp separate simplify situation slick smooth snarl solution solve sort straighten end entangle entwine evolve explanation extend extricate narrow neaten takeout tangle tease tie toward twist accomplishment annul answer apart appearance ascertain get give glossy groom liberate loosen /gnat/]

*disfavor 21-14-2 (n.) 1. the state of being out of favor 2. an inclination to withhold approval from some person or group (v.) 1. put at a disadvantage; hinder, harm [different disapprove discriminate disdain disgrace dislike disposition disruption distaste division idiomatic ignominy inclination indisposition infamy schism scorn separate separation severe sex single split favor fell formal abhor alienate alternative approval attitude aversion obloquy obscurity opprobrium ostracize race reject respect rift rule rupture /ova/] "he is in disfavor with the king"
*disfigure 13-62-11 (v.) 1. mar or spoil the appearance of [damage deface defect deflower deform destroy distortion dwarf impair impaired imperfect inelegant injure scab scar scratch severe split spoil spoilt statue faulty figure flatfooted flaw freakish graceless grotesque ugly unattractive ungainly unlovely unsightly rachitis rickety rift ruin /rug/]
*dishearten 13-41-10 (v.) 1. take away the enthusiasm of [dampen dashed deject deprive deter disappoint disappointing discourage dismay down inadequate incommensurate insufficient intimidate sadden save scary self shake somber spiritless startling stop subdued suicidal hearten heartless help hence hope hopeless hypochondriac embolden encouragement enthusiasm estop exclude alarming anticipate avert awe recreate repel]
*disheveled 19-01-3 (a.) 1. in disarray; extremely disorderly [disarray disorderly scruffy sheet strong hair extremely] "her clothing was disheveled"
*dishonest 11-60-14 (a.) 1. deceptive or fraudulent; disposed to cheat or defraud or deceive 2. capable of being corrupted 3. lacking truthfulness 4. lacking honesty and oblivious to what is honorable [dark deceptive defraud deserve disposed double doubtful dubious duplicity immoral incorrupt indirect insincere integrity scoundrel senator sincerity sinister straight suspicious swindle hollow honest hypocritical oblivious officer empty equivocal evasive express thievish tongue treacherous trick tricky trust truth truthful twofaced] "a dishonest answer"
*disillusion 08-69-28 (n.) 1. freeing from false belief or illusions (v.) 1. free from enchantment [dashed defeat disappoint discontent disenchant disgruntle dishearten dissatisfy dissent down ideal illusion indignation show sophistication sour let letdown low undeceive unfavorable unhappy uplifting objection oppose ostracise /sull/]
*disinfect 18-60-4 (v.) 1. destroy microorganisms or pathogens by cleansing [delouse destroy dirt disease illness infect infection injury sanitize smoke sterilize substance filth free fumigate care carry chlorine cleanse compound taint treatment /nisi/] "disinfect a wound"
*disinfectant 18-65-4 (a.) 1. preventing infection by inhibiting the growth or action of microorganisms (n.) 1. an agent (as heat or radiation or a chemical) that destroys microorganisms that might carry disease [defoliant destructive detergent disease disinfect infection inhibit salt sanitize septic sterilize substance force formaldehyde free fumigate fungicide effect exert carry cation chemical chlorine clean cleanser cresol toxin acaricide agent anthelmintic anti antiseptic /nisi/]
*disingenuous 13-56-11 (a.) 1. not straightforward or candid; giving a false appearance of frankness [deceitful deceptive designing devious disagreeable dishonest distorted duplicity illusive impression inability indirect ingenuous insincere sincerity slick sly smooth straightforward genuine give guile empty excuse underhanded untruthful oblique operator /nisi/] "an ambitious, disingenuous, philistine, and hypocritical operator, who...exemplified...the most disagreeable traits of his time"
*disinherit 21-51-2 (v.) 1. prevent deliberately (as by making a will) from inheriting [death deliberate deprive dispossess divest inherit natural establish right /nisi tire/]
*disinter 21-64-2 (v.) 1. dig up for reburial or for medical investigation; of dead bodies [dead dig disclose divulge investigate sinter tomb turn excavate exhume expose reburial remove reveal /nisi/]
*disinterested 17-51-5 (a.) 1. unaffected by self-interest [dedicated devoted disinterest distant impartial impersonal indifferent insouciance interested sacrifice self show slack sluggish negative neutral numb torpid easygoing equitable evenhanded regardless remote resigned /nisi sere/]
*dislocate 11-61-14 (v.) 1. move out of position 2. put out of its usual place, position, or relationship [detached disarticulate disjoint displace disrupt disturb divided divorce interrupt isolated scattered separate settle shift ship shuffle slip splay surgical litter locate luxate out clutter cockeyed colonist concrete confusion convulse abstract alienate amiss artificial awry throw tousle transfer turbulent estranged /taco/] "dislocate joints"
*dislodge 13-53-11 (v.) 1. remove or force out from a position 2. remove or force from a position of dwelling previously occupied 3. change place or direction [dentist deposit direction disentangle dismount down dwell implant secure send shift side space stick leave leg lift lodge occupy office oust gum earthquake eject employee evict exclude expel extricate /dol/] "The dentist dislodged the piece of food that had been stuck under my gums"
*dismal 07-60-43 (a.) 1. depressing in character or appearance 2. causing dejection [dark day dead death dejection depressing dick dingy dis disconsolate drab dreary dry dull inadequate inane insipid sad sharp show slow sorry spirit street melancholy min miserable moving murky affecting afflict appearance arid lack lamentable landscape lifeless lower]
*dismay 05-53-64 (n.) 1. fear resulting from the awareness of danger 2. the feeling of despair in the face of obstacles (v.) 1. lower someone's spirits; make

downhearted 2. fill with apprehension or alarm; cause to be unpleasantly surprised [daunt deject demoralize deprive desire despair deter disappointment discourage disoriented disquiet distress disturb downhearted dread intimidate intricate sad scare shake sharp shock spirit startling status strike struck sudden superior surprise maze may moider mournful mousy moving mystify affecting affright afraid alarm alarming anticipation anxiety appal aware awe /yam/]

*dismissal 04-35-130 (n.) 1. a judgment disposing of the matter without a trial 2. permission to go; the sending away of someone 3. the termination of someone's employment (leaving them free to depart) 4. official notice that you have been fired from your job [decision decline deem denial depart determination discharge dismiss displace dispose ignore impeach impose inactivate incident intention sabotage sack scouting send separation service slip submit suspension matter military murder abrupt absolution acquittance adjourn advance age approval army arrange authority law layoff liberation liquidate /ass lass lassi/]

*dismount 18-75-4 (n.) 1. the act of dismounting (a horse or bike etc.) (v.) 1. get off (a horse) [demolish depose descend discontinue dislodge downward interruption item separate settle stand support mean motorcycle mount mounting move off unhorse unsaddle unseat uproot necessarily takedown teardown touchdown transport]

*disobedience 15-40-7 (n.) 1. the failure to obey 2. the trait of being unwilling to obey [decline defiance denial disrespect dissent dutiful influence insubordinate interregnum irresponsible slow stubborn submissive sulk obedience obeisance obey obstinate opposition backward bad behavior body naughty nay nix nonobservance children comply contradiction contumacy court cursory]

*disobedient 23-57-1 (a.) 1. not obeying or complying with commands of those in authority 2. unwilling to submit to authority [defiant difficult disagree disregardful dutiful impervious incorrigible instruction intractable involuntary irresponsible self stubborn submit subordinate sulky sullen obdurate obedient obey obstinate obstreperous oppose bad behave bold burke edmund naughty negative non teenager tenacious tractable transgress] "disobedient children"

*disown 15-70-7 (v.) 1. prevent deliberately (as by making a will) from inheriting [decline deliberate deny deprive disclaim discount dismiss dispute ignore impugn inherit scouting sown spurn swallow obtain oppose outcast waive withdrawal nullify]

*disparage 11-43-15 (v.) 1. express a negative opinion of [damage decry defame denigrate deprecate deride derogate despite detractor diminish disapprove discredit disdain disgrace disrespectful down drain impair impudent insolent insult scandalous scoff scorn slander slight sneer stain pejorative perceive abate abstract abusive arrogant reflection remark remove reprobative reputation revile ridicule gibbet effort erode exclusive express /psi/] "She disparaged her student's efforts"

*disparate 09-40-25 (a.) 1. fundamentally different or distinct in quality or kind 2. including markedly dissimilar elements [degree depart describe different disagree dissimilar distinct distinguished idea inadequate include incongruent insufficient irregular separate several skew song para people prayer aggregate assorted asymmetric attraction element /psi/] "such disparate attractions as grand opera and game fishing"

*disparity 09-35-25 (n.) 1. inequality or difference in some respect [departure difference difficulty disappointing discrepancy dissimilarity division imbalance inadequate inconsistency inequality injustice secession separate shortcoming spread parity part people polarize proportion alienate antagonism asymmetry recusant rejection repugnance respect /psi/]

*dispel 08-54-28 (v.) 1. force to go away; used both with concrete and metaphoric meanings 2. to cause to separate and go in different directions, of crowds, for example [die different direction dis disappear disappointed dismiss dissipate division doubt drive idea scatter separate separation shoo soon sun supermarket perish potential purge eliminate emotion erode erroneous exit liquidate /psi/]

*dispensation 17-70-5 (n.) 1. an exemption from some rule or obligation 2. a share that has been dispensed or distributed 3. the act of dispensing (giving out in portions) [direction discipline distribution divine doctrine document due immunity indulgence issue sacrifice sati service share special spread spreading part pepper percentage permit portion practice privilege publication emergency empire epoch evaporation exemption expansion abandon admission affair allowance asset authorize obligation official okay ordain order oversight /psi/]

*displace 07-38-41 (v.) 1. force to move 2. take the place of 3. put out of its usual place, position, or relationship 4. remove or force from a position of dwelling previously occupied 5. move (people) forcibly from their homeland into a new and foreign environment 6. cause to move, both in a concrete and in an abstract sense [deliver depose deracinate disgorge dislodge dismiss disorder distant disturb down issue send separate set shed shift side slop spill splay squeeze succeed supersede support part place position post purge layoff liquidate lock luxate attend can cashier channelize commove cutout eject evict exclude exile expel extirpate /psi/] "the refugees were displaced by the war"

*dispossess 23-85-1 (v.) 1. expel or put out of the possession of real estate [deprive disinherit dislodge disown divest strip possess possession property putout occupancy oust eject estate evict expel /psi sess/]

*disqualify 08-53-29 (v.) 1. make unfit or unsuitable 2. declare unfit [debar declare deprive different disarm

disenable dispose incapacitate income incompetent ineligible invalidate suspend qualify unarmed unfit unqualified unsuitable alter athlete label law legal fit /fila/]
*disquiet 13-84-10 (n.) 1. a feeling of mild anxiety about possible developments 2. the trait of seeming ill at ease (v.) 1. disturb in mind or make uneasy or cause to be worried or alarmed [danger daunt deeply development dislike dismay disorder disturb disturbed dull ill illdefined indicative inquietude say seeming serious shaking shock son startle strained suspense quake quaver quiet uncomfortable uneasy unhappy unhinge unpleasant unrest upset ease electrify embarrassed emotion empty excitement experience temperament tension trait trouble turbulent turmoil]
*disregard 07-48-35 (n.) 1. willful lack of care and attention 2. lack of attention and due care (v.) 1. bar from attention or consideration 2. refuse to acknowledge 3. give little or no attention to [decline defiant defy desert despite disbelieve discredit disdain dismiss disoblige distrust down due ignore importance inadvertent indifference indulgence insouciance interact saucy scoff shrug shunt slack slight snub spare rebuff recant reckless redeem refuse regard reject remit reprieve respect endure error exception excuse exonerate eye giddy give grant absolve accept acknowledge acquit advance airy amuse apathy arrogant aside attention audacious /age drag rag rage/]
*disreputable 18-60-4 (a.) 1. lacking respectability in character or behavior or appearance [damage deserve dirty discredit disgraceful dishonorable dubious ignominious ill infamous inglorious integrity scandalous seamy seedy shabby shady sleazy sloppy sordid sorry squalid raddle reprehensible reputable reputation respect past pitiable unexpected unkempt unsavory untidy unworthy tattered threadbare abject appearance bad base basis bedraggle behavior lack low /tup/]
*disrepute 14-87-9 (n.) 1. the state of being held in low esteem [discredit disgrace dishonor ill scandal school shame repute respect esteem evil public /tup/]
*disrobe 21-55-2 (v.) 1. get undressed [decollete discase disease disinvest divest down strapless strip remove robe everybody]
*disrupt 05-47-81 (v.) 1. throw into disorder 2. make a break in 3. interfere in someone else's activity [dance defeat destroy dis discontinue dish dislocate disorder disturb inject insert interrupt short signal spike spring squash stop stump sudden reception ruin rummage rupture unsettle upc upset usual partner pause perplex phone prevent process progression pulverize punctuate temporary throw thwart trip turn]
*dissatisfy 10-47-18 (v.) 1. fail to satisfy [dashed defeat disappoint discontent disgruntle disillusion displeasure indignant irk satisfy sour sulky against annoy tantalize tease thwart fail faultfinding foil frustrate /ass tass/]
*dissect 13-49-10 (v.) 1. cut open or cut apart 2. make a mathematical, chemical, or grammatical analysis of; break down into components or essential features [decompose detail dichotomize disjoint dismember diss divide down instrument scientific scrutinize sentence separate slice specimen speech split still structure study syntactic essential examine explore carve chemical cleave collect compound constituent cut /cess/] "dissect the bodies for analysis"
*dissection 16-62-6 (n.) 1. a minute and critical analysis 2. cutting so as to separate into pieces 3. detailed part-by-part critical analysis or examination as of a literary work [detailed diaeresis dismember dissect division inspection investigation scientific scrutiny segment separation specimen split study subdivision examine component constituent critical critique cut think observation /cess/]
*dissemble 19-56-3 (v.) 1. make believe 2. hide under a false appearance 3. behave unnaturally or affectedly [dead deceive deception difference disguise distinction dive idea ill imposture incomparable intention seeming semble sham shenanigan show silent simulate simulation speech makeup manner masquerade mislead misleading misrepresent mouth behavior believe bluff boxer bull lip /mess/]
*disseminate 11-37-15 (v.) 1. cause to become widely known [declared delivery diffuse disperse display distribute distribution drill implant import include interchange introduce issue scattered seed semina set signal sough spread stated strew switch environment expansion expel export extradition makeover metathesize metempsychosis migration accessible advertise affirm airing announce around assign attenuate taste televise tell transposition travel turnover /anime mess/]
*dissension 17-18-5 (n.) 1. disagreement among those expected to cooperate 2. a conflict of people's opinions or actions or characters [difference disagreement dispute diss diversity division idea inequality infighting interest irritable secession serious shrewish speech split strife enmity expect negative noncooperation obstinate open opinion opposition /ness/]
*dissent 06-38-51 (n.) 1. (law) the difference of one judge's opinion from that of the majority 2. a difference of opinion 3. the act of protesting; a public (often organized) manifestation of dissent (v.) 1. withhold assent 2. be of different opinions 3. fight back, also metaphorically [deal decline demand demonstration deny departure different disagree disagreement discord disillusion dispute diss dissident doctrine impose indignant inequality infighting inharmonious interference issue sectary show shrill sign speech stop strike structure support establish exclusion express nature nay negate negative non noncooperation nonobservance norm train truth /ness/] "he expressed his dissent in a contrary opinion"
*dissertation 15-36-7 (n.) 1. a treatise advancing a new

point of view resulting from research; usually a requirement for an advanced academic degree [degree descant discourse discussion disquisition diss sketch speak study submit survey essay examination exposition require research theme thesis tract treatment academic advance argumentation article outline note /tres tress/]
*disservice 13-43-10 (n.) 1. an act intended to help that turns out badly [damage difficulty disfavor ill imposition injury injustice intend service] "he did them a disservice"
*dissimilar 14-65-8 (a.) 1. not similar 2. not alike or similar 3. not like; marked by dissimilarity [degree depart differ disagree disparate distinguished divergent inharmonious irreconcilable separate several similar many mark motley multifarious antithetic antonym approach assorted resemblance /miss/] "a group of very dissimilar people"
*dissipate 11-40-16 (v.) 1. move away from each other 2. spend frivolously and unwisely 3. to cause to separate and go in different directions, of crowds, for example 4. live a life or pleasure, esp. with respect to alcoholic consumption [debauched decrease degenerate degraded die different direction disappear disintegrate disperse diss distribute division drive drop impoverish inheritance irretrievable scatter separation shoot short shrink small spend spent split spread squander storm style swing part party perish philander pleasure profligate abandon abate ablate aerosolize alcoholic apart approach attenuate throw erode exhaust exit expend extravagant /piss tapis/]
*dissipation 23-48-1 (n.) 1. breaking up and scattering by dispersion 2. dissolute indulgence in sensual pleasure 3. useless or profitless activity; using or expending or consuming thoughtlessly or carelessly [debauchery degeneracy departure devotion disappear dispersion distribution impoverish incontinent indulgence intemperate scattering sensual sow specific spent spread spreading squander strew passing patio pepper physical pleasure prodigal profligate publication pursuit abandon abate amusement anger anxiety appetite attrition thoughtless occult orgy natural /piss tapis/] "the dissipation of the mist"
*dissolute 19-66-3 (a.) 1. unrestrained by convention or morality [debauched decadent degenerate degraded depraved draw immoral incontinent indulge intemperate self slack society solute overindulge lax libertine light live loose unbridled unprincipled unrestrained taint /loss/]
*dissolution 14-41-9 (n.) 1. separation into component parts 2. the process of going into solution 3. the termination of a meeting 4. the termination of a relationship 5. dissolute indulgence in sensual pleasure [death decompose demise departure destruction disappear disband disintegration division divorce down immoderate inconsistency indulgence institution intent salt sensual separation silence sleep small solid solution split suspension occult overthrow oxidize law leach legal licentiousnes liquid undo termination thaw nature /loss/]
*dissolve 06-44-55 (n.) 1. (film) a gradual transition from one scene to the next; the next scene is gradually superimposed as the former scene fades out (v.) 1. stop functioning, as of organizations or groups 2. pass into a solution 3. terminate (legally) 4. become weaker, as of sound or vision 5. cause to go into a solution 6. lose control emotionally [decline defrost die disappear disband disconcert disintegrate dismissal disperse down ice image incinerate infuse internal separate shoot solid solve sugar organization laugh law leach legal liquidize liquify lose vacate vanish vise void erode evaporate exit expire /loss/] "The recipe says that we should dissolve a cup of sugar in two cups of water"
*dissonance 15-23-7 (n.) 1. a conflict of people's opinions or actions or characters 2. disagreeable sounds 3. the auditory experience of sound that lacks musical quality; sound that is a disagreeable auditory experience [difference disagreement discord displease distinct idea inconsistency inequality inharmony interest irreconcilable separate serious sharp simultaneousl sonance sound stimulus strife odds opposition otherness negation noise nonconformity note antagonism argumentation atonality attribute auditory character clash combination confuse consonance controversy /nano/]
*dissonant 17-22-5 (a.) 1. not musical in nature 2. lacking in harmony 3. (music) characterized by musical dissonance; harmonically unresolved [depart disagree disharmony diss distinguished immiscible incorporate inharmonious irreconcilable separate several sharp sound structure off nature negative non note antagonistic artistic assorted atonal auditory tone tuneless /nano/]
*dissuade 11-52-15 (v.) 1. turn away from by persuasion [deter discourage diss divert intimidate urge admonish adopt advise arm exhort expostulate] "Negative campaigning will only dissuade people"
*distant 04-51-102 (a.) 1. far apart in relevance or relationship 2. separated in space or time or coming from or going to a distance 3. remote in manner 4. far distant in space 5. far distant in time [deep degree detached dignity dim discern diverse icy improbable indistinct intimate isolated sack seclude secret self separate short show situate slight smile soft sound space stan star stiff telephone ten town traffic adjacent aloof apart arrogant away non] "the distant past"
*distemper 23-63-1 (n.) 1. any of various infectious diseases of animals (v.) 1. paint with distemper [disease disorder disturb illness indisposition infirmity sign symptom syndrome temper tempera thinner tincture malaise medium muddle paint pathology peevish pip riot rocky rot /met/]
*distend 21-56-2 (v.) 1. become wider 2. swell from or as if from internal pressure [develop diastole dilate

dilation dimension drench dropsy dumpy imposing increase inflate inflation internal intestine intumescence scope size snowball soak stalwart starve stomach strain stretch swell swollen tend tension testes thickset tight tubby tum tumescent tumor turgid ectasia edema enlarge expand expansive extensive normal]
*distill 15-44-7 (v.) 1. extract by the process of distillation 2. undergo the process of distillation; of liquids 3. remove impurities from, increase the concentration of, and separate through the process of distiilation 4. undergo condensation; change from a gaseous to a liquid state and fall in drops 5. give off (a liquid) [deal decontaminate depurate develop different disinfectant doctor dribble drop due illegal important improve impurity increase infuse sanitize science screen separate slow smoke specific spirit still sublimate substance temperature transude trickle trill try large leach liquify long lose]
*distillation 17-43-5 (n.) 1. the process of purifying a liquid by boiling it and condensing its vapors 2. a purified liquid produced by condensation from a vapor during distilling; the product of distilling [decontamination distill dribble drop image implication infusion intent invention issue separate smoke soul stuff substance summation temperature thermogenesis tincture large leach leak liquor long aerate artifact aspect atomize opera originate outcome narrow nature nub /tall/]
*distiller 16-52-6 (n.) 1. someone who distills alcoholic liquors [distill liquor]
*distinction 05-43-86 (n.) 1. a distinguishing difference 2. a distinguishing quality 3. high status importance owing to marked superiority 4. a discrimination between things as different and distinct [decoration demarcation departure direct dissimilarity distinct division idiosyncrasy illustrious importance individualism inequality separation significance smooth trait natural neat noble note change clear contrast credit odds opposition ornament] "it is necessary to make a distinction between love and infatuation"
*distort 06-45-50 (v.) 1. form into a spiral shape 2. make false by mutilation or addition; as of a message or story 3. distort 4. twist and press out of shape 5. alter the shape of (something) by stress [defective deflect deform deformed different disfigure disguise disorder divert dummy ill illegitimate image imitation impact inaccurate infect influence intend irregular scar scattered shape signal snarl spin spiral split spoil spring squeeze story strain stretch taint tangle thread tin tinge tort torture touch translation travesty twist obfuscate obscure off out overstate rationalize ravage refrangible reproduce /trot/]
*distraught 10-63-19 (a.) 1. deeply agitated especially from emotion [daft deeply dismay disturbed insane irrational senseless sick strange torment touched trouble rambling abroad adrift agitate aught unbalance unsettled upset grief guess hallucinate harass hysterical /guar/] "distraught with grief"
*distress 05-60-64 (n.) 1. a state of adversity (danger or affliction or need) 2. psychological suffering 3. extreme physical pain 4. the seizure and holding of property as security for payment of a debt or satisfaction of a claim (v.) 1. cause mental pain to [damage danger deadly death debt decision deeply deplorable destroy difficulty discomfort disorder disturb down improper infect injury inordinate intolerable isolation sad satisfaction security seizure sharp shock shoot situation social sorrow staggering stress strong struggle suffering symptom taint tenant terribly torment torture touching toxic trial trouble try rack rasp regrettable revelation rigor rub rueful economic embarrassment emotional excessive excruciating execution expropriate extremely] "the death of his wife caused him great distress"
*distrust 09-43-25 (n.) 1. doubt about someone's honesty 2. the trait of not trusting others (v.) 1. regard as untrustworthy; regard with suspicion; have no faith or confidence in [disbelieve discredit dishonest dispute doubt dubious incertitude incredulity invidious shy skepticism suspicious swear trait trust trusting refuse reject reliable rely uncertainty uneasy unlikely unreliable unsure untrustworthy]
*dither 13-76-10 (n.) 1. an excited state of agitation (v.) 1. act nervously; be undecided; be uncertain 2. make a fuss; be agitated 3. shake, as from cold or fear [dally dawdle desire display disturbance dit dot dote drivel drool illusion image indecisive inquietude intermediate involuntarily irritate teeter terrible theft tiny tizzy turbulence turmoil halt heave hesitate emotional equivocate excessive excited extreme reflexive represent restless rictus] "he was in a dither"
*divergence 17-52-5 (n.) 1. the act of moving away in different direction from a common point 2. a variation that deviates from the standard or norm 3. a difference between conflicting facts or claims or opinions 4. degree of spatial separation 5. an infinite series that has no limit [degree departure develop deviation different direction disagreement discrepancy disorder disparity dissimilar distribution diverge divide drift infinite influence instance interest value variation vessel expand expect expression eye rate give net normal claim clash conflict corner current] "an angle is formed by the divergence of two straight lines"
*divergent 15-26-7 (a.) 1. diverging from another or from a standard 2. tending to move apart in different directions [degree depart describe deviate differ direction disagree distinguished diverge idiosyncrasy improve incline increase irregular value various vary eccentric equal erratic exceptional express radiate rebuild revive right rough grating great nature negative nonconformist nutty tend transmute twist] "a divergent opinion"
*diverse 05-42-83 (a.) 1. distinctly dissimilar or unlike

2. many and different [degree depart differ disagree disparate dissimilar distinctly distinguished diver inclusive inharmonious interest irreconcilable various vary verse ethnic separate several sloth socioeconomic student sundry]
*diversion 08-41-27 (n.) 1. an attack calculated to draw enemy defense away from the point of the principal attack 2. a turning aside (of your course or attention or concern) 3. an activity that diverts or amuses or stimulates [dance deflexion departure detail deviation difference digression direction distraction divagate dive double drive improvement infiltrate investment version embezzle enjoyment entertainment reality recreational renewal retreat reverse revolution road romp routine rule rush saltation sheer sport stake step strike sunshine offensive onslaught overthrow] "scuba diving is provided as a diversion for tourists"
*diversity 05-45-67 (n.) 1. noticeable heterogeneity 2. the condition or result of being changed [departure difference discrepancy distinct diver improvement inclusive individuality inequality institution variety ethnic expect extent range renewal revolution separate shift style switch transition turnabout] "a diversity of possibilities"
*divert 06-53-59 (v.) 1. occupy in an agreeable, entertaining or pleasant fashion 2. send on a course or in a direction different from the planned or intended one 3. turn aside; turn away from 4. withdraw (money) and move into a different location, often secretly and with dishonest intentions [deflect delight depart deter detour deviate different digress direction discourage dishonest disport dissuade distract diver draw indispose intention interest veer via violate engage entertainment erratic exhilarate expect recreate redirect regale relax remove repel river route tickle titillate traffic travel turn twist]
*divest 11-33-14 (v.) 1. take away possessions from someone 2. deprive of status or authority 3. take away one's investment [damage death denial denude deny deprive destruction disarm discharge dismantle dispose disrobe dissociate dives down drain draw dry duty impoverish injury investment vest estate exhaust expel expense expose sacrifice separate sex shear showing skin source spoil spoliation status strip supply takeoff tap throne]
*divestiture 03-AA-155 (n.) 1. an order to an offending party to rid itself of property; it has the purpose of depriving the defendant of the gains of wrongful behavior [defendant deprive dispossession divest division impose instance issue sale sell stock subsidiary refrain removal require rid rule] "the court found divestiture to be necessary in preventing a monopoly"
*divination 23-52-1 (n.) 1. a prediction uttered under divine inspiration 2. the art or gift of prophecy (or the pretense of prophecy) by supernatural means [dead discover divine down dowse dream incomplete infallible insight inspiration interpretation intuitive vampirism vatic voodooism nation necromancy alchemy allegorical anticipatory apocalyptic arrange art attempt augury talisman telling thaumaturgy theurgy thrown tide obeah obscure obtain omen opinion oracle oracular]
*divinity 14-38-8 (n.) 1. the quality of being divine 2. any supernatural being worshipped as controlling some part of the world or some aspect of life or who is the personification of a force 3. white creamy fudge made with egg whites 4. the rational and systematic study of religion and its influences and of the nature of religious truth [deal death declared defense deity demigod destiny discipline distinguishing divine doctrine dream idol immortal incorporeal individual infant influence innocent inspiration vegetation victory virtuous voodoo nature nit nut teach tend theology torment truth] "ancient Egyptians believed in the divinity of the Pharaohs"
*divulge 11-46-16 (v.) 1. make known to the public information that was previously known only to a few people or that was meant to be kept a secret [declaration develop diclose directly discover display illuminate impart incarnate indiscretion van ventilate unexpected unfold unintentional utter leak let give giveaway gossip entry evident exclusion exhibit explore expose express]
*docile 16-48-6 (a.) 1. willing to be taught or led or supervised or directed 2. easily handled or managed 3. ready and willing to be taught [direct disposed doc domesticate ductile dutiful obedient old clever command comply consent control impressionable incline instruction intelligent lead eager easy edmund educate enslave enthusiastic /cod/] "the docile masses of an enslaved nation"
*docket 19-13-3 (n.) 1. (law) the calendar of a court; the list of cases to be tried or a summary of the court's activities 2. a temporally organized plan for matters to be attended to (v.) 1. in law: place on the docket for legal action 2. in law: make a summary or abstract of a legal document and inscribe it in a list [delivery detail diary dock document dossier duty organize calendar card carry case certificate chit collection confirm content court credit custom cut keep enroll enter entry tab tag tape temporal ticket timetable try /cod/] "Only 5 of the 120 cases docketed were tried"
*document 02-45-353 (n.) 1. anything serving as a representation of a person's thinking by means of symbolic marks 2. writing that provides information (especially information of an official nature) 3. a written account of ownership or obligation 4. (computer science) a computer file that contains text (and possibly formatting instructions) using 7-bit ASCII characters (v.) 1. support with evidence 2. record in detail [decisive deed demonstrate describe detail down official opus original overwhelming certain chronicle clause confirm convince copy corroborate cum cumulative undergird uphold manuscript material matter minute monument enrol enter essay evidentiary example

expenditure name nonfiction nuncupative telling testimony transcription typescript /cod emu/] "The parents documented every step of their child's development"
*doe 13-48-10 (n.) 1. mature female of mammals of which the male is called 'buck' [dam department drake dromedary okapi economic eland elk energy eutherian ewe except executive expertise]
*doggerel 23-52-1 (n.) 1. a comic verse of irregular measure [ditty dogger dysphemism outlandish garbage gibberish graceless gross rhyme rhythm rubbish rude limerick low /egg god/] "he had heard some silly doggerel that kept running through his mind"
*dogma 14-47-9 (n.) 1. a religious doctrine that is proclaimed as true without proof 2. a doctrine or code of beliefs accepted as authoritative [divided doctrine dog generally gospel group maxim moral accept authoritative axiom /god/] "he believed all the Marxist dogma"
*dogmatic 16-55-6 (a.) 1. characterized by arrogant assertion of unproved or unprovable principles 2. relating to or involving dogma [derive doctrine dogged dogma doubtless obdurate obstinate opinion oracular gospel magisterial moral mulish arbitrary arrogant assertion assured tenacious tenet tolerance twist inflexible influence insistent interested certain church confident convince creed /god/] "dogmatic writings"
*doleful 18-60-4 (a.) 1. filled with or evoking sadness [dejected depressing despondent distress dole downcast dreary lamentable lugubrious evoke experience expression eye fill forlorn funereal unhappy] "the child's doleful expression"
*dolt 23-48-1 (n.) 1. a person who is not very bright [deliberate dol donkey dope dullard dummy oaf offensive lack lightweight loon lout twit]
*domain 07-52-40 (n.) 1. territory over which rule or control is exercised 2. a particular environment or walk of life 3. the set of values of the independent variable for which a function is defined 4. a knowledge domain that you are interested in or are communicating about 5. people in general; especially a distinctive group of people with some shared interest [define demesne direction discipline discourse distinctive dominion duke occupy ology online opinion orb orbit organization orient ownership magnetism main mandatory manor march material mathematics abstract academic acre archduke area arena art atom influence nation nationality /mod/]
*domesticity 17-57-5 (n.) 1. the quality of being domestic or domesticated 2. domestic activities or life [distinguishing domestic married matter essential specific comfort concern creature /mod/] "a royal family living in unpretentious domesticity"
*domicile 16-86-6 (n.) 1. housing that someone is living in (v.) 1. make one's home or live in [desert dig domic domiciliate dwell occupy old inhabit island camp cantonment cohabit crib live locate lodgment look entertain establish /mod/]
*dominance 06-61-51 (n.) 1. the state that exists when one person or group has power over another 2. superior development of one side of the body 3. the power or right to give orders or make decisions [decision deed defeat despotism determine development direct dominion offspring overlord magnetism mastery moment importance insinuation issue nance animal arrest ascendancy ascendant attention attribute authority authorization coercive community complete consequence control credit effective enchantment esteem exclusive exert exist expression /mod/] "her apparent dominance of her husband was really her attempt to make him pay attention to her"
*dominant 04-47-93 (a.) 1. exercising influence or control 2. of genes; producing the same phenotype whether its allele is identical or dissimilar (n.) 1. (music) the fifth note of the diatonic scale [defeat demisemiquaver describe diatonic dissimilar duration official officious offspring opinion ordinary outstanding overriding main major manner marriage master mina minor molding musical identical imperative important incorporate influential normal notation note number absolute allele animal artistic ascendant assertive auditory authoritarian authorize average tone totalitarian triumphant /mod/] "television plays a dominant role in molding public opinion"
*dominate 02-51-313 (v.) 1. be in control; rule the roost 2. have dominance or the power to defeat over 3. be larger in number, quantity, power, status or importance 4. look down on [defeat dictate direct disenfranchise down dwarf obtain occupy outbalance outweigh overtop manage master mesmerize method mina idea important influential neighborhood appear area aspect authority top tower town twist effect element elevated emotion enslave enter enthrall excessive exert /mod/]
*domination 08-57-31 (n.) 1. power to dominate or defeat 2. social control by dominating [defeat despotism dictatorship dominion oppress organization overlord market mastery might moment monopolizatio importance insinuation nation nine absolutism angel ascendancy authority terrorism thrall traditional transcend tyranny /mod/]
*donate 04-41-107 (v.) 1. give to a charity or good cause [death devote dispense offer organ orphanage accord alive allow amount atom award tender tissue treatment earthquake eat electron endow extend /nod/] "I donated blood to the Red Cross for the victims of the earthquake"
*donor 05-44-77 (n.) 1. person who makes a gift of property 2. (medicine) someone who gives blood or tissue or an organ to be used in another person (the host) [deal don donation donator organ necessary negative non relinquish reproductive retail return /nod/]
*dormant 10-41-19 (a.) 1. of e.g. volcanos; temporarily

inactive 2. not active but capable of becoming active 3. (biology) in a condition of biological rest or suspended animation 4. (heraldry) lying with head on paws as if sleeping [deadline deathly describe develop device doldrums dorm droopy drug dry dull oblivious obscure out relaxation responsibility rest resting meditation mental metabolism monotonous moribund mystic abeyance adverse aestivate affection animal animation apathy armorial asleep awaken neutral numb tame temporary torpid trace /rod/] "a dormant volcano"
*dote 14-55-9 (v.) 1. be foolish or senile due to old age 2. shower with love; show excessive affection for [dear decline demonstrate devoted dither dot drivel drool due old thoughtless trusting twin enjoy excessive extreme /tod/] "Grandmother dotes on her the twins"
*doublet 23-81-1 (n.) 1. a man's close-fitting jacket; worn during the Renaissance [derivative design different distortion double dress duet duo optics base both brace language layer lens letter line linguistics eponym error etymon team thin twain two]
*doubly 12-62-13 (ad.) 1. to double the degree 2. in a twofold manner [degree different usual bright] "she was doubly rewarded"
*dowry 19-64-3 (n.) 1. money or property brought by a woman to her husband at marriage [dot dow dower dowery wed woman wry require]
*dragnet 21-21-2 (n.) 1. a conical fishnet dragged through the water at great depths [depth drag draw ransack river rummage abduct across apprehend apprehension game grab great group nab net noose element enclose exploration toil tracking trap trawl]
*dragoon 18-84-4 (n.) 1. a member of a European military unit formerly composed of heavily armed cavalrymen (v.) 1. compel by coercion, threats, or crude means 2. subjugate by imposing troops [demoralize dinner drag railroad regiment retain ruffle armed army origin necessity]
*drainage 11-60-16 (n.) 1. emptying accomplished by draining [debit deplete disburse discharge draft drain drawing remove runoff accomplish aspiration insolation gush eliminate empty evacuation expense]
*dramatist 11-64-15 (n.) 1. someone who writes plays [drama dramaturge review albee anderson annalist monograph tragedian screenwriter scriptwriter storyteller]
*dramatize 10-01-17 (v.) 1. represent something in a dramatic manner 2. add details to 3. put into dramatic form [demonstrate detail develop display drama radio real represent responsibility reveal rollout adapt add adopt affect aggrandize amplify assume attention magnify manifest manner mean mount television theatrical today token truth tryout turn illuminate importance incarnate indite embellish embroider enlarge evidence exaggerate exhibit express /zit/]
*drastic 05-37-60 (a.) 1. forceful and extreme and rigorous [degree desperate dire radical rigorous rough acute amount severe sharp significant strength strong sweep tic tough immoderate intense call consequence considerably crisis cut /tsar/] "drastic measures"
*drawl 13-59-10 (n.) 1. a slow speech pattern with prolonged vowels (v.) 1. in particular, draw out the vowels [deliberation distinctive down draw reluctance roar rumble accent articulate awl wail way whine whisper lazy leisurely lengthen lilt /war ward/]
*droll 14-48-9 (a.) 1. comical in an odd or whimsical manner [rich ridiculous risible roll odd laughable little ludicrous /lord/] "a droll little man with a quiet tongue-in-cheek kind of humor"
*drone 10-53-19 (n.) 1. an unchanging intonation 2. stingless male bee in a colony of social bees (especially honeybees) whose sole function is to mate with the queen 3. someone who takes more time than necessary; someone who lags behind 4. a pipe of the bagpipe that is tuned to produce a single continuous tone 5. an aircraft without a pilot that is operated by remote control (v.) 1. make a monotonous low dull sound 2. talk in a monotonous voice [dawdle descent dragon dull range remote require rise round run one operate orderly necessary nexus noise non note numerous express]
*drought 06-42-44 (n.) 1. a prolonged shortage 2. a temporary shortage of rainfall [dearth defective deficiency deficit dry dryness rainfall relish replenish omission ought grow hungry tapeworm taste temporary thirsty]
*drowsiness 21-60-2 (n.) 1. a very sleepy state [driving dull oscitancy wakeful sleepy somnolent stupor]
*drowsy 17-55-5 (a.) 1. half asleep 2. showing lack of attention or boredom [disturb dope doze dozy dreamy driving drow dull restful ride rock oscitant wakeful weary seem show sleepy slow sluggish snooze somnolent soothe still stretch stupor summer yawn /sword word/] "made drowsy by the long ride"
*drudgery 17-60-5 (n.) 1. hard monotonous routine work [donkeywork drudge routine unpleasant graft grind employment exhaust]
*dubious 06-59-50 (a.) 1. open to doubt or suspicion 2. fraught with uncertainty or doubt 3. not convinced [dark debatable dishonest distrustful doubt doubtful downright unbelievable uncertainty unconvinced undecided unlikely unquestionable unsavory unsure untrustworthy base beguile bio immoral imprecise improbable indeed indicate influential insecure intention open outcome shady shy sinister sure suspicious /bud/]
*duckling 16-49-6 (n.) 1. flesh of a young domestic duck 2. young duck [darling depress doll domesticate duck calf chick colt cub cygnet kid kit kitten lamb lambkin leg leveret litter lover nestle goose gosling grouse /ilk/]
*dud 16-67-6 (a.) 1. failing to detonate; especially not charged with an active explosive (n.) 1. (informal) someone who is unsuccessful 2. an explosion that fails to occur 3. an event that fails badly or is totally

ineffectual [detonate duff dummy unload unsuccessful useless] "he stepped on a dud mine"
*duet 07-38-40 (n.) 1. two items of the same kind 2. a pair who associate with one another 3. a musical composition for two performers 4. two performers or singers who perform together 5. a dance for two people (usually a ballerina and a danseur noble) [dancer danseur deal deuce distich doublet duad due duo dyad ecumenism engage equal terpsichore theatrical trio twain two twosome]
*dulcet 23-55-1 (a.) 1. extremely pleasant in a gentle way 2. pleasing to the ear [desirable unmelodious unpleasant likable like catchy cello cheerful constitute cordial ear engaging enjoyable extremely taste tone tune tuneful /tec/] "the most dulcet swimming on the most beautiful and remote beaches"
*dun 08-35-29 (a.) 1. of a dull grayish brown to brownish gray color (n.) 1. horse of a dull brownish gray color 2. a color varying around light grayish brown (v.) 1. treat cruelly 2. cure by salting 3. make a dun color 4. persistently ask for overdue payment [dark day debt demand demanding dim drab dreary drive dry dull dusky umber unsaturated urge urgent nag nagging needle nerve] "the dun and dreary prairie"
*dupe 11-60-14 (n.) 1. a person who is tricked or swindled (v.) 1. fool or hoax [deception defenseless delude device double duck dup dust unsophisticated untruth pawn pay persuade pigeon prank pull puppet easy exploit] "The immigrant was duped because he trusted everyone"
*duplex 11-36-14 (a.) 1. (used technically of a device or process) having two parts 2. (telecommunication) allowing communication in opposite directions simultaneously (n.) 1. a house with two units sharing a common wall 2. an apartment having rooms on two floors that are connected by a staircase [detached device dichotomy direction distance divide double duple duplicate dwell pair part perform process line living loft efficiency electronics engineering entity entrance equivalent] "a duplex transaction"
*duplicity 15-52-7 (n.) 1. a fraudulent or duplicitous representation 2. acting in bad faith; deception by pretending to entertain one set of intentions while acting under the influence of another [deal deceptive dichotomy dishonesty disloyalty dissemble double unfaithfulnes pair pairing perfidy polarity pretend licit indirection influence insidious intention irony condition conjugation constellation craft cunning treachery twin]
*duration 08-56-28 (n.) 1. the property of enduring or continuing in time 2. continuance in time 3. the period of time during which something continues [dull durable unbroken ration require rigid run age amount antiquity arrange art attribute temporal tenure term tide transient traverse immovable immutable impermanent indefinitely interval inveterate note] "the ceremony was of short duration"
*duress 17-51-5 (n.) 1. compulsory force or threat [detention dint drive dure restraint effect effectual energy steam strength superpower suspect] "confessed under duress"
*dutiful 10-45-17 (a.) 1. willingly obedient out of a sense of duty and respect [deferential devoted devout diligent duteous duty theism instruction faithful filial flexible fulfill little loyal /fit/] "a dutiful child"
*dwarf 07-58-38 (a.) 1. atypically small (n.) 1. a person who is abnormally small 2. a legendary creature resembling a tiny old man; lives in the depths of the earth and guards buried treasure (v.) 1. cast a shadow [deface defect deficiency depth development dictate direct disfigure dole dominate dot down due war wart watery wee whit wizened abnormal abstemious ace animal appear ascetic astronomy atom atypical austere average race reason resemble response rickety rudimentary runty faery fairy fay flatfooted fleck form fragment frugal] "dwarf tree"
*dwindle 06-43-46 (v.) 1. become smaller or lose substance [decline decrease deduct die diminish disappear drop dying wane weaken wilt wind worsen impassive intensity isolated languish lapse lessen little lose lull erode evaporate exit] "Her savings dwindled down"
*dynamics 07-36-34 (n.) 1. the branch of mechanics concerned with the forces that cause motions of bodies [deal different diminuendo dynamic activity actuate aspect mark mechanics moral motion motivation movement moving musical incentive change church concern crescendo science situation soft sphere spiritual statics stirring study subtlety /any man many/]
*dynamo 10-85-17 (n.) 1. generator consisting of a coil (the armature) that rotates between the poles of an electromagnet (the field magnet) causing a current to flow in the armature [direct nam armature machine magnetic mechanical motor /any man many/]
*dyne 21-90-2 (n.) 1. a unit of force equal to the force that imparts an acceleration of 1 cm/sec/sec to a mass of 1 gram [decagram decigram newton energid equal erg]

E

*earnest 05-48-67 (a.) 1. characterized by a firm and humorless belief in the validity of your opinions 2. not distracted by anything unrelated to the goal 3. earnest (n.) 1. something of value given by one person to another to bind a contract [eager ear engrossment enthusiastic entirely escrow excessive exhaustive existence abandon active alert ardent arne assiduous assurance attitude aware relentless remark resolved respect retirement nice niggling note notice security seller serious serve side sincerity sober social solemn spirit steady strong success support surety tenacity thorough thoughtful triviality tyrant] "both sides were deeply in earnest, even passionate"
*earthenware 19-36-3 (n.) 1. ceramic ware made of porous clay fired at low heat [earthen enamelware aegean appliance reddish tableware temperature terra tin tinware hard hardware heat highly hollowware housewares ware white woodenware /awn/]
*ebullient 10-50-19 (a.) 1. joyously unrestrained [energy enthusiastic excite excited exhilarate expression exuberant bake beat boiling bouncy bright brightness brisk bubble bull unrestrained life lively impassioned inflame thrill toast torrid /lube/]
*eccentric 05-61-65 (a.) 1. not having a common center; not concentric 2. conspicuously or grossly unconventional or unusual (n.) 1. a person with an unusual or odd personality 2. a person of a specified

kind (usually with many eccentricities) [elliptical engineering erratic exceptional capable case caution centric character circular clothe combination component conformist conspicuous convert crank natural nut nutty teenager tramp twist type rabbit real reciprocate revolution rich ridiculous rotary rough idiosyncrasy impulsive irresponsible]
*eccentricity 11-61-15 (n.) 1. strange and unconventional behavior 2. (geometry) a ratio describing the shape of a conic section; the ratio of the distance between the foci to the length of the major axis 3. a circularity that has a different center or deviates from a circular path [easily eccentric ellipse engineering equal explain express cast center character circularity conic constant constitution correspond curve nature nutty tendency true twist type ratio restless rich rod rotate roughness round idiosyncrasy inept inferiority inside instance irregularity] "a circle is an ellipse with zero eccentricity"
*eclectic 07-45-35 (a.) 1. selecting what seems best of various styles or ideas (n.) 1. someone who selects according to the eclectic method [electoral empirical existential extensive careful catholic choose collection combined comprehensive taste theism tic idea indicate integrate intricate ironic]
*eclipse 06-63-48 (n.) 1. one celestial body obscures another (v.) 1. cause an eclipse of (a celestial body) by intervention 2. exceed in importance; outweigh 3. cause an eclipse of; of celestial bodies [earth economics eliminate emersion excel extinguish cast celestial clip completely conceal cope cover curtain layover light loss immersion incrustation intervention partial passing performance place plasterwork popular powerful prior putdown screening shadow shining side slump solar stand star status successful sun supply surpass]
*economize 23-01-1 (v.) 1. use cautiously and frugally 2. spend sparingly, avoid the waste of [energy expenditure careful cautious con conserve curtail cut cutback money move /mono/] "I try to economize my spare time"
*ecstasy 10-67-20 (n.) 1. a state of elated bliss 2. a state of being carried away by overwhelming emotion 3. a stimulant drug that is chemically related to mescaline and amphetamine and is used illicitly for its euphoric and hallucinogenic effects; it was formerly used in psychotherapy but in 1985 it was declared illegal in the United States [effect elation emotion euphoric exaltation excite excitement exhilarate experience extreme exuberant carry cheerful chemical cloud consciousness craze self serotonin seventh sexual sexy soul spirit stimulant street stupor sweet thrill transport abandon adam affectionate amorous amphetamine avoid /sat/]
*ecstatic 09-51-23 (a.) 1. feeling great rapture or delight [elated elsewhere emotion entrance euphoric excite excited experience completely sent show spell stargaze static storm thrill trance transported abandon absorbed abstract intense intoxicate]
*ecumenical 14-46-8 (a.) 1. concerned with promoting unity among churches or religions 2. of worldwide scope or applicability [experience catholic christopher church combined comprehensive concern cosmopolitan unbigoted unity universal mix morley move mutual national non ical import inclusive insecta inter international issue applicable /cine emu/] "ecumenical thinking"
*eddy 13-42-11 (n.) 1. founder of Christian Science in 1866 (1821-1910) 2. a miniature whirlpool or whirlwind resulting when the current of a fluid doubles back on itself (v.) 1. flow in a circular current, of liquids [ebullition effervesce deity devotion disturbance doubles dying yeasty]
*edible 12-48-13 (a.) 1. suitable for use as food (n.) 1. any substance that can be used as food [easy eat eatable energy esculent dainty delicious digestible ingesta board build /bid bide/]
*edict 14-52-9 (n.) 1. a formal or authoritative proclamation 2. a legally binding command or decision entered on the court record (as if issued by a court or judge) [enactment encyclical enter enunciate date decision declaration decree deliberation dictum diktat directive divorce document impose instrument issue canon certain character circular codify collection committee communique company couple court trouble /cide/]
*edify 18-57-4 (v.) 1. make understand [educate encourage enhance enlighten enrich demonstrate didactic direct disciplinary illuminate impart improve improvement inform informative instruct intellectual introductory irradiate favor forward foster /fid/]
*editorial 03-13-230 (a.) 1. of or relating to an article stating opinions or giving perspectives 2. relating to or characteristic of an editor (n.) 1. an article giving opinions or perspectives [editor enlighten essay expository express daily demonstrative devoted duty illustrative independent tabloid train opinion remark report reportorial review advertisement analysis annotate article /lair roti tide/] "editorial column"
*efface 13-53-11 (v.) 1. remove completely from recognition or memory 2. make inconspicuous 3. remove by or as if by rubbing or erasing [eliminate eradicate erase erode exclude face formula analogous annul camp cancel completely crossing cut /caff/] "efface the memory of the time in the camps"
*effect 01-48-906 (n.) 1. the central meaning or theme of a speech or literary work 2. an impression (especially one that is artificial or contrived) 3. a symptom caused by an illness or a drug 4. (of a law) having legal validity 5. an outward appearance 6. a phenomenon that follows and is caused by some previous phenomenon (v.) 1. act so as to bring about 2. cause to happen or occur [eff end energy essential figure form found fulfill cause clobber

commodity control core crap credit thing] "the magnetic effect was greater when the rod was lengthwise"
*effective 01-52-581 (a.) 1. existing in fact; not theoretical; real 2. able to accomplish a purpose; functioning effectively 3. exerting force or influence 4. works well as a means or remedy 5. producing or capable of producing an intended result or having a striking effect 6. (military) equipped and ready for service [effect effectual efficient eloquent energy essential excellent fact feasible fervent firm fluent force forcible function championship charming cogent commendable competent control convince cutting technical trenchant imperium important impressive incisive inefficacious influential valid valuable vehement vigorous virtue vital vivid] "an air-cooled motor was more effective than a witch's broomstick for rapid long-distance transportation"
*effeminate 19-63-3 (a.) 1. having unsuitable feminine qualities 2. characterized by excessive softness or self-indulgence [emasculate epicene excessive feminine flimsy fragile frail manly mannish masculinity metaphoricall mina muliebrity absence appearance autoerotic tacky tradition transvestite /anime/] "an effeminate civilization"
*effervesce 21-51-2 (v.) 1. of liquids [eddy eff emit energy enthusiasm escape excite exist exuberant ferment fizz fizzle flurry foam form froth frothy fume refer rhapsodize rhonchus ruffle verve vibrant vitality vivacity vortex simmer sound soup sparkle spirited spit squash stir swirl carbonate commotion consistency]
*effervescent 17-56-5 (a.) 1. used of wines and waters; charged naturally or artificially with carbon dioxide 2. marked by high spirits or excitement 3. (of a liquid) giving off bubbles [effervesce energy enthusiastic excitement fertile fire fizzy foamy form frothy full resilient rouse row vesicular vibrant vivacious volatile scintillating sparkle spirit spirited stimulate carbonate charge cheerleader chiffon chipper conversation naturally thrill tingly tiny]
*effete 18-65-4 (a.) 1. marked by excessive self-indulgence and moral decay [empty erode excessive exhaust fall fete finished flat tasteless tedious tired /teff/]
*efficacious 23-59-1 (a.) 1. marked by qualities giving the power to produce an intended effect 2. producing or capable of producing an intended result or having a striking effect [eff effectual efficient effort enchanting entrance estimable expense force formal functional impel important improve ineffective influential intend capable charming chemical complaint cool cough able active adequate operative useful utile service step stop striking strong substantial successful] "written propaganda is less efficacious than the habits and prejudices...of the readers"
*efficacy 13-57-11 (n.) 1. capacity or power to produce a desired effect [eff effectual capacity]
*efficiency 05-53-86 (n.) 1. skillfulness in avoiding wasted time and effort 2. the ratio of the output to the input of any system [eff effective effectual efficient effort energy expert express facility fitness fitted fuel ingenuity input capacity cognitive command competence control] "she did the work with great efficiency"
*efficient 03-52-151 (a.) 1. able to accomplish a purpose; functioning effectively 2. being effective without wasting time or effort or expense [economical economically eff effectual efficacious effort engine excellent expense expert feasible fit fuel function inexpensive ingenious intend capable capably clever competent convenient cost neat nimble nothing task thrifty] "an efficient production manager"
*effigy 16-65-6 (n.) 1. a representation of a person (especially in the form of sculpture) [eff emperor famous fawkes fellow figurine form frighten icon idol image insult intentional god guy] "the coin bears an effigy of Lincoln"
*efflorescence 23-37-1 (n.) 1. the period of greatest prosperity or productivity 2. the time and process of budding and unfolding of blossoms 3. a powdery deposit on a surface 4. any red eruption of the skin [eruption florescence flourish flowering flush food formation full level literary loss obstruction ontogeny organism reach red response roseola simple skill skin spring substance surface sweat symptom change chemistry complex crystal culmination natural nettle]
*effrontery 23-70-1 (n.) 1. audacious (even arrogant) behavior that you have no right to [face front right obtrusive nerve temerity]
*effusion 21-34-2 (n.) 1. an unrestrained expression of emotion 2. flow under pressure [ebullition emotion excessive explosion expression extravagant fit flare flood flow fluid fusion uncontrollable unrestrained significant speech sudden impulsive inflammation irritate ooze open outburst outflow outpouring overflow neurotic /suff/]
*effusive 14-52-8 (a.) 1. uttered with unrestrained enthusiasm 2. extravagantly demonstrative [ebullient eff emotional energy enthusiasm excessive expansive expression extravagant exuberant female flip frank free friendship full fulsome unchecked undemonstrative unrestrained utter sentimental sloppy smooth sociable speech verbose vociferous voluble /suff/]
*egotism 19-61-3 (n.) 1. an exaggerated opinion of your own importance 2. an inflated feeling of pride in your superiority to others [ego egocentric egoism estimate exaggerate grasping greed opinion otis tendency trait importance individualism inflated interest self speak superiority swell megalomania much /tog/]
*egotist 23-63-1 (n.) 1. a conceited and self-centered person [egocentric egoist egomania exaggerate excessive exhibitionist otis talkative temporize tend think timeserver importance individualist selfish show

soldier speak stock swellhead /tog/]
*egregious 13-26-11 (a.) 1. conspicuously and outrageously bad or reprehensible [enormous error excessive extreme eye gigantic glaring gross rank regio regular remarkable reprehensible right inconspicuous incredible inept infamous injustice intensive obvious offensive outrageous outright outstanding ubiquitous universal utter sad shame signal straight]
*eject 08-38-29 (v.) 1. eliminate, as of bodily substances 2. put out or expel from a place 3. leave an aircraft rapidly, using an ejection seat or capsule 4. cause to come out in a squirt, of liquids [egest egg eliminate emergency emission emit escape evict exclude excrete exile exit exorcize expel jettison job junk cannon capsule cashier cast channel charge chase child chuck classroom clearance cock come commercial competition concrete considerable cough tattoo tenant terminate throw torpedo transude turf turn turnout]
*elaborate 04-31-118 (a.) 1. developed or executed with care and in minute detail 2. marked by complexity and richness of detail (v.) 1. add details, as to an account or idea; clarify the meaning of and discourse in a learned way, usually in writing 2. make more complex, intricate, or richer 3. produce from basic elements or sources; change into a more developed product 4. work out in detail [elegant embellish enlarge enrich evasion exemplify expatiate explanation expound extend extra extravagant labored labyrinthine lace lavish lot lucubration luxury add advance arabesque architecture attention baroque beautify better blossom borate brilliance broad building organize ornate ostentatious outwork overwrought raise rarify rear refine remark resplendent rhythmic rich rise rococo tangle theme thoroughgoing topic transform treatment trimming twist /bale rob taro/] "an elaborate lace pattern"
*elapse 13-57-10 (v.) 1. pass by, as of time [endure expire extinct lapse last advance ago antique apse pass period proceed progress slide slip slow /pal pale spa/]
*elasticity 18-63-4 (n.) 1. the tendency of a body to return to its original shape after it has been stretched or compressed [easy elastic energy exceed extensible lack limber limit lithe absorb adapt adaptable adjust advert agreeable sensitive shape shear size snap soft springy squash stretchy substance supple susceptibility temper tendency tensile tolerance tone impressionable incorporate input capacity characterize circumstance compress /sale/]
*elegy 16-42-6 (n.) 1. a mournful poem; a lament for the dead [eclogue epigram eulogy lament leg limerick line lyric georgic]
*element 02-49-294 (n.) 1. one of four substances thought in ancient and medieval cosmology to constitute the physical universe 2. the most favorable environment for a plant or animal 3. an artifact that is one of the individual parts of which a composite entity is made up; especially a part that can be separated from or attached to a system 4. any of the more than 100 known substances (of which 92 occur naturally) that cannot be separated into simpler substances and that singly or in combination constitute all matter 5. an abstract part of something 6. a straight line that generates a cylinder or cone 7. the situation in which you are happiest and most effective [earth electronic environment essential lawrencium line locale machine magnetic making matter medium mendelevium nature neon neutralize nitrogen nobelium norm table tangent territory thing]
*elicit 08-37-28 (v.) 1. deduce (a principle) or construe (a meaning) 2. call forth; of emotions, feelings, and responses 3. derive by reason [educe effect emotion enkindle evoke excite extract lead licit light likelihood linguistic logical lose love ignite induce infer inflame injure inspire instigate interpret invite irrational call cause chance chord composures construe contrive create criticism curiosity touch]
*eligible 04-36-112 (a.) 1. qualified for or allowed or worthy of being chosen 2. (sports) prohibited by official rules [eli embrace encompass enfranchise entitle establish exertion law legal likely line inclusive incorporate good bachelor bail benefit /big/] "eligible to run for office"
*eliminate 02-22-277 (v.) 1. eliminate from the body 2. dismiss from consideration 3. do away with 4. kill in large numbers 5. terminate or take out 6. math: remove (an unknown variable) from two or more equations 7. remove from a contest or race [eject emission empty eradicate exclude exclusion execution exhaust exile expel exude laxation lift liquidate lop isolate manslaughter murder mutilate negation nip nullification abandon abolish abstract alternative amputate analysis annihilate arrangement assassination takeout throw throwaway transude truncate /mile/] "Let's eliminate the course on Akkadian hieroglyphics"
*elizabethan 12-67-12 (a.) 1. of or relating to Queen Elizabeth I of England or to the age in which she ruled (n.) 1. a person who lived during the reign of Elizabeth I [elizabeth england live individual age art brutalism human neoclassical nouveau]
*elocution 21-63-2 (n.) 1. an expert manner of speaking involving control of voice and gesture [eloquence enunciate expert express language lecture locution oral oratory chatter clearly comment control conversation correct talk /cole/]
*eloquence 13-45-11 (n.) 1. powerful and effective language [effective elocution expressive expressivenes language lecture oratory notable]
*eloquent 07-47-38 (a.) 1. expressing yourself readily, clearly, effectively [easily effective elocution emotion expressive language lofty outspoken talk telling tongue touching]
*elucidate 18-45-4 (v.) 1. make clear and (more) comprehensible 2. make free from confusion or ambiguity; make clear [editorial elaborate enlarge

enlightenment exemplify expatiate explicate expound learn less light lucida lucubration unambiguous unfold unlock unravel clarify comprehensible confusion cracking critical crystallize idea illuminate illustrative interpret death decipher decode demonstrative demythologize detail dilate disambiguate discourse account add allegorize ambiguity annotate /tad/]
*elude 08-47-33 (v.) 1. be incomprehensible to; escape understanding by 2. escape, either physically or mentally 3. avoid or try to avoid fulfilling, answering, or performing (duties, questions, or issues) [escape eschew evade explanation loose lude understand upset defeat defy destroy difficult dodge double duck dumbfound] "The thief eluded the police"
*emaciate 17-58-5 (v.) 1. cause to grow thin or weak 2. grow weak and thin or waste away physically [eat enfeeble excess extremely macerate man marasmus anorexic atrophy attenuate cadaverous cavernous chemotherapy cold concentration consumptive corky illness tabetic thin transform treatment turn /came/] "The treatment emaciated him"
*emanate 09-52-21 (v.) 1. proceed or issue forth, as from a source 2. give out, as of breath or an odor [effuse emit erupt exhale expel exude mana move approach arise attend thick toward track trail travel /name tana/] "Water emanates from this hole in the ground"
*emancipate 19-49-3 (v.) 1. free from slavery or servitude 2. give equal rights to; of women and minorities [easygoing enfranchise equal extricate manumit minority clear convention passive pate position transform turn /name/]
*embargo 08-20-33 (n.) 1. a government order imposing a trade barrier (v.) 1. prevent commerce [enjoin enter exception exclusion measure move movie ban bar barrier block boycott arg reason refuse regulation rejection relegate restrict give government official omit outlaw /grab/] "The U.S. embargoes Lybia"
*embark 04-69-91 (v.) 1. set out on (an enterprise, subject of study, etc.) 2. go on board 3. proceed somewhere despite the risk of possible dangers [enplane enterprise entrain expedite export express mail move bark begin board boarding bus buy aircraft airfreight airmail ashore assume remit resume risk] "she embarked upon a new career"
*embarrass 03-62-186 (v.) 1. cause to be embarrassed; cause to feel self-conscious 2. hinder or prevent the progress or accomplishment of [ease easy effect effort encumber endure enigmatic extravagant maze moment money mortify mystify baffle bewildering block book bother broke brother abash abroad accomplishment adult ankle annoy anxious arise arras attention awkward rattle reach red reduce remark remorse require sale save say self shake shame show slow squeeze street sty]
*embellish 09-43-23 (v.) 1. add details to 2. make more beautiful 3. be beautiful to look at 4. make more attractive by adding ornament, colour, etc. [educate elaborate encrust engild enhance enrich evolve magnify mask mature meliorate mock mordent bard bead beautify bedeck bedight bedizen begild belie bellis better bogus broider lily lush luxury illegitimate illumination imitation improve incrust inlay involve seasoning sham slant smarten smoothen spruce stone strain stud synthetic hyperbole /sill/]
*embezzle 10-28-17 (v.) 1. appropriate (as property entrusted to one's care) fraudulently to one's own use [employer entrust extort misappropriate misconduct mishandle mismanage misuse money bag befoul boost borrow larceny liberation lift loot] "The accountant embezzled thousands of dollars while working for the wealthy family"
*emblazon 11-51-15 (v.) 1. decorate with colors 2. decorate with heraldic arms [embellish embroider enrich exhibit extol magnify manifest beautify bedeck blazon bless brandish bright lacquer laud lead lionize literary add adorn advertise air arm array art artistic attractive ornament]
*emblem 10-36-20 (n.) 1. a visible symbol representing an abstract idea 2. special design or visual object representing a quality, type, group, etc. [eagle ensign equilateral erect example explanation magistrate mantle marking medal medieval membership metal modern moral motif motto badge baton bear bent blade book bundle button lamb leg lesson letter livery logo logotype]
*embody 07-39-42 (v.) 1. represent or express something abstract in tangible form 2. represent, as of a character on stage 3. represent in bodily form [embrace evidence exemplify express mean mirror mix model best blend bodily body breathe buildup objectify occupy organize demonstrate develop display]
*embolden 11-44-14 (v.) 1. give encouragement to [encouragement endorse bold bolster buoy olden nerve /lob/]
*embolism 21-64-2 (n.) 1. an insertion into a calendar 2. occlusion of a blood vessel by an embolus (a loose clot or air bubble or other particle) [emboli embolus enter evil mark matter medicine bar barrier begin block blood bone bottleneck bubble obstruction occlusion length liver lodge long loose impasse impediment infarction injection injure insertion instant interval scuba serious stoppage strangulate stream surgery /lob silo/]
*embrace 03-48-187 (n.) 1. the state of taking in or encircling 2. the act of clasping another person in the arms (as in greeting or affection) 3. a close affectionate and protective acceptance (v.) 1. take up the cause, ideology, practice, method, of someone and use it as one's own 2. hug, usually with fondness 3. include in scope; include as part of something broader; have as one's sphere or territory [eager elbow electoral embosom encircle enclose encompass engage espouse method band become belief bond bosom box brace

range reception roundabout accept address admit adopt affectionate ambient approval artistic assimilate case clasp clench clinch close clutch comfort comprise consider contain cover covering cuddle /carb/] "an island in the embrace of the sea"

*embroil 08-66-28 (v.) 1. force into some kind of situation, condition, or course of action [eddy enmesh ensnare entangle entrap excitement maelstrom malaise melee mix muddle boiling bother broil brush business rage riot row overly imbroglio inquietude involve logomachy]

*emerge 01-60-637 (v.) 1. come up to the surface of or rise, as from water; also used metaphorically 2. become known or apparent 3. come out of 4. come out into view, as from concealment 5. happen or occur as a result of something [early effort egress emission emit emotion enter escape evasion evolve existence exit experience exploit exposure manifestation materialize maturity merge metaphoricall ray realize recent release ripe rise river generation getaway gradual grow growth gum] "Suddenly, the proprietor emerged from his office"

*emergence 06-56-44 (n.) 1. the becoming visible 2. the gradual beginning or coming forth 3. the act of coming (or going) out; becoming apparent 4. the act of emerging [effort egression emanation emit eruption exploit ripe rise gradual growth gum notable catkin come] "figurines presage the emergence of sculpture in Greece"

*emergent 19-53-3 (a.) 1. coming into existence [embryonic emerge eventual existence extrapolate randolph republic root grow nascent near tall transient tree]

*emeritus 08-35-31 (a.) 1. honorably retired from assigned duties and retaining your title along with the additional title 'emeritus' as in"professor emeritus" [elderly man merit reader retain retired imply inactive indicate instructor title tutor specify superannuate /tire/] "professor emeritus"

*emigrant 16-50-6 (n.) 1. someone who leaves one country to settle in another [emigre exile expatriate mig migrant move immigrant intruder goer greenhorn recruit refugee region rookie alien arriviste newcomer tenderfoot traveler trek]

*emigrate 06-39-46 (v.) 1. leave one's country of residence for a new one [evacuate exile expatriate migrate move immigrate region relocate resettle residency run adopt transmigrate travel trek] "Many people had to emigrate during the Nazi period"

*eminence 13-53-11 (n.) 1. high status importance owing to marked superiority 2. a protuberance on a bone especially for attachment of a muscle or ligament [effect esteem excellence mark memorable mine moment muscle illustrious importance insinuation natural noble notable note noteworthy category chief control credit] "a scholar of great eminence"

*eminent 07-52-34 (a.) 1. (used of persons) standing above others in character or attainment or reputation 2. having achieved eminence 3. standing above others in quality or position 4. of imposing height; especially standing out above others [easy eclipse elevation exceptional extension major mark marked member memorable mine mountain iceberg imperative imposing inferior influential noble notable noteworthy noticeable telling throne towering transcend]

*emit 08-47-27 (v.) 1. give off, send forth, or discharge; as of light, heat, or radiation, vapor, etc. 2. expel, as of gases and odors 3. express audibly; utter sounds (not necessarily words) [effort eject eliminate emanate eruct exclamation exhale expel expire express male metaphoricall mew mit moan money monkey imitate impart inarticulate indicate intend issue tell transude trumpet twirp /time/] "The ozone layer blocks some harmful rays which the sun emits"

*emote 19-60-3 (v.) 1. give expression or emotion to, in a stage or movie role [emotionalize exaggerate expression mime mote movie troupe /tom tome/]

*emotive 14-81-9 (a.) 1. characterized by emotion [melodramatic motive move theatrical touching impassioned intend issue visceral /tom tome/]

*emphasis 04-43-127 (n.) 1. special and significant stress by means of position or repetition e.g. 2. intensity or forcefulness of expression 3. special importance or significance 4. the relative prominence of a syllable or musical note (especially with regard to stress or pitch) [excellence mark measure moment paramount period priority has accent accentuate anapest attention significance stress superiority swing importance interest ionic] "the red light gave the central figure increased emphasis"

*emphasize 04-01-122 (v.) 1. give extra weight to (a communication) 2. to stress, single out as important [evince exercise expression extra mark mean move pay pinpoint play point press punctuate highlight home accentuate anew assert attention sentence show single size special spotlight star stress identification important italicize] "Dr. Jones emphasizes exercise in addition to a change in diet."

*emphatic 07-64-43 (a.) 1. spoken with emphasis 2. sudden and strong 3. forceful and definite in expression or action [education emphasize entertain evident exceptional exciting exclamatory expensive expression exquisite extraordinary magical magnificent marked marvelous might particularly phat phatic physical pointed positive prominent pronounced provoke absolute absolutely accent accuracy aggressive amazing apple appropriate ardent assertive astonish auxiliary tell impassioned impressive incline incredible insistent intense categorical certain clear confident conspicuous copious] "an emphatic word"

*empirical 16-43-6 (a.) 1. derived from experiment and observation rather than theory [eclectic empiric ethical existential experimental expression materialistic mechanistic medicine metaphysical model philosophy

pilot posteriori practical pragmatic primarily provisional idealistic instead instrumentalist rationalism realistic rely case characterize concern confirm consideration animism apply archaism law little logic /rip/] "an empirical basis for an ethical theory"
*employee 02-33-502 (n.) 1. a worker who is hired to perform a job [employ member menial mercenary migrant pensioner personnel porter proletarian operative]
*employer 03-62-211 (n.) 1. a person or firm that employs workers [elder employ enjoy establishment excessive exploit manager master paramount patron pay perform proprietor leader leg organization outfit owner rabbi responsible rule]
*emporium 13-39-10 (n.) 1. a large retail store organized into departments offering a variety of merchandise; commonly part of a retail chain [establishment exposition marketplace mart merchandise part place plaza post offering organize outlet retail rialto]
*empower 07-48-38 (v.) 1. give or delegate power or authority to 2. give qualities or abilities to [embolden eminent enable encourage endow endue energize enfranchise entitle excessive mighty mission momentous monocracy paper passive patent permit post power prestigious privilege prominent obligation official warrant weighty ranking ratify render responsibility right rouse ruling /wop/]
*emulate 07-67-40 (v.) 1. strive to equal or match, especially by imitating 2. compete with successfully; approach or reach equality with 3. imitate the function of (another system), as by modifying the hardware or the software; in computer science [engage engineering equality match measure meet mimic modify late look accept achievement admire aid ape appearance approach artist try /alum/]
*enact 05-19-74 (v.) 1. act out; represent or perform as if in a play 2. order by virtue of superior authority; decree [early effect endorse establish evidence express expulsion achieve act affect authorize complete conduct copy table token transact /can cane/]
*enamor 16-AA-6 (v.) 1. attract; cause to be enamored [enchant endear enrapture entrance album allure amor appeal attention attractive man mark mean right rock /man mane roman/]
*encamp 23-41-1 (v.) 1. live in or as if in a tent [near camp circus people place populate position provide /acne mac/]
*encapsulate 11-74-15 (v.) 1. enclose in a capsule or other small container 2. put in a short or concise form; reduce in volume [embrace encase enclose envelop express capture case compress concise condense container cover crate package protective short shroud shut smother sum summarize surround lap late look thin tumor /acne spa talus/]
*encomium 23-44-1 (n.) 1. a formal expression of praise [eulogy expression citation commendation compliment magnification]
*encompass 07-42-41 (v.) 1. include in scope; include as part of something broader; have as one's sphere or territory [embody embrace encircle enclose envelop extend carry ceremony compass comprise contribution couple cover occupy orbit marshal mass mix much pair part pen people plow pocket add address admit artistic associate scope shrine skirt solder sphere surround /sap/] "This group encompasses a wide range of people from different backgrounds"
*encore 10-45-18 (n.) 1. an extra or repeated performance; usually given in response to audience demand (v.) 1. request an encore, from a performer [echo eclat entertainment express extra new newly call core curtain ovation repetition replay reprise request response return]
*encourage 01-57-583 (v.) 1. spur on 2. inspire with confidence; give hope or courage to 3. contribute to the progress or growth of [ease egg embolden endorse enliven exalt exciting exhilarate exhort nerve nourish nurture carry cause caution challenging charge cheer cheery classroom comfort computer conducive confidence console contribute courage course crying urge reassure recreate relieve remonstrate reserved rosy advance advantage advocate aid alluring animate approval assist assure galvanize give gladden goad growth]
*encroach 11-47-16 (v.) 1. advance beyond the usual limit 2. impinge or infringe upon [eat effort entrench entry excessive civil conduct culture cutin resent right roach obtrusion occupy overstep adoption advantage apparent appropriation area assumption authority]
*encumber 19-40-3 (v.) 1. hold back [embarrassed entangle entwine net chain charge clog complicate confine constrain cumber curb mortgage motion block bound bridle burden burthen restrict retard]
*encumbrance 23-53-1 (n.) 1. an onerous or difficult concern 2. a charge against property (as a lien or mortgage) 3. any obstruction that impedes or is burdensome [embarrassment endure nuisance care cause charge claim concern create cross crosswise umbra uncalledfor unhappy unpleasant millstone mind mortgage bale bump bundle burdensome burthen responsibility ridge roadway affliction albatross anxiety]
*encyclical 21-47-2 (a.) 1. intended for wide distribution (n.) 1. a letter from the pope sent to all Roman Catholic bishops throughout the world [edict enunciate newsletter nixie notify catholic circular communique concentrate cyclical letter instruction intend issue address aerogram announcement annunciation] "an encyclical letter"
*encyclopedia 13-20-11 (n.) 1. a reference work (often in several volumes) containing articles on various topics (often arranged in alphabetical order) dealing with the entire range of human knowledge or with some

particular specialty [elementary entire calendar casebook comprehensive concordance cyclo cyclopedia literature lore offering polyglot publication database deal directory index almanac alphabetical area arrange article atlas authoritative /aide/]
*endanger 05-35-75 (v.) 1. put in a dangerous, disadvantageous, or difficult position 2. pose a threat to; present a danger to [effect existence expose extant danger dangerous difficult disadvantageous disrepute affect risk] "The pollution is endangering the crops"
*endear 13-68-10 (v.) 1. make attractive or lovable [enamor enrapture dear delight affectionate allure attractive recommend] "This behavior endeared her to me"
*endearing 09-60-23 (a.) 1. lovable especially in a childlike or naive way [earing engage naive delight adorable affection appealing attractive]
*endemic 11-62-14 (a.) 1. (of disease or anything resembling a disease) constantly present to greater or lesser extent in a particular locality 2. originating where it is found 3. (ecology) native to or confined to a certain region (n.) 1. a disease that is constantly present to a greater or lesser degree in people of a certain class or in people living in a particular location [ecology epidemic epiphytotic epizootic extent natal native northernmost defect define degree demi describe disease disorder distribute malaria medicine illness impair include infirmity inoculate interest island catching certain class community complication concern condition confined constant cosmopolitan] "diseases endemic to the tropics"
*endorse 04-31-129 (v.) 1. guarantee as meeting a certain standard 2. give support or one's blessing to 3. be behind; approve of 4. of documents or cheques [elect encourage endo engage ensure exponent negotiable nod nominate notarize defend defender deign dependence document office okay ratify receipt recipient recommend reliance report respect root sanction second secure show side signature specific sponsor standard star strong subscribe support supporter sympathy /rod/]
*endow 10-40-18 (v.) 1. furnish with an endowment 2. give qualities or abilities to [enable endo endue enfeoff enhance enrich equip excessive deputize desirable donate dot dower dowry occupy organize outfit own worth]
*endurance 09-62-25 (n.) 1. the power to withstand hardship or stress 2. a state of surviving; remaining alive [earn energy engrossment environmental exertion extension decisive despite diligence distress durance duration unfavorable unhappy ravage remain resolution robust run runner acceptance age alive ancient animation application capacity concentration condition constant continuance continuity] "the marathon tests a runner's endurance"
*enduring 05-58-63 (a.) 1. unceasing 2. patiently enduring continual wrongs or trouble [element exist experience day defy despite die difficulty disposition dress driver durable during unceasing uncomplaining undergo unpleasant unprofessional usable race remark run impatient impermanent]
*energetic 06-52-54 (a.) 1. working hard to promote an enterprise 2. possessing or exerting or displaying energy [ebullient effectual enterprising enthusiastic erg exert raise rattling ready relentless require robust ruling great group gump telling tireless trenchant imagination incisive indefatigable industrious initiative intense irresistible challenging chipper cogent college /cite teg/] "an energetic fund raiser for the college"
*enervate 19-51-3 (v.) 1. weaken mentally or morally 2. disturb the composure of [eat emasculate encumber enfeeble eviscerate exhaust nerve nerveless numb rapscallion rarefy rascal rattle reduce rogue valetudinary vegetative vigor villain vitality abate adynamic afflict age apathetic asthenic attenuate tire toilworn torpid tucker]
*enfeeble 21-56-2 (v.) 1. make weak [effete emasculate enervate eviscerate exhaust extenuate faint fatigue feeble flagging blunt bugger lame languid lessen /bee beef/]
*enfranchise 23-52-1 (v.) 1. grant freedom to; as from slavery or servitude 2. grant voting rights [election eligible emancipate empower enable entitle naturalize fit fitted formerly franchise freedom ratify release rescue right acceptable accord admissible allow authorize century certify charter city sanction servitude set slavery suitable] "Slaves were enfranchised in the mid-19th century"
*engender 11-52-15 (v.) 1. call forth 2. make children [establish evolve excite existence gender generate gestate get give grow design develop discover realize recognize rise rouse]
*engrave 09-44-23 (v.) 1. write upon; engrave a pen, for example 2. make an engraving of (an image) [earmark embed emboss emotional enroll enter entrench establish etch etching needle negative nick notch gash gem glass gouge graphic grave gravure groove ground rabbet raise recordist registrar reproduce reproduction rifle rooted ruck run rut abstraction accountant acid affect amanuensis archivist art artistic assemble vested videotape vignette]
*engross 18-55-4 (v.) 1. engross (oneself) fully 2. engage or engross wholly 3. enclose or envelop completely, as if by swallowing [eat ecstatic edit elsewhere enchant enclose engage engaged engulf enough enthrall envelop excite exercise nap nod give grab grip gross rapt record revise rewrite rivet running oblivious obsess occupy osmose scriptural scroll set shortly shut sink soak speak spellbind spellbound sponge steep story study swallow]
*engrossing 13-62-11 (a.) 1. capable of arousing and holding the attention [eat enchanting enclose engage engaging engross engulf enthral envelop exciting gripping obsessive occupy shortly shut sink soak

spellbind steep stimulate story study swallow immerse interesting intrigue]
*engulf 08-57-28 (v.) 1. flow over or cover completely 2. engross (oneself) fully [eat enclose enfold engorge engross envelop enwrap gobble great grief gulf underwater light fascinate flood floodwater flow focus fully /flu lug/]
*enhance 03-51-188 (v.) 1. make better or more attractive 2. increase [educate effective electronic enjoy enrich exaggerate excess expansion extended extreme nurture hance headway heighten hike huckster acceleration add advancement alter ameliorate amend amendment annoy appearance attractive augment civilized clarity computer concentration consolidation convert culture] "This will enhance your enjoyment"
*enigma 11-61-14 (n.) 1. something that baffles understanding and cannot be explained 2. a difficult problem [embarrassment esoterica explain nature node nonplus get mystery mystify arcanum /gin/]
*enjoin 18-28-4 (v.) 1. give instructions to or direct somebody to do something 2. issue an injunction [encourage enjoy exact join occupy order outlaw own impose incite induce injunction instruction interdict issue]
*enlighten 08-51-30 (v.) 1. make understand 2. make free from confusion or ambiguity; make clear 3. give spiritual insight to; in religion [editorial educate elucidate enhance enrich experience explain learn lecture lift light lighten lit luminous illuminate illustrate inspiration instruct introductory guide highly homiletic teach tell train transform tutor] "Can you enlighten me-- I don't understand this proposal"
*enlist 06-34-54 (v.) 1. engage somebody to enter the army 2. as of aid, help, services, or support 3. join the military [effort employ engage engagement enroll enrollment enter entry lead levy list lobby lure impress inauguration index influence inscribe intention invest secure seek sell service sign solicit special spent stretch summon support sway tempt term time tour]
*enmity 14-53-9 (n.) 1. a state of deep-seated ill-will 2. the feeling of a hostile person [economic emotion end enemy envy estrange exist express extreme nature nausea negative noncooperation main malevolent malignity manifest mischief mity ill illwill incompatible inharmony international tension toward try]
*ennoble 18-52-4 (v.) 1. confer dignity or honor upon 2. give a title to someone; make someone a member of the nobility [elevate enshrine erect nobility noble baronet beatify bestow lionize lord /bonne/]
*enormity 17-56-5 (n.) 1. the quality of being outrageous 2. (informal) vastness of size or extent 3. an act of extreme wickedness 4. the quality of extreme wickedness [error evil expanse expression extent extreme nefarious nonfeasance obnoxious offensive omission outrageousnes rank recognize magnitude massive mean mighty mity monstrous moral idea imitate immense indecent inhumanity insult intensity task taunt trespass trip /one/] "in careful usage the noun enormity is not used to express the idea of great size"
*enormous 02-51-236 (a.) 1. extraordinarily large in size or extent or amount or power or degree [excessive experience extent extraordinary extreme nasty nefarious noise norm notorious offensive outrageous outsize rank regrettable rotten magnitude mammoth massive mighty monstrous monumental unbridled unconscionable undue unusual sad size steep stiff sweep /one/] "an enormous boulder"
*enrage 09-56-23 (v.) 1. put into a rage; make violently angry [enkindle excite extreme rage rouse accident anger annoy arouse attached]
*enrapture 19-59-3 (v.) 1. hold spellbound [ecstatic elate enchant enthrall entrance rage rant rapture ravish rejoice roaring abandon allure amaze attract awed pleasure popeyed possessed puzzle tempt thrill thunderstruck transport transported uncontrollable]
*enshrine 11-57-15 (v.) 1. enclose in a shrine, as of an object for religious purposes 2. hold sacred [elevate enclose encompass exalted sacred saint shrine shut special stable surround hallowed hearse hold raise religious respect reverence imprison include inter]
*ensign 18-39-4 (n.) 1. a person who holds a commissioned rank in the United States Navy or Coast Guard; below lieutenant junior grade 2. colors flown by a ship to show its nationality 3. an emblem flown as a symbol of nationality [eagle emblem nationality naval navy service ship show sign skipper staff standard symbol idea indicate insignia grade guard guidon]
*ensnare 17-51-5 (v.) 1. take or catch as if in a snare or trap 2. catch in or as if in a trap [enmesh entangle entice entrap escape nail net noose sack seduce situation snare spear sport allure animal]
*entail 08-51-27 (n.) 1. land received by fee tail (v.) 1. impose, involve, or imply as a necessary accompaniment or result 2. have as a logical consequence [estate express extensive necessitate note tail testify transmit absolute accompaniment acre affect argue assume identify imperative impose indicate inevitable inheritance instruction involve irrevocable land leave legacy limit line logical long]
*entangle 10-41-17 (v.) 1. entrap 2. twist together or entwine into a confusing mass [embarrassment embroil enclosure engage engagement enmesh ensnare ensnarl escape extricate nail net noose take tangle trap triangle trick trip twine twist absorb adultery affair allure animal association gin glacis land liaison lime loophole lunette lure /gnat/]
*enthrall 23-34-1 (v.) 1. hold spellbound [enchant engage engross enrapture enslave enthral entrance exercise thrall thrill titillate transport hold hypnotize ravish rivet arrest attention legal literary]
*enthrone 19-69-3 (v.) 1. provide with power and authority 2. put a monarch on the throne [elevate

ennoble enshrine throne raise remove office ordain ordinate] "The Queen was enthroned more than 50 years ago"
*enthuse 10-92-19 (v.) 1. cause to feel enthusiasm 2. utter with enthusiasm [effuse elicit excite express talk thus utter say show speak stimulate stir]
*enthusiastic 04-53-109 (a.) 1. having or showing great excitement and interest [eager earnest enthusiast evangelistic excitement exciting express nutty tickle titillate trenchant hearty heated hot unqualified unrestrained urgent show spirited stimulate stirring street strong impassioned incline interest interested active afire aflame aggressive animation ardent ardor attract avid concerned content crazy crowd curious] "enthusiastic crowds filled the streets"
*entice 06-52-49 (v.) 1. provoke someone to do something through (often false or exaggerated) promises or persuasion [effect effort enchantment ensnare enthrall entrap exaggerate exciting exotic taking tantalizing tease tempt tempting tend toll trap tree ice imitate incentive induce inducement influence interesting intrigue inveigle invite inviting cajole cajolery call captivate catching charming coax cognitive come conduct]
*entirety 13-50-11 (n.) 1. the state of being total [entire everything exhaustive extent thorough totality tote treatment inclusive intact integrity /rit/]
*entity 06-39-52 (n.) 1. that which is perceived or known or inferred to have its own physical existence (living or nonliving) [early earth enclosure ens essential existence existent extent nature non tangible thing tit totality individual infer integrate]
*entomology 17-29-5 (n.) 1. the branch of zoology that studies insects [ecology ethology taxidermy taxonomy termite ology ornithology malacology mammalogy]
*entrails 21-66-2 (n.) 1. internal organs collectively (especially those in the abdominal cavity) [trail try abdominal ancient animal inn inner inside intestine sacrificial situate /liar/]
*entreaty 18-36-4 (n.) 1. earnest or urgent request [earnest emotion entreat thanksgiving treaty rank request rogation rosary address adjure affection appeal application authority] "an entreaty to stop the fighting"
*entree 08-01-29 (n.) 1. the principal dish of a meal 2. something that provides access (entry or exit) 3. the act of entering 4. the right to enter [eleanor enclose enter entry equip escape exit extend nature nibble theater threshold tradition tree reception refuse removal right roast room]
*entrench 09-46-26 (v.) 1. fix firmly or securely 2. occupy a trench or secured area 3. impinge or infringe upon [embed encroach ensconce entrance establish establishment etch excessive night nobility trench trespass troop trough tunnel right root rooted cement channel confirmation constitute cut cutin hard hold]
*entwine 15-46-7 (v.) 1. tie or link together 2. spin or twist together so as to form a cord [embarrass enlace entangle entrap net noose tangle thread tie tissue twine twist wattle weave web wind wreath wreathe impede interweave involve]
*enumerate 18-16-4 (v.) 1. specify individually 2. determine the number or amount of [effect ejaculate election encounter enroll enter estimate experiment nose number numerate numeration measurement mention miscount recite reckon red refer register registry relate remain repertory resolve response accounting add additional amount arbitrary array ascertain tabulate tale tally telling topic tot total tote /emu tare/] "She enumerated the many obstacles she had encountered"
*enunciate 16-38-6 (v.) 1. express or state clearly 2. speak, pronounce, or utter in a certain way [eat edict emit encyclical explain express nasal notify nuncupative ukase unwritten utter careful certain certify chord circular clarify clearly click closer communicate complicate conclusion consonant contend convey creed curl impart indistinct insist intelligible involve accentuate advance affirm alleged alveolar announcement argue articulation aspect aspiration assertion attack audible audience tongue trill twang]
*enzyme 12-53-12 (n.) 1. any of several complex proteins that are produced by cells and act as catalysts in specific biochemical reactions [egg elastin epinephrine essential esterase exist nitrogen nucleotide mammal meat microorganism milk monosaccharide]
*eon 18-50-4 (n.) 1. the longest division of geological time; two or more eras 2. (in Gnosticism) a divine power or nature emanating from the Supreme Being and playing various roles in the operation of the universe 3. an immeasurably long period of time [early earth element emanate era eternity evidence old operation organism orientation nature]
*ephemeral 14-41-9 (a.) 1. enduring a very short time [enduring ephemera episodic eternal evanescent evergreen passing perennial period perishable permanent plant hardy mayfly momentary mortal mutable leave live] "the ephemeral joys of childhood"
*epic 05-67-80 (a.) 1. constituting or having to do with or suggestive of a literary epic 2. surpassing the ordinary especially in size or scale (n.) 1. a long narrative poem telling of a hero's deeds [eclogue elegy elevated empire epi epigram epos expensive extent palinode pentameter poem poetry production proportion prothalamion provide iambic idyll illustrious imposing impressive canso celebrate chanson characterize chronicle cinema classic comedy comm composition constitute cover] "an epic voyage"
*epicure 23-45-1 (n.) 1. a person devoted to refined sensuous enjoyment (especially good food and drink) [eater enjoy expert picnic pleasure collector connoisseur consumer critic cure refined]
*epicurean 21-56-2 (a.) 1. of Epicurus or epicureanism 2. furnishing gratification of the senses 3. devoted to

pleasure (n.) 1. a person devoted to refined sensuous enjoyment (especially good food and drink) [enjoy epicure expert philosophy piggish pleasure porcine immoderate indulgent intemperate chandelier chinchilla collector connoisseur critic crystal unconfined unending unrestrained refined remainder robe rug amateur appetite authority]
*epidemic 06-48-47 (a.) 1. (especially of medicine) of disease or anything resembling a disease; attacking or affecting many individuals in a community or a population simultaneously (n.) 1. a widespread outbreak of an infectious disease; many people are infected at the same time [endemic epizootic eruption exhaustless expect extent extravagant exuberant pandemic people pestilential plague plenty population present prevalent productive proportion inexhaustible infectious infective influenza inoculate irruption deal demi develop diffuse disease dominant many meaty medicine much card catching civil community compact condition constant crime current /dip/] "an epidemic outbreak of influenza"
*epidermis 23-64-1 (n.) 1. the outer layer of the skin covering the exterior body surface of vertebrates [ectoderm endothelium envelope exterior external palm parallel periphery pinprick plant protective immediately innermost integument invertebrate dead dermis die replace rete rind mantle material mesoderm mollusk move secrete site skin slight slough stratum substance surface /dip/]
*epigram 21-36-2 (n.) 1. a witty saying [elegy epic expression paradox people phrase poem poetry pun idea idyll georgic gibe gnome gram remark retort rhyme riposte adage ana aphorism axiom maxim mode moral motto /gip/]
*epilogue 18-37-4 (n.) 1. a short speech (often in verse) addressed directly to the audience by an actor at the end of a play 2. a short passage added at the end of a literary work [effect end epi eventually express passage payoff period play point prologue infix interpolate introduction last letter literature omega give goal /lip/] "the epilogue told what eventually happened to the main characters"
*epiphany 12-47-13 (n.) 1. a divine manifestation 2. twelve days after Christmas; celebrates the visit of the three wise men to the infant Jesus [emerge evidence expression presentation proof publication indication infant inspiration issue holiday holy any apocalypse appear appearance arise year /pipe/]
*episode 03-56-175 (n.) 1. a brief section of a literary or dramatic work that forms part of a connected series 2. a happening that is distinctive in a series of related events 3. a part of a broadcast serial 4. film consisting of a succession of related shots that develop a given subject in a movie [epi event excursus experience particular period picture plan plot incident injection introduction scene section show spell story subject occasion occurrence outbreak design development device /sip/]
*epistle 23-56-1 (n.) 1. especially a long, formal letter [epi provide instruction intend letter literary long /sip/]
*epitaph 15-62-7 (n.) 1. an inscription on a tombstone or monument in memory of the person buried there 2. a summary statement of commemoration for a dead person [engrave epigraph piece pita inscription tombstone /pat tip/]
*epithet 13-37-10 (n.) 1. a defamatory or abusive word or phrase 2. descriptive word or phrase [earn epigraph eponym expletive part picture pith inscription insult tag tautonym taxonomy title traduce handle hatchet highlight honorific hurt hyponym /tip/]

*epitome 12-65-13 (n.) 1. a standard or typical example 2. a brief abstract (as of an article or book) [elegance embodiment essence exemplar paradigm parent pattern personification piece point precis prototype provide idealize telescope theory tome truncate original outline overview main mirror model /tip/]
*epoch 14-47-9 (n.) 1. a period marked by distinctive character or reckoned from a fixed point or event 2. a unit of geological time 3. (astronomy) the precise date that is the point of reference for which information (as coordinates of a celestial body) is referred [earth eocene eon era even existence extensive period periodical pleistocene pliocene point position precise present prior pulse occur oligocene oscillate calendar calif celestial century christ circle climate community consequential cool coordinate cyclic head holocene human /cop cope/]
*equable 23-77-1 (a.) 1. not varying 2. not easily irritated [easily easygoing equal even unbroken unflappable uniform able alike automatic balance] "an equable climate"
*equalize 18-01-4 (v.) 1. compensate; make the score equal 2. make equal, uniform, corresponding, or matching [electronics employee equal equation equivalent exchange quality uniform accord achieve adapt adjust align alter amplitude layout level lie line liquid interchange] "let's equalize the duties among all employees in this office"
*equanimity 17-58-5 (n.) 1. steadiness of mind under stress [emotion equable equipoise even quiet uniformity unity usual accept accordance aplomb assured imperturbable mind mity mood temperament tranquillity /mina/] "he accepted their problems with composure and she with equanimity"
*equestrian 11-67-16 (a.) 1. of or relating to or composed of knights 2. of or relating to or featuring horseback riding (n.) 1. a man skilled in equitation [early employ equestrienne equitation quest ungulate saddle show skill soldier statue steeplechase swinish travel race ride rider roughrider ruminant animal aristocrat asinine near /airt/]
*equilibrium 13-51-10 (n.) 1. a stable situation in which forces cancel one another 2. a chemical reaction and its reverse proceed at equal rates 3. equality of distribution 4. a sensory system located in structures of the inner ear

that registers the orientation of the head [emotional entity equality equation equivalency even unchanged uniformity unity unstable identity imperturbable inner interact invariable involve labyrinthine level libri likeness location long loss balance beauty biological body rate reaction reduce register regularity reliable remain reversible rhythm rotate maintain mass mechanism mental metabolic move mutuality]
*equitable 08-47-29 (a.) 1. implying justice dictated by reason, conscience, and a natural sense of what is fair to all [equal ethical evenhand unbiased unbigoted uncolored unjust identical impartial imply indifferent table tolerant toward treatment applicable balance law lawful legal level] "equitable treatment of all citizens"
*equity 02-69-263 (n.) 1. the difference between the market value of a property and the claims held against it 2. the ownership interest of shareholders in a corporation 3. conformity with rules or standards [earn entitle equi estate ethics even evenhandedne exchange quality unfair use useful utility identity impartial inadequate influence interest involve temper tenant title tolerance treatment trust]
*equivalent 03-63-215 (a.) 1. essentially equal 2. equal in amount or value 3. being essentially equal to something (n.) 1. a person or thing equal to another in value or measure or force or effect or significance etc 2. the atomic weight of an element that has the same combining capacity as a given weight of another element; the standard is 8 for oxygen [effective element energy equation ersatz essential even exchange quantity unanimous understudy unequal uniform image imitation interchange valent value vicarious visa volume admission agent agree amount answer area atomic attorney learn less light likeness logic noes temporary trade twin] "send two dollars or the equivalent in stamps"
*equivocal 18-60-4 (a.) 1. open to two or more interpretations; or of uncertain nature or significance; or (often) intended to mislead 2. open to question 3. uncertain as a sign or indication [eclectic enigmatic erratic evasive questionable uncertain unclear undecided univocal unsure incalculable intricate ironic vague varied vocal oblique obscure changeable combined compound confusing agnostic amalgamate ambivalent lying] "an equivocal statement"
*equivocate 21-41-2 (v.) 1. be deliberately ambiguous or unclear in order to mislead or withhold information [elude escape exaggerate quibble unclear vacillate vague vary obscure oscillate cate cavil change choplogic address alternate ambiguous answer avoid teeter tergiversate topic totter /taco/]
*eradicate 08-59-31 (v.) 1. kill in large numbers 2. destroy completely, as if down to the roots [eliminate entire evocative except exile exterminate exterminatory extirpate extort recur remove return rid roman root abate abolish abstract annihilate army arouse death decimate democracy deport destruction die disentangle dock down intentional isolate carry cate chuck completely crop cut takeout ten truncate /acid dare/]
*errant 11-52-15 (a.) 1. capable of making an error [erratic erring error rambling range rant reach right roam romance route rowdy abroad accept adrift adventure awry naughty nomadic traipse turning twist]
*erratic 07-51-36 (a.) 1. liable to sudden unpredictable change 2. having no fixed course 3. likely to perform unpredictably [eccentric err establish exceptional expect extraordinary random regular reliance restless rock rough adrift alteration alternate ambiguous temperamental tendency trust turning twist ice idiosyncrasy impulsive instrument intermittent irresponsible carry casual change character comet cool course] "an erratic comet"
*erroneous 10-28-20 (a.) 1. containing or characterized by error [errant erring right roneo off out uneven unfinished unfounded untrue short sketchy specious stray] "erroneous conclusions"
*error 03-48-228 (n.) 1. departure from what is ethically acceptable 2. (baseball) a failure of a defensive player to make an out when normal play would have sufficed 3. a misconception resulting from incorrect information 4. inadvertent incorrectness 5. a wrong action attributable to bad judgment or ignorance or inattention 6. (computer science) the occurrence of an incorrect result produced by a computer 7. part of a statement that is not correct [embarrass engineering enormity err erroneous establish ethical evil report rock run runner observe occurrence offense official opinion outrage oversight]
*erudite 15-60-7 (a.) 1. having or showing profound knowledge [educate encyclopedic read deep dit intellectual /dure/]
*erudition 18-51-4 (n.) 1. profound knowledge [education encyclopedism erudite read depth dit instruction intellectuality /dure/]
*eschew 09-64-24 (v.) 1. avoid and stay away from deliberately; stay clear of [elude evade sacrifice shun shy spare stay chew clear course holdback way withhold]
*esoteric 12-47-12 (a.) 1. confined to and understandable by only an enlightened inner circle [eerie enlighten eric exceptional exoteric express secret several sibylline specific suitable obfuscate obscure occult orphic otherworldly theory theosophy transmundane recondite resident respective restricted impenetrable individual initiate inner inside intend internal cabalistic certain circle close compilation concrete confined /cire/] "a compilation of esoteric philosophical theories"
*espouse 10-44-17 (v.) 1. choose and follow; as of theories, ideas, policies, strategies or plans 2. take up the cause, ideology, practice, method, of someone and use it as one's own 3. take in marriage [embrace ethnic seize select social splice spouse stick strategy supporter

sustain sweep partner pass perform pick plan policy practice promote purpose unify unite unsuitable uphold]
*espy 21-25-2 (v.) 1. catch sight of [encounter eye see sense sight spot spy sudden perceive pickup]
*esquire 16-31-6 (n.) 1. (in medieval England) an attendant and shield bearer to a knight; a candidate for knighthood 2. (British) a title of respect for a member of the English gentry ranking just below a knight; placed after the name (v.) 1. accompany as an escort [earl english escort europe scotland seduce serve shepherd shield squire stage swell quire unite usher inamorato ireland isle italian ranking renaissance respect]
*essence 05-45-67 (n.) 1. the choicest or most essential or most vital part of some idea or experience 2. the central meaning or theme of a speech or literary work 3. any substance possessing to a high degree the predominant properties of a plant or drug or other natural product from which it is extracted 4. a toiletry that emits and diffuses a fragrant odor [effect element embody emit esse existence experience express extract sense soul space speech spice spirit story stuff substance sum nature nitty nub nucleus case central chemical child choice city cologne communicate component constituent content cook core cosmetic critical crux /ness/]
*esthetic 10-AA-20 (a.) 1. concerning or characterized by an appreciation of beauty or good taste 2. relating to or dealing with the subject of aesthetics 3. aesthetically pleasing (n.) 1. a philosophical theory as to what is beautiful [ethics existence sensuous show success tasteful theory het illustration investigate concerning conform cosmetic /cite/] "the aesthetic faculties"
*estimable 18-38-4 (a.) 1. deserving of respect or high regard 2. may be computed or estimated 3. deserving of esteem and respect [elegant esteem exceptional extraordinary scorn sound special strong telling immaculate important incalculable influential marked merit model moral able admiration admire asset august benevolent blameless bonny laudable /amit bam/]
*estrange 08-52-27 (v.) 1. remove from customary environment or associations 2. arouse hostility or indifference in where there had formerly been love, affection, or friendliness [eject environment exacerbate expel scattered schedule schism segregated separate separation set sever split spouse stop strange sympathetic tear toward tradition transform turn reconciliation remove rupture abrupt affection aggravate alienate alone alter apart arouse association aversion group]
*estuary 11-77-14 (n.) 1. the wide part of a river where it nears the sea; fresh and salt water mix [earth england escape exhaust exit salt scotland sea section sound spout strait stream stu surface tap tide trent uruguay argentina arm armlet avenue reach rio river roadstead]
*eulogize 21-03-2 (v.) 1. praise formally and eloquently [eloquent emblazon exalt express extol laud lionize log glorify idolize /zig/] "The dead woman was eulogized at the funeral"
*eulogy 14-54-8 (n.) 1. a formal expression of praise [elegy encomium exaltation exhortation expression lionize logy obsequies oration glory great]
*euphemism 11-55-16 (n.) 1. an inoffensive expression that is substituted for one that is considered offensive [elegant euphuism expression exquisite understatement unnatural unpleasant pedantry people place pretentious purist harsh hemi mannerism might mild military mincing mitigate inadvertent indirect inflict inoffensive saying simper situation substitute substitution synonym]
*euphoria 10-55-18 (n.) 1. a feeling of great (usually exaggerated) elation [ease ecstasy elation entertainment exaggerate excite exhilarate extreme exult phoria pleasure preoccupation pride happy high hypochondria hysteric obsession rapture reconciliation relish resignation indifference insensible intoxicate abnormal acceptance alienate amusement]
*eureka 17-54-5 (n.) 1. a copper-nickel alloy with high electrical resistance and a low temperature coefficient; used as resistance wire 2. a town in northwest California on an arm of the Pacific Ocean [earthquake electrical express unite urban resistance roll rug alloy area arm /rue/]
*euthanasia 15-63-7 (n.) 1. the act of killing someone painlessly (especially someone suffering from an incurable illness) [execution exterminate terminate than asia assist sacrifice shoot stone suffering illegal illness immolate incurable injury]
*evade 07-51-34 (v.) 1. escape, either physically or mentally 2. avoid or try to avoid fulfilling, answering, or performing (duties, questions, or issues) 3. practice evasion 4. use cleverness or deceit to escape or avoid [elude equivocate escape eschew evasion explanation victimize abstain achieve ade answer avoid deal deceit difficult directly ditch dodge double duck /ave/]
*evanescent 19-31-3 (a.) 1. tending to vanish like vapor [embryonic ephemeral evanesce evaporate vanish vapor volatile atomic short soon subatomic capricious changeable corruptible temporary tend tenuous thin transient /ave nave/] "evanescent beauty"
*evangelical 08-56-28 (a.) 1. relating to or being a Christian church believing in personal conversion and the inerrancy of the Bible especially the 4 Gospels 2. of or pertaining to or in keeping with the Christian gospel especially as in the first 4 books of the New Testament 3. marked by ardent or zealous enthusiasm for a cause [eager emphasize enthusiastic evangelistic excitement accept acceptance angelic angelica approve ardent authority gospel great literalism ideal inerrant inspired interest christian church conversion correct customary /ave leg nave/] "evangelical Christianity"
*evangelist 11-47-15 (n.) 1. a preacher of the Christian gospel 2. any of the spiritual leaders who re assumed to be authors of the New Testament Gospels [epistle evangel extravagant venerate votary adore affair apostle

assume author noted gathering graham guru leader luke lyman idolater sacred sage saint say second sermonize service spiritual swami television testament third traditional try /ave leg nave sile/]
*evasion 09-39-25 (n.) 1. a statement that is not literally false but that cleverly avoids an unpleasant truth 2. the act of physically escaping from something (an opponent or a pursuer or an unpleasant situation) by some adroit maneuver 3. nonperformance of something distasteful (as by deceit or trickery) that you are supposed to do 4. the deliberate act of failing to pay money [elusive emerge equivocation eva excuse expression vent abstention artifice shift shy slip impartial independence issue outguess outlet outwit neutrality nonaligned /ave save/] "his evasion of all his creditors"
*evasive 14-54-9 (a.) 1. deliberately vague or ambiguous 2. skillful at eluding capture 3. avoiding or escaping from difficulty or danger especially enemy fire [elude elusory enemy equivocal equivocate escape eva vague achieve adapt afford ambiguous amoral answer arch artful artless attack avoid shifty significance sinister skillful sliding slippery statement suspicious immoral indirect insidious interpretation issue /ave save visa/] "his answers were brief, constrained and evasive"
*eventual 06-49-50 (a.) 1. expected to follow in the indefinite future from causes already operating [ending ensue event expect extreme terminal trend ultimate unavoidable utmost already anticipate last later latest likely /neve/] "hope of eventual (or ultimate) rescue"
*evert 17-23-5 (n.) 1. United States tennis player who won women's singles titles in the United States and at Wimbledon (born in 1954) (v.) 1. turn inside out; turn the inner surface of outward [ever eyelid resupinate retroversion reverse tennis title transpose turn] "evert the eyelid"
*evict 07-40-42 (v.) 1. expel or eject without recourse to legal process 2. expel from one's property or force to move out by a legal process [eject exclude expel expropriate expulsion vic insult chase chuck comply cutoff tenant throw title turf turn turnout] "The landlord wanted to evict the tenants so he banged on the pipes every morning at 3 a.m."
*evidential 23-95-1 (a.) 1. serving as or based on evidence [effect entry epiphany evident exploratory expository expressive valid value identify important individual insignificant investigatory irresistible designate display document documentary name nuncupative telling theophany typical absolute appear authentic law /dive lait/] "evidential signs of a forced entry"
*evince 17-40-5 (v.) 1. give expression to [emphasize evidence exhibit expression ventilate vince voice illustrate impart imply important indirect involve necessary call cause clearly confirm connote consequence convey]
*evoke 05-35-86 (v.) 1. call forth 2. call forth; of emotions, feelings, and responses 3. deduce (a principle) or construe (a meaning) 4. evoke or call forth, with or as if by magic 5. call to mind or evoke [educe effect element elicit emotion engage evil evince excite expression extract objection obtain offend out outline overtake kick kindle]
*evolution 05-47-67 (n.) 1. a process in which something passes by degrees to a different stage (especially a more advanced or mature stage) 2. (biology) the sequence of events involved in the evolutionary development of a species or taxonomic group of organisms [early effective elaborate emission entirely equation era essential evolve exercise extend vapor variation verdict violate vitality volute operation organism later law lead level life living long lower unfold upgrowth taxonomy teach tennessee theory trait transformation trial idea induce interpolate inversion involution ion natural notation /love/]
*evolve 04-41-102 (v.) 1. acquire or build up traits or characteristics 2. undergo development or evolution 3. work out; as of a theory or an idea [early elaborate emit environment eradicate erect essence expansion experience explicate vapor via vol obtain ontogeny original originate leadership long lose /love/]
*exacerbate 07-68-34 (v.) 1. make worse 2. exasperate or irritate [enhance enlarge exaggerate exasperate excite excitement explosion abnormal acceleration acerb acerbate alienate already alter anger animation annoy arouse chafe cheapen complicate concentration condition consolidation contentious rasp redouble reduce reinforcement bad bitter blowup buildup tighten transform triple /axe tab/]
*exaggerate 05-53-86 (v.) 1. do something to an excessive degree 2. to enlarge beyond bounds or the truth [embellish embroider emphasis engage enhance enlarge enormous excessive exhaust explosion extreme eye abandon abnormal acceleration add affectation agger aggrandize aggravate amount amplify appear garble gas gasconade gigantic give gluttony grandiloquence great radicalism reasonable redouble reinforce report represent rhetoric romanticize tale tout trick triple true twist /axe egg tare/] "tended to romanticize and exaggerate this ``gracious Old South" imagery"
*exasperate 08-54-32 (v.) 1. exasperate or irritate 2. make furious 3. make worse [embitter enhance enlarge enrage exacerbate excite excitement exercise exhilarate abnormal aggravate agitation alter anger animation annoy arouse asper setup sharpen sour stimulus pain passive peeved persecution pesky pique placate plague problem provoke reduce repeat resentment ride rile roil round ruffle tease tiresome torment transform trial trouble /axe sax tare/]
*excavate 11-51-16 (v.) 1. lay bare through digging 2. form by hollowing 3. find by digging in the ground 4. remove the inner part or the core of [earth effort

eradicate evolve exhume expose careful cava cavity clear come company concrete condition core countersink cut cutout abstract archaeology artifact valuable view visible team tooth tree trench trough tunnel turn /vac/] "Schliemann excavated Troy"
*exceed 04-40-133 (v.) 1. be or do something to a greater degree 2. go beyond 3. go beyond [eclipse evil exaggerate excel expectation cap cee circumvent clever come competition conflict cost cruelty crush dare degree distinguish dollar draw] "Their loyalty exceeds their national bonds"
*excel 06-66-48 (v.) 1. distinguish oneself [eclipse exceed cap] "She excelled in math"
*excellence 05-67-61 (n.) 1. the quality of excelling; possessing good qualities in high degree 2. something in which something or some one excels [elegance elevation ellen eminence essential choice civilization class cuisine culture lead lofty nicety nobility note] "the use of herbs is one of the excellences of French cuisine"
*excellency 16-91-6 (n.) 1. a title used to address dignitaries (such as ambassadors or governors); usually preceded by Your or His or Her [ellen clergy course]
*excellent 02-66-294 (a.) 1. of the highest quality [elegant ellen expert extremely capital champion choice laudable lofty neat nice noble teacher terrific top transcend tremendous] "made an excellent speech"
*excerpt 06-11-52 (n.) 1. a passage selected from a larger work (v.) 1. take out of a literary work in order to cite or copy [extract choose citation cite clipping collection composition copy cut read recording particularly passage passive past philosophical pick piece press prophet take torah track] "he presented excerpts from William James' philosophical writings"
*excess 03-55-137 (a.) 1. more than is needed, desired, or required (n.) 1. immoderation as a consequence of going beyond sufficient or permitted limits 2. a quantity much larger than is needed 3. excessive indulgence 4. the state of being more than full [embarrassment employment enhance enough enthusiasm exorbitance expansion extreme capacity caricature cess cheese child condition consequence constitute crapulous sensationalism social spare spoil stretch sufficient supernumerary surfeit surplus surplusage] "trying to lose excess weight"
*excitable 14-78-8 (a.) 1. easily excited 2. (physiology) capable of responding to stimuli [easy edgy emotional eruptive explosive capable cranky cross crusty impulsive inflammable insensitive irascible irritable table temperamental testy tissue touchy apprehensive bearish biological bitchy branch liable]
*exclamation 14-42-8 (n.) 1. an abrupt excited utterance 2. an exclamatory rhetorical device 3. a loud complaint or protest or reproach [effect ejaculate emotion emphatic excited expletive express call clam comment communication complaint confusion create cry language literary loud abrupt address allegation anger answer auditory mention more tempo thought interjection observation outburst outcry note] "she gave an exclamation of delight"
*exclude 03-54-154 (v.) 1. prevent from entering; keep out 2. lack or fail to include 3. prevent from entering; shut out 4. prevent from being included or considered or accepted 5. put out or expel from a place [eject elide eliminate employee enter ethnocentrism except exercise exile exorcize expel xenophobia celebrate certain chuck church clip consider cost country crop curse cut lack leave legal less liquidate list lockout look lop lude unimaginable unless unthinkable deal debar decline deny deport disallow discount dislodge dismiss displace disregard door dwell] "The bad results were excluded from the report"
*exclusion 07-56-34 (n.) 1. the state of being excluded 2. the act of expelling someone 3. a deliberate act of omission 4. the state of being excommunicated [eject eliminate embargo exception excommunicate exile expel expulsion censure certain child circumstance combination complaint consent contradiction country coventry law leave lockout undesirable unfrock unhappy sanction scouting segregation statute strip ignore indignation injunction ion objection omission ostracize ouster negative neglect]
*excruciate 12-59-13 (v.) 1. torment emotionally or mentally 2. subject to torture [emotional enough exquisite extremely consuming cramp cringe cruciate cruel curling rack rend unbearable unendurable inflict infuriate injury insufferable intense irritate acute afflict agonizing anguish awful tearing terrible toe tor torment torture torturous]
*exculpate 24-57-1 (v.) 1. pronounce not guilty of criminal charges [excuse exemption exonerate explanation charge clear clearing compurgation condone criminal label let pardon pate perfunctory presentation pro proof prove purge absolve accusation acquit acquittance amnesty assoil]
*excursion 08-49-31 (n.) 1. a journey taken for pleasure 2. wandering from the main path of a journey [episode equilibrium examination excursus expedition campaign cautious corner course cover cur unsuccessful rambling red regular rest return ride run sail sashay sheer shoot short summer indirect obliquity open orbit organ oscillate outing nonconformity] "many summer excursions to the shore"
*excusable 24-74-1 (a.) 1. capable of being overlooked 2. easily excused or forgiven [easily error explicable capable understandable unpardonable admit allowable]
*execrable 21-79-2 (a.) 1. of very poor quality or condition 2. unequivocally detestable 3. deserving a curse [edmund error evil evoke extremely city condition crime criminal crude cursed curst rank repellent reptile repulsive revolting abhorrent abject able abominable accuse appalling atrocious awful bad base behavior black bless burke little loathsome lovable low

/bar/]
*executor 15-52-7 (n.) 1. a person appointed by a testator to carry out the terms of the will [effector engineer exec carry conceive construct court creator task testator trust operator organizer originator raise realize]
*exegesis 21-41-2 (n.) 1. an explanation or critical interpretation (especially of the Bible) 2. critical interpretation of a text (especially of the Bible) [edit enlightenment exemplify explanation gloss god good sacred scholium scripture simplify solution specific illustration interpret]
*exemplar 17-51-5 (n.) 1. something to be imitated [example exemplify explanation major masterwork mirror modern pacesetter paradigm paragon pattern percept perfect prototype lar lead literary archetype attain representative] "an exemplar of success"
*exemplary 09-62-22 (a.) 1. worthy of imitation 2. serving to warn 3. being or serving as an illustration of a type [emblematic estimable excellent exemplar exhibit expert masterly mature merit model monitory perfect persuasive polished praiseworthy prototype punishment pure laudable admirable admonitory archetype atypical realistic regular representative] "exemplary behavior"
*exemplify 09-43-22 (v.) 1. clarify by giving an example of 2. be characteristic of [edit elaborate embody enlarge enlightenment epitomize example except excuse expatiate expound map mirror model particular personify plan point popularize portray project law leader learn legal letter light limn lucubration idea illustrate image instance few figure flesh foreshadow free fugue]
*exempt 05-32-70 (a.) 1. (of persons) freed from or not subject to an obligation or liability (as e.g. taxes) to which others or other things are subject 2. (of goods or funds) not subject to taxation (v.) 1. grant relief or an exemption from a rule or requirement to 2. grant exemption or release to [enforce ensure entitle exam except excuse exonerate experience mean military pass payment permit poor privilege process purge tax] "She exempted me from the exam"
*exert 07-51-40 (v.) 1. make a great effort at a mental or physical task 2. of power or authority 3. put to use [effect effort employ endeavor excessive exercise expend task tell throw toil try /rex/] "exert one's power or influence"
*exhale 16-44-6 (v.) 1. expel air 2. give out, as of breath or an odor [emanate emit exhaust expel expire hack hale hard hiccup huff aerate atomize lift literary lung]
*exhaust 04-57-105 (n.) 1. gases ejected from an engine as waste products 2. system consisting of the parts of an engine through which burned gases or steam are discharged (v.) 1. deplete 2. use up, as of resources or materials 3. wear out completely 4. create a vacuum in (a bulb, flask, reaction vessel, etc.) 5. use up the whole supply of [eat eject eliminate emotional empty enervate enfeeble entirely erode escape eviscerate excess expand expend extent hack harass hard harsh heavy huff abate absorb acoustic apparatus arduous arid artifact automobile avenue unfruitful unhealthy unplowed unused unwanted sap saving shape silencer skin smoke spatial spent steam sterile strain stress supply tap tax temporal tired travel try tubular tucker tyranny] "This kind of work exhausts me"
*exhaustion 09-60-21 (n.) 1. extreme fatigue 2. serious weakening and loss of energy 3. the act of exhausting something entirely [eliminate empty enervate enfeeble entirely exhaust extremely hard heat hour hypochondriasis abate absorption affect agency aid attrition unhealthy unload unsound serious soften spend squander stock strength temporary thin tired imminent impoverish inanition infirmity ingest neurasthenia]
*exhaustive 10-48-17 (a.) 1. very thorough; exhaustively complete [egregious entire exhaust extensive hand heavy holistic absolute account aggregate all author ubiquitous universal utter search serious step straight strong study sweep thorough thoroughgoing total inclusive incomplete intensive irresistible veritable] "an exhaustive study"
*exhibitionist 18-68-4 (a.) 1. compulsively attracting attention to yourself especially by boasting or exaggerated behavior (n.) 1. someone with a compulsive desire to expose the genitals 2. someone who deliberately behaves in such a way as to attract attention [egotist erotomania exaggerate exhibition expose eye habitual himself hot inconspicuous behavior boast braggart bugger transvestite obvious naked narcissism necrophilia nymphomaniac sadist satyr self showboat showoff spectator sst stunt swellhead]

*exhilarate 07-58-37 (v.) 1. fill with sublime emotion; tickle pink (exhilarate is obsolete in this usage) [ebullient elate emotion encourage enliven entertain exalt excite exuberant happy heady hearten heaven high hilar hopeful impassioned impressive incite inebriate infection inflammatory inform inject inspiration intoxicate intrigue invigorate laughing lift liven activate adrenaline aggravation agitation agog alive amuse animate archaism arouse rack rapture recreation refreshing rejuvenate relax renew revive roller thrill tickle tingly titillate tonic]
*exhume 14-57-9 (v.) 1. dig up for reburial or for medical investigation; of dead bodies [excavate hume unearth medical /emu/]
*exigency 21-41-2 (n.) 1. a pressing or urgent situation 2. a sudden unforeseen crisis (usually involving danger) that requires immediate action [emergency extreme extremity immediate impulsion insistent gen necessity never clutch constraint cope course crisis crucial crunch] "the health-care exigency"
*existence 04-52-132 (n.) 1. everything that exists anywhere 2. the state or fact of existing [endurance entity essence exist experience immediate immortal

individuality something soul survival thing timeless nebula continuation cosmos creature critter /six/]
*exit 04-58-135 (n.) 1. an opening that permits escape or release 2. the act of going out 3. euphemistic expressions for death (v.) 1. move out of or depart from 2. pass from physical life and lose all all bodily attributes and functions necessary to sustain life 3. lose the lead, in card games [early egress eject emerge end enter escape euphemism exodus expire expressway ingress inlet intersection issue tap termination theater transform trench tunnel turn]
*exodus 08-52-27 (n.) 1. a journey by a large group to escape from a hostile environment 2. the second book of the Old Testament: tells of the departure of the Israelites out of slavery in Egypt led by Moses; God gave them the Ten Commandments and the rest of Mosaic law on Mount Sinai during the Exodus [egypt emigration environment escape evacuation exit old outgoing decamp departure divertissement division sacred scene scripture second sinai sketch skit slavery /udo/]
*exonerate 10-50-17 (v.) 1. pronounce not guilty of criminal charges [excuse exemption explain obligation official nonpros rate redemption release relieve remit reprieve reputation responsibility absolve accusation acquit acquittance allow amnesty assoil /nox tare/]
*exoneration 21-41-2 (n.) 1. the condition of being relieved from blame or obligation 2. the act of vindicating or defending against criticism or censure etc. [excuse exemption explain obligation reasoning reestablishment release relieve reputation absolution acquittal]
*exorbitant 13-51-10 (a.) 1. greatly exceeding bounds of reason or moderation [enormous entertain excessive extortionate extreme orbit outrageous overprice overwrought rate rent ridiculous rigorous rough ballyhoo beyond bound boundless immoderate inflated inordinate insistent instant interest tall tough tout towering abandon acute amount amplify] "exorbitant rent"
*exorcise 15-62-7 (v.) 1. expel through adjuration or prayers; of evil spirits; in certain religions [eject evil exclude expel express oppressive orc religious rid ritual certain chuck clear influence institution intention send spirit suppose /cro/]
*exotic 04-55-94 (a.) 1. being or from or characteristic of another place or part of the world 2. strikingly strange or unusual [ecology engaging entrance exceptional excite odd originate other otic outlandish outside taking tease tempting tropical import independent interesting introduce catching charming colorful costume country crazy culture custom]
*expand 02-38-296 (v.) 1. exaggerate or make bigger 2. grow stronger 3. make bigger or wider in size, volume, or quantity 4. become larger in size or volume or quantity 5. extend in one or more directions 6. add details, as to an account or idea; clarify the meaning of and discourse in a learned way, usually in writing 7. expand the influence of [elaborate enlarge evolve expatiate expound extend parlay particularize prolong pyramid abridge aggrandize ahead amplify and augment deploy detail development dilate] "The dough expands"
*expanse 10-44-19 (n.) 1. the extent of a 2-dimensional surface enclosed within a boundary 2. a wide scope 3. a wide and open space or area as of surface or land or sky [enclose enormousness entity erase existence expansion extent pan perceive place plain power prodigious proportion purpose acreage amplitude area non nothingness scope sea size sky space span spread square staff stretch surface sweep /snap/]
*expansion 03-45-170 (n.) 1. the act of increasing in size or volume or quantity or scope 2. a discussion that provides additional information 3. adding information or detail [elaborate enhance extent extreme peak proportion publication addition amplification appreciation area note nothingness size space spreading subjunction increment inflation inordinate ion opening overstate /snap/]
*expatriate 08-38-30 (n.) 1. voluntarily absent from home or country (v.) 1. expel from a country 2. move away from one's native country and adopt a new residence abroad [eliminate emigrate exclude exile expel pariah patriate people period prolong proscribe punishment purge abroad absent abstract admit adopt throw transport trek refugee relegate remove run immigrate /airt/]
*expect 01-54-2149 (v.) 1. look forward to the birth of a child 2. look forward to the probable occurrence of 3. consider obligatory; request and expect 4. be pregnant with 5. consider reasonable or due 6. regard something as probable or likely [eager envisage envision esteem estimate excited explanation parturient pass pec perceive phone plan predict pregnant prepared presume probably progressive project promise promotion proof prospective calm carry case certain child compose conclude confident conjecture consider contemplate cool count teem tense tentative theorize think third threaten tomorrow toward true trust turn] "The meteorologists are expecting rain for tomorrow"
*expectancy 10-71-19 (n.) 1. something expected (as on the basis of a norm) 2. pleasurable expectation [excited expect picture pleasurable probability prospect calculation climax crowd amount anticipation approach aware nervous norm]
*expediency 16-51-6 (n.) 1. the quality of being suited to the end in view [effective excellence expedient pleasant position practicality pragmatism pregnancy profitable propriety desert design die immediate nice careworn class cogency consider convenience course crisis]
*expedient 16-50-6 (a.) 1. serving to promote your interest 2. appropriate to a purpose; practical (n.) 1. a means to an end; not necessarily a principled or ethical

one [effective effort emergency ervin ethical excellent express plot politic possible practical pragmatic principle promote prudent purpose decent desirable device die improvise influence interest intrigue necessary nice noble tactics timely trump] "was merciful only when mercy was expedient"
*expedite 13-14-10 (v.) 1. speed up the progress of; facilitate 2. process fast and efficiently [edit eff efficient encourage ensure explain express place post press process progress promote deal dispatch institute transaction transmit try /tide/] "This should expedite the process"
*expeditious 18-19-4 (a.) 1. characterized by speed and efficiency [edit eff effective effectual efficient effort express passing precipitate prompt pronto punctual dashing decisive delay diligent directly double immediately instantly tenacious tight trippingly once urgent secure sharp slow smart speedy steady swift /tide/]
*expend 12-48-12 (v.) 1. pay out 2. use up, consume fully [eat economize effort employ end energy erode exchange exhaust extravagant pass pay payout pend penny pervert place possible postpaid prepay purpose put normal deplete devote digest disburse discharge dissipated distribute drop] "The legislature expended its time on school questions."
*expense 02-41-254 (n.) 1. money spent to perform work and usually reimbursed by an employer 2. a detriment or sacrifice 3. amounts paid for goods and services that may be currently tax deductible (as opposed to capital expenditures) [employer evaluate expenditure pay payment pen perdition performance period personal premium preserve prevention price privation problem promote property purpose necessary sacrifice score service specify spent strip] "at the expense of"
*expertise 05-57-87 (n.) 1. skillfulness by virtue of possessing special knowledge [efficiency epicure expert polymath possess privity proficiency prowess ready tactful technique time information intelligence intimacy savvy seaman skillful special style]

*expiate 24-42-1 (v.) 1. make amends for [eat pay payback penance propitiate punishment indemnity injury abye amend amends apology appease atone] "expiate one's sins"
*explicate 19-17-3 (v.) 1. make palin and comprehensible 2. elaborate, as of theories and hypotheses [elaborate elucidate evolve exemplify experience expound particularize physics plainplicate popularize law literary idea illuminate illustrate impart implication improve inform interpret interpretation clarify clear comprehensible conjecture construe crack acquire affair allegorize amplify tentative theme theory thesis]
*explicit 05-43-69 (a.) 1. precisely and clearly expressed or readily observable; leaving nothing to implication 2. in accordance with fact or the primary meaning of a term [entire evident exact express perfect perspicuous plain portray positive power precise precisely primary lead leave licit limited limpid literal lucid luminous imply independent indisputable ingenuous inherent instruction interpretation candid categorical certain clearly complete conclusion correct cover tangible total] "explicit instructions"
*explode 04-48-111 (v.) 1. "I could hear rifles explode" 2. be unleashed; burst forth with violence or noise, as of an emotion or an expression of emotion 3. show a violent emotional reaction 4. burst outward, usually with noise 5. cause to explode 6. cause to burst as a result of air pressure; of stop consonants like /p/, /t/, and /k/ 7. destroy by exploding 8. drive from the stage by noisy disapproval 9. increase rapidly and in an uncontrolled manner 10. show to be baseless, or refute and make obsolete, as of a new theory or claim [emotional enemy enunciate erupt expose expression part pop position provide puncture link lode loose obsolete oil outward overturn deflate deny destroy detonate direction discredit dispute doubt drawing /dol/] "We exploded the nuclear bomb"
*exploit 03-62-151 (n.) 1. a notable achievement (v.) 1. draw from; make good use of (resources) 2. use or manipulate to one's advantage 3. work excessively hard [earth easy effort egress emerge employ equalize excavation excessive excite exercise exhume expect extract parent passage perform performance permission persuadable pliable practical production profit propulsion provoke purpose operation overwork implement ingenuous inherent interest tap taxation touch tour transaction turn] "He exploit the new taxation system"
*explosion 04-44-126 (n.) 1. the act of exploding or bursting something 2. a violent release of energy caused by a chemical or nuclear reaction 3. the terminal forced release of pressure built up during the occlusive phase of a stop consonant [effusion enhance eruption expansion exposure paddy paroxysm pickup plosion plosive pop leap outburst scene shot sound strengthen stroke increase intensify invalidate negation] "the explosion of the firecrackers awoke the children"
*explosive 04-46-123 (a.) 1. liable to lead to sudden change or violence 2. tending or serving to explode or characterized by explosion or sudden outburst 3. sudden and loud (n.) 1. a chemical substance that undergoes a rapid chemical change (with the production of gas) on being heated or struck [edgy eruptive excitable peak plastic plosive pop lateral lingual liquid occlusive sensitive serious short stop iffy irascible irritable voice volatile volcanic] "an explosive device"
*exposition 10-21-19 (n.) 1. a systematic interpretation or explanation (usually written) of a specific topic 2. a collection of things (goods or works of art etc.) for

public display 3. an account that sets forth the meaning or intent of a writing or discourse [edit elucidate enlighten essayist exercise exhibition explanation explicate expound expressive part performance period position preacher publicist ornament ostentation outline scholiast section sermonize serve set showcase statue study illustrative informative instructive interpretive talk task theme trade translator note /itis/] "we would have understood the play better if there had been some initial exposition of the background"
*expository 24-20-1 (a.) 1. serving to expound or set fourth [enlighten expositor serve set informative instructive /roti/] "clean expository writing"
*expostulate 24-60-1 (v.) 1. reason with (somebody) for the purpose of dissuasion [earnest encourage except excited exhort express persuasion postulate present prompt protest purpose objection opposition scruple squawk strike talk urge utterance abrupt admonish argument attempt]
*exposure 04-51-122 (n.) 1. aspect re light or wind 2. the disclosure of something secret 3. the act of subjecting someone to an influencing experience 4. vulnerability to the elements; to the action of heat or cold or wind or rain 5. abandoning without shelter or protection (as by leaving as infant out in the open) 6. presentation to view in an open or public manner 7. the act of exposing film to light 8. the intensity of light falling on a photographic film or plate 9. a picture of a person or scene in the form of a print or transparent slide; recorded by a camera on light-sensitive material 10. the state of being vulnerable or exposed [emerge experience explosion expo performance production publishing open orientation outlook scandal scene section set shelter shock strip sun sunlight uncover unearth unmask unveiling radiation rain range ray record reduce region report rise risk] "exposure to the weather"
*expressive 08-36-28 (a.) 1. (usually followed by 'of') giving expression to 2. characterized by expression [emotional explicit express extension pointed pregnant presentational realistic represent representative revelation rich sensitive showing signify speak striking substantial idea identify indicative individual interpretation vivid] "an expressive glance"
*expulsion 09-46-21 (n.) 1. the act of expelling someone 2. the act of expelling or projecting or ejecting 3. squeezing out by applying pressure [eject eliminate emesis eruct evict exclusion exile expel export extrusion party perfusion phlegm place political projection propulsion proscription puke punishment purge undesirable unfrock unseat leave liquidate lung saliva school society spit spreading spurt squeeze stomach suspension impeach import interchange ion ostracise oust ouster outburst negative noisy]
*expunge 18-54-4 (v.) 1. remove by erasing or crossing out [edit end eradicate erase excise exclude extinct perfect pung purge unwanted]
*extant 19-43-3 (a.) 1. still in existence; not extinct or destroyed or lost [exist extinct topical actuality alive ant around art new] "extant manuscripts"
*extemporaneous 24-09-1 (a.) 1. with little or no preparation or forethought [excuse extemporize extra tempora temporary toast makeshift measure perform piano poor precipitate prepare offhand offthecuff reassure recital redan advance note unorganized unplanned unrehearsed unstudied say show skill skit snap sound speak spontaneous surprise /met/]
*extension 03-49-140 (n.) 1. act of stretching or straightening out a flexed limb 2. an educational opportunity provided by colleges and universities to people who not enrolled as regular students 3. act of expanding in scope; making more widely available 4. the spreading of something (a belief or practice) into new regions 5. a mutually agreed delay in the date set for the completion of a job or payment of a debt 6. an addition that extends a main building 7. an addition to the length of something 8. amount or degree or range to which something extends 9. an additional telephone set that is connected to the same telephone line 10. the most direct or specific meaning of a word or expression; the class of objects that an expression refers to [effect elongation enlargement expansion extent extra tailpiece telephone telephony tenor tension nothingness sense series space idea impact import instruction offshoot orbit overtone] "they applied for an extension of the loan"
*extensive 03-39-167 (a.) 1. great in range or scope 2. large in number or quantity (especially of discourse) 3. having broad range or effect 4. large in spatial extent or range 5. of agriculture; increasing productivity by using large areas with minimal outlay and labor [effect enormous expansive experience extension tall technological tensive titanic treatment tremendous national non northwest note scarce scope selection set settlement sewage significantly size social spatial spreading structure substantial sweep immense include inconsiderable increase infinite input intensive international vast vocabulary voluminous] "an extensive Roman settlement in northwest England"
*extenuate 21-46-2 (v.) 1. lessen or to try to lessen the seriousness or extent of [ease eat excuse exhaust explain tame temper try underplay unman unnerve abate alleviate alter apologize appear assuage authority] "The circumstances extenuate the crime"
*exterior 07-42-39 (a.) 1. situated in or suitable for the outdoors or outside of a building (n.) 1. the outer side or surface of something 2. the region that is outside of something [envelope epidermis exotic ext external threedimensi top townscape triviality twodimension region represent rind riverscape roundabout image inner inside interior open out outer outside outstanding outward] "an exterior scene"

*external 05-64-63 (a.) 1. exogenous 2. coming from the outside 3. from or between other countries 4. happening or arising or located outside or beyond some limits or especially surface 5. purely outward or superficial (n.) 1. outward features [endogenous enjoy envelope environment essential exist exogenous exotic exterior extern extrinsic top trade true reality relation religion reputation rind roundabout nation nature near affair alien apparent appearance arise aspect auditory light limit lineament locate] "the external auditory canal"
*extinct 10-41-20 (a.) 1. no longer in existence; lost or especially having died out leaving no living representatives 2. of a fire; being out or having grown cold 3. of e.g. volcanos; permanently inactive [end energy erupt exert existence expire extant extinguish temporary terminate tinct inactive inexistent irrecoverable nonexistent candle capacity case cease cigarette civilization clod cold complete conclude custom] "an extinct species of fish"
*extinguish 10-42-19 (v.) 1. put an end to; kill 2. kill in large numbers 3. put out, as of fires, flames, or lights 4. extinguish by crushing [eclipse eliminate enemy entire eradicate except exclude takeout ten terminate throttle ting turn turnout ignite intentional invalid isolate necessary nip nullify gag give great uproot show silence smother snuff squash stamp start stub suppress surpass survivor switch halt heat hope]
*extol 11-45-16 (v.) 1. praise, glorify, or honor [elevate emblazon ensky enthusiasm eulogize exalt express ext treat trumpet language laud lift lionize /lot/] "extol the virtues of one's children"
*extort 14-25-8 (v.) 1. obtain through intimidation 2. obtain by coercion or intimidation 3. get or cause to become in a difficult or laborious manner [embezzle evil exact executive extract take thieve threat tort obtain overcharge rack requisition reveal rip rob rustle /trot/] "They extorted money from the executive by threatening to reveal his past to the company boss"
*extortion 10-26-17 (n.) 1. an exorbitant charge 2. the felonious act of extorting money (as by threats of violence) 3. unjust exaction (as by the misuse of authority) [exaction excessive exorbitant exploitation extort tax tearing threat tribute obtain official order overcharge rend ripping rob illegal impost indent notice /trot/] "the extortion by dishonest officials of fees for performing their sworn duty"
*extradite 10-52-17 (v.) 1. hand over to the authorities of another country [exclude exile expel export extra throw transfer transpose trial turnover refugee relegate repatriate restore return accuse assign authority deliver deport different disseminate impart import /dart/]
*extradition 09-54-23 (n.) 1. the surrender of an accused or convicted person by one state or country to another (usually under the provisions of a statute or treaty) [exclusion exile export expulsion tradition transposition travel treaty trial relegate repatriate restore return accuse arrest authority delivery deport deprivation different import interchange osmosis outlawry /dart/]
*extrajudicial 24-42-1 (a.) 1. beyond the usual course of legal proceedings; legally unwarranted [rule accept judicial jurisdiction unwarranted usual illegal court law legal /jar laic/] "an extrajudicial penalty"
*extraneous 17-37-5 (a.) 1. not essential 2. not pertinent to the matter under consideration 3. coming from the outside 4. not belonging to that in which it is contained; introduced from an outside source [exist exotic external extra extrinsic relevant removed rest add additional adulterate apart applicable arise needless nonessential objective originate other outside ulterior unconnected unearthly unimportant unnecessary unrelated segregate separate source spoil strange struck superfluous] "an issue extraneous to the debate"
*extraordinary 02-53-301 (a.) 1. (of an official) serving an unusual or special function in addition to those of the regular officials 2. far more than usual or expected 3. beyond what is ordinary or usual; highly unusual or exceptional or remarkable [esteem exceptional express exquisite exuberant telling terrific rare remarkable respective richly abnormal absolute acute amazing appalling astonish odd ordinary outlandish outstanding detailed different distinguished impressive incomparable incredible individual inner inordinate intense negotiate noble notably noticeable /oar rani roar/] "extraordinary authority"
*extravagance 12-64-13 (n.) 1. something that is an indulgence rather than a necessity 2. excessive spending 3. the trait of spending extravagantly [economic enhance enough exaggerate excessive expansion expensive extra thoughtless tirade today tout trait travesty treat truth rampant rank redundancy resource abandon abundance affluent appropriate verbosity generous glitter gorgeous nature necessity needless non numerous car careless caricature climate colorful condemn consuming crude /nag/]
*extravagant 07-59-40 (a.) 1. recklessly wasteful 2. unrestrained in especially feelings [elaborate elegant enormous exaggerate excessive exist expenditure expensive extra exuberant tall tend terribly tough tout reasonable reckless restraint richly ridiculous riotous rough abandon abundant acute affluent ambition awfully vehement violent vulgar gaudy generous glorious grand great greed gross nakedly noble nonsensical numerous /nag/] "extravagant praise"
*extremist 06-61-55 (a.) 1. (used of opinions and actions) far beyond the norm (n.) 1. a person who holds extreme views [education extreme extremis terrorist traitor radical reasonable rebel red revolutionary malcontent maverick moderate mutineer idea inordinate intemperate irrational subversive syndicalism] "extremist political views"
*extremity 16-59-6 (n.) 1. an external body part that projects from the body 2. an extreme condition or state

(especially of adversity or disease) 3. that part of a limb that is farthest from the torso 4. the greatest or utmost degree 5. the outermost or farthest region or point [edge egg emergency end except external terminal terrorism thumb tip toe top torso region release remit rescue roughness manus march margin mark measure member middle misfortune mitt modify mouth impasse important incontinent indicate insect intensity interface /time timer/]
*extricate 14-53-8 (v.) 1. release from entanglement of difficulty [emerge entangle eradicate evolve expression extract takeout task recovery release remove rescue issue capable cate clearing complicate constraint contract cutout avulsion] "i cannot extricate myself from this task"
*extrovert 14-66-9 (a.) 1. characterized by extroversion (n.) 1. (psychology) a person concerned more with practical realities than with inner thoughts and feelings [effusive expansive external talkative tend reality open outgoing outside outspoken outward overt]
*extrude 24-34-1 (v.) 1. form or shape by forcing through an opening; as of metal [elaborate elect emerge through turnout raise reject remove rude defenestrate devise dismiss]
*exuberance 09-54-21 (n.) 1. joyful enthusiasm 2. overflowing with enthusiasm [ebullient emotion energy enthusiasm era exaggerate excitement expression unrestrained animation apathy cheerful]
*exuberant 06-49-54 (a.) 1. joyously unrestrained 2. unrestrained in especially feelings 3. produced or growing in extreme abundance [ebullient ecstatic elaborate emotion energetic energy enthusiastic excite excited exhaustless exhilarate expression extreme unrestrained blessed blissful blooming blossom boisterous bonanza boom buoyant burn rampant rank rant redundancy reiterate restraint rich riotous abandon abundant affluent ambition ample animation apathy numerous teem thick thrive]

F

*fabricate 10-33-18 (v.) 1. put together out of components or parts 2. make up something artificial or untrue [fabric fact fake falsify fancy fantasy fashion feign forge form formulate frame accuse artificial assemble beget breed bring build raft raise rear refined replace imagine incorporate invent car cast charge combine component concoct confabulate construct contrive cook counterfeit craft create think toy true trump turnout elaborate engineer erect evidence evolve extract]
*fabulous 05-75-75 (a.) 1. extremely pleasing 2. barely credible 3. based on or told of in traditional stories; lacking factual basis or historical validity [fab fable factual fancy fantastic fascinating abandon ace acknowledge almost amazing barely base basis beguile belief bewildering beyond boundless unbelievable understand unicorn unique unprecedented unreal lack legend legendary look outfit outlandish outrageous outstand satisfaction signal story strange striking substance sum] "a fabulous vacation"
*facet 10-40-18 (n.) 1. a distinct feature or element in a problem 2. a smooth surface (as of a bone or cut gemstone) [face factor feature figure flat form anatomy anterior area arthropod article aspect case compound contrast count covering cut effect element external eye thing tooth top twist /tec/] "he studied every facet of the question"
*facetious 18-45-4 (a.) 1. cleverly amusing in tone [facet flippant foolish frivolous full funny advice amusing clever comical time tone tongueinche ill inane inappropriate intend saltine sharp silly smart sparkle suppose /tec/]
*facial 07-67-38 (a.) 1. of or concerning the face (n.) 1.

cranial nerve that supplies facial muscles 2. care for the face that usually involves cleansing and massage and the application of cosmetic creams [face facia follow forehead front application care chin cleanse concerning cosmetic cranial cream involve /laic/] "a facial massage"
*facile 15-54-7 (a.) 1. arrived at without due care or effort; lacking depth 2. performing adroitly and without effort 3. expressing yourself readily, clearly, effectively [facetious flippant flow fluent formative adaptable adroit affecting apparently apt arrive articulate care casual clearly clever complex concern cursory impressionable inane intelligent language light limber lithe easy educate effective effortless elegant eloquent emotional expressive] "too facile a solution for so complex a problem"
*facilitate 08-57-32 (v.) 1. make easier 2. physiology: increase the likelihood of (a response) 3. be of use [favor forward further accelerate accident advantage aid alleviate assistance conduce contribute impulse intentional likelihood loose lubricate tate ease easy enable encourage expedite explain] "you could facilitate the process by sharing your knowledge"
*facility 02-53-270 (n.) 1. a building or place that provides a particular service or is used for a particular industry 2. skillful performance or ability without difficulty 3. a service that an organization or a piece of equipment offers you 4. services and space and equipment provided for a particular purpose 5. a natural effortlessness [facility feature field firm fixture flair flow force forum furniture ability address adept adroit advantage agency appliance appointment aptitude armament capacity concern control convenience corporation impedimenta ingenuity institution intelligence landing lavatory lean lit lodge loft tackle talent technique thing toilet] "the assembly plant is an enormous facility"
*facsimile 14-31-8 (n.) 1. an exact copy or reproduction 2. duplicator that transmits the copy by wire or radio (v.) 1. send something via a facsimile machine [fax apparatus autotype clone coin communicate copy counterpart secondary selfsame send simile synonym idem imitation machine material model likeness longdistance equivalent exact /misc/]
*faction 05-34-68 (n.) 1. a clique that seeks power usually through intrigue 2. a dissenting clique [fellowship flak fleet abortion accept action affiliate antagonism argue argumentation cabal camarilla camp church circle clique community conflict conservatism contention coterie crowd team tribe troop idea induce inequality infighting inner interest intrigue offshoot order organization outfit negation]
*fallacious 24-40-1 (a.) 1. containing or based on a fallacy 2. intended to deceive 3. based on an incorrect or misleading notion or information [fact fall false fantastic faulty flaw force fraudulent abroad adrift advert airy argument legal loose casuistic catchy cheat cogency conformity corrupt ice idea imaginary inconsistent intend invalid irrational off ostensible out unfounded unreasonable untrue scheme seeming senseless shin sole stray /call calla ical/] "fallacious reasoning"
*fallacy 17-54-5 (n.) 1. a misconception resulting from incorrect reasoning [fall false falsity faulty follow fool friendly aberration antinomian argumentation assumption attribute line logical circumvent claptrap conclusion condition conn /call calla/]
*fallible 14-72-8 (a.) 1. likely to fail or be inaccurate 2. having the attributes of man as opposed to e.g. divine beings [failure fall faulty form frail frailty adulterate animal attribute lacking liable likely imperfect imperfection inaccurate inadequate incapable incomplete indicate blemish err errant erring error /bill/] "everyone is fallible to some degree"
*fallow 17-51-5 (a.) 1. left unplowed and unseeded during a growing season 2. undeveloped but potentially useful (n.) 1. cultivated land that is not seeded for one or more growing seasons [fertility flat force free future agriculture allow anemic arable arid available land left lemon list location ocher off orchard weak white work /olla/] "fallow farmland"
*falter 06-51-53 (n.) 1. the act of pausing uncertainly (v.) 1. speak haltingly 2. walk unsteadily 3. move hesitatingly, as if about to give way 4. be unsure or weak [fade fail fear feet flagging flutter fumble abate advance alter amble apology labor lag last lazy limp linger lose loss lumber lurch tail talk temporary tentative timid totter trail trip trudge tumble easy enthusiasm express relaxed reluctant retreat rock roll] "Their enthusiasm is faltering"
*famish 24-48-1 (v.) 1. be hungry; go without food 2. deprive of food 3. die of food deprivation [fast feel food function attribute mis impoverish starve suffering sustain hungry hurt]
*fanatic 08-60-29 (a.) 1. marked by excessive enthusiasm for and intense devotion to a cause or idea (n.) 1. a person motivated by irrational enthusiasm (as for a cause) [fan fana fervent fervor fiend fixate follower freak frenzy fury fuss addicted aficionado agitation ardent ass authoritarian natural nearsighted neophyte nut tenacity tramp trust turbulence turmoil type idea idiot indifference infatuation insular intense intolerant intransigent irrational isolationist cacophony cant case chaos character churchill commotion convert /tana/] "A fanatic is one who can't change his mind and won't change the subject"
*fancier 15-33-7 (n.) 1. a person having a strong liking for something [fan flamboyant florid fussy admire adorn animal aureate castle clothe crackle crenelate indent interested intricate elaborate embattle enthusiastic expensive extravagant rhetorical rich rococo]
*fastidious 13-54-10 (a.) 1. giving and careful attention to detail; hard to please; excessively concerned with

cleanliness 2. (microbiology) having complicated nutritional requirements; especially growing only in special artificial cultures [faddy fair fasti fine finicky fresh fussy accurate appearance appreciative artificial assiduous attention sensitive small specialize squeamish strict study sweet tactful tidy immaculate incisive intellect dainty delicate demanding detail difficult discriminative disgust old overnice unadulterated unspotted /dit/] "a fastidious and incisive intellect"
*fathom 12-57-13 (n.) 1. a linear unit of measurement (equal to 6 feet) for water depth 2. (mining) a unit of volume (equal to 6 cubic feet) used in measuring bodies of ore (v.) 1. come to understand 2. measure depths with a sounding line, as of a body of water [fat feet figure follow absorb answer apprehensible articulate assess average think triangulate ore origin main master measure measured mensurable meter mystify]
*fatuous 17-67-5 (a.) 1. complacently or inanely foolish [fat fond foolish futile absurd airy asinine tenuous tranquil trivial unaware unintelligent unoccupied unthinking useless oblivious otiose show silly slight stupid subtle /out outa/]
*faulty 09-47-25 (a.) 1. characterized by errors 2. having a defect [fallible fault flaw abroad accurate adrift appliance awry uneven unfinished unreasonable lacking logic loose twist] "he submitted a faulty report"
*faun 21-37-2 (n.) 1. ancient Italian deity in human shape, with horns, pointed ears and a goat's tail; equivalent to Greek satyr [ancient]
*fawn 14-58-9 (n.) 1. a color varying around light grayish brown 2. young deer (v.) 1. show submission or fear 2. have fawns, of deer 3. tray to gain favor by cringing or flattering [farrow favour fear feet first flattery fledgling flex flunky form fulsome abase abject adulate affection animal antelope antler attention awn walk walnut wear wheedle win woman woo nestle]
*fealty 21-20-2 (n.) 1. the loyalty that citizens owe to their country (or subjects to their sovereign) [faithful feudal fidelity firm ethics acquiesce allegiance alt attachment literary lord loyalty tenant tie true]
*feasible 09-46-26 (a.) 1. capable of being done with means at hand and circumstances as they are (ad.) 1. in a practicable manner; so as to be feasible [fit fitting flexible effect effectual efficient enough executable exist expedient accept achieve act appropriate sensible sort suitable becoming befitting believe beneficial likely]
*feckless 14-72-8 (a.) 1. not fit to assume responsibility 2. generally incompetent and ineffectual [fatuous feck feeble fruitless futile easygoing effete empty careless counterproductive lack lackadaisical shiftless show spineless start sterile suit superfluous /elk/] "feckless attempts to repair the plumbing"
*fecund 21-59-2 (a.) 1. capable of producing offspring or vegetation 2. intellectually productive [fertile flourish fruitful effusive extravagant exuberant capable conceptual copious creative unproductive notional different diffusive]
*federate 14-08-9 (a.) 1. united under a central government (v.) 1. enter into a league for a common purpose 2. unite on a federal basis or band together as a league [federalize fuse enter entity derate divide reciprocate republic affiliate allied ally amalgamate associate team /def rede tare/] "The republics federated to become the Soviet Union"
*feign 13-62-11 (v.) 1. make believe 2. make a pretence of [fabricate fake false falsify fictitious fictive form framework embellish embroider ersatz ignorance ill illegitimate imitate imitation indifference insincere intent invent game gammon garble genuine] "He feigned that he was ill"
*feint 18-56-4 (n.) 1. any distracting maneuver (as a mock attack) (v.) 1. deceive with a feint [face fake feign football force fraud front encircle end enemy excuse expedient infiltrate intend intrigue investment tactical tactics thrust trick trickery true]
*felicitous 18-29-4 (a.) 1. exhibiting an agreeably appropriate manner or style 2. marked by good fortune [fine fit fitting fortune elicit eloquent enjoy exhibit expedient life likable likely lucky inspired choice civil congratulate convince correct tailored telling timely opportune outcome unexpected urbane useful satisfy show sort speaker style suitable sweet /otic/] "a felicitous speaker"
*felicity 12-56-12 (n.) 1. pleasing and appropriate manner or style esp of expression 2. state of well-being characterized by emotions ranging from contentment to intense joy [finish fitness fitting fortunate fortune ease ecstasy elegance elicit emotion expression exuberant lean luck lucky luxury inappropriate inclination intense intoxicate choice clear combination comfort contentment correct create tasteful tendency timeline transport]
*felon 14-13-9 (n.) 1. someone who has committed (or been legally convicted of) a crime 2. a purulent infection at the end of a finger or toe in the area surrounding the nail [fel fester fight find finger firebug fistula fraud fugitive elude embarrass eschar evil evildoer expose extort later law lawbreaker lead leader legal lesion liquor obtain offender outlaw nail novel]
*felonious 24-17-1 (a.) 1. involving or being or having the nature of a crime [felon fishy flaw fraudulent evasive evildoer excessive law lawless offense official outlaw outrageous nature illegitimate illicit immoral indirect iniquitous intent irregular unconstitutional unlawful unofficial scandalous senseless sinful sinister slippery suspicious]
*felony 08-06-28 (n.) 1. a serious crime [failure fault felon force engage enormity enter error evil extortion lapse law lawbreaker offering omission outrage nonfeasance]
*feminine 09-61-25 (a.) 1. of grammatical gender 2.

associated with women and not with men 3. (music or poetry) ending on an unaccented beat or syllable 4. befitting or characteristic of a woman especially a mature woman (n.) 1. a gender that refers chiefly (but not exclusively) to females or to objects classified as female [fair female fer form effeminate effete end exclusive maidenly majority man manner masculine matronly mature mini music inanimate include incorporate indoeuropean inflect intuition neuter] "feminine intuition"
*feral 15-72-7 (a.) 1. wild and menacing [fatal fell ferine ferocious fierce ecstatic enrapture epitaph era rage rear regressive roaring ruthless abandon animal atrocious lethal live]
*ferment 11-45-14 (n.) 1. a state of agitation or turbulent change or development 2. a substance capable of bringing about fermentation 3. a chemical phenomenon in which an organic molecule splits into simpler substances 4. a process in which an agent causes an organic substance to break down into simpler substances; especially, the anaerobic breakdown of sugar into alcohol (v.) 1. be in an agitated or excited state 2. work up into agitation or excitement 3. cause to undergo fermentation 4. go sour or spoil [fan fire fit function eddy emotional enough enzyme evolve excitement extreme raise rise row maelstrom malaise mass matter mayhem milk mind molecule mother nature nervous nettle nitrate temperature throw tickle top transform trouble tumult turbulent turmoil turn] "the political ferment produced a new leadership"
*ferocious 06-65-54 (a.) 1. marked by extreme and violent energy [fell fiendish fierce fighting force furious fury ecstatic emotional enemy energy enrapture extreme rage relentless roaring roc ruthless offensive orgasm orgiastic combative contentious cruel cruelty implacable inhuman intensity intoxicate uncivilized uncontrollable unfriendly unruly unstoppable sadistic savage soldierly strong /core/] "a ferocious beating"
*ferocity 11-63-14 (n.) 1. the property of being wild or turbulent [fierce furious fury extreme city cruelty intensity turbulent /core/]
*ferret 14-44-9 (n.) 1. ferret of prairie regions of United States; nearly extinct 2. domesticated albino variety of the European polecat bred for hunting rats and rabbits (v.) 1. hound or harry relentlessly 2. hunt with ferrets 3. search and discover through persistent investigation [family fitch flush food foul foumart fur eagle err eurasia european extinct rabbit raccoon rat relentless rummage run threaten track truth] "She ferreted out the truth"
*fervent 09-47-23 (a.) 1. characterized by intense emotion 2. sincerely or intensely felt 3. extremely hot [faithful fanatical felt fervid fiery fluent forceful france frantic eager effective emotion emotional enthusiastic exciting express extremely relentless religious resolute vehement vent vigorous visitor vivid nathaniel telling temperature tender tireless torrid transported trollope]
*fervid 21-32-2 (a.) 1. characterized by intense emotion 2. extremely hot [faithful fervent feverish fiery france eager earnest emotion enthusiastic excite express extremely resolute vehement vigorous impassioned intense intent intoxicate itch dedicated desire devoted devout drunk]
*fervor 12-AA-13 (n.) 1. feelings of great warmth and intensity 2. the state of being emotionally aroused and worked up [face faithful fancy fire flush eager emotion energy enthusiasm excessive excitement extremely regard relish resolution vehement verve]
*fester 13-55-11 (n.) 1. a sore that has become inflamed and formed pus (v.) 1. ripen and generate pus [felon fiery fistula form foul fret eject eliminate embitter enter envenom eschar ester excruciate expel sensitive skin smart sore stab sting suppurate swell tender tension tingle torment torture tubercle twist rack rankle red release rile ripen rise rotten run] "her wounds are festering"
*festive 07-66-37 (a.) 1. offering fun and gaiety [feast fest full fun excite suitable inauguration]
*fete 13-63-10 (n.) 1. an elaborate party (often outdoors) 2. an organized series of acts and performances (usually in one place) (v.) 1. have a celebration [fair family feast feature festivity fiesta film forum eisteddfod elaborate engage entertainment exam turnout]
*fetid 19-56-3 (a.) 1. offensively malodorous [filthy foetid foul funky fusty egregious enormous execrable terrible icky ignoble infamous decay dire dirty disgusting dreadful /dit/]
*fetter 19-60-3 (n.) 1. a shackle for the ankles or feet (v.) 1. restrain with fetters [fasten feet freedom embarrass entangle entwine tangle tie toil trammel reins restrict rope rule]
*fetus 13-01-10 (n.) 1. an unborn or unhatched vertebrate in the later stages of development showing the main recognizable features of the mature animal [feature foetus eight enclose expel unborn segment show skeleton skull spinal stage structural]
*feud 06-52-51 (n.) 1. a bitter quarrel between two parties (v.) 1. carry out a feud [family fee fence fuss engage enmity estrange differ disagreement dispute /due/] "The two professors have been feuding for years"
*feudal 14-61-9 (a.) 1. of or relating to or characteristic of feudalism [feud feudatory fief dependent dictatorial domineering arbitrary arrogant authoritative liege lordly /due lad/]
*feudalism 21-62-2 (n.) 1. the social system that developed in Europe in the 8th C; vassals were protected by lords who they had to serve in war [fascism federalism feudal economic enslavement enthrall europe exchange exist develop disenfranchise disfranchise domination absolutism land legal lord imperialism service servitude slavery society structure medieval military monarchism /due lad/]

*fez 18-46-4 (n.) 1. a city in north central Morocco; religious center 2. a felt cap (usually red) for a man; shaped like a flat-topped cone with a tassel that hangs from the crown [fedora felt france eastern]
*fiasco 09-72-24 (n.) 1. a sudden and violent collapse [failure fall flop foil frustration abortion setback shamble straw sudden cave cock collapse comedown cover]
*fickle 10-65-17 (a.) 1. marked by erratic changeableness in affections or attachments 2. liable to sudden unpredictable change [fade faithless flirt fly fragile frequently friend frivolous ickle impetuous impulsive indecisive intention irresponsible capricious changeful character cogent cool coquette corruptible liable light likely loyalty lubricious eccentric ephemeral erratic /elk/] "fickle friends"
*fictitious 12-52-12 (a.) 1. formed or conceived by the imagination 2. adopted in order to deceive [fabricate fact fake fancy fantastic fashion form imagination imagine imitative improvise interest invent character cheerful childish colored conceive confront corresponding counterfeit create criterion tin tinsel titi true twist unnatural unreal untrue sham simulate story substance superior sympathy synthetic]
*fidelity 08-48-32 (n.) 1. accuracy with which an electronic system reproduces the sound or image of its input signal 2. the quality of being faithful [factual faithful fidel fine fire firm image industry input insistency intent dedication dependable detail device devotion devout diligence distinguishing earnest electronics endurance essential exact extent literal loyalty television tenacity tie true trustworthine truth /led tile/]
*fidget 16-53-6 (n.) 1. a feeling of agitation expressed in continual motion (v.) 1. move restlessly [fast fear fid fiddle flirt flurry flutter fret fuss idle inquietude itch dabble dally desire disorder disturbance dither get give glass glow ebullition excitement express throb tinker toy tumble turbulence turmoil twiddle twitch /teg/] "he's got the fidgets"
*fief 21-12-2 (n.) 1. a piece of land held under the feudal system [farmer fee feoff feudal fie field formerly estate extensive]
*figment 19-57-3 (n.) 1. a contrived or fantastic idea [fabrication fancy fantasy fiction fig idea illusion imagination imagine invention maggot main myth eidolon exist extravaganza nightmare think trip] "a figment of the imagination"
*figurehead 14-76-9 (n.) 1. a person used as a cover for some questionable activity 2. figure on the bow of some sailing vessels [figure figurine follower form front frontman full institution gillie goon understudy uniform real representative responsibility ring rose eagle effigy emblem exponent half head henchman heraldry advocate alternate apparent attorney authority deceive decoration deputy dress /her rug/]
*filibuster 14-09-9 (n.) 1. a legislator who gives long speeches in an effort to delay or obstruct legislation that he (or she) opposes 2. a tactic for delaying or obstructing legislation by making long speeches (v.) 1. obstruct deliberately by delaying; of legislation [file foreign frustrate impede inactivity introduction invective irrelevant later law legislate legislator logrolling long blockade buster until say screed serve speech stop table tactic thwart tirade try effort embarrass enact eulogy exhortation read recitation revolutionary]
*finale 06-50-57 (n.) 1. the concluding part of any performance 2. the closing section of a musical composition 3. the temporal end; the concluding time [fate final finish intermission introduction number act afterpiece apodosis last effect end entertainment /elan/]
*finality 18-37-4 (n.) 1. the quality of being final or definitely settled [fate final finish fixed further immutable indisputable inevitable irrevocable apodosis terminus] "the finality of death"
*finally 01-52-607 (ad.) 1. the item at the end 2. as the end result of a succession or process 3. after a long period of time or an especially long delay [family final firstly further inevitable inexorable introduce irrevocable item necessarily net next absolutely accordingly arrive ask attempt lastly length long yet]
*financial 01-51-944 (a.) 1. involving financial matters [fin fiscal commercial connect /laic/]
*financier 07-50-40 (n.) 1. a person skilled in large scale financial transactions (v.) 1. conduct financial operations, often in an unethical manner [fin industrialist investor account angel capitalist cooke economist entrepreneur rhodes]
*finery 18-53-4 (n.) 1. especially fine or decorative clothing [festoon fine frippery fuss elaborate rag raiment regalia]
*finesse 09-33-25 (n.) 1. subtly skillful handling of a situation [facility feeling flair fool ingenuity intervene intrigue inventive negotiation nicety elegant engineering esse expert exploit sensitivity sequence sharp show situation skillful strategy style subtle]
*finicky 19-24-3 (a.) 1. exacting especially about details [fastidious fine fini food full fussy narrow nice niggling careful choosy cleanliness close clothe complicate concern critical] "a finicky eater"
*finite 14-55-8 (a.) 1. bounded or limited in magnitude or spatial or temporal extent 2. (grammar) of verbs; relating to forms of the verb that are limited in time by a tense and (usually) show agreement with number and person [figurative fini fixed form frail imaginary impermanent impossible integral narrow negative neither nite numeric tellurian temporal tense terminable transcendental earthy element even exact exhaust]
*fiscal 03-17-154 (a.) 1. involving financial matters [financial fisc commercial cost lucrative] "fiscal responsibility"
*fishmonger 17-77-5 (n.) 1. someone who sells fish

[florist food furnish furrier inventory ironmonger saddler sell haberdasher maintain monger newsdealer good greengrocer]
*fission 21-44-2 (n.) 1. a nuclear reaction in which a massive nucleus splits into smaller nuclei with the simultaneous release of energy 2. reproduction of some unicellular organisms by division of the cell into two more or less equal parts [fork fragment fusion induce ion ionization schism scission section separation significant simultaneous single slice small split spontaneous sporozoan structure surgery organism nucleus]
*fissure 16-42-6 (n.) 1. a long narrow depression in a surface 2. a long narrow opening 3. (anatomy) a long narrow slit or groove that divides an organ into lobes (v.) 1. break into fissures or fine cracks [faction fairly fatigue fault flaw fracture furrow impression incision interval schism scissure see separate shift side slit space split start structure sure surface undergo regular rent respect rift rip rock earth empty enter erupt excavation excise exfoliate]
*fitful 14-53-8 (a.) 1. occurring in spells and often abruptly 2. intermittently stopping and starting [fire fit fitting flicker fluctuate flutter impulsive infrequent instance interrupt irregular irresponsible tremulous twitchy unbroken uncertain uneven unpredictable lurch] "fitful bursts of energy"
*fixate 14-56-8 (v.) 1. attach (oneself) to a person or thing in a neurotic way 2. pay attention to exclusively and obsessively 3. make fixed, stable or stationary 4. become fixed (on) [fascinate fix focus form frame freeze immobilize advert age attached attention tie totally ear eat emotional exclusive eye /tax taxi/] "He fixates on his mother, even at the age of 40"
*fixture 04-82-134 (n.) 1. a object firmly fixed in place (especially in a household) 2. the quality of being fixed in place 3. a regular patron 4. the act of putting something in working order again [facility fastness feature firm fit fix function furniture immovable improve increment instrument inveterate tableware tackle temporary thing thread upkeep utensil utility racetrack rearrange regular reinforcement reparation restore rig equipment establish event extension]
*flag 03-54-186 (n.) 1. plants with sword-shaped leaves and erect stalks bearing bright-colored flowers composed of three petals and three drooping sepals 2. emblem usually consisting of a rectangular piece of cloth of distinctive design 3. a conspicuously marked or shaped tail 4. stratified stone that splits into pieces suitable as paving stones 5. a rectangular piece of fabric used as a signalling device 6. flagpole used to mark the position of the hole on a golf green (v.) 1. provide with a flag 2. communicate or signal with a flag 3. become less intense 4. decorate with flags, as of buildings 5. droop, sink, or settle from or as if from pressure or loss of tautness [fade failing fall figure file flash foetid label lag lazy lessen limp linger loss lumber abate adobe adorn africa amble america asphalt gem gentle gesture gladwyn glance glory grace gradual group /gal/]
*flagrant 13-36-11 (a.) 1. conspicuously and outrageously bad or reprehensible [flaring forward foul frightfully fume lamentable lie little live loathsome loser low lurid abject absolute agonizing ardent awfully glaring gorgeous grant grave gross rank regular reprehensible rotten nasty notably notorious tawdry terribly tolerate total treachery /gal/]
*flak 12-77-13 (n.) 1. a slick spokesperson who can turn any criticism to the advantage of their employer 2. artillery designed to shoot upward at airplanes 3. intense adverse criticism [fault fire firework flack litigious abuse advantage adverse advocate aggravation aircraft arrival artillery aspersion attack automatic knock]
*flamboyant 07-56-43 (a.) 1. elaborately or excessively ornamented 2. richly and brilliantly colorful (n.) 1. showy tropical tree or shrub native to Madagascar; widely planted in tropical regions for its immense racemes of scarlet and orange flowers; sometimes placed in genus Poinciana [fancy fine flashy florid flower frilly lofty loud loudness lurid luxurious affected africa ambo appearance arabesque architecture audacious aureate madagascar magniloquent meretricious moresque baroque blare blatant brazen bright brilliant busy obtrusive orange ornament ornate ostentatious outrageous ovary overwrought ovule native noted tall tortuous tree tropical /nay yob/] "flamboyant handwriting"
*flatulence 21-64-2 (n.) 1. a state of excessive gas in the alimentary canal 2. pompously embellished language [function language alimentary turgid embellish excessive canal condition]
*flax 19-59-3 (n.) 1. fiber of the flax plant that is made into thread and woven into linen fabric 2. plant of the genus Linum that is cultivated for its seeds and for the fibers of its stem [fabric family fibre flowering lack lax leaf light linac linen linum]
*fledged 11-40-15 (a.) 1. (of birds) having developed feathers or plumage; often used in combination 2. (of an arrow) equipped with feathers [feather fell flight fully embellish equip dart decorate develop grace grow]
*fledgling 09-35-23 (a.) 1. young and inexperienced 2. of a young bird just having acquired its flight feathers (n.) 1. any new participant in some activity 2. young bird that has just fledged or become capable of flying [feather fellow field firsthand flee fly force freshman lack lad lawyer learn learner litter eaglet enterprise entrant evergreen experience deb develop dove duckling gosling green inexpert infant initiate intact neophyte new newbie newcomer novice] "a fledgling robin"
*fleet 04-56-107 (a.) 1. moving very fast (n.) 1. group of aircraft operating together under the same ownership 2. a group of steamships operating together under the same ownership 3. a group of warships organized as a

tactical unit 4. group of motor vehicles operating together under the same ownership (v.) 1. move along rapidly and lightly; skim or dart 2. disappear gradually; as of emotions, for example [fade fast flee flight flit flotilla flutter fly foot force freight frigate lightly line lively lose emotion enemy enterprise evanesce evaporate eventually exchange expeditious explanation express tactical task taxicab team transport travel tribe troop /eel tee teel/] "fleet of foot"
*flexible 03-57-152 (a.) 1. able to adjust readily to different conditions 2. bends and snaps back readily without breaking 3. able to flex; able to bend easily 4. extended meanings; capable of change 5. making or willing to make concessions [facility feasible feature fit flex fluidity flute formative lack limber line literal lithe lively easy elastic elasticity enjoy extend extensible impermanent impressionable incapable influence injury interpretation becoming bend bendy bent biddable birch bouncy break buoyant] "a flexible character"
*flimsy 11-63-16 (a.) 1. having little substance or significance 2. lacking solidity or strength 3. resembling cardboard especially in flimsiness 4. very thin and insubstantial (n.) 1. a thin strong light-weight translucent paper used especially for making carbon copies [feeble foolish fragile furniture futile lack lightweight limp link little loose low idle implausible inadequate incredible inferior insubstantial makeshift misty section significance slight small solidity spiritual strength strong substance subtle suitable summer superior surface] "a flimsy table"
*flinch 13-55-10 (n.) 1. a reflex response to sudden pain (v.) 1. draw back, as with fear or pain [fade falter fear frighten funk inch involuntary non calf confront cower cringe hesitate] "she flinched when they showed the slaughtering of the calf"
*flippant 17-64-5 (a.) 1. showing inappropriate levity [facetious flip fool fresh frivolous lack lazy leer levity lightness lip impertinent impish inappropriate indifferent insouciance irreverent pan perfunctory pert playful airy attitude negligence nervy nonobservance taunt tease thoughtless]
*floe 21-54-2 (n.) 1. a flat mass of ice (smaller than an ice field) floating at sea [field firn flat flo floating frazil lolly]
*flop 06-61-47 (ad.) 1. with a flopping sound 2. (informal) exactly (n.) 1. an arithmetic operation performed on floating-point numbers 2. a complete failure 3. the act of throwing yourself down 4. (informal) someone who is unsuccessful (v.) 1. fall suddenly and abruptly 2. fall loosely 3. fail utterly; collapse [face failure fall fan feature fell fiasco flat flo founder land lemon let lie limp literally location loose lop lose loss lower operation perform piece play point present produce project purpose] "He flopped into a chair"
*flora 09-54-23 (n.) 1. all the plant life in a particular region 2. a living organism lacking the power of locomotion [flo life rural accumulation area]
*floral 08-52-32 (a.) 1. resembling or made of or suggestive of flowers 2. of or relating to the plant life in a particular region 3. relating to or associated with flowers [flora florid flowery life oral organ region accumulation aggregation alpine angiosperm assemblage] "an unusual floral design"
*florid 15-47-7 (a.) 1. elaborately or excessively ornamented [fancy fantastic fine flamboyant flo flowery luscious lush luxurious ornate ostentatious outlandish overly red rich rococo rosy ruddy declamatory decorative]
*florist 14-47-9 (n.) 1. a shop where flowers and ornamental plants are sold 2. someone who grows and deals in flowers [fishwife floriculture flower furrier landscapist loris ornamental retail ironmongery saddlery sale sell service shopkeeper store sweetshop tradesman] "the florist made up an attractive bouquet"
*flourish 04-54-97 (n.) 1. a showy gesture 2. a display of ornamental speech or language 3. an ornamental embellishment in writing 4. the act of waving 5. (music) a short lively tune played on brass instruments (v.) 1. gain in wealth 2. grow stronger 3. move or swing back and forth [fanfare fat flight float flour fly fruit large leave live lush luxuriant ornament ornamentation outgrow overrun undulation rank reveal rich root rosy run impenetrable increase indicate involve score shaking shoot showy sleek state strain successful swagger halcyon heavy high highlight histrionics holdup hypertrophy] "she entered with a great flourish"
*flout 11-60-15 (v.) 1. treat with contemptuous disregard 2. laugh or scoff at [foolery laugh law lout obey offense openly out outrage tantalize taunt tease transgress treat trespass twit] "flout the rules"
*fluctuate 07-46-35 (v.) 1. cause to fluctuate or move in a wave-like pattern 2. be unstable; have ups and downs 3. move or sway in a rising and falling or wavelike pattern [fall fickle fitful flicker flounder flow flurry flutter form level libration life line low lurch uncertainty undergo undulation uneven unpredictable unstable unsteady capricious careen catchy change chemical choppy circumstance concrete cycle teeter tide toss totter trade transform turn twinkle abstract adrift afloat alternate alternation arrhythmia atmosphere eat ebb equivocate /taut/]
*fluctuation 21-38-2 (n.) 1. a wave motion 2. the quality of being unsteady and subject to fluctuations 3. an instance of change; the rate or magnitude of change [fall fixed flow flux form fortune life undulation uneven unsteady changeable chemical circumstance composition crystalline cycle tide trade transposition twinkle atmosphere increase instance interval irregularity oscillation next norm] "the fluctuations of the sea"
*flue 21-53-2 (n.) 1. flat blade-like projection on the

arm of an anchor 2. a conduit to carry off smoke 3. organ pipe whose tone is produced by air passing across the sharp edge of a fissure or lip [fairy feather fireplace fissure flat flu fluke fur furnace labial lamp lint lip edge eiderdown electric ether]
*fluent 07-67-36 (a.) 1. easy and graceful in shape 2. expressing yourself readily, clearly, effectively 3. smooth and unconstrained in movement [facile fervent flow flue fluid fly forceful form frank language liquid literary long loquacious unconstrained upward ease easily easy effective effortless elegant eloquent expressive natural newsy talky telling tidal tongue tripping] "a yacht with long, fluent curves"
*fluke 11-50-14 (n.) 1. a stroke of luck 2. a barb on a harpoon or arrow 3. either of the two lobes of the tail of a cetacean 4. flat blade-like projection on the arm of an anchor 5. parasitic flatworms having external suckers for attaching to a host [facing favorable fin fish flatworm flue fortune freak freeliving lead limb line liver lobe lucky luke unexpected unknown unpredictable eastern elongate external]
*fluster 16-55-6 (n.) 1. a disposition that is confused or nervous and upset (v.) 1. be flustered; behave in a confused manner 2. cause to be nervous or upset [feel fit flap flurry flutter frenzy full fuss lack lather luster uneasy unrest unsettled upset scramble seek shake shock shuffle side sodden speak state temperament thrown tiddly tipsy tizzy trouble turbulent turmoil embarrassment entangle excite excitement expression rattle reel restless rock row ruffle]
*flux 13-43-11 (n.) 1. a flow or discharge 2. the rate of flow of energy or particles across a given surface 3. a substance added to molten metals to bond with impurities that can then be readily removed 4. excessive discharge of liquid from a cavity or organ (as in watery diarrhea) 5. in constant change 6. (physics) the number of flux changes per unit area 7. the lines of force surrounding a permanent magnet or a moving charged particle (v.) 1. move or progress freely as if in a stream 2. mix together different elements 3. become liquid or fluid; of a solid substance, when heated [faint fall fat field flight flow flu fluctuate fluid following force form freely frequency frozen fundamental fuse fusion leach line liquid lose lux uncertainty undergo undertow undulate unfreeze unify unite unrest] "his opinions are in flux"
*foggy 14-47-8 (a.) 1. filled or abounding with fog or mist 2. indistinct or hazy in outline 3. stunned or confused and slow to react (as from blows or drunkenness or exhaustion) 4. obscured by fog [faint feeble fill fog fuddle full fuzzy obscure opaque outline general groggy]
*foible 15-55-7 (n.) 1. a behavioral attribute that is distinctive and peculiar to an individual 2. the weaker part of a sword's blade from the forte to the tip [failure fault flaw forte idiosyncrasy imperfection inadequate bad behavior blade blemish brand bug less long eccentricity /bio/]
*foil 06-52-51 (n.) 1. a piece of thin and flexible sheet metal 2. a light slender flexible sword tipped by a button 3. anything that serves by contrast to call attention to another thing's good qualities 4. picture consisting of a positive photograph or drawing on a transparent base; viewed with a projector 5. a device consisting of a flat or curved piece (as a metal plate) so that its surface reacts to the water it is passing through (v.) 1. hinder or prevent (the efforts, plans, or desires) of 2. enhance by contrast 3. cover or back with foil [fail fence figure film fin fish flat flexible forbid forestall form frame friend frustrate offset oil opponent outreach outwit overhead icon image impede ingenue interest invent inverse lap layer lead leaf let letdown light] "In this picture, the figures are foiled against the background"
*foist 17-64-5 (v.) 1. to force onto another 2. insert surreptitiously or without warrant [finagle force obtrude overreach impose inferior inflict insert intervene introduce invade sandwich stick surreptitious swindle thrust trench trespass trick] "He foisted his work on me"
*foliage 09-55-25 (n.) 1. (architecture) leaf-like architectural ornament 2. the main organ of photosynthesis and transpiration in higher plants [fern fig floating flower folia form fruit functional fungus organ ornamentation leaf life lily lobe improve incise indent add almost apex appearance aquatic architectural arrange assume gnaw grass great greenery ground grow early]
*folio 19-61-3 (n.) 1. the system of numbering pages 2. a book (or manuscript) consisting of large sheets of paper folded in the middle to make two leaves or four pages 3. a sheet of any written or printed material (especially in a manuscript or book) [face film first flap flyleaf foil folder foldout foreword four front octavo octodecimo olio once opuscule lamina language large law leaf ledger legal length letter imperial index inserted introduction /oil/] "the first folio of Shakespeare's plays"
*foment 14-43-8 (v.) 1. try to stir up public opinion 2. bathe with warm water or medicated lotions [fan fire for forward foster further fury fuss omen opinion overheat medicate mentation motivate move mull encourage enrage exasperate excitement exhilarate nervous nurse nurture tickle treatment trigger trouble try turbulence turmoil /nemo/] "His legs should be fomented"
*fondle 18-51-4 (v.) 1. touch lightly and with affection, with brushing motions [favorite feed feel fond foster necking nestle nose nurse nurture nuzzle dalliance dandle darling lap lick lightly long lovemaking loving ear embosom embrace endearing entertain]
*foolproof 16-48-6 (a.) 1. not liable to failure (v.) 1. proof against human misuse, error, etc. [face failure fallible feasible fireproof flexible function leakproof liable perfect pliant practical proof properly reliable

resistant risky rustproof /loo loof/] "a foolproof identification system"
*foppish 24-59-1 (a.) 1. affecting extreme elegance in dress and manner [preen inelegant self style]
*forage 13-50-11 (n.) 1. animal food for browsing or grazing 2. the act of searching for food and provisions (v.) 1. collect or look around for (food) 2. hunt for food or provisions 3. wander and feed; of animals [fad feed fodder food fora foray fuel oat obtain oil rage raid raven research root rummage run age animal gas give grain grass grazing grow eat eatage engage ensilage exploration explore]
*forbear 21-72-2 (n.) 1. a person from whom you are descended (v.) 1. not do something [failure father forebear forgo oneself refrain relax remote reserve restrain root bear behind benevolent bridle easygoing effort endurance enduring escape evade abstain accepting alone antecedent ascendant avoid]
*forbearance 21-43-2 (n.) 1. good-natured tolerance of delay or incompetence 2. a delay in enforcing rights or claims or privileges; refraining from acting [fact favor feeling forbear forgiving formal obliging overlook refrain reply resignation respond restraint right ruth benevolent easy elusive enforce escape exercise abandon abeyance acceptance alarming nature neutrality charity cheerful claim compassion constraint] "his forbearance to reply was alarming"
*forcible 11-52-16 (a.) 1. impelled by physical force especially against resistance [for full obstinate operative real reminder removal resistance robustious rugged ruling cogent compulsory convince cop corrosive cutting impel impressive influential intense irresistible biting bouncing brisk lively living lock lusty effective energetic enough enthusiastic entry /cro/] "forcible entry"
*ford 03-51-188 (n.) 1. United States film maker (1896-1973) 2. a shallow area in a stream that can be forded 3. son of Henry Ford (1893-1943) 4. English writer and editor (1873-1939) 5. the act of crossing a stream or river by wading or in a car or on a horse 6. 38th President of the United States; appointed Vice President and succeeded Nixon when Nixon resigned (1913-) 7. American manufacturer of automobiles who pioneered mass production (1863-1947) 8. grandson of Henry Ford (1917-1987) (v.) 1. cross a river where it's shallow [ferry filmmaker financial flat flow for ocean office opening outer outlet outward overstride reef resigned ride river rudolph run deep defile depth downward drive]
*forebode 16-53-6 (v.) 1. make a prediction about; tell in advance [fateful fearful forbidding forewarn forward omen ominous outcome outguess reaction refute response reveal election encourage engage ensure evil experience bad behavior bet black bludgeon bode boding bother bulldoze dark denounce dismiss disturbed divine doubt dread]
*forecast 02-63-293 (n.) 1. a prediction about how something (as the weather) will develop (v.) 1. indicate by signs 2. judge to be probable 3. predict in advance [figure financial flow forewarning form frame omen opinion organize outlook radio rationalize recast reckon early estimation expect calculation climatology conclude condition conjecture coordination count accounting advance aerology ahead analysis anticipate apocalypse arrange augur auspicate shape soothsayer speculation statement steer suggest symptom tell /ace cero/]
*foreclose 15-09-7 (v.) 1. subject to foreclosing procedures; take away the right of mortgagors to redeem their mortgage 2. keep from happening or arising; have the effect of preventing [fend foil forbid forestall formal obstruct obviate occurrence redeem repel repossess resolve right effect effort embarrass evict exclusive exile expenditure expropriate claim close cross cutoff save scotch settle shut spoil stave stop /cero/]
*forecourt 15-95-7 (n.) 1. the outer or front court of a building or of a group of buildings [front open outer railroad concourse court courtyard tennis /cero/]
*forefather 18-56-4 (n.) 1. the founder of a family 2. person from an earlier time who contributed to the tradition shared by some group [faith family father forth founder office originator race remote root early ancestor antecedent architect ascendant author tradition hold human] "keep the faith of our forefathers"
*forego 18-41-4 (v.) 1. be earlier in time; go back further [first fore former further old relinquish remain early elder evident exist give grab]
*foreground 14-39-9 (n.) 1. the part of a scene that is near the viewer 2. (computer science) a window for an active application (v.) 1. move into the foreground to make more visible or prominent [facade facet focal focus foreword front obverse operate receive rectangular region rest electronicall engineering environs ground understate near neighborhood different direct display distinguished downplay draw]
*forehead 09-57-25 (n.) 1. the part of the face above the eyes 2. the large cranial bone forming the front part of the cranium: the forehead and the upper part of the orbits [face fore form forward frontal orbit ridge ear earlobe eminence enclose eye eyebrow hairline head develop /her hero/]
*foreign 01-43-702 (a.) 1. not belonging to that in which it is contained; introduced from an outside source 2. relating to or originating in or characteristic of another place or part of the world 3. not contained in or deriving from the essential nature of something 4. of concern to or concerning the affairs of other nations (other than your own) [far form free observation odd office originate other outburst outlandish outside overseas reign remote removed repellent repugnant economic essential establish exotic external exterritorial extrinsic import impure independent indigenous international

introduce isolated native nature] "foreign trade"
*foreigner 05-50-83 (n.) 1. a person who comes from a foreign country; someone who does not owe allegiance to your country 2. someone who is not a member of a group [citizen family feel foreign outlander outlaw outsider owe refugee reside return emigre englishman environment exclude exile expel immigrant import italy greek gringo group national newcomer non]
*foreman 10-36-18 (n.) 1. a person who exercises control over workers 2. a man who is foreperson of a jury [factory floorwalker overseer recognitor reman early exercise manager member monitor african ask auditor /name/] "if you want to leave early you have to ask the foreman"
*foresee 06-47-54 (v.) 1. act in advance of; deal with ahead of time 2. picture to oneself; imagine possible 3. realize beforehand [face fair faith farsighted fore forewarning form oracular overdue ready realize envision espy expect sagacious see soothsayer speculate]
*foreshore 24-96-1 (n.) 1. the part of the seashore between the high-water and low-water marks [feature formation ocean rock earth economically exploit sand sea seacoast shingle shore]
*foresight 14-60-8 (n.) 1. providence by virtue of planning prudently for the future 2. knowing in advance; foreseeing [farsighted figure forethought forward front future futurity observation obstacle omen organization outlook rationalization read ready resource early enterprise envision eventuality exercise expectation safeguard sagacious sagacity see sight speculation strategy survey idea incisive instance insurance intention intuition intuitive game graph guideline hereafter tactics think tomorrow trenchant]
*forestall 14-26-9 (v.) 1. keep from happening or arising; have the effect of preventing 2. act in advance of; deal with ahead of time [fend foil forbid forbidding forest forewarn frustrate obstruct obviate occurrence optimistic outreach outwit ready refrain repel eager effect effort embarrass engross envision escape estop exclude expenditure sale save scotch slow snow spoil stave stay stop sure tact thwart trick accomplishment advance agape agog ahead answer anticipate arise avert avoid await letdown]
*foretell 17-45-5 (v.) 1. foreshadow or presage 2. indicate by signs 3. make a prediction about; tell in advance [forewarn forward omen outcome outguess refute retell retold reveal review election expect tea tell tense threaten leaf let likely literary loom]
*forethought 24-52-1 (n.) 1. planning or plotting in advance of acting 2. judiciousness in avoiding harm or danger [farsighted figure future open organization rationalization rethink enterprise exercise tactics think handle happening harm heedful game good graph guideline]
*forfeit 09-49-21 (a.) 1. surrendered as a penalty (n.) 1. something that is lost or surrendered as a penalty; 2. a penalty for a fault or mistake that involves losing or giving up something 3. the act of losing or surrendering something as a penalty for a mistake or fault or failure to perform etc. (v.) 1. lose or lose the right to by some error, offense, or crime [failure faith fault fee fine forgo forsake fulfil offense orfe outside relinquish require right robbery ruin erode error expense inheritance injury instance involve irretrievable task throw title /fro tie/] "the contract specified forfeits if the work was not completed on time"
*forge 04-51-90 (n.) 1. furnace consisting of a special hearth where metal is heated before shaping 2. a workplace where metal is worked by heating and hammering (v.) 1. come up with (an idea, plan, explanation, theory, or priciple) after a mental effort 2. make a copy of with the intent to deceive 3. of metals 4. make out of components (often in an improvising manner) 5. move ahead steadily 6. move with increasing speed 7. make something, usually for a specific function [face faker falsify fantastic farrier fashion few figure financial finish flat foil for form formulate forward frame function furnace one operate ore oven raise raw recreate refine reflect refuse relation repeat reproduce reshape rice roughly rounded gain gather genuine great grow echo effort elevation enchant enclose energy ersatz establish excogitate explanation extract]
*forgery 12-50-12 (n.) 1. a copy that is represented as the original 2. criminal falsification by making or altering an instrument with intent to defraud [fake falsify fiction financial following forge fraudulent onomatopoeia rendering represent resemblance romance gain genuine emulate evil extravaganza]
*forgo 09-35-23 (v.) 1. do without or cease to hold or adhere to 2. lose or lose the right to by some error, offense, or crime 3. refrain from consuming [for forbear fore forfeit formality forsake forsworn offense old omit refrain release relinquish renounce reserve resign right give]
*formation 05-52-73 (n.) 1. the act of forming something 2. a particular spatial arrangement 3. natural process that causes something to form 4. the fabrication of something in a particular shape 5. the geological features of the earth 6. an arrangement of people or things acting as a unit 7. creation by mental activity [fashion figure flank format fountain order organization organize outpouring raise range realize regularity machine making manufacture affair appearance architecture assembly texture turn type impression incorporate institution] "a defensive formation"
*formidable 05-57-83 (a.) 1. inspiring fear 2. extremely impressive in strength or excellence [fanatic fantastic fatal fearsome fell forbidding frighten onerous opponent outstanding overwhelming redoubtable remarkable respect rigorous rough marked mean menace imposing impressive incredible inspire intimidate daunt deal

delicate demanding difficult disposal dreadful able admirable adversary alarming amazing appalling arduous army astound awesome awful brain brutal burdensome laborious effort exceptional extraordinary /bad dim/] "a formidable opponent"
*formula 03-58-144 (n.) 1. something regarded as a normative example 2. a conventionalized statement expressing some fundamental principle 3. a representation of a substance using symbols for its constituent elements 4. directions for making something 5. a group of symbols that make a mathematical statement 6. a liquid food for infants 7. (mathematics) a standard procedure for solving a class of mathematical problems [fact factor fighting food form function observance office ordinance race raise ratio recipe recognize regulation relation repeat replace represent require root rule main math means measure member message method milk modus molecular upper law legislation liquid liturgy logic act algorithm alternative analysis argument arrange atom attack axiom /alum/]
*forswear 19-32-3 (v.) 1. formally reject or disavow a formerly held belief, usually under pressure [false forgo formerly oath oppose rebuff recant refuse reject release religion repudiate resign resort retract sacrifice scout spare statement stop strong surrender swear waive withdraw early evidence except exclude abandon abdicate abjure]
*forte 11-61-14 (a.) 1. used chiefly as a direction or description in music (ad.) 1. used as a direction in music; to be played relatively loudly (n.) 1. an asset of special worth or utility 2. the stronger part of a sword blade between the hilt and the foible 3. (music) with great loudness [faculty failing field finger foible form fort full oyster really resounding ring ritardando talent thing thrust thumb tone type effective efficiency equipment] "the forte passages in the composition"
*forth 04-32-100 (ad.) 1. out into view 2. forward in time or order or degree 3. from a particular thing or place or position [for formal fort forward forwards obsolete off onward out region teacher thence thereof hence]
*forthright 10-54-19 (a.) 1. characterized by disconcerting directness in manner or speech; without subtlety or evasion (ad.) 1. directly and without evasion; not roundabout [face farmer forth frank free openhearted opinion outspoken responsibility right roundabout rude talk think timid transparent honest indirect ingenuous genuine give]
*fortify 09-51-23 (v.) 1. make strong or stronger 2. prepare oneselg for a military confrontation 3. add nutrients to; as of foods 4. enclose by or as if by a fortification 5. add alcohol beverages [fence firm flavor food fort furnish further rally rampart ready rearm recruit refresh reinforce relation revive rough ruggedize temper toughen transform trench improve increase ingredient invigorate /fit/]
*fortitude 14-64-8 (n.) 1. strength of mind that enables one to endure adversity with courage [face faith fear fearless force fort four obstinate resilience resolution robust rugged temperance tenacity toughness indulgence intrepid danger dauntless decisive derive determination difficult enable endure energy]
*foster 03-53-150 (a.) 1. providing or receiving nurture or parental care though not related by blood or legal ties (n.) 1. United States songwriter whose songs embody the sentiment of the South before the American Civil War (1826-1864) (v.) 1. promote the growth of 2. bring up under fosterage; of children 3. help develop, help grow [father force form further oblige sentiment serve songwriter south stand stephen stuff substitute support surrogate temporary tend tie train transform education embody embrace encourage exercise raise ready rear receive regular related] "foster parent"
*foursome 14-56-9 (n.) 1. four people considered as a unit 2. the cardinal number that is the sum of three and one [figure form four race rectangle runoff singles sport square sum man match meet element ensemble event]
*fracas 15-68-7 (n.) 1. noisy quarrel [feud fight fuss raca riot roar row runin ado affray altercation angry argument calm charivari clap controversy scrap scuffle silly squabble stir]
*fractious 12-54-13 (a.) 1. stubbornly resistant to authority or control 2. easily irritated or annoyed 3. unpredictably difficult in operation; likely to be troublesome [feisty force fretful rebellious refractory reluctant require resistant restless rival act adverse alien animal annoy averse comprehend control countryman cross techy testy tetchy touchy troublesome ill incorrigible intractable irrepressible irritate obedient obey object obstructive operation ornery ugly unpleasant unpredictable unruly unwilling spiteful stubborn submit sulky sullen] "a fractious animal that would not submit to the harness"
*fracture 05-55-68 (n.) 1. breaking of hard tissue such as bone 2. (geology) a crack in the earth's crust resulting from the displacement of one side with respect to the other 3. the act of cracking something (v.) 1. violate or abuse 2. become fractured 3. break into pieces 4. break, as of a bone 5. interrupt, break, or destroy 6. fracture a bone of [fault fissure flaw fray relax rent repair run rupture abuse abyss act amuse arroyo check chip cleft cracking crevice cut tear tickle trench enliven entertain exhilarate] "it was a nasty fracture"
*fragile 05-53-80 (a.) 1. vulnerably delicate 2. easily broken or damaged or destroyed 3. lacking solidity or strength [fade feeble flimsy fly frail frailty friable fugitive rickety robust rugged agile gossamer illness impetuous impulsive indecisive infirm injury insubstantial invalidity irresolute lack languish lightweight link little easy effeminate ephemeral evanescent exquisite]
*fragment 05-42-60 (n.) 1. a broken piece of a brittle

artifact 2. a piece broken off or cut off of something else 3. an incomplete piece (v.) 1. break or cause to break into pieces [face fall file fire flake fleck flour flower frag friction reduce remnant rend restriction rive rock rub abrade ace ana anthology apart artistic atomize glowing gob grain grate grating grinding group mash material matter metal mill minimum edge element end enzyme excerpt extract nation natural nutshell tatter thin thrown total trivia] "a fragment of rock"
*fragrant 10-49-18 (a.) 1. pleasant-smelling [flowery fruity redolent rose ambrosial aromatic grant]
*frailty 12-74-13 (n.) 1. the state of being weak in health or body (especially from old age) 2. moral weakness [failing failure fear feeble fine flaw fragility frail rarity reduction resist rift abnormal abulia age airy arise astheny attenuate avoid ill imperfection inadequate indecisive infirmity inherent languish lead liability lightness loss taint temptation tenuity thin /liar/]
*frankincense 24-78-1 (n.) 1. an aromatic gum resin obtained from various Arabian or East African trees; formerly valued for worship and for embalming and fumigation [formerly fumigate religious resin african arabian aromatic native incense ceremony certain east embalm exude substance]
*frantic 06-58-51 (a.) 1. marked by uncontrolled excitement or emotion 2. excessively agitated; transported with rage or other violent emotion [fan fear ferocious feverish fierce follow frenzied frenzy frustration furious rabid rage rant restraint riotous roaring abandon accident agitate anger antic anxious nervous tame tempestuous transported trouble tumultuous turbulent impossible infuriate insane insensate intrusive chaotic characterize confused control corybantic crowd] "frantic with anger and frustration"
*fraternal 15-31-7 (a.) 1. of or relating to a fraternity or society of usually men 2. like or characteristic of or befitting a brother 3. (of twins) derived from two separate fertilized ova [familial favorable felt fertilize frater friendship affectionate agreeable amiable amicable tenderhearted tie twin egg embryology exist neighborly nice loving] "a fraternal order"
*fraudulent 08-44-31 (a.) 1. intended to deceive [fair fake fallacious falsify felonious flam flimflam forge fraud racket rotten advantage advert amoral artful unconscionable unethical unscrupulous untrue dark deception deceptive defraud deliberate design devious dishonor dishonorable disposed dodge doubtful dubious dupe duplicity larceny later escape evasive extract tax testimony thievish thin treacherous tricky true]
*fray 07-53-40 (n.) 1. a noisy fight (v.) 1. wear away by rubbing 2. cause friction [fall fighting file fra fracas fracture frazzle friction raggedy ratty ray rent rope row rub ruffle run abrasion action adjoin already altercation anger apart area argument] "The friction frayed the sleeve"
*freemason 21-83-2 (n.) 1. a member of a widespread secret fraternal order pledged to mutual assistance and brotherly love [fellow fraternity religion male masonry member mutual assistance secret]
*freethinker 24-46-1 (n.) 1. a person who believes that God created the universe and then abandoned it [conformist rationalism refuse religion establish teach thinker toleration humanist independent individualist isolationist neutral non nonpartisan /tee/]
*frenetic 09-58-21 (a.) 1. excessively agitated; transported with rage or other violent emotion [feverish follow frantic frenzied frustration furious rabid rage rant rene emotional excessive eye transported trouble infatuated insane intense intrusive calm chaotic characterize confusion corybantic /cite tene/]
*frequency 07-42-42 (n.) 1. the ratio of the number of observations in a statistical category to the total number of observations 2. the number of observations in a given statistical category 3. the number of occurrences within a given time period (usually 1 second) [fact fluctuate friend radio range rate ratio ray receive reciprocal recur regular reinforcement repeat resonance electromagnetic element establish express quantity quotient node nutation cardinal category continuous count crest cycle] "the frequency of modulation was 40 cycles per second"
*fresco 09-71-22 (n.) 1. a mural done with watercolors on wet plaster 2. a durable method of painting on a wall by using watercolors on wet plaster (v.) 1. paint onto wet plaster on a wall [face frieze rapid reproduction res emblazon enamel engrave shadow significant smear stain surface ceiling collage copy covering creation /serf/]
*freshness 10-51-17 (n.) 1. originality by virtue of being refreshingly novel 2. the property of being pure and fresh (as if newly made); not stale or deteriorated 3. the trait of being rude and impertinent; inclined to take liberties 4. an alert and refreshed state 5. originality by virtue of being new and surprising [firm flavor free revive rude sparkle surprising healthy hutzpah new novelty] "she loved the freshness of newly baked bread"
*fret 08-59-30 (n.) 1. agitation resulting from active worry 2. a small bar of metal across the fingerboard of a musical instrument; when the string is stopped by a finger at the metal bar it will produce a note of the desired pitch (v.) 1. be agitated or irritated 2. worry unnecessarily of excessively 3. become or make sore by or as if by rubbing 4. be too tight; rub or press 5. gnaw into; make resentful or angry 6. remove soil or rock, as of wind or water 7. carve a pattern into 8. cause annoyance in 9. decorate with an interlaced design 10. wear away or erode 11. cause friction [fastening field file flap fleck form fracture fray friction furnish fuss raddle rag rage raise rankle rasping relief remove render repeat resentful restless ret ridge rigid rile rock rose rub run rust eager eagle edgy embellish emotional entwine erode erosion etching exam excessive excite excitement exercise extreme tear terrace textile tight torment torture

touch trouble troublesome twine twist]
*fretful 19-64-3 (a.) 1. unable to relax or be still 2. habitually complaining [fidgety flutter fret fussy relax resentment restless eager easy edgy excite excitement express testy touchy turbulent unable uncomplaining uneasy unquiet unrest unsettled upset lather] "a constant fretful stamping of hooves"
*frightful 18-69-4 (a.) 1. (informal) extreme in degree 2. provoking horror 3. extremely distressing [face farm fearful formidable foul frighten remarkable repel repulsive rightful rousing imitate indicate ghastly good great grisly gruesome hideous highly horror howling hurry terrify thirst thumping turn ugly undesirable unpleasant unspeakable usual loathsome lose lurid]
*frigid 14-22-9 (a.) 1. extremely cold 2. sexually unresponsive 3. devoid of warmth and cordiality; expressive of unfriendliness or disdain [face failure forbidding force formality freezing friendly frosty frozen frustrate raw react reception reciprocate refrigerate removed reply reserved respond rigid room ice impotent inability inadequate indifferent inside intercourse gelid give glacial greeting guarded day detached devoid disdain distant dull /dig/]
*fringe 05-62-86 (a.) 1. at or constituting a border or edge (n.) 1. a part of the city far removed from the center 2. the outside boundary or surface of something 3. edging consisting of hanging threads or tassels (v.) 1. adorn with a fringe 2. decorate with or as if with a surrounding fringe [factory far field finance finish fling flock form forward frame front frontier radical ravel reed relation remove representative require resemble residential rim role roundabout ruffle rug idea important inge interference galloon golf grace grow edge embellish encircle envelope establish extend external extremist] "fur fringed the hem of the dress"
*frivolity 17-56-5 (n.) 1. the trait of being frivolous; not serious or sensible 2. something of little value or significance 3. acting like a clown or buffoon [feature flirt fluff folly foolish fri frippery fun rice roguish idle importance impulsive inconsequential indulgence inept insanity value vanity vapidity volatility laughter lightness little lunacy tomfoolery trait tricky trifle trite triviality]
*frivolous 10-44-17 (a.) 1. not serious in content or attitude or behavior [featherbrain flippant flutter flyaway foolish fri frolicsome futile random rejoicing remark risible idle important inconsequential insignificant intellectual irresponsible vague vain volatile otiose lack light unclassified unimportant unorganized seriously shallow silly slight substance superficial surface system] "a frivolous novel"
*frizz 24-84-1 (v.) 1. curl tightly, of hair [form friz refer ringlet roll]
*frontier 06-42-50 (a.) 1. on the American frontier (n.) 1. a wilderness at the edge of a settled area of a country 2. an international boundary or the area (often fortified) immediately inside the boundary 3. an undeveloped field of study; a topic inviting research and development [field finish floor fortify fringe front full furthest real remote research riddle rim rural open outlandish outpost outskirt nowhere terminus threshold timber topic town traffic immediately individualism inside international inviting edge end enigma expand extent extremist extremity /reit/] "one of the last real frontier towns"
*frugal 12-49-12 (a.) 1. avoiding waste [farmer father forbearance forehanded frug reasonable reluctance remember renounce renunciation resource restraint gift great abnegate abstemious affair ascetic austere avoid lean light limited little low lunch /lag/]
*fruition 14-62-9 (n.) 1. the condition of bearing fruit 2. something that is made real or concrete [fruit fulfill fun ready realize relish right ripe implement intend titillate tree outcome own]
*fulcrum 17-65-5 (n.) 1. the pivot about which a lever turns [fin fish uphold lever cane carrier crook radiant reinforcer retail revolving rig rigid rum maintain major mandrel mast]
*fulminate 18-61-4 (n.) 1. a salt or ester of fulminic acid (v.) 1. criticize severely 2. cause to explode violently and with loud noise 3. come on suddenly and intensely [feed fire forceful form frightened unacceptable likely loud medicine mercury metal mina intense noise acid appear arm article attack thunder thunderous ester existence explosive express] "He fulminated against the Republicans' plan to cut Medicare"
*fulsome 21-73-2 (a.) 1. unpleasantly and excessively suave or ingratiating in manner or speech [fawn flashy flatter foul frugal unctuous unpleasant lack lavish little low lush luxury sad self shabby shock sincerity smarmy smug some speech suave superficial sycophant obscene offensive oily oleaginous outrageous overgenerous manner mean miserable monstrous earnest effusive embarrass enormous excessive express exuberant]
*fumble 07-28-38 (n.) 1. dropping the ball (in baseball or football) (v.) 1. handle clumsily 2. make one's way clumsily 3. feel about uncertainly or blindly 4. make a mess of, destroy or ruin 5. drop or juggle or fail to play cleanly a grounder in baseball [flounder flub fluff football foulup fuck uncouth ungainly unwieldy maladroit mar mess miscarry misconduct misguided mishandle misstep mistake muff murder baseball blow blunder blundering boner boob botch bumble bungle bungling butcher loutish lubberly lumber error]
*fumigate 21-33-2 (v.) 1. treat with fumes, expose to fumes, esp. with the aim of disinfecting or eradicating pests [fluidize fractionate fume microorganism improve incense gasify gate aerate aim antisepsis atomize autoclave treatment emit eradicate evaporate exhale expose /tag/]
*functionary 18-33-4 (n.) 1. a worker who holds or is invested with an office [factor feed fighter function newsagent clerk commissioner conductor tool

implement instrument official officiary operator agent amanuensis runner]
*fundamental 03-47-175 (a.) 1. far-reaching and thoroughgoing in effect especially on the nature of something 2. being or involving basic facts or principles 3. serving as an essential component (n.) 1. the lowest tone of a harmonic series [fact factor farreaching first focus frequency fundament ultimate uncluttered underwent unequivocal uniform utterly nascent nature necessary note nucleus deep dominant downright aboriginal absolutely affect argument austere axiom major materially meat mere milestone most effect element elixir embryonic essential extravagance extremely teach theorem thoroughgoing tone totally truth landmark law /mad/]
*fungus 14-43-8 (n.) 1. a parasitic plant lacking chlorophyll and leaves and true stems and roots and reproducing by spores [flora fun neoplasm nevus germ growth gymnosperm sarcoma smut staphylococcus]
*furlong 08-75-33 (n.) 1. a unit of length equal to 220 yards [feet furl racetrack length linear]
*furlough 17-02-5 (n.) 1. a temporary leave of absence from military duty (v.) 1. dismiss, usually for economic reasons 2. grant a leave to [fire flee force unemployment unfrock reason reduce release remove replace reward rush layoff leave let liberty lie lough off official give good grant holiday hooky] "The prisoner was furloughed for the weekend to visit her children"
*furrier 21-21-2 (n.) 1. someone whose occupation is making or repairing fur garments [fitter fleecy florist fur furnish fuzzy repair ironmonger establishment]
*further 01-66-996 (a.) 1. more distant in especially degree 2. existing or coming by way of addition (ad.) 1. to or at a greater distance in time or space ('farther' is used more frequently than 'further' in this physical sense) 2. in addition or furthermore 3. to or at a greater extent or degree or a more advanced stage ('further' is used more often than 'farther' in this abstract sense) (v.) 1. contribute to the progress or growth of 2. promote the growth of [far farther favor forward foster frequently fresh fur future ulterior uncertainty remote renew research then thither too travel truth happen hasten help home education else encourage excuse exist expect extent extra] "further complicated by uncertainty about the future"
*furtherance 24-41-1 (n.) 1. encouragement of the progress or growth or acceptance of something 2. the advancement of some enterprise [flowering forwarding foster further upbeat uplift upward recovery rise rush travel headway elaborate encouragement enhance enterprise expansion experience expression acceptance advance advancement advocate aid approval career championship course]
*furtive 14-56-8 (a.) 1. marked by quiet and caution and secrecy; taking pains to avoid being observed 2. secret and sly or sordid [false feline footstep foxy fraudulent fur unconcealed unobtrusive treacherous tricky impression indirection insidious intend intimacy engage escape exchange] "a furtive manner"
*fuse 08-52-30 (n.) 1. electrical device that can interrupt the flow of electrical current when it is overloaded 2. any igniter by which an explosive charge is ignited (v.) 1. become plastic or fluid or liquefied from heat 2. mix together different elements 3. equip with a fuse; provide with a fuse 4. make liquid or plastic by heating [federate fender ferocity fill fire fit flow fluid flux fuel fusible fuzee umbrella unfreeze unify unite united use safety saturate screen screw serenity shape socket solid solve specific storm substance surge switch syncretize synthesize easily eclectic electricity element embody encompass equip exceed explode explosive]
*futile 09-48-23 (a.) 1. unproductive of success 2. producing no result or effect [failing fond foolish frivolous fruitless function unavailing undertake unfortunate unhappy unproductive unsuccessful useless therapy thoughtless tile trite trivial idle improper incapable insufficient lack lame light loony effect effete effort empty errand etiolated] "a futile effort"
*futurist 18-40-4 (a.) 1. of or relating to futurism (n.) 1. someone who predicts the future [fantast foresight fulfil unusual theology revelation rist scripture seer speculate] "futurist art"

G

*gaffe 11-68-14 (n.) 1. a socially awkward or tactless act [gaff gaucherie awkward faux flub foulup embarrass error etiquette /fag/]
*gaiety 17-65-5 (n.) 1. a gay feeling 2. a festive merry feeling [gay glad gleeful good gorgeous great animation appearance inappropriate intensity intoxicate emotion entertainment exhilarate experience exuberant transport trap trickery]
*gaily 19-52-3 (ad.) 1. in a gay manner [gail garish gaudy gay airily insouciance lighthearted] "the scandals were gaily diverting"
*gainsay 24-67-1 (v.) 1. take exception to [gain good abjure argue impugn naysay negate negative not nullify sincerity statement]
*gait 14-60-8 (n.) 1. the rate of moving (especially walking or running) 2. a horse's manner of moving 3. a person's manner of walking [gallop ground ait alternate amble injure threatening travel tread trot two]
*galaxy 09-56-25 (n.) 1. a splendid assemblage (especially of famous people) 2. tufted evergreen perennial herb having spikes of tiny white flowers and glossy green round to heart-shaped leaves that become coppery to maroon or purplish in fall 3. (astronomy) a collection of star systems; any of the billions of systems each having many stars and nebulae and dust [galax garden gas gathering glossy gravitation green grouping accumulation across aggregation arm army assembly asymmetric attractor lack leaf legion light lion luminary year young /lag/] "`extragalactic nebula' is a former name for `galaxy'"
*gallant 12-63-13 (a.) 1. unflinching in battle or action 2. having the qualities of gallantry attributed to an ideal knight 3. lively and spirited 4. having or displaying great dignity or nobility (n.) 1. a man who is much concerned

with his dress and appearance 2. a man who attends or escorts a woman [gay gentleman george glorious good gracious grand great abandon accomplishment admire adore adult affect allan alpine animation appearance attack attribute leader libertine literary lively lofty lothario lover nobility noble tend thoughtful tiger toward /lag/] "a gallant warrior"
*galore 14-66-9 (a.) 1. in great numbers 2. existing in abundance [generous great abound abundant affluent amount ample aplenty largely lavish liberal lore opulent overflow rampant rich rife everywhere exhaustless exist exuberant /lag/] "daffodils galore"
*galvanize 12-02-13 (v.) 1. to stimulate to action 2. cover with zinc; as of steel, for example 3. stimulate by administering a shock; as of muscles [generate great aback activate administer ani animate arouse awake liven vitalize nerve impel incite inflame invigorate iron zinc electrify enliven excite exhilarate /lag/]
*gamble 03-54-179 (n.) 1. money that is risked for possible monetary gain 2. a risky act or venture (v.) 1. take a risk in the hope of a favorable outcome 2. play games for money [gain game gamester give great guess adventure adventurer amble amuse assay attempt money back bet bettor big bootleg break broke buy lady lie life long lose loss lot luck effort endanger essay expectation expose /mag/]
*gambol 19-63-3 (n.) 1. gay or light-hearted recreational activity for diversion or amusement (v.) 1. play boisterously [gambado garden gay glory glow ambo amuse antic arouse meadow beam behavior bob boisterous bound lamb lark laugh leap lighthearted lunacy /lob mag/]
*gamut 14-41-9 (n.) 1. a complete extent or range: "a face that expressed a gamut of emotions" 2. (music) the entire scale of musical notes [gam gradation accord ambit area array artistic auditory manner monotone musical thread tier tone train /mag tum uma/] "a face that expressed a gamut of emotions"
*garble 19-40-3 (v.) 1. make false by mutilation or addition; as of a message or story [garb gibberish gild gobbledygook adulterate affected alter argot artificial assume represent riffle babble belie biased bogus burlesque butcher lack logical lop embellish embroider empty exaggerate /bra brag rag/]
*garner 07-52-39 (n.) 1. a storehouse for threshed grain or animal feed (v.) 1. acquire or deserve by one's efforts or actions 2. store grain 3. assemble or get together [gain gather glean good grain granary abstract accumulate acquire amass animal arne arrange assemble athletic rake rally ready reap refuse reserve natural nest nut effort elevator entrepot extract /rag/]
*garnish 09-28-23 (n.) 1. something (such as parsley) added to a dish for flavor or decoration 2. any decoration added as a trimming or adornment (v.) 1. decorate (food), as with parsley or other ornamental foods [garni garniture gold grace gravy accompaniment add adorn appearance array attach attractive authority redecorate redo refurbish relish nationalize illumination impound impress sauce savory security seize sequester sequestrate side socialize spangle stud support /rag/]
*garrison 10-26-20 (n.) 1. a fortified military post where troops are stationed 2. the troops who maintain and guard a fortified place 3. United States abolitionist who published an anti-slavery journal (1805-1879) (v.) 1. station in a fort or garrison, as of troops [george goaltender gordon guard guardsman abolitionist acropolis agency arm armed armor army arris assign rank rearguard reformer regiment installation section security send service slavery soldiery squadron station supply organization outfit outpost national /rag/]
*garrote 24-49-1 (n.) 1. an instrument of execution for execution by strangulation [gag garotte gas guillotine asphyxiate rote obstruct throttle tighten electrocute execution /orra rag torr/]
*garrulous 17-56-5 (a.) 1. full of trivial conversation [gabby gar gaseous gassy glib gossipy gregarious gush ready long loquacious smooth sociable speech /rag/]
*gaseous 21-30-2 (a.) 1. existing as or having characteristics of a gas [garrulous gas gasiform gassy gossamer gush aeriform aerosolize aerostatic airy shape slight smoky solid sparkle steamy subtle effervescent effusive ethereal evaporate exist expand oxyacetylene unreal unsubstantial /sag/] "steam is water is the gaseous state"
*gastric 19-73-3 (a.) 1. relating to or involving the stomach [gast abdominal anal splanchnic stomachic tummy rectal ileac intestinal cardiac colonic coronary /sag/] "gastric ulcer"
*gastronomy 18-63-4 (n.) 1. a particular style of cookery (as of a region) [good gourmet appreciation art artistic astronomy significant style region manner /mono sag/]
*gauge 06-42-53 (n.) 1. a measuring instrument for measuring and indicating a quantity or for testing conformity with a standard (v.) 1. form an opinion about; judge tentatively; form an estimate of, as of quantities or time [gage gap gas great groove grouping guess gun accept account accurate adapt add adjust amount amplitude analyze approximate area assessment atmospheric aug axle udometer uncertain uniform element ensure estimate evaluate example experiment express extent]
*gendarme 21-69-2 (n.) 1. a French policeman [general group gumshoe enforce narc detective dick arm armed reeve responsibility marshal member]
*genealogist 24-54-1 (n.) 1. an expert in genealogy [expert skillful special]
*genealogy 14-46-8 (n.) 1. successive generations of kin [gene group early expert ancestry lineage origin]
*generality 19-32-3 (n.) 1. an idea having general application 2. the quality of being general or widespread or having general applicability [general generalization

gist gravamen essential everywhere everywoman exist normal reasoning remark ruck rule run abstraction accept amorphous application aspect attribute average axiom law laxity loose idea important imprecise inaccuracy incoherent indiscriminate instance think thrust true truism]
*generalize 16-01-6 (v.) 1. draw from specific cases for more general cases 2. become systemic; spread throughout the body; of diseases and infections 3. speak or write in generalities 4. cater to popular taste to make popular and present to the general public; bring into general or common use [general give globalize evidence expand express extend extrapolate range rationalize reasoning analyze around author limit logic incomplete inference instance intellectualize]
*generally 02-40-364 (ad.) 1. without distinction of one from others 2. without regard to specific details or exceptions 3. usually; as a rule [general exception naturally normative rain rarely regular roundly routine rule about altogether largely law life loose]
*generate 02-50-307 (v.) 1. make children 2. produce (energy) 3. give or supply 4. bring into existence [galvanize genera gestate get give gradual effect electricity energy engender enough entire establish estate evolve existence realize recognize render return revenue rule accomplish achieve application arise author /tare/] "The new manager generated a lot of problems"
*generic 07-45-36 (a.) 1. (biology) relating to or common to or descriptive of all members of a genus 2. (of drugs) not protected by trademark 3. applicable to an entire class or group [generalize genus group entire eric nebulous neutral non nonspecific range run indeterminate category class collective common copyright /cire/] "the generic name"
*generosity 08-61-33 (n.) 1. the trait of being willing to give your money or time 2. acting generously [generous give goodwill gracious effort elevation eros evidence extravagance exuberant nobility noble numerous receptive repletion riotous openhandedne outpouring overflow share shower size stream substantial sympathetic idealism temperament trait yourself /sore/]
*genesis 11-50-16 (n.) 1. a coming into being 2. the first book of the Old Testament: tells of creation; Adam and Eve; the Fall of Man; Cain and Abel; Noah and the flood; God's covenant with Abraham; Abraham and Isaac; Jacob and Esau; Joseph and his brothers [gene generation god grassroots esau eve nativity noah sacred scripture source stage start stock subsequent inception incipiency infancy intend isaac /sene/]
*genial 10-56-19 (a.) 1. diffusing warmth and friendliness 2. conducive to comfort; beneficial 3. of or relating to the chin or median part of the lower jaw [gathering gen genetic gentle glowing good gracious grateful greeting growth enjoyable exalted exhilarate nature neighborly nice inferior influence intimacy irrepressible affable agreeable amiable approachable ardent laughing liberality life light lineament lower lukewarm /lain/]
*geniality 24-57-1 (n.) 1. a disposition to be friendly and approachable (easy to talk to) [gracious inferior affable amiable approachable light talk temporary]
*genital 17-58-5 (a.) 1. of or relating to the external sex organs [gamete gen genetic genitive epigenetic external iliac testicle abiogenesis lumbar /tine/] "genital herpes"
*genteel 11-51-16 (a.) 1. marked by refinement in taste and manners [gent gentleman good gracious elegant exalted exquisite narrow neat noble taste title tony trim lady ladylike /lee leet/]
*gentile 16-32-6 (a.) 1. belonging to or characteristic of non-Jewish peoples (n.) 1. a person who does not acknowledge your God 2. a person who is not a member of one's own religion; used in this sense by Mormons and Hindus 3. in this sense ‘Gentile' denotes a Christian as contrasted with a Jew; ‘goy' is a derogatory word for Christians used by Jews [genetic gent give god goy grammar ethnic national non totem tribal idol infidel lineal]
*geology 10-39-20 (n.) 1. a science that deals with the history of the earth as recorded in rocks 2. the geological features of the earth [generate geography geomorphology geophysics give glacier gravel grinding ground earth eastern eccentric economically elevation erode erosion exceed exposure extend ology once origin overlie lake land layer leaf leap less level line long loose low]
*germane 21-40-2 (a.) 1. having close kinship and appropriateness [german enate related relevant material affiliate apply appropriate apropos ask] "he asks questions that are germane and central to the issue"
*germinate 15-53-7 (v.) 1. produce buds, branches, or germinate; of plants 2. work out; as of a theory or an idea 3. cause to grow or sprout [gather gemmate germ grow evolve rain reproduce riot root mature mental mind mushroom idea increase incubate natural new abstract artistic theory thrive tower]
*gestation 17-60-5 (n.) 1. the period during which an embryo develops (about 266 days in humans) 2. the conception and development of an idea or plan 3. the state of being pregnant; the period from conception to birth when a woman carries a developing fetus in her uterus [gravid growth early ectopic embryo extrauterine section shed sluggish stage station surgery symptom synthesis tension thicken thrombosis travail abdominal aid amniotic implant incubation inflammation offspring ovum narrow nausea normal]
*gesticulate 17-70-5 (v.) 1. show, express or direct through movement [gest god greeting express extend shake shout show shrug signal signify speak spit stance stretch thrust transmit indifference call carriage catholic charade clap cognitive communicate consecrate cross leave lower acclaim approval arm]
*gesture 04-43-130 (n.) 1. something done as an

indication of intention 2. the use of movements (especially of the hands) to communicate familiar or prearranged signals 3. motion of hands or body to emphasize or help to express a thought or feeling (v.) 1. show, express or direct through movement [gambit gest gesticulate god gracious greeting guise elation emotion emphasize entail expression extend salutation shake shame sharp shout showy shrug signify slap spit stretch style submission suggest symbol tactics thrust token tone track transmit raise religious reminder resignation reverence right ritual] "He gestured his desire to leave"
*ghastly 09-83-24 (a.) 1. shockingly repellent; inspiring horror 2. gruesomely indicative of death or the dead [ghost gray grim grisly gross gruesome haggard hair hast hideous horror human aftermath age ailing alarming appalling awful sacrifice scary sepulchral shadowy shock shriek sick smell tale task terrible terrify toneless torture tremendous lackluster last literary lurid luster] "ghastly wounds"
*gibe 16-78-6 (n.) 1. an aggressive remark directed at a person like a missile and intended to have a telling effect (v.) 1. be compatible, similar or consistent; coincide in their characteristics 2. laugh or scoff at [gib gird gun identical indignity injury inspection insult intend bait barb barrack bear belief beseem brickbat effect enormity epigram equal evidence express /big/]
*giddy 10-40-20 (a.) 1. having or causing a whirling sensation; liable to falling 2. lacking seriousness; given to frivolity [gaga gay gid giggle give glorious good ill impulsive intoxicate irresponsible dated dizzy down drench drunken yeasty /dig/]
*gigantic 09-51-25 (a.) 1. so exceedingly large or extensive as to suggest a giant or mammoth [gangly gargantuan giant gluttonous great immense infinite inordinate abandon antic astronomical average awesome tall task tiny titanic towering tremendous cargo colossal corporation cosmic cyclopean /nag/] "a gigantic redwood"
*gist 17-63-5 (n.) 1. the central meaning or theme of a speech or literary work 2. the choicest or most essential or most vital part of some idea or experience [general gold gravamen ground idea impact important intend inward issue sense short signify soul speech spirit story stuff substance sum text theme topic] "the gist of the prosecutor's argument"
*giver 18-45-4 (n.) 1. someone who devotes themselves completely 2. person who makes a gift of property [gift give good great increase institution intend relinquish return] "there are no greater givers than those who give themselves"
*glacial 14-54-8 (a.) 1. relating to or derived from a glacier 2. extremely cold 3. devoid of warmth and cordiality; expressive of unfriendliness or disdain [gelid geology greeting look low absence advance algid aloof arctic characterize climate cold contemptuous cool cordiality cover crisp cutting ice icily icy inadequate indifferent inside /ical laic/] "glacial deposit"
*glacier 11-57-15 (n.) 1. a slowly moving mass of ice [glaciate growler lolly accumulate alaska almost alpine calf central compact continuous ice iceberg icecap icicle earth /ical/]
*gladden 19-49-3 (v.) 1. make glad or happy 2. become glad or happy [glad gratify last liven animate death delight elate encourage enliven exhilarate /dal/]
*glazier 21-58-2 (n.) 1. someone who cuts flat glass to size [glasswork artificer install]
*glean 11-54-17 (v.) 1. gather, as of as crops [gain garner gather gathering get grabble grain lean learn left link lucre earnings employ excerpt extract accumulate accumulator amass amount anthology area assemble natural net nut]
*glib 13-49-11 (a.) 1. marked by lack of intellectual depth 2. artfully persuasive in speech 3. having only superficial plausibility [garrulous generalization gossipy graphic gregarious gushy lack lib light loquacity implausible incense induce ingratiating insincere intend belief bigmouth bland buttery] "glib generalizations"
*glimmer 11-57-15 (n.) 1. a flash of light (especially reflected light) (v.) 1. shine brightly, like a star or a light [gesture glance glitter glow light limmer look idea implication index indication inkling intermittent intimate emit energy extent radiate ray reflect]
*glimpse 04-52-93 (n.) 1. a brief or incomplete view 2. a quick look 3. a vague indication (v.) 1. catch a glimpse of; see briefly [gander glim glimmering glint lake look incomplete indistinct mean peek peep perceive percept pointer power preview professor prospect scene see serve side sight sign spot stare suggest espy eye] "from the window he could catch a glimpse of the lake"
*gloat 13-59-10 (n.) 1. malicious satisfaction (v.) 1. dwell on with satisfaction 2. gaze at or think about something with great self-satisfaction, gratification, or joy [gas gasconade gawk gaze glare glee gratification great line look oat off ogle achievement attention think tout toward triumph]
*glorious 04-73-94 (a.) 1. bringing great happiness and thankfulness 2. having or worthy of pride 3. having or deserving or conferring glory 4. characterized by or attended with brilliance or grandeur 5. having great beauty and splendor [golden good grace grandeur great lasting laud lovely loving lustrous luxurious omniscient one outstand radiant reason redoubtable reel renowned resplendent illustrious immense imposing impressive incandescent inspire intellectual ubiquitous ugly unbounded unlimited scholar self shameful shape simplicity soar splendor strong sublime sunset superb supreme] "a long and glorious career"
*glut 10-47-20 (n.) 1. the quality of being so overabundant that prices fall (v.) 1. overeat or eat immodestly; make a pig of oneself 2. supply with an excess of [give gobble gorge gormandize gourmand guzzle large lead lower tennis]

*glutinous 21-65-2 (a.) 1. having the properties of glue [gelatinous gluey glut gooey gummy tacky tenacious tend thicken tough inspissate non obstinate sticky stodgy stubborn]
*glutton 18-58-4 (n.) 1. a person who is devoted to eating and drinking to excess 2. wolverine of northern Eurasia [gal gigantic give glut gorge gourmand gourmet greedy groundhog unbridled undue unlimited trencherman omnivorous opossum outrageous overeat overweening northern nourishment nutritious]
*gluttonous 21-49-2 (a.) 1. given to excess in consumption of especially food or drink [gal give glutton greedy scavenge show sparing swinish] "over-fed women and their gluttonous husbands"
*gnash 19-62-3 (v.) 1. grind together, of teeth [gnaw grating grinding grit gum nash nibble nip anger ash snap sound swallow /sang/]
*gnaw 13-53-10 (v.) 1. become ground down or deteriorate 2. bite or chew on with the teeth [galling gradual grate grave grinding grip ground gum nag nettle nip ache afflict aggravate ail annoy anxiety away wave wear well wind worry wound wrench wring /wan wang/] "gnaw an old cracker"
*goad 13-57-11 (n.) 1. a pointed instrument used to prod into motion 2. a verbalization that encourages you to attempt something (v.) 1. urge with or as if with a goad 2. give heart or courage to 3. prod or urge as if with a log stick 4. goad or provoke,as by constant criticism [gad gadfly get give goa onward actuate animal animate annoy approval assault attempt desire develop dig driving drove]
*gordian 24-45-1 (a.) 1. extremely intricate; usually in phrase"gordian knot" [interconnecte intricate] "gordian knot"
*gorge 10-67-19 (n.) 1. a deep ravine (usually with a river running through it) 2. a narrow pass (especially one between mountains) 3. the passage between the pharynx and the stomach (v.) 1. overeat or eat immodestly; make a pig of oneself [gap gastrointestinal geologic gill glut gormandize gourmand grand greedy gulch gulf gullet obstruction opening organism outwork overindulge overweight range ravine rear rent replete rift rise river rocky run rupture early eat eliminate embolus enormous entrance esophagus excavation excess extend /grog/]
*gosling 19-80-3 (n.) 1. young goose [gander goner goose gregarious owlet shoat sling lamb lambkin large less leveret litter long immature nestle]
*gossamer 19-42-3 (a.) 1. characterized by unusual lightness and delicacy 2. so thin as to transmit light (n.) 1. a gauze fabric with an extremely fine texture 2. filaments from a cobweb [gaseous gauzy girlish goss ground gruel open opposite section see seethrough shade sheer silk slender slight small smooth stock strand subtle surface susceptible synthetic air airy attenuate matchwood misty mote moth mousse effeminate ethereal exquisite extent extremely rarefied reed refined reveal robust rugged /ass mass/]
*gouge 13-41-11 (n.) 1. an impression in a surface (as made by a blow) 2. and edge tool with a blade like a trough for cutting channels or grooves 3. the act of gouging (v.) 1. obtain by coercion or intimidation 2. make a groove in 3. force with the thumb [gash gazump geology glare good gore grinding groove obscure obtain out outrageous overcharge overtax unearth unravel unreasonable edge evolve excessive executive exorbitant exploit extort eye] "gouge out his eyes"
*gourd 19-28-3 (n.) 1. bottle made from the dried shell of a bottle gourd 2. any of numerous inedible fruits with hard rinds 3. any vine of the family Cucurbitaceae that bears fruits with hard rinds [glass green oblong old orange our unite red reproductive rind ripen round decoration derive different dry]
*gourmand 21-55-2 (n.) 1. a person who is devoted to eating and drinking to excess [gastronome glutton greedy gut mand nourishment devoted drink]
*graceless 19-65-3 (a.) 1. lacking graciousness 2. lacking social polish 3. lacking grace; clumsy [gauche gawky good grace gross refinement reprobate room rude awkward charm clumsy coarse conversation crude elegant excellent lack leave lose low lumber scott sir skill sloppy social stature stiff] "a totally graceless hostess"
*gradation 21-32-2 (n.) 1. relative position in a graded series 2. a vowel whose quality or length is changed to indicate linguistic distinctions (such as sing sang sung song) 3. the act of arranging in grades [gamut geography grad graduation grouping range round run ablaut accord arrange array assortment degree deposition difference discrete distinction tense thread tier tone train imperceptible indicate orthoepy nexus nuance /tad/]
*gradient 19-84-3 (n.) 1. a graded change in the magnitude of some physical quantity or dimension 2. the property possessed by a line or surface that departs from the horizontal [glacis grad grade gravity growth railroad rake ramp rate relational rise road abrupt alteration altitude ascent degree depart descent deviation different dimension distance downward incline increase even non talus tangent temperature tilt] "a five-degree gradient"
*granary 19-76-3 (n.) 1. a storehouse for threshed grain or animal feed [garner good grain grana grow region abundant animal /rana/]
*grandeur 08-52-27 (n.) 1. the quality of being exalted in character or ideals or conduct 2. the quality of being magnificent or splendid or grand [generous glory good graceful grand grande great refined regality respect resplendent amplitude austerity nobility noble nobleminded note deserve dignity distinction effect elaborate elevated exalted excellence extensive /rue/]
*grandiloquent 24-50-1 (a.) 1. lofty in style 2. puffed up with vanity [gobbledygook really rhetorical appearance

never newsweek distinction importance lofty oratory orotund undeserved unpretentious effect engage talk]
*grandiose 10-47-18 (a.) 1. impressive because of unnecessary largeness or grandeur; used to show disapproval 2. affectedly genteel [garish gaudy genteel glorious grand rhetorical ritzy royal affected ambitious appearance august noble declamatory deluxe disapproval distinction impenetrable imposing impressive inflated orotund ostentatious overwrought show splendid stately strong sumptuous swell elaborate elegant elevated excessive extravagant]
*granular 21-38-2 (a.) 1. composed of or covered with relatively large particles 2. having a granular structure like that of chondrites [grainy gran gritty gross rough appear atomic ultramicroscopic unrefined /lunar/] "granular sugar"
*granulate 21-40-2 (v.) 1. form into grains 2. form granulating tissue, as of wounds and ulcers 3. become granular [give gnarl grainy gran grate gritty gross rank reinforce rough abrade appearance assume atomize ulcer uneven unkempt unrefined levigate texture thicken tissue tooth toughen triturate effloresce /lunar/]
*granule 21-63-2 (n.) 1. a tiny grain [geology grain gran gravel grit region ace animal approximate astronomy atom nutshell /lunar/]
*grapple 08-41-33 (n.) 1. a tool consisting of several hooks for grasping and holding; often thrown with a rope 2. a dredging bucket with hinges like the shell of a clam 3. the act of engaging in close hand-to-hand combat (v.) 1. to grip or seize, as in a wrestling match 2. come to terms or deal successfully with [gallon gas get government grab graft grasp grasping grip ground raise ras ring riot rope abduct accomplish amateur anchor apple arm attach pair part perform player position practice prehend pull purchase putto lift loaf lose economic effort embrace engage engraft existence]
*gratification 13-52-10 (n.) 1. the act or an instance of satisfying 2. state of being gratified; great satisfaction [give gratuity great gusto ratify relish repetitious return reward achieve amusement appetite arrive titillate trip immense indulge indulgence instance intellectual favor fruition fulfill full fun comfort compensation condition cozy cultural obliging /fit/] "dull repetitious work gives no gratification"
*gratify 10-42-21 (v.) 1. make happy or satisfied 2. yield (to); give satisfaction to [genial give gladden good gracious grass grateful graze ratify recompense regale rejoicing restraint rewarding acceptable agreeable allay amiable appease assuage indulge favorable feed feel felicitous fine flush food fulfill yield /fit/]
*gratuitous 12-55-13 (a.) 1. without cause 2. costing nothing 3. unnecessary and unwarranted [give given grant groundless random rat receive redundant remark require return rude accord allow arbitrary tautology tent ticket toll uncalledfor unfounded unjustified unmerited unneeded unpaid unreasonable unwarranted independent insult irrational irregular obligation offer optional smart spare striker superfluous system] "a gratuitous insult"
*gratuity 18-33-4 (n.) 1. a relatively small amount of money given for services rendered (as by a waiter) 2. an award (as for meritorious service) given without claim or obligation [gift give gravy grease rat remainder render reward right amount appreciation award tip token type incidental inducement year]
*grave 03-52-137 (a.) 1. causing fear or anxiety by threatening great harm 2. dignified and somber in manner or character and committed to keeping promises 3. of great gravity or crucial import; requiring serious thought (n.) 1. a place for the burial of a corpse (especially beneath the ground and marked by a tombstone) 2. death of a person 3. a mark (') placed above a vowel to indicate pronunciation (v.) 1. shape (a material like stone or wood) by whittling away at it 2. write upon; engrave a pen, for example [gloomy glyptic grand gray great grievous grim groove ground rave raven record rectangular regal region release require responsibility roof rooted royal accent anaglyph ancient anxiety assemble august awful value vault venerable verge vested videotape vital vowel earnest egyptian embed emergency end enter entrench establish etch] "a grave God-fearing man"
*gravity 07-48-37 (n.) 1. (physics) the force of attraction between all masses in the universe; especially the attraction of the earth's mass for bodies near its surface 2. a manner that is serious and solemn 3. a solemn and dignified feeling [gloomy grandeur grim regality remote reserve responsible rice rigid acute affective affinity allure amount astronomical attitude attract venerable immediate impersonality importance inappropriate inverse temperance thoughtfulnes traction trait tug] "the more remote the body the less the gravity"
*graze 08-54-28 (n.) 1. a superficial abrasion 2. the act of grazing (v.) 1. break the skin (of a body part) by scraping 2. feed as in a meadow or pasture 3. eat lightly, try different dishes 4. let (animals) feed in a field or pasture or meadow 5. scrape gently [gentle get give glancing gobble grass green grinding rake range rap raze read regular relish rub ruffle ruminate ablate abrasion abrasive afield allow animate appetite appetizer area attrition eat entr erase erode excoriate]
*gregarious 14-48-9 (a.) 1. seeking and enjoying the company of others 2. tending to form a group with others of the same kind [gari genial glib gossipy group grow effusive enjoy expansive expressive extrovert affable amiable animal avoid organize outgoing unreserved urbane seek smooth social solitude species swarm /age rag rage/] "gregarious bird species"
*grenadier 18-87-4 (n.) 1. an infantryman equipped with grenades 2. deep-sea fish with a large head and body and long tapering tail [gadid gadoid giant grunt rattail red regiment rifleman eastern equip exceptional arm assign deepsea die dogface infantryman /dan/]

*grief 06-58-57 (n.) 1. intense sorrow caused by loss of a loved one (especially by death) 2. something that causes great unhappiness [get give great grievous regret rue ruth infelicity injury intense emotion extremity fail] "her death was a great grief to John"
*grievance 08-48-30 (n.) 1. a complaint about a (real or imaginary) wrong that causes resentment and is grounds for action 2. an allegation that something imposes an illegal obligation or denies some legal right or causes injustice 3. a resentment strong enough to justify retaliation [gall gripe groan ground grudge grumble rally rancor reason receive remonstration resentment retaliate right rigor ill illegal illwill imaginary impose infection inflict infringe injustice encumbrance enough evil exception expression vance venom vexation visitation accusation affront allegation anger atrocity nemesis care cause charge complaint court criticism cross /ave nave/]
*grievous 13-67-11 (a.) 1. causing fear or anxiety by threatening great harm 2. shockingly brutal or cruel 3. of great gravity or crucial import; requiring serious thought 4. causing or marked by grief or anguish [good granddaughter gravity great grieve gross rank regrettable require responsibility rotten rueful illness important improper infamous inordinate intolerable irreparable egregious emergency enormous evil exacting excess excruciating experience express extremely value verge vile villainous offense openly operation oppressive outrageous ugly unashamed unbearable uncomfortable unduly unfortunate sad serious severe shameful sharp shock sigh significant situation sorrowful staggering]
*grimace 12-58-13 (n.) 1. a contorted facial expression (v.) 1. contort the face to indicate a certain mental or emotional state [gesture gloom glower grim rant recoil roar indicate mental mop mow mug muscle ache ail amount angry anguish certain close communicate configuration contort contorted emotional execute expression eye /amir/] "He grimaced when he saw the amount of homework he had to do"
*grindstone 24-50-1 (n.) 1. a revolving stone shaped like a disk; used to grind or sharpen or polish edge tools [grind revolving rock implement industry definite disk sharper special steel stone tool edge]
*grisly 11-62-16 (a.) 1. shockingly repellent; inspiring horror [ghastly grim gruesome repel repellent repugnant repulsive revolting inspire sacrifice shock sickening sly livid loathsome lurid]
*grotesque 08-59-29 (a.) 1. ludicrously odd 2. distorted and unnatural in shape or size; abnormal and hideous (n.) 1. art characterized by an incongruous mixture of parts of humans and animals interwoven with plants [gnarled gross grot gruesome realistic reflection revolting rickety ridiculous rococo odd offbeat ordinary outlandish outrageous teratoid truncate twist eerie eight extreme sea seeming serpent shadow shape size slight statue strange study style surreal queer ugly uncanny unexpected unnatural unusual /set/] "tales of grotesque serpents eight fathoms long that churned the seas"
*grotto 16-62-6 (n.) 1. a small cave (usually with attractive features) [garden grot ground ornamental tunnel]
*ground 01-58-976 (a.) 1. broken or pounded into small fragments; used of e.g. ore or stone (n.) 1. the part of a scene (or picture) that lies behind objects in the foreground 2. a relation that provides the foundation for something 3. a position to be won or defended in battle (or as if in battle) 4. a rational motive for a belief or action 5. the loose soft material that makes up a large part of the land surface 6. the solid part of the earth's surface 7. the first or preliminary coat of paint or size applied to a surface 8. (art) the surface (as a wall or canvas) prepared to take the paint for a painting 9. a relatively homogeneous percept extending back of the figure on which attention is focused 10. a connection between an electrical device and the earth (which is a zero voltage) 11. material in the top layer of the surface of the earth in which plants can grow (especially with reference to its quality or use) (v.) 1. dance by rotating the pelvis in an erotically suggestive way 2. confine or restrict to the ground 3. instruct someone in the fundamentals of a subject 4. place or out on the ground 5. work hard 6. reduce to small pieces or particles by pounding or abrading 7. make a grating or grinding sound by rubbing together 8. fix firmly and stably 9. press or grind with a crunching noise 10. use as a basis for; found on 11. connect to a ground, of electrical connections for safety reasons 12. hit (a baseball) onto the ground 13. hit a groundball, in baseball 14. throw (a football) to the ground in order to stop play and avoid being tackled behind the line of scrimmage 15. bring to the ground, as of vessels 16. hit or reach the ground 17. cover with a primer; apply a primer to [gain game given good radical reach realty reason right round run obligation observation occasion ultimatum undercoat necessary data deposit domain]
*grove 06-51-58 (n.) 1. garden consisting of a small cultivated wood without undergrowth 2. a small growth of trees without underbrush [gap garden gill glen group growth ravine rove orange orchard vale valley]
*grovel 18-71-4 (v.) 1. show submission or fear [genuflect ground grove gumshoe rake recline recumbent reposing respect roll obsequious exaggerate lackey lickspittle lie literary loll lounging low lying /levo/]
*guess 03-47-209 (n.) 1. an estimate based on little or no information 2. a message expressing an opinion based on incomplete evidence (v.) 1. put forward, of a guess 2. form an opinion about; judge tentatively; form an estimate of, as of quantities or time 3. guess correctly; solve by guessing 4. expect, believe, or suppose [gamble gauge get give good guilty undo

unlock unravel unusual upset earn element embarrassed enough estimate estimation evidence expect explain expression set shell shot signal solution solve speculation spite stand steak substantiate successful sufficient supposition surmise suspicion]

*guile 14-79-9 (n.) 1. shrewdness as demonstrated by being skilled in deception 2. the quality of being crafty 3. the use of tricks to deceive someone (usually to extract money from them) [gain gamesmanship underhanded indirect ingenious insidious intend inventive lack extract]

*guileless 19-44-3 (a.) 1. free from guile 2. free of deceit [guile unassuming unflattering unguarded upright ingenuous innocent expect simple sincere straightforward]

*guinea 07-76-43 (n.) 1. a former British gold coin worth 21 shillings 2. W African bird having dark plumage mottled with white; native to Africa but raised for food in many parts of the world 3. a republic in eastern Africa on the Atlantic; formerly a French colony; achieved independence from France in 1958 4. ethnic slur; offensive terms for a person of Italian descent [gallinaceous gold greaseball independence indian inhabitant italy napoleon native niger eagle eastern equivalent ethnic europe achieve african amount atlantic]

*guise 09-56-23 (n.) 1. an artful or simulated semblance [gear gesture getup gloss idea imago impression intention investment semblance shape show side simulate style system effect eidolon excuse] "under the guise of friendship he betrayed them"

*gullible 14-69-8 (a.) 1. naive and easily deceived or tricked 2. easily tricked because of being too trusting [game green guile gull unaffected unsophisticated unwary lack love immature inexperienced innocent believe early easy experience exploit /bill lug/] "at that early age she had been gullible and in love"

*gumption 21-50-2 (n.) 1. sound practical judgment 2. (informal) fortitude and determination [game get give good green grit gump gut guts mettle mind mother moxie perspicacity pluck police practicality presence trouble try imitate initiative nerve nous /mug/]

*gush 10-65-20 (n.) 1. a sudden rapid flow (as of water) 2. an unrestrained expression of emotion (v.) 1. praise enthusiastically 2. gush forth in a sudden stream or jet of liquids 3. issue in a jet; come out in a jet; stream or spring forth [gain gas growth gus uncontrollable unctuous unrestrained upcoming uprise say self sentimental set simply sluggish smooth soft speak spout spread spring spurt squirt stream sudden surface surge swell hear hike honeyed]

*gust 11-48-14 (n.) 1. a strong current of air [gale gus upheaval sand shape short spirit squall strong sudden sweet taste tongue tree trick] "the tree was bent almost double by the gust"

*gusto 11-65-14 (n.) 1. vigorous and enthusiastic enjoyment [gayness glow good gust satisfaction soul spirit taste titillate]

*guy 01-44-545 (n.) 1. (British) an effigy of Guy Fawkes that is burned on a bonfire on Guy Fawkes Day 2. an informal term for a youth or man 3. a rope or cable that is used to brace something (especially a tent) (v.) 1. subject to laughter or ridicule 2. steady with a guy [gazebo gee gentleman great group unite uphold youth] "a nice guy"

*guzzle 12-69-12 (v.) 1. drink greedily or as if with great thirst [gargle gobble gorge great greedy gulp lap libation liquid eat engorge esophagus]

*gynecology 13-01-10 (n.) 1. the branch of medicine that deals with the diseases and hygiene of women [geriatrics gerontology gynaecology neurology non ecology cardiology chiropody obstetrician ophthalmology organ orthopedic]

*gyrate 17-44-5 (v.) 1. to wind or move in a spiral course:" the muscles and nerves of his fine drawn body were coiling for action,", "black smoke coiling up into the sky" 2. revolve quickly and repeatedly around one's own axis [grow gyre young rate reel repeatedly revolve rise rotate round run abstract advance around ascend axis travel turn twirl twist ebb]

*gyroscope 21-31-2 (n.) 1. rotating mechanism in the form of a universally mounted spinning wheel that offers resistance to turns in any direction [governor reduce reel resistance rolling rotate rotor offer orientation scope screw ship side space spin spit spring stabilize centrifuge chuck circular compass counterweight pendulum pivot propeller extractor /sory/]

H

*habitable 16-68-6 (a.) 1. fit for habitation [habit house livable liveable lot /bah/] "the habitable world"
*habitual 10-66-18 (a.) 1. commonly used or practiced; usual 2. made a norm or custom or habit 3. having a habit of long standing [habit hardened harmonious household accept accordance accustomed addicted arrange average beat behavior bring businesslike ingrained instinctive inveterate involuntary tackle tendency traditional trite uniform universal usual long /bah/] "his habitual practice was to eat an early supper"
*hack 06-68-48 (n.) 1. one who works hard at boring tasks 2. a car driven by a person whose job is to take passengers where they want to go in exchange for money 3. a horse kept for hire 4. a saddle horse used for transportation rather than sport etc. 5. a mediocre and disdained writer 6. an old or over-worked horse 7. a politician who belongs to a small clique that controls a political party for private rather than public ends (v.) 1. cut with a tool 2. cut away 3. kick on the arms; in basketball 4. kick on the shins; in rugby 5. informal: be able to manage or manage successfully 6. significantly cut up a manuscript 7. fix a computer program piecemeal until it works 8. cough spasmodically [halve hard herbivorous hew hire hit hoe hold hoop horizontal horse hour hunter abrupt access adapt amble antiquated arm article aspiration automobile axe cab call cant car careless carve chop chunk clique commit computer congestion control cope cough court cruise cut keep kerf kick knife] "I can't hack it anymore"
*hackney 11-96-17 (n.) 1. a carriage for hire 2. a compact breed of harness horse [hack harness hire horse automobile carriage compact equipage /yen/]
*hackneyed 17-67-5 (a.) 1. repeated too often; overfamiliar through overuse [habitual hackney household answer antiquated archaic automatic axiom commonplace constant conventional current nail notorious everyday /dey yen/]
*haggard 16-58-6 (a.) 1. very thin especially from disease or hunger or cold 2. showing the wearing effects of overwork or care or suffering [hawk henry howling hunger hysterical abandon adult adventure amok angular

anxiety appearance article gar gaunt ghastly gray grim gruesome raddle rage ravage reach rest rider ring roaring romantic dark deplete describe dick dim disease draw dull /drag rag/]
*halcyon 17-64-5 (a.) 1. idyllically calm and peaceful; suggesting happy tranquillity 2. marked by peace and prosperity 3. joyful and carefree [hal happy heavenly hush ancient atmosphere literary calm carefree clear clipper cool youth old orderly nest /noy/] "a halcyon atmosphere"
*hale 10-45-20 (a.) 1. exhibiting or restored to vigorous good health (n.) 1. American Revolutionary soldier hanged as a spy by the British; his last words were supposed to have been"I only regret that I have but one life to give for my country" (1755-1776) 2. prolific United States writer (1822-1909) 3. United States astronomer who discovered that sunspots are associated with strong magnetic fields (1868-1938) (v.) 1. to cause to do through pressure or necessity, by physical, moral or intellectual means :"She forced him to take a job in the city" 2. draw slowly or heavily [hang hardy haul healthy hearty heat heavy ale american apply article astronomy last leader life lug lusty elle exert exhibit] "hale and hearty"
*hallow 19-70-3 (v.) 1. render holy by means of religious rites [holy honor allow anew authoritative observe worship /olla/]
*handwriting 13-47-11 (n.) 1. something written by hand 2. the activity of writing by hand [hand art arthritis note decline disaster document down wall way write writing rapid read recognize represent run illegible implement imprint guest] "she recognized his handwriting"
*hangar 13-49-10 (n.) 1. a large structure at an airport where aircraft can be stored and maintained [hang hayloft house accommodation aircraft airdrome airfield airlock airport arsenal geometer grain granary repair /rag/]
*hapless 08-69-28 (a.) 1. deserving or inciting pity [help homeless accompany appeal pathetic piteous pity poor less life limb luckless extraordinary sad shabby star struck] "a hapless victim"
*harangue 16-55-6 (n.) 1. a loud bombastic declamation expressed with strong emotion (v.) 1. deliver a harangue to; address forcefully [hara homework homily address allocution angry argue assignment rant rave read recite give emotion exercise explain expound express]
*harass 07-39-36 (v.) 1. annoy persistently 2. cause to suffer 3. annoy continually or chronically 4. challenge aggressively [hara harry hassle haunted heckle hector hound humiliate hunt hurt abuse afflict aggressive annoy anxious attack rag repeatedly ride rile roil ruffle staff stammer strain stress suffer surround]
*harbinger 14-31-9 (n.) 1. an indication of the approach of something or someone (v.) 1. foreshadow or presage [herald ancestor announcer annunciate antecedent anticipate approach bellwether binge bushwhacker indication innovate notify groundbreaker guide evangelist explorer /bra/]
*harbor 05-04-82 (n.) 1. a place where ships can take on or discharge cargo (v.) 1. keep in one's possession; of animals 2. secretly shelter (as of fugitives or criminals) 3. hold a thought or feeling of 4. maintain; as of a theory, thoughts, or feelings [habitat hardship haven hide hold home house accommodate anchor ancient animal arbor arm asylum attack reach refuge repair resistant retain roman room base bear bed board boat body /bra rob/]
*harmonious 12-46-12 (a.) 1. exhibiting equivalence or correspondence among constituents of an entity or between different entities 2. musically pleasing 3. suitable and fitting 4. existing together in harmony [habitual harmon harmonize honeyed accord affable agreement amicable appropriate arrange regular relation rewarding routine match meeting melodious methodical military musical orderly orthodox neighborly nice normal incongruous inharmony instep unanimous unbalance uniform show sounding square straight suitable sweet symmetrical symphonious systematic] "the tailored clothes were harmonious with her military bearing"
*harrow 10-95-19 (n.) 1. a cultivator that pulverizes or smoothes the soil (v.) 1. draw a harrow over (land) [heckle hector hurt husbandry aerate afflict agonized agriculture ail angle arrow rack raise rip rub oil weed work wound wring /orra/]
*haughty 14-55-8 (a.) 1. having or showing arrogant superiority to and disdain of those one views as unworthy [hauteur highfalutin aerial aristocrat arrogant aspire aught unworthy uplift uppity upstage usual toplofty topping toward trait]
*havoc 08-57-28 (n.) 1. violent and needless disturbance [harm harry hurt abomination atrocity avo vandalism venom vexation violent outrage condition confusion consumption control corruption /ova/]
*hawthorn 13-94-10 (n.) 1. a spring-flowering shrub or small tree of the genus Crataegus [hair haw hazel heather hedge hydrangea acid aestival almost american apple azalea whitethorn wide witch woody woolly thorn thorny tome tree orange red rhododendron rose north]
*hazard 05-38-60 (n.) 1. an unknown and unpredictable phenomenon that causes an event to result one way rather than another 2. a source of danger 3. an obstacle on a golf course (v.) 1. put forward, of a guess 2. take a risk in the hope of a favorable outcome 3. put at risk [handbook health hitch hope hurdle accident advance adventure alcohol anticipate area assay assume attempt avoid racket reach real reasoning receiver refute rely remove reputation resemble rise risk roulette rub run damage damocles dangerous dare deathtrap deterrent dice difficulty doubt downfall /raza/] "drinking alcohol is a health hazard"

*haze 11-46-17 (n.) 1. confusion characterized by lack of clarity 2. atmospheric moisture or dust or smoke that causes reduced visibility (v.) 1. harass by imposing humiliating or painful tasks, as in military institutions [harass harry hassle hazy humid humiliate abstraction academy aerosol annoy atmospheric embarrassment]
*heartrending 24-84-1 (a.) 1. causing or marked by grief or anguish [harrowing ending excruciating experience express extreme affecting afflict agonizing anguish rack regrettable rend torment torturous touching tragic desolate dire distress intense irreparable granddaughter grievous]
*heed 07-52-35 (n.) 1. paying particular notice (as to children or helpless people) (v.) 1. pay close attention to; give heed to [hearing hedge hesitation ear eye earnest environment exclusion execution diligence discretion]
*heedless 19-32-3 (a.) 1. marked by or paying little heed or attention 2. characterized by careless unconcerned [haphazard hasty heed hurried easygoing economics edith extravagance danger deaf desperate detached disinterested disregard lack lackadaisical lazy listless little self shiftless slapdash sloppy spasmodic squander stolid suppress] "We have always known that heedless self-interest was bad morals; we know now that it is bad economics"
*hegemony 14-57-9 (n.) 1. the domination of one state over its allies [government group member mony organization nation /nome/]
*heifer 24-53-1 (n.) 1. young cow [hen hind hoyden ewe fawn female filly fledgling foal frail roe romp /fie/]
*heinous 15-53-7 (a.) 1. shockingly brutal or cruel [hateful horrid egregious enormous evil excess ignoble improper infamous nasty naughty notorious nous obscene odious offense outrageous unforgivable unspeakable unworthy utterly sad scandalous shock small]
*heir 06-52-55 (n.) 1. a person who is entitled by law or by the terms of a will to inherit the estate of another 2. a person who inherits some title or office [heritor hold effect entitle estate expect immediate inherit issue receiver recipient relict remainderman replacement right]
*hemorrhage 15-01-7 (n.) 1. flow of blood from a ruptured blood vessels (v.) 1. lose blood from one's body [haemorrhage heavily hurt hyp hypertension hypotension ecchymosis edema eject eliminate emaciate etch excessive experience external extravasate eye marasmus massive menstruation money month outflow outpouring rash reaction release rheum rupture accident age allergic asphyxiate asthma atrophy growth gum]
*henchman 15-67-7 (n.) 1. someone who assists in a plot [heavy heeler help hen high hold hooligan entourage collaborate commit confederate confidant creature criminal crony man member minion myrmidon accessory adherent assist associate attendant]
*herbaceous 16-77-6 (a.) 1. (botany) characteristic of a nonwoody herb or plant part [herb herby radicular rhizoid biology botany branch bulbous appearance aromatic cereal color oppose sage season stem study]
*hereditary 13-68-11 (a.) 1. tending to occur among members of a family usually by heredity 2. inherited or inheritable by established rules (usually legal rules) of descent [hand heritable hold home edit estate relation right rule descent disease down impose inborn inbred indigenous inherit innate instinct temperamental tend tradition traditional trait transmit ancestral atavistic authority /dere tide/]
*heredity 14-09-8 (n.) 1. the biological process whereby genetic factors are transmitted from one generation to the next 2. the total of inherited attributes [hair heritage edit endowment essential eugenics extraction replication right root descent determiner diathesis inherit total transmit /dere tide/]
*heresy 14-59-8 (n.) 1. any opinions or doctrines at variance with the official or orthodox position 2. a belief that rejects the orthodox tenets of a religion [hamartia here heterodoxy heterogeneity hippie hiss hold holy human element equivocal errancy error establish evil exterminate radical real reject release religious revisionism roman sacrilege schism science separate set sin sinful single son source southern spiritual /sere/]
*heretic 18-63-4 (n.) 1. a person who holds religious beliefs in conflict with the dogma of the Roman Catholic Church 2. a person who holds unorthodox opinions in any field (not merely religion) [here hippie hold home establish extremely recusant refuse reject religious renegade revisionist roman teach theory iconoclast infidel ishmael catholic church conduct conform consider contradict /cite iter/]
*heritage 04-57-116 (n.) 1. any attribute or immaterial possession that is inherited from ancestors 2. practices that are handed down from the past by tradition 3. hereditary succession to a title or an office or property 4. that which is inherited; a title or property or estate that passes by law to the heir on the death of the owner [heir heredity endowment entail estate replication reversion rita inheritance traditional allelomorph genetics /tire/] "a heritage of freedom"
*hermetic 17-42-5 (a.) 1. completely sealed; completely airtight [hard heavy herm hide enigmatic esoteric exclude existence recluse resistant restricted magic manner mysterious tight impermeable influence interference close completely conceal construction /cite item/]
*hernia 14-78-8 (n.) 1. rupture in smooth muscle tissue through which a bodily structure protrudes [hern hiatus enter region rupture navel near inguinal injury intestine abdominal]
*hesitancy 18-54-4 (n.) 1. a feeling of diffidence about doing something 2. a certain degree of unwillingness [exert self slothful indecision indisposition tentative

timidity trait agree caution certain commit yourself]
*hesitant 09-43-24 (a.) 1. lacking decisiveness of character; unable to act or decide quickly or firmly 2. acting with uncertainty or hesitance or lack of confidence [halting heedful hesitate effort equivocal erratic exert safe say self shrink shy slothful slow strain sure incalculable indecisive indemonstrable indicate indisposition inspiration tentative thorough timid timidity trait afraid agree ambivalent ant assurance averse noncommittal]
*hesitation 10-56-21 (n.) 1. the act of pausing uncertainly 2. a certain degree of unwillingness 3. indecision in speech or action [hedge hesitate holiday exert shall shill slothful speech stall stay suspension inactivity incalculable indecisive indisposition interval ion irresolute temporary tentative thorough trait truce abeyance agree alternative averse objection]
*heterogeneous 21-26-2 (a.) 1. consisting of elements that are not of the same kind or nature 2. originating outside the body [hetero homogenous eclectic element equivocal originate outside nature non unconformable unequal unlike unrelated scramble separate several species substance sundry /ego rete/] "the population of the United States is vast and heterogeneous"
*hew 11-39-14 (v.) 1. make or shape as with an axe 2. strike with an axe; cut down, strike [hack halve hand excise weapon whittle wood work] "hew out a path in the rock"
*hexagon 20-52-3 (n.) 1. a six-sided polygon [equal agon geometric /axe nog/]
*hiatus 12-44-12 (n.) 1. an interruption in the intensity or amount of something 2. a natural opening or perforation through a bone or a membranous structure 3. a missing piece (as a gap in a manuscript) [hemisphere hole hollow inlet interventricular abate abrupt amount anatomy aperture arrearage artistic third ullage uncork unexpected unstop separation shortage side space spinal split structure subsidence suspension syllable]
*hideous 09-76-24 (a.) 1. so extremely ugly as to be terrifying 2. grossly offensive to decency or morality; causing horror [hateful hear heinous hide horror inadmissible industry injustice damnable deal decency dire disgusting displease dreadful dreadfully exceptionable execrable extremely odious offensive outrageous ugly undesirable unpleasant unsightly unspeakable scar shock shriek sickening suffer]
*highbrow 15-64-7 (a.) 1. (informal) highly cultured or educated (n.) 1. a person of intellectual or erudite tastes [imitate interest genius ballet bookish brainy brow opera way write] "highbrow events such as the ballet or opera"
*hilarious 07-64-41 (a.) 1. marked by or causing boisterous merriment or convulsive laughter [hilar humour hysterical incongruous laughter ludicrous absurd amusing rejoicing rich ridiculous riotous uproarious scream side split story] "hilarious broad comedy"
*hillock 21-57-2 (n.) 1. a small natural hill [hammock hill hummock land last local knob knoll]
*hinder 08-51-29 (a.) 1. located at or near the back of an animal (v.) 1. put at a disadvantage 2. hinder or prevent the progress or accomplishment of 3. be a hindrance or obstacle to [hamper hamstring handicap happening harm heavy hind hockey hold ice impede inhibit interference intervene near delay deliberate deter development disadvantage discussion disfavor down drag effect embarrass encumber enjoin reach rear rebuff rescue resist return]
*hindrance 16-64-6 (n.) 1. something immaterial that interferes with or delays action or progress 2. any obstruction that impedes or is burdensome 3. the act of hindering or obstructing or impeding [halt hamper handicap happen hind hitch holdup immaterial impede incumbrance inhibition injunction instill interruption negative delay deterrent difficulty discourage doubt drag drawback ration rein respite roadway afterthought anxiety check chemical circumvent complication confine control crosswise curb effort encumbrance /nard/]
*hirsute 20-79-3 (a.) 1. having or covered with hair [hairy head hispid hoary shaggy shock shorthaired stiff stubble stud unshorn]
*hoard 13-56-10 (n.) 1. a secret store of valuables or money (v.) 1. save up as for future use 2. get or gather together [heap hide hive hoar hold abundance accumulation amass amount aside assemble available recurrent repertory reserve resource retain return rick roll data debt discharge dividend dump]
*hoarse 16-46-6 (a.) 1. deep and harsh sounding as if from shouting or illness or emotion [harsh hawk husky arse rasp raucous rough rude shaky shout sounding stifle strangle emotion euphonious]
*hoax 11-55-15 (n.) 1. something intended to deceive; deliberate trickery intended to gain an advantage (v.) 1. subject to a palyful hoax or joke [hoodwink humbug hypnotize offer outreach outwit overreach actor advantage]
*hollow 06-46-49 (a.) 1. devoid of significance or point 2. deliberately deceptive 3. as if echoing in a hollow space 4. not solid; having a space or gap or cavity (n.) 1. a depression hollowed out of solid matter 2. a small valley between mountains 3. a cavity or space in something (v.) 1. remove the inner part or the core of 2. remove the interior of [hand heavy high hillside hold hole hollo horizontal hungry opening orifice otiose out outlet lack lake land last laugh leak lifeless lift long low wall want way wear weathering well white wild withdraw wood wooden worm worthless] "a hollow wall"
*holster 20-37-3 (n.) 1. a sheath for a handgun; usually leather [handgun hip holder hols leather loop saddle sheath shoulder slot tie tool]
*homage 07-53-42 (n.) 1. respectful deference [honor

obligation observance ought mage magnification mission must acceptance acknowledgment admiration allegiance approval genuflection glory emperor esteem ethics eulogy expression]
*homogeneity 21-41-2 (n.) 1. the quality of being similar or comparable in kind or nature 2. the quality of being of uniform throughout in composition or structure [harmony heterogeneous oneness monism gene equality equanimity equivalence even nature identity indistinguishable integrity /ego tie/] "there is a remarkable homogeneity between the two companies"
*homogeneous 18-31-4 (a.) 1. all of the same or similar kind or nature [harmonize heterogenous homespun orderly measured mere mock gene group element equal essential even nature unbroken uncluttered uniform unruffled similar simple single smooth solid standardize structure /ego/] "a close-knit homogeneous group"
*hone 07-61-34 (n.) 1. a whetstone made of fine gritstone; used for sharpening razors (v.) 1. sharpen with a hone 2. make perfect or complete [hard head hole one optimize edge enhance excellence] "hone a knife"
*honorarium 21-10-2 (n.) 1. a fee paid for a nominally free service [honor nominal redress render return reward address allowance amends amount atonement indemnity inducement meed money]
*hoodwink 20-69-3 (v.) 1. influence by slyness 2. conceal one's true motives from esp. by elaborately feigning good intentions so as to gain an end [heathen hoax hood humbug obscure outwit darken dazzle deceive delude deprive dim dupe well wool illiterate influence intention nose know]
*horde 09-60-22 (n.) 1. a vast multitude 2. a moving crowd 3. a nomadic community [heap host huddle hunt rendezvous rout ruck date deluge drove eastern europe]
*hosiery 21-31-2 (n.) 1. socks and stockings and tights collectively (the British include underwear as hosiery) [hose hosier occupy scotland shoe sock stocking support include inside ireland isle england europe reach /reis/]
*hospitable 14-47-9 (a.) 1. favorable to life and growth 2. disposed to treat guests and strangers with cordiality and generosity 3. ('hospitable' is usually followed by 'to') having an open mind [handsome hearty open openhearted sociable social stranger sufficient suggestion supportive sympathetic pleasant princely profuse provide idea ingest invitation inviting table tear tolerant treat agreeable amiable ardent assure befitting bountiful lavish liberal life live encourage environment /tip/] "soil sufficiently hospitable for forest growth"
*hospitality 07-71-34 (n.) 1. kindness in welcoming guests or strangers [hearty homey hospital offer open service sociable sociality soft stranger subdivision suite peaceful provide inconsiderate industry intimacy tract treatment affable amiable amicable largesse lodgment luxurious /tip/]
*hostility 05-52-62 (n.) 1. a hostile (very unfriendly) disposition 2. violent action that is hostile and usually unprovoked 3. acts of overt warfare 4. a state of deep-seated ill-will 5. the feeling of a hostile person [hate hatred horror host obstinate official open opposition outbreak overt say scrap showdown social steal strong struggle suspect tension toward truculent ill illwill inconsistency inimical injury international intimidate legal litigation loathing logomachy long] "he could not conceal his hostility"
*hubris 13-56-11 (n.) 1. overbearing pride or presumption [hardihood haughty hauteur hero heroic highhandedne hub unwary belief bold brass rash imposition imprudent indiscretion inferior security superior surety]
*huckster 20-33-3 (n.) 1. a seller of shoddy goods 2. a person who writes radio or tv advertisements (v.) 1. sell or offer for sale from place to place 2. wrangle (over a price, terms of an agreement, etc.) [haggle hawk heighten higgle huck underbid cadge caricature chaffer chapman charlatan cheat con copywriter costermonger salesperson seller sellout service shoddy street stretch superlative tout trade trafficker travesty trickster enhance exchange expansion extreme radio retail]
*humane 08-43-28 (a.) 1. pertaining to or concerned with the humanities 2. marked or motivated by concern with the alleviation of suffering 3. showing evidence of moral and intellectual advancement [high human humanitarian understanding mane mark melt mercy mild minimal moderate moral motivate accepting advance affectionate alleviate altruistic animal area art aspect attribute necessary nice non easygoing education eleemosynary emphasis evidence]
*humanitarian 07-48-40 (a.) 1. marked by humanistic values and devotion to human welfare 2. of or relating to or characteristic of humanitarianism (n.) 1. someone devoted to the promotion of human welfare and to social reforms [harmful help humane mark member motivate affect aid alleviate almoner almsgiver altruistic anita improve inhumane institution theory reason reform]
*humanize 18-01-4 (v.) 1. make more humane [human mayor modify alter anthropomorphize nature improve] "The mayor tried to humanize life in the big city"
*humbug 20-73-3 (n.) 1. pretentious or silly talk or writing 2. something intended to deceive; deliberate trickery intended to gain an advantage (v.) 1. trick or deceive [hamper hinder hoax hogwash hokum hooey hypocrisy masquerade mean message mislead misleading misrepresent mock money balls baloney betray bluff boloney bosh bug bunkum gain garbage gibberish gilt gloss group guile gull]
*humiliate 06-66-57 (v.) 1. cause to fee shame; hurt the pride of [hangdog housebreak humble hurt unbecoming unfrock unman unspeakable master mock mortify ilia injure insolent insulting letdown lower abase abash abusive affront ashamed atrocious awkward tame taunt tyrannize embarrass embarrassed /tail/]

*hurl 07-64-35 (n.) 1. a violent throw (v.) 1. make a thrusting forward movement 2. throw forcefully 3. utter with force; utter vehemently [heave hurtle utter rapid lance launch lob lunge] "hurl insults"
*hush 09-53-24 (n.) 1. (poetic) tranquil silence (v.) 1. cause to be quiet or not talk 2. become quiet or still; fall silent 3. run water over the ground to erode (soil), revealing the underlying strata and valuable minerals; in mining 4. wash by removing particles; in mining 5. become quiet or quieter [halcyon hide hissing underlie undisturbed unmoved untroubled usual utter shout shut silent sleek smooth soap soften sound stable stamp steady still strata stream subdue suppress] "hush my babay!"
*husk 18-38-4 (n.) 1. material consisting of seed coverings and small pieces of stem or leaves that have been separated from the seeds 2. outer membranous covering of some fruits or seeds (v.) 1. remove the husks from, as of ears of corn [hogwash holdover hull useful seed separate serve shadow sheath shell shuck sift skin stalk stem straw structure stubble]
*hussar 20-90-3 (n.) 1. a member of a European light cavalry unit; renowned for elegant dress [horseback uniform soldier adopt renowned /ass/]
*hustle 09-38-22 (n.) 1. a swindle in which you cheat at gambling or persuade a person to buy worthless property 2. a rapid bustling commotion (v.) 1. move or cause to move energetically or busily 2. cause to move furtively and hurriedly 3. sell something to or obtain something from by energetic and esp. underhanded activity [head hula hurry hurtle underhanded urge sale scheme secret sell service shady sharp shift shock shoulder shove solicit speaker spirit sport steal sting stir stole swindle tear technique theft thrust trick tumult twist late leap legislation limbo lindy lively look eject elbow energy engage exciting execute expeditious] "The secret service agents hustled the speaker out of the amphitheater"
*hybrid 06-48-47 (a.) 1. produced by crossbreeding (n.) 1. a word that is composed of parts from different languages (e.g., 'monolingual' has a Greek prefix and a Latin root) 2. a composite of mixed origin 3. an offspring of genetically dissimilar parents or stock; especially offspring produced by breeding plants or animals of different varieties or breeds or species [hellenic hinny homozygous yield balkan bastard better biology blend botany breed republic rid rome root run identify independent interbreed intercrossed derive describe develop dialect different dissimilar distinct] "the vice-presidency is a hybrid of administrative and legislative offices"
*hydra 21-54-2 (n.) 1. (Greek mythology) monster with nine heads; when struck off each head was replaced by two new ones 2. small tubular solitary freshwater hydrozoan polyp 3. a long faint constellation in the southern hemisphere near the equator stretching between Virgo and Cancer [head difficulty dominant renowned replace ancient aspect]
*hydraulic 14-43-8 (a.) 1. moved or operated or effected by liquid (water or oil) 2. of or relating to the study of hydraulics [hydra device driven rise apply large liquid compound] "hydraulic erosion"
*hydroelectric 15-27-7 (a.) 1. of or relating to or used in the production of electricity by waterpower [dynamoelectric electric electricity electrothermal convert couple turbine] "hydroelectric power"
*hygiene 10-72-20 (n.) 1. a condition promoting sanitary practices 2. the science concerned with the prevention of illness and maintenance of health [health hygienics surgical illness epidemiology non] "personal hygiene"
*hyperbole 13-51-11 (n.) 1. extravagant exaggeration [heighten huckster hyper hypertrophy perversion prodigal profuse effect embellish enhance exaggerate excessive expansion extravagant radicalism ballyhoo boundless burlesque obvious overstate language litotes /lob/]
*hypnosis 18-58-4 (n.) 1. a state that resembles sleep but that is induced by suggestion [hyp hypnotism yourself people practice psychological psychotherapy samadhi sleep suggestion susceptible induction /son/]
*hypnotic 12-57-13 (a.) 1. attracting and holding interest as if by a spell (n.) 1. a drug that induces sleep [hold hop horse painkiller people pill piquant pleasing poppy presence produce narcotic nightcap obsessive opiate opium otic tablet taking tease tempting induce interest intrigue inviting capsule catching charm charming completely consuming /ton/] "read the bedtime story in a hypnotic voice"
*hypnotism 24-71-1 (n.) 1. the act of inducing hypnosis [people practice psychology psychotherapy otis theory induce suggestion marathon mesmerism mesmerize /ton/]
*hypnotize 21-05-2 (v.) 1. induce hypnosis in [hold hyp popeyed preoccupy puzzle narcotize obsess overwhelm thunderstruck tranquillize transport immerse induce infatuate intrigue enchant enthral enthrall entrance exercise /ton zit/]
*hypocrisy 09-57-23 (n.) 1. insincerity by virtue of pretending to have qualities or beliefs that you do not really have 2. an expression of agreement that is not supported by real conviction [high humbug hypo piety pious pretense pretension principle oily oleaginous open cant claim conviction craft criticize cunning really religiose run image indirection insincerity instance intention sanctimonious self service sham sheer show smug sorrow stylish support /cop copy/]
*hypocrite 15-60-7 (n.) 1. a person who professes beliefs and opinions that they do not hold [high hold humbug parrot phony piety play polly pretend principle professe protagonist opinion outwardly canter charlatan cheat counterfeit crit cuckoo ranter religious imitate

impersonate impostor ingratiate inwardly talk tartuffe trickster true evil /cop copy/]
*hypodermic 20-20-3 (a.) 1. relating to or located below the epidermis (n.) 1. a piston syringe that is fitted with a hypodermic needle for giving injections [hit hollow hypodermis yourself piston derm dermatologica dermic ectoderm epidermis mainline medical implant injection inoculate instrument internal connective cortical cover cutaneous cutis /dopy redo/] "hypodermic needle"
*hypothesis 11-44-14 (n.) 1. a tentative theory about the natural world; a concept that is not yet verified but that if true would explain certain facts or phenomena 2. a proposal intended to explain certain facts or observations 3. a message expressing an opinion based on incomplete evidence [position possibility premiss presupposition theory thesis speculation statement supposition surmise inference /top/] "a scientific hypothesis that survives experimental testing becomes a scientific theory"
*hysteria 10-61-21 (n.) 1. excessive or uncontrollable fear 2. state of violent mental agitation 3. neurotic disorder characterized by violent emotional outbreaks and disturbances of sensory and motor functions [hypochondriasis hysteric scandal sensory show specific stupor symptom tend tic transport traumatic twitch ecstasy elation emotional euphoria exaggerate excessive excite exhibit experience extreme rage rapture ravish respond indifference insensible instability intoxicate abandon abstraction accompany affective agitation alienate anticipation anxiety attribute /aire/]

I

*icily 21-55-2 (ad.) 1. in a cold and icy manner [icy industry child coldly comment coolly] "Mr. Powell finds it easier to take it out of mothers, children and sick people than to take on this vast industry,' Mr Brown commented icily"
*icon 05-63-79 (n.) 1. (computer science) a graphic symbol (usually a simple picture) that denotes a program or a command or a data file or a concept in a graphical user interface 2. a conventional religious painting in oil on a small wooden panel; venerated in the Eastern Church 3. a visual representation of an object or scene or person produced on a surface [ideal idol ikon illustration image incarnation input inset instead interface camera carve church click color command companion compute con concept continuous conventional copy creation cross observe oil one organ osculate ostensorium numeral]
*iconoclast 13-37-10 (n.) 1. someone who tries to destroy traditional ideas or institutions [idea image individualist institution challenging clast conservative convention custom oppose orthodox overturn nihilism lie annihilate arsonist attack subversive syndicalism terrorist think traditional try /con/]
*idealize 15-01-7 (v.) 1. consider or render as ideal 2. form ideals [ideal ideality ignore illusive imagine immaterialize imperfection impractical interpret invent death deem deify delusive dematerialize devise disembody dream elevate ennoble etherealize exaggerate exist airy apotheosize appearance] "She idealized her husband after his death"
*ideology 07-36-43 (n.) 1. imaginary or visionary theorization 2. an orientation that characterizes the thinking of a group or nation [idealistic imaginary immoderate imperial impossibly independent individual industry interest ism democratic divine doctrine dogma elite ethos ology opinion oppose organize orientation orle ownership left less liberalism line gospel group]
*idiom 10-30-18 (n.) 1. the style of a particular artist or school or movement 2. the usage or vocabulary that is characteristic of a specific group of people 3. a manner of speaking that is natural to native speakers of a language 4. an expression whose meanings cannot be inferred from the meanings of the words that make it up

[identify imaginative immigrant infer isogloss deal decorative deduce develop dialect diction difficult distinguished odd orchestral originate ornamentation manner mastery member misspell mode motivation move music]
*idiosyncrasy 08-48-29 (n.) 1. a behavioral attribute that is distinctive and peculiar to an individual [identify image implicative impression individual irregular denote designate discriminative disposition distinguishing divergence drug odd oddball oddity odor shape signify singular specialty strange style sync name nature nonconformity nutty cast characteristic characterize connotation constitution cranky response abnormal allergy anomaly attribute]
*idolatry 21-53-2 (n.) 1. religious zeal; willingness to serve God 2. the worship of idols; the worship of images that are not God [iconolatry idol idolize image desire devotion duty obsession libido like lord love admiration adore adulation affection approval title top tribute truelove regard religious respect reverence yearning]
*idolize 20-02-3 (v.) 1. love unquestioningly and uncritically or to excess; venerate as an idol [iconolatry idol intense deify desire devotion disapprove dote duty laud libido like lionize love emblazon envy esteem exalt excess extol] "Many teenagers idolized the Beatles"
*idyll 13-74-11 (n.) 1. an episode of such pastoral or romantic charm as to qualify as the subject of a poetic idyll 2. a short descriptive poem of rural or pastoral life 3. a musical composition that evokes rural life [idealize idyl innocent depict descriptive dirge distinctive dithyramb life limerick literary lyric]
*ignoble 21-53-2 (a.) 1. completely lacking nobility in character or quality or purpose 2. not of the nobility [ignominy immoral indicative infamy inferior inglorious integrity government gross nasty nauseous nobility noble notorious noxious obscenity offensive oliver ordinary origin base beastly beggarly belonging birth lack less loathsome low lowborn lowly lowness elevated escape evil execrable expect /bong/] "something cowardly and ignoble in his attitude"
*ignominious 15-76-7 (a.) 1. (used of conduct or character) deserving or bringing disgrace or shame [illegal improper incorrect ineffective inglorious integrity island greed notorious oceanic opprobrium mini monument undue unlawful unsuitable self shabby shady shameful shameless /mong/]
*iliad 20-61-3 (n.) 1. a Greek epic poem (attributed to Homer) describing the siege of Troy [long deed describe]
*illegal 02-43-279 (a.) 1. prohibited by law or by official or accepted rules [illgotten illicit immigrant improper inappropriate incorrect ineligible irregular law lawless legal embezzle enter establish evil game general abnormal accept allow amerce anarchist atrocious /age gell lag/] "an illegal chess move"
*illegible 20-51-3 (a.) 1. (of handwriting, print, etc.) not legible [impossible incomprehensible indecipherable legible easily /big gell/] "illegible handwriting"
*illegitimate 11-51-14 (a.) 1. contrary to or forbidden by law 2. of marriages and offspring; not recognized as lawful (n.) 1. the illegitimate offspring of unmarried parents [illicit imitation immediate improper incorrect invalid issue law lawful lawless lefthand legal legitimate love embellish embroider endow ersatz garble govern tin tinsel trade twist marry measure misbegotten miscreate mock accept accordance adulterine affected artificial assume /amit gell tig/] "an illegitimate seizure of power"
*illiberal 20-85-3 (a.) 1. narrow-minded about cherished opinions [idea insular intolerant lack liberal little bear behavior biased bigoted breadth broad racist reactionary rigid rigorous authoritarian avaricious /bill/]
*illicit 09-48-25 (a.) 1. contrary to accepted morality (especially sexual morality) or convention 2. contrary to or forbidden by law [illegitimate improper irregular law lawless licit chargeable clandestine consider contrary convention criminal custom taboo trade triable /cill/] "an illicit association with his secretary"
*illiterate 10-43-18 (a.) 1. ignorant of the fundamentals of a given art or branch of knowledge 2. not able to read or write (n.) 1. a person unable to read [ignorant lack language literate little lowbrow tenderfoot enough error read rude alphabet art /tare till/]
*illogical 14-61-8 (a.) 1. lacking in correct logical relation 2. lacking orderly continuity [illogic inconsistent instruction intuitive invalid irrational irreconcilable lack logical loose ludicrous off orderly out garble give good capable coherent confused connection consistent contradictory correct corrupt abroad absurd adrift apparently awry /cig/]
*illuminate 05-44-63 (v.) 1. make free from confusion or ambiguity; make clear 2. make lighter or brighter 3. paint, as of medieval manuscripts [illustrate improve indicate inform informative instructive intellectual introductory irradiate lacquer lamp lecture letter light lighter lit literary loaded look lumina luminous understand understandable unfold unlock unravel manifest manuscript mature mean medieval moonlit muzzy ablaze add adorn affect afflict alight allegorize ambiguity animate annotate art artistic attractive autodidact tanked teach theater tight tinge tinsel token tone easy element elevated elucidate embellish enlighten evidence exhibit explain express]
*illusion 05-48-62 (n.) 1. the act of deluding; deception by creating illusory ideas 2. something many people believe that is false 3. an erroneous mental representation 4. an illusory feat; considered magical by naive observers [idea ill imagine impression incorrect invention irradiation legerdemain limb unorthodox semblance sensory shadow sleight smoke spirit still stimulus observer obsession outwit overreach naive /sull/] "they have the illusion that I am very wealthy"

*illusory 16-41-6 (a.) 1. based on or having the nature of an illusion [illogical imagine immaterial lack unfounded unorthodox unreal untrue seeming sham sory staple stray substance subtle off offer open ostensible out rarefied reality /sull/]
*illustrious 10-75-19 (a.) 1. having or conferring glory 2. widely known and esteemed 3. having or worthy of pride [important inglorious lofty lust lustrous unknown scholar scientist self signal striking sublime radiant reason redoubtable renowned respect resplendent outstanding /sull/]
*imaginable 11-53-14 (a.) 1. possible to conceive or imagine [meal able answer assume likely /ban bani/]
*imaginary 08-50-28 (a.) 1. not based on fact; dubious [ideal illusory imagine impossible invent mind misleading mythological abstract agin airy autistic gaseous genuine gossamer negative nonexistent notional numeric radical rational reality /rani/]
*imbibe 18-63-4 (v.) 1. take in, also metaphorically 2. take into solution, as of gas, light, or heat 3. take in liquids 4. receive into the mind and retain [idea imbue incorporate infiltrate ingest mental metaphoricall mind minister moisture mop mouth become bib blot bolt booze eat engross engulf entirely ethical experience]
*imbroglio 20-38-3 (n.) 1. an intricate and confusing interpersonal or political situation 2. a very embarrassing misunderstanding [interpretation intrigue involve messy mistake misunderstand mix morass bicker bind brawl row logomachy /oil/]
*imitation 09-45-25 (a.) 1. not genuine or real; being an imitation of the genuine article 2. artificial and inferior (n.) 1. copying (or trying to copy) the actions of someone else 2. a copy that is represented as the original 3. the doctrine that representations of nature or human behavior should be accurate imitations 4. a representation of a person that is exaggerated for comic effect [idea identity image impersonate impression incongruity inferior ingenuity instrument intend ion melody message metaphor mimic mock mockery model motif much musical takeoff taking teeth temporary travesty try twin accept accurate agent agreement alligator alternative animal art artificial authoritative original nature near]
*imitator 24-39-1 (n.) 1. someone who (fraudulently) assumes the appearance of another 2. someone who copies the words or behavior of another [impersonate impressionist individual inferior mimic mortal musician trickster true actor actress ape apery appearance artist assume]
*immaculate 07-75-34 (a.) 1. completely neat and clean 2. without fault or error 3. free from stain or blemish [ideally imperfect impurity infallible innocent maculate manly meticulous modest moral absolutely apartment cap chaste clean cleanly completely condition conscientious creditable unadulterated undefiled uniform unimpeachable upright upstanding logic taintless technique thorough tidy time totally entirely erect error ethical exquisite] "the apartment was immaculate"
*immaterial 18-61-4 (a.) 1. of no importance or relevance especially to a law case 2. not pertinent to the matter under consideration 3. lacking importance; not mattering one way or the other; often followed by"to" 4. not consisting of matter 5. without material form or substance [incorporeal independence indifferent inferior insubstantial intangible invisible irrelevant issue marginal material matter metaphysical minor minute misty adrift aerial airy altogether apparition appearance technical tenuous theophany thin think trifling trivial eidolon entity ephemeral ethereal evanescent extraneous rare rarity revenant lack larva law lemures light little /aire lair/] "an objection that is immaterial after the fact"
*immature 12-59-13 (a.) 1. lacking in development 2. characteristic of a lack of maturity 3. not fully developed or mature; not ripe 4. not yet mature 5. (of birds) not yet having developed feathers 6. (used of living things especially persons) in an early period of life or development or growth [ignorance imperfect inadequate inchoative inexperience infant innocent intact maidenhood mature maturity mediocrity minority missing mixed acquire adolescent adult adulterate amateurism teenage tender tenure tomato unbeaten undeveloped uneven unfamiliar unfinished unfledged unripe unsophisticated unusual raw rawness reach recent ripe roughness rudimentary early embryonic emotional erroneous /ruta/] "immature behavior"
*immeasurable 14-62-9 (a.) 1. impossible to measure 2. beyond calculation or measure [measurable /bar/]
*immense 05-61-62 (a.) 1. unusually great in size or amount or degree or especially extent or scope [immeasurable incalculable incomprehensible infinity innumerable magnitude mammoth marvelous massive mense mighty monstrous mountain education endless enormous enormousness estate exception exhaust expanse expense extent scope sensational sheer show size snake space spend staggering sterling strength]
*immerse 09-53-26 (v.) 1. engross (oneself) fully 2. Thrust or throw into 3. enclose or envelop completely, as if by swallowing 4. cause to be immersed [inundate macerate meditation merge mesmerize monopolize eat enchant enclose energy engage engaged engross engulf entirely envelop exercise rapt resistance rivet saturate shortly shut sink soak solution souse spellbound sprinkle steep study submerse surface surround swallow swamp sword]
*immersion 14-42-8 (n.) 1. sinking until covered completely with water 2. complete attention; intense mental effort 3. a form of baptism in which part or all of a person's body is submerged 4. (astronomy) the disappearance of a celestial body prior to an eclipse 5. the act of wetting something by submerging it [infusion ingress intense intent involve ion meditation mental

method moisten monomania move eclipse education effort emersion energy engage engagement engrossment engulf entangle reappearance rebirth rinse sacrament shadow signify sink soak spiritual spray steep study submerse obscure obsession occupy]
*immigrant 03-33-150 (n.) 1. a person who comes to a country where they were not born in order to settle there [incomer intruder mig migrant move greenhorn recruit refugee region rookie alien animal arriviste national newcomer tenderfoot traveler trek]
*immigrate 14-03-9 (v.) 1. migrate to a new environment, of plants and animals 2. come into a new country and change residency 3. introduce or send as immigrants [introduce migrate move refer region resident animal arrive enter environment establish] "Britain immigrated many colonists to America"
*imminence 21-63-2 (n.) 1. the state of being imminent and liable to happen soon [impendent intimacy main mine muggy near chummy confidence contact convenience]
*imminent 05-63-78 (a.) 1. close in time; about to occur [immediate impending inevitable intimidate main menace minatory mine momentary muggy near nigh element eventuality expect extrapolate terrorize threaten]
*immoral 10-52-18 (a.) 1. not adhering to ethical or moral principles 2. violating principles of right and wrong 3. characterized by wickedness or immorality 4. marked by immorality; deviating from what is considered right or proper or good 5. morally unprincipled [impurity incorrupt indecent indirect iniquitous insidious integrity mark moral motive obscene recidivism reprobate righteous riotous rotten abandon accept adhere amoral aristocrat lack law lewd libertine life loyalty lust]
*immortalize 18-01-4 (v.) 1. be or provide a memorial to a person or an event 2. make famous for ever [immortal magnify memory mighty mind modify monumental mortal movie raise remind reproduce throne transform aggrandize alter apotheosize art awesome lasting life lionize live lofty long elevate elevated eminent enshrine eternize exalt excellent extol]
*immovable 18-67-4 (a.) 1. not able or intended to be moved [icy incapable inflexible intend iron mobile motionless movable move obdurate objective obstinate obtuse opinion adamant anchor arctic autistic blunt building land law loyal emotionless /avo/] "the immovable hills"
*immune 05-41-71 (a.) 1. relating to the condition of immunity 2. (usually followed by 'to') not affected by a given influence 3. secure against 4. relating to or conferring immunity (to disease or infection) (n.) 1. a person who is immune to a particular infection [immunize impervious individual infection influence insusceptible intact invulnerable irresponsible mortal unaffected undergo unharmed unscathed untouched natural not endure except excuse exempt] "the immune system"
*immutable 18-47-4 (a.) 1. not subject or susceptible to change or variation in form or quality or nature [insistent intact iron irreversible making measured mechanical mutable ubiquitous unalterable unbroken unchanging undaunted tenacious tend timeless tough absolute aged ancient antique balance boundless level loving loyal enduring equal even /tum/] "the view of that time was that all species were immutable, created by God"
*impair 11-43-17 (v.) 1. make imperfect 2. make worse or less effective [immaturity imperfect incomplete infect inflict injury irritate mar mediocrity menace mess mischief molest pair patchy place poison pollute prejudice abstract abuse adulterate afflict appearance attrition reduction remission remove retrench ruin] "His vision was impaired"
*impale 17-60-5 (v.) 1. pierce with a sharp stake or point 2. kill by piercing with a spear or sharp pole [instrument intentional macerate pale passive penetrate pierce piercing pin pink point pole punish agonize arm auger lacerate left empale enemy excruciate /lap/] "impale a shrimp on a skewer"
*impartial 09-55-23 (a.) 1. showing lack of favoritism 2. free from undue bias or preconceived opinions [impersonal independent indifferent interest involve midway mild moderate mugwump pacifism partial passive preconceived prejudice prudent abnegate abstinence apathetic appraisal repose restraint rule temperate tranquillity lack lofty /lait trap/] "the cold neutrality of an impartial judge"
*impassable 20-42-3 (a.) 1. impossible to pass [ice impenetrable impossible inaccessible pass passable peace snow solve bad block /ass bass sap/]
*impassive 14-50-8 (a.) 1. having or revealing little emotion or sensibility; not easily aroused or excited 2. deliberately impassive in manner [icy incline incommunicative indifference inexpressive interest isolated manner matter mindless modest molder pacific passive patient peaceful plight poker positive aloof arctic arouse autistic sensibility show shrink sign silent smooth steady vacant verdict easy ebb emotion empty excited expressionless /sap/] "her impassive remoteness"
*impatience 11-47-14 (n.) 1. a restless desire for change and excitement 2. a lack of patience; irritation with anything that causes delay 3. a dislike of anything that causes delay [ill impetuosity impulsive incompetent irritation malevolent motion patience pique psychological agitation annoy anxiety tolerance touchy eager edgy enthusiasm exasperate excitement express nature cause continual]
*impeccable 07-63-36 (a.) 1. without fault or error 2. not capable of sin [ideal immaculate impoverish moral peccable perfect proper pure error exact excellent exquisite cable capable character chaste clean complete

correct criticism absolute accurate beyond blameless blemish logic]
*impecunious 21-78-2 (a.) 1. not having enough money to pay for necessities [impoverish indigent insolvent money pay penniless penurious pinch poor possession poverty embarrassed enough circumstance clean comfortable unable underprivileged unio narrow necessity needy skin squeeze strap strike struggle]
*impede 09-39-22 (v.) 1. block passage through 2. be a hindrance or obstacle to [imp impair inhibit interfere intervene involve meddle moderate move passage path prevent progress project earth embarrass encumber entangle enter entwine dam delay detain development down drag]
*impediment 12-37-13 (n.) 1. something immaterial that interferes with or delays action or progress 2. any structure that makes progress difficult [impair impasse inconvenience incumbrance inhibition interfere interruption marriage metal millstone mountain pack pediment penalty pipe place positive prevent produce progress embarrassment embolus encumbrance enter delay detain deterrent difficult difficulty disable disorder drawback negative negativism tend thrown top trouble tube tumbler]
*impel 16-39-6 (v.) 1. urge or force (a person) to an action; constrain or motivate 2. cause to move forward with force [imp impulsive incentive incite induce inspire instigate intentional issue make mobilize moral motivate motive motor move pole possess power press pressure project promote propel protest provide punt push energize enforce launch light]
*impending 07-56-36 (a.) 1. close in time; about to occur [immediate imminent incumbent menace pending people prepare project element near danger day distant gathering]
*imperative 08-55-32 (a.) 1. requiring attention or action 2. (grammar) relating to verbs in the imperative mood (n.) 1. a mood that expresses an intention to influence the listener's behavior 2. some duty that is essential and urgent [immediate important impose incline inevitable influence insistent instant intention mission modality mode moral must peremptory place potential powerful press prevent priority proliferate effective era essential ethics exigent regulation require responsibility rule absolutely acute adjure aggressive arrogant assertive attention authoritative authorize telling tenet vital /tare vita/] "as nuclear weapons proliferate, preventing war becomes imperative"
*imperceptible 17-47-5 (a.) 1. impossible or difficult to perceive by the mind or senses [impalpable impossible inaudible indiscernible indistinguishable insensible insignificant invisible microscopic mind minute molecular perceptible ear embryonic ephemeral evanescent eye camouflage capable cognoscible conceal corpuscle temperature thin tiny touch trivial barely latent light /bit/] "an imperceptible drop in temperature"
*imperil 13-20-11 (v.) 1. pose a threat to; present a danger to [menace pass peril pinch plight pollution pose present emergency endanger existence expose extant risk /lire/]
*imperious 11-67-14 (a.) 1. able to deal authoritatively with affairs [imperial insistent instant majestic mandatory masterful matter must peri pivotal pressing purple elitism exigent require restrain royal obligatory oppressive overrule urgent severe sovereign stringent submissive superior] "dismissed the matter with an imperious wave of her hand"
*impermeable 24-39-1 (a.) 1. preventing especially liquids to pass or diffuse through [impassable impervious massive packed passage permeable permit prevent rainproof resistant rubberize admit affect allow layer liquid] "impermeable stone"
*impermissible 20-15-3 (a.) 1. not permitted 2. not allowable [impossible inadmissible intolerable permissible permit prohibit proscribe endure rule behavior] "impermissible behavior"
*impersonal 14-37-9 (a.) 1. having no personal preference 2. not relating to or responsive to individual persons [icy ignore impassive inaccessible indifferent inhospitable inhuman monolithic pedantic people personal prim private emotion equal equitable external refer reflect remark remote removed report reserved responsive shrink soulless stiff objective outside outward neutral nominal abstract alienate aloof lack legalism life lofty] "an impersonal corporation"
*impersonate 08-50-27 (v.) 1. assume or act the character of 2. represent another person with comic intentions 3. pretend to be someone you are not; sometimes with fraudulent intentions [illegal illustrate image imitate impostor impression incarnation incognito intention manner masquerade mime mimic mirror mockery monkey musician parrot part pass perform performance personate play portray pose pretend project public ecdysiast elderly embody emulate enactment entertain entertainer exemplify realize reflect repetition represent representation require ringer role satirize sham sheep simulation singer skill slapstick stunt support onomatopoeia overact act acting actor adumbrate ape appearance art artiste assume astray takeoff thespian trouper] "She impersonates Madonna"
*impertinence 21-74-2 (n.) 1. an impudent statement 2. the trait of being rude and impertinent; inclined to take liberties 3. inappropriate playfulness [impolite impudent inappropriate incline insolent insulting manner mouth pert playful expression rejoinder respect rude talk trait cause cheeky chutzpah crust]
*impertinent 17-75-5 (a.) 1. characterized by a lightly pert and exuberant quality 2. not pertinent to the matter under consideration 3. improperly forward or bold [impolite improper impudent inappropriate incline independence insolent insult insulting intrusive irrelevant irreverent issue malapert manner matter

meddle modesty mouth pert pertinent playful point presumptuous price prying pushy ease effrontery expression extraneous extrinsic exuberant rejoinder relevant respect restraint ridicule rude talk temperament trait nervy nonessential nosy /nitre/]
*imperturbable 21-53-2 (a.) 1. not easily perturbed or excited or upset; marked by extreme calm and composure [icy impassive inhospitable manner mark patient peace perform perturb poise predictable easy equanimity excited extreme rawness reliable reserve tranquillity unflinching unmoved unruffled unsociable untouched upset balance bovine absence agitation alarm aloof assurance level /brut/] "hitherto imperturbable, he now showed signs of alarm"
*impervious 15-51-7 (a.) 1. not admitting of passage or capable of being affected [inaccessible inflexible insensitive invulnerable material pachydermatous passage penetration people pervious prevent proof property entrance remain resentment resistant responsiveness rigid run rustproof obdurate obstinate opinion unaffected unapproachable unbending unmoved unreceptive unwavering unyielding solid solidity soundproof staff steely stony suggestion] "a material impervious to water"
*impetuosity 24-65-1 (n.) 1. rash impulsiveness [imp impulsive moment perform tendency trait spontaneity spur sudden /out sou/]
*impetuous 17-48-5 (a.) 1. characterized by undue haste and lack of thought or deliberation 2. marked by violent force [imp impatient impulsive incautious intense irresponsible mad madcap madly mark moment moody mortal move passionate peppy physical plump pop precipitous eager emotion energy enthusiastic escapade excited tearaway temporary tornado trenchant unawares uncertain undue uneasy unexpected unthinking offhand sharp spend spontaneous spur stranger strength strong sudden surprise /out/]
*impetus 08-57-27 (n.) 1. a force that moves something along 2. the act of applying force suddenly [imp impulsion incentive incite influence inspiration maintain mettle momentum motivation move physics pickup power produce propel push encouragement energy enthusiasm thrust undertake spirited spur stimulus sudden]
*impinge 15-60-7 (v.) 1. impinge or infringe upon 2. advance beyond the usual limit [impact impi impose infringe interrupt intervention intrude invade invasion march matter maul meeting metaphor move pass percussion progress noise nudge glance graze eardrum encounter encroach entrench excessive] "This impinges on my rights as an individual"
*implacable 13-58-10 (a.) 1. impossible to placate [ice impossible inexorable inflexible iron mercy mortal pacify pitiless placable placate punitory adamantine appease avenge callous calm cold cruel enemy] "an implacable enemy"
*implausible 11-68-15 (a.) 1. having a quality that provokes disbelief 2. highly imaginative but unlikely [imaginative improbable inconceivable incredible plausible preposterous problematic provoke puzzling likely little absurd apparently unbelievable unconvinced understand unlikely unreliable suspicious believe beyond excuse explanation] "gave the teacher an implausible excuse"
*implicate 08-42-31 (v.) 1. bring into intimate and incriminating connection 2. impose, involve, or imply as a necessary accompaniment or result [identify imply impose included interweave intimate involve ironic mean metaphor parallel part participate point possible presuppose link closely comprise connection connotation consequence contain crime criminal accompaniment accuse affect associate assume task tax tie embroil engaged entangle error evidential] "He is implicated in the scheme to defraud the government"
*implicit 08-39-32 (a.) 1. implied though not directly expressed; inherent in the nature of something 2. being without doubt or reserve [imply indirect inexplicit inherent inner internal manner material mathematics part patient perfect perfectly positive power practice precisely private pure latent leave licit certain clearly complete completely connotation covert criticism tacit telling total totally trust] "an implicit agreement not to raise the subject"
*implosion 17-66-5 (n.) 1. a sudden inward collapse 2. the initial occluded phase of a stop consonant [ing initial insolvency internal inward manage mishap phase plosion plosive point political poor pressure produce light occlusion small sound speech star stock stop structure subsidence sudden] "the implosion of a light bulb"
*imply 04-49-109 (v.) 1. have as a logical consequence 2. suggest as a logically necessary consequence; in logic 3. express or state indirectly 4. have as a necessary feature or consequence; entail 5. suggest that someone is guilty [imp import impressive include incriminate indirect infer intimate involve manifest mark mean method mind paint part picture pinon ply point possibility postulate precondition predicate presuppose prompt proper logical long]
*impolitic 24-25-1 (a.) 1. not politic [ill imprudent inappropriate inept inexpedient injudicious irrational issue mark misconduct misguide misguided murder politic prudent likely tactless thoughtless] "an impolitic approach to a sensitive issue"
*importation 18-35-4 (n.) 1. the commercial activity of buying and bringing in goods from a foreign country 2. commodities (goods or services) bought from a foreign country [ingress introduction mercantilism prohibit purchase objective trade transaction article]
*importune 24-35-1 (v.) 1. beg persistently and urgently [immoral implore import insistent invoke irk irritate persistent pester plague pray press pressure provoke

pursue push overture recommend relation repeat request tease torment trouble troublesome urgent nag entreat exasperate exchange exhort /nut/] "I importune you to help them"
*impose 02-45-341 (v.) 1. impose and collect 2. impose something unpleasant 3. compel or impose [imperial impressive inconvenience increase inflict infringe insist intervene intrude invade irrevocable majestic makeup mandatory manner mansion material minister misuse monarch moving must page pass payment people peremptory persuade plump policeman pose posh prescribe presume principal print prorate proud punishment put oblige officiate screw serious set sounding strength strike strong superior swell enact encroach enforce entail exact execute exploit] "Social relations impose courtesy"
*impotent 10-66-19 (a.) 1. lacking power or ability 2. (of a male) unable to copulate [inadequate incapable incompetent ineffectual inept infertile intercourse issue male marriage meaningless menopausal morality penis perform physiological pointless potent powerless purpose otiose triviality easy easygoing effective emasculate empty erection etiolated exhaust negligent nerveless neutral /top/] "Technology without morality is barbarous; morality without technology is impotent"
*impoverish 07-49-38 (v.) 1. make poor 2. take away [impecunious ingest insolvent meager mean milk miserly modest paltry part passive pauperize pinch pluck poor over vocabulary eat empty erode establish exhaust reduce rich ruin sink skin slight small smash soil spent spoil status substance /sire/]
*impracticable 24-68-1 (a.) 1. not capable of being carried out or put into practice [impossible impractical inconvenient infeasible possible practicable practice prevailing prove reform accomplish awkward capable carry circumstance condition troublesome effective /carp/] "refloating the sunken ship proved impracticable because of its fragility"
*imprecation 24-53-1 (n.) 1. the act of calling down a curse that invokes evil (and usually serves as an insult) 2. a slanderous accusation [implore impute inflict insult invoke malediction malison mob petition plea power prayer profanity rogation entreaty evil excommunicate execration expletive calling cation charge condemn cry curse cuss accusation anathema appeal application thundering oath /ace/] "he suffered the imprecations of the mob"
*impregnable 18-72-4 (a.) 1. able to withstand attack 2. impossible to take by storm [immortal immune impenetrable impossible indestructible indomitable inexpugnable inviolable invulnerable irresistible mighty protect redan resistless enter guarded able attack break /anger ban bang banger/] "an impregnable fortress"
*impregnate 17-59-5 (v.) 1. fill, as with a certain quality 2. fertilize and cause to grow 3. make pregnant 4. infuse or fill completely [imbue implant impression infuse injection instill macerate manure marinate penetration permeate pervade program pulp rinse enrich gnat grease temper tincture tinge /anger tang/]
*impromptu 10-49-18 (a.) 1. in response to an unforeseen need (ad.) 1. without advance preparation (n.) 1. an extemporaneous speech or remark 2. a short musical passage that seems to have been made spontaneously without advance preparation [interpolate makeshift measure musical party passage piece plan popular precipitate premeditated prior prompt redan remark response riff offhand offthecuff unforeseen unorganized unplanned unrehearsed unstudied] "an impromptu speech"
*improper 05-25-63 (a.) 1. not suitable or right or appropriate 2. not conforming to legality, moral law, or social convention 3. not appropriate for a purpose or occasion [ill illegal inadequate inappropriate incorrect indelicate informal inopportune inordinate intolerable malevolent manner miserable misplace monstrous morality painful peccant piteous practice premature profession proper propriety purpose rank regular reprehensible require roughly rude rule obscene occasion offensive openly outlandish outoftheway erroneous evil excessive excruciating extravagant /repo/] "slightly improper to dine alone with a married man"
*impropriety 12-31-13 (n.) 1. an improper demeanor 2. an act of undue intimacy 3. an indecent or improper act [improper inappropriate incorrect indelicate intimacy irrelevant misbehavior misconduct misdeed mismatch mistake moral people pompous pop prematurity propriety roughness rowdy rude obscene offensive omission outrage error evil excess tasteless tort toward trait trespass]
*improvise 06-36-58 (v.) 1. perform without preparation 2. manage in a makeshift way; do with whatever is at hand [improve incapable incompetent invent inventive makeshift makeup manage material mature means measure mint move music perform performance piece plan play precipitate preparation present procreate provisional resource riff rig offhand originate vamp vulnerable shift sketch snap solution song spawn speak spot stand step stopgap substitute successful surprise engender evolve execute extemporize]
*imprudent 18-38-4 (a.) 1. not prudent or wise 2. lacking wise self-restraint [idea ill illjudged immaturity impulsive incautious indiscreet injudicious insane insensitive irrationality irresponsible mad mindless misguided perverse policy pompous promiscuous provide prudent puerility rash reckless remark romantic unreasonable unsound unwary unwise devoid discretion encourage tactless talk temerarious thorough thoughtless] "very imprudent of her mother to encourage her in such silly romantic ideas"
*impudence 24-60-1 (n.) 1. an impudent statement 2. the trait of being rude and impertinent; inclined to take

liberties [impertinent impolite incline insolent insulting manner mousy mouth presumption unbelievable den discourtesy disrespect effrontery expression nerve cheeky chutzpah crust /dup/]
*impudent 18-59-4 (a.) 1. improperly forward or bold 2. marked by casual disrespect [ill impertinent impolite improper imprudent incline indiscretion insolent insult insulting irreverent malapert manner mark modesty mousy mouth mouthy pert presumptuous unbelievable unblushing uncivil unwary daring defiant defy dent despite discourtesy disrespectful effrontery excessive exhibit expression nervy temerarious temperament /dup/]
*impugn 20-44-3 (v.) 1. attack as false or wrong [imp implicate indict involved issue motive protest puncture untrue upset gainsay negative nullify]
*impulse 07-36-42 (n.) 1. the act of applying force suddenly 2. (electronics) a sharp transient wave in the normal electrical state (or a series of such transients) 3. the electrical discharge that travels along a nerve fiber 4. a sudden desire 5. an instinctive motive 6. an impelling force or strength [impetus incentive incite inclination instinctive itch manpower motive passion pressure propulsion pulse push untimely urge urgency libido lust signal spur stimulus stress echopraxia excitant exigency] "profound religious impulses"
*impulsive 13-49-11 (a.) 1. proceeding from natural feeling or impulse without external stimulus 2. determined by chance or impulse or whim rather than by necessity or reason 3. having the power of driving or impelling 4. characterized by undue haste and lack of thought or deliberation 5. without forethought [immediate imp impatient impetuous imprudent impulse inconstant inherent instability irresponsible madcap mechanical moody motive moving passing plump pop precipitate precocious prematurity pressing previous prompt uncertainty unequal uneven unexpected unsettled untimely unwary libido sharp snap speed spontaneous sudden surprise swift variety eccentricity emotional erratic expeditious] "an impulsive gesture of affection"
*impunity 13-51-10 (n.) 1. exemption from punishment or loss [immunity punishment unity unpleasant]
*impure 21-46-2 (a.) 1. combined with extraneous elements 2. used of persons or behaviors; not morally pure 3. (religion) ritually unclean or impure [improper inadequate incorrect inferior maculate makeshift mediocre mix moral muddy partial patchy plat poison pollute power pure unchaste unclean uneven unfinished unprocessed unseemly untouchable raw religious ritual rotten rude element erring erroneous evil extraneous] "impure thoughts"
*impute 21-35-2 (v.) 1. attribute or credit to 2. attribute (responsibility or fault) to a cause or source [imp impeachable implicate imply incorporate indictment information insinuation internalize intimate mean pass personify pester pinon placement project prosecution put putative undesirable taint tarnish task tax taxing toward traceable twit explicable externalize /tup/]
*inaccessible 13-48-11 (a.) 1. capable of being reached only with great difficulty or not at all 2. not capable of being obtained [icy impassive impenetrable impervious impossible island isolated abstruse accessible achieve afford almost aloof antipodean attain available capable challenging chilly cold confidential cool earth elitism esoteric exclusive expressionless shrink solitary subdued suppress backward backwood bashful blank bury lonely /can/] "a rare work, today almost inaccessible"
*inaccurate 08-47-28 (a.) 1. containing or characterized by error 2. not precisely accurate 3. not accurate [impaired imprecise inadequate incorrect inexact negligent nonspecific accurate almost amiss amorphous answer awry chaotic cold conclusion conformity confused correct uneven unfaithful unfinished untrue random right thermometer total translation truth error exactly /can/] "an inaccurate translation"
*inactive 11-53-16 (a.) 1. (pathology) not progressing or increasing; or progressing slowly 2. not participating in a chemical reaction 3. temporarily inactive 4. not in physical motion 5. of e.g. volcanos; temporarily inactive 6. of e.g. volcanos; permanently inactive 7. lacking activity; lying idle or unused 8. not active or exerting influence 9. not active physically or mentally 10. not engaged in full-time work 11. not engaged in military action 12. lacking in energy or will [idle immobile immobility indolent inert inoperative neutral abeyance active apathetic asleep catatonic comfort contemplative tame torpid torpor tranquillity vegetative easy /can/] "desired amounts of inactive chlorine"
*inadequate 05-47-83 (a.) 1. (sometimes followed by 'to') not meeting the requirements especially of a task 2. not sufficient to meet a need [imperfect inability incapable incompetent incomplete inefficient inept infant inferiority injustice insufficient need nugatory adequate adulterate arrest asymmetry damage decline defective deficient deficit derisory difference disappointing embryonic empty enough erroneous experience quantity unable unapt understaffed unequal uneven unsatisfactory unskillful unsound unsuitable useless trivial /dan/] "inadequate training"
*inadmissible 20-46-3 (a.) 1. not deserving to be admitted [impermissible impossible improper irrelevant narrow nonessential admissible admit adrift allowable deserve disallow malapropos misplace segregate selective snobbish ban bar law ethnocentrism evidence exceptional exclude extrinsic /dan/] "inadmissible evidence"
*inadvertent 16-36-6 (a.) 1. without intention; especially resulting from heedless action [ignore inattentive inconsiderate incurious indifferent intention involuntary negligent nonfeasance nonobservance nonrestrictive notice accidental advert arbitrary attention automatic

default deliberate dereliction disregardful distrait vase enough error reflexive regardless relaxed responsibility table think thoughtless trait trip /dan/] "with an inadvertent gesture she swept the vase off the table"
*inadvisable 24-67-1 (a.) 1. not prudent or wise; not recommended 2. not advisable [ice impolitic imprudent inept injudicious irrational advisable advise devoid senseless suggest suitable bad expedient /dan/] "running on the ice is inadvisable"
*inane 17-61-5 (a.) 1. complacently or inanely foolish [idle immature inadequate inexperienced insubstantial irritate naive nan nuts nutty absurd airy asinine awkward effete elephantine empty]
*inanimate 20-41-3 (a.) 1. (linguistics) belonging to the class of nouns denoting nonliving things 2. appearing dead; not breathing or having no perceptible pulse 3. not endowed with life [immobile impassive inactive inert inorganic insensate neuter non numb abiotic animate apathetic appear martyr masculine mute torpid endow energetic enervate expect extinct /mina/] "the word `car' is inanimate"
*inarticulate 18-57-4 (a.) 1. without or deprived of the use of speech or words [imply inaudible incline incomprehensible indistinct irrational nasal numinous ambiguous aphasic aphonic articulate awkward rage rambling right talk thick timid tongue tonguetied choke choose class clearly clumsy confused conscious cry unclear uncommunicative unconnected understandable unfathomable unintelligible unspoken lack language lisp emotion expressive /rani/] "inarticulate beasts"
*inaudible 18-50-4 (a.) 1. impossible to hear; imperceptible by the ear [imperceptible impossible infrasonic noiseless audible ultrasonic unheard unpronounced unsound unvoice uproar difficult breathe little loud low ear enough /bid/] "an inaudible conversation"
*inborn 24-22-1 (a.) 1. normally existing at birth 2. present at birth but not necessarily hereditary; acquired during fetal development [inbred indigenous inherit instinct instinctive intuitive natural necessarily non normal bear birth bodily organic /rob/]
*inbred 21-50-2 (a.) 1. produced by inbreeding 2. normally existing at birth [inborn indigenous ingrained inherit innate instinct interbreed naturally normal bear birth bodily breed endogamy exist exogamy deep different]
*incandescent 16-52-6 (a.) 1. emitting light as a result of being heated 2. characterized by ardent emotion or intensity or brilliance [ignite inflame inglorious intensity irradiate candent confer consequence ablaze aglow alight anger ardent dark descent deserve display effulgent emit emotion shin show smoke spark sunny temperature] "an incandescent bulb"
*incapacitate 14-51-8 (v.) 1. make unable to perform a certain action 2. injure permanently [illness immobilize impair ineligible injury invalid invalidate nobble capa capacitate car castrate certain close command computer confine cripple cut accident afflict alter paralyze perform permanent pinion power prostrate put transform effective emasculate enfeeble eviscerate exhaust /cap capa/]
*incapacity 17-82-5 (n.) 1. lack of intellectual power 2. lack of physical or natural qualifications [inability inadequate incompetency ineffective injury intellectual natural caducity capacity challenge pedestrian perform physical powerless produce task /cap capa/]
*incarcerate 10-47-20 (v.) 1. lock up or confine, in or as in a jail [immure impose imprison inclusion intern cabin cage captivity cera chamber collection confinement contain cordon authority away rail remand rest restrained rule enclosure encompass enshrine envelop torment torture trial /tare/]
*incendiary 13-50-10 (a.) 1. involving deliberate burning of property 2. capable of catching fire spontaneously or causing fires or burning readily 3. arousing to action or rebellion (n.) 1. a criminal who illegally sets fire to property 2. a bomb that is designed to start fires [incentive inflammatory instigate catalyst crook enkindle exciter demon devil diary dragon aggressive agitprop arsonist rapist revolutionary rouse /raid/] "an incendiary fire"
*incense 09-63-23 (n.) 1. a substance that produces a fragrant odor when burned 2. the pleasing scent produced when incense is burned (v.) 1. perfume esp. with a censer 2. make furious [incite indignant infuriate ingredient irate ireful irritate nettle nosegay celebrate cense censer chemical chinese collection compound confirmation cross element enrage exasperate excite sacrifice scent slender smelly smoke smooth soap sore spice stick substance sweet] "incense filled the room"
*incentive 03-45-144 (n.) 1. an additional payment (or other remuneration) to employees as a means of increasing output 2. a positive motivational influence [impetus incent increase induce influence interest invitation negative carrot catalyst clout efficient employee encourage encouragement entice exceed extra thrust]
*inception 11-45-17 (n.) 1. an event that is a beginning; a first part or stage of subsequent events [inauguration incept infancy initiation institution introduce nativity childhood commencement conception constitution effectuate emanation enrollment establishment part parturition pentecost precede pregnancy preliminary procession provide taproot organization origin originate overture]
*incessant 11-51-16 (a.) 1. occurring so frequently as to seem ceaseless or uninterrupted 2. uninterrupted in time and indefinitely long continuing [immutable indefinitely indestructible infinity interruption isolation neverending noise non nonstop ceaseless cess chatter chiefly child city closely complaint connected constant continuity continuous endless equilibrium eternity

search seeming series smooth space standard steady stop straight struggle successive surf sustain ageless always articulate thematic thunder timeless together /ass/] "a child's incessant questions"
*inchoate 21-39-2 (a.) 1. only partly in existence; imperfectly formed [idea immature imperfect inaugural inch inform inventive nascent natal nondescript casual chaotic civil confused creative haphazard hazy obscure organization original aboriginal aimless anarchic tumor early elementary embryonic emergent erratic existence]
*incidence 09-55-22 (n.) 1. the relative frequency of occurrence of something 2. the striking of a light beam on a surface [impact instance number category cide common confused contingent degree different disease extent] "he measured the angle of incidence of the reflected light"
*incident 02-53-311 (a.) 1. falling or striking on something 2. (sometimes followed by 'to') minor or casual or subordinate in significance or nature or occurring as a chance concomitant or consequence (n.) 1. a single distinct event 2. a public disturbance [imaginary importance infectious instance investigate nature nightclub case cide circumstance clash color condition confrontation crisis design development device different disease disorderly disruption disturbance duty episode eventuality expansion expense experience theme todo tone touch transmit tumult twist] "incidental expenses"
*incidentally 08-59-30 (ad.) 1. in an incidental manner 2. introducing a different topic 3. by the way [incidental influence introduce casual chance different topic accidental achievement additional apropos lend]
*incinerate 15-40-7 (v.) 1. become reduced to ashes 2. cause to undergo combustion [integrity car cine combustion completely condemn confound consume cracking cremate cremation engorge ravage reduce refine riddle ash thermogenesis /tare/] "The paper incinerated quickly"
*incipient 17-39-5 (a.) 1. only partly in existence; imperfectly formed [idea imperfect inaugural inc initial introductory inventive nascent natal civil creative partly place pregnant prenatal procreate early elementary elfin embryonic emerge existence tumor] "incipient civil disorder"
*incise 21-24-2 (v.) 1. make an incision into by carving or cutting [imprint inc index injure insert instrument interrupt invitation nick notch nutrient carve channel character chisel chop circulation compound cut score scratch sculpture see separate sharp simple slit stamp surface surgery edge emblazon enchase engrave enroll enter etch excise]
*incisive 11-67-17 (a.) 1. having or demonstrating ability to recognize or draw fine distinctions 2. very penetrating and clear and sharp in operation 3. suitable for cutting or piercing [impressive inc insightful intelligent intense ironical needle nervous capacity characterize clearly comment critical cut cynical severe sharp stroke strong suitable violent vital vivid edge effective enthusiastic express]
*incisor 24-61-1 (n.) 1. a tooth for cutting or gnawing; located in the front of the mouth in both jaws [inc canine chew crown cuspid cut cutter sharp snaggletooth structure]
*incite 08-58-28 (v.) 1. provoke or stir up 2. give an incentive for action 3. urge on; cause to act [impact incentive induce inflame influence inspire instigate intentional interest investigate needle nettle career carrot cause caution charge cite clout cognitive communicate compassion compulsion talk team temptation thrust tickle egg emotional encouragement energy enrage enthusiasm exciting exhilarate expression]
*incitement 16-74-6 (n.) 1. needed encouragement 2. an act of inciting 3. the act of exhorting; an earnest attempt at persuasion 4. something that incites or provokes; a means of arousing or stirring to action [improper induce instill intend investigate communicate talk team earnest encouragement energy enthusiasm exhort expression mean motivation]
*inclined 06-52-54 (a.) 1. (often followed by 'to') having a preference, disposition, or tendency 2. used especially of the head or upper back 3. having made preparations 4. at an angle to the horizontal or vertical position [interested naturally nervous nod cant corpulent course language lean lecture let liable line listen lower lowpitched ear erect excuse diagonal direction disapproval disposition down dress] "wasn't inclined to believe the excuse"
*incoherence 20-58-3 (n.) 1. lack of cohesion or clarity or organization 2. nonsense that is simply incoherent and unintelligible [illogicality inarticulate non clarity cohesive confusion convey organization hear]
*incoherent 13-58-10 (a.) 1. without logical or meaningful connection 2. unable to think or express your thoughts in a clear or orderly manner 3. unable to express yourself clearly or fluently [illogical inaccurate inarticulate interrupt irrational non nonlinear nonspecific numinous change chaotic choppy clarity clearly coherent cohesive confused confusion connection consistent convey correct obscure off open orderly organization hazy hear electromagnetic embarrassment episodic express rambling random rant rational reason talk tenuous think turgid] "a turgid incoherent presentation"
*incomparable 14-57-9 (a.) 1. such that comparison is impossible; unsuitable for comparison or lacking features that can be compared [immortal impossible independent inimitable invincible isolated nonpareil comparable computer only other outlandish outstand matchless paramount peerless pleasure positive proceed prominent alien alltime alone apart remarkable removed report rest basis best beyond breakdown lack logic early efficiency equal exceptional exotic extraneous /bar/] "an

incomparable week of rest and pleasure"
*incompatible 11-53-17 (a.) 1. not compatible 2. used especially of drugs or muscles that counteract or neutralize each other's effect 3. of words so related that one contrasts with the other 4. not compatible with other facts 5. not easy to combine harmoniously 6. not in keeping with what is correct or proper 7. (computers) incapable of being used with or connected to other devices or components without modification 8. used especially of solids or solutions; incapable of blending into a stable homogeneous mixture 9. not suitable to your tastes or needs [icy inequality inhospitable irreconcilable negative noncooperation close cold compatible conflict contrast cross odds opposition oxymoron machine many mischief mismatch mixture morose motley paradox processor abnormal absurd ambivalence assorted asymmetry autism tension bashful /bit/] "incompatible personalities"
*incompetence 09-67-23 (n.) 1. lack of physical or intellectual ability or qualifications 2. inability of a part or organ to function properly [impair inability ineffective inept intellectual close competence completely condition organ male part perform physical power prep properly testosterone trunk]
*incompetent 06-62-45 (a.) 1. not qualified or suited for a purpose 2. showing lack of skill or aptitude 3. not meeting requirements 4. not doing a good job (n.) 1. someone who is not competent to take effective action [in competent] "an incompetent secret service"
*incomplete 08-28-31 (a.) 1. not complete or total; not completed 2. (botany) lacking one or more of the four whorls of the complete flower--sepals or petals or stamens or pistils 3. not yet finished [imperfect impoverish inadequate incompetent infant insufficient intermittent irregularity need callow complete crude off omission only mediocre merely mild missing mixed modest parenthesis partly patchy piecemeal purely lacking leastwise embryonic episode erroneous tolerable] "an incomplete account of his life"
*incomprehensible 11-57-14 (a.) 1. difficult to understand 2. incapable of being explained or accounted for [immense impenetrable impossible incredible indecipherable inscrutable insoluble numinous comprehensible countless cryptic obscure opaque outlandish marvelous miraculous miss morn mystify paradox perplex puzzling rambling rare remarkable endless enigmatic enunciate error exceptional explicable extraordinary house self sensational strange striking baffle beguile bewildering beyond limitless lose /her/]
*inconceivable 11-62-14 (a.) 1. totally unlikely [imagine implausible impossible incapable incredible conceivable conceive consider outlandish overwhelming exceptional exclude extremely absurd accept antic bar beguile belief bewildering /vie/]
*incongruous 11-58-17 (a.) 1. lacking in harmony or compatibility or appropriateness [improper inappropriate inept inharmonious ironical irrational character clash compatible conflicting congruous context contrast conversation corresponding odd reason rich ridiculous risible unfit unfortunate unhappy unlike unsuitable scream separate set several specific strange /our/] "a plan incongruous with reason"
*inconsequential 14-53-8 (a.) 1. lacking worth or importance 2. not following logically as a consequence [illogical important inappropriate inconsistent inferior insignificant irrelevant negligible nonessential nugatory consequential correct cursory seem short slight small quite unconnected unreasonable unscientific technical tiny triviality absonant lack little logical loose low /lait/] "his work seems trivial and inconsequential"
*inconsiderable 21-76-2 (a.) 1. too small or unimportant to merit attention [inferior influence insignificant irrelevant negligible nonessential considerable cursory shallow short size small sum degree dinky dispensable duty extent amount attention life little low /bar bare/]
*inconsistent 08-45-31 (a.) 1. not capable of being made consistent or harmonious 2. displaying a lack of consistency 3. not in agreement [impossible invalid irrational irreconcilable irresponsible nonconformist nonstandard capable capricious change changeable compatible conflict confront congruous consistent contradictory contrast correspond obverse odd open separate set several shift shuffling situation spotty statement temperamental tenuous ticklish eccentric element equation erratic expectation] "inconsistent statements"
*inconstant 24-50-1 (a.) 1. likely to change frequently often without apparent or cogent reason; variable [inconsistent indefinite instability intermittent irregular irresponsible negligent nonconformity nonstandard capricious cogent constant coquette corruptible obligation shuffling skittish sporadic spotty stability staggering steadfast temperature temporary tendency ticklish transitory adrift afloat alteration alternate ambivalence apparent arrhythmia] "inconstant affections"
*incontrovertible 18-67-4 (a.) 1. impossible to deny or disprove 2. necessarily or demonstrably true [implicit impossible incapable indisputable indubitable innocence irrefutable irresistible necessarily nuncupative certain confirm contest controvert convince open overwhelming telling test true real reliable valid verify establish evidentiary /bit/] "incontrovertible proof of the defendant's innocence"
*inconvenient 12-60-13 (a.) 1. not suited to your comfort, purpose or needs 2. not conveniently timed [improper irrelevant irritate clumsy comfort contrary convenient cumbersome onerous opportune early effort embarrass extra telephone time tiresome troublesome] "it is inconvenient not to have a telephone in the kitchen"
*incredulous 13-57-10 (a.) 1. not disposed or willing to

believe; unbelieving [inconvincible irreligious cautious characterize completely credulous evidence disbelieve disposed distrustful doubt dubious unable unbelieving uncertain unconvinced understand unwilling leery little sceptical show skeptical suspicious /lude/]
*incriminate 12-38-13 (v.) 1. suggest that someone is guilty 2. bring an accusation against; level a charge against [impeach imply inadequate inculpate indict involve call censure charge claim convict criminate criticism return mind misbehavior mistake mutual abuse accuse appear arraign assail attack tax toward engage entangle error evoke express]
*inculcate 20-59-3 (v.) 1. teach and impress by frequent repetitions or admonitions [implant impress indoctrinate infuse instruct irreversible cate catechize chronic coach condition confirmed constant admonition teach thorough train engrave establish etch]
*incursion 12-49-12 (n.) 1. the act of entering some territory or domain (often in large numbers) 2. the mistake of incurring liability or blame 3. an attack that penetrates into enemy territory [ignorance inattention incur infiltrate ingress injection inroad interpenetrate intervention intrusion invasion night conquest unpleasant unwelcome usurp raid scale short sortie spread sudden obtrusion offensive onrush onset onslaught overstep] "the incursion of television into the American livingroom"
*indefatigable 14-60-9 (a.) 1. showing sustained enthusiastic action with unflagging vitality [indomitable inexorable insistent invincible never defat determined diligent display dogged effort enduring energy enthusiastic equal excellence exert faithful fervent abiding achieve advocate ardent assiduous attentive tenacious tireless laborious lasting lazy lethargic loyal /agita bag git/] "an indefatigable advocate of equal rights"
*indefensible 15-60-7 (a.) 1. (of theories etc) incapable of being defended or justified 2. incapable of being justified or explained [impossible inadmissible incapable inexcusable insupportable intolerable invalid defensible exceptionable excuse explain expose fact shaky show sound bad base blame]
*indefinitely 07-40-35 (ad.) 1. to an indefinite extent; for an indefinite time [immeasurable imprecise incalculable infinite dead definitely downright essential extent extremely fixed forever fundamental totally length life] "this could go on indefinitely"
*indelible 11-46-14 (a.) 1. cannot be removed, washed away or erased [immortal impossible impression ingrained ink invincible nagging deathless deep deli destroy enduring eradicate erase lasting /bile led/] "an indelible stain"
*indemnify 21-45-2 (v.) 1. secure against future loss, damage, or liability; give security for 2. make amends for; pay compensation for [illness incur indemnity insure never damage deliver exchange expiate meed money fee financial fully future /fin/]
*indescribable 18-60-4 (a.) 1. defying expression or description [impossible incommunicable indefinable ineffable inexpressible intense noteworthy defy description difficult dramatic ecstasy exceptional expression extreme sensation splendor stupendous contempt remarkable beauty able anguish legendary]
*indestructible 16-63-6 (a.) 1. not easily destroyed 2. very long lasting [immortal imperishable impossible incessant infinite non nonstop dateless deathless destructible difficult durable easy endless enduring eternal sempiternal shatterproof spine steady timeless reinforce resistant rock unbreakable unending uninterrupted unremitting unyielding ceaseless constant continent continuous lasting long /bit curt/]
*indicator 05-45-71 (n.) 1. a device for showing the operating condition of some system 2. a signal for attracting attention 3. a number or ratio (a value on a scale of measurement) derived from a series of observed facts; can reveal relative changes as a function of time 4. (chemistry) a substance that changes color to indicate the presence of some ion or substance; can be used to indicate the completion of a chemical reaction or (in medicine) to test for a particular reaction [image index indicate needle note device dial differentia display cato characteristic critic arbitrator test thermocouple trait reaction referee representative /acid rota/]
*indict 06-14-57 (v.) 1. accuse formally of a crime [impeach imply incriminate involved damn decry denounce censure charge cite claim commission condemn crime task tax twit]
*indifferent 09-55-26 (a.) 1. (usually followed by 'to') unwilling or refusing to pay heed 2. lacking importance; not mattering one way or the other; often followed by"to" 3. showing no care or concern in attitude or action 4. marked by a lack of interest 5. fairly poor to not very good 6. marked by no especial liking or dislike or preference for one thing over another 7. neither too great nor too little 8. neither good nor bad 9. characterized by a lack of partiality 10. (chemistry) having only a limited ability to react chemically; not active [icy immaterial immoderate inert inferior interested intermediate invitation natural negligent neither neutral numb dead deaf detached different differentiate dull fade fairly family flat flavorles follow friendly easygoing equitable everyday reactive reasonable refuse rejection reluctant removed resigned tedious think thoughtless tissue tolerable trivial /fid/]
*indigenous 09-52-26 (a.) 1. originating where it is found [inborn include inherit innate instinct island natal native naturally northernmost nous genetic grow endemic ethnic organic originate /gid one/]
*indigent 16-10-6 (a.) 1. poor enough to need help from others [impecunious impoverish necessitous needy deprive destitute disadvantaged gent enough extremely /gid/]

*indigestible 21-74-2 (a.) 1. digested with difficulty [impenetrable impossible incomprehensible inedible dense difficulty digestible dry stodgy suitable /bit gid/]
*indigestion 17-71-5 (n.) 1. a disorder of digestive function characterized by discomfort or heartburn or nausea [inflammation irregularity itch nausea necrosis diarrhea difficulty digestion digestive discomfort disease disorder dizzy dysentery dyspepsia gastritis gripe growth eat edema emaciate experience seizure sensation shock sore symptom tachycardia trot tumor obstipation /gid/]
*indignant 12-57-13 (a.) 1. angered at something unjust or wrong [incense irate ireful irritate denial disapprove disbelief disgruntle disillusion against anger annoy ant apparent territory /gid/] "an indignant denial"
*indignity 12-59-13 (n.) 1. an affront to one's dignity or self-esteem [ignominy injustice insult deliberate despite dignity disgrace dishonor dump gibe grievance taunt /gid ting/]
*indiscreet 20-76-3 (a.) 1. lacking discretion; injudicious [imprudent inappropriate incautious indelicate injudicious insensitive irrational naive nosy discreet discretion secret self senseless separate sound careless casual confuse rare rash reckless tactless talkative temerarious thoughtless /tee/] "her behavor was indiscreet at the very best"
*indiscriminate 12-48-13 (a.) 1. failing to make or recognize distinctions 2. not marked by fine distinctions [inattention incurious inexplicable intricate ironic negligence dapple detachment diffuse discriminate disinterest disproportionate distinction sloth style sweep carelessness choice color combined compound random read reckless recognize mark meaningless mindless mingle mix aimless assorted tactless eclectic erratic extensive] "indiscriminate reading habits"
*indispensable 10-46-19 (a.) 1. absolutely necessary; vitally necessary 2. not to be dispensed with; essential 3. unavoidable [imperative important indicate necessary necessity needful nutrition desirable dispensable dispense duty substantive prerequisite project essential extremely absolutely basic bedrock binding legal /psi/] "foods indispensable to good nutrition"
*indistinct 20-40-3 (a.) 1. not clearly defined or easy to perceive or understand [imprecise inaccurate inarticulate inaudible indefinite indistinguishable interchange nasal nebulous nonspecific notion dark define dim distinct see shadowy shape slur soft standard stated sweeping thick transcendent twangy chaotic choke clearly cloudy confused] "indistinct shapes in the gloom"
*indistinguishable 13-44-10 (a.) 1. exactly alike; incapable of being perceived as different 2. not capable of being distinguished or differentiated [identical impossible inarticulate inaudible incapable indefinite interchange dark differentiate dim distinguish distinguished duplicate same specimen standard stereotype tantamount tell twin uncertain understand undistinguish undistinguished uniform unintelligible hard hazy hear homogeneous homoousian actually alike almost apart bleary blurry license like low equal except /bah/]
*indivisible 21-45-2 (a.) 1. impossible of undergoing division [impossible individual infusible inseparable integral nation divisible division separate severe simple spare bare basic blend leave liable lone either essential exclusive] "an indivisible union of states"
*indolence 21-68-2 (n.) 1. inactivity resulting from a dislike of work [idle inactivity inert initiative disposition lack lassitude lethargy energy consequence]
*indolent 18-65-4 (a.) 1. disinclined to work or exertion 2. (pathology) of tumors e.g.; slow to heal or develop and usually painless [idle inactive inactivity increase indifference indole inert infectious initiative interest nature necessarily deadline deliberation describe develop dilatory dish disincline disposition dormant oscitancy otiose lack languish lassitude lax lay lazy leisurely lethargic lethargy limp listless lumber easygoing effect effort employee energy entropy exertion tentative torpid totter trudge tumor]
*indomitable 14-62-8 (a.) 1. impossible to subdue [impossible insistent intrepid invincible irresistible never defeat defiant determined dogged doughty obstreperous overcome overwhelming mettlesome table tenacious tireless assiduous brave lasting loyal enduring /mod/]
*induct 13-29-11 (v.) 1. place ceremoniously or formally in an office or position 2. accept young people into society, usually with some rite [idea ignoramus impart inaugurate include initiate institute instruct interaction introduce invest invite neophyte newcomer novitiate draftee duct catechumen ceremonious chair christen conscript crown current teach tenderfoot throne train trainee tyro] "We were inducted into the honor society"
*indulge 05-70-64 (v.) 1. yield (to); give satisfaction to 2. enjoy to excess 3. give free rein to 4. treat with excessive indulgence [immoderate interact dear debt degree deplete desire devote devour dispensation disregard domesticate drink language leniency like live look love luxuriate gentle give good gratify eat endure engage enjoy enjoyable entirely excessive excuse exhaust exonerate experience] "The writer indulged in metaphorical language"
*indulgence 09-67-22 (n.) 1. an inability to resist the gratification of whims and desires 2. foolish or senseless behavior 3. the act of indulging or gratifying a desire 4. a disposition to yield to the wishes of someone [immunity incontinent indiscipline indulge delicacy disregard drunken understanding liberty license luxury gambol generous grant gratification easy endurance excessive extravagance caper charity church clemency clown concern consideration crazy] "too much

indulgence spoils a child"
*indulgent 10-70-21 (a.) 1. tolerant or lenient 2. showing or characterized by or given to indulgence 3. being favorably inclined [incline incontinent indulge inordinate intemperate non decadent decent delicate discipline dissipated drink unbridled understand unfavorable unlimited lax lenient libertine luxurious gamble gay generous give gluttonous gracious grant easygoing effete encourage epicurean excess excuse extreme tactful tend thoughtful tolerant tolerate] "indulgent grandparents"
*inebriate 18-70-4 (n.) 1. a chronic drinker (v.) 1. fill with sublime emotion; tickle pink (exhilarate is obsolete in this usage) 2. make drunk (with alcoholic drinks) 3. become drunk; drink excessively [imbibe insobriety intoxicate nappy eat effect elate emotion exalt excessive excite exhilarate beatify become befuddle bemuse besot beverage boozer reel revel rummy addle affect alcoholic alky archaism temporary thrill tickle tiddly tippler tipsy toper /ben/]
*inedible 20-56-3 (a.) 1. not suitable for food [indigestible noxious eat eatable edible difficulty digest disgusting bad /bid bide den/]
*ineffable 17-43-5 (a.) 1. defying expression or description 2. too sacred to be uttered [ideal indescribable inexpressible inviolate noteworthy numinous ecstasy effable ethereal exceptional expression extraordinary fabulous abstract anguish awesome awful beauty beyond legendary /baff fen/]
*inefficiency 12-48-12 (n.) 1. unskillfulness resulting from a lack of efficiency [inability inadequate incompetency inept efficiency effort cognitive competence /fen/]
*inefficient 10-43-19 (a.) 1. not producing desired results; wasteful 2. lacking the ability or skill to perform effectively; inadequate [inadequate incompetent inept inferior intend effective efficient effort expense fail campaign careless task thoughtless /fen/] "an inefficient campaign against drugs"
*ineligible 11-36-16 (a.) 1. not eligible 2. (sports) prohibited by official rules [illegal eligible entitle establish exertion law legal ban bar benefit /big/] "ineligible to vote"
*ineluctable 21-46-2 (a.) 1. impossible to avoid or evade:"inescapable conclusion" [impossible incapable inescapable inevitable inexorable necessary evade evitable unavoidable unequivocal unmistakable unpreventable casualty certain conclusion conclusive table absolute accident apodictic avoid bound]
*inept 08-57-30 (a.) 1. generally incompetent and ineffectual 2. not elegant or graceful in expression 3. revealing lack of perceptiveness or judgment or finesse [ignorance ill inability inapt incapable incompetent incongruous ineffectual inefficient inexpert infelicitous inferiority insane irrelevant nutty eccentricity elegant expression pedestrian perceptivenes plumbing poorly proper prose purpose tactless task thoughtless totally training triviality true /pen/]
*ineptitude 14-61-9 (n.) 1. unskillfulness resulting from a lack of training [incompetent ineffective training unskillful useless]
*inert 16-43-6 (a.) 1. (chemistry) having only a limited ability to react chemically; not active 2. unable to move or resist motion 3. slow and apathetic [idle immobile impotent inactive indifferent indolent natural neutral noble non numb energy enervate reactive ready resist tame torpid] "inert matter"
*inestimable 24-62-1 (a.) 1. beyond calculation or measure [immeasurable incalculable incomputable inescapable infinite invaluable necessary enormous estimable tremendous measure measureless amount beyond /amit bam/]
*inevitable 02-63-267 (a.) 1. invariably occurring or appearing 2. incapable of being avoided or prevented (n.) 1. an unavoidable event [imperative impossible incapable ineluctable inescapable inexorable inflexible invariably necessary necessity end enforce evitable expect table therefore truth absolute accept accordingly apodictic appear appointed argue assured astrology avert avoid binding bound lot] "the inevitable result"
*inexcusable 16-51-6 (a.) 1. without excuse or justification 2. not excusable [impermissible impossible improper indefensible insupportable interested intolerable nakedly excessive excruciating excuse extravagant capable censure confounded cruel uncalled uneven unfair unjustifiable unjustified unpardonable unreasonable untenable unwarranted usable sad shock staggering abominable admit agonizing awfully bitter blame blatant brash lamentable]
*inexhaustible 17-47-5 (a.) 1. that cannot be entirely consumed or used up 2. incapable of being entirely consumed or used up [immense impossible incapable incomprehensible infinite innumerable never numberless numerous end endless entirely everlasting exhaust exhaustless extent exuberant abound affluent ample unfailing universal unlimited untold shoreless show sign space superabundant supply teem termless tire tireless bottomless boundless bountiful lavish liberal limit limitless /bit/] "an inexhaustible supply of coal"
*inexorable 10-56-18 (a.) 1. not capable of being swayed or diverted from a course; unsusceptible to persuasion 2. not to be placated or appeased or moved by entreaty [implacable impossible incapable inescapable inevitable inflexible necessity non entreaty extend obdurate obstinate oppose orthodox refusal relentless rigorous ruthless able adamantine appease approach attempt liberal /bar baro/]
*inexpensive 07-23-37 (a.) 1. relatively low in price or charging low prices [nickel nominal easy economical economy expensive popular price sensible shabby shoddy sixpenny]
*inexperience 12-62-12 (n.) 1. lack of experience and

the knowledge and understanding derived from experience [ignorance immaturity increase infancy ingenuous innocence naivety nonage experience participation rawness callow]
*inexplicable 08-59-30 (a.) 1. incapable of being explained or accounted for [incomprehensible indiscriminate inextricable inscrutable insoluble enigmatic error explicable explicate paradox peculiar perplex purpose puzzling capable casual cause confound cryptic curious account admit aimless baffle bewildering bizarre] "inexplicable errors"
*inexpressible 24-56-1 (a.) 1. defying expression [impossible indescribable ineffable inviolate numinous express religious sacrosanct spiritual beyond]
*infallible 15-59-7 (a.) 1. incapable of failure or error [ideal immaculate impeccable incapable ineluctable inerrant inevitable necessity nice failure faithful fallible faultless fine finish flawless foolproof absolute acceptable accurate agreeable antidote assured likely effective erring error even exact express /bill/] "an infallible antidote"
*infamous 07-73-43 (a.) 1. having an exceedingly bad reputation [ignoble ignominious ill illegal imprison improper incorrect inglorious iniquitous insidious nasty naughty nauseating nefarious notorious fame famous filthy flagrant formerly foul fraudulent abnormal abominable appearance atrocious awfully miscreant monstrous obnoxious offensive outrageous underhanded unhealthy unlawful unsuitable sad savage scandalous serious shameful shock sorry suspicious]
*infamy 18-62-4 (n.) 1. a state of extreme dishonor 2. evil fame or public reputation [ignominy ill imprison incur infamous iniquity notorious fame favorable formerly abhorrence abomination acclaim amy atrocity monstrosity] "a date which will live in infamy"
*inference 14-47-9 (n.) 1. the reasoning involved in drawing a conclusion or making a logical judgment on the basis of circumstantial evidence and prior conclusions rather than on the basis of direct observation [illation imply import indicative inductive infer innuendo insinuation interpretation intimate ironic notice nuance fact follow future entail evidence extrapolate ratiocinate read reasoning reckon referential respect circumstantial coherent conclusion conjecture connotation corollary]
*infernal 18-65-4 (a.) 1. expletives used informally as intensifiers 2. extremely evil or cruel; expressive of cruelty or befitting hell 3. characteristic of or resembling hell 4. being of a lower world of the dead 5. relating to or inhabiting hell (n.) 1. an inhabitant of hell [idiot imaginary infer influence informal inhabit inhumane iniquitous instrument intensifier nature nether noise nuisance fell ferocious fiendish fierce fire fool earth everlasting evil execrable expletive expressive extremely region roar ruthless absolute alive animal annoy atrocious lit long lower] "infernal heat and noise"
*inferno 15-54-7 (n.) 1. any place of pain and turmoil 2. a very intense and uncontrolled fire 3. (Christianity) the abode of Satan and the forces of evil; where sinners suffer eternal punishment [imagination infer intense nether netherworld fiction fiery firestorm flame force full furnace earth embody emphasize engine envisage equator eternal evil exist extend rage rapid red region religious reminiscent role room old oven]
*infest 09-50-22 (v.) 1. invade in great numbers, as of pests 2. live on or in a host, as of parasites 3. occupy in large numbers or live on a host [infiltrate inhabit inside inundate invade north fest fill flood force site spread table territory threaten]
*infidel 16-67-6 (n.) 1. a person who does not acknowledge your God [idol non faithless fidel freethinker deity devotion disbelieve ethnic /led/]
*infidelity 12-64-13 (n.) 1. the quality of being unfaithful [inconstant incredulity intrigue faithless false fickle fidelity flirtation denial disapprove disbelief discredit disloyalty distinguishing entangle essential liaison treachery triangle /led tile/]
*infinite 07-61-38 (a.) 1. having no limits or boundaries in time or space or extent or magnitude 2. too numerous to be counted 3. total and all-embracing 4. (grammar) of verbs; having neither person nor number nor mood (as a participle or gerund or infinitive) [imaginary immense immensely immortal impossible incalculable incessant incomprehensible inestimable inexhaustible ingenuity interminable negative neither never nonstop noticeable numberless numerous figurative finite forever form fractional fundamental temporal tense thick thousand timeless total totally towering tremendous end endless enormous essential even extent extreme] "the infinite ingenuity of man"
*infinity 14-56-9 (n.) 1. time without end [immense impair impose incessant fall far figure fini first forever formidable fullness future timeless trillion yardage]
*infirm 17-54-5 (a.) 1. confined to bed (by illness) 2. weak and feeble 3. lacking physical strength or vitality 4. lacking firmness of will or character or purpose [ill insecure invalid irresponsible failing fall feeble firm fragile frail resolute restless risky robust rusty mental mercurial mind moody moribund]
*infirmary 12-80-12 (n.) 1. a health facility where patients receive treatment [incompetent infant infectious infirm injure insane institution newborn nurse facility for form foundling receive recuperate room medicine mental military area asylum]
*infirmity 20-49-3 (n.) 1. the state of being weak in health or body (especially from old age) [ill inadequate indisposition infirm failing failure fault fear feeble flaw frailty reduction rift rocky malady malaise medical mind minor taint ticklish treachery]
*inflammable 24-65-1 (a.) 1. possible to burn [ignite incendiary irascible irritable isooctane item nervous non fiery fire fireball flammable alcohol angry methanol

mettlesome briquette burn butane easy edgy eruptive explosive /bam/]
*inflammation 12-58-13 (n.) 1. a response of body tissues to injury or irritation; characterized by pain and swelling and redness and heat 2. the state of being emotionally aroused and worked up 3. the act of setting on fire or catching fire 4. arousal to violent emotion [ignition incite infection infuriate irritation nausea necrosis nephritis faint fervour fever fire flam laryngitis light animation arouse asthma marasmus meningitis myelitis tachycardia tender tumor ophthalmia osteomyelitis otitis]
*inflexible 13-58-11 (a.) 1. extended meanings; incapable of change 2. literal meanings 3. incapable of adapting or changing to meet circumstances 4. not making concessions [impossible incapable inertia inescapable inevitable inexorable invincible ironclad irrevocable necessity fateful firm fixed flexible flexile flinty fossilize frozen fundamentalism law literal loyalty easily elastic establish extend bar blade brassbound] "a man of inflexible purpose"
*influence 02-50-447 (n.) 1. a cognitive factor that tends to have an effect on what you do 2. causing something without any direct or apparent effort 3. the effect of one thing (or person) on another 4. a power to affect persons or events especially power based on prestige etc 5. one having power to influence another (v.) 1. shape or influence; give direction to 2. have and exert influence or effect 3. induce into action by using one's charm [impact importance inspiration inspire factor favoritism flue forward leverage lobbyist lure upon upshot effect encroach energy engage enlist entice change control court] "The artist's work influenced the young painter"
*influential 04-56-113 (a.) 1. having or exercising influence or power [imperative important influent instrumental newspaper fluential forceful lead leading effective eminent empower enchanting exercise telling totalitarian absolute authoritative authorize autocratic /lait/] "an influential newspaper"
*influx 08-48-32 (n.) 1. the process of flowing in [increase incursion inpouring inrush intervention invasion flood flow flux uninterrupted]
*infrequent 11-39-14 (a.) 1. not frequent; not occurring regularly or at short intervals [infrequency instance interval irregular niggardly few fitful frequent random rare rarely recurring regular encounter exceptional exiguous uncommon uncommonly unique unpredictable unusual temper thin tight] "infrequent outbursts of temper"
*infringe 07-54-37 (v.) 1. go against, as of rules and laws 2. advance beyond the usual limit [imitate impinge injury interfere intervention intrude invade invasion naughty noncooperation fail flout forward freedom fringe froward recusant regulation right rule run gradual encroach entrench]
*infuriate 07-65-39 (v.) 1. make furious [incense incite indifference inflame irritate nettle fan fire flame furious umbrage rile rouse alienate anger annoy tumult eat enrage exacerbate exasperate excite extremely]
*infuse 09-40-25 (v.) 1. teach and impress by frequent repetitions or admonitions 2. fill, as with a certain quality 3. sit or let sit in a liquid to extract a flavor or to cleanse [imbue immerse impart implant impress inculcate inform inspire instill introduce invest fill fire flavor flush fortify full fuse saturate season soak solve souse steep suffuse enliven exhilarate express]
*infusion 11-17-15 (n.) 1. a solution obtained by steeping or soaking a substance (usually in water) 2. (medicine) the passive introduction of a substance (a fluid or drug or electrolyte) into a vein or between tissues (as by gravitational force) 3. the act of infusing or introducing a certain modifying element or quality [ill impression injection inspiration instilment insufficient intimate introduction necessary non feed ferment fire fishnet fluid font force formerly frequently fusion sail saline science secretion soak solution specialty spirit steady steep substance success sucrose suggestion obtain] "the team's continued success is attributable to a steady infusion of new talent"
*ingenious 08-49-32 (a.) 1. (used of persons or artifacts) marked by independence and creativity in thought or action 2. skillful (or showing skill) in adapting means to ends 3. showing inventiveness and skill [imaginative independence inge innovative inspire inspired inventive neat nifty notional gadget gifted graceful guile effective excellent expert originative uncreative scheme selfish sensitive shape sharp show skillful solution some story success]
*ingenuity 10-48-19 (n.) 1. the power of creative imagination 2. the property of being ingenious [imagination inge ingenious initiative inventive genius gift grace great efficiency expertise unusual talent technique thinking time] "a plot of great ingenuity"
*ingenuous 20-23-3 (a.) 1. characterized by an inability to mask your feelings; not devious 2. lacking in sophistication or worldliness [inability inexperienced inge innocent intact naif naive natural genuine give green growing guile gullible easy experience explanation exploit unaffected unchecked undistorted unequivocal uninhibited unsophisticated unworldly open openhearted outspoken seeming show simplicity sincere soft sophistication stare straightforward] "an ingenuous admission of responsibility"
*ingest 13-45-10 (v.) 1. take up, as of knowledge or beliefs 2. serve oneself to, or consume regularly [imbibe imbibition impoverish ingurgitate inhale nibble nutrition gain gest gobble grazing gulp eat engulf erode erosion esophagus excess exhale exhaust expenditure sample sate satisfaction serve sip skill smoke solid sop soup spend spoon squander substance suck sugar sup surround swallow swig taste touch try]
*inglorious 20-75-3 (a.) 1. (used of conduct or

character) deserving or bringing disgrace or shame 2. not bringing honor and glory [ignominious infamous innocuous integrity island nameless notorious glorious glory greed lack least literary low obscure oceanic opprobrium rache receive record rest retreat unknown unnoticed unpopular unsung shabby shameful simple small]
*ingratiate 15-41-7 (v.) 1. gain favor with somebody by deliberate efforts [influence insinuate gain give glib grovel represent reveal abject adulate advantage approval arm attempt tend timeserver toady top truckle try eat effort]
*ingratitude 24-63-1 (n.) 1. a lack of gratitude [gratitude rude affective appreciation thankless unappreciativ ungratefulnes emotional experience express]
*ingredient 04-54-121 (n.) 1. an abstract part of something 2. a component of a mixture or compound 3. food that is a component of a mixture in cooking [include index inside intermixture item nutritive gelatinous geometric grammatical guts recipe relation require effective egg element endall entity essential extension detail die dish dissolve divided division dry thick tomato /eider/]
*inherent 06-42-51 (a.) 1. existing as an essential constituent or characteristic 2. present at birth but not necessarily hereditary; acquired during fetal development 3. in the nature of something though not readily apparent [immediate imply inability inborn individual inhere integral internal intrinsic invest native nature necessarily non normal hereditary elementary esoteric essential exist explicit express extrinsic ready regular resident risk tell truth typical]
*inhibit 10-44-19 (v.) 1. limit the range or extent of 2. to put down by force or authority [impede impound interfere intervene nascent hamper hide hinder hold holdup hush ban bar behave bite blinking bodily bound burke taboo talk temper threat throttle trammel troublesome]
*inhospitable 16-58-6 (a.) 1. unfavorable to life or growth 2. not hospitable [icy ill incompatible harsh hospitable hostile stark stranger tense treat area bare barren bleak life live extremely /tip/] "the barren inhospitable dessert"
*inhuman 14-58-8 (a.) 1. belonging to or resembling something nonhuman 2. without compunction or human feeling [implacable impression infernal insensitive noise non heartless hellish human humanity uncanny unearthly unfeeling unkindly unrelenting malignant merciless murderous animal anthropophagus appropriate atrocious]
*inimical 22-50-2 (a.) 1. not friendly [ical icy ill inconsistent negative noncooperation martial military miserable cold contrary contrast critic cross adverse aggression aggressive alien amicable antagonistic /mini/]
*inimitable 16-57-6 (a.) 1. defying imitation; matchless [imitate imitation immortal impossible incomparable invincible irreproducible matchless /mini/] "an inimitable style"
*iniquity 20-76-3 (n.) 1. absence of moral or spiritual values 2. morally objectionable behavior 3. an unjust act [immoral impropriety indiscretion injustice nonfeasance quit unfair unjust unlawful tort transgression treacherous trespass trip]
*initiate 05-38-67 (a.) 1. having been introduced to something new (n.) 1. someone new to a field or activity 2. people who have been introduced to the mysteries of some field or activity 3. someone who has been admitted to membership in a scholarly field (v.) 1. accept young people into society, usually with some rite 2. take the lead or initiative in; participate in the development of 3. bring into being 4. bring up a topic for discussion 5. prepare the way for [include induct insider institute introduce invest neophyte new newbie newcomer newly novitiate talk teach technical topic trade train transplant trigger tyro accept actuate admit architect arrange artist associate attack attempt author eat enroll enterprise entrant establish experience] "He initiated a new program"
*inject 05-58-63 (v.) 1. to introduce (a new aspect or element) 2. give an injection to 3. feed intravenously 4. take by injection 5. force or drive (a fluid or gas) into by piercing 6. to insert between other elements [immunize increase infect inform infuse injury inoculate insert instill insulate interrupt introduce join element enclose enliven exhilarate cavity clever combine come confined cure cut therapeutic throw training trajectory] "We injected the glucose into the patient's vein"
*injunction 08-43-31 (n.) 1. a formal command or admonition 2. (law) a judicial remedy issued in order to prohibit a party from doing or continuing to do a certain activity [impose inadmissible inhibition instruction issue narrow notify judicial junction until cease certain charge collection command commission completion continue control court taboo teach temporary trial omission order over]
*inkling 14-62-9 (n.) 1. a slight suggestion [idea impression index indication intimate nod notion nudge kick ling look gesture give glimmer glimmering /ilk/] "he had no inkling what was about to happen"
*inland 07-72-42 (a.) 1. situated away from an area's coast or border (ad.) 1. towards or into the interior of a region [inshore internal intestine inward inwards native near land landlocked locate area] "the town is five miles inland"
*inlet 15-32-7 (n.) 1. an arm off of a larger body of water (often between rocky headlands) [ingress inland intake interval island narrow nearly nether northwestern norway lake land lane large leak let liquid loch long earth enclose england enter entryway european exit extra tunnel]

*innocuous 11-58-15 (a.) 1. not injurious to physical or mental health 2. unlikely to harm or disturb anyone 3. lacking intent or capacity to injure 4. not causing disapproval [inglorious injurious inn innocent inoffensive insipid intent noxious old capacity comment uncontroversi undistinguished unimportant unlikely unobjectionab unpretentious safe sapless simple small strong /con/]
*innovate 10-50-19 (v.) 1. bring something new to an environment [idea initiative introduce invent inventor open originate originator ovate vanguard agent architect area author trailblazer transform try environment /avo von/]
*innuendo 13-54-11 (n.) 1. an indirect (and usually malicious) implication [implication import impropriety incriminate index indirect inference information interpretation intimate nod nuance nudge undertone endo entend explanation denounce denunciation double obvious overtone]
*innumerable 13-46-10 (a.) 1. too numerous to be counted [immeasurable immense incalculable incomprehensible inestimable numberless numerable numerous uncounted universal unlimited untold measureless multitudinous myriad endless eternal exhaustless reason rich boundless limitless /bar bare emu/]
*inoffensive 18-67-4 (a.) 1. not causing anger or annoyance 2. of an inoffensive substitute for offensive terminology 3. giving no offense 4. not offensive 5. causing no harm 6. morally respectable or inoffensive [injurious innocuous noxious offensive forgive euphemism excuse exempt safe savoury scarcely stimulant substitute venial vindicate] "inoffensive behavior"
*inopportune 22-37-2 (a.) 1. not opportune [ill improper inappropriate inconvenient inept irrelevant opportune premature purpose time unfortunate unhappy unlucky unpropitious unseasonable untimely /nut troppo/] "arrived at a most inopportune hour"
*inquire 07-51-38 (v.) 1. have a wish or desire to know something 2. inquire about 3. conduct an inquiry or investigation of [inquisitorial inspect instance intercommunicate interview investigate investigative irregularity itch nosey query questioning quidnunc quire quiz union report request research rich rubbernecker eavesdrop engage enquire espionage examine expect explore]
*inquisition 15-66-7 (n.) 1. a former tribunal of the Roman Catholic Church (1232-1820) created to discover and suppress heresy 2. a severe interrogation (often violating the rights or privacy of individuals) [inquiry interrogatory investigation ion questioning until sentence severe spain suppress torture tribunal organization orthodoxy /itis/]
*inquisitive 15-65-7 (a.) 1. showing curiosity 2. inquiring or appearing to inquire [interfere intrusive investigate investigative itch nosy questioning quizzical searching see show sit snoop snoopy speculative voyeuristic eager explore eyebrow /itis vitis/] "if someone saw a man climbing a light post they might get inquisitive"
*inquisitor 18-66-4 (n.) 1. a questioner who is excessively harsh 2. an official of the ecclesiastical court of the Inquisition [inquisitive interview investigator querist query question quidnunc quiz sampler search sightsee sit snoop spain official relentless rubbernecker /roti/]
*inroad 11-52-16 (n.) 1. an encroachment or intrusion 2. an invasion or hostile attack [improve infiltrate injury intervention intrusion invasion night raid right road obtrusion advance army arrival attack damage destruction detriment] "they made inroads in the United States market"
*insatiable 12-62-12 (a.) 1. impossible to satiate or satisfy [impossible insistent intemperate satisfy sordid stuffing swinish able acquisitive appetite avaricious avid bolt bottomless limitless edacious esurient exigent /bait/] "an insatiable appetite"

*inscribe 11-46-16 (v.) 1. write upon; engrave a pen, for example 2. mark with one's signature 3. convert ordinary language into code 4. register formally; as a participant or member 5. address, as a work of literature, in a style less formal than a dedication 6. draw within a figure so as to touch in as many places as possible 7. write, engrave, or print as a lasting record [imprint incise index initial insert score scratch scribe scriptural sculpture security set sign square stamp style surface calligraphy carve character chip chisel cipher circle code compliment confirm consecrate curve cut cypher reason record recruit register root running bed book edit encrypt engage engrave engross enlist enrol enroll enter establish etch]
*inscrutable 14-57-8 (a.) 1. of an obscure nature [impenetrable impossible inarticulate incapable incomprehensible indecipherable insurance interpret investigate nature numinous scrutable secret sphinx cabalistic carson clarity clearly cryptic rache rambling unaccountable unconnected unfathomable unknowable unreadable thus totally account ambiguous arcane land life encompass enigmatic explicable expression]
*insecure 10-61-18 (a.) 1. not firm or firmly fixed; likely to fail or give way 2. not financially safe or secure 3. lacking self-confidence or assurance 4. lacking in security or safety 5. not safe from attack [infirm nervous secure shaky shifty slippery expose uncertain unreliable unsure rickety risky rocky] "the hinge is insecure"
*insensible 24-65-1 (a.) 1. incapable of physical sensation 2. barely able to be perceived 3. unresponsive to stimulation 4. (followed by 'to' or 'by') unaware of or indifferent to [impassive imperceptible impossible

inappreciable incapable indiscrimination indistinguishable inert intangible intent invisible nap nearsighted numb secret sedate senseless sensible sensory shift shroud stimulus stoicism stolid submerge suffer earth elation emotionless emphasis engross envelop euphoria barely benumb blind bloodless blunt lack latent lethargy lie lifeless] "insensible to pain"
*inseparable 14-47-9 (a.) 1. not capable of being separated [impartible impossible indivisibility indivisible inextricable infrangible infusible insoluble intimate near see seem separable separate set share solidify spell stick piece accretion adhesion agglutinate attached rock link /ape bar pes rape/] "inseparable pieces of rock"
*insidious 12-51-12 (a.) 1. beguiling but harmful 2. intended to entrap 3. working or spreading in a hidden and usually injurious way [indirect ingenious injurious ins intend inventive safe seductive sharp sinister slow smooth sneaky spread stealthy strategic subtle dangerous dark deceptive deep desire destructive devious disease unconscionable underhand unethical unsafe unscrupulous] "insidious pleasures"
*insight 04-59-118 (n.) 1. a feeling of understanding 2. the clear (and often sudden) understanding of a complex situation 3. clear or deep perception of a situation 4. grasping the inner nature of things intuitively [impression incisive inner inspiration instinctive interest intuitive nature note notice sage savvy schizophrenia self sensitivity sharp shrewd sight situation sixth solution sudden suggestive symptom gain gnostic grasping hallucination tell thank trenchant]
*insignificance 18-79-4 (n.) 1. the quality of having little or no significance [important inconsequential influence irrelevant note significant great effect]
*insignificant 10-53-21 (a.) 1. of little importance or influence or power; of minor status 2. signifying nothing 3. not worthy of notice 4. not large enough to consider or notice 5. not important or noteworthy [idle immaterial imperfect important inane inappreciable inconsequential indifference inferiority influence irrelevant negligible niggling noise nonsensical note noteworthy nothing noticeable nullity scarcely secondary shallow short significant signify slight small sound status superficial garble great faint feeble few footle frivolous futility casual considerable cursory aimless attention technical tiny trifling trivial /fin/] "insignificant sounds"
*insinuate 14-38-8 (v.) 1. introduce or insert (oneself) in a subtle manner 2. give to understand [imply indicative indirect inference influence ingratiate insert intimate introduce involve ironic nasty nearby sandwich silky sinuate smooth subtle suggest suggestive suppose unctuous understand unpleasant accuse adulate adumbrate allude article assume table task tax trench try eat encroach entail entrench environment] "He insinuated himself into the conversation of the people at the nearby table"
*insipid 15-71-7 (a.) 1. lacking taste or flavor or tang 2. lacking significance or impact 3. lacking interest or significance 4. not pleasing to the sense of taste [impact inane indecisive indifferent injurious innocuous ins interest neutral novel noxious savour significance slight slow soft supermarket pale pedestrian personality physical plain pleasing diet dilute dry dull /dip/]
*insistence 06-46-47 (n.) 1. continual and persistent demands 2. urgently demanding attention 3. the state of urgently demanding notice or attention [imperativenes importance instancy necessity notice speedy earnest considerable continual]
*insistent 05-46-67 (a.) 1. demanding attention 2. persistently continual [imperative importance incessant industry inexorable insist insistency instant interruption invincible nagging necessity needle notice seeming series space speedy sporadic spur stable steady stubborn tease tenacity tireless earnest emphatic encouragement enduring exacting exigent] "the bluejay's insistent cry"
*insolence 24-60-1 (n.) 1. the trait of being rude and impertinent; inclined to take liberties 2. an offensive disrespectful impudent act [impertinent impudent incline insulting show offensive lack liberty cheeky chutzpah crust]
*insolent 20-57-3 (a.) 1. unrestrained by convention or propriety 2. marked by casual disrespect [impertinent impudent incline indiscretion insole insulting irreverent nose saucy scurrilous serious shame show side speech student success superior obdurate offensive outrageous lack liberty lofty lying exhibit temerarious tourism trick]
*insomnia 13-65-11 (n.) 1. an inability to sleep; chronic sleeplessness [inability indigestion inflammation ins itch nausea necrosis normal sentient shock sleepless slumber sore stay stress marasmus alert asleep asphyxiate asthma awake]
*insouciant 18-60-4 (a.) 1. marked by blithe unconcern [indifferent interest seasonal slapdash spontaneous student occasional offhand unexpected unintentional unplanned unpremeditated utterly calm car careless casual cavalier chance cold concern cool abandon tease temporary]
*inspector 04-58-133 (n.) 1. a high ranking police officer 2. an investigator who observes carefully [inspect investigator narc scrutinize search sergeant sheriff supervisor surveyor patrolman policeman policewoman proctor election examine canvass captain care check clue commissioner compliance controller cor correct taskmaster tester trooper observe observer official overseer ranking reeve rule]
*instance 02-40-307 (n.) 1. a single item of information that is representative of a type 2. an occurrence of something (v.) 1. clarify by giving an example of [idea illustration incidental insistent intend item name natural needle say self serve single situation stance study suggestion symbol syndrome thing type account acquire

add adduce article aspect case circumstantiate citation cite clarify class clip conform count elaborate enlarge event example excuse expatiate experience explanation expound]
*instant 04-58-103 (a.) 1. occurring with no delay 2. demanding attention 3. in or of the present month (n.) 1. a particular point in time 2. a very short time (as the time it takes to blink once) [immediately imminent imperative indefinitely insistent intermediate item near new novel season second short slow split stage stan sudden suitable swift taxing temporal threatening tick trice truth twinkle achieve actual alert approach appropriate arrive attention] "relief was instantaneous"
*instantaneous 14-43-8 (a.) 1. occurring with no delay [immediately indicate infinitesimal instant instantly slow spontaneous sudden summary swift transitory alert almost apt average expeditious express] "relief was instantaneous"
*instigate 09-66-22 (v.) 1. provoke or stir up 2. serve as the inciting cause of [impulse incentive incite induce initiate initiator inspire institute introduce nettle sag scheme serve set shape sire smith specify spur start stimulate stimulus stir stirring suggest tickle trouble troublemaker gate generator get goad great grow guide activate agitation architect arouse artist assertive author effect evoke excite /git tag/]
*instigator 20-56-3 (n.) 1. someone who deliberately foments trouble 2. a person who initiates a course of action [illicit incite initiator inspire sag stir trouble guide assertive ringleader rule] "she was the instigator of their quarrel"
*instill 11-56-16 (v.) 1. impart gradually 2. fill, as with a certain quality 3. make a deep and indelible impression on someone 4. teach and impress by frequent repetitions or admonitions 5. enter drop by drop, as of medication into an eye [idea imbue impart implant impression imprint inculcate indelible infix infuse ingrain inject insert introduce school season self soak stamp steep still strike student suffuse teach temper tincture tinge traffic transfuse try leaven lend liquid love] "Her presence instilled faith into the children"
*instructive 12-47-13 (a.) 1. serving to instruct of enlighten or inform 2. tending to increase knowledge or dissipate ignorance [ignorance illuminate illustrative imperative increase inform informative insight instruct interpretive sententious serve standard statutory teach tend recommend regulation reveal useful cautionary clarify compel convey cultural edify educate elucidate enlighten explanatory expository /curt/]
*insufficiency 24-40-1 (n.) 1. a lack of competence 2. (pathology) inability of a bodily part or organ to function normally 3. lack of an adequate quantity or number [inability inadequate inefficiency inferiority injustice nature scant scarcity science shortfall slight slump small study sufficiency sufficient unemployment uneven unfit unsuitable failure fewness flaw flow function cause competence contrariety coronary effect eliot excretion exiguity exiguous expect]
*insufficient 06-53-45 (a.) 1. of a quantity not able to fulfill a need or requirement [inadequate incomplete inferior satisfy scant scarce short shy skimpy small sufficient uneven unqualified unsatisfactory unskillful failing fulfill fund enough extent trivial] "insufficient funds"
*insular 13-49-11 (a.) 1. relating to or characteristic of or situated on an island 2. suggestive of the isolated life of an island 3. narrowly restricted in outlook or scope [inaccessible independent insula insulation inward island islet isolate narrow nearsighted scope separation situate small solo stranger suggestive sympathy unaccompanied unattended unconnected land leonard life limit limited little local lonesome alien alone anatomy apartheid attitude authoritarian reef regional reminiscent restricted retired] "insular territories"
*insularity 22-49-2 (n.) 1. the state of being isolated or detached [isolated narrow separation]
*insulate 09-39-26 (v.) 1. place or set apart 2. protect from heat, cold, noise, etc. by surrounding with insulating material [inmate insula island isolation noise screen seclude segregate separate sequestrate set sex shelter shield single soundproof strand surround undesirable unpleasant lag leave line alter apart thrash thresh transform treat electricity enforce enisle /talus/] "We had his bedroom insulated before winter came"
*insuperable 22-73-2 (a.) 1. impossible to surmount 2. incapable of being surmounted or excelled [impenetrable impossible incapable insurmountable irresistible successful super superable surmount unable unassailable unbeatable unconquerable unworkable excel redan resistless rid battle /bar bare/] "insuperable odds"
*insurgent 06-47-49 (a.) 1. in opposition to a civil authority or government (n.) 1. a person who takes part in an armed rebellion against the constituted authority (especially in the hope of improving conditions) 2. a member of an irregular armed force that fights a stronger force by sabotage and harassment [nonconformist seditious subversive surgent rebellious revolutionist riotous rise government guerrilla traitorous treasonable turbulent]
*insurrection 15-41-7 (n.) 1. organized opposition to authority; a conflict in which one faction tries to wrest control from another [inequity ins insurgent intifada israel numerous seaman seditious sepoy soldier strip struggle subversion subversive suppress sweeping radical rebellion rebellious revolution revolutionary rise ruler england catastrophic civil clash conflict constitute control country tax traitorous treasonable try turbulent officer open opposition oppress organize overthrow]
*intangible 13-35-10 (a.) 1. (of especially business assets) not having physical substance or intrinsic productive value 2. hard to pin down or identify 3.

incapable of being perceived by the senses especially the sense of touch 4. lacking substance or reality; incapable of being touched or seen (n.) 1. assets that are saleable though not material or physical [identify immaterial imperceptible impossible imprecise incapable incorporeal indefinite indescribable insubstantial intrinsic invisible non tangible tenuous thin touched transmundane abstract acquire advantage airy aspect asset astral atomic germinal ghostly good granular benefit bodiless lack elude elusive enterprise ethereal exist /big gnat/] "intangible assets such as good will"

*integral 08-54-32 (a.) 1. constituting the undiminished entirety; lacking nothing essential especially not damaged 2. existing as an essential constituent or characteristic (n.) 1. the result of a mathematical integration; F(x) is the integral of f(x) if dF/dx = f(x) [important impossible inability inbuilt include indefinite inherent intact integrate intrinsic involve nature necessary negative nothing numeric teg totality transcendental truth either entire essential even exception exist extent extrinsic gross radical rational real reckoning all amount any anyone lack lifetime local logarithmic lone /get large/]

*integrity 05-47-86 (n.) 1. moral soundness 2. an unreduced or unbroken completeness or totality [identity imperfect incomplete inherent intact integration nation nobility nominalism nonconformity territorial thorough togetherness totality truthful embodiment entire erect ethical exhaustive goodness grit reaction reliable reputable respect respectable righteous /get/]

*intellect 10-59-18 (n.) 1. the capacity for rational thought or inference or discrimination 2. knowledge and intellectual ability 3. a person who uses the mind creatively [ideation illuminate important improve individual inference inherent intel intuition theorize thinker trust egghead einstein elixir endow erudite esprit exceptional exercise experience explain expound learn life literate capacity clever cognitive comprehend consciousness creative curious /cell/]

*intellectual 03-48-157 (a.) 1. appealing to or using the intellect 2. of or associated with or requiring the use of the mind 3. of or relating to the intellect 4. involving intelligence rather than emotions or instinct (n.) 1. a person who uses the mind creatively [ideation illumination individual innate intellect internal noetic technology thinking thoughtful einstein elitism emotional erudition expert learned letter literation capacity characteristic conceptual constitutional culture understanding academic academician affective apprehension authority /cell/] "his intellectual career"

*intelligence 02-49-244 (n.) 1. a unit responsible for gathering and interpreting information about an enemy 2. the ability to comprehend; to understand and profit from experience 3. the operation of gathering information about an enemy 4. secret information about an enemy (or potential enemy) 5. new information about specific and timely events [information insight instruction intel newsworthy notify nous technique television transmission espionage evidence expertise language light gen genius grip capacity clever community consciousness /gill/] "we sent out planes to gather intelligence on their radar coverage"

*intelligible 18-45-4 (a.) 1. capable of being apprehended or understood 2. well articulated or enunciated, and loud enough to be heard distinctly [incomprehensible indicative intel interpret noise transfer ease easy effortless enough enunciate exoteric expressive extension legible logical loud lucid luminous grasp barely /big gill/] "intelligible pronunciation"

*intensive 05-50-77 (a.) 1. characterized by a high degree or intensity; often used as a combining form 2. of agriculture; intended to increase productivity of a fixed area by expending more capital and labor 3. tending to give force or emphasis (n.) 1. a modifier that has little meaning except to intensify the meaning it modifies [increase insane intensify tend tensive terrific thoroughgoing topping total true effort egregious emphasize entirely exaggerate except exhaustive expend expression extent extremely scientific sentence serious severe sheer short simply sincerely speaker straight superb sweeping veritable] "the questioning was intensive"

*intention 03-57-211 (n.) 1. (usually plural) the goal with respect to a marriage proposal 2. an anticipated outcome that is intended or that guides your planned actions 3. an act of intending; a volition that you intend to carry out [idea ideal immediate inspiration intent tactics target terminate translation end enough enterprise entirely objective obtain once organization outcome]

*interact 09-44-25 (v.) 1. act together or towards others or with others [inmesh inter telepathy responsive act answer conversational /care/] "He should interact more with his colleagues"

*intercede 18-24-4 (v.) 1. act between parties with a view to reconciling differences [inter intervene negotiate talk reconcile referee represent difference discuss dispute] "He interceded in the family dispute"

*intercept 07-41-43 (n.) 1. the point at which a line intersects a coordinate axis (v.) 1. seize on its way 2. tap a telephone or telegraph wire to get information [impede include inhibit inter intervene take tap target transmission trap eavesdrop element enter extent radio reach repress resist restrain room calculate capture catch check communicate coordinate country cross curb curve cut part people phone plane point position possession prevent progress] "The fighter plane was ordered to intercept an aircraft that had entered the country's airspace"

*intercession 22-39-2 (n.) 1. a prayer to God on behalf of another person 2. the act of intervening (as to mediate a dispute) [implore incarnate intervention involution

involve negotiate negotiation thanksgiving translator treat try empyrean engagement entrepreneur reach reconcile redemptive resolve reverent rogation rosary celestial cession chosen collect communion conciliator conflict connection contemplate counselor saint salvation second settle share solicitor speaker spokeswoman suit ombudsman orison /secret/]
*interdict 18-19-4 (n.) 1. an ecclesiastical censure by the Roman Catholic Church withdrawing certain sacraments and Christian burial from a person or all persons in a particular district (v.) 1. destroy by firepower, such as an enemy's line of communication 2. command against [inhibition injunction inter notify taboo embargo enjoin exclusion refuse rein rejection restriction debar deny disallow check compel control court curb]
*interim 04-62-110 (a.) 1. serving during an intermediate interval of time (n.) 1. the time between one event, process, or period and another [impermanent instant inter interval temporary tentative truce effect elect establish recess reign replacement rest room margin mark measure moratorium /mire/] "an interim agreement"
*interlocutor 20-51-3 (n.) 1. the performer in the middle of a minstrel line who engages the others in talk 2. a person who takes part in a conversation [inter negro talk troupe engage line ceremony comic converse]
*interlude 12-47-14 (n.) 1. an intervening period or episode 2. a brief show (music or dance etc) performed between the sections of another performance (v.) 1. occur as an interlude 2. perform an interlude, as on a musical instrument [idyll incorporate inter interval number timeout tone truce turn entertainment entracte epilogue episode exhibition exodus relief response rest routine lapse layoff length long lull dance definite development different division drop]
*intermediate 08-32-28 (a.) 1. around the middle of a scale of evaluation of physical measures 2. lying between two extremes in time or space or degree (n.) 1. a substance formed during a chemical process before the desired product is obtained (v.) 1. act between parties with a view to reconciling differences [inter mediate /aide idem/] "going from sitting to standing without intermediate pushes with the hands"
*interminable 12-65-12 (a.) 1. tiresomely long; seemingly without end [immensely incessant incomprehensible indicate infinite never nonstop noon tall temporal terminable termless timeless tiresome together end endless enduring eternal everlasting exhaustless extensive recurrent repetitive running marathon measureless monotonous morning ageless articulate average boring boundless lasting lengthy limitless link long /ban bani/]
*intermission 10-07-18 (n.) 1. the act of suspending activity temporarily 2. a time interval during which there is a temporary cessation of something [inactivity inadvertent instant interval introduction number temporary theatrical timeout truce turn epilogue exodus radio relaxation release relief respite rest routine mark mission movie musical scene second show sound spell stay suspension occurrence]
*intermittent 09-44-22 (a.) 1. stopping and starting at irregular intervals 2. stopping and starting at regular intervals [inconstant infrequent instance interval irregular nonlinear timeout truce eccentricity episode erratic even rain random recurring regular relief return roughness measured meter methodical metronome mitten /nett/] "intermittent rain showers"
*interpose 24-34-1 (v.) 1. to insert between other elements 2. introduce 3. be or come between 4. get involved, usually so as to hinder or halt an action [infringe inject insert inter intervention into intrude invasion involve negotiate nose tamper tangent thicket threat throw toss toward trade trench trespass early element encroach entrench environment establish excursus referee remark represent right parenthesis people place placement poke position proper obtrusion sandwich say shove situation soliloquy step]
*interpreter 08-42-33 (n.) 1. someone who uses art to represent something 2. someone who mediates between speakers of different languages 3. (computer science) a program that translates and executes source language statements one line at a time 4. an advocate who represents someone else's policy or purpose [individual interpret tin translator editor execute explicate exponent expound road painting perform person player programme /rete/] "his paintings reveal a sensitive interpreter of nature"
*interrogate 10-53-19 (v.) 1. transmit (a signal) for setting off an appropriate response, as in telecommunication 2. pose a series of questions to [inquisitor inter interview investigate television test threaten transmit examine expect explosion radio raise reach request response rubberneck gape gawk grill address aggressive airwave answer approach appropriate ask /ago tag/]
*interrupt 05-47-79 (v.) 1. interfere in someone else's activity 2. destroy the peace or tranquility of 3. make a break in 4. end prematurely [impede imposing incoherent inhibit inject insert instruction inter intervene intrude intrusive invasive irregular natural nonlinear temporary terminate throw tranquillity trip troublesome turn early element end episodic read reception remark repressive resist restrictive unconnected upc utterance parenthetic partner patchy pause phone plan postpone pregnancy premature prevent processor program punctuate /purr/] "We interrupt the program for the following messages"
*intersect 14-24-8 (v.) 1. meet at a point [inter interlock nip tally taper traverse encounter run see set check coincide come cooperate cross]
*intersperse 11-49-15 (v.) 1. place at intervals in or among 2. introduce one's writing or speech with certain

expressions [illustration insert inter introduce enclose exclamation expression recording scatter sector set speech spread sprinkle stick store surface pattern pepper place pose position protective punctuate put] "intersperse exclamation marks ina the text"
*intervene 04-55-89 (v.) 1. get involved, usually so as to hinder or halt an action [influence infringe inter intervention into intrude invade involve negotiate nose tamper temporary tend third threat top toward trade trench trespass early economics effect elapse encroach ensue enter entrench extend reach recess referee resist right river] "Why did the U.S. not intervene earlier in WW II?"
*intervention 04-57-104 (n.) 1. the act of intervening (as to mediate a dispute) 2. (law) a proceeding that permits a person to enter into a lawsuit already in progress; admission of person not an original party to the suit so that person can protect some right or interest that is allegedly affected by the proceedings 3. a policy of intervening in the affairs of other countries [impose influence injection institution inter intrusion invasion involve trend trespass economic encroach engagement enter entry relation right rule obtrusion original] "the purpose of intervention is to prevent unnecessary duplication of lawsuits"
*intestate 24-90-1 (a.) 1. (law) having made no legally valid will before death or not disposed of by a legal will [impose testate end estate assign authority /set/] "he died intestate"
*intestine 14-56-9 (n.) 1. the part of the alimentary canal between the stomach and the anus [include inland inside internal native test thorax throat ticker tongue tract embryo emunctory end endocardium entrails esophagus excrete situate spleen stomach sweetbread /set/]
*intimacy 08-50-31 (n.) 1. close or warm friendship 2. a usually secretive or illicit sexual relationship 3. a feeling of being intimate and belonging together [illicit informal information intercourse intima involve inward near night technique tender tie mate meat mysterious absence accord affair affaire affectionate amour association atmosphere care close confidence congress connection create /amit/] "the absence of fences created a mysterious intimacy in which no one knew privacy"
*intimidate 04-51-101 (v.) 1. to compel or deter by or as if by threats 2. make timid or fearful [imminent inadequate inspire instill nerve terrorize threat threaten timid timorous toward try mean menace minatory monitory mousy danger dash daunt deliberate demoralize denounce denunciation deprive desire deter discourage dismay dissuade dissuasive abusive accompany admonitory affright afraid alarm alarming anticipation appal around awe awed enslave expostulate /dim tad/] "Her boss intimidates her"
*intolerable 10-60-18 (a.) 1. completely unacceptable 2. impossible to tolerate or endure [impermissible impossible improper inadmissible indefensible inexcusable inordinate insupportable nakedly noise terribly thoroughgoing tolerable tolerate total objectionable odious openly outright lamentable egregious endure excessive excruciating extravagant rank regular abhorrent abominable absolute acceptable agonizing annoying arrant awfully bad bear bitter blatant brash /bar bare lot/] "an intolerable degree of sentimentality"
*intolerance 12-53-13 (n.) 1. impatience with annoyances 2. unwillingness to recognize and respect differences in opinions or beliefs [illiberal narrow tenacity tolerance obdurate obstinate racism restive ageism attitude chauvinism classism /lot/] "his intolerance of interruptions"
*intolerant 15-62-7 (a.) 1. unwilling to tolerate difference of opinion 2. narrow-minded about cherished opinions [idea impatient indignant ingredient irritable narrow narrowminded tenacious thrive tolerant tolerate twist obstinate opinion opinionated outrage own lack lifestyle love easy eat environment racist reaction read refuse respect restive right rigid accept ageist allergic anger annoy antipathetic averse /lot/]
*intoxicate 09-48-23 (v.) 1. fill with high spirits; fill with optimism 2. have an intoxicating effect on, of a drug 3. make drunk (with alcoholic drinks) [impassioned impressive inebriate infatuate inflammatory inspire toxic optimism orgasm orgiastic orgy overjoy overwhelming can compulsive conceited concerned craze create affect agitate alcoholic animate ardent arouse effect elate emotion enthusiastic entrance exalt excite excited exhilarate exuberant]
*intramural 22-02-2 (a.) 1. carried on within the bounds of an institution or community [inner institution internal intra tissue member /arum mart rum uma/] "most of the students participated actively in the college's intramural sports program"
*intransigence 15-50-7 (n.) 1. the trait of being intransigent; stubbornly refusing to compromise [idea inflexible narrow trait refuse resolute adhere self stubborn compromise]
*intransigent 13-46-10 (a.) 1. not capable of being swayed or diverted from a course; unsusceptible to persuasion [idea incapable inexorable inflexible intra iron irreconcilable narrow naysayer negativism non tendency toughness trait refuse relentless resist resolute rigid rigorous adamantine adhere ass attitude self steely stern stiff stubborn sway grim extend]
*intrepid 11-53-15 (a.) 1. invulnerable to fear or intimidation [invulnerable tenacious timid trepid reporter resolute explorer photograph pioneer plucky daring dashing dauntless doughty /dip pert/]
*intricacy 12-41-12 (n.) 1. marked by elaborately complex detail [incredible intricate involution involve tangle technicality toughness tri ramification rigorous rugged carve character compound convoluted

convolution crabbed abstruse arduous arrange artful aspect]
*intricate 07-39-42 (a.) 1. highly involved or intricate [implicate interrelated involved ironic needlework negotiation tangle tax tortuous tough tricky reason refined resolve rich rigorous rough rugged cate combine combined complicate compound convoluted critical ambivalent amphibious arduous artful eclectic elaborate element embarrass]
*intrigue 03-56-137 (n.) 1. a crafty and involved plot to achieve your (usually sinister) ends 2. a clandestine love affair (v.) 1. cause to be interested or curious 2. form intrigues (for) in an underhand manner [illegal imagination importance infidelity influence interest intimacy inviting irresistible tactic taking tease thrilling transport triangle trickery trig racket ravishing reference relationship rig romance rope ruse gambit game gimmick glamorous great underhand underplot engineering entrance excite /girt/]
*intrinsic 11-59-17 (a.) 1. belonging to a thing by its very nature 2. (anatomy) situated within or belonging solely to the organ or body part on which it acts [inalienable inbuilt incapable inherent inherit innate inner ins inside internal intimate native nature transfer treat real repudiate resident respect secret singular situate solely statement structure subjective surface central characteristic congenital constitutional core] "form was treated as something intrinsic, as the very essence of the thing"
*introductory 12-46-14 (a.) 1. serving to open or begin 2. serving as a base or starting point 3. serving as an introduction or preface [illuminate inaugural initial intermediate inventive nascent natal necessary teach tool train raw recruit remark rudimentary opening original degree didactic disciplinary ductor understand chapter close come communicate course creative cultural /udo/] "began the slide show with some introductory remarks"
*introspection 14-50-9 (n.) 1. the contemplation of your own thoughts and desires and conduct [intent introspect navel reflexion ruminate search solipsism penetrating examination calm conduct consideration contemplate /sort/]
*introvert 15-66-7 (a.) 1. characterized by introversion (n.) 1. (psychology) a person who tends to shrink from social contacts and to become preoccupied with their own thoughts (v.) 1. fold inwards, of certain organs 2. turn inside [icy ill impersonal inaccessible individual inner inside interested intro intussuscept invaginate invert inward tend think timid toward transform transpose turn reality reclusive removed reserved reticent retract reverse revolve rotate offish organ ease ectomorph evert examine experience expressionless extrovert] "He introverted his feelings"
*intrude 11-40-17 (v.) 1. enter unlawfully on someone's property 2. enter uninvited 3. thrust oneself in as if by force [impose inflict infringe intervene invade irrupt noise thrust transgress trench trespass rock rude rule unauthorized uninvited unlawful unpleasant unwelcome upon usurp dinner disregard disturb down effect encroach enter entry] "They intruded on our dinner party"
*intrusion 09-47-23 (n.) 1. entrance by force or without permission or welcome 2. any entry into an area not previously occupied 3. rock produced by an intrusive process 4. the forcing of molten rock into fissures or between strata of an earlier rock formation 5. entry to another's property without right or permission [igneous illegal import imposition incoming incursion ingress inroad intervention invasion inward ion irrelevant natural nonconformity tourist transgresse transgression trespass reception right rock unlawful unsuitable untimely unwelcome upset usurp sandwich seepage solid stone strata subsequent occupy old overstep]
*intuition 14-51-9 (n.) 1. an impression that something might be the case 2. instinctive knowing (without the use of rational processes) [idea immediate impression inkling inner insight instinctive intimate nature notion truth tuition understand obtain opinion] "he had an intuition that something had gone wrong"
*inundate 11-55-16 (v.) 1. fill quickly beyond capacity; as with a liquid 2. fill or cover completely, usually with water [image immerse inroad invade underwater undone date deal deluge dip dribble drown duck afflict afloat aggrieve anguish awash torment embitter engulf escalade /tad/] "the basement was inundated after the storm"
*inundation 24-57-1 (n.) 1. the rising of a body of water and its overflowing onto normally dry land 2. an overwhelming number or amount [ice immersion ion irrigation natural deal deluge dip dry duck duration abuse accumulation alluvion alluvium amount annual aspersion avalanche tidal tidy torrent tumultuous overwhelming /tad/] "plains fertilized by annual inundations"
*inure 20-48-3 (v.) 1. cause to accept or become hardened to; habituate [impervious indurate insensitive naturalize unaccustomed unblushing unpleasant upset use usual regular effect emotional endure equable establish experience exposure /run/] "He was inured to the cold"
*inured 20-49-3 (a.) 1. made tough by habitual exposure [indurate unaccustomed usual regular endure enure equable exposure dark]
*invalid 11-50-16 (a.) 1. having no cogency or legal force 2. no longer valid (n.) 1. someone who is incapacitated by a chronic illness or injury (v.) 1. force to retire, remove from active duty, as of firemen 2. injure permanently [ill illegitimate illness inadequate incapacitate incorrect infirm injury nugatory nullify vain valid vicious victim void acceptable accident afflict ailing arthritic languish legal license logic loner long loose debilitate disable disorder drain driver duty]

"invalid reasoning"
*invalidate 13-30-11 (v.) 1. declare invalid 2. of cheques or tickets 3. show to be invalid 4. take away the legal force of or render ineffective [impugn incapacitate ineffective negative neutralize nullify vacate valid validate value vitiate void abate abolition abrogate alter annul avoid legal declare defeasance deflate deletion deny deprive different discredit dismiss dispute disqualify down thwart ticket transform explode expose /tad/]
*invaluable 08-69-27 (a.) 1. having incalculable monetary worth [important incalculable inestimable instrumental irreplaceable valuable value vital unique useful exchange extremely /aula/]
*invariable 24-66-1 (a.) 1. not liable to or capable of change [inert inflexible irrevocable never noble variable vary abiding affection agreement alike automatic regular rigid rule balance blah lasting level liable enduring equal even] "an invariable temperature"
*invasion 04-51-115 (n.) 1. any entry into an area not previously occupied 2. the act of invading; the act of an army that invades for conquest or plunder 3. (medicine) the spread of pathogenic microorganisms or malignant cells to new sites in the body [incursion infiltrate infringe injection interfere intervention intrusion inward ion non violation aggressive annex area armed army arrival assault assumption attack attempt science seizure site space species spoil spread stifling storm structure subjugation surround swarm obtrusion occupy offensive onslaught organism] "an invasion of tourists"
*invective 17-51-5 (n.) 1. abusive or venomous language used to express blame or censure or bitter deep-seated ill will [ill innuendo insult intend inveigh irony venomous vilify violent vitriol vituperation eulogy execrate execration exhortation expression caustic censure condemn counterblast criticism cynicism talkathon tirade truculent]
*inveigh 22-29-2 (v.) 1. complain bitterly 2. speak against, in an impassioned manner [impassioned express]
*inventive 06-50-45 (a.) 1. (used of persons or artifacts) marked by independence and creativity in thought or action [imaginative independence ingenious ingenuity innovative inspired invention nascent natal newness notional novelty vision vulpine elementary embryonic tactical teem tricky turn]
*inverse 17-54-5 (a.) 1. reversed (turned backward) in order or nature or effect 2. inversely related 3. (mathematics) varying in a manner opposite to that of another quantity (n.) 1. (math) one of a pair of numbers whose product is 1: the reciprocal of 2/3 is 3/2; the inverse of 7 is 1/7 2. something inverted in sequence or character or effect [inconsistent increase inimical invert nature negative variable vary verse vice effect element entity rather rear reciprocal relation repugnant reverse revert science sequence set setoff shape sum] "1/2 is the inverse of 2"
*inversion 20-53-3 (n.) 1. the layer of air near the earth is cooler than an overlying layer 2. the reversal of the normal order of words 3. (genetics) a kind of mutation in which the order of the genes in a section of a chromosome is reversed 4. abnormal condition in which an organ is turned inward or inside out (as when the upper part of the uterus is pulled into the cervical canal after childbirth) 5. the act of turning inside out 6. turning upside down; setting on end [interpolate involution notation version equation evert evolution extrapolate reduction reversion subtraction overturn]
*invert 13-52-11 (v.) 1. make an inversion (in a musical composition) 2. turn inside out or upside down [image incorporate inside interval introvert intussuscept invaginate inverse isomer nance negate note vert vice vocal evert resupinate retroversion reverse revert revolve rotate theme tone top transform transpose tribade turn] "here the theme is inverted"
*investigator 03-26-162 (n.) 1. a police officer who investigates crimes 2. someone who investigates 3. a scientist who devotes himself to doing research [inspector invest narc visitor examine eye scrutineer settlement sleuth tec tester gumshoe adjuster agent observer operative revenuer /git rota tag/]
*investor 01-56-561 (n.) 1. someone who commits capital in order to gain financial returns [income institution interest invest issue nominee venture expect saver security sell share sponsor stakeholder stockholder option organization outlook own rent resale return rise]
*inveterate 17-54-5 (a.) 1. having a habit of long standing [immovable immutable implant imprint incorrigible incurable ingrained instil venerable vested vital elder embed enduring entrench establish establishment thorough torpor tough traditional rate receive recognize remain rigid acknowledge adamant addicted admit age ancient antiquity /arete rete tare/]
*invidious 20-63-3 (a.) 1. containing or implying a slight or showing prejudice [imply impossible iniquitous insult nasty noxious vilify defame detestable difficult discriminatory distinction distrustful obnoxious odious offensive ornery undesirable unenviable unfavourable unjust unpleasant scandalous show sideline slander slight spiteful suspicious]
*invigorate 10-55-18 (v.) 1. heighten or intensify 2. make lively 3. impart vigor, strength, or vitality to 4. give life or energy to [imagination impart inflame infuse inspire inspirit interest nerve viable vigor vitality vitalize vivify galvanize ginger gird give gladden orate rally refresh refreshing reinforce rejuvenate renew revitalize revive room activate alert analeptic animate arouse temperate tonic toughen emotion encourage energy enliven exalt excite exhilarate /taro/]
*invincible 11-63-16 (a.) 1. incapable of being overcome or subdued [immortal impossible impregnable indestructible indomitable ingrained

insistent insurmountable invulnerable irrepressible irresistible valid vanquish vinci vincible calculable capable conquer constant continue lasting loyal enduring] "an invincible army"
*inviolable 22-38-2 (a.) 1. that cannot be transgressed or dishonored 2. not capable of being violated or infringed 3. able to withstand attack 4. must be kept sacred [immune impenetrable impregnable incapable indomitable infringe irresistible numinous venerable violate violence vulnerable oath old overwhelming long alienable attack awesome awful blessed breach broken] "the person of the king is inviolable"
*invoke 06-32-49 (v.) 1. cite as an authority; resort to 2. evoke or call forth, with or as if by magic 3. request earnestly (something from somebody); ask for aid or protection [idea image implore importune imprecate incite indent kick earnest effect emotion entreat evil evoke express]
*involuntary 13-38-10 (a.) 1. not subject to the control of the will 2. (physiology) controlled by the autonomic nervous system; without conscious control [incline inevitable inherent instinct instinctive natural necessary nervous vegetative volition voluntary obligatory oppose lack libido uncontrolled unintentional unplanned unthink unwilling unwitting toward asleep autonomic averse aware recalcitrant reflex reluctant require resistant] "involuntary manslaughter"
*involve 01-50-1417 (v.) 1. require as useful, just, or proper 2. have as a necessary feature or consequence; entail 3. engage as a participant 4. contain as a part 5. connect closely and often incriminatingly 6. make complex or intricate or complicated 7. occupy or engage the interest of 8. wrap [identify immerse imply include]
*invulnerable 18-42-4 (a.) 1. immune to attack; impregnable [immortal immune impenetrable impregnable indestructible indomitable injury inviolable irresistible vanquish vulnerable unable unassailable unbeatable unconquerable untouchable unyielding loss entrench rake redan reliable resistless risk airtight armed attack beach bombproof /bar bare/] "gunners raked the beach from invulnerable positions on the cliffs"
*inwardly 20-72-3 (ad.) 1. with respect to private feelings [injustice inland inside interior internal intimate inward naturally appearance rage respect deeply yourself /awn draw drawn/] "inwardly, she was raging"
*iota 20-58-3 (n.) 1. a tiny or scarcely detectable amount 2. the 9th letter of the Greek alphabet [indefinite ounce thimbleful tiny tittle trivia ace alphabet amount ancient atom average]
*irascible 16-62-6 (a.) 1. quickly aroused to anger 2. characterized by anger [ill infighting inflammable ira irritable response anger arouse sensitivity show snappy stuffy sullen cantankerous commander contrary cross crusty bearish belligerence bicker bitchy litigious easygoing edgy eruptive explosive /sari/]
*irate 13-52-10 (a.) 1. feeling or showing extreme anger [incense indicate indignant infuriate ireful irritate rage rate anger annoy enrage extreme] "irate protesters"
*ire 09-74-24 (n.) 1. a strong emotion; a feeling that is oriented toward some real or supposed grievance 2. belligerence aroused by a real or supposed wrong (personified as one of the deadly sins) [ill incense indignation infuriate intense ira irade irritation rage real resentment righteous emotion enrage entail]
*iridescent 17-40-5 (a.) 1. varying in color when seen in different lights or from different angles 2. having a play of lustrous rainbow-like colors [rainbow ready reflect dazzle delicate descent different dragonfly dull eggshell emit sad see shimmer shiny shot silk simple slick sparkle striking sweet chatoyant cloud colorful continuum creamy nacreous taffeta tender]
*irk 13-51-11 (v.) 1. irritate or vex [inconvenience irritate rankle resentful ride rile roil ruffle]
*irksome 18-65-4 (a.) 1. so lacking in interest as to cause mental weariness [importune interest irk irritate routine slight some speaker onerous oppressive mark mental edmund effect exasperate excitement exhaust]
*irony 05-62-81 (n.) 1. incongruity between what might be expected and what actually occurs 2. witty language used to convey insults or scorn 3. a trope that involves incongruity between what is expected and what occurs [ignorance image inappropriate inconsistency ingenuity innuendo insincerity insult invective involve iron remark opposite oxymoron nation non normal /nori/]
*irradiate 22-36-2 (v.) 1. give spiritual insight to; in religion 2. cast rays of light upon 3. expose to radiation [illumine improve infect inform insight inspire instruct intelligible radiate radiation ray ready refrigerate religion remedy reveal ripen rot ablaze activate aim alight dehydrate desiccate deteriorate divine down dry tinsel treatment electromagnetic embalm enlighten evaporate explain expose /darr/] "irradiate food"
*irrational 09-53-25 (a.) 1. not consistent with or using reason 2. (math) real but not expressible as the quotient of two integers [ignorance illogical impossible incoherent inconsistency inept infinite injury instead integer integral irregularity rabid radical rational real reasonless reckless relation ridiculous aberration abnormality absurd algorithm alienate aliquot animal thinker thoughtless touched transcendental odd oddness off ordinal negative non normal numeric lack loco logical long loose lunatic] "irrational fears"
*irreducible 24-42-1 (a.) 1. incapable of being made smaller or simpler [impossible inherent inner internal intricate radical rational reducible requisite resident edmund either essential exclusive expression decrease degree describe difficult uniform unique unquestionable capable chaste complicate bare basic lesser lone] "an irreducible minimum"
*irrelevant 06-59-56 (a.) 1. having no bearing on or connection with the subject at issue [immaterial

impertinent important improper inapt independence inept inferiority issue relevant extraneous extrinsic late little abnormality adrift alien allegation anomaly applicable negligible nonessential tangential technical /ave nave navel/] "an irrelevant comment"
*irreligious 24-73-1 (a.) 1. hostile or indifferent to religion [impious incredulous indifferent irreverent recidivism recreant religious renegade reverence lack lapse godless oppose unbelieving ungodly unholy sacrilegious show sinful]
*irreparable 14-46-8 (a.) 1. impossible to repair, rectify, or amend [impossible incurable irrevocable rectify reparable ruin amend beyond lasting lose /ape bar rape/] "irreparable harm"
*irrepressible 12-59-12 (a.) 1. impossible to repress or control [impossible incorrigible indomitable indulgent intractable rampant rein repress resist restrain ebullient enthusiastic exhilarate permissive pleasant smile sparkle sunny beam bubble buoyant laughter lax loose] "an irrepressible chatterbox"
*irresistible 06-60-46 (a.) 1. impossible to resist; overpowering 2. overpoweringly attractive [immovable impossible impulse inevitable interesting intrigue relentless reliable resistible resistless ruling effective entice entrance exciting eye seductive serious significant strong successful taking tantalizing telling tempting total beauty beguile bewitching blandish lovely luxurious /bit/] "irresistible (or resistless) impulses"
*irresolute 24-35-1 (a.) 1. uncertain how to act or proceed 2. lacking decisiveness of character; unable to act or decide quickly or firmly [impulsive incapable incertitude indecisive indeterminism infirm insipid inspiration irresponsible rambling random resolute resolve restless roving eccentric effeminate equivocation erratic settle shifty shuffling skeptical sleazy slight lack lightness luck unable unaccountable uncertain uncertainty undetermined unpredictable unsettled unsteady unsure tasteless tentative timid trait /lose loser/] "the committee was timid and mediocre and irresolute"
*irresponsible 07-52-39 (a.) 1. showing lack of care for consequences [idiot idle immature immune imprudent impulsive incapable ineffectual rash reckless release require responsible restless eccentric excuse exempt scatterbrain shifty show shuffling slaphappy spare permit personal privilege negligent lack lawless legal licentious loose] "behaved like an irresponsible idiot"
*irreverence 18-43-4 (n.) 1. an irreverent mental attitude 2. a disrespectful act [immoral impertinent impudent iniquity respect reverent ridicule value violation certain character cheek complex contempt]
*irreverent 10-48-18 (a.) 1. showing lack of due respect or veneration 2. not revering god 3. characterized by a lightly pert and exuberant quality [immoral impertinent impious impudent insolent insulting recidivism recreant renegade respect revere reverent ridicule rude ease exhibit exuberant value veneration vigor violation tourist /ever/] "irreverent scholars mocking sacred things"
*irreversible 12-47-12 (a.) 1. impossible to reverse or be reversed 2. impossible to reverse or undo [implant impossible incapable ingrained instil retract reverse reversible revolution rooted ruin establish set shakespeare straightway lasting lose /ever/] "irreversible momentum toward revolution"
*irrevocable 13-51-10 (a.) 1. impossible to retract or revoke [immutable imperative impossible inescapable inevitable inexorable relentless require retract revocable revoke right ruin enduring entail establish obligatory capable certainly clean compulsory conclusive constant absolutely annul binding lasting lose /cove cover over/] "firm and irrevocable is my doom"
*irrigate 12-42-14 (v.) 1. supply with water, as with channelsor ditches or streams 2. supply with a constant flow or sprinkling of some liquid, for the purpose of cooling, cleansing, or disinfecting [immersion inundation rarefy reduce refresh reveal rinse run gargle gate ground grow ablution adulterate agriculture area aspersion attenuate thin treatment tub erode /tag/]
*irritable 12-69-12 (a.) 1. easily irritated or annoyed 2. (physiology) capable of responding to stimuli 3. (pathology) abnormally sensitive to a stimulus [ill impatient incorrigible inflammation insensitive irascible itch raspy refined responsive table techy temper temperamental tender testy tetchy touchy abnormal aggressive allergic annoy apprehensive bad bearish belligerent bicker biology branch least litigious easy edgy effect eruptive exasperate excitable explosive extremely]
*irritant 14-57-9 (n.) 1. something that causes irritation and annoyance [inflict irascible responsive rita temper testy thorn touchy trouble abnormal aggravation annoy ass neck nuisance]
*irritate 05-67-61 (v.) 1. excite to an abnormal condition, of chafe or inflame 2. cause annoyance in; disturb, esp. by minor irritations 3. physiology and biology: excite to some characteristic action or condition, as motion, contraction, or nervous impulse, by the application of a stimulus [impulse increase inflammation infuriate injure intensify irk irksome irritative itch rack rag rankle rasping raw reaction really red relieve rent resentful response rile rita rough rub ruffle tear tease tender tog torment trouble try twist abnormal acerbic acid aggravate alienate anger annoy antagonize enhance enlarge exacerbate exasperate excessive excite exercise extreme]
*isle 05-87-79 (n.) 1. a small island [insular island sandbar southern surround land literary english]
*islet 20-68-3 (n.) 1. a small island [island isle southern spain surround land let english]
*isolate 04-46-123 (v.) 1. set apart from others 2. obtain in pure form, in chemistry or medicine 3. place or set

apart 4. psychology: separate (experiences) fromt he emotions relating to them [ignore independent individual insulate interior island screen secret segregate separate sequestrate set sort special split strange ostracize other outlandish late leave life lonesome lop abandon abstract alone apart avoid takeout thrash transport eliminate exceptional exclude exile exotic] "They isolated the political prisoners from the other inmates"
*itinerant 14-47-8 (a.) 1. traveling from place to place to work 2. working for a short time in different places (n.) 1. an itinerant laborer who works for a short time in various places [india itinerary tour traipse travel trek troubadour nomad nomadic non northern engage errantry establish expeditionary rambling range rant road roam rom romany rover roving ambulatory australian] "itinerant labor"
*itinerary 09-56-24 (n.) 1. an established line of travel or access 2. a guidebook for travelers 3. a proposed route of travel [index intend tine tour track trader traffic transport traverse newspaper northern nucleus east electron elliptical record regular revolution rocket round route run access advance aircraft airline airport airway america approach atlantic atom /rare/]

J

*jabber 22-57-2 (n.) 1. rapid and indistinct speech (v.) 1. talk in a noisy, excited, or declamatory manner [jargon jaw jay jib abb absurdity amphigory babble blabbermouth blather bombast bullshit excite express rabbit ramble rant rapid rattle rave rigmarole rubbish /ebb/]
*jagged 11-48-15 (a.) 1. having a sharply uneven surface or outline 2. having an irregularly notched or toothed margin as though gnawed [jag angular gnaw edge erose distant draw /egg/] "the jagged outline of the crags"
*jargon 10-58-20 (n.) 1. a characteristic language of a particular group (as among thieves) 2. specialized technical terminology characteristic of a particular subject 3. a colorless (or pale yellow or smoky) variety of zircon [jabberwocky jumble abracadabra absurdity argon argot rant refer rhyme ripoff road rod rot rubbish gab gangster garble gibberish offensive noise nonsense /nog raj/]
*jaundice 17-59-5 (n.) 1. yellowing of the skin and the whites of the eyes caused by an accumulation of bile pigment (bilirubin) in the blood; can be a symptom of gallstones or liver infection or anemia 2. a sharp and bitter manner (v.) 1. distort adversely 2. affect with, or as if with, jaundice [jalousie jealousy judgment abnormal accumulation acerbity acrimony adverse affect alter amount anemia asphyxiate asthma atrophy attitude unfavorable unfriendly nausea necrosis neon nerve newborn damage deform diarrhea dice disapprove disease dishonest disposition distort distrustful dizzy duct icterus illness illtempered immature inclination infant infection invidious itch chill cirrhosis colored condition convulsion corrupt cough critical cynical edema emaciate embitter envy eye] "Jealousy had jaundiced his judgment"
*jeopardize 09-AA-25 (v.) 1. put at risk 2. pose a threat to; present a danger to [jeopardy endanger entire existence expose extant pard peril pollution pose present adventure reputation risk damage danger destroy imperil indiscretion]
*jettison 12-54-14 (v.) 1. throw away, of something encumbering 2. throw as from an airplane [jilt junk eliminate encumber equipment exclude expel thrown toss turnout idea iso scrap shed ship slough obtrusion oust]
*jibe 15-66-7 (n.) 1. an aggressive remark directed at a person like a missile and intended to have a telling effect (v.) 1. be compatible, similar or consistent;

coincide in their characteristics 2. shift from one side of the ship to the other [jib identical improve inspection insult intend intersect barb bear behind belief beseem boat break effect equal evidence express]
*jocular 18-54-4 (a.) 1. characterized by jokes and good humor (ad.) 1. with humor [jesting jocose joke jokey jolly josh jovial joy ocular clever comical laughter levity lighthearted ludicrous amusement rejoicing risible roguish] "they tried to deal with this painful subject jocularly"
*joust 14-56-9 (n.) 1. a combat between two mounted knights tilting against each other with blunted lances (v.) 1. joust against somebody in a tournament by fighting on horseback [jostle oust unseat scramble series spar squabble strive struggle televise test tilt tournament trial try]
*jovial 14-62-9 (a.) 1. full of or showing high-spirited merriment [jocund jolly josh joy joyful joyous old vial affable amiable amusement lark laughter levity lighthearted]
*jubilant 12-49-13 (a.) 1. joyful and proud especially because of triumph or success 2. full of high-spirited delight [joy joyful joyless joyous achievement ant thrill transported triumphant]
*jubilation 16-56-6 (n.) 1. a feeling of extreme joy 2. a joyful occasion for special festivities to mark some happy event 3. the utterance of sounds expressing great joy [joy joyful joyous jubilee uninhibited utter banquet ion affair auditory treat triumph occasion /tali/]
*judgment 03-55-197 (n.) 1. the legal document stating the reasons for a judicial decision 2. the capacity to assess situations or circumstances shrewdly and to draw sound conclusions 3. the act of judging or assessing a person or situation or event 4. the cognitive process of reaching a decision or drawing conclusions 5. (law) the determination by a court of competent jurisdiction on matters submitted to it 6. an opinion formed by judging something 7. ability to make good judgments [judicious justice decision decree default desert determination discrimination dismissal document good gumption mind mystique ethos evaluation eye nature nemesis new notion theory thinking] "he was reluctant to make his judgment known"
*judicial 05-43-74 (a.) 1. decreed by or proceeding from a court of justice 2. expressing careful judgment 3. belonging or appropriate to the office of a judge 4. relating to the administration of justice or the function of a judge [judgment judgmental judi judicious jurist just decision decree dennet discriminatory distinguishing duty impartial careful censure constitutional court critical accept adjudicate administration analytic applicable appropriate authorize law lawmaker legal legitimate /laic/] "a judicial decision"
*judiciary 07-31-44 (n.) 1. persons who administer justice 2. the system of law courts that administer justice and constitute the judicial branch of government [judgment judgmental judi judicious justice unify unite department dispense independent inquisition interrelated central committee comprise concern constitute country court critical curia administration authority regime responsible]
*judicious 12-48-12 (a.) 1. characterized by good judgment or sound thinking 2. proceeding from good sense or judgment 3. marked by the exercise of good judgment or common sense in practical matters [journalism judgment judgmental judi judiciary juristic just uncommunicative understanding decision delicacy diplomatic discriminating discriminative dispassion impartial imprudent inadvisable insightful intelligent irresponsible calm careful cautious choice clever consider control critical objective safe sagacious sensible sensitivity show shrewd smart soft sound stability steady suggest] "judicious journalism"
*juggle 08-56-33 (n.) 1. the act of rearranging things to give a misleading impression 2. throwing and catching several objects simultaneously (v.) 1. influence by slyness 2. deal with simultaneously 3. juggle an account, for example, so as to hide a deficit 4. throw, catch, and keep in the air several things simultaneously [job jug gammon give grip guile gull letdown life load entertainment extract] "She had to juggle her job and her children"
*jugular 20-65-3 (a.) 1. relating to or located in the region of the neck or throat (n.) 1. veins in the neck that return blood from the head 2. a vital part that is vulnerable to attack [join junction gula locate lower anatomy arise attack auricular region rest retro return /lug/] "jugular vein"
*juicy 08-53-29 (a.) 1. (informal) lucrative 2. having strong sexual appeal 3. full of juice 4. suggestive of sexual impropriety [job joke unfledged unformed unprofitable unripe unsex icy imitate immaturity impropriety inexperience infancy innocent interesting intrigue callow colloquial colorful communicate contract yielding yummy] "juicy barmaids"
*junction 09-69-26 (n.) 1. the place where two or more things come together 2. a place where two things come together 3. the shape or manner in which things come together and a connection is made 4. an act of joining or adjoining things 5. something that joins or connects 6. the state of being joined together [joint jointure juncture unction unification union unite natural neuron cable circular close colligate conductor confluence conjugation connection connexion construction continuous convergence crossway thermocouple topography touch traffic trot tubular incorporate increase inosculate intersection inventory island]
*juncture 13-38-11 (n.) 1. an event that occurs at a critical time 2. the shape or manner in which things come together and a connection is made 3. a crisis situation or point in time when a critical decision must be made [joint jun junction unfold union unique

unstable natural neck nuclear climax combination come company conceive condition confluence connection course crisis critical crucial terminal tide turn rabbet reaction realize recognize elbow embrace emergency epithelium esophagus extreme] "at such junctures he always had an impulse to leave"
*junta 13-31-10 (n.) 1. a clique that seeks power usually through intrigue [jun junction junto unification union team tribunal troop addition agreement assembly association]
*juridical 24-36-1 (a.) 1. of or relating to the law or jurisprudence 2. relating to the administration of justice or the function of a judge [judge judgmental judicial judicious just righteous rightful ical day competent constitutional critical actionable administration applicable authorize law lawmaker legal legitimate /acid/] "juridical days"
*jurisdiction 06-30-47 (n.) 1. (law) the right and power to interpret and apply the law 2. in law; the territory within which power can be exercised [judgment justiciar range reach record region right rule imperium impose influence interpret say string subdivision supervise delegation department diction diocese district dominion caliph care charge circuit collection commit control task territory trial tutelage office orbit oversight] "courts having jurisdiction in this district"
*jurisprudence 18-41-4 (n.) 1. the branch of philosophy concerned with the law and the principles that lead courts to make the decisions they do 2. the collection of rules imposed by authority [remit impound intern prude /psi/]
*juror 07-22-43 (n.) 1. someone who serves (or waits to be called to serve) on a jury [judge jurywoman oath]
*justification 07-57-43 (n.) 1. a statement in explanation of some action or belief 2. something (such as a fact or circumstance) that shows an action to be reasonable or necessary 3. the act of defending or explaining or making excuses for by reasoning [just saint sanctify show sin slug space statement structure support imposition fact furniture canonize cation cause censure circumstance comprehensible condition confirmation consider criticism absolve account adjustment alignment apologia attitude operation necessary nemesis /fit/] "he considered misrule a justification for revolution"
*juvenile 07-42-42 (a.) 1. of or relating to or characteristic of or appropriate for children 2. displaying or suggesting a lack of maturity (n.) 1. a youthful person [jejune joke junior juvenescent unfledged unripe unsophisticated villain volume earth nestle nile nipper notebook novel immature individual infantile ingenue innocent insecurity intend lack life /lin line/] "juvenile diabetes"
*juxtapose 10-34-20 (v.) 1. place side by side [join junction union unite abstract accumulate addition adjacent adjoining alongside amass apposition assembly association pair partner pattern perihelion physical place pose position put occupy set shape side space strong suffix suggest supplement survey emphasize endwise /pat/] "The fauvists juxtaposed strong colors"
*juxtaposition 12-34-13 (n.) 1. the act of positioning close together (or side by side) 2. a side-by-side position [apposition association pattern physical placement portion position occupy shape sidebyside space /itis pat/] "it is the result of the juxtaposition of contrasting colors"

K

*keepsake 22-43-2 (n.) 1. something of sentimental value [keep entity evoke party physical sentimental shadow souvenir /asp peek/]
*ken 03-52-149 (n.) 1. range of what one can know or understand 2. the range of vision [knowledge expertise eye eyesight notice] "beyond my ken"
*kerchief 24-12-1 (n.) 1. a square scarf that is folded into a triangle and worn over the head or about the neck [chief head fold]
*kernel 15-40-7 (n.) 1. the inner and usually edible part of a seed or grain or nut or fruit stone 2. a single whole grain of a cereal 3. the choicest or most essential or most vital part of some idea or experience [kerne key keystone kind edible electron element elixir epicenter equator essential experience range reality reside resource root nature navel never nitty nub nucleus nut landmark learn linseed lose] "black walnut kernels are difficult to get out of the shell"
*kiln 18-52-4 (n.) 1. a large oven for firing or burning or drying such things as porcelain or bricks [kitchen industrial inner insolate lime low naturally]
*kilometer 10-46-19 (n.) 1. a metric unit of length equal to 1000 meters (or 0.621371 miles) [kiloliter klick inch league length linear link meter metric micron mile myriametre ell equal term thousand rod /mol rete/]
*kilowatt 17-22-5 (n.) 1. a unit of power equal to 1000 watts [kilo ohm watt across ampere]
*kimono 16-46-6 (n.) 1. a loose robe; imitated from robes originally worn by Japanese [imitate mono origin negligee]
*kingship 24-70-1 (n.) 1. the dignity or rank or position of a king [king knighthood imperium influence say sovereignty status supremacy sway hegemony height high palm position power presidency]
*knead 16-48-6 (v.) 1. make uniform 2. usually for medicinal or relaxation purposes [knockout nose nuzzle ease emulsify admix alloy amalgamate dough down] "knead dough"
*knickknack 22-15-2 (n.) 1. miscellaneous curios [kickshaw knack nicknack notion novelty inexpensive cent class club collect cosmetic curiosity agate artifact /can ink/]
*knight 03-72-138 (n.) 1. originally a person of noble birth trained to arms and chivalry; today in Great Britain a person honored by the sovereign for personal merit 2. a chessman in the shape of a horse's head; can move two squares horizontally and one vertically (or vice versa)

(v.) 1. raise (someone) to knighthood 2. invest with knighthood; make of knight of [king night nobility noble non idle gallant game gentle give gladiator graduate great group head history hold holy honor hoodlum hooligan horizontal horse horsewoman table templar tenant thug title today tough train travel /gin gink ink/] "The Beatles were knighted"
*knighthood 13-91-10 (n.) 1. aristocrats holding the rank of knight [kingship knight nobility generalship group hereditary heroism hold honor title occupation duke /gin gink ink/]
*knit 06-48-56 (n.) 1. a fabric made by knitting 2. a basic knitting stitch 3. needlework created by interlacing yarn in a series of connected loops using straight eyeless needles or by machine (v.) 1. tie or link together 2. make (textiles) by knitting 3. to gather something into small wrinkles or folds [knot narrow natural neck needlework net nip nit noose infant interweave isthmus item textile texture thickness thread tie tighten tissue trim twist /ink tink/] "knit a scarf"
*knotty 17-36-5 (a.) 1. making great mental demands; hard to comprehend or solve 2. highly involved or intricate 3. used of old persons or old trees; covered with knobs or knots [knob knot knurly needlework negotiation nodal nodose nubby obfuscate obscure old operose tangle tax terrible thorny tie tortuous tough tree tricky /ton tonk/]

L

*laborious 14-50-9 (a.) 1. characterized by toilsome effort to the point of exhaustion; especially physical effort [labor labored lengthy ardent arduous assiduous backbreaking break brutal burdensome onerous oppressive overwork relentless require rigorous rough indefatigable industrious intricate unremitting unsparing unwavering unwelcome uphill sedulous severe show sign speech steady steep strenuous /rob/]
*labyrinth 13-55-10 (n.) 1. complex system of paths or tunnels in which it is easy to get lost 2. a complex system of interconnecting cavities; concerned with hearing and equilibrium [loop lose aby angle apparatus artery artifact auditory basilar bodily bone bony branch build ravel receptor respond right impulse include inner interrelated nearly nerve nose temporal tube tunnel hearing]
*labyrinthine 16-56-6 (a.) 1. relating to or affecting or originating in the inner ear 2. highly involved or intricate 3. resembling a labyrinth in form or complexity [labyrinth language lasting legal lofty lopsided lurid affecting askew asymmetric backstreet bent billowy bow byzantine rambling reason receptor refined rhetorical ruffle indirect inner internal intricate involved needlework negotiation network tall tangle tax tortuous turning twisty highly ear elaborate elevated erratic extremely] "labyrinthine deafness"
*lacerate 15-52-7 (a.) 1. irregularly slashed and jagged as if torn 2. having edges that are jagged from injury (v.) 1. cut or tear irregularly 2. deeply hurt the feelings of; distress [lacer leaf lesion abrasion abrupt abscission afflict aggravate agonized ail amputate check chip chop crack cut edge embitter emotional enucleate exacerbate excision excruciate rack ragged remark rent rip rough rub run rupture tear tearing torment torture trauma twist /tare/] "lacerate leaves"
*lachrymose 24-72-1 (a.) 1. showing sorrow [lachrymal lacrimatory loss cry rheumy mark mournful move sad secrete seminal show sob sorrowful easily excrete experience express]
*lackadaisical 20-40-3 (a.) 1. lacking spirit or liveliness 2. idle or indolent especially in a dreamy way [laissez languorous lax lay lazy lethargic limp linger lively afternoon alert annoying apathetic ataractic attempt careless casual cold cool dais dead deficient delay dull idle impractical inactive indifferent indolent sentimental shuffling slapdash slow spiritless /dak kcal/] "a lackadaisical attempt"

*lackluster 12-AA-12 (a.) 1. lacking brilliance or vitality 2. lacking luster or shine [leaden lifeless light little lively lurid luster lustreless anemic animation ashen ashy cadaverous uncolored undistinguished unexciting uninspiring sallow shine sickly somber tame tarnish tedious toneless emit energy enthusiasm etiolated excite eye reflect respectable rusty /kcal sulk/] "a dull lackluster life"
*laconic 14-59-9 (a.) 1. brief and to the point; effectively cut short [abbreviate abridge almost concise conic contract crisp curt cut]
*lactic 22-75-2 (a.) 1. of or relating to or obtained from milk (especially sour milk or whey) [acid act] "lactic acid"
*laddie 24-82-1 (n.) 1. a male child (a familiar term of address to a boy) [lad add address adolescent /dal/]
*ladle 16-43-6 (n.) 1. a spoon-shaped vessel with a long handle; used to transfer liquids (v.) 1. put (a liquid) into a container by means of a ladle 2. remove with or as if with a ladle; of liquids [lad lade laden lie lift liquid location long abstract appendage decant deep design dip dipper /dal/] "ladle soup into the bowl"
*laggard 18-42-4 (a.) 1. inclined to waste time and lag behind 2. wasting time (n.) 1. someone who takes more time than necessary; someone who lags behind [lag lax lazybones leisurely linger loafer loiter long aimless apathetic appointed gar goldbrick grudging reluctant remiss restive dawdle delay deliberate dilatory doodle drone /drag gal rag/]
*lambaste 12-69-12 (v.) 1. beat with a cane 2. censure severely or angrily [lash lather lecture lick lie admonish aggression angrily apart attack maul mother bang baste batter bawl beat berate best bring scold settle severe slate smear smother soup stranger strong tell thrash thump trim trounce enter excoriate express]
*lament 05-48-60 (n.) 1. a cry of sorrow and grief 2. a song or hymn of mourning composed or performed as a memorial to a dead person 3. a mournful poem; a lament for the dead (v.) 1. express grief verbally 2. regret strongly [lack languish line loud agony ament anguish annoyance memorial metrical misery moan mourning musical mutter elegy emotion expression threnody tirade] "their pitiful laments could be heard throughout the ward"
*landholder 24-29-1 (n.) 1. a holder or proprietor of land [lease lithosphere lordship acre alluvium noble dirt dryland dust hold holder occupant occupy own owner ownership english]
*landlord 05-50-70 (n.) 1. a landowner who leases to others [laird land landowner lease lessor licensee lodge lord accommodation apartment duplex offering organization owner receptionist rent rentier run /old/]
*landmark 04-40-112 (n.) 1. an event marking a unique or important historical change or one on which important developments depend 2. the position of a prominent or well-known object in a particular landscape 3. a mark showing the boundary of a piece of land 4. an anatomical structure used as a point of origin in locating other anatomical structures (as in surgery) or as point from which measurements can be taken [land law life lightship location adam anatomical apostle arrest notable noteworthy nub damascus death depend development disease driving major mark mear measurement meat medical meer merestone milestone momentous monument mythology radical recognize reference represent revolutionary road ruling kernel keystone knowledge] "the church steeple provided a convenient landmark"
*landscape 03-48-205 (n.) 1. painting depicting an expanse of natural scenery 2. a genre of art dealing with the depiction of natural scenery 3. an expanse of scenery that can be seen in a single view (v.) 1. embellish with plants 2. do landscape gardening [lay lookout adorn alter appearance aspect deal decorate design diorama scape scenery seascape shrub sight site situation spent sweep cityscape cloudscape combine contour countryside create panorama perspective plant plot produce prospect embellish environment exterior]
*languid 12-60-12 (a.) 1. lacking spirit or liveliness [lack lazy leisurely lethargic limp lively lumber afternoon alert aloof amble anemic attempt nap nod numb gentle gesture gradual guid unconcerned unhurried uninterested unnerve idle impotent indifferent indolent dead deficient deliberate droopy drowsy dull]
*languor 22-42-2 (n.) 1. a relaxed comfortable feeling 2. a feeling of lack of interest or energy 3. inactivity; showing an unusual lack of energy [lack languish lassitude lazy leisurely lethargy listless abeyance absence anemia apathy atmosphere unusual oppressive refreshing relaxed reluctance remain]
*lapse 06-49-54 (n.) 1. a failure to maintain a higher state 2. a break or intermission in the occurrence of something 3. a mistake resulting from inattention (v.) 1. end, at least for a long time 2. drop to a lower level; as in one's morals or standards 3. go back to bad behavior 4. pass into a specified state or condition 5. pass by, as of time 6. let slip [law layoff least less let letter level long lose lower lull advance antique apostate apse assumption atheistic atrocity attribute participle pass past pause period physical plunge point practice previous proceed profane progress property sacrilegious set significance sink slide slip space spatial specify standard stay stop suspension swinish earthy end erring error erstwhile evil exercise expire /pal spa/] "a lapse of three weeks between letters"
*larceny 13-15-10 (n.) 1. the act of taking something from someone unlawfully [less locale actually amount appropriation arc article avoid awful removal robbery care cattle collection corporation crime embezzle entrust]
*largess 20-02-3 (n.) 1. a gift or money given (as for service or out of benevolence); usually given

ostentatiously 2. extremely liberal generosity of spirit [liberal acquire generous gift give extremely service spirit]
*lascivious 18-66-4 (a.) 1. driven by lust; preoccupied with or exhibiting lustful desires [lewd libidinous lover lurid lust animal appetite ardent arouse secular sensual sensuous sex sexy show somatic carnal coarse concupiscence corporeal impassioned indecent interest itch vile voluptuous obscene offensive orgastic orgy unsex]
*lassie 22-61-2 (n.) 1. a girl or young woman who is unmarried [lady lassi adolescent sexual sock]
*lassitude 24-47-1 (n.) 1. a state of comatose torpor (as found in sleeping sickness) 2. weakness characterized by a lack of vitality or energy 3. a feeling of lack of interest or energy [lack lassi lethargy liability lifeless listless absence accompany anemia apathy atony sensibility sickness sleeping slow sluggish soft strain stress suspension impotent inactivity inanition indifference inertia insouciance interest tedium tired torpor unconcern depression disregard dull emotion enfeeble ennui enthusiasm exhaustion]
*latent 14-52-8 (a.) 1. not presently active 2. potentially existing but not presently evident or realized [late leaden lifeless lurk abstruse actual apathetic arcane talent tame tent torpid eclipse embryonic enigmatic esoteric evident exist express non] "a latent fingerprint"
*later 01-52-1554 (a.) 1. more advanced in time or nearer to the end in a sequence 2. coming at a subsequent time or stage 3. at or toward an end or late period or stage of development (ad.) 1. at some eventual time in the future 2. happening at a time subsequent to a reference time 3. comparative of the adverb 'late' [language last late latish latter lineal literature advance afterward age alive antecedent apologize appointment approach argument arrear attendant tardy then therewith tomorrow toward train trip ensue enter eventual expect extrapolate recent reference ripe]
*lateral 12-63-13 (a.) 1. situated at or extending to the side 2. lying away from the median and sagittal plane of a body (n.) 1. a pass to a receiver upfield from the passer [later lee lemniscus light locate low lying accent adjacent affect alveolar appendage aspiration assimilation teammate tennyson thick throw tip tongue top toss touch transfer tree edge explosive extend receiver retroflex ridge rounded] "the lateral branches of a tree"
*lattice 17-49-5 (n.) 1. an arrangement of points or particles or objects in a regular periodic pattern in 2 or 3 dimensions 2. framework consisting of an ornamental design made of strips of wood or metal 3. small opening (like a window in a door) through which business can be transacted [lace lantern light arabesque arrange atom attic texture thin tissue tracery transact trellis interweave ion cadre cancellation classify climb compose crisscross crystal cycle /citta/]
*laud 07-51-35 (v.) 1. praise, glorify, or honor [lift lionize literary lofty acclaim admire advance answer approval aside august day deify distinguished doxology /dual/]
*laudable 14-60-9 (a.) 1. worthy of high praise [able admirable advantageous auspicious unexceptionable unworthy useful deserve benevolent bonny braw effort elegant environment excellent exemplary /bad dual/] "applaudable efforts to save the environment"

*laudatory 22-28-2 (a.) 1. full of or giving praise [laud acclamation admiring approve uncomplimenta raving remark /dual rota tad/] "a laudatory remark"
*laundress 24-31-1 (n.) 1. a working woman who takes in washing [live undress dated earn]
*laureate 09-55-23 (a.) 1. worthy of the greatest honor or distinction (n.) 1. someone honored for great achievements; figuratively someone crowned with a laurel wreath [leader leaf librettist lie literary accomplishment ace achievement appointed art aureate award recipient recognition rhapsodist royal ruler elegist] "The nation's pediatrician laureate is preparing to lay down his black bag"
*lavish 05-55-76 (a.) 1. very generous 2. characterized by extravagance and profusion (v.) 1. expend profusely; also used with abstract nouns [landslide leader liberal lot lush luxurious luxury abstract abundant accord affluent aid allow aplenty attention avalanche avis award vouchsafe immoderate impart imposing incontinent inexhaustible intemperate issue serve share shower slip snow spend squander stingy stream substantial suggestive sumptuous half hand handsomely heap hospitable] "distributed gifts with a lavish hand"
*lawmaker 05-04-83 (n.) 1. a maker of laws; someone who gives a code of laws [law lawgiver leader legislator legislature act alderman almost assemblyman athenian authority way whip maker enact execution representative rule]
*lax 10-42-19 (a.) 1. lacking in rigor or strictness 2. lacking in strength or firmness or resilience 3. tolerant or lenient 4. (phonetics) pronounced with muscles relatively relaxed (e.g., the vowel sound in 'bet') 5. not taut or rigid; not stretched or held tight 6. emptying easily or excessively [lack lapse last lay lenient light limp liquid little long loose low abandon accept acceptance acoustics admission allow analysis attend] "such lax and slipshod ways are no longer acceptable"
*laxative 22-63-2 (a.) 1. stimulating evacuation of feces (n.) 1. a mild cathartic [lax lower acid agar alkalinity aloes aperient titration trade indicator irritate various emetic evacuation /tax vita/]
*lea 10-78-18 (n.) 1. a unit of length of thread or yarn 2. a field covered with grass or herbage and suitable for grazing by livestock [land last lengthy ley lifer linear literary livestock earth equal area average]

*leaflet 08-70-29 (n.) 1. a thin triangular flap of a heart valve 2. a small book usually having a paper cover 3. part of a compound leaf [lamina leaf lemma advert flag flap flier flow flyer folder foliage free tear thin ticket tissue tract transpire triangular]
*leaven 16-44-6 (n.) 1. a substance used to produce fermentation in dough or a liquid 2. an influence that works subtly to lighten or modify something (v.) 1. cause to puff up with a leaven; of dough [leave lift lighten limit liquid literary lower effect elevate enliven abate accurate add agent assess assuage atmosphere various narrow] "unleavened bread"
*leeward 22-57-2 (a.) 1. on the side away from the wind (ad.) 1. toward the wind (n.) 1. the direction in which the wind is blowing 2. the side of something that is sheltered from the wind [lateral lee lees leftward earthward expose ward widdershins wind windward alee anticlockwise aweather relation rightward direction downwind /drawee/] "on the leeward side of the island"
*legacy 04-54-114 (n.) 1. (law) a gift of personal property by will [law leftover leg effect entail estate generation gift acquire authority codicil collection compensation consequent corollary currency /age cage/]
*legalize 11-AA-17 (v.) 1. make legal [law lawful legal legitimize let license enable enact entitle establish give govern allow authorize introduce /age lag/] "Marijuana should be legalized"
*legerdemain 24-28-1 (n.) 1. an illusory feat; considered magical by naive observers [leger entertainment execution resourceful dazzle deception deft dexterous display magical manual music acuity adroit agility art illusory ingenuity naive nimble /dreg/]

*legging 17-66-5 (n.) 1. a garment covering the leg (usually extending from the knee to the ankle) [laborer leather leg lower egg elastic extend gaiter garment instep insulate]
*legible 18-43-4 (a.) 1. (of handwriting, print, etc.) able to be read [enough gib intelligible /big/] "legible handwriting"
*legislate 11-58-15 (v.) 1. make laws, bills, etc. or bring into effect by legislation [law legalize legitimize logroll effect enact establish sanction slate spend superior amend authorize table]
*legislative 04-14-98 (a.) 1. of or relating to or created by legislation 2. relating to a legislature or composed of members of a legislature [law lawmaker legal legitimate enact general government sanction senatorial slat solution statutory actionable applicable assembly authorize valid /vita vital vitals/] "legislative council"
*legislator 05-07-86 (n.) 1. someone who makes or enacts laws [law lawgiver lawmaker leader long lower effort elder elect enact enforce engage give government impose induna selectman senate senator slat speech strategy supervisor administration alderman appointed archon assembly assemblyman authority obstruct opposition organize reeve regular representative rule /rota/]
*legitimacy 09-42-25 (n.) 1. lawfulness by virtue of being authorized or in accordance with law 2. undisputed credibility [law lawful legality legit genuine trustworthy mccoy acceptable accordance attribute authorize conform correct credible /amit tig/]
*legitimate 04-43-126 (a.) 1. authorized, sanctioned by, or in accordance with law 2. in accordance with recognized or accepted standards or principles 3. in accordance with reason or logic 4. of marriages and offspring; recognized as lawful (v.) 1. make legal 2. make (an illegitimate child) legitimate; declare the legitimacy of (someone) 3. show or affirm to be just and legitimate [land law lawful lawmaker lefthand legal legit legitimize let licit literal logical endow excuse exempt genuine good government ground inoffensive invalid tax tender theatrical thespian true trustworthy marry mccoy melodramatic milk modify monetize morganatic movie accept acceptable accordance acknowledge admissible advert affirm allow allowable alter applicable appropriate art attribute authorize /amit tig/]
*leisure 04-79-98 (a.) 1. free from duties or responsibilities (n.) 1. freedom to choose a pastime or enjoyable activity 2. time available for ease and relaxation [lack last left liberty little lumpen ease engage enjoyable ida idle inactive sculptor semiretired spare strain sure unemployed unhurried unoccupied relaxation relief require responsibility rest resting retired] "he writes in his leisure hours"
*leniency 14-45-9 (n.) 1. mercifulness as a consequence of being lenient or tolerant 2. a disposition to yield to the wishes of someone 3. lightening a penalty or excusing from a chore by judges or parents or teachers [len lessen lightening loosen lull ease endurance excuse negligence impotent indifference indulgence calm charge charity child choice chore clemency compassion concern consequence yield]
*lenient 11-54-15 (a.) 1. tolerant or lenient 2. not strict 3. characterized by tolerance and mercy [lax len light little loose easy easygoing effort enduring negligent impotent incline indifferent indulgent tactful teacher temperate thoughtful tolerant tolerate]
*leonine 24-53-1 (a.) 1. of or characteristic of or resembling a lion [leo leon lion imposing impressive]
*lethargic 15-51-7 (a.) 1. deficient in alertness or activity [lackluster languorous lazy lifeless listless logy energy enervate exert exhaust tired torpid heartless hopeless alert aloof apathetic arg resigned groggy idle inactive indifferent indolent catalepsy cold comatose /cig/] "bullfrogs became lethargic with the first cold nights"
*lethargy 16-61-6 (n.) 1. weakness characterized by a lack of vitality or energy 2. a state of comatose torpor (as found in sleeping sickness) 3. inactivity; showing an

unusual lack of energy [lack languor lassitude lazy liability lifeless listless elation enthusiasm euphoria exhaustion tired torpor trance twitch heavy high hopeless abstraction alienate aloof arg remain gross yawn]
*levee 17-32-5 (n.) 1. a barrier constructed to contain the flow of water or to keep out the sea [land large logjam low earthwork egypt eisteddfod embankment erect eve]
*lever 09-54-23 (n.) 1. a rigid bar pivoted about a fulcrum 2. a simple machine that gives a mechanical advantage when given a fulcrum 3. a flat metal tumbler in a lever lock (v.) 1. to move or force, esp. in an effort to get something open [last lid lift limb load lock log early effort elevator engine erector ever valve vehicle raise resistance rigid ripping rocker roll rudder /revel/]
*leviathan 18-74-4 (n.) 1. the largest or most massive thing of its kind 2. monstrous sea creature symbolizing evil in the Old Testament [large levi literary lusus elephantine enormous evil extremely vessel immense animal argosy assign testament textbook titan troll tub hobgoblin hooker huge hulk hull nat] "it was a leviathan among redwoods"
*levity 20-51-3 (n.) 1. feeling an inappropriate lack of seriousness 2. lightness of manner [lack laughter leer levi levitation lightness emotional empty ethereal experience vanity vapidity volatility idle inanity inappropriate indifference intend taunt tender trait tricky yeasty]
*levy 05-52-81 (n.) 1. a charge imposed and collected 2. the act of drafting into military service (v.) 1. impose and collect 2. cause to assemble or enlist [last legal lev liability lie list engage enhance enlist enrollment enter execution] "levy a fine"
*lewd 15-55-7 (a.) 1. suggestive of or tending to moral looseness 2. driven by lust; preoccupied with or exhibiting lustful desires [language lascivious lecherous lechery lew libertine libidinous limerick loose lubricity lurid lust lusty erotomania exhibit way whisper wild debauched desire dirty dissolute driven] "lewd whisperings of a dirty old man"
*lexicographer 24-46-1 (n.) 1. a compiler or writer of a dictionary; a student of the lexical component of language [language larousse linguistics lit editor emerson emile english etymology expression italian component consistent craig oxford reference remember accuse alexander augustus paul philology pierre plagiarism henry]
*lexicography 20-36-3 (n.) 1. the act of writing dictionaries [language lexigraphy linguistics lit edit editor english epigraphy etymology exegetics expound expression interpreter italian clarify commentator composition consistent create criticism cryptology orthoepy oxford graphy guide reference remember accuse alexander allegory annotate author paleography pen philology phonology physiognomy pierre plagiarism henry hermeneutics]
*lexicon 14-54-9 (n.) 1. a language user's knowledge of words 2. a reference book containing an alphabetical list of words with information about them [language learn lexis list electronic enough entire entry equivalent icon idiolect cant carry catch checker claim communicate complete concordance convenient origin noes nomenclator]
*liable 06-67-47 (a.) 1. subject to legal action 2. (often followed by 'to') likely to be affected with 3. at risk of or subject to experiencing something usually unpleasant 4. held legally responsible [legal likely lose incline able accountable affect age answerable apt assail blame bound exempt expose /bail/]
*liaison 07-53-36 (n.) 1. a channel for communication between groups 2. a usually secretive or illicit sexual relationship [line link liquid love illicit infidelity intergroup intimacy intrigue iso access accord affaire agent amour association sauce secretive sexual silent similarity soup speak splice sympathy near] "he provided a liaison with the guerrillas"
*libel 09-57-23 (n.) 1. a tort consisting of false and malicious publication printed for the purpose of defaming a living person (v.) 1. make slanderous statements against [law lie live impose include innuendo insinuation intent base bel belittle besmirch blacken blot bring ecclesiastical explain] "The paper was accused of libeling him"
*liberalism 12-48-13 (n.) 1. an economic theory advocating free competition and a self-regulating market and the gold standard 2. a political orientation that favors progress and reform [laissez liberal libertine ideology individualism intellectual isolationism begin belief blend broad reform regulation reject religious right advocate authoritarian self speech standard stress market matter minded minimal moderation moral move]
*liberate 04-44-126 (v.) 1. grant freedom to; free from confinement 2. give equal rights to; of women and minorities 3. grant freedom to [libertine lifestyle lift line loose impose independence issue bail belong berate bondage boost bound breakout ease easygoing effort emancipate emancipation embezzle emerge enfranchise enlighten equal evasion extricate reaction recovery redeem release remove rescue restraint right appropriation arise toleration transform turn /tare/] "The students liberated their slaves upon graduating from the university"
*libertine 16-81-6 (a.) 1. unrestrained by convention or morality (n.) 1. a dissolute person; usually a man who is morally unrestrained [lady lewd like live lover lust immoral independent individualist indulge bert bestial blood engage rake rakish randy ravish relationship right riotous rip roue rounder toleration tramp neutral nonpartisan /nitre/]
*licentious 22-66-2 (a.) 1. lacking moral discipline; especially sexually unrestrained [lack lax loose lust

immoral indulgent irresponsible candid carnal cent chaste corrupt natural nonrestrictive open outgoing overt unbridled unchecked unconstrained unrestrained unruly salacious satyr selfish sensual sex spontaneous] "coarse and licentious men"
*liege 24-64-1 (a.) 1. owing or owed feudal allegiance and service (n.) 1. a person holding a fief 2. city in eastern Belgium; largest French-speaking city in Belgium [lackey large law leading lie light lord loyal luminary include independent inferior eastern elder employer european guru] "one's liege lord"
*lien 17-22-5 (n.) 1. the right to take another's property if an obligation is not discharged 2. a large dark-red oval organ on the left side of the body between the stomach and the diaphragm; produces cells involved in immune responses [landlord last law left legal lie lymphoid immune interest enforce erect /neil/]
*lieu 12-37-12 (n.) 1. the function or position properly or customarily occupied or served by another [last lie location locus emplacement expect express]
*lifelike 18-41-4 (a.) 1. unaffected and natural looking 2. evoking lifelike images within the mind [legitimate life literal living look image faithful free evoke exposition express expressive]
*lifelong 06-53-48 (a.) 1. continuing through life [lasting long indicate felon friend enduring great] "a lifelong friend"
*lifetime 04-56-118 (n.) 1. the period during which something is functional (as between birth and death) [length life lifelong live livelong living long immortal favorable functional epoch era existence expect extremely /emit mite/]
*ligament 07-64-36 (n.) 1. a sheet or band of tough fibrous tissue connecting bones or cartilages or supporting muscles or organs 2. any connection or unifying bond [labia ligature line link liver inguinal abdominal ament attachment major mesoderm metal musculature nexus tendon tie tissue tough tube twist /mag/]
*likelihood 06-54-58 (n.) 1. the probability of a specified outcome [improbable eventuality expectation happen hood hope obligation odds outcome outlook degree]
*likely 01-61-1055 (a.) 1. likely but not certain to be or become true or real 2. has a good chance of being the case or of coming about 3. expected to become or be; in prospect 4. within the realm of credibility (ad.) 1. with considerable certainty; without much doubt [liable like limb little long loss imaginable improbable income incredible indubitable investigate ironical earthly encourage excuse exist expect expedient extent young] "these services are likely to be available to us all before long"
*liking 09-66-22 (n.) 1. a feeling of pleasure and enjoyment [last like incline novel gin good great] "I've always had a liking for reading"
*limitation 05-34-73 (n.) 1. the greatest amount of something that is possible or allowed 2. the quality of being limited or restricted 3. a principle that limits the extent of something 4. (in law) a time period after which suits cannot be brought 5. an act of limiting or restricting (as by regulation) [law legal less level line load imitation imperfection impose inadequate inferior interface march mark maximum memory modification move terminate threshold title trust accept accord allow allowance amount armament armed authority narrow near]
*limn 24-11-1 (v.) 1. trace the shape of 2. make a portrait of [likeness lipstick image interpret map mistress notate]
*limp 06-64-46 (a.) 1. not firm 2. lacking in strength or firmness or resilience (n.) 1. the uneven manner of walking that results from an injured leg (v.) 1. proceed slowly or with difficulty 2. walk impeded by some physical limitation or injury [lack lame lax lazy leg lettuce lifeless limitation little loose lumber lunge lurch idle imp impede impotent incapacitate indolent ineffectual injury maim manner material moderate mosey move muddle muscle pace paddle paperback peg physical poke poky power proceed]
*limpid 18-53-4 (a.) 1. clear and bright 2. transmitting light; able to be seen through with clarity 3. (of language) transparently clear; easily understandable [language light linguistic liquid lucid luculent luminous luster impi intelligible mean melt mind morn pass perspicuous plain polished pool prose pure definite diaphanous direction distinct /dip/]
*linear 11-40-15 (a.) 1. (mathematics) directly proportional 2. of or in or along or relating to a line; involving a single dimension 3. (electronics) of a circuit or device having an output that is proportional to the input 4. of a leaf shape; long and narrow 5. measured lengthwise [last leaf lengthwise level line lineal logic long lumber input narrow near effect electron elongate emission equation even extend additive amplifier approach art rectilinear relation rely represent right run] "a linear foot"
*liner 06-44-48 (n.) 1. (baseball) a hit that flies straight out from the batter 2. a piece of cloth that is used as the inside surface of a garment 3. a large commercial ship (especially one that carries passengers on a regular schedule) [last line living luxury inlay insert inside insole interline equip regular room run] "the batter hit a liner to the shortstop"
*lingo 16-41-6 (n.) 1. a characteristic language of a particular group (as among thieves) [language langue last lawyer learn leg ling lingua locution idiom illegal important inferior narcotic native neighborhood nervous niff non gangster gibberish girlfriend gobbledygook good grand group occasion offensive omit organ outside] "they don't speak our lingo"
*lingua 22-50-2 (n.) 1. a mobile mass of muscular tissue

covered with mucous membrane and located in the oral cavity [ling locate lung neck glossa animal]
*linguist 15-53-7 (n.) 1. a specialist in linguistics 2. a person who speaks more than one language [lexicology ling individual]
*linguistics 18-42-4 (n.) 1. the scientific study of language 2. the humanistic study of language and literature [language lexical linguistic grammatical graphemics semantics speaker structuralism study syntax tonal tone topic]
*lionize 22-01-2 (v.) 1. assign great social importance to [laud lion idolize immortalize importance ionize observe elevate enshrine extol /oil/]
*liquefy 15-63-7 (v.) 1. become liquid 2. become liquid or fluid; of a solid substance, when heated 3. make (a solid substance) liquid, as by heating [leach liquidize infuse interaction undergo unfreeze energy fall fat fluid fluidize flux frozen fuse]
*liqueur 15-52-7 (n.) 1. strong highly flavored sweet liquor usually drunk after a meal [layer licorice inebriant intoxicant italian elderberry ratafia remain /rue/]
*liquidate 08-37-29 (v.) 1. get rid of; kill 2. convert into cash 3. settle the affairs of by determining the debts and applying the assets to pay them off 4. eliminate by paying off; as of debts [liability lift liquid lynch ill immolate impeach informer insolvency insurance intentional quit quittance unfrock unlawful unload unseat uproot death debar debt deport deprivation devastate die discharge dismissal dispose disposition down dump abolition abstract acquit affair amortize annihilate annul ante assassinate asset taboo termination threat trade eject eliminate end exchange exclude execute exile exterminate /tad/] "The mafia liquidated the informer"
*liquor 08-16-33 (n.) 1. a liquid substance that is a solution (or emulsion or suspension) used or obtained in an industrial process 2. distilled rather than fermented 3. the liquid in which vegetables or meat have be cooked [latex left lotus lush industrial inebriant infusion intoxicant obtain opiate opium originate rainbow red reduce room root rum russia] "waste liquors"
*listless 13-50-10 (a.) 1. lacking zest or vivacity 2. marked by low spirits; showing no enthusiasm [lack languid languor lassitude less lethargic lethargy lifeless limp low lukewarm impotent inactive indiscrimination indolent inert initiative insouciance interest show slow sluggish soft spent spirit tepid thoughtless torpor trait easygoing effete effort emotion enervate ennui enthusiasm etiolated] "he was listless and bored"
*literacy 10-52-21 (n.) 1. the ability to read and write [learn learned letter level liter intellectuality three training erudition read accomplishment acquisition area attainment classicism computer culture /care/]
*literal 09-42-22 (a.) 1. without interpretation or embellishment 2. being or reflecting the essential or genuine character of something 3. limited to the explicit meaning of a word or text 4. lacking stylistic embellishment 5. of the clearest kind; usually used for emphasis 6. (of a translation) corresponding word for word with the original (n.) 1. a mistake in printed matter resulting from mechanical failures of some kind [lack lawful legitimate letter lifelike limited liter ideograph incident inexact infertile interpretation invest tedious textual traditionalism translation trueful typographic elaborate erratum error essential evangelical exactly explicit express real realistic receive reflect rhetorical rightful russell accept account accurate actual adhere approve authoritative awkward]
*literature 03-26-214 (n.) 1. the profession or art of a writer 2. published writings in a particular style on a particular subject 3. the humanistic study of a body of literature 4. creative writing of recognized artistic value [language leaflet letter liberal liter longueur lore information tendency theatrical theory transition treat typescript early education effect element encyclopedia erotica essay expose express read recension recognize redact reference require acceptable alphabet art artistic aspect autograph /ruta tare/] "he took a course in French literature"
*lithe 14-54-8 (a.) 1. gracefully slender; moving and bending with ease [lean lightly limber lissome lith loose impressionable thin tractile ease elastic extensible]
*lithograph 16-24-6 (n.) 1. a print produced by lithography 2. duplicator that prints by lithography; a flat surface (of stone or metal) is treated to absorb or repel ink in the desired pattern (v.) 1. make by lithography [linocut image ink inscription treat type graph repel absorb apparatus art artistic pattern photographic picture print production]
*litigant 16-54-6 (n.) 1. (law) a party to a lawsuit; someone involved in litigation [law lawsuit legal litigious lower impose indict informer institution intransigent irreconcilable talebearer tattletale telltale grass accessory accuse actionable ant appellant authority narc naysayer negativism notice /git nag/] "plaintiffs and defendants are both litigants"
*litigate 14-28-8 (v.) 1. engage in legal proceedings 2. institute legal proceedings against; file a suit against [law lawsuit legal impeach implead institute issue gate accuse arraign attorney efficient engage /git tag/]
*litigious 18-56-4 (a.) 1. of or relating to litigation 2. inclined or showing an inclination to dispute or disagree, even to engage in law suits [law lawyer legal lit incline irascible irritable tend give scrappy show shrewish spirit style suit /git/]
*littoral 24-35-1 (a.) 1. of or relating to a coastal or shore region (n.) 1. the region of the shore of a lake or sea or ocean [lake lido limbic limiting lit live low terminal threshold tidal tide ocean oral region rim riverside riviera aquatic]
*liturgy 15-62-7 (n.) 1. a Christian sacrament

commemorating the Last Supper by consecrating bread and wine 2. a rite or body of rites prescribed for public worship [last laud lay lit lord inauguration initiation institute institution tierce traditional unction receive religious rite ritual roman god grace]
*livelihood 10-54-18 (n.) 1. the financial means whereby one lives [living long income earn ease emolument employment endowment expect handicraft hood occupation draw /evil/]
*livid 16-72-6 (a.) 1. (informal) furiously angry 2. (of a light) imparting a deathlike luminosity 3. ash-colored or anemic looking from illness or emotion 4. discolored by coagulation of blood beneath the skin [lackluster lavender lightning lip look luminosity lurid illness imitate impart incense indignant injury invalid irate ireful violet dark day death deep dim discolor drain dull]
*loam 22-54-2 (n.) 1. a rich soil consisting of a mixture of sand and clay and decaying organic materials [lowdown organic material matter mix moist muck mud]
*loath 13-48-11 (a.) 1. unwillingness to do something contrary to your custom 2. (usually followed by 'to') strongly opposed [laggard loth oath oppose admit afraid antipathetic apathetic averse toward hesitate]
*loathe 07-74-38 (v.) 1. find repugnant [loath odium abhor abominate abomination allergy antipathy aversion toward hate hatred horror hostility execrate] "I loathe that man"
*loch 10-92-19 (n.) 1. a long narrow inlet of the sea in Scotland (especially when it is nearly landlocked) 2. Scottish word for a lake [lagoon lake landlocked large last linn long lough ocean central cistern coast cove creek harbor highland]
*locomotion 24-44-1 (n.) 1. the power or ability to move 2. self-propelled movement [lap limb location once change circuit commutation course crawl creep crossing manner mobility mode motion motivity movement moving transit travel trot /tom/]
*lode 20-24-3 (n.) 1. a deposit of valuable ore occurring within definite boundaries separating it from surrounding rocks [layer load ode ore definite deposit dike /dol/]
*lofty 08-52-28 (a.) 1. of imposing height; especially standing out above others 2. of high moral or intellectual value; elevated in nature or style 3. having or displaying great dignity or nobility [leading liberal lift loft lordly low oliver orotund ostentatious overwrought false famous fancy flashy flatulent frank tall telling tony towering tumid turgid]
*logic 05-54-71 (n.) 1. the principles that guide reasoning within a given field or situation 2. a system of reasoning 3. reasoned and reasonable judgment 4. the branch of philosophy that analyzes inference [law log logistic lucidity observation ontology operation gain general give good govern guide gumption idea inductive inference influence instance intelligence interaction introduce investigate capable casuistry certain circuit commonsense computer conclusion conjunction copula cosmology criterion /cig/] "it made a certain kind of logic"
*logical 06-49-59 (a.) 1. marked by an orderly, logical, and aesthetically consistent relation of parts 2. in accordance with reason or logic 3. capable of or reflecting the capability for correct and valid reasoning 4. capable of thinking and expressing yourself in a clear and consistent manner 5. based on known statements or events or conditions [lack lawful legal legitimate likely logic lucid observation obvious give good ground independent inductive inference intelligent invalid irrational capable circumstance clear cogent coherent commonsensica compel conclusion condition consistent correct credible accident accord accordance act admissible aesthetic analytic argument authoritative /cig/] "a logical mind"
*loll 16-62-6 (v.) 1. hang loosely or laxly 2. be lazy or idle [last lax laze lazy lean lie linger loaf loose lounge lounging lying] "His tongue lolled"
*loneliness 09-52-22 (n.) 1. sadness resulting from being forsaken or abandoned 2. the state of being alone in solitary isolation 3. a disposition toward being alone [emotion experience isolation sad seclusion separation solitude]
*longevity 09-58-23 (n.) 1. duration of service 2. the property of being long-lived [length life lifetime lively living longe oldness opposite elderly employment endurance existence extension viable vigorous vitality immortal young /veg/] "her longevity as a star"
*loot 07-49-44 (n.) 1. informal terms for money 2. goods or money obtained illegally (v.) 1. take illegally; of intellectual property 2. steal goods; take as spoils [law lawbreaker legal lettuce lift lolly loo lot lucre obtain occasion onslaught owner take tender throttle till /tool/]
*lope 14-50-9 (n.) 1. a slow pace of running 2. a smooth 3-beat gait; between a trot and a gallop (v.) 1. run easily [lane leap list long lop outing pace paddock path pen plunge prance easy enclosure excursion]
*loquacious 18-51-4 (a.) 1. full of trivial conversation [open qua candor chatty communicative conversation conversational smooth sociable speech]
*lough 17-95-5 (n.) 1. a long narrow (nearly landlocked) cove in Ireland 2. Irish word for a lake [lake landlocked last loch long lou]
*louse 24-57-1 (n.) 1. wingless usually flattened blood-sucking insect parasitic on warm-blooded animals 2. wingless insect with mouth parts adapted for biting; mostly parasitic on birds 3. any of several small insects especially aphids that feed by sucking the juices from plants 4. has a nasty or unethical character undeserving of respect [leap leech leg lice live lou oak offensive organism undeserving unethical unpleasant use scrounge shaft skunk snake sponger stinker sucking]
*lovable 13-41-10 (a.) 1. having characteristics that

attract love or affection [likable likeable lovely able acceptable achieve admirable adorable affable affection amiable amicable angelic attractive bewitching enchanting endearing engage engaging entrance evoke exciting /avo/] "a mischievous but lovable child"
*lowly 11-67-17 (a.) 1. inferior in rank or status 2. low or inferior in station or quality 3. of low birth or station ('base' is archaic in this sense) 4. used of unskilled work (especially domestic work) [least length low lowborn lower obsequious officialdom ordinary origin way withdraw work workday wretch young]
*lucid 11-48-17 (a.) 1. (of language) transparently clear; easily understandable 2. capable of thinking and expressing yourself in a clear and consistent manner 3. transmitting light; able to be seen through with clarity 4. having a clear mind [language light linguistic logical lucent luculent luminous lustrous unambiguous understood unequivocal unmistakable capable cid clarity classic clear cloudy cogent coherent cold communicate compo connected consistent conventional correct incandescent insight intelligible intuition irrational definition delirium direct direction disorder distinct]
*lucrative 04-62-95 (a.) 1. producing a good profit [compensatory rat remunerative repay retribution rewarding advantageous /vita/]
*ludicrous 07-74-40 (a.) 1. broadly or extravagantly humorous; resembling farce 2. completely devoid of wisdom or good sense [laughable ludic universal unsuitable utterly daft derisory devoid dog droll dull idiotic impractical incongruous incredible interest call child clown cockamamie cockeyed comical completely conceited contribution cottage crazy rich ridiculous risible outrageous outre scream silly stupid]
*lugubrious 17-66-5 (a.) 1. excessively mournful [lamentable loss gloomy glum grievous black bleak brio rueful irreparable oppressive sad somber sorrow sorrowful sullen /bug/]
*lull 10-49-21 (n.) 1. a pause during which things are calm or activities are diminished 2. a period of calm weather (v.) 1. become quiet or less intensive 2. calm by deception 3. make calm or still [lapse last layoff leniency lenify less letup lie loosen unpleasant] "the fighting lulled for a moment"
*lumber 08-34-30 (n.) 1. the wood of trees cut and prepared for use as building material 2. an implement used in baseball by the batter (v.) 1. move heavily or clumsily 2. cut lumber, as in woods and forests [land lazy leisurely length lignify limp load log umber ungainly unhurried unpleasant unwanted unwieldy maladroit mar march material moderate move muddle murder backpack ball bark baseball bat batter beam blow blundering board building bulky burden easy elephantine embarrassment entangle entwine equipment rack reforest region reject relaxed reluctant responsibility roll room] "The heavy man lumbered across the room"
*luminary 12-57-13 (n.) 1. a celebrity who is an inspiration to others [lamp lantern leading light lion literary lumina match moon idol illuminate immortal inspiration nabob name notable achiever actinic astronomical /rani/]
*luminescence 22-48-2 (n.) 1. light not due to incandescence; occurs at low temperatures 2. light from nonthermal sources [level light low luciferin luminesce luster mean incandescence non electromagnetic emission emit sensation shin source chemical]
*luminescent 24-47-1 (a.) 1. emitting light not caused by heat [light emit shin]
*luminosity 22-42-2 (n.) 1. the quality of being luminous; emitting or reflecting light [level light lum measure illumination incandescence incident non second sheen shine source strength sun /son/] "its luminosity is measured relative to that of our sun"
*luminous 10-47-18 (a.) 1. softly bright or radiant [lambent light lighten lit loving lucent ubiquitous understandable unlimited majestic making measure merciful moon illuminate immortal incandescent infinite inspire nous numinous observer omniscient one orange orient sensation shape sharp shimmer shin simple sky soft startling]
*lunacy 15-66-7 (n.) 1. obsolete terms for legal insanity [legal lighthearted luna unintelligent never nutty aberration absurdity alienate amusement caper care clown clownish context cranky crazy /can/]
*lunar 13-54-10 (a.) 1. of or relating to or associated with the moon [luna lunate lunulate uranic nebulous asteroid astrophysics relation] "lunar surface"
*lunatic 11-66-15 (a.) 1. (informal) some insane and believed to be affected by the phases of the moon (n.) 1. an insane person 2. a reckless impetuous irresponsible person [loco loony luna unbalance unhinge unsettled neurotic nut abnormal absurd affect afflict ass tetched thoughtless tomfool touched idiot illness imitate impetuous insane insult irrational irresponsible clown colloquial communicate consider crank crazy]
*lurid 10-67-21 (a.) 1. shining with an unnatural red glow as of fire seen through smoke 2. glaringly vivid and graphic; marked by sensationalism 3. horrible in fierceness or savagery 4. ghastly pale [lackluster life light lofty loud luminance unattractivel uncanny unearthly unnatural unprintable raw ready red reflect rid ruby impure inflame infrared interest detail devastate dim dirty dull] "lurid crimes"
*lurk 06-64-46 (v.) 1. be about 2. lie in wait, lie in ambush, behave in a sneaky and secretive manner 3. wait in hiding to attack [latent lie linger loaf loiter lollygag loom lounge lower lurch underlie unsuspected upcoming read]
*luscious 12-51-13 (a.) 1. having strong sexual appeal 2. extremely pleasing to the sense of taste [likable lush luxurious unsex scrumptious sensual sexual sexy strong style succulent sumptuous sweet choice cloy interest

opulent]
*lustrous 16-51-6 (a.) 1. made smooth and bright by or as if by rubbing; reflecting a sheen or glow 2. reflecting light 3. brilliant [lambent light lucent luminous lust unpolished until sheeny shimmer shiny silver smooth soft sunny sunshine swim radiant ready reflect refulgent resplendent rub orient]
*luxuriant 17-55-5 (a.) 1. marked by complexity and richness of detail 2. produced or growing in extreme abundance [lace lavish liberal lot lush rampant rank rich riotous impenetrable inexhaustible abundant adequate adorn affluent ample ant numerous teem thick thrive]
*luxuriate 18-59-4 (v.) 1. become extravagant; indulge (oneself) luxuriously 2. enjoy to excess 3. thrive profusely or flourish extensively [leave like love relish revel riot root run indulge ahead appetite appreciate teem thrive eat enjoy excess exhaust expand extensive extravagant]
*lying 04-61-132 (a.) 1. given to lying (n.) 1. the deliberate act of deviating from the truth (v.) 1. be and remain in a particular state or condition 2. originate (in) 3. assume a reclining position 4. have a place in relation to something else 5. be lying, be prostrate; be in a horizontal position 6. tell an untruth; pretend with intent to deceive 7. be located or situated somewhere; occupy a certain position [lie locate yin injustice insincere intent give] "a lying witness"
*lyre 22-42-2 (n.) 1. a harp used by ancient Greeks for accompaniment [lute rome electric euphonium]
*lyric 04-47-130 (a.) 1. (music; of a singer or singing voice) being light in volume and modest in range 2. expressing deep personal emotion 3. (music) relating to or being musical drama 4. (poetry) "lyric poetry" (n.) 1. the text of a popular song or musical-comedy number 2. a short poem of songlike quality (v.) 1. write lyrics for (a song) [language libretto light lilt limerick line literature liturgical love lyre range rapturous rhapsodic rhyme rhythmical rich romantic roundelay idiosyncrasy idyllic impassioned incorporate indite individual inspire canso cantabile catchy category chanson choral classical clerihew colloquial coloratura communicate complimentary composition constitute continuous corresponding] "the dancer's lyrical performance"

M

*macabre 12-60-13 (a.) 1. shockingly repellent; inspiring horror [madman morbid mortuary murder aftermath age alarming appalling awesome awful cab cadaverous chilling conceive corpse blue bomb bury redoubtable repellent eerie eldritch evidence]
*macerate 24-51-1 (v.) 1. separate into constituents by soaking 2. become soft or separate and disintegrate as a result of excessive soaking 3. soften, usually by steeping in liquid, and cause to disintegrate as a result 4. cause to grow thin or weak [macer marinate mash masticate agonize attenuate chew component constituent consume crush emaciate enfeeble excessive excruciate rack reduce rinse rip thin tissue torment torture treatment /tare/] "the tissue macerated in the water"
*machination 14-47-9 (n.) 1. a crafty and involved plot to achieve your (usually sinister) ends [maneuver manipulate move achieve affair artifice collusion complicate conspiracy control crafty cuning illegal influence intrigue nation tactics trickery]
*machinery 06-36-49 (n.) 1. a system of means and activities whereby a social institution functions 2. machines or machine systems collectively [machine mean means mechanism medium modify movement moving action agent aggregate apparatus appointment arrange assist channel cog collective combine command comprise convenience harrow header hoist human implement independent innards institution interrelated navvy negotiation edge effect electrical element energy engine equipment expedient resolve resort rig roller] "the complex machinery of negotiation"
*machinist 14-14-8 (n.) 1. a craftsman skilled in operating machine tools [maker mechanic artificer assign chin craftsman handicraft involve naval ship shop skill technician tool trade]
*madden 13-35-11 (v.) 1. cause to go crazy; cause to lose one's mind 2. drive up the wall; go on someone's nerves 3. make mad [mad mental mind move add alienate anger animal annoy derange distract drive dun enrage exacerbate exasperate excite extremely nerve /dam/] "His behavior is maddening"
*madonna 07-70-43 (n.) 1. the mother of Jesus; Christians refer to her as the Virgin Mary; she is especially honored by Roman Catholics 2. United States pop singer and sex symbol during the 1980s (born in 1958) [mary mother address artistic donna /dam nod/]
*maelstrom 16-64-6 (n.) 1. a powerful circular current of water (usually the resulting of conflicting tides) [malaise mark moil mythology ado agitation ebullition eddy exception excitement lying scramble scylla ship

side situation spin steady storm strait stream strong surge tide tumult turbulent turmoil turn reel rom round row /lea leam mort/]

*magician 10-55-18 (n.) 1. someone who performs magic tricks to amuse an audience 2. one who practices magic or sorcery [magic marvel medium musical musician accomplice ace airy alchemist ale amuse ancient appearance art artist audience genius giuseppe great guiser idealize illusionist immaterial impersonate italian cag chain charm clever conjurer container count crackerjack necromancy /cig/]

*magisterial 16-64-6 (a.) 1. of or relating to a magistrate 2. offensively self-assured or given to exercising usually unwarranted power 3. used of a person's appearance or behavior; befitting an eminent person [main majestic manner masterly monarch accept adjudicate aggressive agist aloof approve arrogant august authority autocratic grand grave great imperious imposing ingenious scholarly self show some standard star stately submissive superior swaggering tactful tend topflight tyranny elitism eminent excellent expert express ready receive regal reign royal leading lordly /aire lair/] "official magisterial functions"

*magnanimous 18-67-4 (a.) 1. noble and generous in spirit 2. generous and understanding and tolerant [magical magna magnificent majestic marvelous mind munificent acute altruistic amazing astonish august generous give glaring glorious grudge noble notably idealistic impressive incredible indicative indulgent intense openhearted uncommonly understand unselfish unsparing unstinting unusual upright show singular soar spirit striking sublime superb surprise /mina/]

*magnate 10-64-20 (n.) 1. a very wealthy or powerful businessman [manager marquis mogul affair agnate archduke aristocrat gentleman grandee name nobleman notable thoroughbred top tycoon earl elder engage entrepreneur executive /tang tanga/]

*magnet 08-45-29 (n.) 1. a device that attracts iron and produces a magnetic field [mag material matter metal mounting move ambition apply aspect attract general great needle earth electric end energy entice temporary temptation toward trophy]

*magnificence 18-62-4 (n.) 1. splendid or imposing in size or appearance 2. the quality of being magnificent or splendid or grand [magnific majesty marvelous appearance architecture glory good gorgeous graceful grand great nobility imposing impressivenes indicate conspicuous effect elaborate elegance excel exquisite /fin/]

*magnificent 04-73-104 (a.) 1. characterized by or attended with brilliance or grandeur [magical magnanimous magnific majestic marvelous acute amazing art astonish attend august awful generous glorious golden good grand grandeur great noble notably immense imposing impressive incredible intense famous fancy fine cathedral ceremony commanding conspicuous copious coronation court elaborate elegant exception exceptional terrific towering tremendous /fin/]

*magnitude 08-37-32 (n.) 1. relative importance 2. a number assigned to the ratio of two quantities; two quantities are of the same order of magnitude if one is less than 10 times as large as the other; the number of magnitudes that the quantities differ is specified to within a power of 10 3. the property of relative size or extent [mag mass matter mighty moment amount amplitude area gauge girth grand great neighborhood note number immense importance intensity tune degree depth diameter dimension earthquake enormousness expansion extent /ting/] "they tried to predict the magnitude of the explosion"

*maintain 01-45-550 (v.) 1. supply with necessities and support 2. keep in safety and protect from harm, decay, loss, or destruction 3. of power or authority 4. state categorically 5. keep in a certain state, position, or activity; e.g., "keep clean" 6. maintain by writing regular records 7. maintain for use and service 8. state or assert 9. observe correctly or closely 10. support against an opponent [main mainstay manage manifesto affirm allege announce answer asseverate assume aver avow imagine inhibit insistent invest nurture tarry testify think]

*maintenance 04-42-121 (n.) 1. means of maintenance of a family or group 2. activity involved in maintaining something in good working order 3. court-ordered support paid by one spouse to another after they are separated 4. the act of sustaining [machine maintain manual mean meat mending money month mother age aid allowance improve inhibition interference introduce nance necessity nourishment nurture team tenacity treat endowment endurance enough ensure equipment extension camera car care carry child condition constant continue contribution]

*maize 17-77-5 (n.) 1. tall annual cereal grass bearing kernels on large ears: widely cultivated in America in many varieties; the principal cereal in Mexico and Central and South America since pre-Columbian times 2. a strong yellow color [market mexico millet america animal annual indian zea ear eat evert expose]

*makeup 08-07-31 (n.) 1. cosmetics applied to the face to improve or change your appearance 2. the way in which someone or something is composed [make making manner maqui mind miss accessory actor alter appearance architecture arrangement assembly kidney kind eccentricity embodiment ethos eye eyebrow eyelid unlike page paint pencil pink plan powder preparation product property]

*maladroit 24-61-1 (a.) 1. not adroit [manner mean mediocre move adept adroit awkward lack lefthand little loutish lumber deficient oafish inadequate incompetent inelegant inept insensitive insufficient tactless translation trivial /dal/] "a maladroit movement of his hand caused the car to swerve"

*malady 17-28-5 (n.) 1. impairment of normal physiological function affecting part or all of an organism 2. any unwholesome or desperate condition [malaise medicine motility move multiple myeloma abnormal abrupt absorption aeroembolism affecting affection afflict ailment aircraft allergy amyloid anuria arthritis lady lead decompression defect deposit desperate disease disorder doctor /dal/]
*malapropism 24-60-1 (n.) 1. the unintentional misuse of a word by confusion with one that sounds similar [malaprop metaphor metonymy mispronounce mistake misuse allusion analogy antithesis litotes logogriph parenthesis pun regression repetition ridiculous onomatopoeia oxymoron infelicity instance inversion irony sarcasm solecism sound statement synecdoche /pal sip/]
*malaria 11-62-15 (n.) 1. an infective disease caused by sporozoan parasites that are transmitted through the bite of an infected Anopheles mosquito; marked by paroxysms of chills and fever [madness malar malignant mark measly meningitis mosquito afterdamp ague allergic anemic anopheles anthrax arthritic laryngitis leprous leptospirosis lockjaw rabies rachitis recur reek region rheumatic rickety ringworm illness infective influenza]
*malcontent 20-63-3 (a.) 1. discontented as toward authority (n.) 1. a person who is discontented or disgusted [maverick mortal mourn mutter agitator alienate anarchist authority lament longing chronic complain content continually crabby cranky croak oppose nonconformist toward traitor envious establish estranged experience extremist /clam/]
*malefactor 24-33-1 (n.) 1. someone who has committed (or been legally convicted of) a crime [malevolent miscreant mobster law lawbreaker faction factor felon criminal crook culprit thief transgress offend outlaw racketeer rascal rogue /cafe/]
*malevolence 20-65-3 (n.) 1. wishing evil to others 2. the quality of threatening evil [malignity mean moral annoyance emotion evil venom vindictivenes virtue nasty catty cruelty]
*malevolent 13-62-11 (a.) 1. wishing or appearing to wish evil to others; arising from intense ill will or hatred 2. having or exerting a malignant influence 3. extremely malevolent or malicious [maleficent malign malignant mean misanthropy mischievous misogyny moral acrid annoyance antagonistic antipathy appear arise aversion lent lethal loathing effect emotion evil evoke execration exert extremely venomous vicious vindictive virtue virulent odium old ominous nasty nature noisome noxious tongue toward toxic /love/] "a gossipy malevolent old woman"
*malice 13-57-11 (n.) 1. feeling a need to see others suffer 2. the quality of threatening evil [male malevolent mean mischievousne misogyny moral alice annoyance antagonism antipathy aversion law lice loathing intention invidious catty clash commit conflict contention cruelty enmity evil execration]
*malicious 10-60-18 (a.) 1. having the nature of or resulting from malice 2. wishing or appearing to wish evil to others; arising from intense ill will or hatred [malevolent malic malignant mean mischievous motivate acrid antagonistic antipathetic appear arise leer ill influence iniquitous intent invidious catty clash collide conflicting cruel old ornery sore spiteful successful] "malicious gossip"
*malign 11-61-17 (a.) 1. evil or harmful in nature or influence 2. having or exerting a malignant influence (v.) 1. speak unfavorably about [malevolent mean mislead mortal motive mud murderous align antagonistic antipathetic appear arise asperse atrocious attack lack language lesion lethal libel look ill influence inhuman injurious intention internecine invidious good nasty nature negative noisome noxious] "prompted by malign motives"
*malignant 15-57-8 (a.) 1. (pathology) dangerous to health; characterized by progressive and uncontrolled growth (especially of a tumor) 2. extremely malevolent or malicious [malevolent malign mean medicine menace mischievous mortal murderous allergic arthritic atrocious laryngitis leprous lethal liable likely influence inhuman iniquitous injurious internecine invade invidious gossip growth nasty nature noisome noxious tabetic tissue tongue treat tuberculous tumor] "the malignant tongues of gossipers"
*malinger 22-59-2 (v.) 1. avoid responsibilities and duties, e.g., by pretending to be ill [military miss mountebank abandon assign avoid linger idler ill impersonate impostor incapacity negligent goldbrick elusory evade responsibility ringer]
*malleable 17-47-5 (a.) 1. easily influenced 2. capable of being shaped or bent or drawn out [manage manipulate metal mobile modify mold molten motivate able accessible acquiesce adjust alloy apt leather limber lissome lithe easy educate elastic extensible bend bendy bent biddable break bright butler]
*mallet 15-54-7 (n.) 1. a sports implement with a long handle and a head like a hammer; used in sports (polo or croquet) to hit a ball 2. a light drumstick with a rounded head that is used to strike percussion instruments 3. a tool resembling a hammer but with a large head (usually wooden); used to drive wedges or ram down paving stones or for crushing or beating or flattening or smoothing [mall marimba material metal molding musical large last light long tool /tell/]
*maltreat 20-65-3 (v.) 1. treat badly [maul menace misuse molest abuse afflict aggrieve animal threaten torment torture toward treat envenom]
*manacle 22-54-2 (n.) 1. shackle that consists of a metal loop that can be locked around the wrist; usually used in pairs (v.) 1. confine or restrain with or as if with manacles or handcuffs [makefast metal moor muzzle

acle anchor chain check confine control crime cuff lash leash lock loop enchain /can/]
*mandate 04-26-91 (n.) 1. a document giving an official instruction or command 2. (politics) the commission that is given to a government and its policies through an electoral victory 3. a territory surrendered by Turkey or Germany after World War I and inhabited by people not yet able to stand by themselves and so put under the tutelage of some other European power (v.) 1. assign under a mandate; of nations 2. assign authority to [mandatory mark mediterranean member mission mittimus must absolute administrative agree ally assignment authorize nation nationality notify date decisive declare decree decretory delegate depute designate dictate directive divided document dominion duke task tenure territory title track turkey tutelage earl east effective electorate embassy empire entail european /tad/]
*mandatory 06-35-50 (a.) 1. required by rule (n.) 1. a territory surrendered by Turkey or Germany after World War I and inhabited by people not yet able to stand by themselves and so put under the tutelage of some other European power 2. the recipient of a mandate [mand mandate mark mediterranean moral must absolute administrative authorize necessitous needful decisive demand dictate divided dominion territory turkey tutelage obligatory official read receiver recipient region regulation require requisite resemble rubric rule yet /rota tad/]
*mane 16-58-6 (n.) 1. long coarse hair growing from the crest of the animal's neck 2. growth of hair covering the scalp of a human being [male man mat member mop africa amount animal neck encolure extinct]
*maneuver 06-AA-51 (n.) 1. a military training exercise 2. an action aimed at evading an enemy 3. a deliberate coordinated movement requiring dexterity and skill 4. a move made to gain a tactical end 5. a plan for attaining a particular goal (v.) 1. direct the course; determine the direction of travelling 2. perform a movement in military or naval tactics in order to secure an advantage in attack or defense [machine malleable manageable mane manipulate manoeuvre means measure military mobile movement act action adaptable advantage art artifice attack naval navigate negotiable effort engineering enterprise exercise expedient undaunted undertake undulate valiant valorous viable ready resource reverse rig right roll run ruse /revue/]
*mania 11-54-16 (n.) 1. an irrational but irresistible motive for a belief or action 2. a mood disorder; an affective disorder in which the victim tends to respond excessively and sometimes violently [madness major melancholia mental mood motive aberration abnormality absence abstraction affective agitation alcoholism alienate alone ani attraction idea impulsive inconsistent indifference interest irrational irrationality irresistible itch]
*maniac 15-62-7 (a.) 1. wildly disordered (n.) 1. an insane person [mad madman mania manner mental affect afflict appear nut idiot illness insane interested crackpot crazy] "a maniacal frenzy"
*manifesto 08-80-33 (n.) 1. a public declaration of intentions (as issued by a political party or government) [manifest marx move accord affirmation allegation announcement authority notify intention issue edict emphatic encyclical engel enunciate exercise explicit say socialist stand statement strategy /fin/]
*manifold 18-60-4 (a.) 1. many and varied; having many features or forms (n.) 1. a pipe that has several lateral outlets to or from other pipes (v.) 1. make multiple copies of 2. combine or increase by multiplication [main manage many material metal miscellaneous multiply multitudinous allotropic analogue assorted numerous increase inlet intake feature fivefold fluid fold form fourfold fuel oil open opportunity outlet lateral letter lightweight long derive different dimension distribute diverse duplicate /fin/] "manifold reasons"
*manliness 24-54-1 (n.) 1. the trait of being manly; having the characteristics of an adult male [machismo male man manful manhood masculinity adult]
*mannerism 14-43-9 (n.) 1. a behavioral attribute that is distinctive and peculiar to an individual 2. a deliberate pretense or exaggerated display [manner marking mold affected appearance architecture art artificial attitude attribute nature earmark eccentricity effect elongate exaggerate radical rhetoric idiosyncrasy image impression index seal shape show simulation specialty speech stylize /sire siren/]
*manor 06-63-49 (n.) 1. the mansion of the lord of the manor 2. the landed estate of a lord (including the house on it) [mano mansion medieval messuage acre area asset noble owner realty residence retain right royal]
*mantel 18-25-4 (n.) 1. shelf that projects from wall above fireplace [ante last] "in England they call a mantel a chimneypiece"
*mantle 10-48-21 (n.) 1. the cloak as a symbol of authority 2. anything that covers 3. a sleeveless garment like a cloak but shorter 4. hanging cloth used as a blind 5. shelf that projects from wall above fireplace 6. the layer of the earth between the crust and the core 7. United States baseball player (1931-1997) 8. (zoology) a protective layer of epidermis in mollusks or brachiopods that secretes a substance forming the shell (v.) 1. spread over a surface, like a mantle 2. cover like a mantle [man mannitol marking marten masked medal muffle accessory aerate ancient ant apparel appliance arbitrary arborvitae architecture arm armory array assume athlete audience authority natural tartan tented theatre thistle tie tired trim trouser lamp layer light line livery lobe look loop loose lower lying eagle earth eclipse emblem encase envelop epidermis] "The ivy mantles the building"

*manufacturer 02-40-254 (n.) 1. someone who manufactures something 2. a business engaged in manufacturing some product [machine maker manager manufacture material mccormick mechanical mercer mother munition alcoholic architect arm armourer artist author unite fabricate factory father finish firearm food founder calico car chain cloth commercial computer concern construct cotton creator cyrus raise raw realize effector engage engineer enterprise /fun/]
*marine 03-38-151 (a.) 1. of or relating to the sea 2. of or relating to military personnel who serve both on land and at sea (specifically the U.S. Marine Corps) 3. native to or inhabiting the sea 4. relating to or involving ships or shipping or navigation or seamen (n.) 1. a member of the United States Marine Corps [machine marin maritime member merchant military achieve alaska american amphibious animal aquatic argosy armada armed art republic independence inhabit insurance island native nautical naval navigation northwest escadrille exploration] "marine explorations"
*maritime 08-58-30 (a.) 1. relating to or involving ships or shipping or navigation or seamen 2. bordering on or living or characteristic of those near the sea [mari marine meteorology region influence inland insurance temperature thalassic transport /emit/]
*maroon 11-62-17 (a.) 1. dark brownish to purplish red (n.) 1. an exploding firework used as a warning signal (v.) 1. leave stranded; put ashore on a desolate island and abandon 2. isolate without resources [mar mean misfortune mutinous abandon achromatic aground apart area ashore rate red remote rescue resource ruby rusty] "The mutinous sailors were marooned on an island"
*martial 07-45-41 (a.) 1. (of persons) befitting a warrior 2. of or relating to the armed forces 3. suggesting war or military life (n.) 1. Roman poet noted for epigrams (first century BC) [marti mettlesome military aggressive antagonistic armed reserved roman truculent troup inimical law life /lait tram/]
*martian 16-56-6 (a.) 1. of or relating to the planet Mars (or its fictional inhabitants) (n.) 1. imaginary people who live on the planet Mars [mar marti myth alien terrestrial imagination inhabitant invade /tram/]
*martyrdom 15-58-8 (n.) 1. death that is imposed because of the person's adherence of a religious faith or cause 2. any experience that causes intense suffering [misery murder adhere agony religious ritual torment torture death decease departure distress dying]
*marvel 07-50-44 (n.) 1. something that causes feelings of wonder (v.) 1. express astonishment or surprise about something 2. be amazed at [machinery marv miracle modern ace admiration amazement ancient articulate astonishment astound awe rarity reaction response exception express eyeful last linguistic looker lovely] "We marvelled at the child's linguistic abilities"
*masonry 13-37-10 (n.) 1. structure built of stone or brick by a mason 2. Freemasons collectively 3. the craft of a mason [mason member mixture mortar mud mutual adobe apply ashlar assistance sandstone secret side skill smooth society spackle stone stonework structure surface occupation ornamental roofing]
*masquerade 12-51-13 (n.) 1. a party of guests wearing costumes and masks 2. a costume worn as a disguise at a masquerade party 3. making a false outward show (v.) 1. pretend to be someone or something that you are not 2. take part in a masquerade [mask masque mime mixer modify motley act acting appearance attire seeming serious show shower silly simulation subterfuge suit uniform enactment entertainment equip expert representation rig ruse dance deception disappear disguise dress /dare/] "a beggar's masquerade of wealth"
*massacre 06-50-51 (n.) 1. the savage and excessive killing of many people (v.) 1. kill a large number of people indiscriminately [massa mission montana mow murder anna annihilation antonio assault attack sacking santa savage sioux slaughter slay stand carnage cavalry cheyenne rape rebel riot eliminate eradicate excessive execution exterminate /ass/] "The Hutus massacred the Tutsis in Rwanda"
*massive 03-75-195 (a.) 1. imposing in size or bulk or solidity 2. being the same substance throughout 3. consisting of great mass; containing a great quantity of matter 4. imposing in scale or scope or degree or power [magnitude mammoth mass matter mighty monolithic monumental mortal amount architecture astronomical average awesome awkward scale scope sculpture silver size solidity sound steady strong substantial immense imposing increase incumbent infinite inside internal vast viscous voluminous enduring enormous entirely excellent extensive extent extremely] "massive oak doors"
*masterpiece 05-59-66 (n.) 1. an outstanding achievement 2. the most outstanding work of a creative artist or craftsman [magnum maker manufacture master medieval mirror mobile movie accomplishment achievement agency archetype artist show stabile statue study earn effect effort essence exception extract recognition result pastiche performance piece product production prototype ideal invention issue child classic consider creative creature]
*mastery 10-47-19 (n.) 1. power to dominate or defeat 2. great skillfulness and knowledge of some subject or activity 3. the act of mastering or subordinating someone [master might moment most address adept artful ascendancy authority say sea skillful social strict style subordinate success superiority supremacy surpassing total transcend effective efficiency excel exist expert ready record regulation restraint rule]
*material 02-42-465 (a.) 1. concerned with or affecting physical as distinct from intellectual or psychological well-being 2. directly relevant to a matter especially a law case 3. derived from or composed of matter 4. concerned with worldly rather than spiritual interests 5.

having material or physical form or substance 6. having substance or capable of being treated as fact; not imaginary (n.) 1. information (data or ideas or observations) that can be used or reworked into a finished form 2. artifact made by weaving or felting or knitting or crocheting natural or synthetic fibers 3. a person judged suitable for admission or employment 4. things needed for doing or making something 5. the tangible substance that goes into the makeup of a physical object [major mark materia matter means molecule moment mote abrasive accent air apply appropriate tangible toughness earth eat element emphasis equipment essential existence radical reality regard reliable respect important information interest involve lace lie life literature /aire lair/] "material possessions"
*materialize 11-01-17 (v.) 1. come into being; become reality [manes manifestation material mean accident affect appear approach arise arrive assume telesthesia theophany token transmigration turn typify emerge enter evidence exist expression really represent reveal rise immaterial incorporate indication institution issue larva lemures levitation loom zombie /aire lair/] "Her dream really materialized"
*maternal 10-48-19 (a.) 1. characteristic of a mother 2. related on the mother's side 3. relating to or derived from one's mother 4. relating to or characteristic of or befitting a parent [marriage mater matriarchy melt mother motherly adore affectionate ancestral tender romantic nurture languish love] "warm maternal affection for her guest"
*matinee 11-24-17 (n.) 1. a theatrical performance held during the daytime (especially in the afternoon) [matin afternoon theatrical]
*matriculate 24-41-1 (n.) 1. someone who has been admitted to a college or university (v.) 1. enroll as a student [matric meeting membership academic accept admit tabulate recruit register registry require index inscribe inscription inventory chronicle college course university listing log education enlist enrol enter]
*matrimony 22-57-2 (n.) 1. state of being husband and wife 2. the ceremony or sacrament of marriage [marital marry match mint misalliance miscegenation monogamy mony accept agreement alliance allow authority temporary traditional tribe receive relationship religious require rite ritual roman rule impose institute intermarriage iran orthodox nuptial year]
*matrix 11-64-15 (n.) 1. a rectangular array of elements (or entries) set out by rows and columns 2. an enclosure within which something originates or develops (from the Latin for womb) 3. mold used in the production of phonograph records, type, or other relief surface 4. the formative tissue at the base of a nail 5. the body substance in which tissue cells are embedded [main makeup mass mat material mathematical medium mesoderm metal milieu mint model mold mostly mould absorb adult alloy archetype array art atmosphere template tendon tissue tough turn type record rectangular relief rigid rock row impression intaglio interconnecte]
*maudlin 18-53-4 (a.) 1. effusively or insincerely emotional [mad maud mawkish merry muddle mushy addle affect alcohol apish asinine usual dizzy drippy drunken dumb lachrymose last loony inept insane insincere intoxicate nappy novel nutty]
*maul 09-87-25 (n.) 1. a heavy long-handled hammer used to drive stakes or wedges (v.) 1. split (wood) with a maul and wedges 2. injure badly by beating [mangle manus mar meat merciless mitt molest movie mug mutilate abuse animal appearance assault attack lambaste lash last limb log longhand loot]
*mausoleum 16-53-6 (n.) 1. a large burial chamber, usually above ground [maha marker memory mogul monument mound agra arch sepulcher sepulture shah shrine stone obelisk obituary oleum oppressive ornate ossuary library elaborate emperor expensive]
*maverick 07-53-40 (a.) 1. independent in behavior or thought (n.) 1. someone who exhibits great independence in thought and action 2. unbranded range animal especially a stray calf [malcontent misfit mother mutineer accept agitator alien animal ass aver view eccentric establish exhibit extremist range rebel refuse revolutionist riot rule independent individualist informal intransigent calf case cattle character conduct conform conventional cow kine kinky kook /cire/]
*mawkish 17-71-5 (a.) 1. effusively or insincerely emotional [maggoty maudlin mushy way weepy weevily kish icky insincere saccharine self sentimental sloppy slushy smell soap soft song soppy sticky sympathy syrupy high hokey]
*maxim 10-56-19 (n.) 1. a saying that widely accepted on its own merits 2. English inventor (born in the United States) who invented the Maxim gun that was used in World War I (1840-1916) [maxi merit moral mot motto accept adage aphorism apophthegm apothegm axiom imperative instructive inventor /mix/]
*maze 09-50-25 (n.) 1. complex system of paths or tunnels in which it is easy to get lost 2. something jumbled or confused [maze mesh mess might minotaur mist muddle animal area arrive artifact astonish easy embarrassment entangle entity]
*mead 11-45-17 (n.) 1. United States anthropologist noted for her claims about adolescence and sexual behavior in Polynesian cultures (1901-1978) 2. made of fermented honey and water 3. United States philosopher of pragmatism (1863-1931) [margaret medicate melon add adolescence alcoholic anthropology dilute distill drink]
*meager 13-01-11 (a.) 1. deficient in amount or quality or extent 2. barely adequate [malnutrition marginal mean measly mere minimum miserable eager effective elfin enough entertain exiguous extent abstemious

adequate allowance amount ample ascetic austere gangly gaunt gawky generous rare require resource restricted rudimentary] "meager resources"
*meander 10-49-20 (n.) 1. a curve in a stream (v.) 1. to move or cause to move in a sinuous, spiral, or circular course [maunder maze mean meandrous mesh mess migratory motion move earth elaborate entangle entire err erratic affluent aimless amble ancient anfractuosity architecture art natural nomadic deflection depart design devious direction divagate double drift duct range reflection relaxed river roam round route rove run]
*mechanics 08-45-32 (n.) 1. technical aspects of doing something 2. the branch of physics concerned with the motion of bodies in a frame of reference [mechanic mechanism method microphysics craft cryogenics crystallography acoustics art astrophysics science skill statics]
*medallion 13-20-11 (n.) 1. any of various large ancient Greek coins 2. an award for winning a championship or commemorating some other event 3. a circular helping of food (especially a boneless cut of meat) 4. an emblem indicating that a taxicab is registered [mask material meal meat medal member meritorious metal microchip money emblem emboss enemy ensign extraordinary decorative disc disk drink abstract acorn aerial allegory anaglyph ancient appearance approval army award oak order ornament oval navy neck /lad lade oil/] "medallions of veal"
*meddlesome 22-44-2 (a.) 1. intrusive in a meddling or offensive manner [manner meddle self snoopy offensive officious old]
*medial 18-62-4 (a.) 1. dividing an animal into right and left halves 2. relating to or situated in or extending toward the middle [mean media medium mesial mid middle midline midmost midway morpheme mouth equatorial equidistant exceptional extend dial direct distal divide indifferent inner intervene amidship animal area average language last left len linguistics /aide idem laid/]
*mediate 07-33-34 (a.) 1. acting through or dependent on an intervening agency 2. being neither at the beginning nor at the end in a series (v.) 1. act between parties with a view to reconciling differences 2. occupy an intermediate or middle position or form a connecting link or stage between two others [machinery mechanism media mesne middle minister moderate mollify employ expedient extreme degree depend detente device difference direct discuss disease dispute idea instrumentality intervene intervention achieve adjust advance age agency agreement appeasement arbitrate arrange assist attempt awkward talk /aide idem/] "the disease spread by mediate as well as direct contact"
*medicine 02-39-261 (n.) 1. something that treats or prevents or alleviates the symptoms of disease 2. the learned profession that is mastered by graduate training in a medical school and that is devoted to preventing or alleviating or curing diseases and injuries 3. the branches of medical science that deal with nonsurgical techniques 4. punishment for one's actions (v.) 1. treat medicinally, treat with medicine [medici mixture mycology elixir embryology epidemiology dentistry drop drug immunology inhalant cancer cardiology chiropody cure neurosurgery nostrum nutrition /cide idem/] "he studied medicine at Harvard"
*medieval 05-64-68 (a.) 1. as if belonging to the Middle Ages; old-fashioned and unenlightened 2. relating to or belonging to the Middle Ages 3. characteristic of the time of chivalry and knighthood in the Middle Ages [middle early enlighten eval dark date industry age attitude lack long /ave idem lave/]
*mediocre 08-50-27 (a.) 1. moderate to inferior in quality 2. of no exceptional quality or ability 3. poor to middling in quality [mean med merit mid middling moderate modest equatorial erroneous everyday exceptional damage deficient degree dull improve inadequate inferior insufficient off ordinary caliber central commonplace core respectable routine /idem/] "they improved the quality from mediocre to above average"
*meditation 07-46-40 (n.) 1. continuous and profound contemplation or musing on a subject or series of subjects of a deep or abstruse nature 2. contemplation of spiritual matters (usually on religious or philosophical subjects) [matter meditate mental mind monomania motionless muse ecstatic empty engagement engrossment entreaty extend deep deliberation deliberative destiny develop devotion dormant dreamy idle inactivity instance intent introspection introspective involve thanksgiving think thoughtfulnes absorption abstruse aid appeal application obsession nature /idem tide/] "the habit of meditation is the basis for all real knowledge"
*medley 11-44-16 (n.) 1. a musical composition consisting of a series of songs or other musical pieces from various sources [match member mess miscellany mix musical eclectic equivocal dapple dichromatic different divertissement last length ley]
*mellifluous 18-59-4 (a.) 1. pleasing to the ear [mell mellow melody musical ear enjoyable likable liquid listen felicitous fine flow satisfy silky sing smooth soothe sweet sweetish /fill fille/]
*melodious 20-42-3 (a.) 1. having a musical sound; especially a pleasing tune 2. containing or constituting or characterized by pleasing melody [meadowlark mellow melodic musical euphonious lack lyric odious dulcet interest silvery sing song sound sweet /dol dole idol/] "the melodious song of a meadowlark"
*melodrama 09-50-26 (n.) 1. an extravagant comedy in which action is more salient than characterization [masque monologue morality musical emotion emotive end exaggerate extravagant extravaganza language light

literary operatic demonstrative dialogue display drama dramatic duologue recite review revue romantic ruckus accompany antimasque /dol dole/]
*memento 12-49-12 (n.) 1. a reminder of past events [meme memory monument mound experience necrology tablet token trace trophy obelisk obituary]
*memorable 04-59-102 (a.) 1. worth remembering [marked momentous easy esteem exceptional excite extraordinary observable outstand rare remarkable remember reputable able likely /bar baro/]
*menace 05-59-65 (n.) 1. a threat or the act of threatening 2. something that is a source of danger (v.) 1. express a threat either by an utterance or a gesture 2. pose a threat to; present a danger to 3. act in a threatening manner [maltreat manager manner minatory mistreat molest money emergency endanger envenom evil evince existence explosive expression extant near nuisance abusive ace actual alarming annoyance approach arise asiatic await certain chancy civilization coming comport compromise conduct confront constant crisis critical crop /can cane/]
*menagerie 15-39-7 (n.) 1. a collection of live animals for study or display 2. the facility where wild animals are housed for exhibition [menage museum enclosure entertain exhibition exotic accumulation aggregation ana animal anthology aquarium assemblage garden group industry installation]
*mendacious 22-67-2 (a.) 1. given to lying 2. intentionally untrue [mend mislead equivocate erroneous express deceitful deliberate dishonest accordance actuality child inaccurate intentional unreliable untruthful shifty spurious statement /cad/]
*mendacity 22-59-2 (n.) 1. the tendency to be untruthful [mythomania equivocation exaggerate deception deliberate dishonesty dodge cavil city inaccuracy tale taradiddle tell tendency yarn /cad/]
*mentality 07-61-41 (n.) 1. mental ability 2. a habitual or characteristic mental attitude that determines how you will interpret and respond to situations [mental mindset esprit experience nous temperament think acumen approach attitude learn ideation inclination interpret]
*mentor 05-56-67 (n.) 1. a wise and trusted guide and advisor (v.) 1. serve as a teacher or trusted counselor [mandarin mani mastermind mind monitor mythology educator expert teacher thinker topic tor trainer trust tutor oracle rabbi renowned rishi] "The famous professor mentored him during his years in graduate school"
*mercantile 10-17-20 (a.) 1. of or relating to the economic system of mercantilism 2. of or relating to or characteristic of trade or traders 3. profit oriented [manage militant moneymaker economy engage enterprise commercial connected ahead anti theory trade /acre nacre/] "mercantile theories"
*mercenary 11-61-15 (a.) 1. marked by materialism 2. profit oriented 3. used of soldiers hired by a foreign army (n.) 1. a person hired to fight for another country than their own [mark martial materialistic member merc militant miserly motivate myrmidon employee engage enjoy enterprise espionage esurient rapacious ravenous reception rent risk charter commercial connected corruptible country covet nin acquisitive adventurer army art assassination assistant avaricious avid]
*merciful 18-59-4 (a.) 1. showing or giving mercy 2. characterized by mercy, and compassion 3. used conventionally of royalty and high nobility [making mark merci mercy metaphoricall mild moderate motivate easy easygoing everlasting radiant royalty captive charm clement compassionate concern considerate conventionall creative immortal incline indulgent infinite inhumane forbear forgiving fortunate ubiquitous understand ungracious unlimited unpleasant laxness lenient liberal loving lucky] "sought merciful treatment for the captives"
*merciless 11-65-17 (a.) 1. having or showing no mercy [malevolent merci metaphoricall mortal murderous enemy relentless remorseless rough ruthless callous clemency cold compassion continue cover critic crude cruel cutthroat implacable impossible inclement indifferent inexorable insensitive lack level sanguinary savage severe shakespeare show] "the merciless enemy"
*mercurial 12-60-13 (a.) 1. liable to sudden unpredictable change 2. relating to or containing or caused by mercury 3. relating to or having characteristics (eloquence, shrewdness, swiftness, thievishness) attributed to the god Mercury 4. relating to or under the (astrological) influence of the planet Mercury [mark metallic militant mobile moment moody mouth eccentric element energetic erratic express rapid rough running canal change changeful clever cool copper curia uncertain unchangeable uneven unpredictable utterly impulsive inconstant inferior influence ingenious irresponsible activism alive alteration animate atomic attribute leaden liable lively lubricious /lair/]
*meretricious 24-70-1 (a.) 1. (archaic) like or relating to a prostitute 2. tastelessly showy 3. based on pretense; deceptively pleasing [manner mean mere miserable misleading earthy elevated extravagant raw ring rotten rough rude tacky tall tart tasteless tatty tawdry tortuous trashy trollop inkhorn insincere inwardly car cheap cocotte color common costume crude cyprian obscene ornament ostentatious overwrought sad seeming shirt showy significant sincerity social specious spectacular stylish superficial sway] "meretricious relationships"
*meritorious 22-40-2 (a.) 1. deserving reward or praise [medal merit model esteem estimable excellent exemplary recognition reputable respect reverend reward outstanding unexceptionable unworthy service show /roti tire/] "a lifetime of meritorious service"
*mesmerize 13-02-10 (v.) 1. attract strongly, as if with a magnet 2. induce hypnosis in [magnetize marvel

method mislead monopolize enchant enthral enthrall entrance excite exercise sedate sedative seduce speaker spellbind stagger stare strong surprise rivet immerse induce infatuate influence intrigue involve]
*metal 03-42-195 (a.) 1. containing or made of or resembling or characteristic of a metal (n.) 1. any of several chemical elements that are usually shiny solids that conduct heat or electricity and can be formed into sheets etc. 2. a mixture containing two or more metallic elements or metallic and nonmetallic elements usually fused together or dissolving into each other when molten (v.) 1. cover with metal [marshal mass matter meet mercury mineral mixture motto einsteinium element erbium escutcheon europium tar temperature thermal tin titanium achievement alloy aluminum americium argentiferous arm asphalt auriferous label lighter lithium luster /late/] "a metallic compound"
*metallurgy 18-34-4 (n.) 1. the science and technology of metals [material metal mineral molten engineer extraction technology alloy lower raw reduction ref rod ground /late/]
*metamorphosis 15-40-7 (n.) 1. the marked and rapid transformation of a larva into an adult that occurs in some animals 2. a complete change of physical form or substance especially as by magic or witchcraft 3. a striking change in appearance or character or circumstances [magic mark metathesis metempsychosis modification morphosis mutation tadpole translation transubstantiation adult alter animal appearance avatar old organism overnight rapid reincarnation revise partial permutation physical pond power process hem hol house shape sport striking structure substance supernatural suppose ice insect /mat mate prom/] "the metamorphosis of the old house into something new and exciting"
*metaphor 05-43-68 (n.) 1. a figure of speech in which an expression is used to refer to something that it does not literally denote in order to suggest a similarity [makeshift mannered match mean meaty meet mimic modality effect emblematic equal exchange exploit expression extension token transfer trope tropology agent allegory allusive alternative association peculiar pointed produce proportion proxy hide hypallage hyperbole occur once opposition ornament oxymoron readable real refer referential relation represent reserve /pat pate/]
*metaphysical 14-42-9 (a.) 1. without material form or substance 2. pertaining to or of the nature of metaphysics 3. highly abstract and over-theoretical [materialistic mechanistic mystic eclectic esoteric existential theism theosophy abstract anagogic animism physical positivism pragmatist preternatural hedonist humanist hypothetical scholastic speculative spiritual supernatural idealistic incorporeal instrumentalist insubstantial cabalistic conjecture /pat pate/] "metaphysical philosophy"
*metaphysics 22-40-2 (n.) 1. the philosophical study of being and knowing [mechanics epistemology essential ethics existence existentialism theory think abstract aesthetics axiology phenomenology philosophy physics principle hypostasis sophistry space study investigate casuistry causality concern cosmology /pat pate/]
*meticulous 07-54-43 (a.) 1. marked by precise accordance with details 2. marked by extreme care in treatment of details [mark methodical mindful minute earnest etiquette exact excessive exquisite extremely taste textualism thorough toughness treatment trivial imprecise careful cleanliness close concern conscientious correct craftsman critical cul unsparing literal loyal observe okay orderly scrupulous sensitivity severe sharp specific stern straight stringency /cite item/] "was worryingly meticulous about trivial details"
*metric 13-26-10 (a.) 1. based on the meter as a standard of measurement 2. (prosody) the rhythmic arrangement of syllables [math matter maximize measure meet mensuration meter much multiple element energy equal estimate exchange express temperature throb topology trochaic radian recurring regularity relation rhythmic rhythmical iambic interaction capacity choice chorography concentration coordinate] "the metric system"
*metronome 18-55-4 (n.) 1. clicking pendulum indicates the exact tempo of a piece of music [mark mean measured metro monochord mounted music mute epochal even exact teeterboard tempo temporal timer reciprocal recur recurring regular rhythmic oscillate /mono/]
*metropolis 11-51-16 (n.) 1. a large and densely populated urban area; may include several independent administrative districts 2. people living in a large densely populated municipality [magistracy megalopolis metro municipality electorate exurbia territory town region ride oblast outskirt parish port precinct province important stake state suburbia /port silo/]
*metropolitan 03-29-196 (a.) 1. relating to or characteristic of a metropolis (n.) 1. a person who lives in a metropolis [metro municipality eastern ecclesiastical equivalent territory title resident occupy official orthodox out patriarch period place position prolong province live include inhabitant internal archbishop area /port/] "metropolitan area"
*mettle 14-68-9 (n.) 1. the courage to carry on [makeup meet mental mind mold eccentricity elan emotional enable enthusiasm temperament tendency twist type lean life lively]
*microbe 15-31-7 (n.) 1. a minute life form (especially a disease-causing bacterium); the term is not in technical use [micro minute minutiae mite mold individual iota coccus creature crumb reovirus rhinovirus rickettsia organism organization bacterium being bug echovirus enterovirus]
*microcosm 14-48-9 (n.) 1. a miniature model of

something [micro microscopic miniature model molecular imperceptible intangible invisible college community copy corpuscle representative stand subatomic]
*microphone 07-46-43 (n.) 1. device for converting sound waves into electrical energy [mean micro mike move capacitor cartridge cassette compact condenser contact convert crystal record phone piezoelectric plate head hide electrical energy]
*microscope 12-44-12 (n.) 1. magnifier of the image of small objects [magnify micro modify much illuminate image instrument invention capillary cell reflect resolve observer obtain optical scientific simultaneousl sketch study surface parallel power produce purpose electron enable] "the invention of the microscope led to the discovery of the cell"
*microscopic 13-41-11 (a.) 1. of or relating to or used in microscopy 2. infinitely or immeasurably small 3. extremely precise with great attention to details 4. too small to be seen except under a microscope [macroscopic magnitude mathematical micro mini minute molecular immeasurable infallible infinitesimal intangible invisible care close constant corpuscle refined research rigid rigorous scale see severe sharp square strict sub subatomic pinpoint precise protoplasm] "microscopic analysis"
*middling 17-60-5 (a.) 1. of no exceptional quality or ability (ad.) 1. to a moderately sufficient extent or degree (n.) 1. any commodity of intermediate quality or size (especially when coarse particles of ground wheat are mixed with bran) [medium merit mix modest mood intermediate degree lie ling live neither novel good ground /dim/]
*midsummer 10-50-19 (n.) 1. June 21, when the sun is at its northernmost point [middle month day distance dog dramatist say season set smooth solstice sprite summer summertime sun unfortunate effect equator equinox extend rehearse resolved run /dim/]
*midwife 12-75-12 (n.) 1. a woman skilled in aiding the delivery of babies [mechanism medium minion implement instrument delivery device dummy dupe wife woman existence /dim/]
*mien 20-46-3 (n.) 1. dignified manner or conduct [manner method mood move indication expression]
*migrant 08-61-30 (a.) 1. habitually moving from place to place especially in search of seasonal work (n.) 1. traveler who moves from one region or country to another [menial mobile move mover improve itinerant goer gold grant gypsy ratite region roustabout rover rush animal avifauna avoid navvy nestle nomadic temporary territory toil traveler trek] "appalled by the social conditions of migrant life"
*migrate 09-42-25 (v.) 1. move from one country or region to another and settle there 2. move periodically or seasonally [mid move grate growth range region relocate residency response roam rove run affiliate travel trek tribe economic embryo employment environment expatriate] "Many Germans migrated to South America in the mid-19th century"
*migratory 16-40-6 (a.) 1. used of animals that move seasonally 2. habitually moving from place to place especially in search of seasonal work [meander migration mobile move itinerant gad rambling range region resident roam achieve animal avoid tend tory traipse transitory travel year /rota/] "migratory birds"
*mileage 10-56-20 (n.) 1. distance measured in miles 2. a travel allowance at a given rate per mile traveled 3. the ratio of the number of miles traveled to the number of gallons of gasoline burned [magnitude margin measured milage mile much infinity leeway length lengthy liter longtime emolument emotional employer express extent account advantage allow allowance amazing amount assessment assistance gain gallon gas gasoline give good]
*militant 04-52-110 (a.) 1. showing a fighting disposition without self-seeking 2. engaged in war (n.) 1. a militant reformer [malcolm martial mel member mercurial military motion movement inimical largely leader little thug tough truculent activist activity advocate aggressive alive american animate ant antagonism nation]
*militarism 20-36-3 (n.) 1. aggressiveness that involves the threat of using military force [maintain meritocracy mobocracy monarchy ideal imperialism influence interest internationalism invest involve ism isolationism level theocracy threat triumvirate tyranny aggressivenes aim antagonism aristocracy armed autonomy regency republic strengthen strong]
*militate 22-68-2 (v.) 1. have force or influence; bring about an effect or change [influence inspire tate tell tick act affect aid effect exert express] "Politeness militated against this opinion being expressed"
*militia 06-45-48 (n.) 1. civilians trained as soldiers but not part of the regular army [machine member mercenary law legionnaire lit territorial tie train troop america army]
*milky 13-54-10 (a.) 1. resembling milk in color or cloudiness; not clear [marble milk moisture mushy indecisive insipid irresolute lactiferous leukoderma light liquid]
*millet 18-58-4 (n.) 1. any of various small-grained annual cereal and forage grasses of the genera Panicum, Echinochloa, Setaria, Sorghum, and Eleusine 2. small seed of any of various annual cereal grasses especially Setaria italica 3. French painter of rural scenes (1814-1875) [maize mil mill mush important include italic last loblolly east economically edible europe extensive tropic /tell/]
*mimic 08-47-29 (a.) 1. constituting an imitation (n.) 1. someone who mimics (especially an actor or actress) (v.) 1. imitate (a person, a manner, etc.), esp. for satirical effect [manner mark match mime mimi mirror mock

mum imitate impersonate impressionist caricature colonial comic constitute copy correspond counterfeit] "the mimic warfare of the opera stage"
*mince 08-40-30 (n.) 1. food chopped into small bits (v.) 1. make less severe or harsh 2. cut into small pieces 3. walk daintily [material matter meat mitigate moderate modify mushroom ignore ince negative nice nourishment nutrition chop color crash crumble crush cut ease eat extenuate] "a mince of mushrooms"
*miniature 06-43-49 (a.) 1. being on a very small scale (n.) 1. copy that reproduces something in greatly reduced size 2. painting or drawing included in a book (especially in illuminated medieval manuscripts) [magnitude manuscript match medieval middle mini minute model icon illustration image include initial inside italian negligible abstraction age altarpiece animal antiquity apply art artistic average tiny toy twin usual reduce reflection renaissance reproduce reproduction resemblance effigy engrave extent /ruta tain/] "a miniature camera"
*minimize 08-01-32 (v.) 1. represent as less significant or important 2. make small or insignificant 3. belittle [mini minify misestimate misprize image impart important influence inform insignificant negative erode express extent /mini/] "Let's minimize the risk"
*minion 18-59-4 (n.) 1. a servile or fawning dependant [man mechanism medium mini minus idol implement important inion instrument organ]
*ministration 22-36-2 (n.) 1. assistance in time of difficulty [ministry nurture service servitude show slavery solace succour support tend therapy toward treatment ration religious remedy rescue administer affliction aid alleviate assistance attention office /tart/]
*ministry 03-53-184 (n.) 1. building where the business of a government ministry is transacted 2. religious ministers collectively (especially Presbyterian) 3. a government department under the direction of a minister [management mean medium mini instrumentation service slavery stand steward structure support tend them they transact relation religious remedy rescue roof]
*minority 03-35-235 (n.) 1. being or relating to the smaller in number of two parts 2. a group of people who differ racially or politically from a larger group of which it is a part 3. any age prior to the legal age [main manage marginal mean member minor much inability inadequate incompetency indefinite inhabit insufficient national non nonage offensive organization racial rawness relation religious rest total year young /iron tiro/] "when the vote was taken they were in the minority"
*minute 01-59-1447 (a.) 1. infinitely or immeasurably small 2. immeasurably small 3. characterized by painstaking care and detailed examination (n.) 1. a particular point in time 2. an indefinitely short time 3. a unit of time equal to 60 seconds or 1/60th of an hour 4. distance measured by the time taken to cover it 5. a short note 6. a unit of angular distance equal to a 60th of a degree [memorial meticulous microscopic min miniature minor modern month index individual infinitesimal inner insignificant instant new nice notation note now tally technical term tiny transaction trice twinkle enter entry exact exhaustive express extraordinary eye /tun/] "two minute whiplike threads of protoplasm"
*mirage 12-41-13 (n.) 1. an optical illusion in which atmospheric refraction by a layer of hot air distorts or inverts reflections of distant objects 2. something illusory and unattainable [merely messina mira misconception morgan illusion illusory imagine impression incorrect invert rage real reflection refraction alternate apparition appear appearance arthur atmospheric ensnare entangle entrap /gari rim/]
*misadventure 16-49-6 (n.) 1. an instance of misfortune [mischance misfortune mishap misstep injury inoperative instance shipwreck shock slip accidental adventure avoid death disaster down error threatening tire tragedy trouble uncontrollable unfortunate unlucky untoward]
*misanthrope 20-54-3 (n.) 1. someone who dislikes people in general [malcontent malevolent malignity mankind misogyny mistrust sardonic sexist spiteful strong abomination anchorite antipathy aversion avoid tend hate hatred hermit humanity racist recluse reclusive repugnance rope odium people person pessimist philanthropy]
*misanthropic 20-67-3 (a.) 1. believing the worst of human nature and motives; having a sneering disbelief in e.g. selflessness of others 2. hating mankind in general [mankind motive irritable sardonic self sexist show sneer solitary standoffish anthropic antisocial nature trustful hate human reclusive reserved pessimistic philanthropic cynical]
*misanthropy 24-56-1 (n.) 1. hatred of mankind 2. a disposition to dislike and mistrust other people [mankind mistrust sardonic strong hate hatred reclusive ropy people pessimism philanthropy]
*misbehave 16-63-6 (v.) 1. behave badly [misconduct misdemean morn move improper silly bad behave behavior] "The children misbehaved all morning"
*misbehavior 17-58-5 (n.) 1. improper or wicked or immoral behavior [malicious mature minor misconduct misdeed immoral impropriety indecent indiscretion infantile intimacy shenanigan behavior breach etiquette abnormality act annoyance antisocial violent rascality reckless roguish rule]
*mischievous 09-64-22 (a.) 1. badly behaved 2. naughtily or annoyingly playful 3. deliberately causing harm or damage [malevolent malign malignant mean misbehave misc much ill imp impish inclination injury insidious intention irk irritate saucy scamp school serious sly spirit spiteful sportive capable color corruptive counterproductive harmful hazardous high

hurtful elfish elvish evil express venomous vicious virulent odious offensive ominous undesirable]
*miscreant 17-72-5 (n.) 1. a person without moral scruples [malefactor malevolent malicious misc mischievous moral mug infamous infidel iniquitous insult scalawag scamp scapegrace scoundrel scruple sexual sheep civil contemptible corrupt criminal crook rascal reckless religious reprobate rogue rowdy evil acceptable nefarious thug transgresse trollop troublemaker]
*misdeed 16-31-6 (n.) 1. improper or wicked or immoral behavior [malefactor malfeasance malicious mature minor misbehavior misconduct immoral impropriety indecent indiscretion infantile injustice intimacy shenanigan sin slip deed delinquency dereliction deviltry discomfort enormity error etiquette evil]
*misdemeanor 10-14-20 (n.) 1. a crime less serious than a felony [malfeasance malpractice misbehavior misconduct misdemean misrepresent molest illegal impropriety indiscretion infringe inhabitant injustice sin slip defraud delinquency deprive dereliction disruptive enormity error evildoer exposure agitate arouse atrocity authority naked naughty nonfeasance nudity oath obtain offensive omission outrage overthrow repose resistance roughhouse rowdy ruffian]
*miser 22-60-2 (n.) 1. a stingy hoarder of money and possessions (often living miserably) [magpie mean mise money muckworm saver scrooge selfish skinflint spend squirrel stiff stingy exciseman]
*mishap 11-52-17 (n.) 1. an unpredictable outcome that is unfortunate 2. an instance of misfortune [misadventure mischance misfortune misstep move injury inoperative instance science set sharp shipwreck shock slip smashup sudden hap hazard hole accidental adversity airplane avoid phenomenon piece pileup pressure]
*misinterpret 12-50-13 (v.) 1. interpret falsely 2. interpret in the wrong way 3. interpret wrongly [misapprehend misconstrue misjudge misread misrepresent miss mistake misunderstand misuse idea illusion impression injudicious interpret interpretation screwup see sin slant squeeze stick strain torture err errancy explanation read remark peccant pervert point /nisi/]
*mislay 20-86-3 (v.) 1. place (something) where one cannot find it again [misplace miss islay sacrifice set slay leave lie location losel abstract]
*mismanage 09-37-23 (v.) 1. manage badly or incompetently [malpractice manage mess misconduct misguided mishandle misspell misuse murder impolitic incompetent inexpedient spoil abuse negligent nonfeasance embezzle] "The funds were mismanaged"
*misnomer 18-51-4 (n.) 1. an incorrect or unsuitable name [incorrect nome /mons/]
*misogynist 20-65-3 (n.) 1. a misanthrope who dislikes women in particular [male misanthrope miso mother general]
*misogyny 14-64-9 (n.) 1. hatred of women [malevolent misanthropy miso monasticism monk mother sex sexist single spinster spiteful strong odium general group nun]
*misplace 09-61-24 (v.) 1. place or position wrongly; put in the wrong position 2. place (something) where one cannot find it again [malapropos mislay modifier improper inept irrelevant set shuffle perturb place pose position put leave lie location losel abstract amiss askew awry certain cockeyed confidence convulse eyeglass /psi/] "I misplaced my eyeglasses"
*misrepresent 10-42-21 (v.) 1. represent falsely 2. fake or falsify [mangle manipulate mask mean message misconstruction misdirect misuse move mutilate inaccurate intention sentimentality serve sham simulate slant statement story strain represent representative embellish embroider engage equivocation exaggerate express parody pass perjury pervert practice pretend prevaricate nature tale torture travesty trickery true turn twist] "This statement misrepresents my intentions"
*misrule 22-54-2 (n.) 1. government that is inefficient or dishonest [maladministration misconduct misgovern mishandle mismanage muddle inefficient inexpedient snafu syndicalism rebellion revolution riot rule unjust unruly lawless license exercise]
*missile 03-32-142 (n.) 1. a weapon that is thrown or projected 2. rocket carrying passengers or instruments or a warhead [metal miss mortar infrared instrument internal shaft shape shell shot signal slug snake solid sound sphere spinner spitball stabilize stick stone straight launch light ejective emission emit engine equip explore]
*missive 17-71-5 (n.) 1. a written message addressed to a person or organization [mail mark matter mean memorandum message miss multiple indignant intention screen sent serve sign successive symbolic editor encyclical epistle exchange express]
*mistrust 11-49-17 (n.) 1. doubt about someone's honesty 2. the trait of not trusting others (v.) 1. regard as untrustworthy; regard with suspicion; have no faith or confidence in [misgiving incertitude shy skepticism suspicious swear trait trust trusting refuse reject rely reservation unable uncertainty unsure untrustworthy]
*misty 12-55-14 (a.) 1. filled or abounding with fog or mist 2. wet with mist [mist morn mountain muddy murky indeterminate indistinct indistinguishable inform sad slight small soak spray steamy subtle surround tenuous thread transcendent]
*misunderstand 07-53-44 (v.) 1. interpret in the wrong way [mean misapprehend misconstrue miscue misjudge misprint misread mistake mistreat inaccurate incorrect interpret see sister sorely squabble squeeze sympathetic understand undervalue unpopular unsung disagreement dislike dispute distorted division embarrass erratum

error explanation remark rift row teenager tense true twist admit amiss argument assign]
*misuse 08-51-31 (n.) 1. improper or excessive use (v.) 1. apply to a wrong thing or person; apply badly or incorrectly 2. change the inherent purpose or function of something [manipulate milk million mis misappropriate mismanage money much ill illegal improper inappropriate incorrect infelicity inherent intend investigate say secret sentence service slant strain stroke substance ulcerate usage use utilize employment error excessive exercise expend exploit]
*mite 15-63-7 (n.) 1. a slight but appreciable addition 2. any of numerous very small to minute arachnids often infesting animals or plants or stored foods [magnitude minimum minute mit molecule money monkey indefinite infest inhale innocent insect invertebrate iota tad tarantula terrestrial tetra tick tinge tiny touch trapdoor tree trivia early]
*miter 24-01-1 (n.) 1. a liturgical headdress worn by bishops on formal occasions (v.) 1. bevel the edges of, to make a miter joint 2. confer a miter on, as of a bishop 3. fit together in a miter joint [main material meet mitre mortise indicate interface iter tack tall tiara top edge elbow embrace rabbet ribbon ring rivet]
*mitigate 08-61-27 (v.) 1. lessen or to try to lessen the seriousness or extent of 2. make less severe or harsh [mercy mince minify moderate moderator modify modulate mollify ignore impose improvement inanition tack tame temper thin tone transition try gate gild gloss grace gruel abate accommodation adaptation adjustment allay alleviate alter anodyne apologize assuage authority ease enfeeble eviscerate excuse exhaust explain extenuate /git tag/]
*moat 15-70-8 (n.) 1. ditch dug as a fortification and usually filled with water [mine moa mole mound oat opening abyss access animal aqueduct arroyo attack trench trough tunnel]
*moccasin 22-34-2 (n.) 1. soft leather shoe; originally worn by native Americans [material mukluk mule origin oxford clog court cowboy cross american ankle asin sand seam shoe side slingback slipper sneaker soft sole stiletto stitch native]
*mockery 11-64-17 (n.) 1. showing your contempt by derision 2. a composition that imitates somebody's style in a humorous way 3. humorous or satirical mimicry [mimicry miscarriage mock mocker monkey offense outrage caricature cent charade comic composition contemptuous cut kickshaw effect empty enormity exaggerate rap ridiculous rush]
*moderation 11-49-15 (n.) 1. quality of being moderate and avoiding extremes 2. a change for the better 3. the action of lessening in severity or intensity 4. the trait of avoiding excesses [mean measure medium denial diminution discipline equable ration reasonable relief renounce renunciation restriction abnegate temperance temperate immoderate /redo tare/] "the object being control or moderation of economic depressions"
*moderator 15-36-8 (n.) 1. any substance used to slow down neutrons in nuclear reactors 2. someone who mediates disputes and attempts to avoid violence 3. someone who presides over a forum or debate [magistrate maintain mediator meeting minister moderato modulate officer oxide debate denomination deuterium diplomat discussion dispute emcee reactor referee representative retard absorb administrator agent alleviate apparatus arbitrator artificial assembly assuage atom avoid temper toastmaster tranquilizer /redo rota tare/]
*modernity 12-56-14 (n.) 1. the quality of being current or of the present [mall modern innovativenes instill trendy /redo/] "a shopping mall would instill a spirit of modernity into this village"
*modernize 08-01-31 (v.) 1. become technologically advanced 2. make repairs or adjustments to [mod modern modernistic modish old original overhaul develop different engine equipment essence rapid rebuild reestablish reform regenerate remodel renew renovate repair revolution revolutionize nature new novel now improve innovation /redo/]
*modicum 15-56-7 (n.) 1. a small or moderate or token amount [magnitude measure mess minimum mite moderate modi ounce deal degree dividend drop indefinite interest iota commission cut] "England still expects a modicum of eccentricity in its artists"
*modification 09-35-23 (n.) 1. slightly modified copy; not an exact copy 2. the act of making something different (as e.g. the size of a garment) 3. an event that occurs when something passes from one state or phase to another 4. the grammatical relation that exists when a word qualifies the meaning of the phrase [mitigate moderation mutation mute occlusive overthrow death deteriorate discrimination division improvement individuation fitting cation check concession conversion accommodation adjustment alteration analysis temper transmogrify turnabout nasal nascent nativity /fid/] "a modification of last year's model"
*modify 05-39-67 (v.) 1. (grammar) add a modifier to a constituent 2. make changes to [malleable mitigate mobile moderate modi modification modulate movable mutate opalize overthrow decrease degenerate deviant distinguish divergent divide impermanent improve individuate inseminate fit flexible fluid freshen /fid/] "please modify this letter to make it more polite"
*modish 17-80-5 (a.) 1. in the current fashion or style [mod mode modernize dashing dish smart streamline stylish]
*modulate 15-34-8 (v.) 1. change the key of, in music 2. of one's speech, varying the pitch 3. adjust the pitch, tone, or volume of 4. vary the frequency, amplitude, phase, or other characteristic of (electromagnetic waves) 5. fix or adjust the time, amount, degree, or rate of [measure melody mitigate moderate modify mollify

mouth move musical obtund oral orchestrate overthrow deal degree deteriorate device different diversify down due dull underplay upheaval utter language late leniency lessen lie lilt limit loosen loudness lower accent accord accuracy achieve adapt adjust alleviate alter alteration amend amount amplitude anodyne arrangement assuage tack talk tame temper temperature tonal tone transmit turnabout essence express extenuate /ludo udo/] "modulate the melody"

*mollify 16-36-6 (v.) 1. cause to be more favorably inclined; gain the good will of 2. make less rigid or softer 3. make more temperate, acceptable, or suitable by adding something else; moderate [manage mash massage mellow moderate moll lenify lessen lie loosen lull incline intense irenic favor fluff foment /fill/] "She managed to mollify her angry boss"

*molt 24-03-1 (n.) 1. periodic shedding of the cuticle in arthropods or the outer skin in reptiles (v.) 1. cast off hair, skin, horn, or feathers; of animals [mol moulting outer lose loss throw]

*momentary 14-44-9 (a.) 1. lasting for a markedly brief time [markedly meet menstrual moment monthly mortal ephemeral evanescent temporary transitory triennial annual association yearly /nemo/]

*momentous 10-62-18 (a.) 1. of very great significance"deciding to drop the atom bomb was a very big decision" [major material meaningful mighty momento official earth effect eminent empower enchanting extremely name telling totalitarian senior serious shatter significant strong /nemo/]

*momentum 04-57-120 (n.) 1. the product of a body's mass and its velocity 2. an impelling force or strength [mass measure meteorite moment motion move omentum element energy equal essential express thrust /mut nemo/] "the car's momentum carried it off the road"

*monarchy 10-66-18 (n.) 1. an autocracy governed by a monarch who usually inherits the authority [meritocracy mobocracy monarch monarchism ochlocracy oligarchy nation neocolonialism aristocracy autarchy authority autocracy autonomy regency republic royal royalist rule colonialism commonwealth country head heteronomous hierocracy /cran/]

*monastery 10-59-21 (n.) 1. the residence of a religious community [monk observe origin nun nunnery abbey abbot aster seclusion religious residence room rule]

*monetary 04-47-97 (a.) 1. relating to or involving money [medium monet economic exchange receive regulate reward /rate/] "monetary rewards"

*mongrel 20-70-3 (a.) 1. of inferior or mixed breed (n.) 1. derogatory term for a variation that is not genuine; something irregular or inferior or of dubious origin 2. an inferior dog or one of mixed breed [member mix mong mulatto mule mutt octoroon offensive origin owner nervous norm genus racial reptile ladino liger little lurcher]

*monogamy 17-57-5 (n.) 1. having one wife at a time [marry mate matrimony monandry monogyny multiple gamy anthropology]

*monogram 18-46-4 (n.) 1. a graphic symbol consisting of 2 or more letters combined (usually your initials); printed on stationery or embroidered on clothing [mark gram graphic acquire arbitrary autograph /argon gon gono/]

*monograph 18-39-4 (n.) 1. a detailed and documented treatise on a particular subject [memoir morceau outline note graph article paper paragraph piece profile homily /argon gon gono/]

*monolith 17-51-5 (n.) 1. a single great stone (often in the form of a column or obelisk) [marker massive material megalith menhir monument mound obelisk obituary organization natural necrology lava level limestone lith long immovable inscription tablet tall testimonial trophy headstone hew human]

*monologue 09-38-26 (n.) 1. speech you make to yourself 2. a (usually long) dramatic speech by a single actor 3. a long utterance by one person (especially one that prevents others from participating in the conversation) [masque melodrama mimic mono monotony motion mouth movie mummer opera oral oration orderly language lecture line long gasser giveaway uninterrupted utterance entertainer entire epilogue extravaganza]

*monomania 22-53-2 (n.) 1. a mania restricted to one thing or idea [mania meditation motive obsessive absorption application idea immersion interest involve irrational irresistible /mono/]

*monopoly 06-51-57 (n.) 1. (economics) a market in which there are many buyers but only one seller 2. exclusive control or possession of something 3. (trademark) a board game in which players try to gain a monopoly on real estate as pieces advance around the board according to the throw of a die [management manipulate manufacturer marketplace mono monopolize ownership personal piece player political pool possession power price production prohibition proprietor provider law legal] "a monopoly on silver"

*monotone 18-49-4 (a.) 1. (mathematics) of a sequence or function; consistently increasing and never decreasing or consistently decreasing and never increasing in value 2. sounded or spoken in a tone unvarying in pitch (n.) 1. an unchanging intonation [math melody modulate mono monotony musical mutter orderly overtone owl never nexus non notation note thread tier tone train exactly expression /ton/]

*monotonous 15-50-7 (a.) 1. tediously repetitious or lacking in variety 2. sounded or spoken in a tone unvarying in pitch [mechanical melody mono monotonic ordinary owl nonstop tedious tire tiresome together tone unbroken unceasing uniform uninterest uninterrupted unmelodious unmusical unvarying utter sea smooth sound speak steady straight /ton/] "the owl's

faint monotonous hooting"
*monotony 17-51-5 (n.) 1. the quality of wearisome constancy and lack of variety [mono music orderly overtone never nothing tedium tone treadmill trot /ton/] "he had never grown accustomed to the monotony of his work"
*monsieur 15-76-8 (n.) 1. used as a French courtesy title; equivalent to English 'Mr' [male mons oppose english equivalent /rue/]
*monstrosity 18-59-4 (n.) 1. something hideous or frightful 2. a person or animal that is markedly unusual or deformed [malformation markedly massive mess misc mons monstrous mutation mutilate oddity organism outrage overwhelming nat sight size sport strangely strangeness superiority teratology torticollis truncate immense inferiority irregularity /sort/] "they regarded the atom bomb as a monstrosity"
*moonbeam 24-60-1 (n.) 1. a ray of moonlight [milky night beacon beam]
*morale 06-65-49 (n.) 1. the spirit of a group that makes the members want the group to succeed 2. a state of individual psychological well-being based upon a sense of confidence and usefulness and purpose [member mental mind mood moral motivation octet optimism rale reciprocity rectitude righteous affect angelic assurance attitude level ecumenism emotion esprit ethical]
*moralist 15-41-7 (n.) 1. a philosopher who specializes in morals and moral problems 2. someone who demands exact conformity to rules and forms [manner martineta monitory moral recommend regulate righteous rule academic admonitory advisory alist axiology lace insist instructive saint seek sententious serious specialize standard stickler strait strict study teacher tyrannical]
*morality 07-51-37 (n.) 1. motivation based on ideas of right and wrong 2. concern with the distinction between good and evil or right and wrong; right or good conduct [matter melodrama monologue moral mores motive opera organism reason respect review revue right accept accord adhere admirable angelic antimasque arouse assignment attribute lecture lesson light logical idea ideal inner instruction integrity task teach toward]
*moralize 22-02-2 (v.) 1. interpret the moral meaning of 2. improve the morals of 3. speak as if delivering a sermon; express moral judgements [moral reclaim rectify reform regenerate review right abandon adopt advise advocate analyze annotate argue lead lecture life improve interpretation evil explanation expound express] "moralize a story"
*moratorium 10-22-18 (n.) 1. a legally authorized postponement before some obligation must be discharged 2. suspension of an ongoing activity [meeting obligation obliterate obstruction ongoing orator reprieve respite retardation right abeyance afterthought agree allow authorize await temporary interim /rota taro/]
*morbid 13-61-10 (a.) 1. suggesting an unhealthy mental state 2. caused by or altered by or manifesting disease or pathology 3. suggesting the horror of death and decay [macabre maleficent manifest medicine melancholic melancholy mental mind monstrous moody moral morose murder offensive ominous redoubtable bad baleful bid blue body illness infect inspire interested itch dark death decay depressed detail disease disgusting] "morbid interest in death"
*mordant 17-42-5 (a.) 1. harshly ironic or sinister (n.) 1. a substance used to treat leather or other materials before dyeing; aids in dyeing process [material medicine metal mordacious moxa radium range redo ridicule rigorous roughness dichromate driving droll dye acerbic acid acrid acrimony aid alum ant apply area art asperity astringent nervous tan tart tartrate telling textile treat trenchant]
*moribund 13-48-11 (a.) 1. not growing or changing; without force or vitality 2. on the point of death; breathing your last [obsolete inert infirm invalid bad becoming blase bore breathing bun unhealthy unsound nearly nonviable numb dead death decline dilapidate dying dynamic /biro nub/] "a moribund patient"
*morose 17-54-5 (a.) 1. showing a brooding ill humor [manner melancholy misanthropic miserable moody mopey rose sad saturnine scowl show shrug sickly silence sit snug sour sullen]
*motley 13-51-10 (a.) 1. consisting of a haphazard assortment of different kinds (even to the point of incongruity) 2. having sections or patches colored differently and usually brightly (n.) 1. a collection containing a variety of sorts of things 2. a garment made of motley (especially a court jester's costume) 3. a multicolored woolen fabric woven of mixed threads in 14th to 17th century England (v.) 1. make something more diverse and varied 2. make motley; color with different colors [many match material medieval melange menu minglemangle miscellany mishmash mix multicoloured music odd oddment omniumgatherum outfit tattoo textile thread tights tone last ley eclectic element england equivocal erratic /tom/]
*motto 09-57-24 (n.) 1. a favorite saying of a sect or political group [marshal maxim metal moral mott music oracle ordinary orle teach text tincture /tom/]
*mountaineer 14-57-9 (n.) 1. someone who climbs mountains (v.) 1. climb mountains for pleasure, as a sport [mariner mountain upward nor ten tourist transient traveler adventurer alpinist area astronaut athletics attain inhabitant edmund enjoy everest excursionist exertion explorer redneck require rock rubbernecker]
*mountainous 11-50-16 (a.) 1. containing many mountains 2. like a mountain in size and impressiveness 3. having hills and crags [magnitude massive mighty monstrous monumental mountain outsize overgrown upland tall terrain titanic towering tremendous alpine astronomical average awesome immense impressivenes

infinite irregular ship size smooth spacious staggering steep surface]
*mouthful 14-73-9 (n.) 1. the quantity that can be held in the mouth 2. a small amount eaten or drunk [magnitude meal meaningful morsel mouth munch unfamiliar taste tirade harangue hard hold hunk fill food fork lade last lecture liquid little load lump]
*muddle 09-62-26 (n.) 1. a confused multitude of things 2. informal terms for a difficult situation (v.) 1. make into a puddle 2. mix up or confuse [mar mare marriage mellow merry mess mind mire mix much mud multitude murder mystify unclear unconnected understand unorganized unsettle upheaval upset dazzle deal difficult dinner disarray disaster disguise disk disorganization disturbance dizzy dog drink drunken license lick limp litter look easy effort embarrassment entangle expect]
*muffle 13-42-10 (n.) 1. a kiln with an inner chamber for firing things at a low temperature (v.) 1. conceal or hide 2. deaden (a sound or noise), esp. by wrapping [mantle masked material mellow muff mute muted uncover film fire flame flat floor force form latent layover less loud low lurk ear eclipse enclose enfold envelop esoteric express eyebrow]
*muffler 22-15-2 (n.) 1. a tubular acoustic device inserted in the exhaust system that is designed to reduce noise 2. a device that decreases the amplitude of electronic, mechanical, acoustical, or aerodynamic oscillations 3. a scarf worn around the neck [mantilla masquerade mechanical move muffle mute universal facade fan felt fill fur liquid electronic energy engine exhaust radiator reduce ruff]
*mulatto 24-29-1 (n.) 1. an offspring of a Black and a White parent [mestizo mixed mongrel mule ladino lat liger ancestor tangelo tigon octoroon offensive offspring /alum/]
*multifarious 22-59-2 (a.) 1. having many aspects [manifold many manysided million miscellaneous mix myriad unconformable undertake unequal unlike labyrinthine legion tangle thousand twist implicate include interest intricate involved far allotropic aspect assorted ramify roundabout separate several subtle /fit/]
*multiplicity 18-42-4 (n.) 1. the property of being multiple 2. a large number [magnitude mass mess molecule moment much large lashings level licit lot total indefinite infinitude influence innumerable interaction particle peck people physics plenty possessed power property collection complexity considerable /pit/]
*mundane 08-51-29 (a.) 1. found in the ordinary course of events 2. belonging to this earth or world; not ideal or heavenly 3. concerned with the world or worldly matters [materialistic matter monotonous unblessed unexciting unholy unimagined uninteresting unremarkable unworldly nothing dane day degree diamant dreary dry dull affair animal anita arid earthly earthy everyday]
*municipal 04-11-102 (a.) 1. relating or belonging to or characteristic of a municipality 2. of or relating to the government of a municipality [metropolitan midtown muni uptown urban nation native inland internal intestine city civic civil community concerning council parish park public punish affair assemblage authorize law local /lap/] "municipal government"
*municipality 09-07-25 (n.) 1. an urban district having corporate status and powers of self-government 2. people living in a town or city having local self-government [megalopolis member metropolis ministry municipal urban include independent center city constabulary constitute conurbation corporate people polis populate power purpose administrative appointed area assemblage live local territorial township /lap/]
*munificence 24-70-1 (n.) 1. extremely liberal generosity of spirit [magnanimousne misericord charity extremely]
*munificent 22-66-2 (a.) 1. very generous [magnanimous misericord money mother unselfish unsparing unstinting father freehand freeness cent charitable charity critic extremely too /fin/]
*muster 07-51-40 (n.) 1. a gathering of military personnel for duty 2. compulsory military service (v.) 1. call to duty, military service, jury duty, etc. 2. gather or bring together [machine mass masse match meeting member military miss mobilize must unite selective send service soldier strength summon surge survey thrown turnout emergency enlist enrollment evoke raise rally ready recall request return roll /sum/] "muster the courage to do something"
*mutation 13-50-10 (n.) 1. (biology) an organism that has characteristics resulting from chromosomal alteration 2. a change or alteration in form or qualities 3. (genetics) any event that changes genetic structure; any alteration in the inherited nucleic acid sequence of the genotype of an organism [markedly material metamorphosis metathesis metempsychosis modification modify monstrosity umlaut unusual trait transform transubstantiation turn accord acid alter alteration animal anomaly avatar independent inherit initial innovation ion organism orthoepy nat neutral normal novelty nucleic /tum/]
*mutilate 11-54-17 (v.) 1. destroy or injure severely 2. alter so as to make unrecognizable 3. destroy, as of a limb [madman maim mangle mar maul mayhem message mischief monstrous movie murder unsex takeout tattered tear tearing thumb tourist traumatize truncate impaired important incise inflict infringe injury inroad irritate isolate lacerate lame language late leave lesion limb lop loss abrasion aggravate alter amputate animal annihilation art eliminate embitter exacerbate except exclude /tali tum/] "The madman mutilates art work"
*mutiny 13-59-11 (n.) 1. open rebellion against constituted authority (especially by seamen or soldiers against their officers) (v.) 1. engage in a mutiny against

an authority [mutineer unaccountable uprise tiny try indiscipline insurrection irresponsible /tum/]
*myriad 08-46-27 (a.) 1. too numerous to be counted (n.) 1. a large indefinite number 2. the cardinal number that is the product of ten and one thousand [magnitude many million much multitudinous yard reason repletion rich riotous incalculable indefinite innumerable integer abundance affluent amount avalanche average detail difficulty diverse /airy dairy/] "he faced a myriad of details"
*mystic 11-48-16 (a.) 1. having an import not apparent to the senses nor obvious to the intelligence; beyond ordinary understanding 2. relating to or characteristic of mysticism 3. relating to or resembling mysticism (n.) 1. someone who believes in the existence of realities beyond human comprehension [magical mahatma market meister ment modern mystagogue secrete security sid sorcery spiritual style supernatural supernaturalism symbol symbolic taoism teach theosophy think tic transcendentalism imaginary impenetrable import influence inner inscrutable intelligence intuition cabalistic cerebration circle comprehension confined]
*mystification 24-57-1 (n.) 1. confusion resulting from failure to understand 2. something designed to mystify or bewilder 3. the activity of obscuring people's understanding, leaving them baffled or bewildered [manmade mental specific stupefaction incomprehension failure clear confusion artifact obfuscate obscure orderly]
*myth 04-58-93 (n.) 1. a traditional story accepted as history; serves to explain the world view of a people [maggot mistake thriller traditional trip turn twilight hallucination hero history hold human]
*mythology 10-49-19 (n.) 1. myths collectively; the body of stories associated with a culture or institution or person 2. the study of myths [much mythos tell teuton thriller thunder traditional treasure true hero him history hoard human ology land legend lightning lore love germany god great greek group guard]

N

*nadir 14-75-9 (n.) 1. an extreme state of adversity; the lowest point of anything 2. the point below the observer that is directly opposite the zenith on the imaginary sphere against which celestial bodies appear to be projected [adversity affliction apparent appear dado deep depth despair directly imaginary rock /dan rid/]
*nameless 15-48-7 (a.) 1. being or having an unknown or unnamed source [abominable accurate amel anonymous author awful mention mysterious entitle lack legal shadowy source /leman man/]
*narcissus 20-56-3 (n.) 1. bulbous plant having erect linear leaves and showy yellow or white flowers either solitary or in clusters 2. (Greek mythology) a beautiful young man who fell in love with his own reflection [narc narrow native naturalize numerous ancient anemone reflection central cluster crocus crown cultivate cup cyclamen imaginary individualist iris showy snowdrop solitary southern spring swellhead /cran suss/]
*narrate 10-40-21 (v.) 1. provide commentary for a film, for example 2. narrate or give a detailed account of [novelize account affair allegorize rate recite recount relate report reveal review rhapsody television tell expatiate]
*narration 13-33-11 (n.) 1. a message that tells the particulars of an act or occurrence or course of events 2. (rhetoric) the second section of an oration in which the facts are set forth 3. the act of giving an account describing incidents or a course of events [narrative account actor amuse anecdote arouse radio ration recitation recount relation report review rhetoric rhyme rule tale technique television tell improbable incident incredible inform interest occurrence oration]
*narrative 04-47-101 (a.) 1. consisting of or characterized by the telling of a story (n.) 1. a message that tells the particulars of an act or occurrence or course of events [narration account amuse anecdotic arouse art radio rat relation report review rhyme tale television tell tend idyllic improbable incident incredible interest verse version elegiac entertain epic epos excessive /vita/] "narrative poetry"
*narrator 07-35-37 (n.) 1. someone who tells a story [novelist account africa anecdote annalist author raconteur rat recite refer relator reporter taleteller talk television tell tradition oral /rota/]
*nasal 13-53-10 (a.) 1. sounding as if the nose were pinched 2. of or in or relating to the nose (n.) 1. a continuant consonant produced through the nose with the mouth closed 2. an elongated rectangular bone that forms the bridge of the nose [narrow nosepiece accent adenoidal anterior articulate aspiration assimilation sal

skeleton slur sound speech stop stress strong suture letter light liquid low] "nasal passages"
*nascent 12-48-13 (a.) 1. coming into existence [nascent natal nativity abo aboriginal accouchement antenatal ascent autochthonous scent start childhood come confinement cradle create creative elementary embryonic existence] "a nascent republic"
*natal 15-71-8 (a.) 1. relating to or accompanying birth 2. of or relating to the buttocks (n.) 1. a region of eastern South Africa on the Indian Ocean 2. a port city in northeastern Brazil [nascent nativity natural negroid northern abecedarian aboriginal accompany achieve administrative africa airport alteration american area ass autochthonous tail tall territory true tug large last latin lead leap leave living locate] "natal injuries"
*nationality 07-66-36 (n.) 1. the status of belonging to a particular nation by birth or naturalization [national nativity naturalize aboriginal ally territory tradition tribe independence internationalism origin land language large live]
*naturally 04-63-134 (ad.) 1. according to nature; by natural means; without artificial help 2. in a natural or normal manner 3. through inherent nature 4. as might be expected [natural necessarily normal normative absolutely accord actually aid artificial artless assured talent therefore treatment truly unaffected unassuming unnatural unofficial unpretentious unsurprisingl usual rather realistic really regular represent lawyer lazy legitimate logical yea yeah yes /ruta/] "naturally, the lawyer sent us a huge bill"
*nausea 12-55-12 (n.) 1. the state that precedes vomiting 2. disgust so strong it makes you feel sick [nasty nauseous necrosis abhorrence accompany angst anguish anxiety aversion uneasy unhappy unsettle urge sea seizure sensation shampoo shock sickness soap solvent sore squeamish stomach strong symptom early emetic empty enema enmity ennui experience]
*nauseate 18-59-4 (v.) 1. upset and make nauseated 2. cause aversion in; offend the moral sense of [nasty nausea nauseous noisome noxious abhorrent abominable accompany airsickness anguished anxious appall aversion uneasy unfulfilled unhappy unsettle upset urge sad scandalize shock sicken sickening sloppy smell spoil squeamish stomach strike execrable experience try turn]
*nauseous 20-78-3 (a.) 1. causing or able to cause nausea [nasty nauseating noisome noxious abhorrent accompany anguished anxious uneasy unhappy unpleasant unsettle unwell unwholesome upset urge use sad seasick sickening smell spoil stench stomach suffer emetic offal offensive overripe]
*nautical 12-57-13 (a.) 1. relating to or involving ships or shipping or navigation or seamen [naval navigation thalassic tical transport insurance chart crew law] "nautical charts"
*naval 05-47-67 (a.) 1. connected with or belonging to or used in a navy [nautical navel navigation navy armed attached val vessel last /lava van/] "naval history"
*navel 15-65-8 (n.) 1. scar where the umbilical cord was attached 2. the center point or middle of something [nave nub nucleus attached axis venter vertebrate epicenter equidistant extremity limited line location /levan van/]
*navigable 22-46-2 (a.) 1. able to be sailed on or through safely [negotiable allow gable boat link enable enough /bag van/] "navigable waters"
*navigate 08-44-30 (v.) 1. travel by boat on a boat propelled by wind or by other means 2. direct carefully and safely 3. act as the navigator in a car, plane, or vessel and plann, direct, plot the path and position of the conveyance [accident aircraft airplane allocate altar area assign vessel volplane volunteer voyage instruction interplanetary gate give glide guide tomorrow traverse triangulate trip effort emplace /tag van/]
*nebula 24-40-1 (n.) 1. a medicinal liquid preparation intended for use in an atomizer 2. (pathology) a faint cloudy spot on the cornea 3. an immense cloud of gas (mainly hydrogen) and dust in interstellar space 4. cloudiness of the urine [nature neb nova effect emit envelope expand experience black bodily bolide branch bright brown urine liquid accord appear asteroid atomizer /ben lube/]
*nebulous 17-57-5 (a.) 1. lacking definite form or limits 2. lacking definition or definite content [neutral nonspecific notion easy empyrean equinoctial extragalactic blind blur broad unclear understand unfix unformulated uranic lack limit lou lunate lunulate obscure opaque ought overcloud shadowy solar stated stormy /ben lube/]
*necessary 02-47-383 (a.) 1. unavoidably determined by prior circumstances 2. absolutely essential (n.) 1. anything indispensable [necessity needful entity essential evitable exigent cardinal certain cess circumstance closet compulsory conclusion condition constrain contact convention crucial self separate shelter significant specific absolute absolutely achieve apodictic authority avoid really relentless requisite requisition resistless /ass rasse/] "the necessary consequences of one's actions"
*necessitate 13-53-11 (v.) 1. cause to be a concomitant 2. require as useful, just, or proper [nerve eliminate entail exact call case certain cess claim climate compel concomitant conservation cry sacrifice skill spectacular suffer imply impose inescapable intervention involve affair ask]
*necessity 06-42-55 (n.) 1. anything indispensable 2. the condition of being essential or indispensable [needy earnest enforce entity essential exigency cause cess circumstance compulsion condition constraint create self separate shelter staff stipulate surety impoverish indispensable inevitable insistent truth]
*necropolis 24-62-1 (n.) 1. a tract of land used for burials [elaborate catacomb cemetery churchyard

resting park people piece place polis land locate indigent site /silo/]
*necrosis 24-57-1 (n.) 1. the localized death of living cells (as from infection or the interruption of blood supply) [nausea noma edema emaciate cell chill convulsion cough cro rank rash rot organism seizure shock sore sphacelus supply infection inflammation injury insomnia interruption itch]
*nectar 17-66-5 (n.) 1. a sweet liquid secretion that is attractive to pollinators 2. (classical mythology) the food and drink of the gods; mortals who ate it became immortal 3. fruit juice especially when undiluted [nice eat enjoyable exquisite candy cell choice consider crush tar tasty thick tidbit titbit toothsome treat agreeable ambrosia ambrosial appreciate assist attractive release roman]
*nectarine 22-51-2 (n.) 1. variety or mutation of the peach bearing smooth-skinned fruit with usually yellow flesh 2. smooth-skinned variety or mutation of the peach [nectar edible cherry coconut temperate tree apple apricot avocado region reproductive rosacea]
*needlework 22-35-2 (n.) 1. a creation created or assembled by needle and thread [needle needlepoint net embroidery existence eye darn decorative lace loop work repair require rib knit knot /owe weld/]
*needy 07-24-37 (a.) 1. poor enough to need help from others [necessitous need emotional enough dead deprive destitute disadvantaged]
*nefarious 18-46-4 (a.) 1. extremely wicked [nasty naughty notorious egregious enormous evil extremely far filthy flagrant foul abject atrocious awful rank regrettable reprehensible rotten immoral improper infamous iniquitous obnoxious offensive outrageous unforgivable unspeakable unworthy utterly sad scheme shock small /fen/] "nefarious schemes"
*negate 13-51-11 (v.) 1. be in contradiction with 2. deny the truth of 3. prove negative; show to be false 4. make ineffective by counterbalancing the effect of [negative neutralize nullify effect effort establish evidence experiment explanation explode expose gainsay gate gloom abate abolish abrogate annul automatic theory thwart traverse truth turndown /age tag/]
*negation 24-45-1 (n.) 1. a negative statement; a statement that is a refusal or denial of some other statement 2. (logic) a proposition that is true if and only if another proposition is false 3. the speech act of negating [nay negative nonexistent nullify eliminate empty existence explosion gainsay gat abolition absence affirm alleged analyze annul antagonism antithesis assertion traverse true turndown imply inequality inference invalidate opposition /age tag/]
*neglectful 22-50-2 (a.) 1. leaving vulnerable 2. failing in what duty requires 3. not showing due care or attention [neglect lack lax leave careless casual concern failing financial forgetful undue] "neglectful of her own financial security"
*negligee 24-41-1 (n.) 1. a loose dressing gown for women [gee gown light loose]
*negligence 09-60-23 (n.) 1. the trait of neglecting responsibilities and lacking concern 2. failure to act with the prudence that a reasonable person would exercise under the same circumstances [non nonconformity nonobservance easy escape evasion exercise gen general giddy goal grubby lack lapse law lax leniency level loosen impotent inattention incorrect injury insouciance intend carelessness casual caution concern consequence contributory culpable]
*negligent 11-46-15 (a.) 1. characterized by neglect and undue lack of concern 2. marked by insufficient care or attention [neglect non nonobservance nonrestrictive easy easygoing general gent grasshopper grubby guilty lack law lax lenient level literary loose inaccurate inattentive incorrect indifferent informal insufficient irresponsible tacky task tattered thorough thoughtless] "negligent parents"
*negligible 11-60-16 (a.) 1. so small as to be meaningless; insignificant 2. not worth considering [niggling nonessential nugatory effect effort excellence gib lack least little live low inferior insignificant irrelevant /big/] "the effect was negligible"
*negotiable 13-62-10 (a.) 1. capable of being passed or negotiated 2. legally transferable to the ownership of another 3. able to be negotiated or arranged by compromise [navigable education establish exchangeable experience extend open ownership table transferable traverse inflexible inheritable instrument able accessible accord achieve act alienable arrange assign bond legal liquid /bait tog/] "a negotiable road"
*nemesis 11-60-17 (n.) 1. (Greek mythology) the goddess of divine retribution and vengeance 2. something causes misery or death [emesis equity evil misery mythology scourge suffering inflict /seme semen/]
*neolithic 20-69-3 (a.) 1. of or relating to the most recent period of the Stone Age (following the mesolithic) [early east eolith eolithic latest implement tool human culture] "evidence of neolithic settlements"
*neophyte 16-21-6 (n.) 1. any new participant in some activity 2. a new convert being taught the principles of Christianity by a catechist [neo nestle newbie newcomer novice novitiate educational enrol entrant organism participant pietism plant postulant power previous principle proselyte pupil yet teach tenderfoot tiro trainee trust tyro]
*nestle 09-46-24 (n.) 1. a close and affectionate (and often prolonged) embrace (v.) 1. move or arrange oneself in a comfortable and cozy position [nest new newcomer nipper nuzzle eaglet early embrace ensure entrant evergreen exchange safe screen seclude secret secure set settle shelter sit situate sleep snuggle soften son spoon still swan tadpole talent tight toddler toward trainee tyro lamb lap last learner leave lie litter location

lose lovemaking]
*nestling 17-88-5 (n.) 1. young bird not yet fledged 2. a young person of either sex (between birth and puberty) [nipper nuzzle early exchange scallywag secret sex shaver sleep snuggle son sprog still talent tiddler tight tike toddler tot tyke lamb leave leveret lose imp infant gosling]
*nettle 13-67-11 (n.) 1. any of numerous plants having stinging hairs that cause skin irritation on contact (especially of the genus Urtica or family Urticaceae) (v.) 1. goad or provoke,as by constant criticism 2. cause annoyance in; disturb, esp. by minor irritations [nag nark needle nett never niggle non northern numerous ear eat enrage establish eurasian european exasperate excite exercise explosive extreme tease temperate textile thistle tog tooth torment touched translucent tropical trouble leaf]
*network 02-43-453 (n.) 1. an interconnected or intersecting configuration or system of components 2. communication system consisting of a group of broadcasting stations that all transmit the same program simultaneously 3. an intricately connected system of things or people (v.) 1. communicate with and within a group [net equipment tangle texture tissue weave web work organization raddle reticulum riddle] "a network of spies"
*neural 18-54-4 (a.) 1. of or relating to the nervous system 2. of or relating to neurons [nervous network ural locate /rue/]
*neurology 08-47-27 (n.) 1. the branch of medical science that deals with the nervous system and its disorders 2. the branch of medicine that deals with the nervous system and its disorders [naturopathy nervous neurosurgery non evoke urology radiology response obstetrician operate ophthalmology orthopedic osteopathy geriatrics gerontology gynecology /rue/]
*neuter 17-67-5 (a.) 1. of grammatical gender 2. having no or imperfectly developed or nonfunctional sex organs (n.) 1. a gender that refers chiefly (but not exclusively) to inanimate objects (neither masculine nor feminine) (v.) 1. remove the ovaries of [neither neutral non nonaligned nonpartisan emasculate epicene even exclusive uncommitted undeveloped uninvolved unsex tepid testicle third toward refer remove] "`it' is the third-person singular neuter pronoun"
*neutral 05-59-75 (a.) 1. lacking hue 2. (physics) having no net electric charge; not electrified 3. not supporting or favoring either side in a war, dispute, or contest 4. (chemistry) having only a limited ability to react chemically; not active 5. having no personal preference 6. neither moral nor immoral; neither good nor evil, right nor wrong 7. lacking distinguishing quality or characteristics 8. of no distinctive quality or characteristics or type (n.) 1. one who does not side with any party in a war or dispute [nebulous neuter nonpartisan electropositive emasculate equitable evenhanded unbiased uninvolved tasteless tepid transmission rack removed reverse abstract aloof amoral autonomous light lofty low lurid]
*nevertheless 03-52-158 (ad.) 1. despite anything to the contrary (usually following a concession) [nohow non nonetheless notwithstanding evert rather regardless though try howbeit however little situation spite stern still /even/]
*newtonian 24-52-1 (a.) 1. of or relating to or inspired by Sir Isaac Newton or his science (n.) 1. a follower of Isaac Newton [ordinary inspired isaac accept]
*nibble 11-52-17 (n.) 1. a small byte 2. gentle biting (v.) 1. bite off very small pieces 2. eat lightly 3. eat intermittently; take small bites of [never nib nip nosh nutrition nybble ingest intermittent bite body bolus byte licking lightly line lion little eat expense expression /bin/] "She nibbled on her cracker"
*niggardly 24-74-1 (a.) 1. petty in giving or spending [narrow niggard illiberal impoverish inadequate infrequent insufficient give grudging abstemious ascetic austere racist rare reason reluctant remain debate derive dwarfish lean limited little /drag gin rag/] "a niggardly tip"
*nihilist 24-59-1 (n.) 1. someone who rejects all theories of morality or religious belief 2. an advocate of anarchism [nicola non idea influential italy later sac soviet spite syndicalism theory tucker]
*nil 10-80-19 (n.) 1. a quantity of no importance [nada naught nix non nothing nought nullity little /lin/]
*nimble 10-51-19 (a.) 1. moving quickly and lightly 2. mentally quick [neat nim nous inactive ingenious intelligent masterful mental mercurial mind move brightness brilliant brisk lightly lightness limber lissome lithe lively energetic esprit expeditious express]
*nit 15-63-8 (n.) 1. a luminance unit equal to 1 candle per square meter measured perpendicular to the rays from the source 2. egg or young of an insect parasitic on mammals especially a sucking louse; often attached to a hair or item of clothing [nagging nay niggling nutritive imago impute insect item thin /tin/]
*nocturnal 13-63-10 (a.) 1. (biology) belonging to or active during the night 2. of or during or relating to the night 3. of or relating to or occurring in the night [open oppose close turn animal appropriate living /con/] "nocturnal animals are active at night"
*noiseless 24-43-1 (a.) 1. making no sound [noise inaudible shakespeare silent soft soundless still little /ion lesion/] "th' inaudible and noiseless foot of time"
*noisome 24-62-1 (a.) 1. causing or able to cause nausea 2. offensively malodorous [nasty nauseous notorious noxious offal offensive ominous outrageous ignoble infamous injurious sad shock sickening smelly some stench stinking strong malevolent mischievous monstrous moral egregious enormous execrable extremely /ion/]
*noisy 06-58-56 (a.) 1. full of or characterized by loud

and nonmusical sounds [non obstreperous intensity scream screeching shout shriek snap sound splutter sputter stertorous strident swaggering swishy yap yell yelp /ion/] "a noisy cafeteria"
*nomad 14-62-9 (n.) 1. a member of a people who have no permanent home but move about according to the seasons [noma mad meander member migrant migratory move accord africa ancient arab desert discursive divagate drift drifter /dam damon/]
*nominal 08-47-27 (a.) 1. insignificantly small; a matter of form only 2. relating to or constituting or bearing or giving a name 3. (economics) being value in terms of specification on currency or stock certificates rather than purchasing power 4. (grammar) "nominal phrase" 5. being such in name only 6. named; bearing the name of a specific person [namely nominative original ostensible major male management matter maximum measured mina minimal minimum minor modest ignore inexpensive inflation insignificant insubstantial accounting adjectival alleged apparently artificial assign language least linguistic link list little low] "the Russian system of nominal brevity"
*nominate 04-51-99 (v.) 1. propose as a candidate for some honor 2. charge with a task or function 3. charge with a function; charge to be 4. put forward; nominate for appointment to an office [name nickname obligation offer office ordain ordinate outcome maker mean mina identify influence institute intend accept adopt alternative anew appointment approve assign award task tender term title election embrace endorse enter entitle espouse establish] "The President nominated her as head of the Civil Rights Commission"
*nomination 04-35-118 (n.) 1. the act of officially naming a candidate 2. an address (usually at a political convention) proposing the name of a candidate to run for election 3. the condition of having been proposed as a suitable candidate for appointment or election [name nation non official order ordination induction institution investiture address appointment assignment audience award tab] "the Republican nomination for Governor"
*nominee 05-24-67 (n.) 1. a politician who is running for public office [office opposition owner main mask mate mine enough entrant estate]
*nonchalance 17-56-5 (n.) 1. the trait of remaining calm and seeming not to care; a casual lack of concern [calm care casual concern lack]
*nonchalant 12-61-14 (a.) 1. marked by blithe unconcern [negligent numb offhand calm car carelessness casual cold collected concern cool heartless heedless hopeless abandon alan aloof apathy ataractic lack languid lay lethargy listless tease together torpid]
*nondescript 14-41-9 (a.) 1. lacking distinct or individual characteristics; dull and uninteresting (n.) 1. a person is not easily classified and not very interesting [novel obscure ordinary degree disorderly distinct drab dress dull easy everyday exceptional script shapeless simple size soul chaotic classify clothe commonplace confused remarkable indeterminate individual inform insipid interest person plain prosy] "women dressed in nondescript clothes"
*nonentity 22-63-2 (n.) 1. the state of not existing 2. a person of no influence 3. a nonexistent thing [negative nobody nonexistent nothing nullity objective obscurity empty entity exist tinhorn title trifle imaginary impossiblenes incapable influence insignificant insubstantial invertebrate]
*nonpareil 24-45-1 (a.) 1. eminent beyond or above comparison (n.) 1. model of excellence or perfection of a kind; one having no equal 2. a flat disk of chocolate covered with beads of colored sugar 3. colored beads of sugar used as a topping on e.g. candies and cookies [non only optimum paragon pare peerless perfection pick point prime print prize ace apotheosis art remarkable rich role ruler elect elite eminent equal excellent exemplar ideal imitation impossible impressive incomparable lack laureate leader /lie lier/]
*norm 06-52-53 (n.) 1. a statistic describing the location of a distribution 2. a standard or model or pattern regarded as typical [nine nor numerical ordinance often random range real reference regulation represent require root rule run magnitude mathematics mean measure median member middleclass model month] "the current middle-class norm of two children per family"
*normalcy 18-09-4 (n.) 1. being within certain limits that define the range of normal functioning 2. expectedness as a consequence of being usual or regular or common [normal observe ordinary range regularity routine mediocrity average limit certain common conformity connotation consequence /clam/]
*norman 04-47-121 (a.) 1. of or relating to or characteristic of Normandy 2. of or relating to or characteristic of the Normans (n.) 1. United States operatic soprano (born in 1945) 2. an inhabitant of Normandy 3. Australian golfer (born in 1955) [nationality neoclassical norma northwestern nouveau operatic raid recess region rococo medieval member modernist architecture area art australian]
*nostrum 22-49-2 (n.) 1. hypothetical remedy for all ills or diseases; once sought by the alchemists 2. patent medicine whose efficacy is questionable [never once scheme scientific seek social solution strum substance successful suggest therapy recipe relieve remedy medicine /son/]
*noticeable 07-53-42 (a.) 1. capable of being detected 2. capable or worthy of drawing attention 3. readily noticed 4. undesirably noticeable [notice /ton/] "noticeable shadows under her eyes"
*notorious 04-69-110 (a.) 1. having an exceedingly bad reputation [nasty not notable noted offensive outrageous outstanding tarnish tenderloin terrible trite truism rank renowned reputation respectable rotten ignominious ill immodest infamous unashamed unclean

undesirable unsavory sad shame striking /roto ton/] "a notorious gangster"
*novice 06-73-46 (a.) 1. at a first stage of development; just becoming familiar with the rudiments or skills or routines (n.) 1. someone who has entered a religious order but has not taken final vows 2. someone new to a field or activity [neophyte newbie newcomer nun outdoor vice vow voyage induct inexperience infant initiate clergywoman colt cook cub early enter entrant expert /von/]
*nowadays 06-65-52 (ad.) 1. in these times (n.) 1. the period of time that is happening now; any continuous stretch of time including the moment of speech [nancy night occasion world ada age almost distinguished solely speech stretch /won/] "it is solely by their language that the upper classes nowadays are distinguished"
*nowhere 04-58-127 (ad.) 1. not anywhere; in or at or to no place (n.) 1. an insignificant place [near obscure outback outpost outskirt way well where remote /won/] "I am going nowhere"
*noxious 16-48-6 (a.) 1. injurious to physical or mental health [nasty nauseous noisome nox obscene offensive ominous idea ignoble injurious innocuous invidious unhealthy unhygienic unpleasant unwholesome smell social spiritual spoil strong stuffy] "noxious chemical wastes"
*nuance 07-38-37 (n.) 1. a subtle difference in meaning or opinion or attitude [nicety notch note understand undertone allusion amount argue artistic assumption attitude aware caliber cant color compass cut enjoy expression extent] "without understanding the finer nuances you can't enjoy the humor"
*nucleus 13-41-10 (n.) 1. a small group of indispensable persons or things 2. the positively charged dense center of an atom 3. a part of the cell containing DNA and RNA and responsible for growth and reproduction 4. (astronomy) the center of the head of a comet; consists of small solid particles of ice and frozen gas that vaporizes on approaching the sun to form the coma and tail 5. any histologically identifiable mass of neural cell bodies in the brain or spinal cord [navel neutron nub umbilicus cell centre centrum core lepton loin egg embryo essential soul spirit stuff synthesis /sue/]
*nude 07-45-34 (a.) 1. completely unclothed (n.) 1. a painting of a naked figure 2. as in the phrase"They swam in the nude" 3. a naked person [naked nature nudity unadulterated unclothe uncovered undress unsophisticated decoration design dishabille ecdysiast evidence /dun/] "They swam in the nude"
*nuisance 09-59-24 (n.) 1. (law) a broad legal concept including anything that disturbs the reasonable use of your property or endangers life and health or is offensive 2. a bothersome annoying person [nag neck unhappy unpleasant unreasonable illegal impose include inconvenience inflict interfere irritation san source aggravation agreeable allow annoy ass attract authority cause children collection concept endanger enjoyment exasperate extinguish]
*numerical 12-46-12 (a.) 1. of or relating to or denoting numbers 2. designated by or expressed in numbers 3. measured or expressed in numbers 4. relating to or having ability to think in or work with numbers [name negative numeric mathematical mathematician measurement medical much enemy engineer equation even explicit exponential express radical rating rational real impossible infinite integral cardinal code connotation consider algebraic algorithm analysis analytic aptitude arithmetic logarithmic /cire emu/] "numerical value"
*nunnery 24-72-1 (n.) 1. the convent of a community of nuns [nun religious residence]
*nuptial 16-68-6 (a.) 1. of or relating to a wedding [undersexed perform potent procession procreate prothalamion amorous animal libido /lait pun/]
*nurture 05-56-60 (n.) 1. the properties acquired as a consequence of the way you were treated as a child 2. raising someone to be an accepted member of the community (v.) 1. help develop, help grow 2. provide with nourishment 3. bring up [nature nourishment nurse upbringing upgrade uphold urbanity useful raise ready rear refinement regular run tender thrive till training transform treat embrace encourage enculturation environmental exercise /run/] "they debated whether nature or nurture was more important"

O

*obdurate 17-78-5 (a.) 1. stubbornly persistent in wrongdoing 2. showing unfeeling resistance to tender feelings [obstinate obtuse old orthodox benumb bony brazen dense dogged dull unbending unnatural unsympathetic untouched unyielding urate reform regenerate relentless resistance rigorous rocky ruthless adamant asleep tender tough easy emotion] "the child's misery would move even the most obdurate heart"
*obelisk 20-47-3 (n.) 1. a stone pillar having a rectangular cross section tapering towards a pyramidal top 2. a character used in printing to indicate a cross reference or footnote [obituary barrow base bel brass build bust lantern lighthouse indicate inscription section shrine side skyscraper speech square stand stone structure support symbol /sile/]
*obese 06-80-48 (a.) 1. excessively fat [overweight beefy bloated blubber bodily body burly excessive extremely serious stalwart stout swollen]
*obesity 08-81-32 (n.) 1. more than average fatness [overweight blubber bodily excessive sit stout thin]
*obfuscate 17-54-5 (v.) 1. make obscure or unclear [obscure overshadow befog befuddle blind blur brown unnecessary scramble screen shadow cate clear cloud comprehensible conceal confused corrupt curtain adumbrate alter transform eclipse elucidate ensconce envelop]
*obituary 03-54-140 (n.) 1. a notice of someone's death; usually includes a short biography [obelisk obit biography brass bust include inscription tablet testimonial trophy adventure archival autobiography record resume ribbon]
*objective 04-51-125 (a.) 1. undistorted by emotion or personal bias; based on observable phenomena 2. belonging to immediate experience of actual things or events 3. emphasizing or expressing things as perceived without distortion of personal feelings or interpretation 4. (grammar) serving as or indicating the object of a verb or of certain prepositions and used for certain other purposes (n.) 1. the goal intended to be attained (and which is believed to be attainable) 2. the lens or system of lenses nearest the object being viewed [object outer outside outward basis bauble bias blunt butt judicious just empirical end equitable experience external eyepiece camera choice cool tangible target test trinket icy impartial independent indifferent influence intention velleity volition] "an objective appraisal"
*objector 22-67-2 (n.) 1. a person who dissents from some established policy [opponent orthodoxy backyard enemy eradicate establish conduct conform conscience contestant refuse]
*obligate 13-07-11 (a.) 1. (biology) restricted to a particular condition of life 2. being under moral or legal

obligation (v.) 1. force or compel somebody to do something 2. commit in order to fulfill an obligation 3. bind by an obligation; cause to be indebted [oblige observance organism betrothed bind biology bound law legal liable life ligate living implement impose independence induce inexorable insistent intellectual intended guarantee absence affiance anaerobe apply apprentice article assured thrust tie training trust enforce engaged ensure environmental establish exist /tag/] "an obligate anaerobe can survive only in the absence of OXYGen"
*obligatory 11-62-16 (a.) 1. morally or legally constraining or binding 2. required by obligation or compulsion or convention [obligato binding bounden law left legal impose incumbent indispensable inevitable absolutely apology religious requisite rig rule /rota tag/] "attendance is obligatory"
*oblique 13-45-10 (a.) 1. slanting or inclined in direction or course or position--neither parallel nor perpendicular nor right-angular 2. indirect in departing from the accepted or proper way; misleading (n.) 1. any grammatical case other than the nominative [objective obtuse offhand orbital ownership backhand banking base behavior bend bias body language late leaf lean length less line imply incline indirect inflection instrument intersect question underhanded equidistant evasive everywhere excursive express extern] "the oblique rays of the winter sun"
*obliterate 11-49-16 (a.) 1. reduced to nothingness (v.) 1. remove completely from recognition or memory 2. make undecipherable or imperceptible by obscuring or concealing 3. mark for deletion, rub off, or erase, as of writings 4. do away with completely, without leaving a trace [oblivious obscure become blackout blot blur leave light line literate imperceptible indistinct terminate trace transform efface eliminate eradicate erase erasure expunction raze recognition reduce remain remove rid rub ruin abolish absolve alter annihilate /tare/]
*oblivion 11-60-15 (n.) 1. the state of being disregarded or forgotten 2. total forgetfulness [oblivious obscurity offense offhand overlook blackout blank law lazy lethe limbo inanity indifference insensible insouciance ion vacancy vacuity void neglectful nepenthe nihility nothingness] "he sought the great oblivion of sleep"
*oblivious 10-54-19 (a.) 1. (followed by 'to' or 'of') lacking conscious awareness of 2. failing to keep in mind [offhand old omit out bemuse block lack lazy ignorant inattentive indifferent insensible insensitive insouciance vacant vacuous unaware unconscious unfamiliar senseless show sleeping suppress] "oblivious of the mounting pressures for political reform"
*oblong 20-49-3 (a.) 1. of a leaf shape; having a somewhat elongated form with approximately parallel sides 2. deviating from a square or circle or sphere by being elongated in one direction (n.) 1. a plane figure that deviates from a square or circle due to elongation [orthogonal leaf length long great]
*obnoxious 14-44-9 (a.) 1. causing disapproval or protest [objectionable offensive open outrageous base blame brutal nasty notorious noxious ignoble infamous insufferable intolerable invidious unbearable unclean unmentionable sad small stench subject]
*obsequious 22-52-2 (a.) 1. attempting to win favor from influential people by flattery 2. attentive in an ingratiating or servile manner [obey oily beggarly behavior blarney bootlick buttery servile shop sincerity smarmy smooth sponge submissive subservient sycophant eager equi excessive unctuous influential ingratiate ingratiating insinuate] "obsequious shop assistants"
*observance 12-20-12 (n.) 1. the act of observing; taking a patient look 2. a formal event performed on a special occasion 3. conformity with law or custom or practice etc. 4. the act of noticing or paying attention [observe occasion office ovation ear enforce enterprise exercise reconciliation rejoicing remark vance adjustment affair agreement aware note notice care celebrate ceremony]
*observant 14-42-9 (a.) 1. paying close attention especially to details 2. (of individuals) adhering strictly to laws and rules and customs 3. quick to notice; showing quick and keen perception [obedient obey observe scrupulous servant sharp show shrewd speed strict earnest ethical eye regardful religious respectful ritual rule vigilant adhere alert allow attentive awake aware nice niggling nothing notice thoughtful]
*observatory 12-32-14 (n.) 1. a building designed and equipped to observe astronomical phenomena 2. a structure commanding a wide view of its surroundings [orrery outlook overlook beacon bleachers bridge building satellite scientific spectroscope stand station structure surround earthquake edifice entity equip expansive reflector refractor roof viewpoint artificial astronomical atop telescope tory tower /rota/]
*obsolescence 20-27-3 (n.) 1. the process of becoming obsolete; falling into disuse or becoming out of date [oldness outmode becoming level lower effective essential] "a policy of planned obsolescence"
*obsolescent 18-33-4 (a.) 1. becoming obsolete [old oldness out outmode becoming belonging scent super level lower effective essential current]
*obsolete 10-35-21 (a.) 1. old; no longer in use or valid or fashionable 2. no longer in use [old organ out outdate outofdate over belonging biology bygone sole still super supersede lapse law locomotive long elapse equipment expire extinct /telos/] "obsolete words"
*obstetrician 13-46-10 (n.) 1. a physician specializing in obstetrics [obstetric ophthalmology orthopedic otology baby branch serology specialize radiology immunology internist cardiology care childbirth chiropody accoucheur anesthesiologist neurology]
*obstetrics 12-21-12 (n.) 1. the branch of medicine

dealing with childbirth and care of the mother [obi obstetric oxytocin baby become birth branch sac science six specialty technique treatment incompetent induce infant canal care cervix children concern]
*obstinacy 22-60-2 (n.) 1. the trait of being difficult to handle or overcome 2. resolute adherence to your own ideas or desires [overcome bullheadednes self stubborn tenacity tina trait idea impenitent influence adhere compromise control /can/]
*obstinate 16-59-6 (a.) 1. stubbornly persistent in wrongdoing 2. resistant to guidance or discipline 3. persisting in a reactionary stand (v.) 1. persist stubbornly [obdurate obedient obey objection opinionated opposition orthodoxy outmode backward balky beefy behavior bigoted blockage self serious slow solve stand steady stop stubborn suggestion tacky temper tenacity tight tina tireless trait idea impenitent inexorable inflexible influence insistent invincible naughty negativism nervy noncooperation adamant adhere adverse alien argument assiduous attitude authority aversion enduring enemy] "he obstinates himself against all rational arguments"
*obstreperous 24-32-1 (a.) 1. noisily and stubbornly defiant 2. boisterously and noisily aggressive [oppose ornery bluster boisterous bold boy brawl brazen scream shout show strep strident strong stubborn terrorist tumultuous turbulent rampant refuse resist revolutionary rough rowdy energetic pursuit unbridled undisciplined unrestrained unruly /pert/] "obstreperous boys"
*obstruct 09-43-23 (v.) 1. block passage through 2. hinder or prevent the progress or accomplishment of [occlude operate oppose overdue backward bar barricade become block bolt bound brake brother serious setback shut sight slow stall stay stifle stop suffocate tardy team thwart tie tone turn reach rebuff relax render repel respiration restrain retarded road unready unsuitable untimely check choke clog close complicate conceal congest constipate costive cover crowd /curt/]
*obstruction 10-40-20 (n.) 1. any structure that makes progress difficult 2. something immaterial that stands in the way and must be circumvented or surmounted 3. getting in someone's way 4. the act of obstructing 5. the state or condition of being obstructed [objection obstruct obstructive occlusion opposition balk bar barrier block bowel squeeze stop stoppage suspension resistance restriction rub catch check closure condition curtain impasse impede incumbrance interruption negativism /curt/]
*obtain 02-36-268 (v.) 1. be valid, applicable, or true 2. receive a specified treatment (abstract) 3. come into possession of [obstacle occur official original bad bag become bill breathe bum business buy tain theory treatment trouble true turn abstract accept achieve acquire admit adoption applicable ascertain ask aspect attain incur induce inspire instigate interpretation nature necessary net nothing] "How did you obtain the visa?"
*obtrusive 22-42-2 (a.) 1. undesirably noticeable 2. sticking out; protruding [obvious officious opinion ostensible outstanding outward bad bald behavior blatant bold busy tawdry tend thrust undesirable unmistakable unwelcome uppity scream sheer spectacular spoil stick striking insulting interfere intrusive invasive vulgar effect extravagant] "the obtrusive behavior of a spoiled child"
*obtuse 20-49-3 (a.) 1. of an angle; between 90 and 180 degrees 2. slow to learn or understand; lacking intellectual acuity 3. of a leaf shape; rounded at the apex 4. lacking in insight or discernment [oafish obdurate objective oligarchy behavior benumb bluff blunt bonehead botany triangle uncommonly understand unemotional untouchable use shape sharp simple slow smooth stupid subdivision emotionless] "too obtuse to grasp the implications of his behavior"
*obviate 20-42-3 (v.) 1. do away with 2. prevent the occurrence of; prevent from happening [occurrence bar beforehand impossible intervene involve anticipate arise ask avert avoid tend eat effect eliminate estop exclude]
*occasion 02-65-314 (n.) 1. reason 2. a vaguely specified social event 3. an event that occurs at a critical time 4. an opportunity to do something 5. the time of a particular event (v.) 1. give occasion to [obligation occur open opening opportunity case cause celebrate ceremony chance circumstance condition contingency create advantage affair author scope season shot show spot stage impulse incident incite instance institute ion necessity]
*occult 18-54-4 (a.) 1. hidden and difficult to see 2. having an import not apparent to the senses nor obvious to the intelligence; beyond ordinary understanding (n.) 1. supernatural forces and events and beings collectively (v.) 1. cause an eclipse of (a celestial body) by intervention 2. become concealed or hidden from view or have its light extinguished 3. hide from view [obfuscate obscure observer operation original orphic otherworldly overshadow overspread capable cast cause celestial chemical circle close cloud collective conceal condition confined cope course cryptic cult curtain customary ultimate understood unknown unspoken untold upholstery latent layover learn lid light lore lose lurk technique temporary test theosophy transmundane] "an occult fracture"
*occupant 08-51-32 (n.) 1. someone who lives at a particular place for a prolonged period or who was born there [occupy owner city coastal colony confined unclaimed pant period position possession prison prolong property addressee american area northern temporary tenant townsman /napu/]
*occurrence 11-47-17 (n.) 1. an instance of something occurring 2. an event that happens [occasion occur opening outburst case chance circumstance condition contingency ubiety rate realize rise emergency ending

energy episode error eventuality existence experience] "a disease of frequent occurrence"
*octagon 16-52-6 (n.) 1. an eight-sided polygon [octosyllabic octuple close agon angle geometric /nog/]
*octave 16-41-6 (n.) 1. a feast day and the seven days following it 2. a rhythmic group of eight lines of verse 3. a musical interval of eight tones [oboe octavo octet organ canto cello chorus christianity church consider count third tone trumpet twelfth alone antistrophe ave verse vibrato viola eighth envoi epode /vat/]
*octogenarian 16-57-6 (a.) 1. being from 80 to 89 years old (n.) 1. someone whose age is in the eighties [old oldster centenarian citizen combine teens thirteen twenty gaffer geezer golden gramps eighty elderly eleven ninety nonagenarian age aria attain indicate /ego got/]
*oddity 11-51-15 (n.) 1. eccentricity that is not easily explained 2. something unusual -- perhaps worthy of collecting 3. a strange attitude or habit [oddment oddness original outsider outstand deviation different distinctive dit duck idiosyncrasy improbable incongruousne irregularity item tangible tic trick twist type]
*ode 12-45-12 (n.) 1. a lyric poem with complex stanza forms [dirge dithyramb drama elegy emotion epic epigram exalted express]
*odious 17-57-5 (a.) 1. unequivocally detestable [obnoxious obscene offensive outrageous deserve detestable dire dirty disgust dislike ignoble infamous inspire intolerable unclean unequivocal unmentionable unpleasant sad shock small]
*odor 13-02-11 (n.) 1. the sensation that results when olfactory receptors in the nose are stimulated by particular chemicals in gaseous form 2. any property detected by the olfactory system [offensive olfactory datum delicious detect differential distinctive dor rank receptor redolent reek resemble /rod/]
*off 01-58-2966 (a.) 1. below a satisfactory level 2. not in operation or operational 3. (of events) no longer planned or scheduled 4. not performing or scheduled for duties 5. in an unpalatable state (ad.) 1. no longer on or in contact or attached 2. at a distance in space or time 3. from a particular thing or place or position [obsolete operational out outside oven over owe face farthest fell field fish flat floor fortieth free from fulltime function future] "the oven is off"
*offhand 16-28-6 (a.) 1. with little or no preparation or forethought 2. casually thoughtless or inconsiderate (ad.) 1. without previous thought or preparation 2. in a casually inconsiderate manner [oblivious offthecuff familiar few figure folksy forethought forgetful hand haphazard heedless homey abrupt affair airy appear attention naturally non nonchalant decide degage disregard distant] "couldn't give the figures offhand"
*officiate 06-22-49 (v.) 1. perform duties attached to a particular office or place or function 2. act in an official capacity in a ceremony or religious ritual, such as a wedding [oversee function impose capacity celebrate ceremony chairman conduct confirm act adjudicate anoint attached tie try eat] "Who officiated at your wedding?"
*officious 22-60-2 (a.) 1. intrusive in a meddling or offensive manner [obtrusive off offensive old forward fussy important insistent interfere intrusive unfinished unofficial unwanted self snoopy]
*offshoot 12-55-13 (n.) 1. a natural consequence of development [order organization origin outcome outgrowth fan fixture follow fruit school shoot social society source spin spread spring sprout stem subsidiary sucker hand harvest heir tendril trident twig]
*ogre 17-67-5 (n.) 1. a cruel wicked and inhuman person 2. (folklore) a giant who likes to eat human beings [ghost giant griffin revenant riddle roc eat evil /ergo/]
*ointment 18-68-4 (n.) 1. semisolid preparation (usually containing a medicine) applied externally as a remedy or for soothing an irritation 2. toiletry consisting of any of various substances resembling cream that have a soothing and moisturizing effect when applied to the skin [obtain oil irritation itch nard non technique therapy tin toiletry treat mazuma medicine menthol mercury mix moist moola effect embrocation emollient ester external extract]
*olfactory 22-57-2 (a.) 1. of or relating to olfaction [factory]
*ominous 07-47-41 (a.) 1. threatening or foreshadowing evil or tragic developments 2. presaging ill-fortune [omen oracular meaningful menace minatory mischievous ill imminent inauspicious indicate intimidate noisome nous noxious ugly unfortunate unhappy unlucky unpropitious sad shake silence sinister situation smile somber storm suggest]
*omission 08-62-27 (n.) 1. something that has been omitted 2. any process whereby sounds are left out of spoken words or phrases 3. a mistake resulting from neglect 4. neglecting to do something; leaving out or passing over something [offense omit outrage oversight malpractice mishandle mismanage mission mistake ignorance impoverish inadvertent inattention initial injustice interval search sentence skip slight slip sound speak striking stumble suppression syllable narrow need neglect negligence next non notice] "she searched the table for omissions"
*omnipotence 24-57-1 (n.) 1. the state of being omnipotent; having unlimited power [main might influence invincible powerless control]
*omnipotent 18-55-4 (a.) 1. having unlimited power [omniscient one main majesty making merciful might numinous immortal immutable infinity influence invincible permanent perpetual plenipotentiary possess potency potent powerless timeless effect eternity everlasting /pin top topi/]

*omniscience 24-42-1 (n.) 1. the state of being omniscient; having infinite knowledge [main ignorance infinite insight sagacity sapient]
*omniscient 20-37-3 (a.) 1. infinitely wise [omnipresent one main majesty making mindful numinous ignorance immutable infinite infinity insightful intelligent sagacious sagacity sapient scient seeming sensible shape sovereignty supreme comprehend conscious creative eternity everlasting expertise timeless]
*omnivorous 22-42-2 (a.) 1. feeding on both plants and animals [meat mensal mercenary miserly nourishing nutritious include insatiate insect insectivore interest ivor vegetarian venal voracious range rapacious ravenous undiscriminat scavenge sordid stuffing swinish /vin/]
*onerous 12-54-14 (a.) 1. not easily borne; wearing [obligation operose oppressive nero easily effort exacting exhaust represent return unruly unwieldy uphill sad schedule strained strenuous superincumbent]
*onrush 20-63-3 (n.) 1. a forceful forward rush 2. an offensive against and enemy (using weapons) [objective offensive ongoing onset onslaught operation originate outflow nation naval race rapid regain rise run rush undertow seize service set soar soldier spate strafe sudden surge surprise /urn/]
*onset 10-57-19 (n.) 1. the beginning or early stages 2. an offensive against and enemy (using weapons) [objective offensive oncoming onrush onslaught opening operation originate outbreak nation naval sally seize service set stage start storm strafe strike surprise early edge enemy establishment territory toward troop] "the onset of pneumonia"
*onslaught 09-60-23 (n.) 1. an offensive against and enemy (using weapons) 2. a sudden and severe onset of trouble 3. the rapid and continuous delivery of linguistic communication (spoken or written) [objective offensive onrush onset operation originate outpouring overkill overwhelm naval sally seize service severe slaughter strike surprise loot abuse accompany advance airplane ambush armed artillery assault attack aught unruly ground hammer territory thrust tirade toward trouble]
*onus 13-75-11 (n.) 1. an onerous or difficult concern [obligation odium offensive onerous oppressive ought uncalledfor unhappy unpleasant settlement source spot stain /sun/]
*opaque 11-55-17 (a.) 1. not clear; not transmitting or reflecting light or radiant energy 2. not clearly understood or expressed [obfuscate obscure obscurity obtuse opacity pass passage perplex photographic physics pigment puzzling allow ambiguous amorphous arcane attribute quality uncertain unclear unco understood unfathomable unintelligible einstein elusive energy enigmatic equivocal essential express] "opaque windows of the jail"
*operate 01-43-743 (v.) 1. handle and cause to function 2. happen 3. perform a movement in military or naval tactics in order to secure an advantage in attack or defense 4. perform as expected when applied 5. direct or control; projects, businesses, etc. 6. keep engaged 7. perform surgery on [ongoing opera operational ordain organize perform pilot place plot practice employ engineer exert react rig run act active angle aviate tick trade /repo tare/]
*operative 06-60-47 (a.) 1. being in force or having or exerting force 2. of or relating to a surgical operation 3. effective; producing a desired effect 4. (of e.g. a machine) performing or capable of performing 5. relating to or requiring or amenable to treatment by surgery especially as opposed to medicine (n.) 1. a person secretly employed in espionage for a government 2. someone who can be employed as a detective to collect information [opera operator perform powerful pro process produce employee engineer eye roustabout ruling running active actor agent telling investigator irresistible valid vigorous vital /repo tare vita/] "operative regulations"
*operator 02-65-243 (n.) 1. (mathematics) a symbol that represents a function from functions to functions 2. (informal) a shrewd or unscrupulous person who knows how to circumvent difficulties 3. someone who owns or operates a business 4. an agent that operates some apparatus or machine 5. a speculator who trades aggressively on stock or commodity markets [obey opera opportunist owner perform pilot place plunger principle producer pull element elevator engage engineer enterprise enthusiast entity equipment expediency exploit expression radio railway relation risk runner actor agent apparatus arrange author telephonist transmitter /repo rota tare/] "the integral operator"
*operetta 15-34-7 (n.) 1. a short amusing opera [oratorio overture pere piano pizzicato pop prelude production punk early end rap reggae requiem rock romantic rondo round theatrical theme tone twelve adagio allegro alto amusing andante anthem aria arpeggio /repo/]
*opinion 02-48-374 (n.) 1. the reason for a court's judgment (as opposed to the decision itself) 2. the legal document stating the reasons for a judicial decision 3. a message expressing a belief about something 4. a belief or sentiment shared by most people; the voice of the people 5. a personal belief or judgment that is not founded on proof or certainty 6. a vague idea in which some confidence is placed [obiter observation outlook perception persuasion pinion place point politics poll position preconception prepossession present pretty pris proof proposal public idea impose impression inion instruction instrument intuition issue notion] "my opinion differs from yours"
*opponent 02-49-369 (a.) 1. characterized by active hostility (n.) 1. someone who offers opposition 2. a contestant that you are matched against [obstinate offer overthrow participate person perverse play pone

progress negative noncooperation enemy enmity technological testament] "opponent (or opposing) armies"
*opportune 17-53-5 (a.) 1. suitable or at a time that is suitable or advantageous especially for a particular purpose 2. at a convenient or suitable time [pat place port profitable propitious prosperous purpose receive recommend relevant right ripe tailored timely useful expedient /nut troppo/] "an opportune place to make camp"
*opportunist 11-68-17 (a.) 1. taking immediate advantage, often unethically, of any circumstance of possible benefit (n.) 1. a person who places expediency above principle [power presumptuous principle profit promote resourceful trade tunis unethical unscrupulous immediate inexpedient scarp scratcher seek self serve shrewd speculator swashbuckler /nut troppo/]
*opportunity 01-58-739 (n.) 1. a possibility due to a favorable combination of circumstances [occasion offering opening opportunist pass period place possibility prejudice prize promotion prospect ras rich ring risk room round tabu true turn unity inning instance /nut troppo/] "the holiday gave us the opportunity to visit Washington"
*opposite 03-59-211 (a.) 1. characterized by opposite extremes; completely opposed 2. altogether different in nature or quality or significance 3. the other one of a complementary pair 4. moving or facing away from each other 5. (botany) of leaves etc; growing in pairs on either side of a stem 6. being directly across from each other; facing (ad.) 1. directly facing each other (n.) 1. a contestant that you are matched against 2. a relation of direct opposition 3. two words that express opposing concepts 4. something inverted in sequence or character or effect [obstinate obverse offset parallel perverse polarize posit separate sinister stressful independent inverse irreconcilable toward troublous trying enemy] "to him the opposite of gay was depressed"
*opprobrium 18-74-4 (n.) 1. state of disgrace resulting from public abuse 2. a state of extreme dishonor [obloquy oceanic odium offensive opp public record reproach reproachful retreat revile behavior belittle black bring byword ignominy infamy insulting integrity invective island mortification]
*optic 13-28-10 (a.) 1. of or relating to or resembling the eye 2. relating to or using sight (n.) 1. the organ of sight ('peeper' is an informal term for 'eye') [oculus opt orb peeper pupil image iris cornea]
*optician 18-83-4 (n.) 1. a worker who makes glasses for remedying defects of vision [optic prescribe train contact corrective acquire]
*optics 15-26-7 (n.) 1. the branch of physics that studies the physical properties of light [oculus optic optometry organ path peeper philosophy photometry physics point produce property telescopy thermodynamics threedimensi image infrared instrument interaction catoptrics clearly coherent condition converge create cryogenics crystallography science sight single spectroscopy statics stereoscopy straight study]
*optimism 04-56-92 (n.) 1. the optimistic feeling that all is going to turn out well 2. a general disposition to expect the best in all things [perfectionism philosophy pleasant positivism positivity possible power propose temperament tendency triumph turn idealism ism millennium mood sanguine side sunny]
*option 01-60-526 (n.) 1. the right to buy or sell property at an agreed price; the right is purchased and if it is not exercised by a stated date the money is forfeited 2. the act of choosing or selecting 3. an alternative action [obverse offer opening oppose package parallel period pick play pleasure politics position possible power preference price process property purchase put takeover incentive index instrument ion item naked nothing] "what option did I have?"
*optometry 24-30-1 (n.) 1. the practice of an optometrist [opto practice prescribe profession examine exercise eye]
*opulence 15-56-8 (n.) 1. wealth as evidenced by sumptuous living [plentiful prosperity pule lavish live luxury evidence]
*opulent 09-52-23 (a.) 1. rich and superior in quality [obvious ostentatious outpouring overflow plentiful plenty possession princely productive profuse prolific property prosperous lavish lent liberal live loaded lot luxurious luxury epidemic evidence exhaustless expense extravagance exuberant numerous teem]
*oral 07-40-40 (a.) 1. using speech rather than writing 2. (anatomy) of or involving the mouth or mouth region or the surface on which the mouth is located 3. (psychoanalysis) a stage in psychosexual development when the child's interest is concentrated in the mouth; fixation at this stage is said to result in dependence, selfishness, and aggression 4. of or relating to or affecting or for use in the mouth (n.) 1. an examination conducted by word of mouth [opposite orderly receive recognize region release require rooted acknowledge administer admit affecting aggressive agreement airstream analysis anatomy animal answer legendary linguistic locate] "an oral tradition"
*oration 20-56-3 (n.) 1. an instance of oratory [ration read recitation rhetorical academic address allocution audience talkathon tirade inappropriate instance invective /taro/] "he delivered an oration on the decline of family values"
*orator 17-49-5 (n.) 1. a person who delivers a speech or oration [overlong rabblerouser raconteur rant rat remember revolution rhetorician roman rule address american angry appeal athenian audience talk train tully /rota taro/]
*oratorio 14-48-9 (n.) 1. a musical composition for voices and orchestra based on a religious text [operetta orator orchestra overture rap recessional reggae

religious requiem rock romantic rondo round adagio allegro alto andante anthem appealing aria arpeggio taste tell theme tone traditional twelve instrument intermezzo introit /rota taro/]
*oratory 12-49-13 (n.) 1. addressing an audience formally (usually a long and rhetorical address and often pompous) [orator outstand rhetorical room run address articulation aside audience technique /rota taro/] "he loved the sound of his own oratory"
*ordeal 07-58-37 (n.) 1. a severe or trying experience [outcome reflect dangerous deal defendant determination determine difficult disaster distress divine due escape essay experience accuse adversity affliction ancient anguish apprehend lasting law life long]
*ordination 10-83-18 (n.) 1. the status of being ordained to a sacred office 2. logical or comprehensible arrangement of separate elements 3. the act of ordaining; the act of conferring (or receiving) holy orders [official ordain order organism organization rabbi rationalization receive regulation routinize dedication designation devotion dna inauguration initiation installation institution investiture invoke name nation nomination non normalize nucleotide acceptance adjustment appointment arrange assignment tab]
*ordnance 15-72-7 (n.) 1. military supplies 2. large but transportable armament [onager responsible rifle department direct nance naval antiaircraft arbalest arm armament army artillery catapult collection engine equipment /and/]
*origin 04-52-117 (n.) 1. the point of intersection of coordinate axes; where the values of the coordinates are all zero 2. an event that is a beginning; a first part or stage of subsequent events 3. properties attributable to your ancestry 4. the place where something begins, where it springs into being 5. the descendants of one individual [opening outbreak outset overture radiation radix rise river root rootage inauguration inception inherit institution intersection introduce issue generative genesis geometric germinate gin good grassroots great group nativity nerve nurture /giro/]
*original 02-51-507 (a.) 1. being or productive of something fresh and unusual; or being as first made or thought of 2. (of e.g. information) not secondhand or by way of something intermediary 3. preceding all others in time or being as first made or performed 4. not derived or copied or translated from something else (n.) 1. an original model on which something is patterned 2. an original creation (i.e., an audio recording) from which copies can be made [oddity offbeat opus origin imaginative informal initial innovative inspired inventive genuine good green native new newfangled novel actual advance archetype article lead letter literature /giro/] "the original inhabitants of the Americas"
*originate 06-40-51 (v.) 1. bring into being 2. come into existence; take on form or shape 3. begin a trip at a certain point, as of a plane, train, bus, etc. [occasion opening opera organize origin original realize relativity religious result rise root idea imagine inaugurate initiate instigate institution interest introduce invention issue genesis gestate gradual grassroots grow nativity alpha apply arise artifact author taproot temporal theory train trip early emerge ephemeral establish evaluative evolve existence /giro/] "A new religious movement originated in that country"
*ornate 09-43-25 (a.) 1. rich in decorative detail 2. marked by elaborate rhetoric and elaborated with decorative details [opera opulent ostentatious over overwrought resplendent rhetorical rich rococo rule adorn arabesque aureate teach eat effect elaborate elegant embellish excessive]
*orthodox 06-46-47 (a.) 1. (religion) of or pertaining to or characteristic of Judaism 2. adhering to what is commonly accepted 3. (religion) of or relating to or characteristic of the Eastern Orthodox Church [obstinate official ordinary receive recognize regular religious resistant right russian textuary tory traditional traditionalism hard harmonious hidebound hod human decent destiny doctrine dour]
*orthodoxy 12-52-13 (n.) 1. the quality of being orthodox (especially in religion) 2. a belief or orientation agreeing with conventional standards [obedience observance obstinate official opinion orientation orthodox reconciliation religious rigid rigorous teach tenet theology traditional traditionalism hardness harmony heterodoxy human destiny doctrine]
*orthopedic 11-45-15 (a.) 1. of or relating to or employed in orthopedics [obstetrician ophthalmology orthodontic osteopathy otology radiology homeopathic hope hydropathy pathology pediatrics practice psychiatrist employ deformity dental dermatology disorder iatric immunology internist chiropractic clinical /cide/] "orthopedic shoes"
*orthopedist 22-AA-2 (n.) 1. a specialist in correcting deformities of the skeletal system (especially in children) [practice deformity skeletal specialist]
*oscillate 17-55-5 (v.) 1. be undecided about something; waver between conflicting positions or courses of action 2. move or swing from side to side regularly [oscillate seasonal seesaw serial set shake shift shuffling side speed steady sway swing swinging change cill circle clock come conflicting course cyclic indecisive intermittent isochronal libration long lurch accept alternate alternation teeter toss total totter turn equivocate extent extreme /tall/] "He oscillates between accepting the new position and retirement"
*ossify 24-50-1 (v.) 1. become bony 2. cause to become hard and bony 3. make rigid and set into a conventional pattern [osseous osteal salt schedule set soft solidify state steel stiff strengthen impregnate incrust indurate inflexible inure firm fix fossilize]
*ostensible 08-45-30 (a.) 1. appearing as such but not

necessarily so 2. represented or appearing as such; pretended [obtrusive obviously open outstanding outwardly seeming striking superior suppose surface ten theory tinsel true emotional erroneous evidently external necessarily notably noticeable notorious illusory imaginary imitative intellectual investigate blatant bold]
*ostentation 22-60-2 (n.) 1. a showy outward display 2. pretentious or showy or vulgar display 3. lack of elegance as a consequence of being pompous and puffed up with vanity [obtrusive openly orotund outward seeming sham showing showy splash splurge stent success swaggering taste tortuous turgidity effort elaborate elegance exhibit exposure extravagant notorious acting affectation appearance attention attract importance imposture impress inappropriate inflation intend]
*ostentatious 12-67-12 (a.) 1. intended to attract notice and impress others 2. of a display that is tawdry or vulgar [ornate orotund overwrought sable sensationalism showy social splashy stent stilted success tall tasteless tawdry theatrical tony elaborate elegant elevated notice aesthetic affected ambitious arabesque attract impress inkhorn intend unpretentious] "an ostentatious sable coat"
*ostracism 22-32-2 (n.) 1. the state of being banished or ostracized (excluded from society by general consent) 2. the act of excluding someone from society by general consent [send shun snub society rid riddance association consent course coventry inclusion isolation member]
*ostracize 20-01-3 (v.) 1. expel from a community or group 2. avoid speaking to or dealing with [omit oppose oust shun shut since snob snub society speaking sponsor spurn taboo throw transport refuse reject relegate repudiate ancient avoid cast coldshoulder colleague community cut cutoff ignore informal isolate enter exclude excommunicate exile expel /cart/] "Ever since I spoke up, my colleagues ostracize me"
*ought 04-50-124 (v.) 1. be logically necessary 2. expresses an emotional, practical, or other reason for doing something [obligation ugh good tell]
*oust 05-47-78 (v.) 1. remove from a position or office 2. remove and replace [obtrude office ostracize out overthrow unchurch unsaddle unseat supervene supplant suspend throw transport turnout typewriter] "The chairman was ousted after he misappropriated funds"
*outbreak 05-65-63 (n.) 1. a sudden violent spontaneous occurrence (usually of some undesirable condition) [occurrence opening originate outset undesirable unpleasant upheaval uprise tempest timer tornado torrent begin blaze break burst rapid rash return rise rush edge epidemic eruption establishment explosion abate alpha] "the outbreak of hostilities"
*outburst 08-55-32 (n.) 1. a sudden violent happening 2. an unrestrained expression of emotion 3. a sudden violent disturbance [occurrence outbreak outpouring uncontrollable unrestrained upheaval upsurge tantrum tornado torrent tumultuous belch blowup blurt bomb burst rain rapid reflexion release rush scene set storm strong sudden surge /rub/] "an outburst of heavy rain"
*outcast 13-45-10 (a.) 1. excluded from a society (n.) 1. a person who is rejected (from society or home) [outlaw outsider undesirable unfortunate unsettled untouchable unwanted tight cast castaway catholic church class conflict abandon alien apartheid avoid segregation separation shari society stranger suffer /act/]
*outcry 09-47-26 (n.) 1. a loud utterance; often in protest or opposition (v.) 1. shout louder than 2. utter aloud; often with surprise, horror, or joy [objection outburst outdo outgo outmatch outstrip owl ululate uproar utter thunderclap tirade tongue tumult turmoil turn call charivari clamour communication complaint contempt crowd cry rally rapid raspberry rattle raucous razz reaction right roar roaring row yawp yell yowl]
*outdo 12-49-14 (v.) 1. be or do something to a greater degree 2. get the better of [out outclass outflank outfox outgrow outmatch outperform outrange outrun outstrip outwit overreach overwhelm undone upset tense than top trickery trim trounce trump defeat degree destroy discomfit distance down draw drub]
*outlandish 12-58-14 (a.) 1. conspicuously or grossly unconventional or unusual [odd off offthewall other out outland outre unconventional unique unknown unusual tasteless teenager troglodyte low affect alien animal antic apart notional design detached different discrete incredible independent isolated separate stage strange striking style harsh hat /alt/]
*outlast 13-33-10 (v.) 1. live longer than [last live long survive /alt salt/]
*outlaw 06-49-54 (a.) 1. contrary to or forbidden by law 2. disobedient to or defiant of law (n.) 1. someone who has committed (or been legally convicted of) a crime (v.) 1. declare illegal; outlaw [ostracize outlander outsider unconstitutional unlawful unofficial taboo thief thug transport triable law lawbreaker lawful lawless leper liquidate abstract actionable alien anarchist anomic wander wrongful /alt/]
*outlive 15-46-8 (v.) 1. live longer than [useful last live long endure exist /evil/] "She outlived her husband by many years"
*outpost 08-44-27 (n.) 1. a settlement on the frontier of civilization 2. a military post stationed at a distance from the main body of troops 3. a station in a remote or sparsely populated location [outback outskirt unfamiliar territory tie timber troop people pioneer place point pole populate position post scout sentry service settlement situation sparse stand station suburb /opt/]
*outrage 04-54-101 (n.) 1. a wantonly cruel act 2. a feeling of righteous anger 3. a disgraceful event 4. the act of scandalizing (v.) 1. strike with disgust or revulsion 2. violate the sacred character of a place or language 3. make furious 4. assault sexually; force to

have sex [obstruction offensive omission oppress threaten torture trip rage rape ravish real resentment resignation revolt revulsion run abuse administration affront anger annoyance appall arouse assault atrocity attack aversion genocide grievance grieve emotional enrage error evil exasperate]
*outrageous 05-56-61 (a.) 1. grossly offensive to decency or morality; causing horror 2. greatly exceeding bounds of reason or moderation [obnoxious obscene odious offensive outrage unbridled unconventional unduly unpleasant unrestrained usury terribly too tough rank rate reasonable rent ridiculous rough abandon acute atrocious awfully gigantic great gross grotesque egregious enormous entertain evil excessive exorbitant extortionate extreme sad savage severe shabby shameful sharp shock spend standard steep] "subjected to outrageous cruelty"
*outreach 12-30-14 (n.) 1. the act of reaching out [outdo outfox outplay outre outsmart outstrip outwit overstretch undo thrust toward trick truth reach read elude evade exceed extent circumvent community conjure crane hoax human humbug] "the outreach toward truth of the human spirit"
*outrigger 24-40-1 (n.) 1. a stabilizer for a canoe; spars attach to a shaped log or pontoon parallel to the hull [oarlock upset trigger rope extend /egg girt/]
*outright 06-48-54 (a.) 1. without reservation or exception (ad.) 1. without restrictions or stipulations or further payments 2. without any delay 3. without reservation or concealment [obvious offer omnipresent openly overt universal unlimited unqualified utter utterly tell thorough total totally transparent radical rank refuse regular reservation restriction right immediately instantly intensive glaring global greet gross /girt/] "buy outright"
*outskirt 07-62-37 (n.) 1. a part of the city far removed from the center [outback outer outlying outpost uptown tenderloin territorial town situation skirt subdivision suburb suburbia reach region remove residential /tri/] "they built a factory on the outskirts of the city"
*outstrip 09-73-22 (v.) 1. be or do something to a greater degree 2. go far ahead of [outclass outdo outdraw outfox outgrow outmatch outperform outrun outwit overtake than top transcend trickery trounce sail sell shell shout soar spearhead speed strip student supply surmount surpass race range rear roar runner pace pass performance praise precede product]
*outweigh 07-54-34 (v.) 1. weigh more heavily 2. be heavier than [offset outbalance outdo outgo outmatch outperform outstrip overshadow overweight top transcend trump weigh exceed excel important great heavily]
*overdo 11-63-17 (v.) 1. do something to an excessive degree [occasion orotund ostentatious over overwrought effect engage exaggerate excessive exhaust extreme really rhetorical ruin declamatory defeat degree disproportionate doneness]
*overdose 10-61-20 (v.) 1. dose too heavily [opera overdo overwhelm engulf enough erupt excessive experience redundancy rock room dangerous death deck dose draft drop drug satisfy shot soap star stuff /sod/] "The rock star overdosed and was found dead in his hotel room"
*overeat 18-65-4 (v.) 1. overeat or eat immodestly; make a pig of oneself [over eat englut engorge estimate tense]
*overhang 12-62-12 (n.) 1. projection that extends beyond or hangs over something else (v.) 1. project over 2. be suspended over or hang over [outcrop outer override eaves edge extent rock roof half hang hangover hold hover huge aft amount approach aviation await near gathering]
*overhaul 05-45-82 (n.) 1. periodic maintenance on a car or machine (v.) 1. make repairs or adjustments to 2. travel past, as of a vehicle [observe old outstrip overtake vehicle verify visitation engine equipment examine extensive ready reestablish refit refurbish regenerate regular release renew repair restore review revise rope haul adjustment advance audit autopsy upkeep lap] "it was time for an overhaul on the tractor"
*overlord 20-67-3 (n.) 1. a person who has general authority over others [elder emperor employer rabbi regime royalty rule ruler lord dynast]
*overpass 18-11-4 (n.) 1. bridge formed by the upper level of a crossing of two highways at different levels [obstacle omit opening outlet over vehicle viaduct voyage exaggerate excess exit railway reconnoiter river road rotary route passage patrol people perfect pontoon prevail access alley allow aqueduct arch avenue section span structure superiority suspension sweep swing /sap/] "an overpass is called a flyover or a flypast in England"
*overpay 10-73-19 (v.) 1. pay too much [offer outdo outspend over exchange pay ante /yap/]
*overpower 13-42-11 (v.) 1. overcome, as with emotions or perceptual stimuli 2. overcome by superior force [outdo overwrought vanquish effect elicit emotion enkindle evoke excessive race raise resist response route ruin panic perceptual physical pleasure power prevail provoke putdown whelm whip worsted /wop/]
*overproduction 22-33-2 (n.) 1. too much production or more than expected [expect production /dorp udo/]
*overreach 16-27-6 (v.) 1. beat through cleverness and wit 2. fail by aiming too high or trying too hard [outdo outfox outgo outmatch outplay outreach outstrip outwit vanquish victimize elude exaggerate exceed extend race reach refer aggrandize aim ambitious amplify caricature circumvent clever come competitor conflict conjure crush hard have high hind hoax horse humbug hurt]
*overrun 08-49-28 (a.) 1. (often followed by 'with' or used in combination) troubled by or encroached upon in large numbers (n.) 1. too much production or more than expected (v.) 1. invade in great numbers, as of pests 2.

occupy in large numbers or live on a host 3. flow or run over (a limit or brim) [occupy outstretch over overwhelm vandalize vegetate victory encroach enemy engulf est estimate exceed excess expand expect extra raid rank rapid ravage rebel root run runway unfold untroubled usurp north]
*oversee 03-39-166 (v.) 1. watch and direct [observe operate order overlook verse run secret supervise survey] "Who is overseeing this project?"
*overseer 16-19-6 (n.) 1. a person who directs and manages an organization [organization overman oversee visitor school sirdar supervisor surveyor]
*overshadow 06-60-51 (v.) 1. exceed in importance; outweigh 2. cast a shadow upon 3. cast a shadow [obfuscate obscure occult outdo outshine outweigh veil visible eclipse excel extinguish reduce right ruin screen shadow smoke stand surpass happy haze house adumbrate appear attention detract dim diminish distinguish dominate down dwarf /dah/] "This problem overshadows our lives right now"
*overthrow 07-37-44 (n.) 1. the termination of a ruler or institution (especially by force) 2. the act of disturbing the mind or body (v.) 1. cause the downfall of; of rulers 2. rule against [office oust outdo overt overwhelm vote ecology end expel expose expulsion ravage reach rebel rebellion reject remove retirement reverse revolution rout route ruin ruler ruling takeover termination throw topple transition trim trounce tumble hard hide honeycomb waste way whip wreck] "The Czar was overthrown"
*overtone 12-33-14 (n.) 1. (usually plural) an ulterior implicit meaning or quality 2. a harmonic with a frequency that is a multiple of the fundamental frequency [one overt value effect essence express extension referent relation relevant tenor tinge tone touch note nuance] "overtones of despair"
*overture 08-40-31 (n.) 1. a tentative suggestion designed to elicit the reactions of others 2. something that serves as a preceding event or introduces what follows 3. orchestral music played at the beginning of an opera or oratorio [offer offering open opera oratorio orchestral originate outline overt vamp verse vocal voice voluntary elicit employment exordium reaction rejection relationship rough taster tender tentative theme tone toward usher]
*overweening 22-67-2 (a.) 1. unrestrained in especially feelings 2. presumptuously arrogant [obtrusive opinion outrageous over vainglorious enormous exaggerate excessive extravagant extreme exuberant rash reassure restraint way witty idea immodest importance incontinent inordinate insulting intolerable gigantic gluttonous greed /nine/]
*overweight 08-74-32 (a.) 1. usually describes a large person who is fat but has a large frame to carry it (n.) 1. the property of excessive fatness [obesity offensive oppress outweigh emphasis encumber engorge excessive repletion rotund weight weighty imposing gigantism give good gorge gravity hamper handicap healthy heavy heavyweight height tax thin tonnage tubby]

P

*pacify 15-55-7 (v.) 1. cause to be more favorably inclined; gain the good will of 2. fight violence and try to establish peace in (a location) [palliate peace people placate propitiatory abate agitate allay alleviate angry appease area array assuage calm cease compose conciliate conciliatory conflict cradle incline irenic favor fight force form /cap/]
*packet 07-77-41 (n.) 1. a collection of things wrapped or boxed together 2. a boat for carrying mail 3. (computer science) a message or message fragment 4. a small package or bundle [pack package parcel participle passenger past piles processe produce provide accumulation aid argosy assemblage carry carton collection communicate compute consider content craft keel engineering envelope transmission travel truss tub /cap/]
*pact 05-28-66 (n.) 1. a written agreement between two states or sovereigns [pacify peace people promise protocol accord achieve act agreement aim alliance arm arrangement association atlantic cease commerce concordat consortium contract convention country talk transaction treaty /cap/]
*pagan 12-63-13 (a.) 1. not acknowledging the God of Christianity and Judaism and Islam (n.) 1. a person who does not acknowledge your God [polytheism power profane acknowledge aga animism atheistic gentile god /gap nag/]
*pageant 12-36-13 (n.) 1. an elaborate representation of scenes from history etc; usually involves a parade with rich costumes 2. a rich and spectacular ceremony [parade perform piece play presentation procession production affair antimasque gala gean giveaway grandeur elaborate equivalent event exposition extravaganza tableau theatrical /gap/]
*painstaking 08-51-28 (a.) 1. characterized by extreme care and great effort [pain particular punctual application assiduous attention industry intense scrupulous sedulous show solicitous taking tender thorough thoughtful great /ikat kat/]
*palate 11-51-17 (n.) 1. the upper surface of the mouth that separates the oral and nasal cavities [part personal pharynx projection adenoid aesthetic aftertaste alate apex appreciative larynx late lingua lip lower taste threedimensi tip tongue tonsil tooth twodimension emerge extend /lap tala/]
*palatial 15-67-8 (a.) 1. relating to or being a palace 2. suitable for or like a palace [plush posh proud ala appropriate awful lavish luscious lush luxurious tower imposing impressive /lait lap tala/] "the palatial residence"
*paleontology 16-03-6 (n.) 1. the branch of archeology that studies fossil organisms and related remains [palaeontology pharmacology physiology plant prehistoric aeon aerobiology anatomy ancient animal archeology astrobiology life living earth ecology embryology enzymology eon evidence ontology origin taxonomy genetics growth /lap lot/]

*palette 10-50-20 (n.) 1. board that provides a flat surface on which artists mix paints and the range of colors used 2. the range of colour characteristic of a particular artist or painting or school of art 3. one of the rounded armor plates at the armpits of a suit of armor [paint pale pastel pencil piece pigment plate power protect provide purpose airbrush area armor armpit arrange art artist assortment literature easel enemy thumbhole traditional tray /lap tela/]
*pall 12-58-12 (n.) 1. a sudden numbing dread 2. hanging cloth used as a blind 3. burial garment in which a corpse is wrapped (v.) 1. become less interesting or attractive 2. cause surfeit through excess, of something that was initially pleasing 3. cause to lose courage 4. lose sparkle or bouquet, as of wine or beer 5. cause to become flat, of beer or wine 6. cover with a pall 7. lose strength or effectiveness; become or appear boring, insipid, or tiresome (to) 8. get tired of something or somebody [part performance peter place pleasing preparation prevailing provide accessory across all allay altar alter anticipation appetite appliance apprehensive archbishop area atmosphere attractive audience less linen livable loop lose lower /lap/]
*pallid 16-53-6 (a.) 1. (of light) lacking in intensity or brightness; dim or feeble 2. abnormally deficient in color as suggesting physical or emotional distress 3. lacking in vitality or interest or effectiveness [pale pall paralyze pasty pedestrian performance physical pointless prose abnormal afternoon anemic appal aria arid ashen awed lackluster late lavender lifeless light little lurid inane insipid interest intimidate invalid dawn deficient dim distress dry dull /dill lap/] "the pallid face of the invalid"
*palpable 08-56-28 (a.) 1. capable of being perceived by the senses or the mind; especially capable of being handled or touched or felt 2. (medicine) can be felt by palpation [patent perceptible physical ponderable positive presence profound abdomen able almost anger apparent appreciable arresting lump barely believe branch easy evident examination explicit express /lap/] "a barely palpable dust"
*palpitate 24-61-1 (v.) 1. cause to throb or beat rapidly 2. beat rapidly 3. shake with fast, tremulous movements [palp patter pitapat pound pulse agitate anxiety involuntarily irregular throb thump ticking tremble tremulous tumble twitch exertion /lap tip/] "Her violent feelings palpitated the young woman's heart"
*palsy 15-53-7 (n.) 1. loss of the ability to move a body part 2. a condition marked by uncontrollable tremor (v.) 1. affect with palsy [pal paralyze paraplegia part patient plexus poliomyelitis priapism affect ague akin apoplexy arm attribute leg limbo loss lower sensation shaking shiver side single slap slight speak stroke symptom /lap slap/]
*pamphlet 10-42-18 (n.) 1. a brief treatise on a subject of interest; published in the form of a booklet 2. a small book usually having a paper cover [page paper political position publish advertisement handbill leaflet let essay tear ticket tract treatise /map/]
*pamphleteer 24-48-1 (n.) 1. a writer of pamphlets (usually taking a partisan stand on public issues) [paine pamphlet partisan past pay playwright political professional public american article author material middleton leader english tom revolutionary /map reet/]
*panacea 15-49-7 (n.) 1. hypothetical remedy for all ills or diseases; once sought by the alchemists [paine problem ace alchemist answer nostrum cure /can/]
*pandemic 14-77-9 (a.) 1. epidemic over a wide geographical area 2. existing everywhere (n.) 1. an epidemic that is geographically widespread; occurring throughout a region or even throughout the world [part people plague population predominate prevalent affecting apply area attack average normal nuclear demi different disease dominant effect endemic epidemic epizootic everywhere exist malaria medicine member murrain illness infectious infective inoculate catching category community condition consider contagion contagious country current currently] "a pandemic outbreak of malaria"
*pandemonium 17-57-5 (n.) 1. a state of extreme confusion and disorder [passion perdition place predictable abyss agitation netherworld demon den disorder disturbance dreamland dystopia ebullition extreme mayhem millennium modern outcry inferno underworld uproar upset utopia /nome/]
*panel 02-42-310 (n.) 1. sheet that forms a distinct (usually flat) section or component of something 2. electrical device consisting of an insulated panel containing switches and dials and meters for controlling other electrical devices 3. (computer science) a small temporary window in a graphical user interface that appears in order to request information from the user; after the information has been provided the user dismisses the box with 'okay' or 'cancel' 4. a committee appointed to judge a competition 5. a group of people gathered for a special purpose as to plan or discuss an issue or judge a contest etc 6. a pad placed under a saddle 7. (law) a group of people summoned for jury service (from whom a jury will be chosen) (v.) 1. decorate with panels, as of walls or ceilings 2. select from a list, as of prospective jurors [pad pane partition peel pick piece plank plate plywood pole post prospective accessory adorn allow architectural area assembly assignation eisteddfod embellish enclose entrance exit lap leaf length list litigate log lumber] "he checked the instrument panel"
*panic 04-65-123 (n.) 1. sudden mass fear and anxiety over anticipated events 2. an overwhelming feeling of fear and anxiety (v.) 1. cause panic in; fill with panic 2. feel panic [pain people period permanent phobia play point possible prisoner accompany afraid alarm ani animal anticipation anxiety anxious appear apprehensive

awe nervous nervy intimidate irritable isolation chaos comedian communist confounded consternation cow cowardly] "panic in the stock market"
*panoply 17-49-5 (n.) 1. a complete and impressive array [pan parade press protect accessory armature armor army array necessary needles orderly legion]
*panorama 08-58-33 (n.) 1. the visual percept of a region 2. a picture (or series of pictures) representing a continuous scene [park percept photograph picture produce prospect abstraction altarpiece altitude area arise art aspect narrow near nora omnibus orbit outlook overall radius reach region represent reproduction middle miniature mosaic mural]
*pantheism 24-43-1 (n.) 1. belief in multiple Gods [pantheism phenomena polytheism positivism pragmatist admit animism antinomian apocryphal naturalistic nominalism theism tolerate tritheism hedonist henotheism heretical humanist hylozoism eclectic error existence existential idealistic instrumentalist scholastic sensationalism syncretism manifestation material misbelief monism monotheism multiple]
*pantheon 11-40-16 (n.) 1. all the gods of a religion 2. (ancient Greece or Rome) a temple to all the gods 3. a monument commemorating a nation's dead heroes [pant part peninsula people period place precede public accumulation age aggregation aspect assemblage nation temple tiber hellenic hero historic edifice empire erect eternal europe oil olives]
*pantomime 12-82-14 (n.) 1. a performance using gestures and body movements without words (v.) 1. act out without words but with gestures and bodily movements only [panto part perform piece play pose abbreviation act acting actor ancient appear apple artist narrate takeoff tell theatrical tradition opera mask melodrama mime monologue move imitation impersonate incarnation eat embodiment enactment entertain expression extravaganza]
*papacy 20-54-3 (n.) 1. the government of the Roman Catholic Church [papa period political pope position power premiership president protector archiepiscopate aristocracy authority catholic chairmanship chancellor christ church consul /cap capa/]
*papyrus 22-58-2 (n.) 1. paper made from the papyrus plant by cutting it in strips and pressing it flat; used by ancient Egyptians and Greeks and Romans 2. a document written on papyrus 3. tall sedge of the Nile valley yielding fiber that served many purposes in historic times [palimpsest pap paper parchment pith place plant pressing provide pulp purpose ancient yielding rag reed resemble rhizome roman umbrella scroll sedge serve solid southern spikelet stem strip]
*parable 12-53-13 (n.) 1. a short moral story (often with animal characters) 2. (New Testament) any of the stories told by Jesus to convey his religious message [piece prodigal progress aesop allegory animal apologue apostle appear arable ascribe religious revelation romance believe bible book bunya legend lesson epistle /bar/] "the parable of the prodigal son"
*paradigm 13-39-10 (n.) 1. a standard or typical example 2. systematic arrangement of all the inflected forms of a word 3. the generally accepted perspective of a particular discipline at a given time 4. the class of all items that can be substituted into the same position (or slot) in a grammatical sentence (are in paradigmatic relation with one another) [para parent pattern perspective philosophy position possible precedent prototype provide psychoanalyti accept accidence antitype archetype arrange attribute relation representative root rule declension derivation discipline idealize image indicate inflection inflexion item generally genotype give good grammatical methodology mirror model /gid/]
*paradox 06-45-56 (n.) 1. (logic) a self-contradiction [para perplexity philosophy problematic prohibit proposition puzzle abnormal absurdity ambivalent analyze asymmetry ridiculous dilemma disproportionate opposite oxymoron]
*paragon 13-59-10 (n.) 1. an ideal instance; a perfect embodiment of a concept 2. model of excellence or perfection of a kind; one having no equal [pearl perfectly pick prime prize such ace agon apotheosis archetype assimilate attain remarkable role ruler gem genius optimum non nonpareil /nog/]
*parallel 04-48-96 (a.) 1. being everywhere equidistant and not intersecting 2. (computer science) of or relating to the simultaneous performance of multiple operations (n.) 1. an imaginary line around the Earth parallel to the equator 2. something having the property of being analogous to something else (v.) 1. make or place parallel to something 2. be parallel to 3. duplicate or match [pair para peer picture accord agree ally analogous apply reach reciprocal register latitude legend link lock echo equal even evoke] "parallel lines never converge"
*paralysis 11-48-15 (n.) 1. loss of the ability to move a body part [pain palsy part plexus procrastinate progress akin arm asphyxiate asthma atrophy attribute rash rheum leg lifeless limbo loss lower lumbago lysis shock side single slight sore still stroke idle immobility inactivity inert injury itch]
*paralyze 09-01-22 (v.) 1. cause to be paralyzed and immobile 2. make powerless and unable to function [pallid palsy para part passive perplex petrify poison powerless prevent affect aghast amaze appal astound awe awed layout lose effective enchain enfeeble entire etherize] "The bureaucracy paralyzes the entire operation"
*paramount 07-40-43 (a.) 1. having superior power and influence [palm pick policymaker power predominate preponderate prime principal priority prize accent acme amount apical arch ascendant authorization ranking

record regulate rule main majesty mark maximum moment mood most optimism optimum overriding overrule ultimate unmatched unparalleled utmost note teacher top topmost /mara/]
*paramour 22-60-2 (n.) 1. a woman's lover 2. a woman who cohabits with an important man [playmate pursue admire adore adulterous amorist amour relationship man marry mistress odalisque ongoing /mara/]
*paraphernalia 13-47-11 (n.) 1. equipment consisting of miscellaneous articles needed for a particular operation or sport etc. [perform plant possession property purposer accessory accouterment appointment appurtenance armament article assorted require rig rope royalty rubbish hern high horse husband effect enterpriser equipment necessary law impedimenta indicative installation item]
*paraphrase 13-44-11 (n.) 1. rewording for the purpose of clarification (v.) 1. express the same message in different words [parody perform phrase pony purpose amplification reiterate repeat rephrase reproduction restate retell reword rewrite say short simplify speak summary explicate express]
*pare 08-38-27 (v.) 1. decrease gradually or bit by bit 2. remove the edges from 3. strip the skin off ("pare apples") 4. cut small bits or pare shavings from [particle peel photograph piece plummet plunge potsherd abridge afterimage amputate annihilate apple are reduce refuse remains remove rend rest retrench roughhewn edge eliminate except exclude]
*parentage 18-61-4 (n.) 1. the state of being a parent 2. the descendants of one individual 3. the kinship relation of an offspring to the parents [parent paternity pedigree people phratry adoption ancestry attain reform relationship responsibility root entire extraction tree geographic]
*parenthesis 18-17-4 (n.) 1. either of two punctuation marks (or) used to enclose textual material 2. a message that departs from the main subject [pair palindrome parent part pause piece print punctuation additional afterthought anastrophe aside remark enclose episode excursus textual thesis tmesis topic hypallage hyperbaton sentence separation shallow sign speech substance incomplete indicate injection insert interval introduction isolated]
*pariah 13-55-10 (n.) 1. a person who is rejected (from society or home) [alien anchorite aria ascetic avoid recluse reject religious ritual roman india invalid ishmael isolationist hobo hold home homebody /hair/]
*parish 06-59-53 (n.) 1. a local church community 2. the local subdivision of a diocese committed to one pastor [pastor people politics power precinct priest province administrative archdiocese area arish arrondissement assembly region ride see society state subdivision hamlet hundred]
*parisian 08-59-28 (a.) 1. of or relating to or characteristic of Paris or its inhabitants (n.) 1. a resident of Paris [paris person resident restaurant inhabitant international nationality]
*parity 11-58-17 (n.) 1. (obstetrics) the number of live-born children a woman has delivered 2. (mathematics) a relation between a pair of integers: if both integers are odd or both are even they have the same parity; if one is odd and the other is even they have different parity 3. functional equality 4. (computer science) an error detection procedure in which a bit (0 or 1) added to each group of bits so that it will have either an odd number of 1's or an even number of 1's; e.g., if the parity is odd then any group of bits that arrives with an even number of 1's must contain an error 5. (physics) parity is conserved in a universe in which the laws of physics are the same in a right-handed system of coordinates as in a left-handed system [pair par param pay period philosophy physics position pregnant price processe proportion abit add agreement aid alike alliance amount arrange arrive rally rate reaction receive relation resemblance righthanded identical identity imitation inequality interchange transmit] "the parity of the mother must be considered"
*parlance 15-45-8 (n.) 1. a manner of speaking that is natural to native speakers of a language [parole people phrase profession rhetoric lance language langue lingua locution native natural composition context conversation expression]
*parley 22-14-2 (n.) 1. a negotiation between enemies (v.) 1. discuss, as between enemies [palaver parle people powwow produce proposal advise advocacy agreement audience reach recommendation remonstrance round lengthy enemy exhortation expostulate]
*parliament 02-64-253 (n.) 1. a legislative assembly in certain countries (e.g., Great Britain) 2. a card game in which you play your sevens and other cards in sequence in the same suit as their sevens; you win if you are the first to use all your cards [play policy procedure amend ament assembly repeal law legislature interpellate ireland irish isle israel monarchy england europe explain northwestern /email mail/]
*parlor 10-AA-21 (n.) 1. a room in a private house or establishment where people can sit and talk and relax 2. reception room in an inn or club where visitors can be received [par people premise private provide abode agency area aside atelier reception relax room living loft lounge organization]
*parody 07-46-37 (n.) 1. a composition that imitates somebody's style in a humorous way 2. humorous or satirical mimicry (v.) 1. make a spoof of; make fun of 2. make a parody of [pale par paraphrase participle pasquinade past pastiche perform perversion pervert piece play poor put amusing anamorphosis ape attempt represent rib ridiculous roast role onomatopoeia overstate deliberate derision disguise distortion dummy]
*paroxysm 22-57-2 (n.) 1. a sudden uncontrollable

attack [pang par pathological pinch prick access arrest attack rage recurrent occurrence onset orgasm outburst outpouring overthrow seizure spasm spell storm stroke sudden symptom] "a paroxysm of giggling"
*parse 20-11-3 (v.) 1. analyze syntactically by assigning a constituent structure to (a sentence) [parenthesize phonology point process punctuate analyze apart arse assign resolve role scansion schematize sentence specific structure study subsequent syntactic enumerate essential explain]
*parsimonious 22-67-2 (a.) 1. excessively unwilling to spend [paltry penny penurious pinch poor prudential abstemious ascetic austere relieve saving simon slight small sparing spend stingy impoverish impulse indulgence manner meager mean miserly narrow niggardly ungenerous unwilling] "parsimonious thrift relieved by few generous impulses"
*parsimony 22-77-2 (n.) 1. extreme care in spending money; reluctance to spend money unnecessarily 2. extreme stinginess [paltry part pennypinchin principle providence prudent puny achieve avoid reluctance simony simple slender slight small spend stingy management meager mean ming misericord money narrow niggardly niggardness]
*participant 04-28-124 (n.) 1. someone who takes part in an activity 2. a person who participates in or is skilled at some game [parti party pin play point pool accomplice actor aide alley american applicant assistant athlete attend receive religious retreat roll team tennis tournament ice implicate important involved card ceremony chess class colleague competition confrere contributor /trap/]
*participate 02-30-275 (v.) 1. become a participant; be involved in 2. share in something [partake parti perform program admission affiliate agreement association race reception toleration treatment inclusive incorporate chip consociation contribute cooperation coverage eager enter /trap/]
*partisan 06-25-56 (a.) 1. affiliated with one party or faction 2. adhering or confined to a particular sect or denomination or party 3. devoted to a cause or party (n.) 1. a fervent and even militant proponent of something 2. an ardent and enthusiastic supporter of some person or activity 3. a pike with a long tapering double-edged blade with lateral projections; 16th and 17th centuries [patron people pikestaff politician prejudice propound protagonist public addiction adhere admire advocate affiliate aggressive arbitrary ardent armed arrogant artisan attached racist regular resistance root tail taper team tendentious twist influence interested involved irrational irregular sectarian shadow spearhead sponsor stubborn supporter narrow neighbor nonobjective /trap/]
*partition 10-42-18 (n.) 1. the act of dividing or partitioning; separation by the creation of a boundary that divides or keeps apart 2. a vertical structure that divides or separates (as a wall divides one room from another) 3. (computer science) the part of a hard disk that is dedicated to a particular operating system or application and accessed as a single unit (v.) 1. divide into parts, pieces, or sections 2. separate or apportion into sections [pad panel parietal parti past peninsula piece plank portion pound previous processe property purpose abstraction access aid alienate apart application apportion architectural area asunder ration removal reserved residence rift room temporary thickness incoherent insular interested isolation off operate /trap/] "The Arab peninsula was partitioned by the British"
*passive 07-43-37 (a.) 1. peacefully resistant in response to injustice 2. lacking in energy or will 3. (grammar) passive voice (n.) 1. the voice used to indicate that the grammatical subject of the verb is the recipient (not the source) of the action denoted by the verb [pain paralyze pass patient perform placid power principle produce abstain accepting actor adjust affect asleep semantic sentence serene solar source still submit supine suspend idle implicit inactive independent indicate inert influence injustice investor involve vacant vacuous violent voice effectuate electronics empty enduring energy even express external /sap/] "Much benevolence of the passive order may be traced to a disinclination to inflict pain upon oneself"
*pastoral 09-49-23 (a.) 1. of or relating to a pastor 2. used of idealized country life 3. relating to shepherds or herdsmen or devoted to raising sheep or cattle 4. suggestive of an idyll; charmingly simple and serene (n.) 1. a musical composition that evokes rural life 2. a letter from a pastor to the congregation 3. a literary work idealizing the rural life (especially the life of shepherds) [pacific pastor piece poem agrarian agricultural arcadian scene show success ode opera opus orderly review rhyme rural landscape letter limerick lyric /sap/] "pastoral work"
*paternal 13-52-10 (a.) 1. belonging to or inherited from one's father 2. related on the father's side 3. relating to or characteristic of or befitting a parent 4. characteristic of a father [parental pater patriarchy patrimony adore affectionate agnate ancestral aunt authoritarian tender trait romantic languish loving] "spent his childhood on the paternal farm"
*paternity 14-70-9 (n.) 1. the kinship relation between an offspring and the father [parent parentage pater pedigree propinquity adoption affiliate alliance ancestry attribute author theory enation establish extraction relationship respect role idea initiation innovation institution introduction]
*pathos 13-49-11 (n.) 1. a quality that arouses emotions (especially pity or sorrow) 2. a feeling of sympathy and sorrow for the misfortunes of others 3. a style that has the power to evoke feelings [painful path people period pity poignant power anguish arouse art attribute tragedy over hardship humanity sad share sharp situation sorrow

style sympathy] "the film captured all the pathos of their situation"
*patriarch 10-46-20 (n.) 1. the head of family or tribe 2. a man who is older and higher in rank than yourself 3. any of the early Biblical characters regarded as fathers of the human race [papa paterfamilias pop predecessor prelate priest ancestor antediluvian antique archbishop atria author teacher traditionalism rabbi rector relic ibrahim inventor israel chef chief color conservative head hierarch him himself husband /airt/]
*patrician 15-50-8 (a.) 1. of the hereditary aristocracy or ruling class of ancient Rome or medieval Europe; of honorary nobility in the Byzantine empire 2. belonging to or characteristic of the nobility or aristocracy (n.) 1. a person of refined upbringing and manners 2. a member of the aristocracy [palsgrave patricia peer people plebeian princess privilege proletarian property address adult ancient archduke aristocrat aristocratic taste thoroughbred title tradition rajah rani refined right rome royal rule include india inspire chivalrous citizen class constitute count cultural nobility noble nobleman]
*patrimony 22-24-2 (n.) 1. a church endowment 2. an inheritance coming by right of birth (especially by primogeniture) [pass primogeniture property provide ancestor title tradition reversion right income inherit institution male mony owner]
*patriotism 10-44-20 (n.) 1. love of country and willingness to sacrifice for it [partisan institution sacrifice motherland]
*patron 05-47-83 (n.) 1. a regular customer 2. (French) the proprietor of an inn 3. someone who supports or champions something [pat pay people possessor present production proprietor prospect provide punt purchase aid analogous ancient angel art attend audience award teacher testatrix theatrical tower rabbi regular relation rely republic retail retain right rock opera overlord owner navigator]
*patronize 14-01-9 (v.) 1. treat condescendingly 2. do one's shopping at; do business with; be a customer or client of 3. assume sponsorship of 4. be a regular customer or client of [patron pride prig promote proud psychological putdown aid angel arch art assist assume attitude toplofty toward treat refinance refuse regular run nurture importance inferior interact encourage] "We patronize this store"
*patter 15-49-8 (n.) 1. plausible glib talk (especially useful to a salesperson) 2. a quick succession of light rapid sounds (v.) 1. rain gently 2. make light, rapid and repeated sounds, as of rain [page pajamas pat patois perform pitch plausible pound precipitate across act acting appear argot audible talk tap tick tiny trip emotionalize rain rap rapid register repeat rhythm road roll row run] "the patter of mice"
*paucity 15-61-8 (n.) 1. an insufficient quantity or number [poor poverty amount uncommon city inadequate infrequency insufficient thin tight]
*pauper 17-66-5 (n.) 1. a person who is very poor [pau penury pinch poor possession poverty privation public aid appal unable eligible exist extreme receive recipient]
*pavilion 07-60-35 (n.) 1. large and often sumptuous tent [park peg pole portable public annex inside lion literary ornate outbuilding outdoor outhouse /oil/]
*peaceable 18-38-4 (a.) 1. inclined or disposed to peace 2. disposed to peace or of a peaceful nature [pacific pastoral peace pleasant prudent easygoing ebb agreeable amiable amicable avoid calm citizen civilian compliant contentious cool bland bloodless broken] "they met in a peaceable spirit"
*peaceful 04-46-97 (a.) 1. not disturbed by strife or turmoil or war 2. (of groups) not violent or disorderly 3. peacefully resistant in response to injustice [pacifist passive peace philosophy placid plain principle prudent easy ebb empathetic absence abstain aggressive agitation agree akin amicable appropriate assertive atmosphere calm collected comfortably constant contemplate convenient cool far fighting free friendly friendship understanding undisturbed united unmoved untroubled lawabiding luxurious] "a peaceful nation"
*peccadillo 22-51-2 (n.) 1. a petty misdeed [peccant petty enormity error evil cadi crime atrocity delinquency dereliction immoral improper impropriety indiscretion indulgence infringe injustice lapse offense omission outrage /lid/]
*pectoral 22-57-2 (a.) 1. of or relating to the chest or thorax (n.) 1. either of two large muscles of the chest 2. an adornment worn on the chest or breast [part pec plain exercise chest color connected corresponding thorax transverse oral organ ornament raise relieve respiratory rib rotate abdominal add adduct adorn arm locate] "pectoral organ"
*pecuniary 24-66-1 (a.) 1. relating to or involving money [pec penalty economic exchange commercial compensation receive reward /rain/]
*pedagogue 24-24-1 (n.) 1. someone who educates [pandit professor pundit educator dewey docent doctor don abecedarian agog augusta guide guru university /gad gade/]
*pedagogy 24-12-1 (n.) 1. the profession of a teacher 2. the activities of educating or instructing or teaching; activities that impart knowledge or skill [prepare edification education effort enlightenment extension department didactic direction agog guidance /gad gade/]
*pedal 08-60-30 (a.) 1. of or relating to the feet (n.) 1. a sustained bass note 2. a lever that is operated with the foot (v.) 1. ride a bicycle 2. operate the pedals on a keyboard instrument [pace piano pipe piston pitch pivot play point pole power prize produce push echo entrain extremity dal damper device down drive duration accelerator advance appendage arrange lever lift limb /lad lade/] "the word for a pedal extremity is `foot'"
*pedant 22-75-2 (n.) 1. a person who pays more attention to formal rules and book learning than they

merit [parrot pay perfectionist person precision purist emphasize euphuism detail discipline display doctrinaire ant attention nitpick teenybopper theoretician trimmer]
*pedantic 18-62-4 (a.) 1. marked by a narrow focus on or display of learning especially its trivial aspects [pedant plastic plod pretentious purist elegant exact exquisite detail diligent display doctrinaire donnish dry dull academic affected arcane arid aspect narrow nitpick nominal tall tortuous traditionalism trivial impersonal inkhorn instep compulsive concern convoluted correct corresponding]
*peddle 10-44-21 (v.) 1. sell or offer for sale from place to place [purchase pitch place promote publicize puny push espouse deal drug livelihood]
*peddler 16-16-6 (n.) 1. someone who travels about selling his wares (as on the streets or at carnivals) 2. an unlicensed dealer in illegal drugs [packman peddle pedlar pitchman place promote purveyor pusher exchange express dealer drug duffer latin legal retail]
*pedestal 12-37-12 (n.) 1. a support or foundation 2. a position of great esteem (and supposed superiority) 3. an architectural support or base (as for a column or statue) [piece pile plain platform plinth podium point post elevate ennoble esteem exalted dado dais deify des device die dish sailing section ship short society stacked staff stand standard statue support surbase tablet tall threelegged treat trunk admire aggrandize apotheosize architectural lamp]
*pedestrian 06-48-52 (a.) 1. lacking wit or imagination (n.) 1. a person who travels by foot [plain pleasure poor progress prosy earthbound effete empty expeditionary dead des driver dry dull saunter slow stagger stiff stock tedious travel trek rambling illegal inefficient inept itinerary amble arid artless /airt/] "a pedestrian movie plot"
*pediatrics 10-05-18 (n.) 1. the branch of medicine concerned with the treatment of infants and children [paediatrics pathology pediatric practice prevention psychiatrist danish deal dermatology develop diagnosis disease doctor immunology infant influence internist anesthesiologist technique treatment radiology cardiology care children chiropody concern science specialty /aide/]
*pedigree 08-71-27 (a.) 1. having a list of ancestors as proof of being a purebred animal (n.) 1. the descendants of one individual 2. line of descent of a pure-bred animal 3. ancestry of a purebred animal [parentage people phratry proof property purebred entire extraction derivation descent directory document domesticate inherit generation gree group record root /gid/]
*peerage 13-94-11 (n.) 1. the peers of a kingdom considered as a group [peer privilege earl elect elite royalty aristocrat give group /gare/]
*peerless 14-75-9 (a.) 1. eminent beyond or above comparison [perfect pick prime elect elite eminent equal excellent lack less scholar select sin supreme]
*peevish 22-54-2 (a.) 1. easily irritated or annoyed [peckish pee pettish petulant plaintive plangent easy envious ill incorrigible irritate sorrowful spiteful splenetic sulky howling huffy /vee veep/]
*pejorative 18-42-4 (a.) 1. expressing disapproval [expression judgmental rat ridicule abusive affix tend intend vilify /taro vita/]
*penalty 02-66-373 (n.) 1. a payment required for not fulfilling a contract 2. the disadvantage or painful consequences of an action or condition 3. the act of punishing [painful passive pay payment penal percentage physical player price prison prohibit punishment embarrassment encumbrance equalize exert extract nemesis abate acquittal agreement allow allowance amendment atone award lawful legal lenient less load lose lumber tare team threat torture trouble yourself /lane/] "neglected his health and paid the penalty"
*penance 18-58-4 (n.) 1. a Catholic sacrament; repentance and confession and satisfaction and absolution 2. remorse for your past conduct 3. voluntary self-punishment in order to atone for some wrongdoing [past pay penalty penitent perform pray price priest pro propitiate protestant punishment eastern eucharist extreme nance absolve accept amend amends apology atonement attrition catholic church commit compunction conduct confirmation contrition]
*penchant 08-48-28 (n.) 1. a strong liking [partiality pleasure predilection preference prejudice proclivity prone eager enchant enjoyment experience cast considerable acquire affinity apt taste tendency turn twist]
*pendant 16-52-6 (a.) 1. supported from above (n.) 1. an adornment that hangs from a piece of jewelry (necklace or earring) 2. branched lighting fixture; often ornate; hangs from the ceiling [pair parallel part pendulum picture piece plain pot provide ear eardrop earring equivalent extension nautical neck necklace dabble dangle decoration drapery drop accessory add adorn ally ant architecture art artificial associate attached await tally train twin]
*pendulous 24-63-1 (a.) 1. (biology) having branches or flower heads that bend downward [panicle pensile periodic position posture end erect nod nutation daffodil dangle decision depend downward droop uncertain unco undulatory unsure upright libration literary living loose oscillate overhang sag science study suspend sway swinging]
*pendulum 13-50-10 (n.) 1. an apparatus consisting of an object mounted so that it swings freely under the influence of gravity [periodicity physical piece plane plenum plumb point position progression earth end equipment exact extreme nexus demonstrate descent design direction drone length lineage long mechanism metal method metronome monotone mounted music]
*penetrate 06-42-49 (v.) 1. become clear or enter one's

consciousness or emotions 2. come to understand 3. pass into or through, often by overcoming resistance 4. enter a group or organization in order to spy on the members 5. insert the penis into the vagina or anus of 6. make one's way deeper into ar through 7. spread or diffuse through [pass percolate perforate permeable permeate pervade physical pierce piercing pinch pink place plunge poke porous powerful probe procure profound progress edge effective encroach enemy enigma enter exoteric nature needle nervous nip numbing tap tart telling temper territory thin throw thrust tinge traitor tunnel rate reach readable riddle rigorous rough absorbing access accessible across acute admit advance affect aim anus apprehend apprehensible arctic articulate attack auger /tart tene/] "The bullet penetrated her chest"
*penetration 11-62-17 (n.) 1. the act of entering into or through something 2. clear or deep perception of a situation 3. an attack that penetrates into enemy territory 4. the ability to make way into or through something 5. the act (by a man) of inserting his penis into the vagina of a woman 6. the depth to which something penetrates (especially the depth reached by a projectile that hits a target) [perception piercing providence puncture enter entry tessellation transplant trenchant ration reception relation access acumen acute admission astute import infiltrate injection input intercourse invasion onrush onset /tart tene/] "the penetration of upper management by women"
*peninsular 22-72-2 (a.) 1. of or forming or resembling a peninsula [project prominent protrude earth extend isolation salient solid stick land] "peninsular isolation"
*penitence 24-70-1 (n.) 1. remorse for your past conduct [past penance compunction conduct contrition]
*penitent 18-59-4 (a.) 1. feeling or expressing remorse for misdeeds (n.) 1. a person who repents for wrongdoing (a Roman Catholic may be admitted to penance under the direction of a confessor) [past penance person pope preside priest purgatory embarrassment episcopal excuse express nite tear touched /tine/]
*penitential 24-52-1 (a.) 1. of or relating to penitence or penance 2. showing or constituting penance [penance penitent penitentiary propitiatory purify expiate express tear touched abject amend apologize letter /lait tine/] "the Day of Atonement is the great penitential day of the Hebrew calendar"
*pennant 09-43-25 (n.) 1. the award given to the champion 2. a flag longer than it is wide (and often tapering) 3. a long flag; often tapering [pendant penna pennoncel penoncel piece emblem ensign narrow nautical approval award tangible taper triangular tricolor]
*pension 02-74-264 (n.) 1. a regular payment to a person that iis intended to allow them to subsist without working (v.) 1. grant a pension to [pay posada pub employer scholarship security service shelve social soldier subsist sum superannuate support sustain income injury inn insurance intend ion off ordinary]
*pentagon 04-23-98 (n.) 1. the United States military establishment 2. a government building with five sides that serves as the headquarters of the United States Department of Defense 3. a five-sided polygon [paisley penta plane polygon pyramid establishment nation non teardrop trapezoid triangle armed globe government oblong official orb oval /nog/]
*pentameter 24-66-1 (n.) 1. a verse line having five metrical feet [pair poetry meter metrical rhythm /mat rete/]
*pentathlon 22-75-2 (n.) 1. an athletic contest consisting of five different events [penta point throw track athletics award hurdle long]
*penultimate 11-88-15 (a.) 1. next to the last (n.) 1. the next to last syllable in a word [phoneme next ultimate language large last inadvertent intermediate murder author /amit lune/] "the author inadvertently reveals the murderer in the penultimate chapter"
*penury 20-79-3 (n.) 1. a state of extreme poverty or destitution [pauperize pen penniless pinch poor possession poverty privation exist extreme necessity needy /run rune/]
*perambulate 24-54-1 (v.) 1. make an official inspection on foot of (the bounds of a property) 2. walk with no particular goal [pace parade patrol place property reconnoiter require advance ambulate ankle measure bound law leg legit look track transit tread /mare/] "Selectmen are required by law to perambulate the bounds every five years"
*perceive 04-49-123 (v.) 1. become conscious of 2. to become aware of through the senses [pain palpable past patent per perceptible pickup pierce possess espy evident experience explicit express eye realize rec recognize regard remark reveal catch certain comprehend conciliatory conclude conscious consideration contemplate idea identify indisputable indubitable inexplicable infer inhale input insight instinctive interpret intuitive via viewable visible visual /vie/] "I could perceive the ship coming over the horizon"
*perceptible 18-42-4 (a.) 1. capable of being perceived by the mind or senses 2. easily seen or detected 3. easily perceived by the senses or grasped by the mind [palpable patent pause perceive percept plain prominent ear easy enough evidently expectation explicit expressly eye recognize reveal calculable capable clearly compute conceivable conspicuous tangible touched traceable indisputable indubitable behavior lie limp /bit/]
*perception 04-46-110 (n.) 1. knowledge gained by perceiving 2. a way of conceiving something 3. the process of perceiving 4. the representation of what is perceived; basic component in the formation of a concept 5. becoming aware of something via the senses

[penetration percept providence purview experience eye eyesight range realize reasoning recognition cogency conception consciousness theory thought trenchant idea impression insight observation opinion note notion] "Luther had a new perception of the Bible"
*percolate 17-28-5 (n.) 1. the product of percolation (v.) 1. permeate; penetrate gradually; of liquids 2. be diffused thoroughly 3. cause to pass through a permeable substance in order to extract a soluble constituent, as of solvents 4. prepare in a percolator, of coffee 5. spread gradually 6. pass through 7. gain or regain energy [pass penetrate perforate perform perk permeate pick place play porous prepare product pulp easy effusion emit endosmosis energy engross enter entire entry extract exude reception recover recuperate refinement regain resistance rinse run charge clarify clear coffee cola condensation constituent convalesce cut ooze operate osmosis outward overcome leach leakage let liquid liquidize lively absorption access act admission assimilate thaw thin tick transude trickle] "Light percolated into our house in the morning"
*percussion 09-34-22 (n.) 1. the act of exploding a percussion cap 2. the act of playing drums 3. tapping a part of the body for diagnostic purposes [part patient percussive play practice presence produce purpose encounter enlarge examination explosive ram rhythm cap class collision create crunch cuss cymbal section shock smashing snapper solidify sound stethoscope strike struck impact impinge include instrument onslaught orchestra organ noise /sucre/]
*peregrination 24-41-1 (n.) 1. travel (especially by foot) [passage pilgrimage place excursion expedition nation across traverse trip /gere/]
*peremptory 20-46-3 (a.) 1. offensively self-assured or given to exercising usually unwarranted power 2. not allowing contradiction or refusal 3. putting an end to all debate or action [perfect power preclude prescriptive employee emptor entire exercise expect explicit express refusal repressive require resolute round magisterial mandatory manner masterful must tend tolerate tone total tyranny obey offensive open oppressive order outcome outright overrule /mere/]
*perennial 06-50-54 (a.) 1. (botany) lasting three seasons or more 2. lasting an indefinitely long time; suggesting self-renewal 3. recurring again and again (n.) 1. a plant lasting for three seasons or more [passage pere permanent perpetual persist persistent plant popular power prickly prolong endless enduring eryngo eternal exotic rapid rattlesnake recur regular remain repeat repetitive restricted return running nonstop immediate immortal incessant indefinitely indicate infinite interruption aged always ancient annual lasting life lifelong link litter living long /inn inner lain/] "the common buttercup is a popular perennial plant"
*perfidious 22-75-2 (a.) 1. tending to betray; especially having a treacherous character as attributed to the Carthaginians by the Romans [promise punic erf roman faithful fierce foe intrigue deceitful dishonest disloyal duty obligation untrue]
*perfidy 20-60-3 (n.) 1. betrayal of a trust 2. an act of deliberate betrayal [promise punic entrap erf estranged recreant roman faithless falsity fierce foe formal infidelity insidious intrigue deceit deliberate design disaffect dishonest dishonesty disloyalty doublecrossi duplicity duty]
*perforate 16-45-6 (a.) 1. having a hole cut through (v.) 1. make a hole into or between, as for ease of separation 2. pass into or through, often by overcoming resistance [paper part pass penetrate percolate permeate pervade physical pierce pink pit plate plunge poke prick probe puncture ear eardrum ease easy edge enemy enter examine resistance riddle fix foray force ooze open orate overcome auger tap tear territory throw thrust transparent transpierce trephine tunnel /taro/] "perforate the sheets of paper"
*perform 01-42-882 (v.) 1. give a performance (of something) 2. perform a function 3. get (something) done 4. to act or perform an action [play pose practise practitioner present producer put enact enactment end entertainer evidence execute execution exercise express react realize rehearse representation responsibility reveal run fabricate fake feasible finish flourish form fraud fulfill function occupation officiate operator overact maker management maneuver manipulate mean medium mime mount]
*perfumery 24-84-1 (n.) 1. perfumes in general 2. an establishment where perfumes are made 3. store where perfumes are sold 4. the art of making perfumes [perfumer place private production public educational emit equipment essence establishment residence retail fragrant manufacture mercantile /emu/]
*perfunctory 15-37-8 (a.) 1. hasty and without attention to detail; not thorough 2. as a formality only [passing pococurante easygoing election establish rapid removed require reveal routine rush fail flaw fleeting force forethought form formal unaware unwilling usual negligent neutral nonchalant careless casual cold consideration convention cool courtesy cursory custom tactless tepid thorough thoughtless token tory obligatory oblivious offhand one oppose]
*perhaps 01-55-939 (ad.) 1. by chance [peradventure perchance possibly public express remark run hap haply happen house hunch appear approximate shot show speculation stab /spa/] "perhaps she will call tomorrow"
*perilous 09-54-26 (a.) 1. fraught with danger [parlous peril precarious provisional explosive exposure extreme recovery risky infirm insecure insubstantial liable life ugly uncertain undersea unsafe unsure sea serious shaky slippery stormy surgery /lire/]
*peripatetic 16-46-6 (a.) 1. traveling especially on foot (n.) 1. a person who walks from place to place 2. a follower of Aristotle or an adherent of Aristotelianism

[passing pate pedestrian philosophy place poor preacher progress establish expeditionary roam rover roving infantryman itinerant itinerary adherent ambulatory aristotle tramp travel trek country /cite tapir/] "peripatetic country preachers"
*perish 10-62-19 (v.) 1. pass from physical life and lose all all bodily attributes and functions necessary to sustain life [pain part pass passover patient peaceful peri physical pip pop position putrefy early end exist exit expire extremely raw rot rust shiver snuff spoil starve state stifle stop submerge succumb suffocate superannuate sustain hard harsh hide hunt /sire/]
*perjure 22-29-2 (v.) 1. knowingly tell an untruth in a legal court and render oneself guilty of perjury [palter per pretend prevaricate equivocate render untruth untruthful]
*perjury 11-26-16 (n.) 1. criminal offense of making false statements under oath [perversion prevaricate equivocation exaggerate jury untruthfulnes]
*permanence 18-39-4 (n.) 1. the property of being able to exist for an indefinite duration [perdurable perpetuity persistence plug power preoccupation property endless enduring eternity exist extremely reliable resistant resolution maintenance mane age antiquity application ceaseless concentration condition constant continuance]
*permanent 02-51-252 (a.) 1. continuing or enduring without marked change in status or condition or place 2. not capable of being reversed or returned to the original condition (n.) 1. a series of waves in the hair made by applying heat and chemicals [perennial perpetual persist place plug position president process endless enduring essential eternal everlasting expect relentless remain resistant return reversible rigid rooted majestic making mane mark merciful mont abiding address aged ageless always ancient antique apply natural never noble nonstop temporary tenacious timeless tough] "permanent secretary to the president"
*permeate 12-40-14 (v.) 1. spread or diffuse through 2. penetrate mutually or be interlocked 3. pass through [part pass penetrate people percolate perforate pervade porous pulp easy engulf enter entire resistance rinse macerate marinate marry meat membrane minute mutual administration affect aspect assault atmosphere awash teem temper territory tincture tinge transfusion] "An atmosphere of distrust has permeated this administration"
*permissible 12-40-12 (a.) 1. that may be permitted especially as according to rule 2. that may be accepted or conceded [pardon permit proper endorse endure excuse rule medicine miss inadmissible sanction school speculation suffer bearable behavior lawful legal legitimate legitimize] "permissible behavior in school"
*permutation 15-58-7 (n.) 1. an event in which one thing is substituted for another 2. act of changing the lineal order of objects in a group 3. complete change in character or condition 4. the act of changing the arrangement of a given number of elements [physical place process element exchange rate rearrange reciprocity reincarnation retaliate magnitude mathematics metempsychosis method miller modification move mutation transposition transubstantiation alternative appearance arrangement avatar innovation instance interplay item operation novelty /tum/]
*pernicious 15-54-7 (a.) 1. exceedingly harmful 2. working or spreading in a hidden and usually injurious way [pern pestilent pestilential physical poison poisonous prejudicial evil exceedingly ruinous noisome noxious injurious innocuous insidious internecine capable corruptive counterproductive ominous savage serious sinister spiteful spread subtle swart]
*perpendicular 20-30-3 (a.) 1. intersecting at or forming right angles 2. extremely steep 3. at right angles to the plane of the horizon or a base line (n.) 1. a straight line at right angles to another line 2. an extremely steep face 3. a Gothic style in 14th and 15th century England; characterized by vertical lines, a four-centered (Tudor) arch, fan vaulting 4. a cord from which a metal weight is suspended pointing directly to the earth's center of gravity; used to determine the vertical from a given point [perp plumb plunge precipitous edge english erect rectangular normal depth diagonal diameter directrix chord upright abrupt airline architecture axis /lucid prep/] "the axes are perpendicular to each other"
*perpetrate 07-59-34 (v.) 1. perform an act, usually with a negative connotation [party pay perform petra produce pull effect effectuate enact execute realize render responsible robbery accomplish achieve agent /prep tart/] "perpetrate a crime"
*perpetrator 16-58-6 (n.) 1. someone who perpetrates wrongdoing [party transgresse agent offend]
*perpetual 07-55-39 (a.) 1. continuing forever or indefinitely 2. uninterrupted in time and indefinitely long continuing 3. occurring so frequently as to seem ceaseless or uninterrupted [pain perennial permanent perp persist place plant prolong endless enduring eternal exhaustless rapid recur regular remain repeat restricted revenge rigid theme thunder timeless torpid tough truth ubiquitous unceasing unending uninterrupted universal unlimited unremitting unwavering abiding aged ageless always ancient answer antique appear lasting live long longevity love /prep/]
*perpetuate 09-38-23 (v.) 1. cause to continue or prevail [perp preserve prevail progression prolong propagate protract embalm endurance eternize extend extension remain remember repetition retain run unaltered uphold /prep taut/] "perpetuate a myth"
*perquisite 20-04-3 (n.) 1. an incidental benefit awarded for certain types of employment (especially if it is regarded as a right) 2. a right reserved exclusively by a particular person or group (especially a hereditary or official right) [percentage perk plus point pourboire

prerogative privilege prize profit earnings eleanor employment exclusive extra receipt render reserved return rightful idea incentive incidental income inducement interest service session site squeeze station store sweetener take thing tip tradition type]
*persecution 09-48-23 (n.) 1. the act of persecuting (especially on the basis of race or religion) [passion people perse power problem punishment pursuit ethnic exasperate race rack religious strong subjugation suffer supernatural suppression claw control crucifixion cruelty unfair torment torture trial trouble tyranny ill illtreatment inhumane intimidate ion irritation oppress organize origin outrage nightmare nuisance]
*perseverance 13-53-10 (n.) 1. persistent determination 2. the act of persisting or persevering; continuing or repeating behavior [people period perpetuate pertinacious pluck point prolong purpose earnest elect endurance extension repeat repetition resolve run salvation serious setback severance stamina steady stubborn acceptance achieve appropriate assiduity commitment concept continue continuity]
*persevere 12-56-14 (v.) 1. be persistent, refuse to stop [patient period permanent persist philosophical plug press problem proceed purposeful earnest endure enduring exact rapt refuse relentless remain resolved revive serious set severe single steady stick stop stubborn suffer support survive]
*persist 05-48-65 (v.) 1. stay behind 2. be persistent, refuse to stop 3. continue to exist [per period persevere plug preserve press prevail problem prolong proof effect embrace endure evidence exist extend refuse remain retain room run set smell sphere stage steady stick stop story stubborn survive sustain inhibit insist tarry toil transfer trouble]
*persistence 10-49-18 (n.) 1. persistent determination 2. the property of a continuous and connected period of time 3. the act of persisting or persevering; continuing or repeating behavior [period permanence persist pertinacious plug point power preservation pressure problem prolong purpose pushy earnest effect enduring even extension remove repeat resist resolve rigid run serious stand steady stubborn importunity indefatigable industry insistency insistent tacky tenacity tight tireless commitment connected constant continuous course]
*personable 15-49-7 (a.) 1. (of persons) pleasant in appearance and personality [persona pleasing polite potent powerful prestigious efficacious enchanting estimable eye reputable slender strong substantial affable agreeable amiable appearance attractive authoritative beauty becoming bonny buxom likable likely /ban/]
*personage 20-29-3 (n.) 1. another word for person; a person not meriting identification 2. a person whose actions and opinions strongly influence the course of events [party persona piece principal earthling elder eminence enchilada role shot side something star one name nose notable actor antagonist antihero galaxy giant groundling gun guy] "a strange personage appeared at the door"
*personal 01-51-726 (a.) 1. intimately concerning a person's body or physical being 2. particular to a given individual 3. of or arising from personality 4. concerning or affecting a particular person or his or her private life and personality 5. indicating grammatical person (n.) 1. a short newspaper article about a particular person or group [particular peculiar persona physical precise private exclusive express extraordinary respective retired rude several singular specific story offensive noteworthy absolute actual anonymous article live] "a personal favor"
*personality 03-52-187 (n.) 1. a person of considerable prominence 2. the complex of all the attributes--behavioral, temperamental, emotional and mental--that characterize a unique individual [party personal prestige purchase effect ego elder reflection reign rule say something soul object one organism name nature nose ascendancy aspersion authority leadership life lion identity individuality interest]
*personnel 03-37-147 (n.) 1. group of people willing to obey orders 2. the division of a business responsible for hiring and training and placing employees and for seting policies for personnel management [paramilitary person phony proxy employee equal exchange relief representative reserve service sign spare staff officer]
*perspective 03-46-141 (n.) 1. the appearance of things relative to one another as determined by their distance from the viewer 2. a way of regarding situations or topics etc. [perception piece position post proportion prospect edge evaluation extent eyesight range ratio reach remote scale scene seat side size space spec survey color command composition technique tone treatment infinity value venue viewer vista]
*perspicacity 24-64-1 (n.) 1. intelligence manifested by being astute (as in business dealings) 2. the capacity to assess situations or circumstances shrewdly and to draw sound conclusions [penetration providence purview enterprise experience eye eyesight range scope see slyness sweep incisive insight city cogency crafty cunning acuity acumen acute astute trenchant]
*perspiration 18-59-4 (n.) 1. salty fluid secreted by sweat glands 2. the process of the sweat glands of the skin secreting a salty fluid [place poly pour process profuse excessive excrete exudate exudation ration release room salty secretion skin solvent specialize substance sudation sweat swelter ice tasteless temperature odorless organic /rip/]
*perspire 20-55-3 (v.) 1. excrete perspiration through the pores in the skin [pass pore eliminate excrete exude secrete skin spire suffer swelter intense /rip/]
*persuade 02-59-304 (v.) 1. cause somebody to adopt a certain position, belief, or course of action; twist somebody's arm 2. win approval or support for [plead

poise position positive preach press prevail prompt proud encourage enjoin exhort reassure remonstrate satisfy score secure stimulate sure sway sweet understand unfaltering unhesitating unwavering urge ade admonish affect agree arrogant assured decided determined dispose doubtless]
*pertain 14-33-9 (v.) 1. be a part or attribute of 2. be about; have to do with; be relevant to; refer, pertain, or relate to [part pert pertinent proportionate refer reference regard relevant revolve talk touch accessory admissible advert affect apply appropriate associate attribute importance include incriminate interest involve novel]
*pertinent 10-60-18 (a.) 1. being of striking appropriateness and pertinence 2. having precise or logical relevance to the matter at hand [pert pertain pith point precise proportionate purport effect essence evocative extension refer regard relative relevant reply respect tenor idea image impact interest involve issue nature /nitre/] "a list of articles pertinent to the discussion"
*perturb 15-63-7 (v.) 1. disturb in mind or make uneasy or cause to be worried or alarmed 2. cause a celestial body to deviate from a theoretically regular orbital motion, esp. as a result of interposed or extraordinary gravitational pull 3. disturb or interfere with the usual path of an electron or atom 4. throw into great confusion or disorder [paddle pass path perplex pert plague previous problematic provoke pull puzzle electron embarrass embroil exciting extraordinary rattle ravishing render restless ripple rock ruffle tantalizing tense threaten throw torment trouble turbulent turn uncomfortable undergo uneasy unhinge unnerve unsettle upset baffle behavior beset bewilder body bother breathtaking bring bug burden /brut/] "She was rather perturbed by the news that her father was seriously ill"
*perusal 22-49-2 (n.) 1. reading carefully with intent to remember [peru pore practice process engrossment examination exercise read remember review understand scrutiny study subject survey application linguistic lucubration /sure/]
*pervade 12-48-14 (v.) 1. spread or diffuse through [pass penetrate penetration percolate perforate permeate perv process entire entrance random resistance administration ammoniac atmosphere diffuse distrust dredge dye]
*pervasive 09-26-24 (a.) 1. spread throughout 2. spreading throughout [perfect perm persistent perv plain prevalent puncture pure egregious everywhere exhaustive extensive radical regular rife veritable absolute affectation allot anxiety apply serve sheer specific spread straight sweeping inescapable intensive irony /visa/] "a pervasive anxiety overshadows the triumphs of individuals"
*perverse 08-61-30 (a.) 1. marked by a disposition to oppose and contradict 2. resistant to guidance or discipline 3. marked by immorality; deviating from what is considered right or proper or good [peevish pertinacious perve perverted petulant plan point ponderous positive proper enemy erring erroneous reason rebellious refuse reprobate resistant reverse revolutionary right rival villainous violent satisfaction seem self snappy sour still stray stubborn stuffy sullen] "took perverse satisfaction in foiling her plans"
*perversion 17-59-5 (n.) 1. an aberrant sexual practice that is preferred to normal intercourse 2. the action of perverting something (turning it to a wrong use) [plausible point poison pollution practice prefer error exaggerate expressionism rationalization reverse version vice violation vitiate sex shape sin situation sodomy squeeze stimulate strain illusion infection injustice intercourse obfuscate obscure oral normal] "it was a perversion of justice"
*perversity 18-55-4 (n.) 1. deliberate unruliness 2. deliberately deviating from what is good [persist perve polarity practice principle prone evil excitable repugnance seem showdown stubborn stuffy sullen inconsistency interest irascible irritable testy trait]
*pervert 13-86-10 (n.) 1. a person whose behavior deviates from what is acceptable especially in sexual behavior (v.) 1. corrupt morally or by intemperance or sensuality 2. change the inherent purpose or function of something 3. practice sophistry; change the meaning of or be vague about in order to mislead or deceive [paederast pain parody partner passive pederast pedophile people perve piece pleasure poison practice profane proper prostitute punishment purpose embezzle embroider engage enjoy evil exaggerate expend rationalize ravage receive refer reprobate respect ruin vague vain value varnish violate vitiate taint teach torture transform travesty twist]
*pest 09-50-26 (n.) 1. a persistently annoying person [persecute pes pill problem epidemic evil exasperate sadist scourge smut thorn torment trial trouble]
*pestilence 22-63-2 (n.) 1. any epidemic disease with a high death rate 2. a pernicious evil influence [pandemic people pernicious effect endemic epidemic epizootic evil scourge serious spread stile tend thorn torment transmit tuberculosis infectious influence nemesis calamity cancer cognitive contagious curse]
*peter 01-62-789 (n.) 1. disciple of Jesus and leader of the apostles; regarded by Catholics as the vicar of Christ on earth and first Pope 2. obscene terms for penis [pecker penis pete phallus pope popularity preach prick putz earth euphemism testament tool tradition /rete/]
*petrify 15-67-7 (v.) 1. cause to become stone-like or stiff or dazed and stunned 2. change into stone 3. make rigid and set into a conventional pattern [pallid paralyze pattern penetrate perplex pet pressure easily eerie teach temper terror terrorist think thunderstruck toughen train turn reassure reinforce rigidify rock immobilize impair incrust indurate inorganic intense intimidate fear fill

firm fix flabbergast force fossilize frighten frozen /fir/]
*petty 07-53-40 (a.) 1. inferior in rank or status 2. (informal terms) small and of little importance 3. contemptibly narrow in outlook [paltry parochialism piece pet picayune piddle piffle poor provincial punk effort enormity enterprise equivocate evasive execrable exiguous expression tenure tight tiny tolerance trifling trivial young]
*petulance 20-77-3 (n.) 1. an irritable petulant feeling [peevish easily tantrum temper testy touchy affable angry cantankerousn choler crabby cross]
*petulant 13-71-11 (a.) 1. easily irritated or annoyed [peckish peevish perverse pettish plaintive plangent protest easily easy envy tantrum techy temperamental testy tetchy touchy uneasy unfulfilled unhappy unpleasant least affable angry annoy ant arbitrary nettle notional /lute/]
*pharmacy 09-47-26 (n.) 1. a retail shop where medicine and other articles are sold 2. the art and science of preparing and dispensing drugs and medicines, [pharma pharmacopoeia place posology prepare profession haberdashery apothecary art article retail medicine mercantile milliner chemist clinic collection confectionery]
*phenomenal 07-69-37 (a.) 1. of or relating to a phenomenon 2. exceedingly or unbelievably great [perceptible phenomena philosophy physical prodigious puzzling highly huge enigmatic exceptional external extraordinary noteworthy objective ordinary outlandish outstand marvelous memory mind miraculous mythical amazing apparent astound least legendary /anemone lane nemo one/] "phenomenal science"
*phenomenon 04-53-90 (n.) 1. a remarkable development 2. any state or process known through the senses rather than by intuition or reasoning [paradox particular people perception phenom portent present prodigy pulsation hap happen happenstance hazard human effect episode event excite experience natural notable occasion occurrence oppose ordinary outcome mark marvelous means miracle mirage /nemo none one/]
*philander 16-58-6 (v.) 1. have amorous affairs; of men 2. talk or behave amorously, without serious intentions [pet play playboy profligate propel pursue heartbreaker husband inamorato interact lady lander lead lecher legendary libertine like lover advance adventure affair aggressive amorous never nobleman noted dally debauchee dissolute engage esquire exchange eye rake relationship rip romance roue rounder runaround]
*philanthropic 13-33-10 (a.) 1. generous in assistance to the poor 2. of or relating to or characterized by philanthropy [people poor public help humanitarian love aid almsgiver altruistic anthropic assistance toward relief openhearted charitable concern contributor]
*philanthropist 12-41-14 (n.) 1. someone who makes charitable donations intended to increase human well-being [patron promoter public hila humanitarian intend trust remember offer orphan sponsor /sip/]
*philanthropy 07-28-41 (n.) 1. voluntary promotion of human welfare [patronage present promotion public help hila humankind impart improve intend largesse liberality love aid altruism amity angel assistance award testatrix toward trust remember offer organization orphan]
*philately 20-38-3 (n.) 1. the collection and study of postage stamps [postage item lately aggregation airmail /tali/]
*philharmonic 07-34-38 (a.) 1. composing or characteristic of an orchestral group 2. devoted to or appreciative of music [perform player promote harmonic instrumental affect appreciative musical orchestral organization choir classical combo compose] "philharmonic players"
*philistine 15-63-7 (a.) 1. smug and ignorant and indifferent or hostile to artistic and cultural values (n.) 1. a person who is uninterested in intellectual pursuits 2. a non-Semitic inhabitant of ancient Philistia [people place plebeian prosaic pursuit homespun hoodwink hooligan hostile ignoramus ignorant illiterate impervious indifferent indwell inhabit insensitive intellectual list looby lout lowbrow secular settle sheep smug square tasteless temporal terrestrial trimmer earthy]
*philology 22-56-2 (n.) 1. the humanistic study of language and literature [paleography people period philosopher phonology pioneer polymath professional propose provide psycholinguistics pundit henry history humanity intend language lexicology liberal linguistics literature occupational old ology orthoepy oxford general genius germany grammar graphemics]
*philosophize 22-03-2 (v.) 1. reason philosophically [part phil power pro inference life logic opinion solution speculate standpoint superficial supposedly ethics exercise existence explain express /soli/]
*philosophy 04-46-123 (n.) 1. any personal belief about how to live or how to deal with a situation 2. the rational investigation of questions about existence and knowledge and ethics 3. a belief (or system of beliefs) accepted as authoritative by some group or school [passivism patience phil physics proof hedonism humanism hylozoism idealism ideology individualism opinion optimism outlook sensationalism sentiment serenity skepticism /soli/] "self-indulgence was his only philosophy"
*phlegmatic 18-78-4 (a.) 1. showing little emotion [passive philosophical phlegm placid heartless heavy hopeless latent lifeless listless little emotional enervate equanimous extrovert generally groggy mindless moderate moribund abeyance aloof apathetic arouse tame temperate tranquil impassive inactive indifferent insensitive calm certainly cold compose control cool] "a phlegmatic...and certainly undemonstrative man"

*phonetic 22-51-2 (a.) 1. of or relating to speech sounds 2. of or relating to the scientific study of speech sounds [philology phone pictograph pitch pronunciation hard heavy high human occlusive ogham open narrow nasalize tense thick tonic transcription ideograph intonate central character close /cite/] "phonetic transcription"
*phosphorescence 24-53-1 (n.) 1. a fluorescence that persists after the bombarding radiation has ceased [persist phosphor heat source stimulate radiation removal electroluminescence emission emit exposure cease chemiluminescence continued]
*physicist 08-37-30 (n.) 1. a scientist trained in physics [philosophy physic carnot charless coulomb crookes curie]
*physics 07-46-42 (n.) 1. the science of matter and energy and their interactions [philosophy physic pressure]
*physiognomy 24-57-1 (n.) 1. the human face ('kisser' and 'smiler' and 'mug' are informal terms for 'face'; 'phiz' is British) [phiz physio pudding head scotland seek smile speak imitate indicator ireland isle occupy outward great northwestern monarchy mug /mong mongo/]
*physiology 12-51-13 (n.) 1. the branch of the biological sciences dealing with the functioning of organisms 2. processes and functions of an organism [particular pharmacology physio pressure prevent principle processe human humor science sensory shape shorten specific spread stimulus impulse inactive include isometric oppose organ len lengthen light live location genetics gradual growth]
*physique 11-74-15 (n.) 1. constitution of the human body 2. alternative names for the body of a human being [person plan property habit habitus hefty hominid homo hue human young shape short size somatotype sort soul spirit squat stout strong structure study system ilk include individual quality elasticity entire ethos extinct]
*picaresque 20-44-3 (a.) 1. involving clever rogues or adventurers especially as in a type of fiction [plot prose impish care cheat clever adventurer rascal roguish episode scoundrel separate simple /sera/] "picaresque novels"
*picayune 24-18-1 (a.) 1. (informal terms) small and of little importance [paltry particular petty pica piddle piece piffle pin police precise puny imitate important indifference inferiority infraction insignificant irrelevant cent childish coin colloquial communicate compare country curio cursory negligible nice niggling effort enterprise equivocate evasive exact expression]
*piccolo 20-39-3 (n.) 1. a small flute; pitched an octave above the standard flute [panpipe penny pianoforte pic pipe pitch post principal instrument castanet celesta cello clarinet clarion clavichord close concertina conga cornet crumhorn cymbal oboe ocarina octave opening organ last lute lyre]
*piece 01-49-731 (n.) 1. a distance 2. an object created by a sculptor 3. a serving that has been cut from a larger portion 4. an item that is an instance of some type 5. a portable gun 6. an artistic or literary composition 7. an instance of some kind 8. a musical work that has been created 9. a portion of a natural object 10. a separate part of a whole 11. game equipment consisting of an object used in playing certain board games 12. a share of something 13. a period of indeterminate length (usually short) marked by some action or condition (v.) 1. to join or unite the pieces of 2. make by putting pieces together 3. eat intermittently; take small bites of 4. join during spinning, as of broken pieces of thread, slivers, or rovings 5. repair by adding pieces [paper patch percentage perspective pick pie identical instrument intermittent invention eat end exercise extent case commission conjoin copy create cup cut] "an important piece of the evidence"
*piecemeal 15-44-8 (a.) 1. one thing at a time (ad.) 1. a little bit at a time [part piece proceeding intermittent asunder little] "the research structure has developed piecemeal"
*pied 15-61-8 (a.) 1. having sections or patches colored differently and usually brightly [paint particoloured patch pie piebald plain daisy dapple desert different dress]
*pillage 16-54-6 (n.) 1. goods or money obtained illegally 2. the act of stealing valuable things from a place (v.) 1. steal goods; take as spoils [people pill pinch piracy place plunder possession practice predation predatory prize profit property illegal invade involve level lift loot appropriate army assault attack attribute author gang good goon great gut earthquake encroach excessive /gal gall lip/]
*pillory 15-73-7 (n.) 1. a wooden instrument of punishment on a post with holes for the neck and hands; offenders were locked in and so exposed to public scorn (v.) 1. expose to ridicule or public scorn 2. punish by putting in a pillory 3. criticize harshly or violently [pan participle passage past penalize penalty perceive pick pill plagiarize point post press public punish punishment impose inflict instrument iron leash lock offend openly real restraint ride ridicule roast yoke /lip roll/]
*pinch 05-46-71 (n.) 1. a painful or straitened circumstance 2. the act of apprehending (especially apprehending a criminal) 3. a sudden unforeseen crisis (usually involving danger) that requires immediate action 4. small sharp biting 5. an injury resulting from getting some body part squeezed 6. a squeeze with the fingers 7. a slight but appreciable addition (v.) 1. make ridges into by pinching together 2. squeeze tightly between the fingers 3. make off with belongings of others 4. irritate as if by a nip, pinch, or tear 5. cut the top off [pain palm pass penetrating piercing pilfer poach pucker puny purloin purse icy illiberal imitation impecunious impoverish impulse inch inclement injury

iota irritate narrow near necessity needy nick nip nobble numbing cabbage catch cheap collar concentrate condition control cramped crisp crop cultivate cut haggard hand hair hibernal hole hook hurt hyperborean] "He pinched her behind"
*pine 05-40-72 (n.) 1. straight-grained durable and often resinous white to yellowish timber of any of numerous trees of the genus Pinus 2. a coniferous tree (v.) 1. have a yen for [pacific paint panel peak pendulous persistent pessimistic pin pinus pinyon pitch plant plate ponderosa prefer present prickly prominent prostrate pung needles northwestern numerous nut eastern elongate endure europe exudate]
*pinnacle 10-61-18 (n.) 1. (architecture) a slender upright spire at the top of a buttress of tower 2. the highest level or degree attainable 3. a lofty peak (v.) 1. set on or as if on a pinnacle 2. raise on or as if on a pinnacle [parapet peak pediment perfection pitch point position principle profession identify noon achieve acle acme add all ambition apex apogee artist attain cap column crest crown landscape lantern level lift lighthouse limit lofty edge elevation end extremity /can/] "pinnacle a pediment"
*pioneer 04-51-136 (n.) 1. one the first colonists or settler in a new territory 2. someone who helps to open up a new line of research or technology or art (v.) 1. open up an area or prepare a way 2. take the lead or initiative in; participate in the development of [past pave penetrate pilot plant point prepare previous prime immigrant include initiative innovate institute introduce invent inventor occur open organize originate originator outpost neer neologize early effort engineer enterprise establish experiment explore railhead revolt revolutionize rubbernecker] "She pioneered a graduate program for women students"
*pious 13-54-11 (a.) 1. having or showing or expressing reverence for a deity 2. devoutly religious [parent people persuade pharisaic pharisaism piety positive praiseworthy prayerful pretended profess purpose insincerity irreligious observance oily unctuous unworldly sacred saintly sanctimonious satisfy secure self sheldon show sincere smug snivel snuffle spiritual strict sure sway] "pious readings"
*piquant 14-42-9 (a.) 1. having an agreeably pungent taste 2. attracting or delighting 3. engagingly stimulating or provocative [piercing pleasing poignant prompt provocative pungent impressive interesting intrigue quant quicken unsettle upset acid agitate agreeable appealing attractive taking tangy tart tasty telling tone trouble] "a piquant wit"
*pique 13-45-11 (a.) 1. of textiles; having parallel raised lines (n.) 1. tightly woven fabric with raised cords 2. a sudden outburst of anger (v.) 1. cause to feel resentment or indignation [parallel passionate peeved personal pet pride produce provoke punch ignite ill indignation insult interest interested invite irk irritate quicken umbrage enthusiastic exasperate excite excited exercise exhilarate]
*piteous 24-63-1 (a.) 1. deserving or inciting pity [painful pathetic pit pity poignant poor ill implore incite tearful touching emotional entreat extraordinary uncomfortable unfortunate sad shabby sharp sore struck /tip/]
*pitfall 09-56-22 (n.) 1. an unforeseen or unexpected difficulty 2. a trap in the form of a concealed hole [pen peril pit positive potential produce intend tend toil trap trouble factor fall firetrap flytrap form achieve animal ledge lure /aft tip/]
*pith 22-57-2 (n.) 1. soft spongelike central cylinder of the stems of most flowering plants 2. the choicest or most essential or most vital part of some idea or experience [part perceive pit plant point primary principle prosecutor pudding pulp pure idea impact important inner inside interior inward issue tenor thin thrust tissue toughness hair heart high hub hypostasis /tip/]
*pithy 15-62-7 (a.) 1. concise and full of meaning (ad.) 1. in a pithy sententious manner [peculiar pith point pointed pregnant prolix prune indicative interpret terse tight transfer tree yet /tip/] "welcomed her pithy comments"
*pitiable 22-48-2 (a.) 1. inspiring mixed contempt and pity 2. deserving or inciting pity [pathetic piteous pity poor ill incite inspire able accompany appeal arouse lack life limb effort estimable evoke exhibition extraordinary /bait tip/]
*pitiful 12-72-13 (a.) 1. inspiring mixed contempt and pity 2. bad; unfortunate 3. deserving or inciting pity [paltry pathetic pit piteous pity poor ill inadequate incite infamous insignificant inspire terrible touching trashy fate favored fellow filthy finance flagrant fortune foul unbecoming unclean undesirable unfortunate unimportant lack lamentable life limb little lousy /fit tip/]
*pitiless 20-56-3 (a.) 1. without mercy or pity 2. deficient in humane and kindly feelings [pity inclement inexorable inhumane inhumanity insensitive intensity terrorism lack less extremely extremity sanguinary savagery severe severity sharp show stony sympathy /tip/]
*pittance 17-56-5 (n.) 1. an inadequate payment [pay payment peanut pinch pitta point inadequate insufficiency iota tittle trace trifle trivia ace amount atom nothing nutshell charity chicken collection contribution /tip/] "they work all day for a mere pittance"
*pivotal 07-54-43 (a.) 1. being of crucial importance [paramount periodic pivot polar pregnant pressing principal progress imperious important insistent invasion vital occasional originative outcome overrule acute axial loaded location] "a pivotal event"

*placate 12-53-12 (v.) 1. cause to be more favorably inclined; gain the good will of [pacify placable please propitiate lenify less lie lull allay angry appease appeasement assuage calm cate comfort conciliate cool tranquillize]
*placid 11-33-16 (a.) 1. not easily irritated 2. without untoward incident or disruption 3. free from disturbance 4. taking life easy [pacific peaceful plague lagoon lake life acid affliction appear calm channel cheerful collected complacent compose contented coolly cross ill impassive imperturbable incident infest invasion irritate isolated deer delay despite detached disease disposition disruption disturbed docile dwindle /ical/] "a ribbon of sand between the angry sea and the placid bay"
*plagiarism 16-58-6 (n.) 1. a piece of writing that has been copied from someone else and is presented as being your own work 2. the act of plagiarizing; taking someone's words or ideas as if they were your own [parody parrot pastiche piece pirate point polly present process letter lift actor adoption alphabet ape appropriation assumption idea imitate imitation impersonate impostor impression infringe ism recur renewal return right secure seduce sheep simulator steal style material mimesis mirror mock /gal/]
*plaintive 13-45-10 (a.) 1. expressing sorrow [peevish petulant pitiful plaint plangent lament loss lugubrious aggrieved anguished irreparable nostalgia tearful elegiac experience express]
*plaque 09-45-26 (n.) 1. (pathology) a small abnormal patch on or inside the body 2. a memorial made of brass [panel part patch pathological piece pin plate prize protein psoriasis abnormal amyloid arch artery atherosclerosis award effect encourage erect]
*plasticity 24-56-1 (n.) 1. the property of being physically malleable; the property of something that can be worked or hammered or shaped under pressure without breaking [physical plastic pliancy pressure property limber lithe adjust allow alter apt sensitive sheet soft squeeze stretch subservient substance supple tensile thin transitory image impermanent impressionable intelligence capable changeful characterize clever condition /salp/]
*platitude 14-66-9 (n.) 1. a trite or obvious remark [personal plain pointless prosaism prose public pungent latitude abstraction aphoristic axiomatic tag terse threadbare tired trite truism truth inanity insipid unoriginal dull empty expression]
*plaudit 11-88-15 (n.) 1. enthusiastic approval [popularity positive praise acclamation acknowledge applause approval audit deserve /dual/]
*plausible 07-55-37 (a.) 1. apparently reasonable and valid 2. appearing to merit belief or acceptance 3. within the realm of credibility 4. likely but not certain to be or become true or real [pat persuasive perversion possible potential presumptive probable proof provoke legitimate likely logical loss absence acceptable acceptance admissible apparently appear arguable unco unexceptionable unimpeachable unquestionable seeming sensible slick smooth sophistry sound speech story subtlety illusive imaginable incredible insincerity intention become believe empty excuse]
*playful 07-42-42 (a.) 1. full of fun and high spirits [pixilated play poke prankish puckish lack let levity life lighthearted lively loose animation antic arch facetious flippant fond foolish frisky frolicsome full fun] "playful children just let loose from school"
*playwright 05-34-70 (n.) 1. someone who writes plays [librettist albee anderson wright gagman tragedian]
*plea 04-41-101 (n.) 1. a humble request for help from someone in authority 2. (law) a defendant's answer by a factual matter (as distinguished from a demurrer) 3. an answer indicating why a suit should be dismissed [petition plaintiff prayer pressure pretext principle process property law lea legal liberty life earnest emotional entreaty establish examination exception excuse explanation extricate alibi allegation answer appeal application appropriate argument assertion authority]
*plead 03-38-164 (v.) 1. make an allegation in an action or other legal proceeding, esp. answer the previous pleading of the other party by denying facts therein stated or by alleging new facts 2. enter a plea, as in courts of law 3. offer as an excuse or plea 4. appeal or request earnestly [party past petition plea pray press pressure proceeding procurator protection proxy push law lawyer lead legal lobby earnest emotional encourage energize enter entreat explain adjure advance advocate agent allege answer apologize appeal ask assert attorney authority aver declare defend defense demand deny deputy] "I pleaded with him to stop"
*pleasant 04-46-110 (a.) 1. pleasant in manner or behavior 2. affording pleasure; being in harmony with your taste or likings [pastoral plea pleasure pretty probably profitable last laughing lightly likable likeable lovely easygoing elegant engaging enjoy enjoyable excellent expediency advantageous affable afford agreeable amiable amusing appearance appropriate ardent attractive satisfy scene sensation smile sound spent sunny superiority sweet nature neighborly nice noble taste toothsome tune tuneful] "a pleasant person to be around"
*pleasurable 13-59-10 (a.) 1. affording satisfaction or pleasure [pleasure praise print likable like enjoyment excite able affable afford agreeable amiable satisfy sweet unpleasant read rewarding blissful book /bar/]
*plebeian 24-48-1 (a.) 1. of the common people of ancient Rome 2. of or associated with the great masses of people (n.) 1. one of the common people [patrician person philistine plebe pop popular position proletarian property public pursuit low lowborn lowbrow lowly educate europe baseborn belonging birth blue bourgeois brand brutish byzantine ignoble ill inferior insult

intermediate ancient aristocracy nobility noble nose /bel/] "a plebeian magistrate"
*plenary 22-34-2 (a.) 1. full in all respects [perfect plena power legislature limit limitless entire exhaustive non absolute attend replete respect round] "a plenary session of the legislature"
*plethora 12-71-14 (n.) 1. extreme excess [part permit plenty prodigal landslide lavish limit engorge enough excessive extreme hora hyperemia overplus overweight redundancy repletion rich ruddy amount amplitude article attribute avalanche]
*pliant 20-41-3 (a.) 1. capable of being influenced or formed 2. capable of being bent or flexed or twisted without breaking 3. capable of being shaped or bent or drawn out 4. able to adjust readily to different conditions [persuade persuasible plastic prompt leather limber lissome lithe impressionable incline inelastic influence accessible accommodate adapt adjust agreeable alloy ant ardent nature tensile tractile tree twist /nail/]
*plod 11-62-16 (v.) 1. walk heavily and firmly, as when weary, or through mud [pace pad paddle pale peg permanent persist physical procrastinate productive laborious labour lack laggard lasting lawrence life limp linger loiter loyalty lumber lurch obstinate dawdle dead dig drag drama drone drudgery dry dull /dol/] "Donkeys that plodded wearily in a circle around a gin"
*pluck 07-60-39 (n.) 1. the trait of showing courage and determination in spite of possible loss or injury 2. the act of pulling and releasing a taut cord (v.) 1. pull or pull out sharply 2. sell something to or obtain something from by energetic and esp. underhanded activity 3. rip off; ask an unreasonable price 4. look for and gather 5. pull lightly but sharply with a plucking motion, as of guitar strings 6. strip of feathers [pick pickup pith play plectrum plume plunk possible price pull lightly liver look loss luck lung uncover underhanded unearth unreasonable unveil capon casual cheat chicken chisel coercion collect consent cord courage cull cut] "pluck the flowers off the bush"
*plumb 13-60-10 (a.) 1. exactly vertical (ad.) 1. (slang) completely; used as intensifiers 2. conforming to the direction of a plumb line 3. (informal) exactly (n.) 1. the metal bob of a plumb line (v.) 1. measure the depth of something 2. adjust with a plumb line so as to make vertical 3. examine thoroughly and in great depth 4. weight with lead [pace patois perfect perpendicular pipe plain plane plum pointing position precisely prize properly puddle language latch lead line lingo load lockup ubiquitous understand universal unpleasant upright utterly measure metal meter middle minutely mysterious ball bar base bear bob bottom burden burthen] "the tower of Pisa is far out of plumb"
*plummet 06-48-46 (n.) 1. the metal bob of a plumb line (v.) 1. drop sharply [parachute perpendicular pessimistic pitch plum plump plunge pointing pounce price lead lessen line lower unexpected market metal earth ebb erode experience totter trim tumble tumbledown] "The stock market plummeted"
*plunge 03-49-153 (n.) 1. a brief swim in water 2. a steep and rapid fall (v.) 1. cause to be immersed 2. drop steeply 3. dash violently or with great speed or impetuosity 4. begin with vigor 5. Thrust or throw into 6. immerse into a liquid 7. fall abruptly 8. engross (oneself) fully [parachute pass pay penetrate perforate place play plummet point pool pore power precipitous price professor progressive put labor launch lead leap liquid long look lower lunge uncertainty unpleasant nosedive gallop gamble gape gravity great gyrate eager ebb embark engross engulf enthusiastical erode]
*plural 13-83-11 (a.) 1. grammatical number category referring to two or more items or units (n.) 1. the form of a word that is used to denote more than one [panty leg ural ankle appointment]
*plurality 18-25-4 (n.) 1. (in an election with more than 2 options) the number of votes for the candidate or party receiving the greatest number (but less that half of the votes) [pack party percent plural political position preponderance purpose landslide legion less lot range receive represent respect rival rout ruck amount army attribute average indefinite throng thrust total]
*pneumatic 17-65-5 (a.) 1. of or relating to or using air (or a similar gas) [personable physics pleasing pouch pressure ethereal expose machine mat mephitic agreeable airy atmospheric tire tool troposphere inflated callipygian cavity comely compress context curvy] "pneumatic drill"
*poetic 07-46-39 (a.) 1. characterized by romantic imagery 2. of or relating to poetry 3. of or relating to poets 4. characteristic of or befitting poetry [pastoral perceptive poesy poet possess profound otherworldly effect elegiac elevated epic expressive transmundane idealistic idyllic imaginative impractical insightful concern /cite/] "poetic works"
*poetics 24-33-1 (n.) 1. study of poetic works [philosophical poem poetic principle prosody technique treatise imaginative compose study /cite/]
*poignancy 14-52-9 (n.) 1. a state of deeply felt distress or sorrow 2. a quality that arouses emotions (especially pity or sorrow) [pathos pity nancy nostalgia arouse attribute capture] "a moment of extraordinary poignancy"
*poignant 06-52-51 (a.) 1. keenly distressing to the mind or feelings 2. arousing affect [painful painless pathos penetrate perceptive physical pity pleasurable pointed powerful psychological punch impressive incisive intense irritate gratitude grave grief grievous grip gutsy nervous nostalgia acrimony acute affecting afflict agonizing ant anxiety arouse asperity astringent attribute tast telling tender touching tragic]
*poise 05-59-82 (n.) 1. a cgs unit of dynamic viscosity equal to one dyne-second per square centimeter; the

viscosity of a fluid in which a force of one dyne per square centimeter maintains a velocity of 1 centimeter per second 2. great coolness and composure under strain 3. a state of being balanced in a stable equilibrium (v.) 1. prepare (oneself) for something unpleasant or difficult 2. cause to be balanced or suspended 3. be motionless, in suspension 4. hold or carry in equilibrium [perform persuade place poi pose position positive practice prepare prepared price prime purpose overweening identity imperturbable integrate sangfroid security self set situation social square stable stand steady steel strain stress style suitable support sure suspend early easygoing edge equanimity equation equip equivalency] "The bird poised for a few moments before it attacked"
*poised 05-60-66 (a.) 1. marked by balance or equilibrium and readiness for action 2. in full control of your faculties [perch placid pose position prepare price prime proper seeming self serene set stress sudden sure suspension early easygoing edge equanimous equilibrium danger dependable difficult dignify discompose] "a gull in poised flight"
*polar 09-67-24 (a.) 1. characterized by opposite extremes; completely opposed 2. having a pair of equal and opposite charges 3. extremely cold 4. being of crucial importance 5. located at or near or coming from the earth's poles 6. of or existing at or near a geographical pole or within the Arctic or Antarctic Circles [pair particle pass periodic permanent physics pivotal planet point pole positive principal obverse opinion opposite orbit lar last limiting literary location low aerospace amount antagonistic antithetic arctic reference refrigerate resolution reverse rotate]
*polemic 11-58-15 (a.) 1. of or involving dispute or controversy (n.) 1. a controversy (especially over a belief or dogma) [partisan passionate pay persuasive polarize pole prickly professional provocative opinion opposition outspoken language less literary litigious logomachy engage enmity eristic express mark mic imbroglio impassioned irascible irritable capable combative conflict contentious controversy critic critical]
*pollen 15-56-7 (n.) 1. a fine powder produced by the anthers of seed-bearing plants; fine grains contain male gametes [plant poll powder produce protein protozoan orchid]
*pollute 08-42-33 (v.) 1. make impure [pervert place plastered poisonous pot prejudice product profligate prostitute oil organize outrage overtake lace lake lit litter loaded lubricate lute ulcerate unclean unhealthy unwashed unwholesome taint tanked threaten tight torture twist elevated embezzle envenom environment] "The industrial wastes polluted the lake"
*polygamy 18-51-4 (n.) 1. having more than one wife at a time [partner people person polygyny lawbreaker life gamy adultery animal marry mate matrimony monandry monogyny multiple /mag/]

*polyglot 18-41-4 (a.) 1. having a command of or composed in many languages (n.) 1. a person who speaks more than one language [poly language lay lecture linguist linguistics gazetteer give greenberg translator traveler trilingual] "a polyglot traveler"

*polygon 14-93-9 (n.) 1. a closed plane figure bounded by straight sides [paisley pentagon plane point poly pyramid oblong orb oval line lozenge geometric globe graphics great nine /nog/]
*polytechnic 12-55-12 (n.) 1. a technical school offering instruction in many industrial arts and applied sciences [offering level teach technic engineering college course industrial instruction /cetyl/]
*pomposity 17-70-5 (n.) 1. lack of elegance as a consequence of being pompous and puffed up with vanity [portentousnes posit positive pretentious pride puff orotund ostentatiousn magniloquent manner security self serious snobbish speech splash stately stiff stylize impersonality inflation taste tortuous trust turgidity /mop/]
*pompous 12-67-14 (a.) 1. puffed up with vanity [persuade pomp pontifical positive pretentious proud puff oratory ornate ostentatious overstate overwrought magisterial magnificent magniloquent manner meretricious undeserved unhesitating unwavering unwieldy secure self serious showy snobbish spectacular speech splendor stately stiff sure /mop/]
*poncho 18-52-4 (n.) 1. a blanket-like cloak with a hole in the center for the head [piece outer cape center cloak cloth head hole hood]
*ponder 06-54-55 (v.) 1. reflect deeply on a subject [pause period perpend place pond power premeditate pullback puzzle observe debate decision deeply deliberate digest discuss doubtful dwell evaluate excogitate exercise express reason reflect retreat roll ruminate]
*ponderous 13-59-11 (a.) 1. having great mass and weight and unwieldiness 2. slow and laborious because of weight 3. labored and dull [pale pedestrian physical pointless pompous ponder prehistoric oafish overweight net dead density dismal disproportionate dry dryness dull ease effete elephantine empty etiolated excitement roughness rude ungainly uninterest unmanageable unseemly unwieldy sag slow speech stiff stone superficial]
*pontiff 17-72-5 (n.) 1. the head of the Roman Catholic Church [pace papal patriarch paul persuade piccolo piu poland politics pope power prig primate napoleon nepotism neutrality temporal tiff title treaty turk independent institute intervention introduction italy faith family fight first fourth france french /fit/]
*populace 15-42-8 (n.) 1. people in general considered as a whole [part people person political population public ordinary lace admass area aristocracy children citizenry collective consider constituency crowd easily

elite entertainment estate everywoman eye]
*populous 12-31-14 (a.) 1. densely populated [packed people prolific occupy overcrowd overflow uninhabited lavish legion live lou settle several solid]
*portend 18-13-4 (v.) 1. indicate by signs [point port precaution predict prefigure presage prognosticate promise omen threaten divine]
*portent 15-61-7 (n.) 1. a sign of something about to happen [phenomenon port pre presage prodigy prognosticate promise prophetic omen ominous threat type experience]
*portfolio 04-61-133 (n.) 1. a case for carrying papers or drawings or maps; usually leather 2. a list of the financial assets held by an individual or a bank or other financial institution 3. the role of the head of a government department [paper part photograph post product offer office ordered organization range represent require responsibility rod role topic truncheon fasces file financial flat folder folio foreign formal function leather listing institution invest item /loft oft oil/] "he holds the portfolio for foreign affairs"
*posit 16-49-6 (n.) 1. (logic) a proposition that is accepted as true in order to provide a basis for logical reasoning (v.) 1. put (something somewhere) firmly 2. take as a given; assume as a postulate or axiom [park philosophy place plan pose postulate premiss probability proposal provide put offer seat sediment seldom set shoulder sit situate soil speculate spot statement station submit suggestion suitcase suppose ignorance theorize thesis true] "She posited her hand on his shoulder"
*position 01-52-1059 (n.) 1. an item on a list or in a sequence 2. a rationalized mental attitude 3. a condition or position in which you find yourself 4. a job in an organization 5. the relative position or standing of things or especially persons in a society 6. position or arrangement of the body and its limbs 7. a point occupied by troops for tactical reasons 8. a way of regarding situations or topics etc. 9. the act of putting something in a certain place or location 10. (in team sports) the role assigned to an individual player 11. the appropriate or customary location 12. the spatial property of a place where or way in which something is situated 13. the particular portion of space occupied by a physical object 14. the act of positing; an assumption taken as a postulate or axiom 15. an opinion that is held in opposition to another in an argument or dispute 16. the function or position properly or customarily occupied or served by another (v.) 1. put into a certain place or abstract location 2. cause to be in an appropriate place, state, or relation [particular pass place plant posit posting prepare principle put office opening order say service set settle situation status storage idea importance instal navigate note notion /itis/]
*positive 02-62-335 (a.) 1. impossible to deny or disprove 2. (medicine) indicating existence or presence of a suspected condition or pathogen 3. formally laid down or imposed 4. involving advantage or good 5. having a positive electric charge 6. characterized by or displaying affirmation or acceptance or certainty etc. 7. marked by excessive confidence 8. persuaded of; very sure 9. granting what has been desired or requested 10. (mathematics) greater than zero 11. of or relating to positivism (n.) 1. a film showing a photographic image whose tones correspond to those of the original subject [posit odd optimistic outright self impossible impression indecisive inevitable electron encourage even express /itis vitis/] "a positive attitude"
*posse 06-61-47 (n.) 1. a temporary police force [pack palm party people perceive pocket policeman poss probe property purpose obtain occupy offensive officer organization outfit own ownership search section secure see seize serve set sheriff show skill speak string embody embrace emotion enjoy enter exploration]
*possess 05-60-78 (v.) 1. have ownership or possession of 2. enter into and control, as of emotions or ideas 3. have as an attribute, knowledge, or skill [person posse property proprietor occupy offensive owner ownership save search seize sex share show skill speak emotion enjoy enter exhibit /sess/] "he possesses great knowledge about the Middle East"
*possession 03-56-155 (n.) 1. anything owned or possessed 2. the act of possessing 3. a mania restricted to one thing or idea 4. being controlled by passion or the supernatural [possess power proprietor province obtain occupy oceania oddness ownership secure settlement state effect empire equipment illusion independence irrationality island nationality /sess/] "they took possession of the ball"
*possessive 18-53-4 (a.) 1. (grammar) serving to express or indicate possession 2. desirous of owning 3. having or showing a desire to control or dominate [parent personalism play possess possessory pride proprietary oblique overbearing overprotectiv own ownership selfish serve share show sole stingy study subordinate suspicious eager egotistic envious exclusive exercise express idea indicate individualist influence /sess/] "possessive pronouns"
*possessor 20-60-3 (n.) 1. a person who owns something [person possess proprietor owner save search share ship slave smile soul ssa /sess/]
*possible 01-53-982 (a.) 1. possible to conceive or imagine 2. existing in possibility 3. capable of happening or existing (n.) 1. something that can be done 2. an applicant who might be suitable [poser positive poss potential practice prime problem promising proper purpose obfuscate obscure odd opening seek sleeping submultiple suitable surd imagine infinite integral breakthrough latent likely lurk earthly employment esoteric even exist express] "a breakthrough may be possible next year"
*posterior 20-68-3 (a.) 1. (zoology) at or near the hind end in quadrupeds or toward the spine in primates (n.)

1. the fleshy part of the human body that you sit on 2. a tooth situated at the back of the mouth [part plant poster postpositive prat primate proximate puisne occiput organism science seat sit situate spine stem stern structure study subsequent successive tail tailpiece too tooth toward trunk tush ensue exclude extremity rear ret retrograde reverse rump]
*postgraduate 11-81-15 (a.) 1. of or relating to studies beyond a bachelor's degree (n.) 1. a student who continues studies after graduation [pedagogic professional sophomoric study graduate graduation great research academic advance alumnus amount autodidact degree doctoral undergraduate university education]
*postscript 16-61-6 (n.) 1. a note appended to a letter after the signature 2. textual matter that is added onto a publication; usually at the end [part peroration play postlude prefix publication organization script sequel short signature story subscript suffix supplement tag tail textual chorus collected comment conclusion consequence continue refrain rider infix instruction interpolate]
*potency 13-68-11 (n.) 1. capacity to produce strong physiological or chemical effects 2. the state of being potent; a male's capacity to have sexual intercourse 3. the inherent capacity for coming into being [physiological possibility pot powerful produce pull purchase push obstinate toughness toxin true tuck effect efficiency energy esteem evident exist capacity chemical cold come condition control credit yet /top/] "the toxin's potency"
*potent 06-54-55 (a.) 1. having a strong physiological or chemical effect 2. having or wielding force or authority 3. having the power to influence or convince 4. (of a male) able to copulate [persuasive physiological political possess powerful prestigious problem produce prominent puissant obstinate official operative tea telling tent totalitarian toxin eat effectual efficacious ejaculate eminent empower energetic erection exert nervy nuptial /top/]
*potentate 22-46-2 (n.) 1. a ruler who is unconstrained by law [papa paramount pearl political potent powerful president officer oppressive overthrow tetrarch try tyrant emperor empress execute exercise nazi army assume attack authority autocrat /top/]
*potential 01-58-779 (a.) 1. expected to become or be; in prospect 2. existing in possibility (n.) 1. the inherent capacity for coming into being 2. the difference in electrical charge between two points in a circuit expressed in volts [part phenomenon physics point poser possible potent power presently problem produce profitable prospect prospective obfuscate obscure occult talent thinkable true electricity endowment equipment esoteric evident exist expertise express external nervous nuclear imaginable imminent imply impulse income inherent instinct investor ability actual aptitude latent likely lurk /lait top/] "a potential problem"
*potion 15-64-8 (n.) 1. a medicinal or magical or poisonous beverage [philtre poisonous pop portion potable power pull overdose tonic ill injection ion nip /top/]
*powerless 09-58-23 (a.) 1. lacking power [passive physical poop potency power produce overwhelm weakly effect effete engulf etiolated rubbery lack lightweight limp listless little sapless slack soft spiritual strength swamp /wop/]
*practicable 20-66-3 (a.) 1. capable of being done with means at hand and circumstances as they are 2. usable for a specific purpose [perform plan possible practic practical profitable purpose realistic realize accessible achieve act actual attain availability capable carry circumstance compass concern banausic effect effectual efficient employ executable exist /carp/]
*prate 25-50-1 (n.) 1. idle or foolish and irrelevant talk (v.) 1. speak (about unimportant matters) rapidly and incessantly [palaver patter piffle prat prattle puff rant rapid rate rigmarole rubbish absurdity amphigory talk tattle trash trumpery twaddle express /tarp/]
*prattle 22-49-2 (n.) 1. idle or foolish and irrelevant talk (v.) 1. speak (about unimportant matters) rapidly and incessantly [palaver parole patter piffle prate rap rapid rattle rot rubbish absurdity accent amphigory talk tattle trash twaddle twitter language elocution express /tarp/]
*preamble 17-66-5 (n.) 1. a preliminary introduction to a statute or constitution (usually explaining its purpose) (v.) 1. make a preamble [paper precede preface prelude premise prologue provide purpose exordium explanation amble breakthrough leap]
*precarious 08-51-29 (a.) 1. fraught with danger 2. affording no ease or reassurance 3. dangerously insecure 4. not secure; beset with difficulties [parlous perilous premise problematic provisional reassure recovery risky ease easy equivocal carious chancy critical across afford ambiguous assumption indefensible infirm insecure open uncertain undersea uneasy unjustified unpredictable unsafe unsteady unsure unwarranted safety sea security sensitive shaky shifty stormy surgery /ace race racer/] "a precarious truce"
*precaution 07-51-43 (n.) 1. judiciousness in avoiding harm or danger 2. the trait of practicing caution in advance 3. a precautionary measure warding off impending danger or damage or injury etc. [part portentous possible practice premonition preventive progress protection provision provisional prudent escape espionage exercise care caution cautious circumspect cover advance alert anticipation attention avoid undesirable theft toward trait trouble impending injury insurance open /ace/]
*precede 05-41-69 (v.) 1. move ahead (of others) in time or space 2. be the predecessor of 3. come before 4. be earlier in time; go back further [pace past pioneer position predecessor preface preliminary premise previous prime proceed proclaim prologuize rate recede

relinquish retiring early elder erstwhile exist express certain chief come create document dominion] "Most English adjectives precede the noun they modify"
*precedence 13-55-10 (n.) 1. status established in order of importance or urgency 2. the act of preceding (as in a ceremony) 3. preceding in time [participant personal pharmaceutical place position precede preference primacy priority rank rate reduce rest right early emphasis establish excellence ceremony class come condition consideration deal dean determine note] "...its precedence as the world's leading manufacturer of pharmaceuticals"
*precedent 05-43-62 (a.) 1. preceding in time, order, or significance (n.) 1. (civil law) a law established by following earlier judicial decisions 2. an example that is used to justify similar occurrences at a later time 3. a system of jurisprudence based on judicial precedents rather than statutory laws 4. a subject mentioned earlier (preceding in time) [past pattern perform point practice precede previous property regulation representative require rule early english epitome establish example exist explorer case collection come condemn consideration conversation criterion custom decision determination diagnosis discussion doctrine nation never tenant theme topic trailblazer]
*precipice 16-66-6 (n.) 1. a very steep cliff [peak pice pinnacle point rock escarpment cliff crag crest /pice/]
*precipitate 10-56-19 (a.) 1. done with very great haste and without due deliberation (n.) 1. a precipitated solid substance in suspension or after settling or filtering (v.) 1. bring about abruptly 2. separate as a fine suspension of solid particles 3. fall vertically, sharply, or headlong 4. hurl or throw violently 5. fall from clouds [pita point press project rapid rash reckless running rush effectuate electrify express careless collapse crash crowd impatient impetuous improvise impulsive issue takedown abrupt accelerate advance aftermath /pice tip tipi/] "The crisis precipitated by Russia's revolution"
*precise 04-49-89 (a.) 1. exact in performance or amount; strictly correct 2. sharply exact or accurate or delimited [particular perceive perform pinpoint precis private proper punctilious refer restricted right rigorous easy error even exactly express extraordinary careful clearly close complete conformity correct critical cut idea image indicate inflexible inner instrument intimate scrupulous severe sharp skillful speaker specific square standard strict /sice/] "a precise mind"
*precision 06-48-54 (n.) 1. the quality of being reproducible in amount or performance [perform prude punctual puritan recision reproduce require right rigid rigorous exact explicit exquisite calculation care careful correct critical instrument sensitivity significant specify strict subtlety nicety /sice/]
*preclude 09-38-22 (v.) 1. keep from happening or arising; have the effect of preventing 2. make impossible, esp. beforehand [parochial passover plan prescriptive prevent preventive progress prohibit refuse reject relegate repressive restrictive rid rule effect effort eliminate embargo embarrass enjoin enter estop ethnocentrism exceptional exclude expenditure cease check close company contest cross cutoff lockout lude unless unnecessary debar deflect deny desire deter developing discourage disqualify /ulcer/]
*precocious 10-68-20 (a.) 1. characterized by or characteristic of exceptionally early development or maturity (especially in mental aptitude) 2. (botany) appearing or developing early [physical precipitate premature previous produce reason retard ripen rush early eco emotional exceptional capacity child clever impulsive intelligent unprepared unripe untimely unusual show slow smart soon species stage study] "a precocious child"
*preconceived 18-46-4 (a.) 1. (of an idea or opinion) formed beforehand; especially without evidence or through prejudice [personal predetermine prejudice reflect rigid evidence experience conceptualize create opinion notion idea inflexible define /vie/] "certain preconceived notions"
*precursor 10-50-18 (n.) 1. a person who goes before or announces the coming of another 2. an indication of the approach of something or someone [person pioneer point position predecessor previous priority processe product railhead raise reaction realize early effector effort engineer chemistry come compound conceive connect consider construct context creator cursor understand urgency serve shape sign smith soul space stable substance suggest superiority office omen organism organizer originator outpost]
*predatory 11-67-17 (a.) 1. characterized by plundering or pillaging or marauding 2. living by or given to victimizing others for personal gain 3. living by preying on other animals especially by catching living prey [parasitic party personal peter pillage plunder predator prey prove purpose pursuit rapacious ravage ravening rob ruthless energetic extortionate extremely decency defensive despoil destructive acquisitive aggressive animal attack avaricious taste thieve offal offensive /rota tad/]
*predecessor 04-54-130 (n.) 1. one who precedes you in time (as in holding a position or office) [pioneer point position precursor previous prototype replace early elder existence explorer cess come contribute scout share succeed office /cede secede/]
*predicament 09-56-26 (n.) 1. a situation from which extrication is difficult especially an unpleasant or trying one [pass people pickle place plight problem race rank require risk easy effort embarrass emergency endanger escape estate extricate dangerous deal difficulty dilemma distress division immediate impasse impossible irritation care category class clear concern condition corner adversity affair affliction almost ament annoyance assign awkward mess mix mystery nonplus

threat tight title try /acid cide cider mac/] "finds himself in a most awkward predicament"
*predicate 15-46-8 (a.) 1. (grammar) of adjectives; relating to or occurring within the predicate of a sentence (n.) 1. (logic) what is predicated of the subject of a proposition; the second term in a proposition is predicated of the first term by means of the copula 2. one of the two main constituents of a sentence; the predicate contains the verb and its complements (v.) 1. make the (grammatical) predicate in a proposition 2. involve as a necessary condition of consequence; as in logic 3. affirm or declare as an attribute or quality of [pledge pose proclaim profession pronounce proposition put rank relate rest enunciate establish express declared depose dictum dog imply insist candidate cate center certify conclusion condition consequence contend creed cutting affirm alleged announcement argue asseverate attribute tagmeme /acid cide cider/] "The predicate 'dog' is predicated of the subject 'Fido' in the sentence 'Fido is a dog'"
*predict 02-50-360 (v.) 1. indicate by signs 2. make a prediction about; tell in advance [palm past plan plot point portend possible prefigure presage pretend prognosticate project promise prophesy psychic refute reveal risk edict election emergent envisage envision eventual experience extrapolate desire destine determined divine imminent indication infer inspiration intestine intimate calculate call coming conclude contemplate tea tell think threaten /cide cider/]
*prediction 05-57-80 (n.) 1. the act of predicting (as by reasoning about the future) 2. a statement made about the future [project provision prudent ready eventuality expectation determinism diction discretion imminent intimate calculation cast conjecture contemplate tomorrow offing outlook /cide cider/]
*predilection 15-52-7 (n.) 1. a predisposition in favor of something 2. a strong liking [penchant pleasure preference prejudice prone ready eager eccentricity enjoyment experience delight disposition druthers idiosyncrasy inclination incline individualism interpret ion lean liability like literature car cast character considerable constitution taste tendency thing type nature /elide lid/] "a predilection for expensive cars"
*predominance 22-44-2 (n.) 1. the state of being predominant over others 2. the quality of being more noticeable than anything else [painting patency power preponderance prevalent property easy exist dominance obvious majority noticeable numerous ascendancy control /mod mode moder ode/]
*predominant 14-42-9 (a.) 1. most frequent or common 2. having superior power and influence [painting policymaker popular powerful prevalent prime principal priority property purchase reason reign repute routine rule effect embargo epidemic esteem estuary excellence exercise exist dean dominant dominion obvious optimism ordinary outstanding overriding overrule main major majority mastery moment mood important incomparable influential infrequent inimitable institute interval normal noticeable numerous accomplishment advantage amount arch ascendancy authority average telling topflight topmost /mod mode moder ode/]
*predominate 14-33-9 (a.) 1. having superior power and influence (v.) 1. be larger in number, quantity, power, status or importance 2. appear very large or occupy a commanding position [pre dominate /mod mode moder ode/]
*preempt 25-51-1 (v.) 1. acquire by preemption 2. make a preemptive bid; in bridge [place player pointless possession pree preoccupy prevent public requisition right enslave expropriate monopolize]
*preen 13-60-10 (v.) 1. clean with one's bill, of birds 2. pride or congratulate (oneself) for an achievement 3. dress or groom with elaborate care [paint particularly personal pique plume pree pride primp prink proper redecorate redo refer refurbish remove rig elaborate embellish embroider enrich excessive /neer/]
*preface 12-46-13 (n.) 1. a short introductory essay preceding the text of a book (v.) 1. furnish with a preface [page past piece prayer preamble precede prelude premise priest priority prolusion purpose recto reface remark edition endpaper errata essay exordium express facade facet first foreword formal furnish anterior apology aspect catchword christianity colophon communicate /cafe/]
*prefer 02-57-408 (v.) 1. promote over another 2. select as an alternative; choose instead; prefer as an alternative 3. like better; value more highly 4. give preference to one creditor over another; in law [pass pay people position present priority promotion prosecute put raise rather recommend refer restaurant rule elect elevate enjoyable enter examination exchange extend failing fancy favor fear file fish /refer/] "Some people prefer camping to staying in hotels"
*preferable 10-54-20 (a.) 1. more desirable than another [prefer refer enjoyable achieve better likely /bar bare refer/] "coffee is preferable to tea"
*preference 05-50-78 (n.) 1. a predisposition in favor of something 2. a strong liking 3. grant of favor or advantage to one over another (esp to a country or countries in matters of international trade such as levying duties) 4. the right or chance to choose [payment penchant pick pleasure position priority promotion receive reference right eat eccentricity election elevation enjoyment exercise experience express fancy fascination favoritism fondness nature nepotism cake car chance character choose chosen clearly commerce considerable country course creditor /refer/] "my own preference is for good literature"
*preferential 13-44-11 (a.) 1. manifesting partiality [partisan priority privilege promote rate referential favoritism tariff tax trade treatment international advantageous /lait refer/]

*prefix 18-68-4 (n.) 1. an affix that added in front of the word (v.) 1. attach a prefix to [place plus precede premise priority privative produce radical request rider root element encumber envoi epilogue facade facet fix formal formative front full independent inflect inflection innovation introduction] "prefixed words"
*prejudice 05-63-68 (n.) 1. a partiality that prevents objective consideration of an issue or situation (v.) 1. disadvantage by prejudice; in law 2. influence (somebody's) opinion in advance [parochial partisan poison preconception predisposition preference prone racist ready eager envenom jaundice jinx justice unfair upon damage delight destroy dice disadvantage discrimination doctrinaire dogmatic infect influence injury interested intolerance intolerant cast chauvinism chauvinist colored corrupt]
*prelate 17-30-5 (n.) 1. a senior clergyman [patriarch perform persuade pessimistic poland polish pope priest primate principal prior ralph rector relate religious richelieu rite roman elate english exarch later leader louis abbot abuna administer african allow antiaparthei antipope appointed archpriest article authority theologian turn tutu /tale taler/]
*prelude 09-41-26 (n.) 1. something that serves as a preceding event or introduces what follows 2. music that precedes a fugue or introduces an act in an opera (v.) 1. serve as a prelude to 2. play as a prelude, of musical pieces [part piano piece play preamble precede preface prefix prelusive premise priority prologue purpose replay role run elude employment exordium leading leap long urgency descant dinner dominion]
*premature 05-56-72 (a.) 1. born after a gestation period of less than the normal time 2. uncommonly early or before the expected time 3. too soon or too hasty [period precipitate precocious pregnancy previous rash rush early entire exist expect malapropos mature middle advance advisable uncommonly unfortunate unhappy unlucky unsuitable untimely usual /ruta tame/] "a premature infant"
*premier 03-84-206 (a.) 1. first in rank or degree 2. preceding all others in time (n.) 1. the person who holds the position of head of state in England 2. the person who is head of state (in several countries) 3. the position of the cabinet minister who is in charge of government affairs (v.) 1. be performed for the first time; of a play, ballet, or composition 2. perform a work for the first time [paramount perform play position precede premie president prime principal province public ranking representative require england execute maiden main master minister important intermediate] "an architect of premier rank"
*premise 07-41-37 (n.) 1. a statement that is assumed to be true and from which a conclusion can be drawn (v.) 1. set forth beforehand, often as an explanation 2. furnish with a preface 3. take something as preexisting [position precede prelude proof evidence exhibit exordium manifestation mark mise muniments indication innovation introduction sign statement symptom] "He premised these remarks so that his readers might understand..."
*premonition 18-52-4 (n.) 1. a feeling of evil to come 2. an early warning about a future event [portent portentous predictive prefigure presentiment prophetic psychometry rational early escalate evil expectation mantic meaningful message misfortune misgiving monitory omen ominous impression indication indicative inform insight intervention intimate intuition intuitive ion /nome/]
*preoccupation 09-47-24 (n.) 1. the mental state of being preoccupied by something 2. an idea that preoccupies the mind and holds the attention 3. the act of taking occupancy before someone else does [plug possession prescription processe requisition revert emotional endurance engagement engrossment euphoria exclusion obsession obstinate occupation occupy ordinary own claim cognitive compulsive concern content uneasy unhealthy absentminded abstraction adoption anxiety application assumption attention takeover tenantry tenure think topic idea ignore industry interest involve niggle /tapu/]
*preoccupy 20-52-3 (v.) 1. engage or engross the interest or attention of beforehand or occupy urgently or obsessively 2. occupy or take possession of beforehand or before another or appropriate for use in advance [possibly power prepossess pursue reoccupy requisition response right enchant engage engross enslave exercise obsessive occupy overrun capture catch charm command comp compel concern conquer consume control urgent usurp]
*preordain 20-47-3 (v.) 1. foreordain or determine beforehand [program encode ordain decide decree destine determine divine doom advance arrange /roe/]
*preparation 03-57-164 (n.) 1. the cognitive process of thinking about what you will do in the event of something happening 2. a substance prepared according to a formula 3. the activity of putting or setting in order in advance of some act or purpose 4. the act of preparing something (as food) by the application of heat 5. preparatory school work done outside school (especially at home) 6. (music) a note that produces a dissonant chord is first heard in a consonant chord 7. the state of having been made ready or prepared for use or action (especially military action) 8. activity leading to skilled behavior [plan plot practice product provision put raise ready reparation retail education equipment exercise aforethought alert architecture armament arrangement teach thinking training tuition improvement incorporate intonation investment orchestrate organize outfit nurture /ape perp rape/] "preparations for the ceremony had begun"
*preparatory 12-47-14 (a.) 1. preceding and preparing for something [para precede preliminary primary prior

provisional remark rudimentary education elementary engage essential exist exordium advance anterior open opening year /ape perp rape rota/] "preparatory steps"
*preponderance 17-34-5 (n.) 1. superiority in power or influence 2. exceeding in heaviness; having greater weight 3. a superiority in numbers or amount [pan ponder possession powerful priority prison property purchase reign repute rule effect esteem evidence evil exceed excellence overlord dean dominance dominion accomplishment advantage amount area authority compare consequence control credit /nope perp/] "the preponderance of good over evil"
*preposterous 09-67-22 (a.) 1. completely devoid of wisdom or good sense [page paradox poster problematic prohibitive reasonable ridiculous risible rococo excessive exclude excuse extreme outlandish outrageous outre senseless silly suspicious tall thick thin turn unbelievable universal unreasonable unthinkable /perp/]
*prerogative 13-38-10 (n.) 1. a right reserved exclusively by a particular person or group (especially a hereditary or official right) [people perquisite place position power priority privilege regality reserved restricted right eleanor enjoy entitle excellence exclusive exempt exemption occupy official gat give government great group abstract accomplishment admit adult advantage age allow assembly authorization title tradition idea immunity incomparable interest virtuosity /ago tag vita/] "suffrage was the prerogative of white adult males"
*presage 15-42-8 (n.) 1. a foreboding about what is about to happen 2. a sign of something about to happen (v.) 1. indicate by signs [past picnic point portent pre predict prediction prefigure premonition presa probability prognosticate promise evil experience sign signify sky soothsayer speculation symptom apocalypse apprehensive augury auspice give great guesswork /gas/]
*prescience 20-56-3 (n.) 1. the power to foresee the future [power precognition prediction prevision prophecy retain science significance capacity clairvoyance insight intuition]
*prescient 14-50-9 (a.) 1. perceiving the significance of events before they occur [perceptive place postwar probable prophetic psychic relation revelation scient show significance clairvoyant course insight] "extroardinarily prescient memoranda on the probable course of postwar relations"
*prescription 05-41-62 (a.) 1. (of medicinal drugs) available only with a doctor's written prescription (n.) 1. a drug that is available only with written instructions from a doctor or dentist to a pharmacist 2. directions prescribed beforehand; the action of prescribing authoritative rules or directions 3. written instructions for an optician on the lenses for a given person 4. written instructions from a physician or dentist to a druggist concerning the form and dosage of a drug to be issued to a given patient [power practice preparation prescript principle regulation remedy right rule edict enactment etiquette squat statute sublease charge claim communication injunction instruction interest teach tenantry title occupation ordinance own norma] "a prescription drug"
*preservation 06-22-56 (n.) 1. the activity of protecting something from loss or danger 2. an occurrence of improvement by virtue of preventing loss or injury or other change 3. the condition of being (well or ill) preserved [perpetuate prehension protection providence refuge repression reservation retain eye safeguard safety salvation security shadow support tenacity immortalize improvement inhibition]
*presume 06-46-46 (v.) 1. take to be the case or to be true; accept without verification or proof [perform posit possible postulate premise presumptive pretend probable promising proof prospective provide reasonable reckon regard repute require resume entitle esteem estimate evidence expect exploit say search seem show slight statement stranger suggest suppose suppositive surmise survivor suspect understood unimaginable unscrupulousl mean /emu muse use user/]
*presumption 11-53-15 (n.) 1. an assumption that is taken for granted 2. (law) an inference of the truth of a fact from other facts proved or admitted or judicially noticed 3. a kind of discourtesy in the form of an act of presuming 4. audacious (even arrogant) behavior that you have no right to [position premise promise prospect reaction reliance resumption effrontery evidence expectation eye security speculation supposition meaning mind mystique idea impertinent impression impudent involve observation odds opinion outlook nerve notion nuance /muse use user/]
*presumptuous 17-50-5 (a.) 1. excessively forward [presume pride proud pushy rash restraint rude egotistic entitle excessive saucy servant shameless smug sumptuous supercilious uppity madcap meddle modesty temerarious temperament obtrusive officious outrageous overfamiliar /muse out use user/]
*pretension 11-56-16 (n.) 1. a false or unsupportable quality 2. the advancing of a claim 3. the quality of being pretentious (creating a false appearance of great importance or worth) [people pose posture power prestigious principle produce property refuge representation resort right excuse tension title tortuous town trick naturally negative screen seeming showy status still stylish image importance inflation intend interest orotund] "his pretension to the crown"
*pretentious 10-58-19 (a.) 1. making claim to or creating an appearance of (often undeserved) importance or distinction 2. intended to attract notice and impress others 3. of a display that is tawdry or vulgar [parvenu pedantic pompous pontifical portentous pose precious puff refinement rete rhetorical elaborate

elegance elevated exaggerate extravagant tall tasteless tawdry theatrical notice nouveau imposing impress inflated insincere orotund ostentatious overly overwrought unnatural upstart utopian sable sententious sesquipedalian showy special splash studied superficial swollen] "a pretentious country house"
*preternatural 18-51-4 (a.) 1. surpassing the ordinary or normal 2. existing outside of or not in accordance with nature [physical psychic remarkable eerie esoteric exceptional exist explanation extraordinary extraterrestrial transcendental transmundane natural nature non normal numinous accord acid affable anomalous arcane atypical uncanny unearthly unnatural unworldly usual law literary /rete ruta/] "Beyond his preternatural affability there is some acid and some steel"
*pretext 12-46-12 (n.) 1. something serving to conceal plans; a fictitious reason that is concocted in order to conceal the real reason 2. an artful or simulated semblance [plan plea ploy pose real reason representation rete right ruse excuse explanation token]
*prevalence 13-54-10 (n.) 1. the quality of prevailing generally; being widespread 2. a superiority in numbers or amount 3. (epidemiology) the ratio (for a given time period) of the number of occurrences of a disease or event to the number of units at risk in the population [period pervasive population possessed prison property ratio risk epidemiology express acceptance amount applicable common control] "he was surprised by the prevalence of optimism about the future"
*prevalent 08-48-31 (a.) 1. encountered generally especially at the present time [period plenty population practice predominant present property rampant ratio receive reign religion rich rife risk rule run economy encounter epidemiology establish exist express extensive extravagance exuberant valent accept accompany affluent amount applicable area author average avert landslide lavish leading liberal living lot new non normality numerous teem trade traditional trendy /ave aver lave laver/]
*prevaricate 18-86-4 (v.) 1. be deliberately ambiguous or unclear in order to mislead or withhold information [palter parry perjury perversion pettifogger pussyfoot equivocate evade evasion exaggerate vary account address ambiguous answer avoid canard cate cavil choplogic clear coloring tale taradiddle tell tergiversate topic truthful /ave aver rave raver/]
*prevention 06-40-56 (n.) 1. control by preventing the occurrence of something 2. the act of preventing [participate possess power preclude prevent proceeding proscription refrain refusal rejection restraint effective elusive escape exclusion neutrality non nuclear taboo thwart impede impossible increase influenza inhibition injunction intercept obstruct obstruction obviate opposition /ever neve never/]
*prickle 22-79-2 (n.) 1. a sharp-pointed tip on a stem or leaf (v.) 1. cause a prickling sensation 2. cause a tingling sensation [pain paste perceive plant plaster point process projection remora ickle irritation itch cactus cement cusp leaf leech limpet eye /elk/]
*priggish 22-66-2 (a.) 1. exaggeratedly proper [prim prissy proper prude puritanical right squaretoed straitlaced suitable]
*prim 14-57-9 (a.) 1. affectedly dainty or refined 2. exaggeratedly proper (v.) 1. assume a prim appearance 2. contract one's lips 3. dress primly [pomposity precise press prig prissy proper provide prude puritanical raiment refined right rigid rim impersonality manner mark meticulous mincing miniskirt moralist] "They mince and prim"
*prima 13-65-11 (a.) 1. indicating the most important performer or role (n.) 1. used primarily as eating apples [perform prim raw role important indicate major minor apple /amir/]
*primer 14-27-9 (n.) 1. an introductory textbook 2. the first or preliminary coat of paint or size applied to a surface 3. any igniter by which an explosive charge is ignited [paint pigment preliminary prepare prime principle propellant provide read rudiment ignite induction initiate initiation introductory matter medium edition element explosive /emir/]
*primeval 17-59-5 (a.) 1. having existed from the beginning; in an earliest or original stage or state [past period prehistoric previous prime prior radical recent rudimentary inaugural instinctive introductory intuitive inventive matter middle early earth elementary era erstwhile exist expect aboriginal ancestral ancient appearance arise late life /ave emir lave/]
*primitive 07-43-34 (a.) 1. (anthropology; of societies) preliterate or tribal or nonindustrial 2. little evolved from or characteristic of an earlier ancestral type 3. belonging to an early stage of technical development; characterized by simplicity and (often) crudeness 4. (fine arts) of or created by one without formal training; simple or naive in style (n.) 1. a person who belongs to early stage of civilization 2. a mathematical expression from which another expression is derived 3. a word serving as the basis for inflected or derived forms [past person previous prim prior radical recent root inaugural individual inventive material mortal then troglodyte vernacular early elementary essential] "`pick' is the primitive from which `picket' is derived"
*principal 02-36-272 (a.) 1. most important element (n.) 1. an actor who plays a principal role 2. the educator who has executive authority for a school 3. the original amount of a debt on which interest is calculated 4. capital as contrasted with the income derived from it 5. the major party to a financial transaction at a stock exchange; buys and sells for his own account [particularly people predominantly president prime prominent register resource ruling idol inc interested investment nonpareil central chairman chief chiefly

control corpus ace administrator asset largely laureate luminary /lap/] "she sent unruly pupils to see the principal"
*principality 15-88-7 (n.) 1. territory ruled by a prince [position power premiership president principal region republic ride riviera roman rule russian ireland nationality nine nobility northern cambria capital century chancellor christianity city constitutional control country county ally angel aristocracy ascendancy land leadership lordship territory third tiny traditional /lap/]
*principle 02-52-243 (n.) 1. rule of personal conduct 2. an explanation of the fundamental reasons (especially an explanation of the working of some device in terms of laws of nature) 3. a rule or law concerning a natural phenomenon or the function of a complex system 4. a basic truth or law or assumption 5. a rule or standard especially of good behavior 6. a basic generalization that is accepted as true and that can be used as a basis for reasoning or conduct [philosophy platform prescription procedure proposition pure radical regulation reputable respectable righteous rule immaculate inc induction inspiration interest inviolate irreproachable issue nobility noble norm norma notion nucleus calling campaign cause center character clean code correct course creditable law lifework line lodestar element erect essential estimable ethics] "their principles of composition characterized all their works"
*priory 13-94-10 (n.) 1. religious residence in a monastery governed by a prior or a convent governed by a prioress [place prior religious residence]
*pristine 08-47-27 (a.) 1. completely free from dirt or contamination 2. immaculately clean and unused [patriarchal perfect pregnant primeval pure radical raw reserve rist ruin immaculate impurity initial innocent intact save snow spotless store suspend native natural neat new early element encroach extraneous] "pristine mountain snow"
*privateer 25-61-1 (n.) 1. an officer or crew member of a privateer 2. a privately owned warship commissioned to prey on the commercial shipping or warships of an enemy nation [picaroon pirate position prey private rover run vessel viking armada authorize available tar trade enemy engage english /reet/]
*privilege 04-55-114 (n.) 1. a right reserved exclusively by a particular person or group (especially a hereditary or official right) 2. a special advantage or immunity or benefit not enjoyed by all 3. (law) the right to refuse to divulge information obtained in a confidential relationship (v.) 1. grant a privilege to 2. bestow a privilege upon [penalty permit possess powerful prestige priority protect ratify release rich right rule immunity inclusive incomparable indulgence inner inside irresponsible validate vile virtuosity lack lead leave let license limit elite enable enjoy entitle exception exclusive excuse exempt good grant great group]
*privy 13-70-11 (a.) 1. hidden from general view or use 2. (followed by 'to') informed about something secret or not generally known (n.) 1. a small outbuilding with a bench having holes through which a user can defecate 2. a room equipped with toilet facilities [party personal place plan plumbing pot potty privilege provide public restroom retired romantic room inform interest interior intimate involve isolated ivy view] "a privy place to rest and think"
*probate 18-50-4 (n.) 1. a judicial certificate saying that a will is genuine and conferring on the executors the power to administer the estate 2. the act of proving that an instrument purporting to be a will was signed and executed in accord with legal requirements (v.) 1. put a convicted person on probation by suspending his sentence 2. establish the legal validity of; as of a will, etc. [postpone power proof prorogue prove purport ratify reinforce remit require rule official backup bate bolster buttress accord administer affirm authority table test testament truth estate executor /tab tabor/]
*probation 07-34-39 (n.) 1. a trial period during which your character and abilities are tested to see whether you are suitable for work or for membership 2. (law) a way of dealing with offenders without imprisoning them; a defendant found guilty of a crime is released by the court without imprisonment subject to conditions imposed by the court 3. a trial period during which an offender has time to redeem himself or herself [part period pilot probative process proof prove provisional redeem regular release report role rule offense officer ordeal bat behavior academic assay audition authority test testing touchstone trial try tryout impose improve /tab tabor/] "probation is part of the sentencing process"
*probe 06-53-59 (n.) 1. an inquiry into unfamiliar or questionable activities 2. a flexible slender surgical instrument used to explore wounds or body cavities 3. an exploratory action or expedition 4. an investigation conducted using a probe instrument (v.) 1. examine physically with or as if with a probe 2. question or examine thoroughly and closely [pace pass penetrate perforate physical place poke postmortem prize probing process pump rate read research resistance review robe rummage oppose overcome barometer behavior body enquiry establish estimate examine expedition explore] "probe an anthill"
*probity 18-68-4 (n.) 1. complete and confirmed integrity [rectitude right righteous obit integrity]
*procedure 03-44-207 (n.) 1. a process or series of acts especially of a practical or mechanical nature involved in a particular form of work 2. a particular course of action intended to achieve a results 3. a mode of conducting legal and parliamentary proceedings 4. a set sequence of steps, part of larger computer program [package practice presence process program rationalization routine rule order organization calculation conduct custom enterprise design device drill dure /deco decor rude/] "the procedure of obtaining

a driver's license"
*proceed 04-42-106 (v.) 1. continue a certain state, condition, or activity 2. move ahead; travel onward in time or space 3. follow a certain course 4. follow a procedure or take a course 5. continue with one's activities [pace pass path perform period place play position possible process profit progress ramble remain return riotous rise risk roar room route run onward operate carry carryon cee certain channel choice condition continue course embark endeavor endure ensue exchange expire extend danger desultory develop drag]
*proclamation 13-30-10 (n.) 1. a formal public statement 2. the formal act of proclaiming; giving public notice [people policy premature proclaim profession promulgate prove publicly publishing report rule official ordinance ordonnance circular clam communicate conclusion creed law advertise announce annunciation appointment assertion authoritative manifesto message independence notice notify]
*proclivity 20-40-3 (n.) 1. a natural inclination [penchant preference prejudice pro prone ready cast character constitution lean liability like idiosyncrasy inclination incline individualism taste tendency thing type] "he has a proclivity for exaggeration"
*procrastinate 16-50-6 (v.) 1. postpone doing what one should be doing 2. postpone or delay needlessly [parasitic passive pause permissive plan plod policy postpone practice prolong put rate regular relaxed remiss require omit oversight cadge consequence continue cut abandon absence adjourn almost schedule shillyshally shirk shuffling skip slacker slight slow sluggish snail stall stay suspend table tarry temporize tina tortoise trifle idler inactivity indolent inert needless negligent neutral nonfeasance nonrestrictive easygoing equivocate extend /arco sarco tsar/] "He did not want to write the letter and procrastinated for days"
*procrastination 20-54-3 (n.) 1. the act of procrastinating 2. slowness as a consequence of not getting around to it [postpone rate consequence cunctation absence adjourn shillyshally slow stall inactivity]
*proctor 14-68-9 (n.) 1. someone who supervises (an examination) (v.) 1. as of students taking an exam, to prevent cheating [plead prefect prevent procurator observer octo overseer candidate charge cheat chief controller curator taskmaster television]
*prodigal 15-55-7 (a.) 1. very generous 2. recklessly wasteful 3. marked by rash extravagance (n.) 1. a recklessly extravagant consumer [packed plenty praise prevalent prod productivity profligate provide prudent rampant rank rash reckless reiterate resource return rich opulent outpouring overwrought degree delinquency deluge devotion diffusive dissolute drunken immoral indulgent inflation inordinate intemperate galore generous gift give gluttony good gush abound abundant affluent aid amoral amount avalanche lavish liberal life literary lot lush luxury /dorp gid lag/]
*prodigious 10-62-21 (a.) 1. so great in size or force or extent as to elicit awe 2. far beyond what is usual in magnitude or degree 3. of momentous or ominous significance [phenomenal plenitude power prod profuse puzzling raise rare rarity remarkable outsize overgrown degree demand immense important impressive inconceivable incredible infinite intensity galactic gargantuan giant gigantic gigantism glamorous grand grass great uncommon unique unprecedented unusual seductive significant sizable storm strange strength striking stupendous surpassing surprising /dorp gid/]
*prodigy 10-62-21 (n.) 1. an unusually talented or intelligent child [paragon phenomenon portent pre presage principal prod prognosticate rarity recognize ruler oddity omen originality dean death destruction imitate important impressive improbable indicate infant intelligent genius gifted good great young /dorp gid/]
*productive 05-45-60 (a.) 1. having the ability to produce or originate 2. yielding positive results 3. producing or capable of producing (especially abundantly) 4. marked by great fruitfulness [pay performance plenty positive practical prefix pregnant product profitable prolific raise realize reiterate rewarding rich rise opulent originative outcome outpouring overflow demiurge dynamic useful capable charisma clout competent conceptual copious creative cultivate tautology teem thrive tumescent increment industrious influence inspired inventive value vigorous vision economics efficient energy expansion extension exuberant /dorp udo/] "productive farmland"
*profane 16-36-6 (a.) 1. characterized by profanity or cursing 2. grossly irreverent toward what is held to be sacred 3. not sacred or concerned with religion 4. not holy because unconsecrated or impure or defiled (v.) 1. corrupt morally or by intemperance or sensuality 2. violate the sacred character of a place or language [pagan people pervert physical piety pity place poison pollution prostitution purpose raunchy raw religious renegade respect reverent rite obscenity outrage fane filthy form foul fulminate abomination abusive accuse alter apostate art assault astray atheistic atrocity attack nasty naughty earthly earthy embezzle emotional enter entirely environment ethnic evil /for/]
*profession 04-56-114 (n.) 1. an occupation requiring special education (especially in the liberal arts or sciences) 2. the body of people in a learned occupation 3. affirmation of acceptance of some religion or faith 4. an open avowal (true or false) of some belief or opinion [post practice profess pursuit racket recognition occupation field employment enunciate say stand number /for/]
*professor 02-41-477 (n.) 1. someone who is a member of the faculty at a college or university [patron pedantic preceptorial profess rabbinic rank religious royal owlish

faculty fellow formal full educator school senior staff studious /for/]
*proffer 14-63-9 (n.) 1. a proposal offered for acceptance or rejection (v.) 1. present for acceptance or rejection; [part plan pose possession pour prefer present proposition rain reaction rejection render offer offering optional overture feeler freewill elective elicit extend /for/]
*proficiency 15-32-7 (n.) 1. the quality of having great facility and competence 2. skillfulness in the command of fundamentals deriving from practice and familiarity [paint physical practice preparedness prof progress prowess ready ripe omniscient ongoing facility faculty familiarity fitness fundamental improve ingenuity intellectual capacity cognitive command competency condition control efficiency expert expertise /for/] "practice greatly improves proficiency"
*proficient 14-48-9 (a.) 1. having or showing knowledge and skill and aptitude [perfect practice productive prof professional ready refined require resourceful retouch fancy finished fit ingenious capable classic clean composer effect engineer excellent exercise expert neat tactful talented /for/]
*profile 02-56-298 (n.) 1. biographical sketch 2. a side view representation of an object (especially a human face) 3. a graph representing the extent to which something exhibits various characteristics 4. a vertical section of the Earth's crust showing the different horizons or layers (v.) 1. write about 2. represent in profile, by drawing or painting [pen people perpendicular photograph picture plot predict product recording relief report represent resume obituary outline famous feature figure file fortune identity imagery impression indite interpret investigate itemize legend line list evocation examination experience /for/] "The author of this article profiles a famous painter"
*profiteer 16-55-6 (n.) 1. someone who makes excessive profit (especially on goods in short supply) (v.) 1. make an unreasonable profit, as on the sale of difficult to obtain goods [predator price profit racketeer raptor ration obtain overtax fleece invest embezzle excessive exploit extortion /for reet/]
*profligacy 16-86-6 (n.) 1. the trait of spending extravagantly 2. dissolute indulgence in sensual pleasure [parsimony pleasure prodigal prudent reckless resource lack licentiousnes immoderate indulgence intemperate appetite care]
*profligate 12-76-14 (a.) 1. recklessly wasteful 2. unrestrained by convention or morality (n.) 1. a dissolute man in fashionable society 2. a recklessly extravagant consumer [perversion pimp pleasure pollute principle prodigal promiscuous prudent rake reckless resource right riotous rip rotten roue rounder fashionable fast free lack lavish lewd libertine licentious ligate live loose low immoral improvident incontinent indecent indulgence intemperate gallant gay good abandon amoral appetite aristocratic taint tend thrifty trollop evil excessive expenditure extremely /for tag/]
*profundity 20-51-3 (n.) 1. intellectual depth; penetrating knowledge; keen insight; etc 2. wisdom that is recondite and abstruse and profound 3. the intellectual ability to penetrate deeply into ideas 4. the quality of being physically deep [penetrating perceptivenes perspicacity physical profound property psychological reach recondite require obscurity fathomless fund understood native deal deep degree depth difficulty downward idea immense impress incomprehensible insightful intensity interior intricacy involve inward tall /for/]
*profuse 15-48-8 (a.) 1. produced or growing in extreme abundance [packed particularly plentiful plenty present produce productive prolific prominent pronounced rampant reiterate remarkably richly riotous openhearted opulent overwrought famous fat flush freely fully fuse uncommonly unselfish unsparing unstinting unusual scarce singular stretch striking stud surprise swarm excessive exhaustless express exquisite extreme exuberant /for/]
*progeny 17-52-5 (n.) 1. the immediate descendants of a person [parent plant posterity relation office offspring organism gen grandchild group eldest necessarily young youngster /ego gorp/]
*progression 09-61-22 (n.) 1. a movement forward 2. the act of moving forward toward a goal 3. a series with a definite pattern of advance [pattern place plain predecessor procession professional progress prolong promotion push reciprocal rise round run obtain onward game gamut general geometric goal gradual growth easy effort enhance evolution expansion extension sailing scale sequence series space spreading steady string succession improvement intensify next nexus note /ergo gorp/]
*progressive 05-51-72 (a.) 1. favoring or promoting reform (often by government action) 2. favoring or promoting progress 3. (of taxes) adjusted so that the rate increases as the amount increases 4. advancing in severity 5. gradually advancing in extent (n.) 1. a tense of verbs used in describing action that is on-going 2. a person who favors a political philosophy of progress and reform and the protection of civil liberties [passing piecemeal plunge proceeding progress radical rise running rush oncoming ongoing onward open orthodoxy gradual growing enhance enlighten extremist sink soar successive improve increase /ergo gorp/] "progressive schools"
*prohibition 08-29-28 (n.) 1. the period from 1920 to 1933 when the sale of alcoholic beverages was prohibited in the United States by a constitutional amendment 2. a decree that prohibits something 3. a law forbidding the sale of alcoholic beverages 4. refusal to approve or assent to 5. the action of prohibiting or inhibiting or forbidding (or an instance thereof) [parent

party period policy preclude prevention process prohibit proscription record rejection relegate remedy rescript restrained restriction rule obviate omission oppose order outlaw outlawry halt hindrance ignore impose inferior inhibition injunction interdict ban bar beverage beyond binding taboo trade transport narrow] "in 1920 the 18th amendment to the Constitution established prohibition in the US"
*projection 05-34-62 (n.) 1. a planned undertaking 2. any structure that branches out from a central support 3. the projection of an image from a film onto a screen 4. a prediction made by extrapolating from past observations 5. the act of expelling or projecting or ejecting 6. (psychiatry) a defense mechanism by which your own traits and emotions are attributed to someone else 7. any solid convex shape that juts out from something 8. the representation of a figure or solid on a plane as it would look from a particular direction 9. the act of projecting out from something [plan play point project opening outline overhang jag jut eject estimate exhibition exposure expulsion chart compensation copy illustration impersonate index negativism notation]
*proletarian 18-43-4 (a.) 1. the lowest class of citizens of ancient Rome who had no property 2. belonging to or characteristic of the proletariat (n.) 1. a member of the working class (not necessarily employed) [patrician people person plebeian popular position possess prole rome roustabout ruling occupy origin labor low lowborn employer europe temporary theory title toil ancient aristocracy asset impoverish industrial navvy necessarily nobility /irate rate/]
*proliferate 06-39-47 (v.) 1. grow rapidly 2. cause to grow or increase rapidly [parlor part plant pour procreate propagate propagation pullulate rain raise rapid replicate reproduce reproduction rise offspring outbreed overflow large leap lifer inbreed increase increment inflation intensify father flood flourish flow fructify engender escalate expand expansion extension accumulate addition advance appreciation area arm table thrive tumescent /filo tare/] "Pizza parlors proliferate in this area"
*prolific 07-68-42 (a.) 1. intellectually productive 2. bearing in abundance especially offspring [packed pear period plentiful pregnant pro productive profuse redundant reiterate rich offspring originative overflow lavish life lot lush luxuriant idea imagination imaginative inexhaustible inspired intellectual inventive fecund fertile flourish fox frequently fruitful capable conceptual conducive copious creative crowd /filo/] "a prolific writer"
*prolix 25-54-1 (a.) 1. tediously prolonged or tending to speak or write at great length [pad pleonasm pompous pro prolong protract rambling ready redundant open ornamentation overlap language lecturer length lengthy logorrhea long loquacity luxury invariable irksome] "editing a prolix manuscript"
*prologue 15-43-8 (n.) 1. an introduction to a play [participle passage past performance play poem preamble preface prelude premise routine open overture lead leap line log long epilogue exodus exordium]
*prolong 05-52-69 (v.) 1. lengthen in time; cause to be or last longer 2. lengthen or extend in duration or space [patient payment perpetuate persist place position possible preserve process production progression protract pull recess remain repetition reserve retain rotation run overlong last lasting layby layover lengthen lengthy lineage linger long neg gain good /nolo/] "We prolonged our stay"
*promenade 11-46-16 (n.) 1. a formal ball held for a school class toward the end of the academic year 2. a leisurely walk (usually in some public place) 3. a march of all the guests at the opening of a formal dance 4. a square dance figure; couples march counterclockwise in a circle 5. a public area set aside as a pedestrian walk (v.) 1. march in a procession 2. take a walk [parade past path pedestrian people perambulate perform place pleasure procession prom public regular review run runway omen opening mall march meet mixer move mush esplanade academic advance airing alameda amble american area arrange aside assemble dan dance defile display down /dan nemo/]
*prominence 07-49-34 (n.) 1. relative importance 2. the state of being prominent: widely known or eminent 3. something that bulges out or is protuberant or projects from a form [part plain plant point position professional project protuberant public rank relief reputation rise rounded obscure obvious occipital organ outcrop outer outgrowth mark mine moment mount illustrious important name note noteworthy notorious nubble elevation eminent esteem excellence excrescence extrusion eye celebrity certain chromosphere clarity clear condition conspicuous convex corona]
*prominent 03-33-188 (a.) 1. conspicuous in position or importance 2. having a quality that thrusts itself into attention [particularly popular position powerful price pro project pronounced protuberant prove raise rare recognize remarkably renowned resemblance respect richly rise obvious official ostensible outstanding magical magnificent main major marked marvelous memorable move identify important impressive influential intense nation noble noticeable notorious elevated eminent exceptional exquisite extraordinary eye telling thrust top totalitarian trait]
*promiscuous 15-62-7 (a.) 1. not selective of a single class or person 2. casual and unrestrained in sexual behavior [patchy pattern philander pluralism purpose random relation mark messy mingle misc mix money immoral indiscriminate intricate ironic irresponsible sail scramble selective set sex single slut solicit specific stray system campaign careless casual catch cause chamber chaste choose class combined confused criticize unaccountable unbridled uninhibited

unrestrained] "Clinton was criticized for his promiscuous solicitation of campaign money"
*promissory 22-16-2 (a.) 1. relating to or having the character of a promise [provision miss imply insurance show speech state] "promissory note"
*promontory 20-51-3 (n.) 1. a natural elevation (especially a rocky one that juts out into the sea) [part peninsula pillar point project promo protrude raise reef rocky ocean opposite organ outcrop mediterranean morocco mull musa nasa natural ness northern nova tier tip tongue]
*promoter 06-49-45 (n.) 1. someone who is an active supporter and advocate 2. a sponsor who books and stages public entertainments [patron planner praise promote reliance root organizer maintain tactics tout encourage endorse entrepreneur /tom/]
*promulgate 16-27-6 (v.) 1. put a law into effect by formal declaration 2. state or announce [pro proclaim propagate prosecute publicly publish render rule observe official ordain mandate law gate administer advertise amnesty announce authoritative toot transmit trumpet effect emphatic endorse enforce enjoin exclaim execute /glum tag/]
*prone 06-63-59 (a.) 1. lying face downward 2. having a tendency (to); often used in combination [pliant position posture predispose preference prompt prostrate receptive recline responsive obnoxious obsequious one neap eager enthusiastic erect exaggerate] "a child prone to mischief"
*propaganda 06-51-48 (n.) 1. information that is spread for the purpose of promoting some cause [pagan party political priest promote publicity puffery purpose receive advert art disinformation /gap nag/]
*propagate 12-52-12 (v.) 1. transmit from one generation to the next 2. cause to become widely known 3. cause (plants) to propagate, as by grafting or layering 4. multiply sexually or asexually, in biology 5. transmit or cause to broaden or spread 6. transmit, as in physics 7. travel through the air 8. become distributed or widespread [pepper point printing production proliferate promulgate publicize publishing purpose radiation raise reach reproduce retail observer offspring opening outbreed overspread agate airing apparent around attenuate generation get grow telecast toward transport travel treatment engender /gap tag/] "propagate these characteristics"
*propagation 20-45-3 (n.) 1. the act of producing offspring or multiplying by such production 2. the spreading of something (a belief or practice) into new regions 3. the movement of a wave through a medium [phenomenon physics point practice procreate production proliferate promulgate prop public reach observer offspring opening organism apparent generation toward transmission natural /gap tag/]
*propel 05-54-66 (v.) 1. cause to move forward with force 2. give an incentive for action [pole power press project prompt propulsion punt push pushing rise rocket roll row occur opel emotional energize exhort launch light] "Steam propels this ship"
*propellant 22-29-2 (a.) 1. tending to or capable of propelling (n.) 1. something that propels [personality petrol piston plane pressure project propel provocative pushing release rocket rotor occupy octane oil efficiency ethanol exhaust explosive active aerosol airscrew alcohol anti apply atomic nail napalm neutron nitroglycerin tend thrust torpedo transition travel turf] "propellant fuel for submarines"
*propeller 14-46-9 (n.) 1. a mechanical device that rotates to push against air or water [part pass principle propel push revolving rotate rotor rudder ejector landing]
*propensity 13-59-11 (n.) 1. an inclination to do something 2. a disposition to behave in a certain way 3. a natural inclination [penchant predisposition preference prejudice proclivity prone ready rust open eager eccentricity exaggerate natural nature set spread stamp strain susceptibility idiosyncrasy incline individualism iron tendency toward twist type]
*prophecy 12-50-12 (n.) 1. a prediction uttered under divine inspiration 2. knowledge of the future (usually said to be obtained from a divine source) [prediction pretense prevision priestess project promise prop reasoning reveal revelation obscure obtain omen oracle outlook hereafter epiphany eventuality expectation cast crystal]
*prophesy 20-61-3 (v.) 1. predict or reveal through, or as if through, divine inspiration 2. deliver a sermon [plan plot power preaching prediction prognosticate project promise prop religion revelation oracle happen harbinger herald hereafter hope emergent enlighten evangelize eventual expect extrapolate sermon soothsayer speculate spiritual supposedly]
*prophet 09-57-26 (n.) 1. someone who speaks by divine inspiration; someone who is an interpreter of the will of God 2. an authoritative person who divines the future [parapsycholog people poet predict presage prescient prop protection psychic public rebuke red redeemer religious remember reveal rhapsodist romanticist rome obadiah official old omen oppose oracle haggai haruspex heaven hebrew hide him egypt enthusiast escapist exile exodus ezekiel teacher ten testament thrown]
*propitious 20-47-3 (a.) 1. presenting favorable circumstances [present promote prop prosperous providential reassure ripe rosy omen opportune inspirit tend timely toward useful sort success suitable supportive /tip/] "propitious omens"
*proportionate 12-62-12 (a.) 1. agreeing in amount, magnitude, or degree 2. being in due proportion 3. exhibiting equivalence or correspondence among constituents of an entity or between different entities [par particular pertinent positive price proportion

reconcile refer relation relevant remain respectively rise tie total identical incommensurate indifferently inharmony next adequate agree alike amount apposite enough entity equal equally equivalent exhibit extent]
*propriety 13-34-10 (n.) 1. correct or appropriate behavior [people percentage plain polite politesse prim profitable prop protocol punctilio regularity relevant respectable right rule opportune orderly improper ease elegance equity etiquette exaggerate expectation tasteful timeline toward tradition]
*propulsion 12-29-13 (n.) 1. a propelling force 2. the act of propelling [personality physical plane power pressure process produce projection prop pull pushing raise rapid react reaction repeat rolling opposite launch lift lob seat shell ship shot shove shunt submarine impetus impulsion incentive incite influence newly notable nuclear]
*prosaic 12-65-14 (a.) 1. not fanciful or imaginative 2. not challenging; dull and lacking excitement 3. lacking wit or imagination [pedestrian place plain plot practical pros realistic resemble rhetorical routine rustic open ordinary overdo severe simple stock straightforward subtlety actual arid arouse attention austere imaginative infertile insipid interest irksome candid challenging characterless classical colorless commonplace complication curiosity]
*proscenium 19-26-4 (n.) 1. the part of a modern theater stage between the curtain and the orchestra (i.e., in front of the curtain) 2. the wall that separates the stage from the auditorium in a modern theater [partition people perform pit platform prefix priority project prompter pros obverse open orchestra see separate set shell sit stage stand structure support switchboard coulisse curtain enclose illuminate modern]
*proscribe 19-58-4 (v.) 1. command against [preclude pressure prevent prohibit protect publicly refuse reject relegate require rule ostracize outlaw scribe sentence social spurn suppress call command compel condemn consider convict criminalize cut illegalize inhibit injunction interdict issue ban banish bar boycott embargo enter exclude exile expel]
*proscription 25-53-1 (n.) 1. a decree that prohibits something 2. rejection by means of an act of banishing or proscribing someone [preclude prescription prevention rap refusal rejection rescript order outlaw script sentence statute suppression condemn conviction curse imprecation inhibition injunction interdict taboo thundering]
*prospector 19-42-4 (n.) 1. someone who explores an area for mineral deposits [prospect oil search settler shovel earthmover excavator explore canada crawler]
*prospectus 12-62-12 (n.) 1. a catalog listing the courses offered by a college or university [pamphlet part plan point preliminary project promise propose prospect publication red resolve roster offering official omen organization outline scheme school sec security sell set speculation staff stock study effect enterprise enumerate calendar card catalogue change clearly college counsel course university]
*prostrate 17-68-5 (a.) 1. stretched out and lying at full length along the ground 2. lying face downward (v.) 1. render helpless or defenseless 2. get into a prostrate position, as in submission 3. throw down flat, as on the ground [parasitism physical pine position posture powerless precipitate project prone raze recline render respect reverence rostra ruin obeisance obsequious oppress overexert overwhelm sad short shrub soft spent spread stretch submission throw timeserver toady trail transform truckle abject adore adulation afflict alter anguish assume embitter emotion emperor enemy energy enervate erect exhaust /tart/] "They prostrated the enemy"
*protagonist 07-53-34 (n.) 1. a person who backs a politician or a team etc. 2. the principal character in a work of fiction [patron piece principal reliance role actor admire advocate agonist ingenue singer sponsor star supporter /gator nog/]
*protean 22-37-2 (a.) 1. taking on different forms [permute plastic polymorph protea resilient rubbery transitory twice erratic adaptable adjust allotropic appearance nature never] "eyes...of that baffling protean gray which is never twice the same"
*protection 02-43-332 (n.) 1. the condition of being protected 2. defense against financial failure 3. a covering that is intend to protect from damage or injury 4. the activity of protecting someone or something 5. kindly endorsement and guidance 6. the imposition of duties or quotas on imports in order to protect domestic industry against foreign competition 7. payment extorted by gangsters on threat of violence [pad position protect provision relief rescue resistance office therapy ease extortion care charge control covering immunity injunction insurance nonintervention nullification] "the witnesses demanded police protection"
*protective 06-47-58 (a.) 1. showing a care 2. intended or adapted to afford protection of some kind 3. (usually followed by 'of') solicitously caring or mindful [parental preserve preventive prophylactic protect purpose reputation restrictive tariff tend toward tutelary equipment evasive excessive exercise care careful careless cautionary coating coloring conserve contraceptive country cover covering custody immunize industry intend vigilant] "a protective covering"
*protector 12-45-14 (n.) 1. a person who cares for persons or property [paladin parent peace people period person pillar place practice preserver prominent property protect protectress regent reminder rock officer theft title try escort extinguish care cause champion chaperone charge child consider]
*protege 15-11-8 (n.) 1. a person who receives support and protection from an influential patron who furthers the protege's career [patron pupil receive recipient rote

/get/]
*protestant 07-39-43 (a.) 1. (religion) of or relating to Protestants or Protestantism 2. making a protest (n.) 1. the Protestant churches and denominations collectively 2. an adherent of Protestantism [conformist practitioner presbyterian protest religious england evangelism saint sovereign supernatural supporter adherent anabaptist ancestry anglo approach non /set/]
*protocol 07-57-35 (n.) 1. (computer science) rules determining the format and transmission of data 2. code of correct conduct 3. forms of ceremony and etiquette observed by diplomats and heads of state [piece plan practice preliminary prepare prescribe principle processe promise propriety prospectus proto receipt record roster rule occasion official organization outline transmission treaty trial card ceremony code communicate compute conduct consider control convention conventional copy lineup /cot loco/] "safety protocols"
*prototype 08-43-32 (n.) 1. a standard or typical example [paradigm paragon parent past pattern precursor predecessor primary primitive proto provide referent representative rule original turn epitome essential example exemplar exhibit] "he is the prototype of good breeding"
*protract 08-58-28 (v.) 1. lengthen in time; cause to be or last longer [pad part passage payment physiology plot preserve primarily process produce prolong pull recess reserve retain overlong table taut tedious temporize tense tighten tract adjourn allow argument average chatter continue /cart/]
*protracted 08-58-28 (a.) 1. relatively long in duration; tediously protracted [passage primarily prolong tedious temporal argument average expand extended day delay discussion drawnout duration]
*protrude 13-44-10 (v.) 1. extend out or project in space 2. swell or protrude outwards 3. bulge outward [pop pouch pout project push rock rude obtrude out outward over overhang thrust upward debouch deform different emerge erupt extend eye]
*protrusion 25-38-1 (n.) 1. something that bulges out or is protuberant or projects from a form 2. the act of projecting out from something [part plant project projection prominence protuberancy relief rounded occipital organ outcrop outer overlap tumescent salient shape sharp ski slope solid stick structure surface surround swell ion nubble]
*protuberance 25-55-1 (n.) 1. something that bulges out or is protuberant or projects from a form 2. the condition of being protuberant; the condition of bulging out [palate pile pit plant projection prominence relief rounded occipital organ outer texture tuber belly bold branch bulge bump emboss eminence excrescence extrusion animal nap nub nubble central certain condition convexity /but rebut/] "the protuberance of his belly"
*proverb 19-56-4 (n.) 1. a condensed but memorable saying embodying some important fact of experience that is taken as true by many people [people phrase platitude precept prove obvious offer oracle verse embody epigram experience expression bromide byword]
*provident 12-88-12 (a.) 1. providing carefully for the future 2. careful in regard to your own interests [parsimonious plan prepare presbyopia provide provisional prudent prudential ready reflective resource vigilant incisive interest intuitive develop diligent discriminative distant divination economical economize education enlighten thoughtful thrifty trenchant] "wild squirrels are provident"
*providential 25-50-1 (a.) 1. peculiarly fortunate or appropriate; as if by divine intervention 2. relating to or characteristic of providence 3. resulting from divine providence [peculiar plan portion preordain prepared provident prudent rain ready recovery ripe operate opportune visitation vouchsafe intervention intuitive destiny determined divine earthly expedient nature timely accord advantageous allow appropriate lot lucky /lait/]
*provincial 06-55-51 (a.) 1. characteristic of the provinces or their people 2. of or associated with a province (n.) 1. a country person [pastoral peasant petty province regional rude rural oafish outland vernacular viceroy vinci idiomatic innocent insular naive narrow nearsighted close collector confined agricultural authoritarian awkward limited little lowland /laic/] "provincial government"
*provisional 08-69-32 (a.) 1. under terms not final or fully worked out or agreed upon [pending permanent pilot pinch postage precaution probation provision regular reserve resource risky rough occasional outline validate vicarious imitation impermanent imposing improvise interim schedule spare stamp stated substitute nonessential adventitious agree aleatory alternative]
*proviso 17-69-5 (n.) 1. a stipulated condition [parameter part prerequisite provision require requisite reservation rest rider obligation valid introduce iso specification stipulate string]
*provocation 11-50-17 (n.) 1. unfriendly behavior that causes anger or resentment 2. something that incites or provokes; a means of arousing or stirring to action 3. needed encouragement [patience provoke psychic reason resentment vex vexation vigorous vocation cause criminal criticize actuate affront aggression anger annoyance approval arouse attack taunt twit improper incentive incite indignant induce insult investigate irritation needle niggling /taco/] "the result was a provocation of vigorous investigation"
*provoke 04-58-127 (v.) 1. annoy continually or chronically 2. call forth 3. provide the needed stimulus for 4. call forth; of emotions, feelings, and responses [painful passion peace peeved perceptual persuasion pique pity plague prime produce prompt provo public

rag raise rally reaction readable resentment response ride rile rise roil rouse rousing ruffle objection obtain occur offend overwork vehement vex kick kindle effect elicit emotion encourage engage enhance enlarge erode evoke exaggerate exasperate excite]
*prowess 09-58-22 (n.) 1. a superior skill that you can learn by study and practice and observation [perform practice preaching present proficiency project prow puppet ready return observation oenology operate ordinary wine wit wizardry workmanship efficiency exceptional expertise savvy science seem show skill skin source specious stalwart strengthen study style superior /sew/]
*proxy 09-35-24 (a.) 1. acting as substitute for another (n.) 1. a person authorized to act for another 2. a power of attorney document given by shareholders of a corporation authorizing a specific vote on their behalf at a corporate meeting [personnel placeholder plead poll power pro procurator replacement representative reserve responsibility office organization yea yes]
*prudence 13-59-11 (n.) 1. discretion in practical affairs 2. knowing how to avoid embarrassment or distress [practicality pragmatism providence resource derive discretion distress embarrassment exercise natured calculation careful cautious circumspect]
*prudent 07-50-42 (a.) 1. careful and sensible; marked by sound judgment 2. showing wise self-restraint in speech and behavior especially in preserving prudent silence [peaceful plan practical pragmatic prepared preserve profitable prompt provide provision prude ready reasonable reflective responsible restraint right ruler useful deal decency derive desirable discreet distress divination economize enlighten even exercise expediency natured neutrality noncommittal nonviolence tentative thorough thoughtful trust] "a prudent manager"
*prudential 07-41-42 (a.) 1. arising from or characterized by prudence especially in business matters [partly practical provident prudent reason depend abstain arise /lait/] "he abstained partly for prudential reasons"
*prudery 25-62-1 (n.) 1. excessive or affected modesty [permissivenes prim prissy puritan reserve excessive]
*prudish 22-68-2 (a.) 1. exaggeratedly proper [prig prissy proper puritanical relaxed right squaretoed squeamish starchy straitlaced stuffy suitable]
*prune 08-56-32 (n.) 1. dried plum (v.) 1. cultivate, tend, and cut back the growth of"dress the plants in the garden" 2. weed out unwanted or unnecessary things [pare part peel pithy plant plow plum pointed poll pollard preserve rake rationalize reap reduce remain remove reserved rid rune unnecessary unwanted nip elide eliminate elliptic encourage epigrammatic except exclude]
*prurient 16-62-6 (a.) 1. characterized by lust [passionate pornographic priapic prying randy ribald rooster rouse rubberneck ruttish unhealthy unsex unwholesome uri immodest indecent inquisitive interest interested itch ejaculatory embrace employer erotomania nature nosy nymphomaniac tend thirsty titillate]
*pry 12-28-14 (n.) 1. a heavy iron lever with one end forged into a wedge (v.) 1. search or inquire in a meddlesome way 2. be nosey 3. to move or force, esp. in an effort to get something open 4. make an uninvited or presumptuous inquiry [pail peer people personal pickup pivot poke presumptuous prise private prize probing pull pushy raise research rigid root yenta]
*pseudonym 12-54-13 (n.) 1. a fictitious name used when the person performs a particular social role [pen perform plume pseudo publication social stage original nom /due nod/]
*psychiatry 10-36-20 (n.) 1. the branch of medicine dealing with the diagnosis and treatment of mental disorders [psych specialty hygiene]
*psychic 10-41-20 (a.) 1. pertaining to forces or mental processes outside the possibilities defined by natural or scientific laws 2. affecting or influenced by the human mind 3. outside the sphere of physical science (n.) 1. a person apparently sensitive to things beyond the natural range of perception [paranormal parapsychology perception pertain phenomena philosophical phrenic predict processe psych psychological second sensitive sentient serve shadowy sighted spectral spiritualism stargaze subjective supernatural supernaturalism supposedly cerebral clairvoyant cognitive conceptual haruspex hyperphysical immaterial imponderable impressionable influence insubstantial intangible intermediary internal intuitive] "psychic reader"
*psychopathic 19-69-4 (a.) 1. suffering from an undiagnosed mental disorder [paranoid psychopath psychotic sane schizy suffering catatonic certifiable afflict insane]
*psychotherapy 10-42-19 (n.) 1. the branch of psychiatry concerned with psychological methods 2. the treatment of mental or emotional problems by psychological means [counsel hygiene hypnotism therapy treatment est /pare/]
*pucker 20-50-3 (n.) 1. an irregular fold in an otherwise even surface (as in cloth) (v.) 1. to gather something into small wrinkles or folds 2. draw fabric together and sew it tightly 3. become puckered [perplexity pinch pleat plication puck pull purse uneasy unsettle upc upset care cloth cloud cockle concentration condensation contract cramped crease crimp crinkle crisp curtail knit knot embarrassment reduction ridge ripple rounded ruck rugged rumple run /cup/] "She puckered her lips"
*pudgy 20-32-3 (a.) 1. short and fat [plump podgy portly puffy desirable distended dumpy gross /dup/]
*puerile 19-79-4 (a.) 1. of or characteristic of a child 2. displaying or suggesting a lack of maturity [pompous problem progeny property puerilism unreasonable unsound reach reckless response ridiculous rile

immature immaturity inanity indiscretion infancy infantile insecurity insignificant irrationality irresponsible issue lack /lire/] "puerile breathing"
*pugnacious 15-62-7 (a.) 1. tough and callous by virtue of experience 2. ready and able to resort to force or violence [partisan polarize polemic prospect pug pursuit unfriendly gentle give aggressive antagonistic argumentative attitude callous chauvinist combative confrontation contentious incline inimical intimidate irascible irritable offensive savage scrappy sentimentality show soldierly spirit /can/] "pugnacious spirits...lamented that there was so little prospect of an exhilarating disturbance"
*puissant 25-63-1 (a.) 1. (archaic) powerful [possession potency powerless prestigious prominent important influential irresistible senior strong substantial supreme absolute ant archaism authorize autocratic nervy telling totalitarian /ass/]
*pulmonary 16-45-6 (a.) 1. relating to or affecting the lungs [pant pneumonic puff pulmo lung organ nasal affecting asthmatic respiratory rhinal] "pulmonary disease"
*punctilious 22-75-2 (a.) 1. marked by precise accordance with details [painstaking particular polite practice precise proper punctilio narrow nice careful civil close complex conscientious convention correct courteous critical trivial loyal observant orderly scrupulous seemly sensitive sharp show strict subtle /oil/]
*punctual 15-77-7 (a.) 1. acting or arriving or performed exactly at the time appointed [painstaking particular payment perform place point possess precision prompt property pun uniformity narrow nicety nimble careful close constant correct critical timely accurate active acute alert arrange arrive loyal] "she expected guests to be punctual at meals"
*pundit 08-77-33 (n.) 1. someone who has been admitted to membership in a scholarly field [person philosopher political polymath professor nut dilettante discipline dit doctor don indian initiate instructor teacher technician]
*pungency 22-32-2 (n.) 1. having a sharp bitter flavor 2. having an acrid smell 3. a sharp bitter taste property [pithy pointed power property evoke caustic]
*pungent 10-40-18 (a.) 1. sharp biting or acrid especially in taste or smell 2. capable of wounding [painful part pep peppery pierce piquant pithy plant poignant pointed powerful property uninteresting unripe upset nip garlic gent ginger gnawing grave green elongate epigrammatic evoke exciting excruciating expressive tangy tast tasty torment trenchant] "tasting the pungent wood sorrel"
*punitive 09-40-24 (a.) 1. inflicting punishment [penal penitentiary penology punitory unit implacable impose inflict irreconcilable taxation vengeful vindictive] "punitive justice"
*purgatory 16-59-6 (n.) 1. a temporary condition of torment or suffering 2. (theology) a place where Roman Catholics think those who have died in a state of grace undergo limited torment to expiate their sins [painful passion pen place pound uncomfortable undergo underworld unpleasant until unusual rack rational religious remain repent roman gator grace abuse agony anguish asceticism temporary theology think torment torture truth /rota tag/] "a purgatory of drug abuse"
*purloin 22-48-2 (v.) 1. make off with belongings of others [palm pilfer pinch poach pocket rustle lift loin owner include item nick nip nobble]
*purport 08-46-30 (n.) 1. the intended meaning of a communication 2. general meaning or tenor (v.) 1. propose or intend 2. have the often specious appearance of being, intending, or claiming [people pervade plan point port prediction principal project propose provide undertone upshot utterance rationale reason relation relevant remark research resolve opinion ostensible overall overtone tenor think thrust true] "The letter purports to express people's opinion"
*purvey 20-48-3 (v.) 1. supply with provisions [pass people provide provision publish pur render]
*purveyor 12-46-13 (n.) 1. someone who supplies provisions (especially food) [patron provision purvey retail ridicule vendor victualer outlet]
*pusillanimous 25-69-1 (a.) 1. lacking in courage and manly strength and resolution; contemptibly fearful [poorspirited show sill spineless strength ignoble lack lily liver nervous manly /mina sup/]
*putrid 22-66-2 (a.) 1. of or relating to or attended by putrefaction 2. having undergone infection 3. offensively malodorous 4. in an advanced state of decomposition and having a foul odor 5. morally corrupt or evil [perverse physical punk purulent pussy put putrescent ulcerate undergo unhealthy unpleasant taint rancid rank raw reek rot icky imply incorrupt infection integrity decay decomposition dirty disease disgusting disintegrate /dirt tup/] "putrid decomposition"
*pyre 22-66-2 (n.) 1. wood heaped for burning a dead body as a funeral rite [pile rite roast]
*pyromania 25-60-1 (n.) 1. an uncontrollable desire to set fire to things [passion raise red roast romania madman mania maniac motive arson arsonist ignition immolate incendiarism incinerate insane irrational irresistible]
*pyrotechnic 22-49-2 (a.) 1. of or relating to the draft of making fireworks 2. suggestive of fireworks [paper percussion pinwheel powder project rate remarkable rocket one ordinary technic technique throw trade tube exceptional explosive candle cap case charge circular colored combustion cracker craft cylindrical hard heavy highly noise illuminate] "pyrotechnic smokes"

Q

*quack 17-56-5 (a.) 1. medically unqualified (n.) 1. an untrained person who pretends to be a physician and who dispenses medical advice 2. the harsh sound of a duck (v.) 1. utter quacking noises 2. act as a medical quack or a charlatan [qua qualify unqualified untrained utter advice alleviate artist attract audible call carol certain charlatan cheat chuck claim comport con conduct cure customer] "a quack doctor"
*quackery 25-52-1 (n.) 1. the dishonesty of a charlatan [quack advice charlatan cheat empiricism experience]
*quadruple 09-54-22 (a.) 1. having four units or components 2. four times as great or many (n.) 1. a quantity that is four times as great as another (v.) 1. increase fourfold [quad quantity amount augment describe dosage rhythm part product earn entity expand] "quadruple rhythm has four beats per measure"
*quaff 20-76-3 (n.) 1. a hearty draft (v.) 1. to swallow hurriedly or greedily or in one draught [qua quick alcoholic fast food]
*quagmire 15-50-7 (n.) 1. a soft wet area of low-lying land that sinks underfoot [quag quandary quicksand underfoot unfit area awkward give glade ground marshy mere mess mire mix morass muddle imbroglio embarrassment entangle escape everglade /rim/]
*quail 13-44-11 (n.) 1. (game bird) flesh of quail; suitable for roasting or broiling if young; otherwise must be braised 2. small gallinaceous game birds (v.) 1. draw back, as with fear or pain [quai quake quaver quiff american avoid lassie last]
*quake 11-43-15 (n.) 1. shaking and vibration at the surface of the earth resulting from underground movement along a fault plane of from volcanic activity (v.) 1. shake with fast, tremulous movements 2. shake with seismic vibrations, as of planets [qua quaver quick quiver underground uneasy unrest upheaval agitation ague apoplexy aspen earth]
*qualification 05-82-88 (n.) 1. the act of modifying or changing the strength of some idea 2. an attribute that must be met or complied with and that fits a person for something 3. a statement that limits or restricts some claim [qualify upheaval ability adjustment appropriate limitation improvement instinct facility fit fitness capacity cation color conversion talent term transition overthrow /fila/] "her qualifications for the job are excellent"
*qualify 02-68-361 (v.) 1. make fit or prepared 2. make more specific 3. pronounce fit or able 4. prove capable or fit; meet requirements 5. (grammar) add a modifier to a constituent 6. describe or portray the character or the qualities or peculiarities of 7. specify as a condition or requirement in a contract or agreement; make an express demand or provision in an agreement [qualify quantity undertake university unmitigated unsuitable able accelerate add adequate adjust administer alif alter answer appropriate assuage attribute label legal lessen license life likely limit improve impute include indispose individuate injection instruct farewell fast feature first fit fitting fixed formation fulfill function future /fila/]
*qualm 11-56-15 (n.) 1. uneasiness about the fitness of an action 2. a mild state of nausea [qua queasy queer uncertainty uneasy unpleasant unwilling agitation

airsickness alms anticipation anxious apprehensive march meticulous mild misfortune misgiving modesty]
*quandary 12-34-12 (n.) 1. a situation from which extrication is difficult especially an unpleasant or trying one 2. state of uncertainty or perplexity especially as requiring a choice between equally unfavorable options [uncertainty unfavorable unpleasant unresolvable upset affair almost and awkward node nonplus dangerous deal difficulty dilemma distress disturbance receive require riddle]
*quantity 05-56-77 (n.) 1. an adequate or large amount 2. how much there is of something that you can measure 3. something that has a magnitude and can be represented in mathematical expressions by a constant or a variable [quality quant quantum question universal abstract abundance account adequate alcoholic ammunition amount analogous antiknock area arm assume available nature nest number numerical numerous teem test thousand total twice ictus idea import infer instant interval ionic yardstick] "he had a quantity of ammunition"
*quarantine 12-53-12 (n.) 1. enforced isolation of patients suffering from a contagious disease in order to prevent the spread of disease 2. isolation to prevent the spread of infectious disease (v.) 1. place into enforce isolation, as for medical reasons [unfrequented alien animal anti apart rail reason recess removed retirement retreat narrow thrash thresh tight imprison incarcerate inclusion infectious insulate isolation enclose encompass enforce enter envelop exclusive expose] "My dog was quarantined before he could live in England"
*quarrelsome 22-42-2 (a.) 1. given to quarreling [quarrel querulous unfriendly adverse aggressive antagonistic argumentative rancorous repugnant enemy eristic litigious savage soldierly struggle offensive malevolent martial military]
*quarter 01-47-863 (a.) 1. consisting of one of four equivalent parts (n.) 1. a district of a city having some distinguishing character 2. one of four equal parts 3. (British) a quarter of a hundredweight (28 pounds) 4. a fourth part of a year; three months 5. a quarter of a hundredweight (25 pounds) 6. a unit of time equal to 15 minutes or a quarter of an hour 7. a United States coin worth one fourth of a dollar 8. an unspecified person 9. one of four periods into which the school year is divided 10. one of four periods of play into which some games are divided 11. one of the four major division of the compass 12. piece of leather that comprises the part of a shoe or boot covering the heel and joining the vamp 13. the rear part of a ship (v.) 1. provide housing for, of military personnel 2. pull (a person) apart with four horses tied to his extremities, so as to execute him 3. divide by four; divide into quarters 4. divide into quarters [quadrumanous quarte quarto quinquennium quota unicorn united achievement aim area arm armory ragged range rent rive room rose run tattered tear term tincture tract trend tressure eagle ensconce entertain escutcheon] "a quarter of a pound"
*quarterly 05-41-65 (a.) 1. of or relating to or consisting of a quarter (ad.) 1. in diagonally opposed quarters of an escutcheon 2. in three month intervals (n.) 1. a periodical that is published every quarter [quarter quotidian annual appear arm report review tertian three triennial trim ephemeris escutcheon year yearly] "quarterly report"
*quartet 05-44-71 (n.) 1. the cardinal number that is the sum of three and one 2. a musical composition for four performers 3. four performers or singers who perform together 4. four people considered as a unit 5. a set of four similar things considered as a unit [quadruplet quarte quaternity quatrefoil quintet unaccompanied alliance amalgamation assembly reciprocity rectangle teamwork tee tetrad trio triumvirate troop troupe ecumenism element ensemble /tetra/] "he joined a barbershop quartet"
*quay 11-92-17 (n.) 1. wharf usually built parallel to the shoreline [qua unload access]
*quell 10-53-21 (v.) 1. suppress or crush completely 2. overcome or allay [quash quench quiet unman ease ell extinguish limited lull]
*querulous 22-57-2 (a.) 1. habitually complaining [quarrelsome unco uneasy unfulfilled unhappy envious express rebellious resentment restless lou sorrowful sour sulky /lure/]
*query 07-67-34 (n.) 1. an instance of questioning (v.) 1. pose a question [question quiz quodlibet uncertainty enquiry examine expect express report request reservation rubberneck]
*queue 05-96-82 (n.) 1. a line of people or vehicles waiting for something 2. (information processing) an ordered list of tasks to be performed or messages to be transmitted 3. a braid of hair at the back of the head (v.) 1. form a queue, form a line, stand in line [upright early echelon employment]
*quibble 12-56-12 (n.) 1. an evasion of the point of an argument by raising irrelevant distinctions or objections (v.) 1. evade the truth of a point or question by raising irrelevant objections 2. argue over petty things [question quip quirk unimportant unpleasant impute irrelevant issue belittle bicker boggle brabble literally elude equivocate equivocation evade evasion exception] "Let's not quibble over pennies"
*quiescent 22-37-2 (a.) 1. not active or activated 2. being quiet or still or inactive 3. causing no symptoms 4. marked by a state of tranquil repose [quietude unchecked unfailing unmoved idle inactive inactivity increase inert influence intact interruption isolated ease ebb enduring estivation exert extinct scent slow sluggish solar solidity stay still summer suspension sustain symptom calm centimeter cessation changeless comparable constant continue cool near neutral noiseless temporary torpid town tranquil tumor] "the

quiescent level of centimeter wave-length solar radiation"
*quiet 02-52-424 (a.) 1. in a softened tone 2. without untoward incident or disruption 3. free from disturbance 4. free of noise or uproar; or making little if any sound 5. not showy or obtrusive 6. characterized by an absence or near absence of agitation or activity 7. (astronomy; of the sun) characterized by a low level of surface phenomena like sun spots e.g. (ad.) 1. with little or no activity or especially agitation (n.) 1. the absence of sound 2. an untroubled state; free from disturbances 3. a period of calm weather 4. a disposition free from stress or emotion (v.) 1. make calm or still 2. become quiet or quieter [quell quiescent unassuming uncomplicated understated undisturbed uniformity uninterrupted unobtrusive unofficial unpleasant unruffled idle idyllic impassive imperturbable inaudible intent intimate isolated ease easy ebb elegant excellent tame tasty termination town tranquil tranquillize trouble turbulence] "a quiet life"
*quintessence 09-49-26 (n.) 1. (archaic) the fifth and highest element after air and earth and fire and water; was believed to be the substance composing all heavenly bodies 2. the most typical example or representative of a type 3. the purest and most concentrated essence of something [queen quiddity ultimate unique universe unparalleled ideal idiosyncrasy illustration infusion instance intrinsic inward item naturalistic nitty nonpareil normal nub nucleus typal typical earth elect element elite embodiment epitome essence essential ether experience expert extract say select soul space spirit stuff substance sum supreme center champion chemistry choice compose concentrate constitute core cosmology counteract /ness set/]
*quintet 10-33-21 (n.) 1. a musical composition for five performers 2. the cardinal number that is the sum of four and one 3. a set of five similar things considered as a unit 4. five performers or singers who perform together 5. five people considered as a unit [quartet quint quintuplet instrument teamwork trio triumvirate troop troupe ecumenism element ensemble]
*quirk 05-59-64 (n.) 1. a strange attitude or habit 2. a narrow groove beside a beading (v.) 1. twist or curve abruptly [quality queer quibble quip unconventional unexpected unfamiliar unnatural unpredictable unrestrained unusual idiosyncrasy impression index individual irk irregular record keynote kinky knot kooky] "She quirked her head in a peculiar way"
*quite 01-67-804 (ad.) 1. to the greatest extent; completely 2. of an unusually noticeable or exceptional or remarkable kind (not used with a negative) 3. to a degree (not used with a negative) 4. actually or truly or to an extreme [quality quantity quit understand undoubtedly unusual utterly ill impressive indicate indubitable irrevocable tasty think thorough totally true truly emphasize entirely exactly exceptional expression extent extremely] "quite tasty"
*quixotic 15-44-7 (a.) 1. not sensible about practical matters; unrealistic [unrealistic idealistic impractical impulsive optimistic otherworldly otic overlook tend transmundane chimerical consider] "as quixotic as a restoration of medieval knighthood"
*quotidian 20-50-3 (a.) 1. found in the ordinary course of events [quality quite unremarkable ordinary ian illness daily day degree describe diamant add anita attack nothing /dit/]

R

*rabble 16-67-6 (n.) 1. a disorderly crowd of people 2. disparaging terms for the common people [rag ragtag riffraff robber rout ruck abb army authority bobtail bourgeoisie lack legal legion /bar/]
*rabid 15-50-8 (a.) 1. marked by excessive enthusiasm for and intense devotion to a cause or idea [radical rage rant abandon amok ardent belief bellow berserk bid bigoted blind idea ill infect infuriate insane intense irrational isolationist dedicated derange desperate devotion disease distracted /bar/] "rabid isolationist"
*raconteur 19-63-4 (n.) 1. a person skilled in telling anecdotes [recite relator adventure conte conversationalist narrator novelist taleteller tell entertain exaggerate /rue/]
*racy 12-71-14 (a.) 1. full of zest or vigor 2. suggestive of sexual impropriety [reference rich risky risque root rude run adult anecdote animation arouse asterisk coarse crude curry] "a racy literary style"
*radiance 17-50-5 (n.) 1. the quality of being bright and sending out rays of light 2. the amount of electromagnetic radiation leaving or arriving at a point on a surface 3. an attractive combination of good health and happiness [radian radius range ray receive reflect refulgent region resplendence amount appearance area arrive atmosphere attractive aura delight demeanor diffusion discernible disease dispersion illustrious incandescence intense irradiation nimbus charisma combination continuum corona coruscate countenance eclipse effulgence electromagnetic emanation emit emotion energy envelope] "the radiance of her countenance"
*radiate 11-46-17 (v.) 1. send out real or metaphoric rays 2. send out rays or waves 3. spread into new habitates and produce variety or variegate 4. cause to be seen by emitting light as if in rays 5. esp. of the complexion: show a strong bright color, such as red or pink 6. experience a feeling of well-being or happiness, as from good health or an intense emotion 7. issue or emerge in rays or waves 8. extend or spread outward from a center or focus or inward towards a center [radi radiative ray retail alter approach asymptotic dazzle disseminate distribute incandescence issue tangential transmit twinkle emanate emit] "The sun radiates heat"
*radical 03-56-195 (a.) 1. (used of opinions and actions) far beyond the norm 2. arising from or going to the root 3. markedly new or introducing radical change 4. (linguistics) of or relating to or constituting a linguistic root 5. (botany) especially of leaves; located at the base of a plant or stem; especially arising directly from the root or rootstock or a root-like stem (n.) 1. (chemistry) two or more atoms bound together as a single unit and forming part of a molecule 2. a person who has radical ideas or opinions 3. an atom or group of atoms with at least one unpaired electron; in the body it is usually an oxygen molecule than has lost an electron and will stabilize itself by stealing an electron from a nearby molecule 4. a character conveying the lexical meaning of a logogram 5. a sign placed in front of an expression to denote that a root is to be extracted 6. (linguistics) the form of a word after all affixes are removed [absolutely acid acyl advance agent dead deep digital downright drastic ical immeasurable impossible indefinitely

infinite inherent intensive central character clear completely larboard /acid/] "in the body free radicals are high-energy particles that ricochet wildly and damage cells"
*raffish 19-52-4 (a.) 1. marked by smartness in dress and manners 2. marked by a carefree unconventionality or disreputableness [rakish red roughneck ruffian accordance alienate antic approve fashionable fast fish free individual showy smart snappy society spiffy spirited sporty spruce stylish hat hotel /far/]
*rampant 07-55-34 (a.) 1. unrestrained and violent 2. (heraldry) rearing on left hind leg with forelegs elevated and head usually in profile [rage raise rambling rear rich rife right rise abandon abutment affluent aggression armorial average manner many mounting much multiply pandemic pant plenty popular position posture productive profile proliferate nonrestrictive normal numerous teem terrorist threaten trace] "rampant aggression"
*rampart 16-58-6 (n.) 1. an embankment built around a space for defensive purposes [redan redoubt regular road roadblock roman abatis abutment across arrow artificial average mark meter mile moat mole mound munition palisade parapet part point portcullis protective province purpose tenaille top trumpet tumble /trap/] "they stormed the ramparts of the city"
*rancor 15-18-8 (n.) 1. a feeling of deep and bitter anger and ill-will [rankle resentment retaliate revengeful rich acerbic acrimony admiration amicable anger antagonism antipathy avenge nasty caustic choler clash collide conflicting cor]
*rancorous 19-36-4 (a.) 1. showing deep-seated resentment [rancor resentment rich acrimonious amicable nasty show spiteful splenetic]
*rankle 14-56-9 (v.) 1. gnaw into; make resentful or angry [rack rag rancorous remember resentment rile rub run acerbic acidulous acrimonious anger ankle annoyance arouse nag nark needle nettle nip lacerate eat embitter exasperate excruciate /elk/] "The unjustice rankled her"
*rant 08-75-27 (n.) 1. a loud bombastic declamation expressed with strong emotion 2. pompous or pretentious talk or writing (v.) 1. talk in a noisy, excited, or declamatory manner [rabbit rage rambling ramp rate rave raver read repetitive rhetoric roister ruin abandon act affect aggressive amok announce ant assault attack noisy nonsense talk theatrical threaten tirade tone transported trash trumpet tumultuous]
*rapacious 16-63-6 (a.) 1. living by preying on other animals especially by catching living prey 2. devouring or craving food in great quantities 3. excessively greedy and grasping [rap raptorial ravenous reprehensible abstemious acquisitive aggressive animal appetite avaricious avid parasitic piggish pillage possession predatory prey prowl pursuit catching claim consumption covet cram crapulous craving creditor cupidity idea incontinent insatiable insatiate intemperate obtain offal omnivorous unscrupulous usury shark show sordid stuffing swinish /cap capa/]
*rapid 02-48-284 (a.) 1. done or occurring in a brief period of time 2. characterized by speed; moving with or capable of moving with high speed (n.) 1. a part of a river where the current is very fast [rap rate ready regular repeat ripple rise river rock running rush abrupt agile alacrity always apace pace part perennial period perpetuity plummet pounce precipitous progress prompt property immediate incessant inclination increase instant instantly dashing debacle decisive delay descent despatch dispatch drop /dip/] "a rapid rise through the ranks"
*rapt 15-45-7 (a.) 1. deeply moved 2. wholly absorbed as in thought [rap relentless resolute reverie rhapsodic absorbed abstract admiration apt arrest attentive permanent persist plug tenacious tireless totally transported] "sat completely still, enraptured by the music"
*rash 07-61-34 (a.) 1. imprudently incurring risk 2. marked by unthinking boldness; with defiant disregard for danger or consequences (n.) 1. any red eruption of the skin 2. a series of unexpected unpleasant occurrences [rare reckless red repent response rheum robbery roseola abrupt adventurous affair alacrity allergic ash attempt audacious seize series shock skin speed sudden surface sweat swift symptom happening hasty heat heedless hemorrhage high hijack hubris humidity hurried] "a rash of bank robberies"
*ration 08-62-30 (n.) 1. a fixed portion that is allotted (especially in times of scarcity) 2. the food allowance for one day (especially for service personnel) (v.) 1. restrict the consumption of a relatively scarce commodity, as during war 2. distribute in rations, as in the army [ratio regular rein repertory restrict retardation retrench rick abundance accord adequate administer allowance amass amount apart apportion apportionment army asset assignment available treasury trip troop tucker inhibition injunction interest inventory issue official number nutrition] "the rations should be nutritionally balanced"
*rationalism 19-51-4 (n.) 1. the doctrine that knowledge is acquired by reason without resort to experience 2. the theological doctrine that human reason rather than divine revelation establishes religious truth 3. the doctrine that reason is the right basis for regulating conduct [rational rationalize realistic reason reasoning reference regulate religious resort revelation right accept acquire adherent allegorize animism annotate apologetics authoritative test theism theory truth idealistic illustrative instrumentalist investigate naturalistic nominalism logic school search secularism sensationalism sophistry source syncretism systematics]
*raucous 09-47-25 (a.) 1. disturbing the public peace; loud and rough 2. unpleasantly loud and harsh [ragged

ribald riotous rough rude absonant atonal undisciplined unmusical unpleasant unruly cacophony characterize choke coarse cracked off orderly sharp shout sound sour strangle strident] "a raucous party"
*ravage 08-49-31 (n.) 1. (usually plural) a destructive action (v.) 1. make a pillaging or destructive raid on (a place), as in wartimes 2. devastate or ravage [raid ransack rape rapist ratty raze reduce resolvent rifler rob ruinous ablative abuse adulterate age alloy area army valuable vandalize vaporize village violate grubby gut effect encroach enemy engorge erosive] "the ravages of time"
*rave 08-61-31 (n.) 1. a dance party that lasts all night and electronically synthesized music is played 2. an extravagantly enthusiastic review (v.) 1. participate in an all-night techno dance party 2. talk in a noisy, excited, or declamatory manner 3. praise enthusiastically [rabbit rage rant rare rate raving receive restaurant review rhetoric riot ruin abandon abuse add admiration allnight anarchic angry approval article assault attack audience ave vaporing vehement vilify violent vogue effervesce electronicall enthuse enthusiastical essay evaluation excited explode expression extol extravagant] "raves are very popular in Berlin"
*ravenous 17-56-5 (a.) 1. extremely hungry 2. devouring or craving food in great quantities [ragged rapacious raptorial ravening abstemious acquisitive appetite avaricious avid venal venous voracious vulture vulturine eat edacious empty enemy esurient excess extortionate extremely omnivorous sharpset sleep sordid starve stuffing /one/]
*ravine 16-52-6 (n.) 1. a deep narrow steep-sided valley (especially one formed by running water) [rainfall ravin rent rift river run rupture abyss area arroyo vale valley vine void incision intervale itv narrow notch nullah excavation]
*raze 12-32-12 (v.) 1. tear down so as to make flat with the ground [rase rasp ruin ablate align annihilate erase erode even]
*reaction 02-50-285 (n.) 1. an idea evoked by some experience 2. (chemistry) a process in which one or more substances are changed into others 3. doing something in opposition to another way of doing it that you don't like 4. a bodily process occurring due to the effect of some foregoing stimulus or agent 5. (mechanics) the equal and opposite force that is produced when any force is applied to a body 6. extreme conservatism in political or social matters 7. a response that reveals a person's feelings or attitude [rebuff recession recoil effect experience eye action answer assumption attitude challenge change complaint conclusion idea impact interference objection observation opinion negativism neurosis notion] "he was pleased by the audience's reaction to his performance"
*reactionary 13-57-11 (a.) 1. extremely conservative (n.) 1. an extreme conservative; an opponent of progress or liberalism [reaction rebel returnable revolutionary rightist rightwinger royalist elderly extremely antediluvian antique atavistic cartoon center character clash colonel complain con conservative create tory traditionalism idea illiberal imperialist inimical intellectual intolerant intransigent off opinion oppose opposition orthodox outdate nonconformist]
*readily 05-45-61 (ad.) 1. without much difficulty 2. in a punctual manner [read right eager easily easy effortless enthusiastic enthusiastical anxious ardent avid delay dexterous difficulty identify immediately impatient instantly lightly little /lid/] "these snakes can be identified readily"
*readjust 17-49-5 (v.) 1. adjust anew 2. adjust again after an initial failure [realign rearrange rectify regulate accommodate accuracy achieve adapt adjust alter anew different set settle standard straighten] "After moving back to America, he had to readjust"
*ready 01-52-534 (a.) 1. brought into readiness 2. mentally disposed 3. (of especially money) immediately available 4. completely prepared or in condition for immediate action or use or progress 5. apprehending and responding with speed and sensitivity (n.) 1. poised for action (v.) 1. make ready or suitable or equip in advance for a particular purpose or for some use, event, etc 2. prepare for eating by applying heat [raise rapidity raw read reason repair require resign response ripe roof rot eager ease eat equip exam excellent exercise expert about accessible accord actual address advance agree alert alter ample apt arrange art astute attentive available decisive deep degree delight detonation diplomacy discern disposed doctor dress] "get ready"
*realism 07-49-36 (n.) 1. the philosophical doctrine that physical object continue to exist when not perceived 2. the attribute of accepting the facts of life and favoring practicality and literal truth 3. an artistic movement in 19th century France; artists and writers strove for detailed realistic and factual description 4. the philosophical doctrine that abstract concepts exist independent of their names 5. the state of being actual or real [real reasonable regularity empiricism epiphenomenalism animalism artless authenticity legitimate level literal sane sanity sensible sincerity materialism mechanism movement]
*rearrange 10-48-19 (v.) 1. put into a new order or arrangement [readjust redispose relocate reorganize reposition reschedule reshuffle room adjourn arrange assign] "Please rearrange these files"
*reassure 03-66-138 (v.) 1. give or restore confidence in; cause to feel sure or certain 2. cause to feel sure; give reassurance to [relieve remark restore ease effect encourage ensure establishment afflict agitation aid alleviate anxious ascertain assure auspicious safe settle solace soothe still substantiate support supportive sure sympathy uplift uplifting] "I reassured him that we were

safe"
*rebellious 10-54-20 (a.) 1. discontented as toward authority 2. resisting control or authority 3. participating in organized resistance to a constituted government [rebel recalcitrant refractory reluctant resist restless revolutionary envious estranged experience beef bitch breakaway leader longing loyal iconoclast ill incorrigible insurrectionary object obstructive oppose organize overthrow uncontrollable uneasy unhappy unmanageable unruly seditious show social stubborn submissive subordinate subversive sulky /oil/] "temperamentally rebellious"
*rebuff 07-46-37 (n.) 1. a deliberate discourteous act (usually as an expression of anger or disapproval) 2. an instance of driving away or warding off (v.) 1. reject outright and bluntly 2. force or drive back [reaction rebound recognize refusal rejection repulse resist reverse endure exception exclusion expression baffle beat block blunt bound brush buff upstage failure fight foil force fractious freeze frustration]
*rebuild 03-49-148 (v.) 1. build again [reconstruct recreate reerect reestablish reform remake remodel renew renovate repair repeat restructure revive revolutionary ruin better bomb breakup build building unmitigated imitation improve damage diversify doctor duplication] "The house was rebuild after it was hit by a bomb"
*rebuke 09-49-25 (n.) 1. an act or expression of criticism and censure (v.) 1. censure severely or angrily [rag rap rate real remonstrate rep earful enter expression bawl berate blow bring uke unfavorable upbraid knock] "he had to take the rebuke with a smile on his face"
*rebut 10-35-21 (v.) 1. prove to be false or incorrect 2. overthrow by argument, evidence, or proof [refute reject reply repudiate resistant response rule endorsement espouse evert evidence exception expose behalf belie break buck but undermine uphold upset traverse truth /tub tube tuber/]
*recalcitrant 15-45-8 (a.) 1. marked by stubborn resistance to and defiant of authority or guidance 2. marked by stubborn resistance to authority [rant reaction rebellion rebound refractory refuse reluctant resist revolve rival enemy enmity challenge clash compliant control cooperation cross adamant adverse alien antagonism antipathy authority aversion indomitable influence insubordinate interference intractable irrepressible teenager tractable trait necktie negativism noncooperation nonobservance /ace lace lacer/] "a recalcitrant teenager"
*recant 16-30-6 (v.) 1. formally reject or disavow a formerly held belief, usually under pressure [recall reject release religion renege repudiate resignation retract revoke early error exception exclusion expatriate cancellation cant cassation cast cede connection crossing abandon abjure abolition affirmation annul assertion nay negation nix nullify talk turnout /ace/]
*recapitulate 22-14-2 (v.) 1. summarize briefly 2. repeat stages of evolutionary development during the embryonic phase of life; of animals 3. repeat an earlier theme of a musical composition [reduce reduplicate rehash reiterate repeat replicate reprize resume retail retrograde review run early elide embryonic enumerate epitomize evolutionary capitulate composition contract crop cut abbreviate abridge abstract animal pad perform period phase play practice prune idea inventory itemize iterate telescope theme trim truncate life list /ace pace pacer tip/] "Let's recapitulate the main ideas"
*recapture 08-45-27 (n.) 1. a legal seizure by the government of profits beyond a fixed amount 2. the act of taking something back (v.) 1. capture anew 2. experience anew 3. capture anew 4. capture again, as of an escaped prisoner 5. take back by force, as after a battle [reflect regain remember represent restore retrieval educe emotional escape evoke exist experience express capture catching chase conquer corporation amount anew attempt author part past possession prisoner process profit public trover undergo /ace pace pacer/] "She could not recapture that feeling of happiness"
*recast 12-42-12 (v.) 1. cast again, in a different role 2. cast or model anew 3. cast again [reallocate redistribute redo refashion reforge remake remould reorganize repeat require road role electorate experience cast cracked actor alter anew art assign select skill tour /ace/] "He was recast as Iago"
*recede 09-47-26 (v.) 1. move back and away from 2. pull back or move away or backward 3. retreat 4. become faint or more distant [recession refer regress retiring retrogress return revert early ebb enemy engage essence cede certain close commitment condition curb decline decrease depart different diminish distant down drain draw drop dwindle dying]
*receivable 19-08-4 (a.) 1. awaiting payment [receptive recipient redeemable return revenue royalty earnings commission credit immediately income ingest intake inviting able account amount asset avail await back bill business /vie/] "accounts receivable"

*receptive 11-33-16 (a.) 1. open to arguments, ideas, or change 2. of a nerve fiber or impulse originating outside and passing toward the central nervous system 3. ready or willing to receive favorably [ready reason recept recipient responsive eager educate efferent enthusiastic entrance capable centripetal clever consent content convey pass persuasible pervious physiology plastic prompt proposal teachable tenderhearted toward tractile transmit idea impressive impulse influence interested] "receptive to reason and the logic of facts"
*recidivism 20-41-3 (n.) 1. habitual relapse into crime [reactionary rehabilitate relapse repetition return revert erring carnality cid civil collaborate convict crime criminality immoral impurity infirm irreverent defect

degenerate desertion disenchant vice vicious virtue sacrilege secessionist separatist setback sternway maintain /dice/]
*recidivist 25-53-1 (n.) 1. someone who is repeatedly arrested for criminal behavior (especially for the same criminal behavior) 2. someone who lapses into previous undesirable patterns of behavior [reversion cid civil commit convict criminal crook transgresse /dice/]
*recipient 05-33-68 (n.) 1. a person who gets something 2. the semantic role of the animate entity that is passively involved in the happening denoted by the verb in the clause [realize receive receptive recognition rely return right role entity equivalent estate career clause consign convey court influential ingest inherit intend inviting issue party passive patron pay payee permanent pie procure promise property protege noteworthy take tend title transplant trustee /pice/]
*reciprocal 15-48-8 (a.) 1. concerning each of two or more persons or things; especially given or done in return (n.) 1. (math) one of a pair of numbers whose product is 1: the reciprocal of 2/3 is 3/2; the inverse of 7 is 1/7 [relation requite respect retaliate retribution return reverse effect equal even exchange expression cal changeable character circle club combined communal compliment concern correlative crossing imaginary impossible infinite influence interchange invert pair parallel periodical plant privilege obverse odd opposite oscillate aid ally angle answer arrange associate avenge likeness logarithmic logic /pice/] "reciprocal aid"
*reciprocate 15-59-7 (v.) 1. act, feel, or give mutually or in return 2. alternate the direction of motion of [repay reply respond retaliate retort return empathize engineering equal equivalence exchange cate change combine comeback complementary cooperation correspondence counter interchange interplay invite partner payback perform permute position propeller proportional accept affiliate ally alternate alternation associate teeter totter trade transposition /pice taco/] "We always invite the neighbors and they never reciprocate!"
*reciprocity 20-33-3 (n.) 1. a relation of mutual dependence or action or influence 2. mutual exchange of commercial or other privileges [rapprochement reciprocate recognition relation retaliate return empathy entity equivalence exchange expression charity city commercial complementarity concept cooperative corr correspondence country identity influence interplay part peace people permutation privilege proportional obligation octet oneness tariff teamwork trade trio triumvirate /pice/]
*recitation 17-20-5 (n.) 1. written matter that is recited from memory 2. a regularly scheduled session as part of a course of study 3. systematic training by multiple repetitions 4. a public instance of reciting or repeating (from memory) something prepared in advance [read recital run exercise exhortation exposition citation instruction invective task teach tirade address allocution assignment oration narration] "the program included songs and recitations of well-loved poems"
*reckless 06-50-57 (a.) 1. marked by unthinking boldness; with defiant disregard for danger or consequences 2. characterized by careless unconcerned [rapid rash regardless running easy easygoing edith enough establish expeditious express extravagance careless casual childish climb clumsy consideration cursory lack lackadaisical lazy less listless lively safety seize senseless slapdash sloppy spasmodic speedy squander stuffy sudden swift /elk/]
*reclaim 06-57-51 (v.) 1. claim back 2. overcome the wildness of (an animal); make docile and tractable 3. make useful again; transform from a useless or uncultivated state 4. of materials from waste products 5. bring, lead, or force to abandon a wrong or evil course of life, conduct, and adopt a right one [recovery reform reformed regain regenerate remedy rescue restore retrieve return reuse revival ease claim comfort compromise conduct creature cultivation curable lapse life light aid ameliorate amends assist atonement improvement indemnity mend]
*recline 12-53-12 (v.) 1. move the upper body backwards and down 2. lie in a comfortable resting position [recumbent relax reposing rest ride end cant certain cline comfortable couch crawl lean list location loll lounge lounging lowness lying incline]
*recluse 16-61-6 (a.) 1. withdrawn from society; seeking solitude (n.) 1. one who lives in solitude [rec request eccentric eremite erratic character company crackpot crank life live loner unsocial salome screwball seek sequester society solitudinarian stylite /ulcer/]
*reclusive 12-58-13 (a.) 1. withdrawn from society; seeking solitude 2. providing privacy or seclusion [rec reside rest romantic exclude existence calm cloistered close companion confined life live lone unsocial seek sequester shade society solitude spot isolated /ulcer/] "lived an unsocial reclusive life"
*recognizance 20-01-3 (n.) 1. (law) a security entered into before a court with a condition to perform some act required by law; on failure to perform that act a sum is forfeited [release replevy require rule engagement enter escrow carry case claim cognizance collection commitment condition court creditor obligation gage impose indenture accuse agreement appear arrangement authority /zing/]
*recognize 03-01-223 (v.) 1. perceive to be the same 2. grant credentials to 3. express obligation, thanks, or gratitude for 4. express greetings upon meeting someone 5. detect with the senses 6. be fully aware or cognizant of 7. accept (smeone) to be what is claimed or accept his power and authority 8. show approval or appreciation of [realize receive remember respect reveal right endorse espy establish evident cognizable cognize comprehensible conceive confess conventional correct

credit observe oral orthodox outcrop own glimpse grant grasp greeting nail naked note noticeable identify immemorial insight inveterate /zing/]
*recoil 14-57-9 (n.) 1. the backward jerk of a gun when it is fired 2. a movement back from an impact (v.) 1. draw back, as with fear or pain 2. spring back; spring away from an impact 3. spring back, as from a forceful thrust [react rebound repercussion reply resilience response retreat return ricochet rubber elementary emission evade evasion exchange experience calf clash coil collision comeback cringe objection occurrence impact imprint instinctive interference involve leap location]
*recollect 19-54-4 (v.) 1. recall knowledge from memory; have a recollection [recall reflect refresh remember reminisce retain retrieve review eidetic enduring equanimous evoke call cant cite collect collected compose confident once last lasting love think together /cell cello/]
*recompense 19-78-4 (n.) 1. payment or reward (as for service rendered) 2. the act of compensating for service or loss or injury (v.) 1. make amends for; pay compensation for 2. make payment to; compensate [receive rectify reimburse remuneration render reparation replace restitution return reward right effort emend exchange circumstance comp compensation compromise correction cover offering offset overhaul meed mending mistake money pay payment perform price property punishment never salary satisfy service set square suffer sum]
*reconcile 07-43-34 (v.) 1. come to terms 2. accept as inevitable 3. bring into consonance or accord 4. make compatible with [recon regulate relation resigned resolve return reunite right easygoing equalize equivalent estrange eupeptic euphoric exist capable career century change clan coherent coincide come comfortable compatible compromise concur conform consonance contented cooperative coordinate correct obedient obey observe overlook impossible inevitable inharmony integrate long]
*recondite 25-47-1 (a.) 1. difficult to penetrate; incomprehensible to one of ordinary understanding or knowledge [rebuild recon recover repair require eclipse enigmatic enlighten esoteric exoteric expert circle close complex conceal confined covert obscure opaque ordinary overhaul deal deep degree difficult doctor impenetrable incomprehensible inexplicable inner tend theory transcendental]
*reconsider 06-39-46 (v.) 1. consider again; give new consideration to; usually with a view to changing 2. consider again (a bill) that had been voted upon before, in legislation [reassess recall reckon reevaluate reexamine reflection regard rethink retrace review revision change consider consideration correct see study decision deem] "Won't you reconsider your decision?"
*reconstruct 08-39-33 (v.) 1. build again 2. cause somebody to adapt or reform socially or politically 3. of past events 4. do over, as of (part of) a house 5. return to its original or usable and functioning condition [recover repair repeat change conjecture construct convert copy overthrow speculate subvert theorize /curt/]
*recourse 12-51-13 (n.) 1. act of turning to for assistance 2. something or someone turned to for assistance or security [refuge remedy reserve resource right route effort endorse entree exchange expedient capacity capital choice contribute course court observation option uncle security seek service shadow solution solve source stock sue support] "have recourse to the courts"
*recover 02-60-351 (v.) 1. regain a former condition after a financial loss 2. get over an illness or shock 3. get or find back; recover the use of 4. of materials from waste products 5. cover anew 6. regain or make up for [rebound recapture regain regress release repossess restore return reuse revert extricate claim computer convalesce cover offset vigor]
*recreate 07-48-35 (v.) 1. give new life or energy to 2. give encouragement to 3. engage in recreational activities rather than work; occupy oneself in a diversion 4. create anew [reconstruct refashion refresh reinvent renovate repair resuscitate return revivify embolden energy engage cheer children come confidence consciousness courage create alert amuse anew animate arouse treatment]
*recruit 02-62-312 (n.) 1. any new member or supporter (as in the armed forces) 2. a recently enlisted soldier (v.) 1. cause to assemble or enlist 2. seek to employ 3. register formally; as a participant or member [raise rebellion recent record reform register return rookie ecru employee engage english enlist enroll enrollment enter entrant establish exhortation catchword clothe commandeer company conscription constabulary contribute convert crew uniform unionize untrained upstart improve increase induction inexperience inscribe invest irish tan tenderfoot trainee transaction tyro] "The lab director recruited an able crew of assistants"
*rectify 11-66-16 (v.) 1. math: determine the length of 2. make right or correct 3. convert into direct current 4. set straight or right 5. reduce to a fine, unmixed, or pure state; separate from extraneous matter or cleanse from impurities 6. bring, lead, or force to abandon a wrong or evil course of life, conduct, and adopt a right one [rebuild rec reclaim recoverable reformed regenerate regulate remedy repay resolve restore reverse right edit emend exchange experiment expiation extend extract calculation clear commute compensation convert correct correction counterbalance cover curable cure tailor troubleshoot try tune improve indemnity investigation fit fix follow yield /fit/] "rectify a curve"
*rectitude 19-48-4 (n.) 1. uprightness as a consequence of being honorable and honest [rec reputable respectable right righteous erect estimable character

clean consequence correct immaculate incorruptible integrity upright decency]
*recuperate 10-54-18 (v.) 1. regain or make up for 2. regain a former condition after a financial loss 3. restore to good health or strength 4. get over an illness or shock [rally rate rebound recapture recover recruit regain regress remedy repossess rescue restore retrovert return revert effect energy exercise expect claim comeback conducive convalesce convalescent curative cure uplifting patient percolate perk pick pickup possession power previous promote pull absence abstract ameliorate around trover turn /puce tare/] "recuperate one's losses"
*recur 06-48-50 (v.) 1. return in thought or speech to something 2. happen or occur again 3. have recourse to [ration react reappear recall recourse regular relapse repeat resort resume return round run early echo employ chiefly circle closely come connection continuum course cur cycle undulation utilize] "This is a recurring story"
*recurrent 13-49-10 (a.) 1. recurring again and again [regular repeat require restricted return run effort endless epochal even chiefly chronic circle closely common constant continue current ubiquitous uniform usual nagging nerve nonstop thematic trite turn]
*redeem 08-48-30 (v.) 1. from sins, as in religious dogma 2. exchange or buy back for money; under threat 3. convert into cash; of commercial papers 4. pay off, as of loans or promissory notes [ransom receive recoverable redress refer reform release religious renew reputation rescue restore ease emancipate equivalent evil exchange excuse exonerate express extricate death debt deem deliver discharge disregard divine doctor dogma due manumit martyr mature mend money /meed/]
*redemption 07-56-35 (n.) 1. (Christianity) the act of delivering from sin or saving from evil 2. repayment of the principal amount of a debt or security at or before maturity (as when a corporation repurchases its own stock) 3. purchasing back something previously sold [rebirth reclaim recovery refurbish release religion renovate rescue emancipation emption excuse exemption exonerate expiation delivery pardon propitiate trover immunity improvement indemnity]
*redolent 14-55-9 (a.) 1. serving to bring to mind 2. having a strong distinctive fragrance 3. (used with 'of' or 'with') noticeably odorous [recall reminiscent retentive retrospective emanation essence evocative exhalation detect distinctive dole odorous odour olfactory literary nosegay note noticeable /lode ode/] "cannot forbear to close on this redolent literary note"
*redoubtable 16-75-6 (a.) 1. inspiring fear 2. having or worthy of pride [reason redoubt renowned respect eminent distinguished dreadful unnerve terrible terrific tough tremendous adversary alarming appalling awesome awful /ode/]
*redress 10-68-21 (n.) 1. a sum of money paid in compensation for loss or injury 2. act of correcting an error or a fault or an evil (v.) 1. make reparations or amends for [ready receive recompense rectify reimburse remedy reparation replace restitution return reward right emend equal error evil excessive experience expiation damage different dress salvage satisfaction satisfy service set situation smart soothe square sum sustain]
*redundancy 08-92-27 (n.) 1. the attribute of being superfluous and unneeded 2. repetition of messages to reduce the probability of errors in transmission 3. (electronics) a system design that duplicates components to provide alternatives in case one component fails 4. repetition of an act needlessly [rampant rank robot roundabout embarrassment enough excess extreme exuberant dancy deadwood decode deluge diffusive dismissal needless noise abundance amplitude attribute avalanche channel circumlocution configuration copious create /nude/] "the use of industrial robots created redundancy among workers"
*redundant 08-81-28 (a.) 1. more than is needed, desired, or required 2. repetition of same sense in different words 3. use of more words than required to express an idea [reiterate repetitive roundabout echo employment excess expression extra exuberant deem desire different diffusive dismiss dispensable distribute disuse dresser duplicate uncalled unessential unneeded unwanted needless nonessential abundant account advance amplification ant tautology tedious teem tend terminate true /nude/]
*reestablish 22-60-2 (v.) 1. bring back into original existence, use, function, or position [rebuild recall reconstruct recreate rede regenerate region reinvent remake repeat reproduce return emperor establish existence throne transform alter bring law /bats see seer/]
*refer 02-36-480 (v.) 1. think of, regard, or classify under a subsuming principle or with a general group or in relation to another 2. be about; have to do with; be relevant to; refer, pertain, or relate to 3. have as a meaning 4. seek information from 5. send or direct for treatment, information, or a decision 6. make reference to [racial rain raise recall recommit ref reflect relation relative relevant remember represent research resort respect responsibility return revolve run early emblematize entry error euphemize examine exclaim explicable express extraordinary favourably figure finger focus follow formula forward friendship]
*referee 03-90-233 (n.) 1. (sports) the chief official (as in boxing or American football) who is expected to ensure fair play 2. an attorney appointed by a court to investigate and report on a case 3. someone who reads manuscripts and judges their suitability for publication (v.) 1. be a referee or umpire 2. evaluate professionally a colleague's work [read reasoned ref refer report

represent require rule ensure evaluate exertion expect express fair follow football foul /refer/]
*refine 05-41-74 (v.) 1. make more complex, intricate, or richer 2. improve or perfect by pruning or polishing 3. attenuate or reduce in vigor, strength, or validity by polishing or purifying 4. make more precise or increase the discriminatory powers of 5. treat or prepare so as to put in a usable condition 6. reduce to a fine, unmixed, or pure state; separate from extraneous matter or cleanse from impurities [raise rarify ready rectify reduce remedy remove rhythmic rich rigorous round run ease easy educate effective elaborate elegant eliminate enhance equation even excess excite expert express extraneous fashion filter fine finetune finished focus food form forward idea impair improve impurity increase infuse intricate involve iron irritable itch narrow natural nice nurture nutrient] "refine one's style of writing"
*refinery 08-41-27 (n.) 1. an industrial plant for purifying a crude substance [refine riddle rocker filter finery industrial yard]
*reflection 04-50-89 (n.) 1. a likeness in which left and right are reversed 2. the image of something as reflected by a mirror (or other reflective material) 3. expression without words 4. the phenomenon of a propagating wave (light or sound) being thrown back from a surface 5. a calm lengthy intent consideration 6. a remark expressing careful consideration 7. (mathematics) a transformation in which the direction of one axis is reversed 8. the ability to reflect beams or rays [reaction read recall reflect effect evidence exception fancy fellow flashback likeness lucubration copy counsel criticism icon idea image impression observation opinion outline nagging note notion]
*reflector 22-34-2 (n.) 1. optical telescope consisting of a large concave mirror that produces an image that is magnified by the eyepiece 2. device that reflects radiation [radiation ray record reduce reflect refractor eyepiece focus form furnace lead len light camera center coelostat collector concentrate construct coronograph correct cosmic coud telescope temperature throw tilt observatory off optical orrery]
*reform 02-50-339 (n.) 1. a campaign aimed to correct abuses or malpractices 2. a change for the better as a result of correcting abuses 3. self-improvement in behavior or morals by abandoning some vice (v.) 1. make reforms in by removing abuse and injustices 2. break up the molecules of ("reform oil") 3. improve by alteration or correction of errors or defects and put into a better condition 4. produce by cracking 5. bring, lead, or force to abandon a wrong or evil course of life, conduct, and adopt a right one 6. change for the better [raise reclaim recruit rectify regenerate reorganization restructure return educate effort enhance enrich favor fit form forward overthrow meliorate mend mitigate modify] "reform a political system"
*reformer 09-40-23 (n.) 1. a disputant who advocates reform 2. an apparatus that reforms the molecular structure of hydrocarbons to produce richer fuel [radical reform revisionist revolutionary extremist former meliorism] "a catalytic reformer"
*refract 20-47-3 (v.) 1. subject to refraction, as of a light beam 2. determine the refracting power of (a lens) [energy enter experiment eye act alter appearance ascertain calculation course crook curve turn twist]
*refractory 25-36-1 (a.) 1. resistant to authority or control 2. stubbornly resistant to authority or control 3. marked by stubborn resistance to and defiant of authority or guidance 4. (medicine) not responding to treatment (n.) 1. lining consisting of material with a high melting point; used to line the inside walls of a furnace [rebellious refractor reluctant resistant responsive revolve rival easy enamel enemy fire force form fractious furnace acne adverse alien aluminum animal authority averse case child china clay command complain comply control cooperative corundum cover cross teenager temperature tractable treatment obedient obey object obstinate obstructive ornery oxide] "as refractory as a mule"
*refuge 06-44-52 (n.) 1. a safe place 2. something or someone turned to for assistance or security 3. act of turning to for assistance 4. a shelter from danger or hardship [recess recourse region resort retreat run effort evasion excuse eye facade feint front fuge fulfill furtherance uncle unpleasant geography gloss guard guise]
*refusal 05-53-88 (n.) 1. a message refusing to accept something that is offered 2. the act of refusing [rebut ref rejection reluctance repudiation request resistance embargo exception exclusion first forbidding fractious undercurrent unwilling slow snub statute stubborn substance accept acknowledge antipathy approve assent attitude authority aversion law]
*refute 11-51-15 (v.) 1. prove to be false or incorrect 2. overthrow by argument, evidence, or proof [reason rebut ref rehabilitate rejection rejoin reply repudiate resistant response elenchus error espouse establish evert evidence exception excuse false falsity find finish floor footage forswear undermine uphold upset try] "The speaker refuted his opponent's arguments"
*regale 15-67-8 (v.) 1. provide with choice or abundant food or drink [recreation regal relax relish renewal early eat entertainment entrance exhilarate expensive gale gift give gluttony gobble good grass gratify grazing abundant alcoholize amuse animate appetite licking /age lag lager/]
*regalia 19-46-4 (n.) 1. paraphernalia indicative of royalty (or other high office) 2. especially fine or decorative clothing [raiment regal ring rod rose royalty eagle emblem equipment gear general group apparatus appear appurtenance armory array article attire livery indicative insignia /age lag lager/]

*regenerate 07-86-38 (a.) 1. reformed spiritually or morally (v.) 1. re-establish on a new, usually improved, basis or make new or like new 2. bring, lead, or force to abandon a wrong or evil course of life, conduct, and adopt a right one 3. amplify (an electron current) by causing part of the power in the output circuit to act upon the input circuit 4. be formed or shaped anew 5. become regenerate 6. form or produce anew 7. replace (tissue or a body part) through the formation of new tissue 8. undergo regeneration 9. return to life; get or give new life or energy 10. restore strength [rebuild recover recruit reduce reform refurbish regulate renew renovate repeat revolution extremism generate generative gradualism growth new adoption aggravate amendment anew tissue transformation trouble /renege tare/] "a regenerate sinner"
*regent 08-61-32 (a.) 1. (combining form) acting or functioning as a regent or ruler (n.) 1. members of a governing board 2. someone who rules during the absence or incapacity or minority of the country's monarch [replacement rule effect gent govern great] "prince-regent"
*regime 03-71-195 (n.) 1. (medicine) a systematic plan for therapy (often including diet) 2. the organization that is the governing authority of a political unit [reduce refer reg regulation reign repeal revolution roman routine royal rule elect empire establishment exercise exile exist general goal govern government group impose include industrial manage management matter medication medicine method move]
*regimen 12-29-14 (n.) 1. (medicine) a systematic plan for therapy (often including diet) [recommend regime routine surgical exercise goal government improve include industry intend measure medicine non]
*regiment 06-77-46 (n.) 1. army unit smaller than a division (v.) 1. subject to rigid discipline, order, and systematization 2. assign to a regiment, of soldiers 3. form into a regiment, of military personnel [rally range rank regimen rigid rule entity exercise extent gang garrison give government group imagination impose individuality marshal military mob movement task team train troop] "regiment one's children"
*regional 02-41-257 (a.) 1. related or limited to a particular region 2. characteristic of a region [region extraterritorial geodetic geographic idiomatic navigation area authority limited location] "regional flora"
*regress 17-60-5 (n.) 1. the reasoning involved when you assume the conclusion is true and reason backward to the evidence 2. returning to a former state (v.) 1. go back to a statistical means 2. get worse; fall back to a previous or worse condition 3. go back to bad behavior 4. go back to a previous state [reaction reasoning recall recede recidivate recover regain relapse retrovert revert rise rule run early ebb effect egress emotional essence evidence exhibit generally grow gyrate shape shift soar spin statistics stretch supposedly /serge/]
*regretful 19-55-4 (a.) 1. having regret or sorrow or a sense of loss over something done or undone [regret relate remorseful repentant rueful exam guilty thwart turn felt foil frustrate undone letdown loss] "felt regretful over his vanished youth"
*rehabilitate 04-32-108 (v.) 1. reinstall politically 2. help to re-adapt, as to a former state of health or good repute 3. restore to a state of good condition or operation [rank readapt recover reeducate reestablish reform regenerate reinstate reorient repair replacement repute restoration restore return revitalize right exculpate explanation habilitate health help acclimatize adjustment assimilate backslide building improvement instauration lapse lifetime therapy town train transform turnabout /bah her/] "Deng Xiao Ping was rehabilitated several times throughout his lifetime"
*reign 05-64-87 (n.) 1. a period during which something or somebody is dominant or powerful 2. the period during which a monarch is sovereign 3. royal authority; the dominion of a monarch (v.) 1. be larger in number, quantity, power, status or importance 2. have sovereign power [regimen regulation resemble routine royal rule run effect egotism empire epidemic era excessive exercise extensive imperial important influence insinuation general govern government grip nation neighborhood normality noticeable] "Henry VIII reigned for a long time"
*reimburse 07-20-37 (v.) 1. pay back for some expense incurred 2. reimburse or compensate (someone), as for a loss [reason recover refund remunerate repay return expense imburse incur indemnify money balance satisfaction spent square /rub/] "Can the company reimburse me for my professional travel?"
*rein 07-55-35 (n.) 1. one of a pair of long straps (usually connected to the bit or the headpiece) used to control a horse 2. any means of control (v.) 1. control and direct with or as if by reins; as of a horse 2. stop or check by or as if by a pull at the reins 3. stop or slow up one's horse or oneself by or as if by pulling the reins 4. keep in check [race relax restriction rider right rule running elongate enjoin emperor exercise impede include indri inhibition injunction] "They reined in in front of the post office"
*reinstate 07-39-40 (v.) 1. restore to the previous state or rank 2. bring back into original existence, use, function, or position [recall reconstruct reestablish reform region rehabilitate replace replacement return emperor exculpate existence explanation improvement influence instate instauration throne transform turnabout alter]
*reiterate 06-47-50 (v.) 1. to say, state, or perform again [rank recap reduplicate render repeat repetitive rephrase request response restate resume retail retell review reword echo elaborate express extravagant exuberant imitative ingeminate interpret iterate iterative talkative tautology teem tell tirade tiresome translate twin

abundant amplitude /retie tare tie tier/]
*rejoin 08-51-29 (v.) 1. answer back 2. join again [react repay reply respond retort return riposte echo join organization]
*rejuvenate 09-60-25 (v.) 1. cause (a stream or river) to erode, as by an uplift of the land 2. return to life; get or give new life or energy 3. become young again 4. develop youthful topographical features; of land 5. make younger or more youthful [rebirth recover recruit redevelop reestablish refresh regenerate renew renewal renovate restore resurrect resuscitate return revival revivify river rugged run effective energy enjoyment erode erosion essence undergo unused update uplift vena vigorous vitality nature new animal annual appear area topography] "The contact with his grandchildren rejuvenated him"
*rejuvenation 16-58-6 (n.) 1. the phenomenon of vitality and freshness being restored 2. the act of restoring to a more youthful condition [rebirth recreate refreshment regenerate reinvigoratio relaxation renew renovate restore revival enjoyment vitality natural animal annual] "the annual rejuvenation of the landscape"
*relapse 15-57-8 (n.) 1. a failure to maintain a higher state (v.) 1. deteriorate in health 2. go back to bad behavior [reaction recession recidivism recovery regress rehabilitate retrogress return revert elapse lapse letdown life apostasy apparent patient position previous pullback seeming setback sicken sink sudden /pal pale spa/] "he relapsed"
*relegate 04-90-116 (v.) 1. assign to a lower position; reduce in rank 2. refer to another person for decision or judgment 3. expel, as if by official decree 4. assign to a class or kind [reduce refer reject remit exclude exile expel lag leave legate less lockout lower give accredit alga argue assignment attribute task throw transfer transport trust turnover /age tag/] "She likes to relegate difficult questions to her colleagues"
*relent 12-48-13 (v.) 1. give in, as to influence or pressure [relax reprieve resign rigid rule ebb last lent less thaw]
*relevant 04-66-117 (a.) 1. having a bearing on or connection with the subject at issue 2. having crucial relevance [real regard relative require research respect right effect essence extension lack law learn levant likely linguistics logical value virtue account advantage allowable applicable apply appropriate arrest associate attention tailored testimony /ave nave navel/] "the scientist corresponds with colleagues in order to learn about matters relevant to her own research"
*reliance 07-48-42 (n.) 1. the state of relying on something 2. certainty based on past experience [reception rely elia encourage endorse eventual experience lack leg lover imminent admire advocate aid certainty champion confidence considerable /nail nailer/] "he wrote the paper with considerable reliance on the work of other scientists"
*reliant 10-74-20 (a.) 1. relying on another for support [rely elia trusting /nail nailer/]
*relinquish 07-53-35 (v.) 1. relinquish to the power of another; yield to the control of another 2. part with a possession or right 3. turn away from; give up 4. release, as from one's hands 5. do without or cease to hold or adhere to [reach refrain release remove resign restraint retirement retreat right rope eli end endure entangle layoff leash legal let loose loss idea intent never quit quitclaim unloose sacrifice service spare specific stay stop sudden supersede surrender suspension switch halt hand handover hold house] "I am relinquishing my bedroom to the long-term house guest"
*reliquary 25-26-1 (n.) 1. a container where religious relics are stored or displayed (especially relics of saints) [remain remembrance repository ribbon eli loaded inscription arch]
*relish 05-71-77 (n.) 1. vigorous and enthusiastic enjoyment 2. spicy or savory condiment 3. the taste experience when a savoury condiment is taken into the mouth (v.) 1. derive or receive pleasure from; get enjoyment from; take pleasure in [racy receive ease eat elation eli enhance enjoyment entertainment enthusiastic european excitement experience eye lemon like love luxury incident infatuation interest salt sauce savoury sensation side smack soluble soul spicy spirit stimulus strong sweet heat hotness hungry /sile/] "She relished her fame and basked in her glory"
*reluctance 06-52-49 (n.) 1. (physics) opposition to magnetic flux (analogous to electric resistance) 2. a certain degree of unwillingness [ratio reaction refusal reluct resistance electricity energy equal exert lack languor lazy leisurely unwilling cautious certain challenge circuit close commit complaint tentative trait agree antipathy averse aversion natural negativism noncooperation] "a reluctance to commit himself"
*reluctant 03-52-168 (a.) 1. not eager 2. unwilling to become involved 3. unwillingness to do something contrary to your custom [rebellious relaxed reluct repellent eager easily easy enthusiasm lack languorous lazy leisurely limp linger loath loth lumber unenthusiastic unhurried unwilling unyielding careful cautious circumspect college complain contrary crawl custom tentative totter toward trudge accept admit afraid amble animation averse noncooperation] "a reluctant smile"
*remembrance 11-52-17 (n.) 1. the ability to recall past occurrences 2. a recognition of meritorious service [realize recall recollection remarkable remember reminiscence respect retain retention retrieve engram meditation memento memory meritorious mind monument mound barrow bran brass bust affection anamnesis anniversary approval arch aristocratic art atavism narrator necrology neighbor novel celebrate childhood commemoration cross cup]
*reminiscence 12-40-13 (n.) 1. a mental impression

retained and recalled from the past 2. the process of remembering (especially the process of recovering information by mental effort) [recall recover reflection remembrance reminisce reproduction retain revival rote ruminate effort encounter existence experience memory mental muse idea immediately imperfect impression input nostalgia soul speech stimulus store study suggest cognitive construct]
*reminiscent 06-49-50 (a.) 1. serving to bring to mind [recall recollection redolent remember reminisce resemble resonant restore evocative machine memory mindful mnemonic note serve similarity suggestive campaign characterize childhood close comparison]

*remiss 22-46-2 (a.) 1. failing in what duty requires [regardless relaxed require easygoing expect miss impotent imprecise inattentive inconsistent indifferent shuffling slapdash slipshod slow soft]
*remission 17-60-5 (n.) 1. an abatement in intensity or degree (as in the manifestations of a disease) 2. the act of absolving or remitting; formal redemption as pronounced by a priest in the sacrament of penance 3. the act of remitting (especially the referral of a law case to another court) 4. a payment of money sent to a person in another place [reduction release reprieve respite rest retardation ease emission excuse exemption mitigate modulate mollify immunity indulgence interval slump stay suspension] "his cancer is in remission"
*remodel 10-37-21 (v.) 1. do over, as of (part of) a house 2. cast or model anew [rebuild recast reconstruct redo refashion reforge reform remake renew renovate room electorate model modernize modify different /dome led/] "We are remodeling these rooms"
*remonstrate 20-89-3 (v.) 1. argue in protest or opposition 2. censure severely or angrily 3. present and urge reasons in opposition [rag raise rally real reason rebuke recommend reproof resist revolt encourage enter except exhort expostulatory express march monitory mons moralist mother move objection objurgate opposition outre scold scruple sententious severe soup squabble squawk stranger strong tell trounce admonitory advisory affair angrily apart argue attention /nome tart/]
*remunerate 22-91-2 (v.) 1. make payment to; compensate [rate recompense reimburse render repay reward right effort emend exchange money accord amend award tender /tare/] "My efforts were not remunerated"
*remuneration 11-93-16 (n.) 1. something that remunerates 2. the act of paying for goods or services or to recompense for losses [ration recompense reduce regular reimburse repay return reward rewarding earnings emolument employer enclose engage envelope extra meed merit money union allow amends atonement award tax teacher inconvenience indemnity insurance overtime /tare/]
*renaissance 05-48-67 (n.) 1. the revival of learning and culture 2. the period of European history at the close of the Middle Ages and the rise of the modern world; a cultural rebirth from the 14th through the middle of the 17th centuries [reawaken recovery regenerate ren renewal restoration resurgence return revivify rise rome early era european age aggregate art artistic ignore italy skill start style century close composition content culture /ass/]
*rend 03-46-153 (v.) 1. tear or be torn violently [rage regular rent return rift right rip rive run rupture earn embitter emotion end enter estate exact excavation excise extort national nominal notch nullah demand dismantle disturb divide]
*render 05-46-79 (v.) 1. pass down 2. provide or furnish with 3. give or supply 4. give an interpretation or rendition of 5. cause to become 6. bestow 7. to surrender someone or something to another 8. show in, or as in, a picture 9. give back 10. Law: make over as a return 11. restate (words) from one language into another language 12. melt (fat, lard, etc.) in order to separate out impurities [reach reduce rend repeat report represent return run enforce execute explain express extract naturalize notate declare decree deliver depict describe draw drop] "The shot rendered her immobile"
*rendezvous 13-51-10 (n.) 1. a place where people meet 2. a meeting planned at a certain time and place 3. a date; usually with a member of the opposite sex (v.) 1. meet at a rendezvous [raise reception region rend resort respect eisteddfod engagement dance date diet unite secret session sex sit site social specific spot station surface surge /zed/] "he was waiting for them at the rendezvous"
*rendition 08-45-28 (n.) 1. a performance of a musical composition or a dramatic role etc. 2. an explanation of something that is not immediately obvious 3. the act of interpreting something as expressed in an artistic performance [read realize rend return role edict edition entertainment execution express nation notation decision delivery detail different distinctive dramatic drawing illustration immediately impression influence interpret tablature text theatrical touch translation obvious opinion]
*renovate 03-32-141 (v.) 1. restore to a previous or better condition, as of art works or antiques 2. give new life or energy to 3. make brighter and prettier, as of a house [rebuild recondition recover recreate redecorate reestablish refresh refurbish regenerate remodel renew renewal repair repeat restore resuscitate return revamp revival energy neologize new ovate overhaul vigor vivify alert animate antique arouse art aspiration treatment /avo one von/] "They renovated the ceiling of the Sixtine Chapel"

*renowned 05-66-65 (a.) 1. widely known and esteemed [recognize renown elevated eminent establish esteem exalted expertise noble notable noted notorious

outstanding well wide distinguished /den one won/]
*renunciation 20-34-3 (n.) 1. rejecting or disowning or disclaiming as invalid 2. the state of having rejected your religious beliefs or your political party or a cause (often in favor of opposing beliefs or causes) 3. the act of renouncing; sacrificing or giving up or surrendering (a possession or right or title or privilege etc.) 4. an act (spoken or written) declaring that something is surrendered or disowned [reason recant refute rejection release relinquish repugnant resignation retreat right enunciate eschew expatriate negotiate nullification unsay cause cease claim close contrary crossing interest invalid ion abandon abdicate abnegate acknowledge adversative annul apostasy temperate termination title treaty official oppose]
*reorganize 10-AA-20 (v.) 1. organize anew, as after a setback 2. organize anew [rearrange rebuild regroup repeat reschedule restructure revise revive entity operate ordered organize accord alter anew idea impose improve /nag roe/] "We must reorganize the company if we don't want to go under"
*reparation 16-40-6 (n.) 1. compensation (given or received) for an insult or injury 2. the act of putting something in working order again 3. (usually plural) compensation exacted from a defeated nation by the victors 4. something done or paid in expiation of a wrong [ration receive recompense reimburse repay restore retaliate return revenge reward right exact expiate expiation patch pay price process profitable propitiate punitive achieve adjustment again aid amends apologetic appease atone troubleshoot improve indemnity injury insult offset one original overhaul nation /ape rape/] "an act for which there is no reparation"
*repartee 20-49-3 (n.) 1. adroitness and cleverness in reply [raillery reaction remark reply return echo epigram evoke part patter persiflage pleasantry power acknowledgment adroit answer aphorism talk tease /ape rape trap/]
*repast 25-28-1 (n.) 1. the food served and eaten at one time [refection early eat enjoy entre evening excursion past personnel portion potluck prepare alimentation available salad sandwich satisfy serve snack source spread subordinate substantial sustenance tea teatime tiffin /ape sap/]
*repeal 08-22-31 (n.) 1. the act of abrogating; an official or legal cancellation (v.) 1. annul by recalling or rescinding [recall remove renegue rescind retract reverse revoke effective embargo partial peal petition previous promise abolition abrogate annihilate annul arrange authority law legal lift]
*repel 10-62-20 (v.) 1. reject outright and bluntly 2. be repellent to; cause aversion in 3. force or drive back 4. cause to move back by force or influence 5. fill with distaste [rapid rebuff refuse reject rep repulse repulsive resist revolt revolting revulsion effective endure enemy except excite exclude exert parry physics polarize poohpooh power prevent prohibit psychological pull push language loathsome /leper/] "repel the enemy"
*repellent 13-52-11 (a.) 1. serving or tending to repel 2. highly offensive; arousing aversion or disgust 3. incapable of absorbing or mixing with (n.) 1. a compound with which fabrics are treated to repel water 2. a chemical substance that repels animals 3. the power to repel [rebarbative rebellious reluctant repel repulsive resistant revolting revulsion eat effect element ellen execrable physical pleasant possession powerful prickly proof proportion protest push language literal loathsome nasty nauseous non noxious tend tight treat /leper/] "she knew many repellents to his advances"
*repentance 20-53-3 (n.) 1. remorse for your past conduct [regret remorse past penance penitent atonement conduct contrition]
*repertory 06-11-57 (n.) 1. a storehouse where a stock of things is kept 2. the entire range of skills or aptitudes or devices used in a particular field or occupation [rack range recount repository rick entire enumerate exchequer performance permanent pert pile play plenty production provision tank theater treasury occupation] "the repertory of the supposed feats of mesmerism"
*repetition 08-50-28 (n.) 1. the repeated use of the same word or word pattern as a rhetorical device 2. the act of doing or performing again 3. an event that repeats [regularity repeat run echo epanaphora even extension parody petition progression prolong takeoff tattoo twin imitation impersonate impression onomatopoeia oscillation /tepe/]
*replenish 12-40-14 (v.) 1. fill something that had previously been emptied [refill reform refuel reload replace return empty endow energy please prepare present previous len nourishment invest item stock store supply support /sine/]
*replete 12-42-12 (a.) 1. (informal) having consumed enough food or drink (v.) 1. fill to satisfaction [rampant regular rich rife round eat enough epidemic equip excess exhaustless exuberant pall permeate pleasing plenty possible prevalent productive provide latest lavish let liberal loaded teem throng]
*replica 08-62-31 (n.) 1. copy that is not the original; something that has been copied [repetition reproduction equivalent paraphrase parody photocopylikeness idem imitation carbon clone copy counterpart accurate art artist artwork authorize]
*repository 12-32-12 (n.) 1. a person to whom a secret is entrusted 2. a facility where things can be deposited for safekeeping 3. a burial vault (usually for some famous person) [rack receptacle reclaim record repertory rick room entrust exchequer partisan pick pickup place posit possessor precious prior private provide public origin owner safe sale secretary sepulture service shelf source space sperm stock structure supporter installation intimate island tank till tomb transact treasury /roti/]

*reprehensible 16-45-6 (a.) 1. bringing or deserving severe rebuke or censure [rank rebuke regrettable right rotten egregious enormous evil peccant pitiful hateful heinous hen highly horrid husband nasty naughty notorious sad severe shabby shameful shock improper inexcusable infamous involved bad base black bring lamentable law lousy low /her/]
*repress 19-38-4 (v.) 1. put down by force or intimidation 2. conceal or hide 3. put out of one's consciousness; in psychiatry [reduce refuse reject remember resist restrain reveal rich eff enjoin enslave extinguish painful peasant people population preclude press prevent prohibit psychopathology setback show silence smile smother sound stamp stifle stop strangle subdue subjugate suppress]
*reprieve 10-68-20 (n.) 1. a (temporary) relief from harm or discomfort 2. a warrant granting postponement (usually to postpone the execution of the death sentence) 3. the act of reprieving; postponing or remitting punishment 4. an interruption in the intensity or amount of something (v.) 1. postpone the punishment of a convicted criminal, such as an execution 2. relieve temporarily [relieve remit remove rescue respite rule ease eve evil exculpate excuse execution exemption exonerate pain pardon passive pause perform pity police postpone prorogue provide punishment immunity impose indemnity interrupt]
*reprimand 10-51-18 (n.) 1. an act or expression of criticism and censure (v.) 1. rebuke formally 2. censure severely or angrily [rag rate real rebuke reflection remark remonstrate earful enter expression perceive pick pillory pointing prima impute mild mistake monition mother admonition angrily apart aspersion attaint defame deputy disapproval disapprove disparage down dressing /amir/]
*reprisal 11-38-15 (n.) 1. a retaliatory action against an enemy in wartime [rep repay retaliate return revenge reward enemy payback people prisoner property punishment indemnity injury seizure strong amends avenge]
*reproach 15-56-8 (n.) 1. disgrace or shame 2. a mild rebuke or criticism (v.) 1. utter a reproach to [rap rating rebuke reflect report repro expression pillory plaint president prosecution objurgate onus accuse arraign article ashamed censure charge cite count criminate criticize humiliation] "words of reproach"
*reprobate 25-70-1 (a.) 1. marked by immorality; deviating from what is considered right or proper or good (n.) 1. a person without moral scruples (v.) 1. reject as invalid, as of documents 2. express strong disapproval of 3. Theology: abandon to eternal damnation [racism rank rascal reckless refuse reject religious right eternal evil excoriate execrable express perform perverted pimp pollute pro probate profligate proper objurgate bad base behavior believe blame abandon acceptable accuse acknowledge aristocrat atrocious taint teach temporal theology transgresse troublemaker turndown /tab tabor/] "God reprobated the unrepenting sinner"
*reproduce 07-49-38 (v.) 1. have offspring or young 2. make a copy or equivalent of 3. repeat after memorization 4. recreate an idea, mood, atmosphere, etc. as by artistic means [rebuild repeat revive echo engender parrot produce proliferate outgrow develop double duplicate clone copy /dorp udo/] "reproduce the painting"
*reproduction 08-31-32 (n.) 1. the process of generating offspring 2. copy that is not the original; something that has been copied 3. the sexual activity of conceiving and bearing offspring 4. the act of making copies [recur renewal return echo engrave excrescence photograph picture production outgrowth overgrow development double dummy upgrowth clone copy counterpart tapestry trace twin icon illustration image /dorp udo/] "Gutenberg's reproduction of holy texts was far more efficient"
*repudiate 12-24-13 (v.) 1. refuse to acknowledge, ratify, or recognize as valid 2. cast off or disown 3. refuse to recognize or pay 4. reject as untrue. unfounded, or unjust [ratify rebuff rebut recognize reject reverse exclusion preclude prohibition unbelieving unfounded unjust untrue unwilling debt decline deny dismiss disown dispute ignore impugn inadmissible incredulous injunction invalid irreligious abandon abjure abrogate accusation alienate annul apostatize argument /dup dupe/]
*repugnance 25-44-1 (n.) 1. intense aversion 2. the relation between propositions that cannot both be true at the same time [rank reaction relation resistance revulsion emetic enmity exclusive execration exist perfunctory perversity polarity proposition unwilling gross nance nasty negative noxious abhorrence allergy antithesis aversion clash competition controversy]
*repugnant 17-38-5 (a.) 1. offensive to the mind [recent repellent reverse revolting revolutionary rival enemy execrable extrinsic perverse physical unacceptable unfavorable unfriendly unpleasant ghastly gross gruesome nasty nauseating nauseous novel noxious abhorrent abominable alien ant antagonistic awful terrible]
*repulse 17-47-5 (n.) 1. an instance of driving away or warding off (v.) 1. force or drive back 2. cause to move back by force or influence 3. be repellent to; cause aversion in [rapid reaction rebound refusal rejection repellent resist reverse revolt revulsion endure enemy exception exclusion parry protest pulse push upstage urge sicken slight smoke snub speech spring spurn stop striking strong]
*repulsive 16-64-6 (a.) 1. offensive to the mind 2. so extremely ugly as to be terrifying 3. (physics) possessing the ability to repel [rank recent regrettable repellent revolting rotten egregious energy enormous

execrable extremely philosophy physics pitiful possess property pul pull putrid ugly unpleasant unsavory lamentable loathsome lousy sad scar science shock stomach strong icky ignoble infamous inoffensive interaction vile villainous]
*repute 10-52-21 (n.) 1. the state of being held in high esteem and honor (v.) 1. look on as or consider 2. attribute or credit to [recognize regard report reputation rule rumor effect establish esteem estimation expect eye people popularity power presume prominence public purchase purported put putative understand think thought trade /tup/]
*requiem 13-46-11 (n.) 1. a song or hymn of mourning composed or performed as a memorial to a dead person 2. a Mass celebrated for the dead 3. a musical setting for a Mass celebrating the dead [recessional elegy equi eulogy exequies introit mass memorial monody motet mourning musical]
*requisite 11-48-16 (a.) 1. necessary for relief or supply (n.) 1. anything indispensable [relief requisition rightful entity equi essential ultimatum unnecessary indispensable irreplaceable self separate shelter skill specific stipulate string suitable supply term]
*rescind 11-26-16 (v.) 1. annul by recalling or rescinding [recall remove renegue repeal res retract reverse revoke embargo enactment erase expurgate sentence smoke strike suspend cancel censor countermand cut ineffective invalidate null nullify death decision declare delete dismantle down]
*resemblance 08-48-30 (n.) 1. similarity in appearance or external or superficial details [reflection remarkable representation respect rub effigy equivalence external same semblance shadow similitude simulation superficial symmetrical match mate model liken likeness agreement alike alliance appearance nature near character close community copy]
*resent 07-50-39 (v.) 1. feel bitter or indignant about 2. wish ill or allow unwillingly [rail sent stew toward] "She resents being paid less than her co-workers"
*reservoir 08-41-29 (n.) 1. tank used for collecting and storing a liquid (as water or oil) 2. lake used to store water for community use 3. a large or extra supply of something [rack rainwater recreational resource rick river rock engine entity exchequer extra savings self separate servo shelf source southeastern species store substantial supply surround vat vault vessel oil organism infectious intangible internal inventory] "a reservoir of talent"
*residue 12-39-14 (n.) 1. something left after other parts have been taken away 2. matter that remains after something has been removed [refuse relation remain remains remnant remove rest end estate excess exist scrap scum shadow smoke solid space substance survival include debris debt decease deposit determined detritus distribute dreg dregs due]
*resilience 08-68-27 (n.) 1. the physical property of a material that can return to its original shape or position after deformation that does not exceed its elastic limit 2. an occurrence of rebounding or springing back [rebound rebuff recovery repercussion responsiveness return elasticity exceed extensible setback shape snap speedy spirit springing springy stretch supple impact impermanent irrepressible levity lien limit lively carom changeful chirpy compress]
*resilient 09-63-22 (a.) 1. recovering readily from adversity, depression, or the like 2. rebounds readily [ready rebound recover repercussive responsive resume robust effervescent elastic expansive season setback shape spiritless springy squash stretch stretchy strong sturdy supple impermanent irrepressible lien lightsome lively tennis transitory turf]
*resist 03-49-191 (v.) 1. withstand the force of something 2. stand up or offer resistance to somebody or something 3. fight back, also metaphorically 4. elude, esp. in a baffling way 5. refuse to comply [rebuff refrain refuse repel res restrain elude endure scrapper setback standoff stem stop struggle survive impede inhibit intervene intransigent irreconcilable thwart traverse turndown]
*resistance 04-47-128 (n.) 1. the military action of resisting the enemy's advance 2. a material's opposition to the flow of electric current; measured in ohms 3. any mechanical force that tends to retard or oppose motion 4. the action of opposing something that you disapprove or disagree with 5. (medicine) the condition in which an organism can resist disease 6. (psychiatry) an unwillingness to bring repressed feelings into conscious awareness 7. group action in opposition to those in power 8. the degree of unresponsiveness of a disease-causing microorganism to antibiotics or other drugs (as in penicillin-resistant bacteria) 9. an electrical device that resists the flow of electrical current 10. a secret group organized to overthrow a government or occupation force [rationalization reactance resist escapism impenetrable interruption isolation alienate arrest aversion negativism nonconformity challenge check clash] "he encountered a general feeling of resistance from many citizens"
*resistant 08-45-33 (a.) 1. relating to or conferring immunity (to disease or infection) 2. disposed to or engaged in defiance of established authority 3. incapable of absorbing or mixing with 4. incapable of being affected [compliant reluctant repellent resist revolutionary rocky effect engage establish shed soak solid steam strong sturdy susceptible immunity impervious incapable infection insubordinate intransigent irrepressible tenacious tight absorbing admit affect airtight antagonistic authority averse non noncooperation] "resistant to persuasion"
*resonance 07-46-34 (n.) 1. having the character of a loud deep sound; the quality of being resonant 2. a vibration of large amplitude produced by a relatively

small vibration near the same frequency of vibration as the natural frequency of the resonating system 3. an excited state of a stable particle causing a sharp maximum in the probability of absorption of electromagnetic radiation 4. relation of mutual understanding or trust and agreement between people 5. the quality imparted to voiced speech sounds by the action of the resonating chambers of the throat and mouth and nasal cavities [ray reinforcement ringing sonance sound oscillation node nutation amplitude antinode characteristic crest /nano nose/]
*resonate 09-45-24 (v.) 1. sound with resonance 2. be received or understood [receive reel remind response ring rock roll eat echo effect electrical emotional exhibit extend shake sound support sway swing oscillate noise across apparent approval theater throb toss /nose/] "The sound resonates well in this theater"
*resort 03-57-216 (n.) 1. an area where many people go for recreation 2. a frequently visited place 3. something or someone turned to for assistance or security 4. act of turning to for assistance (v.) 1. have recourse to [ranch ration recourse recreation recur region repair reserve resource retreat effort employ entertain expedient security see sell serve service shadow ski sort source special spot stamp step stock support observation offering option theater toward traveler trick trump turn /rose/] "The government resorted to rationing meat"
*resource 02-48-364 (n.) 1. the ability to deal resourcefully with unusual problems 2. a source of aid or support that may be drawn upon when needed 3. available source of wealth; a new or reserve supply that can be drawn upon when needed [raise ready recourse refuge relief reserve resort responsibility revenue ecology economic efficiency effort enjoy equipment exchequer expense expertise security situation solution source step stock store style substance support sustenance system opportunity unusual useful capacity capitalize cash circumstance control cope corporate creative /ecru/] "the local library is a valuable resource"
*respite 09-62-22 (n.) 1. an interruption in the intensity or amount of something 2. a pause from doing something (as work) 3. a (temporary) relief from harm or discomfort 4. the act of reprieving; postponing or remitting punishment 5. a pause for relaxation (v.) 1. postpone the punishment of a convicted criminal, such as an execution 2. grant a respite to [recovery recuperate relaxation release relief relieve remit removal reprieve rest rule ease execution exertion extension school set shelve short slow space spell spite stay subsidence suspension pause period place postpone prorogue punishment purge impose interval table temporary timeout truce /tip/]
*resplendent 15-61-8 (a.) 1. having great beauty and splendor 2. richly and brilliantly colorful [radiant ravishing refulgent resplendence richly effulgent elaborate elegance emotional envelope exciting simplicity splendor spring stately striking stunning sublimity sumptuous sunrise sunset superb pleasure plush proud lavish lustrous luxury native nimbus nobility numinous dazzle delight dent devastating divine dress]
*respondent 09-49-26 (a.) 1. replying (n.) 1. the codefendant (especially in a divorce proceeding) who is accused of adultery with the corespondent 2. someone who responds [react ready rejoin reply respond return echo emotion examination show single smile suspect people petition plaintiff prisoner proceeding defend direct divorce test]
*restitution 14-22-9 (n.) 1. a sum of money paid in compensation for loss or injury 2. the act of restoring something to its original state 3. getting something back again [ready receive recompense recovery redress refund regain reimburse repay rest retaliate return revert reward right rightful excess expiate expiation salvage satisfaction service smart square sum sustain tongue trivial turnabout improvement indemnity injury instauration occur offset original owner] "upon the restitution of the book to its rightful owner the child was given a tongue lashing"
*restive 15-34-7 (a.) 1. being in a tense state 2. impatient especially under restriction or delay [relaxed reluctant resist rest restless rule eager ease edgy excited set short squirmy strung stubborn suspense temper tenacious tension tolerate twitchy impatient indifferent intractable irrepressible verge] "the government has done nothing to ease restrictions and manufacturers are growing restive"
*restore 02-49-304 (v.) 1. restore by replacing a part or putting together what is torn or broken 2. give or bring back 3. return to life; get or give new life or energy 4. return to its original or usable and functioning condition 5. bring back into original existence, use, function, or position [readapt reestablish rejuvenate repay repeat resto resurrect return right ease enrich existence explain save stir strengthen] "restore the forest to its original pristine condition"
*resumption 11-44-17 (n.) 1. beginning again [recommencement recovery renewal reopen return revival echo salvage start stop sumption plagiarism temporary trover imitation instance negotiation /muse use user/]
*resurgent 12-65-13 (a.) 1. rising again as to new life and vigor 2. surging or sweeping back again [renascent restore resurge revive rise strong surge sweep grow nationalism /ruse use user/] "resurgent nationalism"
*resurrection 11-54-17 (n.) 1. revival from inactivity and disuse [reappearance rebirth rebuild renaissance renewal renovate restoration resurrect revelation revivify rise entomb epistle second soon supernatural christ collection compose copy crucifixion testament third translation imitation inactivity /ruse use user/] "it produced a resurrection of hope"

*resuscitate 11-53-17 (v.) 1. cause to regain consciousness 2. return to consciousness [raise rally reboot recovery recreate recruit regain renew renovate repair restore return revivify round ease emergency energy enliven exhilarate external save sharpen start stimulate stop style undergo callback circulation collapse comatose come comfort consciousness initial injection interest invigorate tate transform treatment turn aid alive animate apparent artificial assist attempt /use user/]
*resuscitation 17-51-5 (n.) 1. act of reviving a person and returning them to consciousness [recovery renewal respiration restore return revive emergency external stop cardiopulmonary circulation collapse consciousness cpr treatment accomplish apparently artificial attempt oxygen] "although he was apparently drowned, resuscitation was accomplished by artificial respiration"
*retaliate 05-33-60 (v.) 1. make a counterattack and return like for like, esp. evil for evil 2. take revenge for a perceived wrong [react redress repay response return returnable revenge revengeful enemy equivalent even evil exchange expiation tali target trade transposition alternate amends army assault atonement avenge logroll implacable impose indemnity inflict interplay irreconcilable /late later tail/]
*retard 19-32-4 (n.) 1. a person of subnormal intelligence (v.) 1. cause to move more slowly or operate at a slower rate 2. slow the growth or development of 3. lose velocity; move more slowly 4. be delayed [range rate reduce relax resist restrict ret enjoin extent thwart transform alter arrest damage dampen deaden decelerate decrease delay detain different diminish down drag drug /drat rate rater/] "The brain damage will retard the child's language development"
*retch 25-77-1 (n.) 1. an involuntary spasm of ineffectual vomiting (v.) 1. eject the contents of the stomach through the mouth 2. make an unsuccessful effort to vomit; strain to vomit [regorge regurgitate reject effort egest eject eliminate etch excrete experience throw case caste cat chuck constriction continuous heave hollow honk]
*retention 10-70-20 (n.) 1. the power of retaining and recalling past experience 2. the act of keeping in your possession 3. the power of retaining liquid [recall recollection refusal rejection remembrance repudiation retain rete excrete experience tenacity tight toughness nay nix nonobservance impermeablene inherent obstinate occurrence ownership]
*reticence 14-55-9 (n.) 1. the trait of being uncommunicative; not volunteering anything more than necessary [reserve restraint taciturnity trait introversion cagey necessary]
*reticent 10-56-21 (a.) 1. temperamentally disinclined to talk 2. cool and formal in manner 3. reluctant to draw attention to yourself [reluctant removed reserved restrained restraint retiring reveal emotion expression expressionless taciturn taciturnity talk temperamental tend timid timidity traditional trait travel icy impersonality inaccessible incline increase introversion cagey cent chilly cold communicate constraint context convey cool nearly necessary never nothing /cite iter/]
*retinue 20-55-3 (n.) 1. the group following and attending to some important person [ret rout employee entourage escort train travel important]
*retort 11-61-17 (n.) 1. a quick reply to a question or remark (especially a witty or critical one) 2. a vessel where substances are distilled or decomposed by heat (v.) 1. answer back [reaction rejoinder remark repay reply response retaliate return riposte echo engine exchange talk talkback teacher tort transformer tube obsolete /rote trot/]
*retouch 22-49-2 (v.) 1. give retouches to; of hair 2. alter so as to produce a more desirable appearance [remove renovate repair restore revive root enhance tint touch occasion colorize cook correct hair] "retouch the roots"
*retrace 15-52-8 (v.) 1. to go back over again, as of a route or steps 2. of past events [reassemble redo reflect remember repeat return review revive route etymologize evoke tentative theorize trace account argument come conjecture construct /cart carte carter/] "we retraced the route we took last summer"
*retract 11-51-17 (v.) 1. formally reject or disavow a formerly held belief, usually under pressure 2. pull inward or towards a center 3. use a surgical instrument to hold open (the edges of a wound or an organ) 4. shrink back, as in fear [recant recoil reject religion relinquish repudiate rescind resign reverse early edge tongue toward tract abandon abjure abolish alter annul apologize apply attribute cancel cant cast cat cede center claw cringe cross /cart carte carter/] "He retracted his earlier statements about his religion"
*retrench 15-28-8 (v.) 1. tighten one's belt; use resources carefully 2. make a reduction, as in one's workforce [ration realize reap reduction rein remove reorganize resource retardation rethink economize epitomize erode extraction telescope tighten trench trim truncate nip careful cautious check company conserve control cost cut hindrance holdup husband] "The company had to retrench"
*retrieve 07-46-41 (v.) 1. get or find back; recover the use of 2. recall knowledge from memory; have a recollection 3. of trained dogs [racket read recall reclaim recover recoverable refresh regain release remedy remember reply repossess request rescue restore return revive right eve extricate tennis think train improve voice]
*retroactive 12-04-14 (a.) 1. (psychology) descriptive of any event or stimulus or process that has an effect on the effects of events or stimuli or process that occurred previously 2. affecting things past [responsive retrospective revulsive early effect expo tax occur active

affecting antiphonal apply concern increase] "retroactive tax increase"
*retrograde 19-64-4 (a.) 1. (astronomy) moving from east to west on the celestial sphere; or--for planets--around the sun in a direction opposite to that of the Earth 2. going from better to worse 3. moving or directed or tending in a backward direction or contrary to a previous direction 4. of amnesia; affecting time immediately preceding trauma (v.) 1. move backward in an orbit, of celestial bodies 2. get worse; fall back to a previous or worse condition 3. move in a direction contrary to the usual one; of stars and planets 4. go back over 5. move back [rearward recapitulate recede regressive rehash retire return returnable revert revolve rot earth ebb effete tabetic tail tend toward trauma travel opposite orbit orf glacier grade grow affect aft aftermost amnesia ante appear argument astronomy atavistic decline descend deteriorate direction drop] "The glacier retrogrades"
*retrospect 10-44-20 (n.) 1. contemplation of things past (v.) 1. look back upon (a period of time, sequence of events, etc.); remember [recapture reconsider reflection reflexion remembrance retain retro revive ruminate evoke think thoughtfulnes sequence study survey past period pride calm cite consideration contemplate /sort/] "in retrospect"
*retrospective 07-49-42 (a.) 1. concerned with or related to the past (n.) 1. an exhibition of a representative selection of an artist's life work [rear reconsider reflective remember restore retrospect review revive ruling early exhibition exposure toward traditional opening ostentation selection self show showing statue style suggestive survey past performance period post present production projection prospective concern conservative vernissage /sort/] "retrospective self-justification"
*reunite 06-63-45 (v.) 1. unify again, as of a country 2. have a reunion; unite again [reconcile resolve unify unite]
*revelation 04-65-106 (n.) 1. an enlightening or astonishing disclosure 2. the speech act of making something evident 3. communication of knowledge to man by a divine or supernatural agency 4. the revelations of Saint John the Divine in the New Testament [realize relevant return ride rise elation elicit emerge enlighten epistle estament evangelistic evidence evil exposure expressive eye visionary law leak litigation location announcement apocalypse apocalyptic apostle apostolic appear astonish attribute talkative tell textuary thunderclap trove indicate inform information insight inspired issue occurrence officer opener opening news /ever lever tale/]
*revere 07-52-35 (n.) 1. American silversmith remembered for his midnight ride (celebrated in a poem by Longfellow) to warn the colonists in Lexington and Concord that British troops were coming (1735-1818) 2. a lapel on a woman's garment; turned back to show the reverse side (v.) 1. regard with feelings of respect and reverence; consider hallowed or exalted or be in awe of 2. love unquestioningly and uncritically or to excess; venerate as an idol [regard remember repair reputable respect restraint revolutionary ride enjoy enshrine envy esteem estimate ever exalted excess value venerate /ever/]
*reverent 16-37-6 (a.) 1. feeling or showing profound respect or veneration 2. showing great reverence for god [religious respectful revere exhibit express veneration theism /ever/] "maintained a reverent silence"
*reverie 15-43-8 (n.) 1. an abstracted state of absorption 2. absent-minded dreaming while awake [reality release engrossment erie exclusion vision idle imaginative incubus indulge /ever/]
*reversion 19-72-4 (n.) 1. (law) an interest in an estate that reverts to the grantor (or his heirs) at the end of some period (e.g., the death of the grantee) 2. a reappearance of an earlier characteristic 3. a failure to maintain a higher state 4. returning to a former state 5. a return to a normal phenotype (usually resulting from a second mutation) 6. turning in the opposite direction [reactionary regression relapse replacement return revert entail eversion version setback succession supinate improvement inheritance inversion /ever/]
*revert 07-67-39 (v.) 1. go back to a previous state 2. undergo reversion, as in a mutation [reacquire reactionary recover reexamine regain regress reinvestigate relapse reopen reparation repeat restore resume retrovert return returnable reverse revisit rule early echo evert topic turn /ever/] "We reverted to the old rules"
*revile 13-55-10 (v.) 1. spread negative information about [rag rail rally rate evil execration vile vilify vituperate vituperation insult invective language libel /live liver/]
*revise 04-41-116 (n.) 1. the act of rewriting something (v.) 1. revise or reorganize, esp. for the purpose of updating and improving 2. make revisions in [realistic record reorganize repeat reread rescript rethink revive rework rewrite early economy edit emend engross estimate vandyke version vise improve incorporate inscribe involve scroll shake slip stage study superscribe swot] "revise a thesis"
*revive 03-49-147 (v.) 1. restore from a depressed, inactive, or unused state 2. be brought back to life, consciousness, or strength 3. give new life or energy to 4. cause to regain consciousness 5. return to consciousness [raise reanimate reawaken reboot rebuild recover recreate recuperate redo reflect refresh regain regenerate reinforce rejuvenate remember renew renovate repair repeat restore resuscitate return round ease echo energy evoke exhilarate expand experience vive vivify imitate improve inactive initial injection invigorate /vive/] "The doctors revived the comatose

man"
*revocation 20-16-3 (n.) 1. the state of being cancelled or annulled 2. the act (by someone having the authority) of annulling something previously done [renounce repeal respect reversal enactment evocation expatriate vocation void official overturn cancel cancellation cassation crossing abolition abrogate annul attribute authority invalidate nullification /cove cover over taco/] "the revocation of a law"
*revoke 09-32-23 (n.) 1. the mistake of not following suit when able to do so (v.) 1. fail to follow suit in a card game when able and required to do so 2. annul by recalling or rescinding [recall remember renegue repeal require rescind retain retract reverse embargo erase evoke exile expunge vacate veto void obligation oppose overturn /over/] "He revoked the ban on smoking"
*rhapsody 15-46-8 (n.) 1. an epic poem adapted for recitation [rant rapture rave recite rhetoric hap heaven hero highfalutin adapt ancient poem poetry professional sinfonietta style symphony deed drool /spa/]
*rhetoric 06-47-48 (n.) 1. using language effectively to please or persuade 2. high flown style; excessive use of verbal ornamentation 3. loud and confused and empty talk 4. study of the technique and rules for using language effectively (especially in public speaking) [rant repetition rhapsody rhetor rodomontade rule high highfalutin homiletics hot humanist elocution emphasis exaggerate excessive exhort expressive extend talk technique tortuous trick oratory ornamentation orotund idiom inconsistency influence insincere introductory claptrap communicate complex composition conclude confused convey convolution /rote/] "mere rhetoric"
*ribald 20-50-3 (a.) 1. humorously vulgar (n.) 1. a ribald person; someone who uses vulgar and offensive language [raw rogue rude imprecate impure indecency ithyphallic bald bawdy behavior blue boor bourgeois abusive arriviste language lewd loud lurid devil dirty display dysphemism]
*riddance 22-63-2 (n.) 1. the act of removing or getting rid of something 2. the act of expelling someone [relegate remove rescue resignation rid issue dance delivery deport destruction detail discard abandon abjure alien negative cession clearance consent country eject eliminate emerge exclusion exile expel expulsion /add/]
*riddle 08-51-32 (n.) 1. a difficult problem 2. a coarse sieve (as for gravel) (v.) 1. set a riddle 2. pierce many times 3. explain a riddle 4. speak in riddles 5. separate with a riddle, as grain from chaff [raise rank resolve rhyme rid rocker imprint infest insulate intercommunicate damage define deliberate device difficult drill drop dumbfound lance last lick line load look lump eject element embarrassment enigma explain] "The bullets riddled his body"
*ridicule 07-54-39 (n.) 1. language or behavior intended to mock or humiliate 2. the act of deriding or treating with contempt (v.) 1. subject to laughter or ridicule [rag railing rally reduce respect rib ride roast rude idea impertinent importance impudent inexperience insolent insult intend irreverent dare debunk defame derision despite discourtesy disdain dismiss disparaging disrespectful caricature catcall chaff cheeky claim cocky comment condemn contemptuous cul lack lampoon language laughter leer libelous lout exchange exclusive expose expression /lucid/] "The satirists ridiculed the plans for a new opera house"
*ridiculous 04-66-92 (a.) 1. completely devoid of wisdom or good sense 2. inspiring scornful pity 3. broadly or extravagantly humorous; resembling farce [rich risible rough idiotic impossible improper incredible inspire interest dash derisory devoid dignity dog doubtful droll dubitable dull call child clown cockamamie cockeyed comical completely conceited contribution cottage crazy cul unbelievable unimaginable universal unreasonable unsuccessful unthinkable lack laughable ludicrous outlandish outrageous outre scornful scream silly suspicious /lucid/]
*rife 10-62-20 (a.) 1. encountered generally especially at the present time 2. excessively abundant [rampant religion report rich ruling inexhaustible factory fat flush frequently full encounter endemic epidemic excessive exhaustless experience extensive exuberant /fir/]
*rift 08-55-30 (n.) 1. a gap between cloud masses 2. a narrow fissure in rock 3. a personal or social separation (as between opposing factions) [relation rent rip rock rupture imperfection inadequate interval faction failure fall fault fissure flaw fracture tap track twist /fir/] "the sun shone through a rift in the clouds"
*righteousness 15-51-7 (n.) 1. adhering to moral principles [rectitude respect good honesty honourablenes evil]
*rightful 11-51-16 (a.) 1. legally valid 2. having a legally established claim [realistic recognize requisite right rightly impartial impersonal inheritance injustice genuine good heir honest fair fairly fit fitting unassuming unflattering unjust unqualified lawful legal legitimate level] "a rightful inheritance"
*rigmarole 22-92-2 (n.) 1. a set of confused and meaningless statements 2. a long and complicated and confusing procedure [rant rigamarole ritual role rubbish intend irritate gammon gibberish gobbledygook meaningless message absurd absurdity academic account achieve amphigory over long excuse explanation] "all that academic rigmarole was a waste of time"
*rigor 13-06-11 (n.) 1. something hard to endure 2. the quality of being logically valid 3. excessive sternness [rawness resolution response restriction rig right rigid rise roughness icy inclement inertia inflexible inhuman insensitive intensity intolerance irritation gelid great grim grip objectivity obstinate onerous onset organ

orthodoxy]
*rigorous 06-53-55 (a.) 1. demanding strict attention to rules and procedures 2. rigidly accurate; allowing no deviation from a standard 3. (of circumstances; especially weather) causing suffering [raw relentless require right rigid rigor rough rule icy inexact inexorable inflexible intense intricate irreconcilable glacial great grim obdurate opposite orthodox outrageous uncompromising undemanding unfavorable unkind unrelenting unyielding uphill safety scope scrupulous security severe sharp skill soft square standard straight strict stringent suffering] "rigorous application of the law"
*ripple 07-47-35 (n.) 1. (electronics) an oscillation of small amplitude imposed on top of a steady value 2. a small wave on the surface of a liquid (v.) 1. flow in an irregular current with a bubbling noise, as of water 2. stir up (water) so as to form ripples [rank rapid regular repercussion resemble ridge riffle rip rise river rock room rough ruck ruffle rugged ice impose increase irregular paddle partly pass peak periodic physics pimply pit pothole progress purse lap last lift liquid lop loudness eagre effect electron emission excite]
*risible 15-91-7 (a.) 1. arousing or provoking laughter [rejoicing rich ridiculous incline incongruous scream shriek snicker snort sober steady story stream stupid surprise bizarre boffola buxom laughter look ludicrous eccentric enable everybody experience]
*rivet 09-45-25 (n.) 1. ornament consisting of a circular rounded protuberance (as on a vault or shield or belt) 2. heavy pin having a head at one end and the other end being hammered flat after being passed through holes in the pieces that are fastened together (v.) 1. focus one's attention on something 2. fasten with a rivet or rivets 3. hold (someone's attention) [rabbet reason recall return reverie ring rive rounded immerse inference insert interesting vault vet engage engross engulf entrance examine excite exercise eye tack testimony think thrilling toggle]
*rivulet 25-37-1 (n.) 1. a small stream [race rill river run let literary little earth]
*robust 04-65-97 (a.) 1. physically strong 2. marked by richness and fullness of flavor 3. rough and crude 4. strong enough to withstand intellectual challenge [recovery refined refusal require rich rough ruby rude rugged obstinate operation beefy behavior big bigboned blunt body boom bouncing brisk build burly bust uncouth unexpected show sound spirited sport square stalwart stamina stout strap strength strong sturdy tale tasteless thrive tough trenchant]
*rondo 20-36-3 (n.) 1. a musical form that is often the last movement of a sonata [rap reggae repeat requiem rock romantic ron round operetta oratorio overture nocturne decrescendo develop diminuendo dub]
*rookery 22-73-2 (n.) 1. a breeding ground for gregarious birds (such as rooks) [rook]
*rotary 15-44-7 (a.) 1. relating to or characterized by rotation (n.) 1. a road junction at which traffic streams circularly around a central island 2. electrical converter consisting of a synchronous machine that converts alternating to direct current or vice versa [recurring revolving rise road rota roundabout route running rush oblique open orbital oscillate tornado traffic transport travel turn accident alternate ascending axial axis] "rotary dial"
*rotate 07-41-38 (v.) 1. exchange on a regular basis 2. perform a job or duty on a rotating basis 3. cause to turn on an axis or center 4. turn on or around an axis or a center 5. plant or grow in a fixed cyclic order of succession [reel regular repeatedly replace resource return revolving rise roast rota run office orientation oscillate outward taxi team temporary travel tread turn twiddle twirl twist abstract advance agriculture alternate around ascend axis ebb ensue exchange exhaust]
*rote 19-34-4 (n.) 1. memorization by repetition [real recall remember repetition review rot rotation routine treadmill]
*rotund 19-61-4 (a.) 1. spherical in shape 2. excessively fat 3. (of sounds) full and rich [resounding rich ringing rot round obese orbicular overweight thickset thin tone tubby deep depth distended dumpy /nut/] "orotund tones"
*rudimentary 12-50-13 (a.) 1. being in the earliest stages of development 2. being or involving basic facts or principles 3. (biology) not fully developed in mature animals [radical rude rudiment unco uncut undeveloped unfinished universe unrefined development dumpy dwarfish imperfect inaugural incidental incomplete inventive mature meager midget early elementary embryonic essential exist nascent natal tail total truth aboriginal animal antenatal arrest]
*rue 09-69-25 (n.) 1. European strong-scented perennial herb with gray-green bitter-tasting leaves; an irritant similar to poison ivy 2. leaves sometimes used for flavoring fruit or claret cup but should be used with great caution: can cause irritation like poison ivy (v.) 1. feel remorse for; feel sorry for; be contrite about [regret remorse repent republic road rut ruth undergo unhappy emotion eurasian experience]
*ruffian 22-41-2 (n.) 1. a cruel and brutal fellow [raffish riot rival rock rogue roughneck rowdy ruff upstart faction fellow fencer foilsman imp improper agent american arriviste assaulter attack naughty /fur naif/]
*ruminate 12-35-13 (v.) 1. (of ruminants) chew the cuds 2. reflect deeply on a subject [reason refer reflect reflective regurgitate religious remarkable retrospective revolve roll uncertain understand mammal matter meditate meditation mina mind morbid mouth mull mumble munch muse infant inference intent introspect nature navel nibble abstruse advance afternoon amount arrive attentive theoretical think thousand turn turnover

eat excogitate exercise exhibit express]
*rumple 16-35-6 (v.) 1. disturb the smoothness of 2. to gather something into small wrinkles or folds 3. become wrinkled or crumpled or creased [ridge ripple ruck ruffle rugged rump unkempt untidy upset matted mess paddle pucker pull purse last lip litter excite]
*rupture 09-48-22 (n.) 1. state of being torn or burst open 2. the act of making a sudden noisy break 3. a personal or social separation (as between opposing factions) (v.) 1. separate or cause to separate abruptly [region relation rift rip rive undergo unjoint painful paper partition physical pierce produce protrude pull tear tissue trauma trench embitter estrange etch exacerbate excavation exfoliate]
*rural 03-57-168 (a.) 1. relating to rural areas 2. living in or characteristic of farming or country life [region road rustic unassuming unpretentious upland ural agrarian agrestic agricultural arable arcadian area life lifestyle live locate lowland] "rural people"
*ruse 14-58-9 (n.) 1. a deceptive maneuver (especially to avoid capture) [racket use scam scheme shift strategy stunt subterfuge expedient]
*rustic 08-49-27 (a.) 1. awkwardly simple and provincial 2. characteristic of rural life 3. characteristic of the fields or country 4. used of idealized country life (n.) 1. an unsophisticated country person [raise rough rube rural rust uncomplicated undignified ungainly unite unsophisticated upland scene set severe simple simplicity southern spare state stone surface tiller title tourist town tranquillity ingenuous chair chaw clothe clown commoner commonplace construction contentment cosmopolitan countryside cracker crude]
*ruth 04-46-94 (n.) 1. American professional baseball player famous for hitting home runs (1895-1948) 2. a feeling of sympathy and sorrow for the misfortunes of others 3. a book of the Old Testament that tells the story of Ruth who was not an Israelite but who married and Israelite and who stayed with her mother-in-law Naomi after her husband died 4. the great-grandmother of King David whose story is told in the Book of Ruth in the Old Testament [recording remorse run rut unite tell testament third trouble half hebrew herman history hit home humanity husband]

S

*saccharine 17-62-5 (a.) 1. overly sweet [saccharin sentimental silky slushy smile sugary sweet syrupy candy cloy honeyed resemble rich ingratiate insinuate excessive]
*sacrifice 04-46-133 (n.) 1. personnel that are sacrificed (e.g., surrendered or lost in order to gain an objective) 2. the act of losing or surrendering something as a penalty for a mistake or fault or failure to perform etc. 3. (in baseball) an out that advances the base runners 4. a loss entailed by giving up or selling something at less than its value 5. the act of killing (an animal or person) in order to propitiate a deity (v.) 1. kill or destroy 2. endure the loss of 3. make a sacrifice of; in religious rituals 4. sell at a loss [scapegoat shoot stone stop abandon altruism appease casualty collection commitment cost ransom release relinquish resign resignation retail immolate incense injury fauna fice forfeiture forgo forswear end execution expense /fir/] "he had to sell his car at a considerable sacrifice"
*sacrificial 17-55-5 (a.) 1. used in or connected with a sacrifice [sac sacrifice slash sumptuous surrender atone conciliatory connected cut reduce rich ritual inflated lamb lavish low luxurious /fir laic/] "sacrificial lamb"
*sacrilege 19-54-4 (n.) 1. blasphemous behavior; the act of depriving something of its sacred character [scandalous shameless shoe show sin sinful abnormal abomination abuse atrocity character consider contamination criminal recidivism recreant renegade respect reverence reverent rile rite ignominy illegal impious improper incorrect infamy irreverent lack lapse enter evil gross]
*sacrilegious 22-54-2 (a.) 1. grossly irreverent toward what is held to be sacred [shoe show respect reverent rile rite impious lack enter gross utterance]
*sacrosanct 17-52-5 (a.) 1. must be kept sacred [sacred sanctify spiritual awesome awful concern criticize regard religious respect rosa numinous tamper /naso/]
*safeguard 06-55-55 (n.) 1. a precautionary measure warding off impending danger or damage or injury etc. 2. a document or escort providing safe passage through a region especially in time of war (v.) 1. make safe 2. escort safely [sabotage save screen security shield accompany advocate arm armament authorization fence flank fuse ensure escort espionage esquire goal goggles governor guard guardsman umbrella undesirable region register damage danger dashboard defend defense destruction device document dodger]
*sagacity 25-59-1 (n.) 1. ability to make good judgments 2. the trait of forming opinions by distinguishing and evaluating [sage sensitivity shrewd sophistication sound acute anticipation apply astute avoid good grasp gumption city cogency comprehension contemplate couple incisive insight intelligence temper trait trenchant /gas/]
*salacious 17-58-5 (a.) 1. suggestive of or tending to moral looseness 2. characterized by lust [sala scandalous sensual sensuous sex sexy show speech spicy succulent suggestive animal arouse language lewd limerick literature little loose lubricious lurid luscious lust call carnal clean concupiscence content crude impure incontinent indecent interesting itch obscenity offensive old orgastic unclean unprintable unrepeatable unsex /alas ical/]
*salient 15-54-7 (a.) 1. having a quality that thrusts itself into attention 2. (heraldry) represented as leaping (rampant but leaning forward) 3. (of angles) pointing

outward at an angle of less than 180 degrees (n.) 1. (military) the part of the line of battle that projects closest to the enemy [semitism service shape ship significant solid space special spectacular statue stick striking surface airspace alien alignment angle area armed armorial arresting attack attention land lead lean leap important impressive intrusive inward emboss eminent enemy esteem exceptional exposure eye nation neighborhood noble notability noteworthy noticeable notorious telling territory theory thrust toward trace trait troop]
*saline 17-41-5 (a.) 1. containing salt (n.) 1. an isotonic solution of sodium chloride and distilled water [salty sodium solution substitute aline alkali line impregnate isotonic] "a saline solution"
*salubrious 20-80-3 (a.) 1. promoting health; healthful 2. favorable to health of mind or body [salutary sanitary sleep stimulate suburb unwholesome beneficial benign body bracing brio refreshing respectable invigorate outlet]
*salutary 15-69-7 (a.) 1. tending to promote physical well-being; beneficial to health [sal salubrious sanitary service serviceable sleep ask useful tend therapeutic tonic refreshing remedial restorative]
*salutation 22-55-2 (n.) 1. an act of honor or courteous recognition 2. (usually plural) an acknowledgment or expression of good will (especially on meeting) 3. word of greeting used to begin a letter [salaam salute scrape signify speech sss statement accost acknowledgment address afternoon approval assist audience left letter lift love tribute inclination indicate initial introduction ion obeisance obsequious one opening nod]
*salvage 06-50-45 (n.) 1. property or goods saved from damage or destruction 2. the act of rescuing a ship or its crew or its cargo from a shipwreck or a fire 3. the act of saving goods or property that were in danger of damage or destruction (v.) 1. save from ruin or destruction 2. collect discarded or refused material [sale save sea shipwreck shot situation spare support abate age allowance amends article assemble lard liberation lifesaver loss volunteer garbage garner gather good guerdon evil extricate]
*salvo 13-55-10 (n.) 1. rapid simultaneous discharge of firearms 2. an outburst resembling the discharge of firearms or the release of bombs 3. a sudden outburst of cheers [sal shot shout shower simultaneous storm sudden surprise allowance anniversary approval artillery last left limitation violent volley observance outburst ovation]
*sanctimonious 16-61-6 (a.) 1. excessively or hypocritically pious [sanctify self show sicken smile smug snuffle stuffy superiority affected narrow canting censorious tokenism impious insincerity mon moral mouthing mummery oily unctuous /omit/] "a sickening sanctimonious smile"
*sanctimony 25-48-1 (n.) 1. the quality of being hypocritically devout [self show sicken smile smug superiority censorious impious insincerity moral]
*sanction 04-45-119 (n.) 1. a mechanism of social control for enforcing a society's standards 2. formal and explicit approval 3. official permission or approval 4. the act of final authorization (v.) 1. give authority or permission to 2. give sanction to 3. give religious sanction to, such as through on oath [second sound sponsor statutory support accept admire advocate affirmation aid applicable approve authorize nod notarize candidate cathedral charter clearance common constitutional illegal imprimatur indorsement initial invest ion official okay oke ordain orthodox]
*sanctity 15-43-7 (n.) 1. the quality of being holy [sacred san spirituality angelic attribute condition consider inviolable]
*sanguine 12-56-14 (a.) 1. confidently optimistic and cheerful 2. inclined to a healthy reddish color often associated with outdoor life [secure shed smile sure anguine aspire assured await gape genial glowing good unhealthy upbeat incline indicate infirmity introvert irrepressible eager enthusiastic expect]
*sanity 11-62-16 (n.) 1. normal or sound powers of mind [sane satisfactory sensible situation sound stability adjustment ani apprehension normal normality ideation]
*sarcasm 15-44-8 (n.) 1. witty language used to convey insults or scorn [salt satire say scorn seem sharp skill stupid swift acerbity acrimony arca asperity rancor remark repartee ridicule caricature caustic comedy convey cut cynicism malevolent malicious mean message mockery /sacra/] "he used sarcasm to upset his opponent"
*sarcophagus 20-54-3 (n.) 1. a stone coffin (usually bearing sculpture or inscriptions) [sarco sculpture stone ancient casket coffin corpse cremate]
*sardonic 12-48-13 (a.) 1. disdainfully or ironically humorous; scornful and mocking [sarcastic satirist scathing scornful sneer rebellion ridicule derisive derisory disdain don dry ironical irwin caustic contemptuous cut cynical /nod/] "his rebellion is the bitter, sardonic laughter of all great satirists"
*sash 13-62-10 (n.) 1. a band of material around the waist that strengthens a skirt or trousers 2. a framework that holds the panes of a window in the window frame [shash shell shoulder side skeleton skirt strengthen strip structure support symbol across admit ash hinge hold]
*satiate 22-60-2 (a.) 1. supplied (especially fed) to satisfaction (v.) 1. fill to satisfaction 2. overeat or eat immodestly; make a pig of oneself [sate sati satisfy scarf serve slake soak stall stuff supply surfeit swollen allay appetite assuage immodest impossible indulge ingest ingurgitate initial irk eat englut engorge enough excess exhaust]
*satire 07-59-38 (n.) 1. witty language used to convey insults or scorn [salt sarcasm sati scorn sendup sharp

skill song spoof stupid swift anacreontic takeoff threnody tire travesty idyll imitation incongruity ingenuity insult invective irony remark rhyme ridicule roundelay elegy esprit evoke exaggerate /rit/]
*satiric 19-15-4 (a.) 1. exposing human folly to ridicule [sarcastic sati sharp ridicule campaign /rit/] "a persistent campaign of mockery by the satirical fortnightly magazine"
*satirical 09-56-22 (a.) 1. exposing human folly to ridicule [sarcastic sardonic satiric spoof sharp abusive irony irreverent ridicule campaign caricature caustic criticize cynical /rit/] "a persistent campaign of mockery by the satirical fortnightly magazine"
*satirize 19-01-4 (v.) 1. ridicule with satire [sati send sharp attack rib ridicule roast /rit/] "The writer satirized the politician's proposal"
*saturnine 25-73-1 (a.) 1. bitter or scornful 2. showing a brooding ill humor [sad sarcastic saturn scornful scowl sensual serious show shrug silence silent sit solemn sour suffer sullen swarthy absorption almost taciturn temper ugly uncommunicative unpleasant unsociable reserved ridicule ill irritable expressive /ruta/] "the face was saturnine and swarthy, and the sensual lips...twisted with disdain"
*satyr 22-50-2 (n.) 1. man with strong sexual desires 2. one of a class of woodland deities; attendant on Bacchus; identified with Roman fauns [sadist seduce service sexual silenus sit sodomite spot strong stud acceptable adultery ancient attendant transvestite rapist ride roman]
*savage 05-70-68 (a.) 1. (of persons or their actions) able or disposed to inflict pain or suffering 2. without civilizing influences 3. wild and menacing 4. marked by extreme and violent energy (n.) 1. a member of an uncivilized people 2. a cruelly rapacious person (v.) 1. attack brutally and fiercely 2. criticize harshly or violently [sack sai second set severe skin slap society soldierly spain stage stick suffering abuse advance africa age animal anthropophagus apart assaulter attack vicious violent voracious gall gathering gaul germanic gorilla great grim group eat efficient emotional empire enemy enrage envenom extreme] "The press savaged the new President"
*savant 20-44-3 (n.) 1. someone who has been admitted to membership in a scholarly field [sage scholarly sharp specialist study admit amateur artist authority avant varied nut technology thinker]
*savor 10-AA-18 (n.) 1. the taste experience when a savoury condiment is taken into the mouth (v.) 1. taste appreciatively 2. have flavor; taste of something 3. derive or receive pleasure from; get enjoyment from; take pleasure in 4. give taste to [sap seafood season sensation sense shape show smack smell soluble stale stimulus adore application appreciate appreciativel aroma attribute avid avo value vanilla vapid vehement verve observe odor receive redolent relish /ova/]
*scarcity 13-38-11 (n.) 1. a small and inadequate amount [shortage slow small supply city copious absence adequate amount rare rarity infrequency insufficient teem thin tight]
*scent 06-67-60 (n.) 1. any property detected by the olfactory system 2. an odor left in passing by which a person or animal can be traced 3. a distinctive odor that is pleasant (v.) 1. cause to smell or be smelly 2. apply perfume to 3. catch the scent of; get wind of [savory sense share sign skin smelly sniff spicy spoor stimulate stink strong suggestion suspicion sweet sweetness care catch censer cent chemical class clue cologne cosmetic course cue embalm essential evidence external extract neaten nod nose nudge telltale toilet track trail]
*schism 15-62-8 (n.) 1. division of a group into opposing factions [school separate set society split chasm chi church community heterodoxy major misbelief mutual] "another schism like that and they will wind up in bankruptcy"
*scholarly 09-31-26 (a.) 1. characteristic of scholars or scholarship [scholar scientific set show study careful cerebral civilized critical culture highbrow owlish learn learned lettered literate abstruse academic accord acquire appealing approach attitude rabbinic rigorous] "scholarly pursuits"
*scholastic 13-16-10 (a.) 1. of or relating to the philosophical doctrine of scholasticism 2. of or relating to schools (n.) 1. a person who pays more attention to formal rules and book learning than they merit [savant seminary sensationalism specialist study chola christianity classroom clerk collegiate concern correct criticize hedonist humanity owlish learn lettered literate long abstruse academic academician animism attention teacher theism theory idealistic insist institution instrumentalist intellectual intramural] "scholastic year"
*scintilla 25-58-1 (n.) 1. a tiny or scarcely detectable amount 2. a sparkling glittering particles [say scarcely scrap shadow shred size sparkle speck structure suggestion suspicion cast coruscate idea indefinite internal intimate iota negligible taste thought till tiny tittle touch trace truth lick look amount average]
*scintillate 14-66-9 (v.) 1. give off 2. physics: fluoresce momentarily when struck by a charged particle or high-energy photon 3. be lively or brilliant or exhibit virtuosity 4. reflect brightly 5. emit or reflect light in a flickering manner; of stars [say scintilla send sharp shimmer shine single sky smart smoke spangle sparkle spirit star stimulate struck substance sun capacity cast charm clever concert constellation conversation coruscate ignite impressive inflame intelligent invigorate natural nimble talented tinsel tree twinkle life light lively living lustrous alight amount amusing animate apt ardent emit entertain excite exhibit /tall/] "the substance scintillated sparks and flashes"
*scope 05-55-86 (n.) 1. an area in which something acts or operates or has power or control: "the range of a

supersonic jet" 2. electronic equipment that provides visual images of varying electrical quantities 3. the state of the environment in which a situation exists 4. a magnifier of images of distant objects [situation source space span standard step sun supersonic surround sweep capacity carry chance choice collect color computer conduction confine control cope cosmic cut occasion opportunity orbit place play point possibility east echo effect environment extent eye]
*scorch 13-55-11 (n.) 1. a surface burn 2. a discoloration caused by heat (v.) 1. make very hot and dry 2. burn slightly and superficially so as to affect color 3. cause to wither or parch from exposure to heat 4. censor and criticize sharply and harshly 5. destroy completely by or as if by fire 6. become superficially burned [sear severe sharp shatter singe sizzle slash slight soil sound speed split stain stick sun superficial surface swinge ceiling char check chemical chip color condition cook cooking countryside cracked criticize cut orch oxidize radiation remark rent roast run rupture handkerchief harm harsh heat highball home hot hurt /cro croc/] "The heat scorched the countryside"
*scoundrel 17-42-5 (n.) 1. a wicked or evil person; someone who does evil deliberately [scallywag scamp shyster sneak cad cheat criminal crook cur unprincipled unreliable deceitful deceive deliberate deserve devil dishonorable dog rapscallion rascal rat reason reprehensible rogue rotter evil louse lowlife]
*scribble 10-58-21 (n.) 1. poor handwriting (v.) 1. write down quickly without much attention to detail 2. write carelessly [scrawl scrivener secretary small squiggle surface cacography calligraphy careless caricature cartoon chicken clerk communicate copier cramped crib illegible incomprehensible indecipherable botch burlesque letter line little look express]
*scribe 17-55-5 (n.) 1. French playwright (1791-1861) 2. someone employed to make written copies of documents and manuscripts 3. informal terms for journalists 4. a sharp-pointed awl for marking wood or metal to be cut (v.) 1. score a line on with a pointed instrument, as in metalworking [score scorer scratch secretary sent sharp surface chase clerk columnist construction copyist crib critic cut religious reporter restore revise rewrite illuminate incise instrument belletrist bibliography book bookkeeping editor employ essayist etch eugene]
*script 04-57-133 (n.) 1. a written version of a play or other dramatic composition; used in preparing for a performance 2. something written by hand 3. a particular orthography or writing system (v.) 1. write a script for [score shot shoulder side calligraphy capital case copy create crip realize roll roman illustration image indite instrument pen penmanship plan point production tablature teleplay text] "The playwright scripted the movie"
*scriptural 22-44-2 (a.) 1. of or pertaining to or contained in or in accordance with the Bible 2. (archaic) written or relating to writing [sacred script shorthand sound standard canonical conventional correct customary receive right running inscribe inspired italicize pen pencil pertain print textuary theological traditionalism accept accordance approve archaism authoritative literal longhand]
*scruple 20-58-3 (n.) 1. a unit of apothecary weight equal to 20 grains 2. an ethical or moral principle that inhibits action 3. uneasiness about the fitness of an action (v.) 1. hesitate on moral grounds 2. have doubts about 3. raise scruples [scrap second speculation spot standard strike suspicion challenge cheat compunction consider continue raise rally refrain regret reluctance restrain retreat rule uncertainty uneasy unnecessary unpleasant pause perjure pharmacy pinch ponder portion pound principle leery lota lying emotion equal ethical exception excessive expostulate express] "The man scrupled to perjure himself"
*scrupulous 11-49-16 (a.) 1. having scruples; arising from a sense of right and wrong; principled 2. characterized by extreme care and great effort [sent severe show slight standard study survey careless case caution cleanliness close conscientious critical religious research right rigid rigorous uncertain upstanding painstaking particular pierce precise principle producer leery lou loyal objective observant orderly overlook] "less scrupulous producers sent bundles that were deceptive in appearance"
*scrutinize 10-01-19 (v.) 1. to look at critically or searchingly, or in minute detail 2. of accounts and tax returns; with the intent to verify [scan searching see size study survey canvass careful check closely consider contemplate critical return review rutin tax inspect intent investigate essential examine eye] "he scrutinized his likeness in the mirror."
*scurrilous 20-64-3 (a.) 1. expressing offensive reproach [scandalous slander sultry censorious coarse cur curse unclean unprintable unspeakable raunchy raw reproach ridicule immoral indecent insulting invective language lewd libelous low lurid obscene offensive opprobrium outrageous]
*scurvy 25-65-1 (a.) 1. of the most contemptible kind (n.) 1. a condition caused by deficiency of ascorbic acid (vitamin C) [sad scorn scummy second shameful shoddy skin skunk small sneak sorry spongy stingy stunt substandard superlative symptom cheap cheesy close common condition contemptible cowardice curvy cut unclean unmentionable rabble rank rate reduce rotten rubbish valueless vile villainous vitamin]
*scuttle 11-46-17 (n.) 1. container for coal; shaped to permit pouring the coal onto the fire 2. an entrance equipped with a hatch; especially a passageway between decks of a ship (v.) 1. to move about or proceed hurriedly [scamper scupper scurry scut sea settle ship side sink skitter slow spoil standardize stymie swing

career coal container cook cover crab crowd undo tear terrify threshold thwart transport trip leap let limp loaded lumber ebb effective emergency end entryway equip escape exit extraordinary]
*scythe 15-86-7 (n.) 1. an edge tool for cutting grass; has a long handle that must be held with both hands and a curved blade that moves parallel to the ground (v.) 1. cut with a scythe, as of grass or grain [sharp sickle single swing sword chisel crop curve cut the tool hand hold horizontal edge]
*seance 22-45-2 (n.) 1. a meeting of spiritualists [sean session sit society speak spiritualist symposium eisteddfod alleged assembly assignation attempt attribute audience necromancy negotiation communicate confrontation congress] "the seance was held in the medium's parlor"
*sear 06-36-55 (a.) 1. (used especially of vegetation) having lost all moisture (v.) 1. make very hot and dry 2. cause to wither or parch from exposure to heat 3. become superficially burned [scallop scar scorch seedling sere shoot shrivel singe sizzle smoke soil solder sound strong sudden sun superficial ear earth edge effect emaciate evaporate exposure extremely adverse agonizing ashen ashy attaint attenuate red remove roast rub]
*secede 19-15-4 (v.) 1. withdraw from an organization or communion [sellout separate split cede communion defect desert different disaffiliate discontinue]
*secession 15-13-7 (n.) 1. an Austrian school of art and architecture parallel to the French Art Nouveau in the 1890s 2. the withdrawal of eleven Southern states from the Union in 1860 which precipitated the American Civil War 3. formal separation from an alliance or federation [schism separation southern style cession civil creative opposition organization nouveau]
*seclude 11-62-15 (v.) 1. keep away from others [screen secret segregate separate sequestrate set sift smooth split spot study ebb eclipse enclose eremite calm cloister closet conceal confine contact cool cut latent little lonely lude undisturbed unknown unmoved detached divide dwindle]
*seclusion 15-50-7 (n.) 1. the quality of being secluded from the presence or view of others 2. the act of secluding yourself from others [separation set shelter social solitude stranger escape ethnocentrism exclusive celibate cocoon company condition cut lonesome incognito insulation ion isolation outcast outsider narrow]
*secondary 04-55-101 (a.) 1. of second rank or importance or value; not direct or immediate 2. inferior in rank or status 3. belonging to a lower class or rank 4. depending on or incidental to what is original or primary 5. not of major importance (n.) 1. the defensive football players who line up behind the linemen 2. coil such that current is induced in it by passing a current through the primary coil [second subordinate employee exchange extra champion coil coming consequential copy ordinary other nonessential deputy derive double agent ancillary assistant attorney relief representative reserve] "the stone will be hauled to a secondary crusher"
*secondly 09-84-26 (ad.) 1. in the second place [second economy consider next discussion]
*secrecy 07-46-34 (n.) 1. the condition of being concealed or hidden 2. the trait of keeping things secret [screening separation silence chest clandestinene cloud conceal condition confidential confidentiali consider rec recess retirement retreat]
*secretary 01-53-676 (n.) 1. an assistant who handles correspondence and clerical work for a boss or an organization 2. a person who is head of an administrative department of government 3. a person to whom a secret is entrusted 4. a desk used for writing [secret supporter administrator assistant /rate rater/]
*secretive 09-59-25 (a.) 1. inclined to secrecy or reticence about divulging information [secret secrete seminal silent enigmatic evasive excrete express cagey cautious closemouthed communicative reserved reticent reveal rheumy taciturn talk tightlipped incline /iter vite/]
*secular 07-49-44 (a.) 1. concerning those not members of the clergy [sacred sing sister sound state earthly earthy education extremely century choir civil clerical collar concerning congregational control course cul unblessed unholy unregenerate laic laity layman laywoman lie long age annual astronomy rational realistic reasonable religious]
*sedate 11-59-15 (a.) 1. characterized by dignity and propriety 2. dignified and somber in manner or character and committed to keeping promises (v.) 1. cause to be calm or quiet as by administering a sedative to [sentence serene serious sleepy slow solemn somber somnolent soporific stately stiff stimulate earnest effect energise entrance date decorous demure detached dignity dope dreamy drowsy drug dull administer alert anesthetize aristocratic arouse august taste temperate thoughtful tranquillize triviality /tad/] "The patient must be sedated before the operation"
*sedentary 16-63-6 (a.) 1. used of persons or actions [seat shellfish sit stand exercise dead dent describe deskbound dormant dull non tame tend torpid abeyance apathetic area attached remain rock year] "forced by illness to lead a sedentary life"
*sediment 16-27-6 (n.) 1. matter deposited by some natural process (v.) 1. deposit as a sediment 2. settle as sediment [salt scum seawater settle silt situate slow soil solid soot space stand stream substance surface suspend ember evaporation debris deposit dime down dreg drift ice mass material matter moraine natural transport /ides/]
*sedition 22-33-2 (n.) 1. an illegal action inciting resistance to lawful authority and tending to cause the disruption or overthrow of the government [seditious serious strike subversion edition estrange extremism

disaffection disruption illegal impose incite infringe instigate intend tend treason troublemaker offense overthrow /ides tide/]
*seditious 22-48-2 (a.) 1. arousing to action or rebellion 2. in opposition to a civil authority or government [serve stimulate subversive edit encourage exciting desert direct disaffect discussion disloyal dissident duty inc incendiary inflammatory instigate insurgent insurrection tend traitorous treasonable trollope turbulent turncoat opposition unfaithful /ides tide/]
*seduce 07-63-39 (v.) 1. induce to have sex 2. lure or entice away from duty, principles, or proper conduct [sex siren squire start sully sway easy educe enchantress encourage endear enslave entice esquire exaggerate excite dally deceptive degrade delude dodger duce charm chat coax conduct coquette corrupt counterfeit course] "Harry finally seduced Sally"
*seer 20-48-3 (n.) 1. a person with unusual powers of foresight 2. an authoritative person who divines the future 3. an observer who perceives visually [sage savant scholar see soothsayer special supernatural suppose enthusiast escapist eyewitness rabbi read religious remote rishi romanticist rome] "an incurable seer of movies"
*seethe 11-62-16 (v.) 1. be noisy with activity 2. be in an agitated emotional state 3. have violent emotions, such as anger or frustration 4. foam as if boiling 5. boil vigorously [see set simmer sit smoke soup sparkle spill steep stir street struggle surge swarm swirl ebullition effervesce emotional enrage erupt excited experience explode extreme teem toast tumble turbulence turmoil heated heave hectic hiss hop horde hot huddle hum /tee/]
*seismograph 25-28-1 (n.) 1. a measuring instrument for detecting and measuring the intensity and direction and duration of of movements of the ground (as an earthquake) [show earthquake extent instrument intensity measure move graph ground record amount presence]
*seize 03-48-203 (v.) 1. take temporary possession of as a security, by legal authority 2. take possession of without permission or take with force, as after a conquest or invasion 3. take or capture by force 4. take hold of; grab 5. seize and take control without authority and possibly with force; take as one's right or possession 6. capture the attention or imagination of 7. hook by a pull on the line 8. affect [salesclerk security see sense sequester shipment snap snatch spasm steal stiffen stimulus stock stop story stuff suspect sweep encroach enemy exert exploit expropriate extract idea illegal imagination immediately immobile impound incident infringe inhabitant interested intrigue invade invasion] "The salesclerk quickly seized the money on the counter"
*selective 06-39-46 (a.) 1. tending to select; characterized by careful choice 2. characterized by very careful or fastidious selection [school select sensitive show strict eclectic elective electoral electronics eliminate exception exceptional exclusive capable careful choice choosy clique constituent critical tactful taste tend inadmissible inclusive indicate insular interference] "an exceptionally quick and selective reader"
*semblance 13-50-11 (n.) 1. outward or token appearance or form 2. an erroneous mental representation 3. picture consisting of a graphic image of a person or thing [same shape side effect effigy excuse manner match model blanc blind bluff law light liken look agreement air appearance near camouflage close community copy] "he tried to give his actions a semblance of authenticity"
*semiannual 20-AA-3 (a.) 1. occurring or payable twice each year [secular semester semiyearly six menstrual momently month monthly issue annual lasting /aim/]
*semicircle 19-29-4 (n.) 1. a plane figure with the shape of half a circle [scythe sector semilunar shape sickle sigmoid sphere spiral square star meniscus moiety circle circumference cone cross cube curve cylinder rectangle rhombus line lozenge lunate lunula]
*seminal 11-62-17 (a.) 1. pertaining to or containing or consisting of semen 2. containing seeds of later development [seed semen semina set sexual shape substance swarm ejaculate elementary embryonic epoch exuberant multiparous idea important influential inspire inspired new notional aboriginal abundant landmark later liquid lush luxuriant /anime/] "seminal fluid"
*seminar 06-41-48 (n.) 1. any meeting for an exchange of ideas 2. a course offered for a small group of advanced students [semina series session share short single specialize specialty study subject supervisor education elective evening examination exchange major meeting minor idea impart industrial instruction investigation academic advance agenda airing analysis application approach area assembly rap regular review roundtable /anime rani/]
*seminary 10-23-19 (n.) 1. a private place of education for the young 2. a theological school for training ministers or priests or rabbis [school seminar support education endowment establish minister institute institution academy rabbi religious run yeshiva young /anime rani/]
*senile 17-50-5 (a.) 1. mentally or physically infirm with age [second senescent seniority shaky shatter show simple specify elder enfeeble neurosis nile indicate infatuation infirm insipid instability inveterate late later less life live long longevity /lin line/]
*sensation 06-59-51 (n.) 1. someone who is dazzlingly skilled in any field 2. a general feeling of excitement and heightened interest 3. an unelaborated elementary awareness of stimulation 4. a state of widespread public excitement and interest 5. the faculty through which the external world is apprehended [sati sight smell star stir success suspicion synaesthesia exception excitement

experience noddle noggin noodle ace adept affection amazement aware taste thrill tingle triumph impression inflammation] "a sensation of touch"
*sense 01-53-880 (n.) 1. a natural appreciation or ability 2. the faculty through which the external world is apprehended 3. the meaning of a word or expression; the way in which a word or expression or situation can be interpreted 4. sound practical judgment 5. a general conscious awareness (v.) 1. perceive by a physical sensation, e.g., coming from the skin or muscles 2. become aware of not through the senses but instinctively 3. comprehend 4. detect some circumstance or entity automatically, as of a machine or instrument [sagacity sane security see self sen sentience short sight signify single situation skin smell sound stimulus substance subtle effect entity essence ethical existence experience expression extension external nature note notice nous nuance nub] "a sense of security"
*sensibility 07-37-44 (n.) 1. refined sensitivity to pleasurable or painful impressions 2. mental responsiveness and awareness 3. (physiology) responsiveness to external stimuli [science scruple selective self sensitivity sentience sentiment situation stimulus susceptibility elasticity emotion emotional energy ethical extensible external extreme nicety note notice impression impressionable incisive insight issue biological body botany branch bright lack less light limber lit literary lithe tactful taste trenchant trouble yourself /ibis/] "cruelty offended his sensibility"
*sensitive 03-49-176 (a.) 1. having acute mental or emotional sensibility 2. responsive to physical stimuli 3. able to feel or perceive 4. used officially of classified information or matters affecting national security 5. hurting [searching secret see sen sharp sticky subject subtle susceptible sympathetic easily eruptive exact explosive expose nervous nice impressionable incline influence irritate tense thin tingle touchy tricky volatile volcanic vulnerable /itis vitis/] "a mimosa's leaves are sensitive to touch"
*sensual 11-54-17 (a.) 1. of the appetites and passions of the body 2. sexually exciting or gratifying [sen sex sexy spirit straight suggest sultry earthy eat enthusiasm epicurean erogenous erotic excess exciting extend nuptial nymphomaniac undersexed abandon animal appetite lip look loose lush luxurious]
*sensuous 12-38-14 (a.) 1. taking delight in beauty [sen sensual stimulate sumptuous sybaritic engaging enjoy entrance esthetical experience exquisite opulent] "the sensuous joy from all things fair"
*sentence 02-45-396 (n.) 1. the period of time a prisoner is imprisoned 2. (criminal law) a final judgment of guilty in a criminal case and the punishment that is imposed 3. a string of words satisfying the grammatical rules of a language (v.) 1. pronounce a sentence on, in a court of law [say see sent single speak specify state string subordinate surprise symbolic emphatic enforce exclamation excommunicate expression note number teach ten term thought topic trial case clause collection community compose condemn construction conviction coordinate county court criminal] "he always spoke in grammatical sentences"
*sentient 20-65-3 (a.) 1. endowed with feeling and unstructured consciousness 2. consciously perceiving [sensitive sent situation sleepless slug smell stage surround susceptive elementary emotion endow external newt taw touch impressive inherent intellectual intolerable] "the living knew themselves just sentient puppets on God's stage"
*sentiment 04-48-109 (n.) 1. a personal belief or judgment that is not founded on proof or certainty 2. tender, romantic, or nostalgic feeling or emotion [sent sex sight soon sop speech sympathy emerge emotional ethos evidence excessive exclusive experience express extravagant eye nostalgia note notion tender theory thinking thought true idea impression incline matter mawkish mental mind mutual mystique /emit/]
*sentinel 16-33-6 (n.) 1. a person employed to watch for something to happen [scout sent spotter stand employ lookout]
*separate 02-46-524 (a.) 1. standing apart; not attached to or supported by anything 2. individual and distinct 3. independent; not united or joint 4. not living together as man and wife 5. have the connection undone; having become separate 6. characteristic of or meant for a single person or thing 7. separated according to race, sex, class, or religion (n.) 1. a separately printed article that originally appeared in a larger publication 2. a garment that can be purchased separately and worn in combinations with other garments (v.) 1. go one's own away; move apart 2. discontinue an association or relation; go different ways 3. force, take, or pull apart 4. make a division or separation 5. become separated into pieces or fragments 6. arrange or order by classes or categories 7. divide into components or constituents 8. come apart 9. separate into parts or portions 10. mark as different 11. act as a barrier between; stand between 12. divide into two or more branches so as to form a fork 13. treat differently on the basis of sex or race [scattering segment select separatist severally singular solely solitude sort specific square strange enclose entropy especially estranged exactly exotic expel expressly extraneous panel para particularly peculiar personally piece point precisely privacy provoke abrupt adrift alienate alone apart apartheid asunder away rank regard release removed retired room rootless tear treat /ape pes rape/] "a problem consisting of two separate issues"
*separatist 08-36-29 (a.) 1. having separated or advocating separation from another entity or policy or attitude (n.) 1. an advocate of secession or separation from a larger group (such as an established church or a national union) [schismatic secessionist separation

service society strikebreaker subdivision subtraction supporter entity establish exponent external para partition people plead policy propound proselyte protest alienate apartheid apostate attitude race racial rebel recidivist recusant religious removal renunciation tergiversate traitor idea incoherent independent isolation /ape pes rape sitar/]
*sequel 07-60-41 (n.) 1. something that follows something else 2. a part added to a book or play that continues and extends it [series shadow story subsequence successor supplement effect end extend upshot legacy lineage]
*sequence 04-61-114 (n.) 1. a following of one thing after another in time 2. film consisting of a succession of related shots that develop a given subject in a movie 3. the action of following in order 4. serial arrangement in which things follow in logical order or a recurrent pattern 5. several repetitions of a melodic phrase in different keys (v.) 1. arrange in a sequence 2. determine the order of constituents in [series set show string survey system effect experiment queue upshot nexus calculation chain chase classification connection course cycle] "the sequence of names was alphabetical"
*sequester 17-23-5 (v.) 1. requisition forcibly, as of enemy property 2. take temporary possession of as a security, by legal authority 3. keep away from others 4. Chemistry: undergo sequestration by forming a stable compound with an ion 5. set apart from others [science seclude secret security segregate seize separate set settle shipment smooth split stable steal study substance support ebb eclipse eject enemy essence estate ester estranged everyday expel quarantine quiet uncouple undergo undisturbed unknown unmoved until unyoke take temporary tooth tranquil reaction removed replevy repossess requisition resting retire retired] "the estate was sequestered"
*serendipity 15-44-8 (n.) 1. pure luck in discovering things you were not looking for [spot strike stroke excavation exhume exposure recognition revelation risk natural destiny determine discovery invention pity pleasant providence pure trove /tip tipi/]

*sergeant 06-48-60 (n.) 1. a lawman with the rank of sergeant 2. any of several noncommissioned officer ranks in the army or air force or marines ranking above a corporal 3. an English barrister of the highest rank [sapper sarge senior serge serjeant serve sheriff speak squad staff station superintendent supporter english enlist ranking reeve regular gendarme guardsman gunner administrative airman appointed army narc non tipstaff trooper]
*sermon 09-54-24 (n.) 1. an address of a religious nature (usually delivered during a church service) 2. a moralistic rebuke [scolding service spanking speak early exercise exhortation exposition rating read rebuke recitation religious major manner member mon moralist mount objurgate oration nature]
*serrated 22-54-2 (a.) 1. notched like a saw with teeth pointing toward the apex [sawtooth scallop see shape smooth edge ragged rough apex teeth toward]
*service 01-51-1941 (n.) 1. employment in or work for another 2. periodic maintenance on a car or machine 3. an act of help or assistance 4. a stroke (in tennis or badminton or squash) that puts the ball in play 5. the act of delivering a writ or summons upon someone 6. the performance of duties by a waiter or servant 7. the act of public worship following prescribed rules 8. a company or agency that performs a public service; subject to government regulation 9. tableware consisting of a complete set of articles (silver or dishware) for use at table 10. a force that is a branch of the armed forces 11. work done by one person or group that benefits another 12. a means of serving 13. (common law) the acts performed by an English feudal tenant for the benefit of his lord which formed the consideration for the property granted to him 14. Canadian writer (born in England) who wrote about life in the Yukon Territory (1874-1958) 15. the act of mating by male animals (v.) 1. make fit for use, as of appliances or cars 2. be used by; as of a utility 3. mate with [sacrament screwball serf servility ease engagement eve evening examination exercise ready repair rescue rite ritual run vice indulgence inferiority intermediate careful ceremony charge check condition couple] "budget separately for goods and services"
*serviceable 16-40-6 (a.) 1. ready for service or able to give long service 2. having a beneficial use 3. intended or able to serve a purpose without elaboration [salutary service shoe stout strong sturdy subservient suitable effective efficient elaborate employ equipment everyday expedient ready remedial repair instrumental intend intermediary capable concern condition conducive constructive contributory convenient actual aid appropriate assist banausic beneficial long lowh] "serviceable equipment"
*servile 22-56-2 (a.) 1. pertaining to or involving slaves 2. involving slaves 3. submissive or fawning in attitude or behavior [salute scrape scrub slavish soul sub subject submissive subordinate subservient sycophant enslavement enthrall regiment resigned restraint reverence vassalage vile vulgar ignoble inclination incurable inferiority ingratiating insurrection lesser low loyalty /livre/] "the servile wars of Sicily"
*servitude 20-41-3 (n.) 1. state of subjection to an owner or master or forced labor imposed as punishment [serf slavery specific status subjugation subordinate subservient employment enslave enslavement enthrall entitle restriction right rule vassalage villeinage impose tend thrall tyranny dependency disenfranchise disfranchise dominate domination] "penal servitude"
*sever 07-48-35 (v.) 1. cut off from a whole 2. set or keep apart [see separate set shear shred slice slit split

stop end ever excise extricate vary ragged relation remove rend rent rive] "sever a relationship"
*severance 11-34-15 (n.) 1. a personal or social separation (as between opposing factions) 2. the act of severing [section separation sever slice social split surgery eliminate employment exile expatriate variation redundancy relation removal rend rift ripping rupture alteration amputate analysis apart available avoid change chop come compensation cut]
*severely 05-45-78 (ad.) 1. causing great damage or hardship 2. with sternness; in a severe manner 3. to a severe or serious degree [say serious spartan stern strict relentless rigorous ruthless]
*sextet 16-29-6 (n.) 1. a musical composition written for six performers 2. a set of six similar things considered as a unit 3. six performers or singers who perform together 4. six people considered as a unit 5. the cardinal number that is the sum of five and one [septet sestet set singer sise six sixer strain string sum ecumenism element ensemble envoi epode ext teamwork trio triumvirate troop troupe]
*shallow 06-54-57 (a.) 1. lacking physical depth; having little spatial extension; downward ("shallow water" 2. lacking depth of intellect or knowledge; concerned only with what is obvious 3. not deep or strong; not affecting one deeply (n.) 1. a stretch of shallow water (v.) 1. make shallow 2. become shallow [seeming short silly slight small superficial surface hallow heedless airy amateurism appearance asinine levity light little low oblivious open otiose outward water wetland windy /olla/] "shallow water"
*shard 12-46-12 (n.) 1. a broken piece of a brittle artifact [scale scrap separate shave shell sherd slice sliver spike splinter sweeping hard hogwash hunk husk abrade animal archaeology artifact atomize rag rasher refuse disintegrate dollop dust]
*sheath 15-30-7 (n.) 1. a dress suitable for formal occasions 2. an enveloping structure or covering enclosing an animal or plant organ or part 3. a protective covering for a knife or sword [saddle scabbard screen secrete seed shell shield shoelace skin skirt stem structure suitable sword handgun hard health heath hide hooded house husk eclipse encase enclose envelop aglet aiglet animal armored attach axon tegument tented thin tube tubular]
*sheer 04-64-108 (a.) 1. very steep; having a prominent and almost vertical front 2. not mixed with extraneous elements 3. complete and without restriction or qualification; sometimes used informally as intensifiers 4. so thin as to transmit light (ad.) 1. straight up or down without a break 2. directly (v.) 1. turn sharply; change direction abruptly 2. cause to sheer [section seethrough sharp she silk simple slew slue square steer step stock straight stupid surface swerve hairpin hat head headlong heel help edge egregious element emphasize endurance exclusive excursus exhaustive explanation extent extraneous race ram rank reference regular restriction right rise rock] "he fell sheer into the water"
*shiftless 25-52-1 (a.) 1. lacking or characterized by lack of ambition or initiative; lazy [shift slack slothful slow sponge student successful suspicious hasty heedless idle improvident indolent inefficient inertia initiative irresponsible faineant feckless thoughtless thriftless lack laggard lax lazy little easy effort] "a shiftless student"
*shrewd 07-56-43 (a.) 1. marked by practical hardheaded intelligence 2. used of persons [scheming selfish sensible sharp show shrew situation slick smart smooth soft sound stupid subtlety hardheaded heady read ready resourceful road wary way wily wise wit deal deep designing devious diplomatic discern discrimination]
*shriek 10-60-20 (n.) 1. a high-pitched noise resembling a human cry 2. sharp piercing cry (v.) 1. utter a shrill cry [say screeching screechy shall sharp shell shout shrill sing snap sound squall sudden hail hear highpitched hiss hollo howling human raw reedy risible rumble exclaim keen kind /keir/]
*shrill 12-51-12 (a.) 1. high-pitched and sharp (v.) 1. utter a shrill cry [say screech sharp shout sound sour squall strident sudden harsh high highpitched hollo howling raucous reedy rill ring inharmonious insistent intense literary loud]
*shrinkage 19-35-4 (n.) 1. process or result of becoming less or smaller 2. the act of stealing goods that are on display in a store 3. the amount by which something shrinks [sale sear ship shoplift shortening shrink shrivel size small steal store reduction remission retrench impair impoverish inch item kiln amount atrophy attenuate attrition good erosion euphemism exhaustion expenditure] "the material lost 2 inches per yard in shrinkage"
*shrivel 15-56-8 (v.) 1. wither, esp. with a loss of moisture 2. decrease in size, range, or extent [sear see shaky shoot shorten shrink shrive size small smoke stunted suffer sun haggard range rickety rub rudimentary rusty incipient ineffectual infirm insolate earn elfin emaciate evaporate extent languish lessen loss] "The fruit dried and shriveled"
*shrug 05-62-78 (n.) 1. a gesture involving the shoulders (v.) 1. raise one's shoulders to indicate indifference or resignation [shoulder show signal stance hand raise resignation rug gesture]
*shuffle 07-54-44 (n.) 1. the act of mixing cards haphazardly 2. walking with a slow dragging motion without lifting your feet (v.) 1. move about, move back and forth 2. walk by dragging one's feet 3. mix so as to make a random order or arrangement [scuffle selection separate shake shamble shifty slack sliding slouch slow sluggish split staggering step half hall halting hand haphazard haywire hear hedge hitch hobble hold huff

uncertain unpredictable unsettled upset falter feet flicker floor fluctuate flurry fluster flutter foot forth frenzy fumble fund fuss lazy lift limp linger litter locate lumber lurch embarrassment equivocation evasive] "he shuffled out of the room"

*shun 07-50-42 (v.) 1. avoid and stay away from deliberately; stay clear of 2. expel from a community or group [scorn shirk shrink shut shy sidetrack slip spare spurn stay hide holdback hun neutrality]

*shunt 13-72-11 (n.) 1. a conductor having low resistance in parallel with another device to divert a fraction of the current 2. a passage by which a bodily fluid (especially blood) is diverted from one channel to another 3. implant consisting of a tube made of plastic or rubber; for draining fluids within the body (v.) 1. transfer to another track, of trains 2. provide with or divert by means of an electrical shunt [send shift shove sidetrack slight sort surgical switch haw heat hunt unconsidered undone unsolicited neglect thrust tissue track train transfer transmit trundle tube turn] "an arteriovenus shunt"

*sidelong 25-41-1 (a.) 1. (used especially of glances) directed to one side with or as if with doubt or suspicion or envy 2. situated at or extending to the side 3. inclining or directed to one side (ad.) 1. on the side 2. with the side toward someone or something 3. to toward or at one side [sidle situate skirting slant slop slope spatial squint stoker straightforward suspicion incline indirect destination devious digressive dimension direct divergent doubt downward edgewise elizabeth envy excursive extend eye lateral lead lean lee lie line listing locate long look lying obliquely nathaniel nearby glance glancing ground /led/] "the plow lay sidelong on the ground"

*sidestep 10-51-20 (n.) 1. a step to one side (as in boxing or dancing) (v.) 1. avoid or try to avoid fulfilling, answering, or performing (duties, questions, or issues) [saltation say series set shy skillful skirt stay step switch ides irrelevant issue dance discuss dodge down drawback duck elude equivocate evade tend tergiversate terpsichore truth try parry perform point prevaricate problem pugilism pullback /pet/]

*siege 06-56-45 (n.) 1. the action of an armed force that surrounds a fortified place and isolates it while continuing to attack [sack san santa seizure service seven sherman spell supply surround syracuse importance imprison inclusion independent indian indochina insurgent investment involve island isolate effort encircle enclosure encompass end enemy english envelop eventually gain grant]

*significance 04-52-90 (n.) 1. the message that is intended or expressed or signified 2. a meaning that is not expressly stated but can be inferred 3. the quality of being significant [sense sign spirit stress substance subtlety idea impact import influence gist grandeur great nicety nobility notability note nuance fatality fateful force communication connotation consequence content credit acceptation authority effect emphasis extension /fin/] "do not underestimate the significance of nuclear power"

*significant 02-54-493 (a.) 1. rich in significance or implication 2. (statistics) too closely correlated to be attributed to chance and therefore indicating a systematic relation 3. fairly large 4. important in effect or meaning [secret sizable sound statistics suggestive superior sure idea identify imply important indicate individual influential interpretation grand great name nod notable noteworthy factual fairly final forceful fundamental cant certain closely collection compel considerable contribution correlate critical absolute amount association attribute authentic tax telling theory transfer typical /fin/] "a significant change in tax laws"

*similar 01-51-724 (a.) 1. having the same or similar characteristics 2. marked by correspondence or resemblance 3. capable of replacing or changing places with something else 4. resembling or similar; having the same or some of the same characteristics; often used in combination 5. (of words) expressing closely related meanings [shape share siamese simulate size standardize synonymous synthetic identical imitation interchange mark match mathematics measure mimic mind mine mock lar like limit look akin alike analogous angle angular antonym ape reciprocal relative replace resemble] "similar food at similar prices"

*simile 20-63-3 (n.) 1. a figure of speech that expresses a resemblance between things of different kinds (usually formed with ‘like' or ‘as') [same semblance sheet simulation speech symbol identity image imitation irony match metaphor mile mimic language liken litotes emphasis exclamation expression]

*simper 20-75-3 (v.) 1. smile affectedly or derisively [say signal simp smile smirk smug sneer spread irritate mincing pedantic pleasure prink purist put elegant euphuism expression exquisite]

*simplify 07-48-41 (v.) 1. make simpler or easier or reduce in complxity or extent [shorten simp smooth solution solve speed straightforward streamline illustration instruction mathematical modify move pare perplex popularize purify less light live loose lower facilitation factor form fraction] "We had to simplify the instructions"

*simulate 09-34-26 (v.) 1. reproduce someone's behavior or looks 2. create a representation or model of 3. make a pretence of [similar sleep steal strive study substitute suggest synthetic identical illegitimate imitate manner mark match mime mimic mirror mock model unnatural unreal like adopt affected ape art artificial assume tin training twist echo effect embellish emulate enact enjoy equal evoke /alum/]

*simultaneous 05-45-87 (a.) 1. occurring or operating at the same time [satisfy straightway subito symbiosis synchronous synergy immediate inphase instantaneous

isochronous momentary mutual union togetherness twin accompany agreement alliance association now equation exist operate]
*sinecure 25-60-1 (n.) 1. a benefice to which no spiritual or pastoral duties are attached 2. an office that involves minimal duties [situation soft spiritual spot income involve easy ecclesiastical endow church cure cushy regular require ride]
*singe 20-53-3 (n.) 1. a surface burn (v.) 1. burn superficially or lightly 2. become superficially burned [scorch sear short slight smoke soil stain superficial surface swinge inge injury edge exposure eyebrow] "I singed my eyebrows"
*sinister 06-69-45 (a.) 1. stemming from evil characteristics or forces; wicked or dishonorable 2. threatening or foreshadowing evil or tragic developments 3. (heraldry) on or starting from the wearer's left [scheme see shameless shield side sin situation slippery start stem storm study suggest suspicious ill improper indirect intelligence near nefarious nigh threatening thundercloud tone trace tragic tricky trying ethnic evasive evil excursive radical rigorous rotten rumbling]
*sinuous 15-46-8 (a.) 1. curved or curving in and out [serpentine sin smooth snaky straight stream supple incurve indirect involutional undulant]
*sinus 20-43-3 (n.) 1. an abnormal passage leading from a suppurating cavity to the body surface 2. any of various air-filled cavities especially in the bones of the skull 3. a wide channel containing blood; does not have the coating of an ordinary blood vessel [scoop secretion shell short shut sigmoid sin sink skull source straight substance suppurate surface indentation nasal natural nose notch unpaired /sun/]
*siren 09-51-24 (n.) 1. a sea nymph (part woman and part bird) supposed to lure sailors to destruction on the rocks where the nymphs lived 2. a woman who is considered to be dangerously seductive 3. a warning signal that is a loud wailing sound 4. an acoustic device producing a loud often wailing sound as a signal or warning 5. eel-like aquatic North American salamander with small forelimbs and no hind limbs; have permanent external gills [sailor salamander sea seaman seductive seductress sexual signal sing sire sit snapper song sound stationary steam suppose interesting intrigue inviting rattlebox ravishing resemble return rhine rock rotate ear eel electronic enchantress entrance exciting exotic external naiad nere nix noisemaker north nymph]
*sisterhood 19-52-4 (n.) 1. the kinship relation between a female offspring and the siblings 2. a religious society of sisters (especially an order of nuns) [sale sect sequence serenity sister society sodality sorority stability succession symmetry imperative instruction tidy tranquillity edict enation regulation relationship requisition harmony orderly organization demand directive]
*skeptic 11-01-15 (n.) 1. someone who habitually doubts accepted beliefs [school keep knowledge evidence expect philosophy physical place possible intellect convince creative cynic]
*skepticism 08-AA-28 (n.) 1. doubt about the truth of something 2. the disbelief in any claims of ultimate knowledge [scepticism scoff skeptic suspicion knowledge philosophy tendency toward true incertitude incredulity cautious claim concern cynicism mark mental misgiving]
*skiff 22-35-2 (n.) 1. any of various small boats propelled by oars or by sails or by a motor [sail sampan schooner scull shallow ski sloop smack speedboat steamer submarine kayak ketch felucca ferryboat flagship flatbottom freighter frigate]
*skirmish 10-40-19 (n.) 1. a minor short-term fight (v.) 1. engage in a skirmish [scrap scuffle strive struggle incident riot rumble melee minor mis]
*skit 15-30-8 (n.) 1. a short theatrical episode [satirize scene sendup short show sketch spoof success kit intermission introduction theatrical turn]
*slack 07-49-35 (a.) 1. not tense or taut 2. lacking in strength or firmness or resilience 3. lacking in rigor or strictness 4. flowing with little speed as e.g. at the turning of the tide (n.) 1. a noticeable decline in performance 2. a cord or rope or cable that is hanging loosely 3. a stretch of water without current or movement 4. the condition of being loose (not taut) (v.) 1. avoid responsibilities and work, be idle 2. become less in amount or intensity 3. be inattentive to, or neglect, as of duties 4. release tension on 5. make less active or fast 6. cause to heat and crumble by treatment with water, as of lime 7. make less active or intense 8. become slow or slower [sag scrap shuffling size skip slake sloppy slovenly slow sluggish lack lazy lessen light limp loose abandon abate aloof careless chamber chicken cut /kcal/] "He slacks his attention"
*slake 22-50-2 (v.) 1. satisfy (thirst) 2. cause to heat and crumble by treatment with water, as of lime 3. make less active or intense [sate satisfy sink slack small soften stuff lake least lessen lie lime loosen abate allay alleviate alter appease assuage engorge exposure extinguish]
*slander 13-27-11 (n.) 1. words falsely spoken that damage the reputation of another 2. an abusive attack on a person's character or good name (v.) 1. charge falsely or with malicious intent; attack the good name and reputation of someone [say scandalous scurrilous seriously slight slur smear smirch speak statement strong strumpet sully lander language libelous abusive accuse argot article aspersion assail assassinate attack damage decry defame denigrate destroy detractor dirt discredit disparage drag rail remark reputation ridicule roorback]
*sleight 15-56-7 (n.) 1. adroitness in using the hands [shift skillful sleigh strategy eight expedient intrigue

gambit game gimmick hand tactic trickery]
*slight 01-52-525 (a.) 1. having little substance or significance 2. being of delicate or slender build 3. almost no or (with 'a') at least some; very little (n.) 1. a deliberate discourteous act (usually as an expression of anger or disapproval) (v.) 1. pay no attention to, disrespect [scarcely self shoot short shoulder shunt sidetrack silent silly size slender slice slim small snub somewhat sparing speak spiritual straight strength strong substantial lack large lean least light limited little look loose idle ignore imperfect inconsequential insignificant insult gauzy girl gossamer hair handle hardly humiliation tad tenuous thin touch trivial]
*slothful 25-70-1 (a.) 1. disinclined to work or exertion [shuffling sloth sluggish staggering languish lazy lethargic limp lumber otiose tentative totter trudge halting hangeron hobble faineant falter flagging form unhurried]
*slur 10-47-18 (n.) 1. (music) a curved line spanning notes that are to be played legato 2. a disparaging remark 3. a blemish made by dirt (v.) 1. play smoothly or legato; of musical passages 2. become vague or indistinct 3. speak disparagingly of; e.g., make a racial slur 4. utter indistinctly [score skate skimp slight smear smirch smoke smooth smudge sound spaning speak spiel splotch spoil spot stain statement structure superficial symbol language lead legato libel line uninterrupted utter race racial recognition refer reflection remark remove rendition repercussion replay] "your comments are slurring your co-workers"
*smolder 15-02-7 (v.) 1. burn slowly and without a flame 2. have strong suppressed feelings [see sensation show sleeping slow smoke smoky smoulder stand storm strong suppress moil molder moment liable lifeless linger live lurk dead dormant dull emotional endure erupt exist experience explode rage ramp reappear reek roast rumble] "a smoldering fire"
*snare 11-43-16 (n.) 1. something (often something deceptively attractive) that catches you unawares 2. a surgical instrument consisting of wire hoop that can be drawn tight around the base of polyps or small tumors to sever them; used especially in body cavities 3. strings stretched across the lower head of a snare drum; they make a rattling sound when the drum is hit 4. a small drum with two heads and a snare stretched across the lower head 5. a trap for birds or small mammals; often has a noose (v.) 1. catch in or as if in a trap 2. entice and trap [sack salesman scheme seize sever sexual side situation slip solicit sound speeder sport steal stretch string struck surgical nail net nip noose abstract across alluring and animal approach appropriate are arrange attractive rattling remove roadway rope rustle embezzle entangle entice entrap escape exaggerate exam]
*snub 09-70-22 (a.) 1. unusually short (n.) 1. an instance of driving away or warding off 2. a refusal to recognize someone you know (v.) 1. reject outright and bluntly 2. refuse to acknowledge [scorn setback short shoulder slight slowdown spatial speech spurn stop stub nip nose nub unusual upstage ban blunt bob bring brushoff /bun/] "a snub nose"
*soar 03-54-197 (n.) 1. the act of rising upward into the air (v.) 1. fly by means of a hang glider 2. fly upwards or high in the sky 3. go or move upward 4. rise rapidly, as of a current or voltage 5. fly a plane without an engine [sailplane set shift shoot size sky spin spring stock stream surge oar ongoing onrush outstrip advance airborne aircraft airline arise ascent aspire august aviation range rapid reach rear rise rocket run] "The stock market soared after the cease-fire was announced"
*sober 06-55-54 (a.) 1. lacking brightness or color; dull 2. dignified and somber in manner or character and committed to keeping promises 3. not affected by a chemical substance (especially alcohol) 4. completely lacking in playfulness (v.) 1. cause to become sober 2. become more realistic 3. become sober after excessive alcohol consumption [sentence serene serious seriously severe simple situation sob solemn sombre sound speculative staid steady stupefy subdued substance ominous opalescent open balance bare base become bed black brightness brown earnest effect eggshell enter equable eschew even excessive excited experience expression rational realistic reasonable recover regal restrained royal] "A sobering thought"
*sobriety 15-47-7 (n.) 1. the state of being sober 2. a manner that is serious and solemn 3. moderation in or abstinence from alcohol or drugs 4. abstaining from excess [sad sedate serious sincerity sober solemnity somber staid steady stuffy balance brie brightness reasonable refrain renounce restraint rice impartial indulge earnest even excesse teetotal temperance temperate thoughtfulnes trait tranquillity]
*sociable 13-77-10 (a.) 1. inclined to or conducive to companionship with others 2. friendly and pleasant (n.) 1. a party of people assembled to promote sociability and communal activity [seek simplicity slush smooth society suitable occasion offering open opportunity organization organize outgoing outspoken outward casual chat civil close clubby community concern conducive congenial convivial cordial courtesy informal interest intimate irregularity able accessible affable agreeable allow amiable assemble association befitting bigmouth brotherly life living loose loquacity love easygoing expansive extrovert] "a sociable occasion"
*socialism 10-44-18 (n.) 1. a political theory advocating state ownership of industry 2. an economic system based on state ownership of capital [sacrifice social stage statism operate organization orientation ownership capitalist centralism change characterize collectivism collegial communism community control ideology imperialism important industry intervention abolish accord achieve advocate allocate law management market mean monarchism move /laic/]

*socialist 05-48-82 (a.) 1. of or relating to or promoting or practicing socialism 2. advocating or following the socialist principles (n.) 1. a political advocate of socialism [six social support oppose overthrow candidate capitalistic castro collectivize communist cuban industrial international advocate argue labor leader leftwinger liberal theft theory thomas /laic/] "socialist theory"
*sociology 07-31-40 (n.) 1. the study and classification of human societies [scientific structure study ology opinion origin classification convention criminal institution law group]
*sodden 15-74-8 (a.) 1. wet through and through; thoroughly wet [saturate shirt shoe soak soppy speaker steep swamp ooze overflow den dip door drench drink drown drunk drunken dull engulf excessive extremely nappy /eddo/]
*soggy 11-48-15 (a.) 1. soaked with moisture 2. having the consistency of dough because of insufficient leavening or improper cooking [soak sodden squelch steep sticky swamp ooze overflow great] "a soggy lawn"
*sol 06-71-45 (n.) 1. a colloid that has a continuous liquid phase in which a solid is suspended in a liquid 2. (Greek mythology) ancient Roman god; personification of the sun; counterpart of Greek Helios 3. the syllable naming the fifth (dominant) note of any musical scale in solmization [scale soh sun suspension syllable last liquid literary]
*solace 10-51-19 (n.) 1. the comfort you feel when consoled in times of disappointment 2. the act of consoling; giving relief in affliction 3. comfort in disappointment or misery (v.) 1. give moral or emotional strength to [sad side silver situation soothe source still strength succour support sympathy lace lessen limited line lull affliction alleviate amusement aspect assistance assure calm comfort console convulse ease emotional empathy encouragement entertainment exhilarate]
*solar 07-52-35 (a.) 1. relating to or derived from the sun or utilizing the energies of the sun [semilunar sidereal sky sola source star starry stellar sun operate originate lar last lunar lunate lunulate asteroid astrophysics radiation reference relation] "solar eclipse"
*solder 20-31-3 (n.) 1. an alloy (usually of lead and tin) used when melted to join two metal surfaces (v.) 1. join or fuse with solder [sculpture sear sell silver span surface oxidize lead league link low dissolve electrical element embrace encompass engrave establish repair] "solder these two pipes together"
*soldier 02-51-327 (n.) 1. an enlisted man or woman who serves in an army 2. a wingless sterile ant or termite having a large head and powerful jaws adapted for defending the colony (v.) 1. serve as a soldier in the military [sapper sergeant spearman squad supporter sweat oldie lafayette lawrence legionnaire dodge drive drudge infantryman intrepid emmet endure recruit regular rifleman] "the soldiers stood at attention"
*solecism 25-75-1 (n.) 1. a socially awkward or tactless act [slip social sole sophistry stupidity syntax lapse embarrass error etiquette catachresis claptrap corruption impropriety inappropriate incorrect indiscretion manner mispronounce mistake moonshine /sice/]
*solemnity 17-43-5 (n.) 1. a trait of dignified seriousness 2. a solemn and dignified feeling [sedate serious service sincerity slow sober solemn somber staid observe occasion office ordinance law leaden legal lifeless lofty earnest effective elevation emotional exercise experience majesty momentous mystery nature nobility importance inauguration institution taciturnity tasteless tedious trait]
*solicitor 04-91-101 (n.) 1. a petitioner who solicits contributions or trade or votes 2. a British lawyer who gives legal advice and prepares legal documents [scotland seek solicit suitor supplicant officer law lawsuit lawyer legal impose intercessor candidate canvass chief city claimant client collection conduct contribution county top tout town trade represent rule /otic roti/]
*solicitous 19-36-4 (a.) 1. full of anxiety and concern 2. showing hovering attentiveness [show solicit strained suspense obliging lenient loving impatient inattentive indulgent inquiry care careful civil concerned consider tender tense trouble uneasy urbane /otic/] "solicitous parents"
*solicitude 25-31-1 (n.) 1. a feeling of excessive concern [show solicit stew strain suspense sympathy obliging leniency indulgence inquietude care careful cautious concern consider consideration tension thorough trouble uneasy upset urbanity discretion disturbance dread excessive express]
*soliloquy 17-34-5 (n.) 1. speech you make to yourself 2. a (usually long) dramatic speech intended to give the illusion of unspoken reflections [section speak oral oration language lilo line long idea illusion intend yourself /lilo/]
*solstice 19-46-4 (n.) 1. either of the two times of the year when the sun is at its greatest distance from the celestial equator [season short southernmost summertime sun sunshine long ice celestial cosmic cover ecliptic equator]
*soluble 19-48-4 (a.) 1. (of a substance) capable of being dissolved in some solvent (usually water) 2. susceptible of solution or of being solved or explained [sol solvent substance susceptible level easily explicate] "the puzzle is soluble"
*solvent 12-36-13 (a.) 1. capable of meeting financial obligations (n.) 1. a liquid substance capable of dissolving other substances 2. a statement that solves a problem or explains how to solve the problem [seek set simple solid solution solve sound statement substance substantial surface obligation obtain odor oil once organic oxybenzene lacquer liquid literary lotion various

volatile emetic enema enough ether expense explain extinguisher nausea non tar tetrachloromethane thin toluene toxicity try turpentine] "the solvent does not change its state in forming a solution"
*somber 11-AA-17 (a.) 1. lacking brightness or color; dull 2. grave or even gloomy in character [sad sepulchral serious simple sober solemn strict subdued suitable obscure occasion ominous overcast mark mat melancholy menace mind mood mournful murky music muted bad black bleak brightness brown earnest eggshell evil]
*somnolent 20-44-3 (a.) 1. inclined to or marked by drowsiness [sleepy slow sluggish slumberous sound stretch opiate oscitant manifest mark moribund nap nod numb lack lassitude leaden lent lethargic lethargy lifeless limited listless little effect enervate ennui eye tend torpid]
*sonata 08-31-28 (n.) 1. a musical composition of 3 or 4 movements of contrasting forms [salsa samba scherzo score self serious sinfonia single ska solo son sonatina song soprano soul spiritual staccato study suite swing symphony operetta opus oratorio orchestrate overture nocturne adagio adaptation allegro alto andante anthem appealing aria arpeggio arrangement taste tone traditional trio twelve]
*sonnet 16-54-6 (n.) 1. a verse form consisting of 14 lines with a fixed rhyme scheme (v.) 1. praise in a sonnet 2. compose a sonnet [satire scheme section sestet sestina set shakespearean short song structure syllable octave ode net elegy english epic epigram express tanka ten threnody triolet /tenno/]
*sonorous 17-45-5 (a.) 1. full and loud and deep [sing sound sounding speak sweet orotund ostentatious overwrought nor rich rolling round uproarious]
*soot 16-37-6 (n.) 1. a black colloidal substance consisting wholly or principally of amorphous carbon and used to make pigments and ink (v.) 1. coat with soot [shadow smoke smudge smut sprinkle substance surface oil organic tar tetravalent]
*soothsayer 22-62-2 (n.) 1. someone who makes predictions of the future (usually on the basis of special knowledge) [seer special speculate sun oracle teller haruspex adumbrate astrology augur /ash/]
*sophisticate 03-45-147 (n.) 1. a worldly-wise person (v.) 1. make less natural or innocent 2. make more complex or refined 3. alter and make impure, as with the intention to deceive 4. practice sophistry; change the meaning of or be vague about in order to mislead or deceive [school season sharp slicker socialite sophistic stylish old pervert polished posh practice hardheaded hep hip intricate involved trendy tricksy trig trim twist chic civilize clever cognoscenti complicate connoisseur convolute cool corrupt cosmopolite cutting cynical adult advance aesthete around educate elaborate elegant erudite experience /tacit/] "Their manners had sophisticated the young girls"
*sophisticated 03-45-144 (a.) 1. ahead in development; complex or intricate 2. marked by wide-ranging knowledge and appreciation of many parts of the world arising from urban life and wide travel 3. having or appealing to those having worldly knowledge and refinement and savoir faire 4. intellectually appealing [sophisticate stylish hight chic classy clever cutting erudite /tacit/] "sophisticated young socialites"
*sophistry 25-53-1 (n.) 1. a deliberately invalid argument displaying ingenuity in reasoning in the hope of deceiving someone [seem sharp shrewd sophist subtlety obfuscate obscure ontology perversion philosophy proof hollow hope illogicality incorrect ingenuity insincerity invalid inventive tricky rationalize ready reasoning]
*soporific 19-73-4 (a.) 1. sleep inducing 2. inducing mental lethargy (n.) 1. a drug that induces sleep [slack sleepy sluggish smack somnific sop speech stimulate substance opiate opium oscitant painkiller passive physiological pill poppy produce psychological rainbow red resigned response indifferent induce insouciance interminable form calm capable capsule catalepsy chemical comatose curiosity /fir/]
*soprano 05-40-67 (a.) 1. having or denoting a high range (n.) 1. a female singer 2. the highest female voice; the voice of a boy before puberty 3. the pitch range of the highest female voice [sacred sax second shrill sill silverman sing soar songstress sound specialize still sutherland swedish operatic part perceive pierce pitch plainsong play power price puberty range register role run accompaniment alto australian nightingale nilsson norman noted] "soprano voice"
*sorcery 20-62-3 (n.) 1. the belief in magical spells that harness occult forces or evil spirits to produce unnatural effects in the world [satan seeming semblance show spell spirit supernatural suppose occult orc originate cantrip clairvoyance conjure effect enchantment evil /cro/]
*sordid 14-53-9 (a.) 1. morally degraded 2. unethical or dishonest 3. foul and run-down and repulsive 4. meanly avaricious and mercenary [sad seamy seedy selfish shock soil squalid obnoxious offensive outrageous rank regrettable rotten rundown decadent degenerate despicable did dire dirty disgusting dreadful ignoble impoverish infamous informal]
*souvenir 08-44-29 (n.) 1. something of sentimental value 2. a reminder of past events [sentimental shadow skill sou occasion value visible engram entity experience recollection relic remembrance reminder]
*sparse 09-44-26 (a.) 1. not dense [scant scarce scattered scrubby seldom skimpy slim slow small space sporadic spread parse passim paucity piddle poor poverty arse rare rarity everywhere exiguous]
*spartan 12-55-13 (a.) 1. of or relating to or characteristic of Sparta or its people 2. practicing great self-denial 3. unsparing and uncompromising in

discipline or judgment 4. resolute in the face of pain or danger or adversity (n.) 1. a resident of Sparta [indulgent self severe simple sixfooter sparta pain parent people pitch plain pointed poor practice prior prowess purpose abstemious accepting adversity ancient ascetic austere authoritarian reason reserved resident resolute rigid rigorous thin tight tough narrow native natural neat nomad non /trap/] "spartan courage"
*spasmodic 22-61-2 (a.) 1. affected by involuntary jerky muscular contractions; resembling a spasm 2. occurring in spells and often abruptly [scattered severe shaky sharp shoot sloppy spasm spell sporadic steady sudden painful patchy periodic poignant promiscuous prone abrupt acute affect afflict alternate meaningless mercurial moody move muscular occasional orgasm outburst desultory different disastrous discontinuous dizzy impulsive instance interval involuntary irregular irresponsible capricious careless casual change chaotic characterize contraction convulsive cruel /sap/]
*specialize 04-01-111 (v.) 1. suit to a special purpose 2. be specific about 3. become more special 4. devote oneself to a special area of work 5. evolve so as to lead to a new species or develop in a way most suited to the environment, of populations of plants and animals [separate set special state study particularize patent precise pursue enlarge enumerate expatiate expound change concentrate condition contain individuate inventory itemize alter analyze anatomize assign limit list lucubration /laic/] "We specialize in dried flowers"
*specialty 05-04-63 (n.) 1. an asset of special worth or utility 2. a distinguishing trait 3. the special line of work you have adopted as your career [seal service shape skill special strong study subject suit peculiarity plant plus point policy practice product property earmark elective element career cast concern cut idiosyncrasy impression index individuation ingredient interest adopt agreement area art aspect asset attribute law legal lifework line long taint tang taste thumb trait /laic/]
*species 04-50-106 (n.) 1. (biology) taxonomic group whose members can interbreed 2. a specific kind of something [science share sort specie stock strain study subdivision plant essential exemplify extinction category chemistry christianity classification coinage collective consider interbreed ion] "a species of molecule"
*specimen 08-52-28 (n.) 1. a bit of tissue or blood or urine that is taken for diagnostic purposes 2. an example regarded as typical of its class [sample serve showpiece sort spec species parade pattern piece protest purpose embodiment example exhibition exposition class collected illustration instance item march material model natural /mice/] "they collected a urine specimen for urinalysis"
*specious 20-42-3 (a.) 1. plausible but false 2. based on pretense; deceptively pleasing 3. plausible but false [seeming sham show sincerity spec spurious superficial perfume phony plausible pleasing pose possible praise presume pretense empty equivocation erroneous ethel external causality cheat circularity claim cogency coloring conceivable idle imaginary imposture inaccurate incorrect inference insincerity interest invalid inwardly obfuscate obscurantist obsolescent ostentation unfounded unreal unsound untrue] "specious reasoning"
*spectator 04-62-91 (n.) 1. a woman's pump with medium heel; usually in contrasting colors for toe and heel 2. a close observer; someone who looks at something (such as an exhibition of some kind) [secret see seek seer sense sex shoe shout spec stand stare swear patron peep people perceive performance pit pump enjoy exhibition eyewitness casual close color compurgation congregation consign contrast take testify theatergoer toe tom trustee acquirer aficionado applaud attend auditory aware observer obtain onlooker orchestra organ receiver recipient /rota/] "the spectators applauded the performance"
*specter 10-02-20 (n.) 1. a ghostly appearing figure 2. a mental representation of some haunting experience [sail see shadow shape ship spec spirit spook supernatural past perception performance phantom possibility presence prospect eidolon exist experience captain condemn confront terror threat revenant review]
*spectrum 06-44-55 (n.) 1. broad range of related values or qualities or ideas or activities 2. an ordered array of the components of an emission or wave [scale scope series spec spirit peacock pendulum progression eidolon carry connection course thread tier train range reach round run megahertz moire monotone]
*speculate 05-41-76 (v.) 1. reflect deeply on a subject 2. talk over conjecturally, or review in an idle or casual way and with an element of doubt or without sufficient reason to reach a conclusion 3. to believe especially on uncertain or tentative grounds 4. invest at a risk [scalp sport study peculate place predict put evaluate excogitate cogitate consider contemplate lot theorize toss]
*speculator 10-41-18 (n.) 1. someone who makes conjectures without knowing the facts 2. someone who risks losses for the possibility of considerable gains [scalp spec sport sportsman stag stock philosophize player possibility price project protect punt effort enjoy entrepreneur exercise capitalist cardsharp casuist commodity conjecture cosmology loss adventurer aggressive available technology theorize thinker tout trade transaction operator opportunist outcome reach resell risk /rota/]
*spinster 16-63-6 (n.) 1. an elderly unmarried woman 2. someone who spins (who twists fibers into threads) [shape silkworm single spider spin never tabby thread throstle twist elderly remain /snip snips/]
*splenetic 25-83-1 (a.) 1. very irritable [sore spiteful spleeny stew pancreas peevish perverse press prickly prostate len lien literary luteal embitter endocrine

exchange excitable extremely testy thymic thyroid ill irascible irk irritable caustic colleague cross crusty /cite tene/]
*splice 14-43-9 (n.) 1. a junction where two things (as paper or film or magnetic tape) have been joined together 2. joint made by overlapping two ends and joining them together (v.) 1. join the ends of 2. perform a marriage ceremony 3. join by interweaving strands 4. join together so as to form new genetic combinations [seam solemnize span spining strand strap structure swathe pairing paper parallel part passive people perform piece plait pleach proper lace lap league lice link loom imperfect include incorporated insert interweave intimate involved capacity ceremony chain collected combination come conjunction connect connection contact cord couple cover edit embrace encompass entwine espouse] "splice film"
*sponge 11-56-17 (n.) 1. a porous mass of interlacing fibers the forms the internal skeleton of various marine animals and usable to absorb water or any porous rubber or cellulose product similarly used 2. a follower who hangs around a host (without benefit to the host) in hope of gain or advantage 3. primitive multicellular marine animal whose porous body is supported by a fibrous skeletal framework; usually occurs in sessile colonies (v.) 1. wipe with a sponge, so as to clean or moisten 2. ask for and get free; be a parasite 3. erase with a sponge; as of words on a blackboard 4. gather sponges, in the ocean 5. soak up with a sponge [sauce screen scrubber slack slow smoke soap parasitism paste percolate pong poriferan present prostrate pudding obliterate obsequious osmosis nekton net gather gauze give grovel guzzle efface eradicate evaporate]
*spontaneous 07-48-36 (a.) 1. happening or arising without apparent external cause 2. said or done without having been planned or written in advance 3. produced without being planted or without human labor [say script self simple snap strawberry subliminal suggestion plant process produce proffer offer offhand optional naturally neo nightstick truncheon abortion advance apparent arbitrary arise artless autonomous elective external unconstrained uncultivated unforced unguarded uninhibited unprompted unrestrained unwitting] "spontaneous laughter"
*sprightly 13-57-11 (a.) 1. full of spirit and vitality [sharp smart spiritless spry step playful pointed pungent rightly rollicksome rompish gay girl good graceful hearty life light lively young] "a sprightly young girl"
*spurious 13-74-10 (a.) 1. plausible but false 2. born out of wedlock 3. intended to deceive [sham spur substitute superior synthetic parent part pass phony plant plausible pretended pseudo unauthentic unfounded unnatural unreliable reason recognize resemble ruler illegitimate imitation imitative inauthentic inference intend invalid obsolescent offspring origin outward]
*spurn 09-60-26 (v.) 1. reject with contempt [scornful scout show slight sniff snub spur pass poohpooh proscribe push unwilling urn rebuff refuse reject relegate repel repulse] "She spurned his advances"
*squabble 08-49-28 (n.) 1. petty quarrel (v.) 1. argue over petty things [scrap spit squab strife quarrel quibble unimportant altercation angry argument beef bicker brabble brawl broil logomachy loud encounter]
*squalid 14-58-9 (a.) 1. morally degraded 2. foul and run-down and repulsive [sad scandal seamy seedy shantytown shock small soil stink quality ugly unclean unpleasant unsightly untidy abject ali apartment appearance atmosphere atrocious awful lack life likely little live loose low ignoble immoral infamous informal insanitary intrigue degraded detail dignity dire dirty dishonest disreputable dreadful]
*squander 07-58-34 (v.) 1. spend thoughtlessly; throw away 2. spend extravagantly 3. spend lavishly or wastefully on [schedule shoot shower shrink spend spent unwise ablate absorb abstract amount and assimilate decrease deplete digest dissipate dissipated drop eat erode exhaust expend extravagant]
*squat 09-61-22 (a.) 1. having a low center of gravity; built low to the ground 2. short and thick; as e.g. having short legs and heavy musculature (n.) 1. exercising by repeatedly assuming a squatting position; strengthens the leg muscles 2. a small worthless amount 3. the act of assuming or maintaining a squatting position (v.) 1. be close to the earth, or be disproportionately wide 2. sit on one's heels 3. occupy (a dwelling) illegally [scrunch seat see seem shit short sit size smokestack sojourn solid square stand stature stocky stop strengthen stubby stumpy sublease superlative quality quantity quat underslung ungainly upward abiding abode adipose amount anchor animal assume average avoid tenantry thickset thigh title tower tubby] "In some cultures, the women give birth while squatting"
*squatter 14-39-9 (n.) 1. someone who settles lawfully on government land with the intent to acquire title to to it 2. someone who settles on land without right or title [seem settle short smokestack squat stowaway stumpy sublease underslung ungainly unlawful upstart acquire animal arriviste tall tenant tenderfoot thick title tower trespass ear emigrant empty recruit red resident right rookie]
*stagnant 12-41-14 (a.) 1. not circulating or flowing 2. not growing or changing; without force or vitality [slow sluggish stag stale stand stationary still stock suspend tame torpid abeyance absence adynamic apathetic groggy grow neutral numb]
*stagnate 09-54-22 (v.) 1. stand still 2. be idle; exist in a changeless situation 3. cause to stagnate 4. cease to flow; stand without moving [service sit situation sleep slug spoil stale stand stifle still stimulate stop torpor trammel agnate around arse art artistic aspect awake game good growth nature necessary economy essence exist /tang tanga/] "Industry will stagnate if we do not

stimulate our economy"
*stagnation 13-49-11 (n.) 1. a state of inactivity (in business or art etc) 2. inactivity of liquids; being stagnant; standing still; without current or circulation [service significant sluggish stand still torpor art artistic aspect good growth immobility inactivity industrial inertia] "economic growth of less than 1% per year is considered to be economic stagnation"
*stagy 22-27-2 (a.) 1. having characteristics of the stage especially an artificial and mannered quality [scenic spectacular stag stellar study suit theatrical thespian affected artificial] "stagy heroics"
*staid 13-46-11 (a.) 1. characterized by dignity and propriety [serious settle sober solemn solid somber steady stiff stolid taste temperament temperate thoughtful aid arid infertile decorous demure dignity dry dull]
*stallion 13-60-11 (n.) 1. uncastrated adult male horse [sexual sow species stag stall steer stot stud suppose tigress tom tomcat tup adult lioness nag nanny /oil/]
*stanch 20-17-3 (v.) 1. as of the flow of a liquid flowing, such as blood from a wound [silence slow stan staunch stay stem stop throttle abrupt anti arrest asphyxiate cease check cover curb curtail cut halt hinder hold]
*stanchion 25-38-1 (n.) 1. any vertical post or rod used as a support [scaffold sponsor staff stanch standard stem substantiate support sustenance timber trunk agriculture aid assistance authentication neck care caryatid colonnade column confirmation corroborate cow help]
*stanza 20-41-3 (n.) 1. a fixed number of lines of verse forming a unit of a poem [scheme screen second section separate seven six stan statement stave strain strophe successive tailpiece tercet textual triplet ababa across alexandrine anacrusis answer antistrophe]
*statecraft 25-44-1 (n.) 1. wisdom in the management of public affairs [trait affair art experience control country craft /far farce/]
*static 08-59-27 (a.) 1. not in physical motion 2. not active or moving 3. showing little if any change (n.) 1. a crackling or hissing noise cause by electrical interference [shortcoming show society stable stagnant stand stat stay still stop tame television torpid trouble abeyance abiding absence acoustic adynamic agriculture angry apathetic idle immobile inertia intact interference invariable central change charge chip community computer concern constant content continue crackle criticism] "a static village community and a completely undynamic type of agriculture"
*stationary 13-49-10 (a.) 1. standing still 2. not capable of being moved [secure set show solid stand station stay still tendency torpid abiding adamantine aren army idle immobile inactive inert intact neutral non remain rigid] "the car remained stationary with the engine running"
*statistician 17-52-5 (n.) 1. a mathematician who specializes in statistics 2. someone versed in the collection and interpretation of numerical data (especially someone who uses statistics to calculate insurance premiums) [skill specialize survey theory analyst apply arithmetic insurance interpretation calculator collection computer concern conduct crunch numerical]
*statuesque 19-66-4 (a.) 1. of size and dignity suggestive of a statue 2. suggestive of a statue [shapely short size slender sober solemn statue suggestive tall trim agreeable aristocratic attractive august elegant queenly]
*statuette 19-53-4 (n.) 1. a small carved or molded figure [sculpture statue]
*stature 07-47-39 (n.) 1. high level of respect gained by impressive development or achievement 2. natural height of a person or animal in an upright position [short size stand stat status sublimity tall toplofty achievement altitude animal attribute authority average upright rank reputation respect elevation eminence exaltation /ruta/] "a man of great stature"
*statute 07-24-44 (a.) 1. enacted by a legislative body (n.) 1. an act passed by a legislative body [separate society stamp stat suppression surveillance taboo act american append apply appropriate assize authorization unite unwritten edict embargo enable enactment enforce establish exclusion] "statute law"
*stealth 10-64-19 (n.) 1. avoiding detection by moving carefully [secretive sharp shrewd slow slyness sneaky steal surreptitious tricky enemy acute aircraft almost art astute avoid likelihood hide highly]
*steeply 13-53-10 (ad.) 1. in a steep manner [sharp street sudden precipitous] "the street rose steeply up to the castle"
*stellar 09-56-22 (a.) 1. indicating the most important performer or role 2. being or relating to or resembling or emanating from stars [shining skater solar spectacular star stature stella terrestrial theatrical twinkle emanate empyrean entertain equinoctial exception extragalactic leading legitimate light luminous arch asteroid astrophysics ranking role ruling]
*stentorian 22-36-2 (a.) 1. used of the voice [sonorous sound stent thin thunderous tone ear earsplitting earthshaking orotund ringing roaring rough]
*steppe 25-59-1 (n.) 1. extensive plain without trees (associated with eastern Russia and Siberia) [saltpan savanna siberia socialist soviet step swale tableland territory tract tree tundra earth eastern esplanade establish europe extensive pampas park plain plane prairie /pet/]
*sterling 06-57-56 (a.) 1. highest in quality (n.) 1. British money; especially the pound sterling as the basic monetary unit of the UK [sensational silver simple social superlative terrific tremendous true ethical exceptional exquisite real realistic record responsibility rightful last lawful legitimate ling literal immaculate

immense incomparable inferior issue national naturalistic noble nonpareil genuine golden good government great]
*stickler 19-61-4 (n.) 1. someone who insists on something [shrink standpatter stick stickle strain strict tentative tickler timid tyrant insist intransigent caesar cautious commissar compunction conformity correct czar last exact rule /elk/] "a stickler for promptness"
*stifle 07-56-41 (n.) 1. joint between the femur and tibia in a quadruped; corresponds to the human knee (v.) 1. smother or suppress 2. conceal or hide [secret severe silence skeleton smother soften sound spark spread squash stamp sticky still stimulant strangulate subdue suffocate sustain tame temperature thick throttle thunderstorm tibia toast troublesome twangy imagination impair impede inarticulate incandescence indistinct inhibit interrupt femur flat flicker flush force forceful fry full function lack latent laugh leg less lie life limb lisp lock lose element enigmatic esoteric excite exit expire extenuate extinguish /fit/]
*stigma 10-53-18 (n.) 1. the apical end of the style where deposited pollen enters the pistil 2. a symbol of disgrace or infamy 3. a skin lesion that is a diagnostic sign of some disease 4. an external tracheal aperture in a terrestrial arthropod [school score set shame significance sinister skin slender spiracle spoil spot stain stalk structure style symbol taint tarnish terrestrial tick tig tip top tracheal impute infamy gash gathering give grain grave macule male mar mark misconduct mole mottle abscess acquire anther aperture apical appearance arbitrary armed arthropod aspersion /git/]
*stigmatize 19-01-4 (v.) 1. to accuse or condemn or openly or formally or brand as disgraceful 2. mark with a stigma or stigmata [score select slur society spot stigma taint tattoo trace imprint iris gash gibbet government mark motley mottle muckrake accuse adulteress assign attaint emblematize engrave /git zit/]
*stiletto 14-75-9 (n.) 1. a small dagger with a tapered blade [saber scimitar short skean stabbing sticker stile sword taper tomahawk tool lance leather]
*stimulant 14-57-9 (a.) 1. that stimulates (n.) 1. a drug that temporarily quickens some vital process 2. any stimulating information or event; acts to arouse action [snow speed spur tea tonic impulse incentive incite input instruction upper urge life activate animator ant antidepressant narcotic nitrite /alum/] "stimulant phenomena"
*stimulate 04-47-98 (v.) 1. stir feelings in 2. of bodily processes such as fever, illness, etc. 3. cause to be alert and energetic 4. stir the feelings or emotions of 5. cause to do; cause to act in a specified manner 6. act as a stimulant 7. provide the needed stimulus for [secure sex shake spark spur stimulus stir strength strengthen striking sweetening target telling thrill tickle tingly titillate tonic trouble impassioned impressive incentive incline increase influence inspire interesting intoxicate inviting maddening minded motivation move unsettle uplift upset urgent late liven lure accelerate activate affright agitation agog animate animation ardent arouse attract ebullient effectuate elate elicit encourage enkindle evoke excited exhilarative /alum/] "The book stimulated her imagination"
*stimulus 11-39-17 (n.) 1. any stimulating information or event; acts to arouse action [spur stimulate strengthen strong study sudden sweetening tonic turn impetus impulse imu incentive incite increase induction instruction interest invitation motivation undesirable urge life loss lure]
*stingy 15-36-7 (a.) 1. not generous 2. selfishly unwilling to share with others [scrim selfish share slight slim small sparing spend sting sup thin thrifty tightfisted tip illiberal impoverish inadequate infrequent narrow near niggardly give grudging yourself] "she practices economy without being stingy"
*stint 06-59-55 (n.) 1. an unbroken period of time during which you do something 2. smallest American sandpiper 3. an individuals prescribed share of work (v.) 1. scratch and scrimp 2. supply sparingly, with a meager allowance [sacrifice sandpiper save scant scrimp service share shift short skimp slender slight slim small sober sparing specific spell spent stoppage stretch subsist supply task temperate term thin time tint turn icebound impoverish interval narrow niggardly notch nuance numerous]
*stipend 15-21-7 (n.) 1. a sum of money allotted on a regular basis; usually for some specific purpose [salary scholarship specific stipe sum support tribute income interval pay payment pension prebend purpose earnings emolument expense dole /epi pit/]
*stipple 25-38-1 (v.) 1. engrave by means of dots and flicks 2. apply in small touches, of paint 3. make by small short touches that together produce an even or softly graded shadow, as in paint or ink 4. produce a mottled effect [score sculpture shadow short significant soft spangle speckle sprinkle streak stroke stud substance sunlight surface tattoo technique texture tinge tipple tone touch tree illuminate imbue ink iris painting passive patchy pepper plaster pointillistic prime printing production lacquer lime line literary effect emblazon engrave etch etching /pit/] "The sunlight stippled the trees"
*stipulate 08-49-30 (v.) 1. specify as a condition or requirement in a contract or agreement; make an express demand or provision in an agreement 2. give a guarantee or promise of 3. make an oral contract or agreement in the verbal form of question and answer that is necessary to give it legal force, in Roman Law [scene selection set settle sign specify state string surety term transaction include indicate insist instruct particularize payment pertinent precision presence price prisoner proceeding promise protocol proviso provisory ultimatum undertake late law legal lie life live accord admit agreement

ancient answer arrange arrangement assign assume engaged enter expense express /pit/] "The will stipulates that she can live in the house for the rest of her life"
*stoic 15-51-8 (a.) 1. seeming unaffected by pleasure or pain; impassive 2. pertaining to Stoicism or its followers (n.) 1. someone who is seemingly indifferent to emotions 2. a member of the ancient Greek school of philosophy founded by Zeno [school seeming show sluggish smooth specialist steady submission suffer theory tolerant tolerate torpid tranquil onward impassive indifferent indulgent isolated calm comatose complain cool courage] "stoic courage"
*stoicism 17-64-5 (n.) 1. the philosophical system of the Stoics following the teachings of the ancient Greek philosopher Zeno 2. an indifference to pleasure or pain [sand school steady stoic stolid teach teetotal theory toleration impassive indifference indulgence intuitionism investigate calm celibate chastity continent cool]
*stolid 16-39-6 (a.) 1. having or revealing little emotion or sensibility; not easily aroused or excited [sensibility show silent slow smooth solemn steady thick tranquil obtuse lethargic lid listless literal little impassive inactive indifferent insensitive interest isolated destitute distant dry dull /lot/]
*strait 09-48-24 (a.) 1. (archaic) strict and severe (n.) 1. a narrow channel of the sea joining two larger bodies of water 2. a bad or difficult situation or state of affairs [sea sound spot squeeze threat throat trait trouble reach restrict risk roadstead arm armlet imbroglio imperil inlet insolvency] "strait is the gate"
*stratagem 20-44-3 (n.) 1. a maneuver in a game or conversation 2. an elaborate or deceitful scheme contrived to deceive or evade [scheming secret sell shift show skill soon step stock strata subterfuge tactic tactical testimony throw track trickery trump racket refuge resource rise ruse accomplish achieve action answer art gain gambit game gimmick gloss goal effort elaborate enemy engineering evade excuse maneuver manipulate manoeuvre means measure military money move /atar mega tart/]
*stratum 25-48-1 (n.) 1. one of several parallel layers of material arranged one on top of another (such as a layer of tissue or cells in an organism) 2. an abstract place usually conceived as having depth [sea section sedimentary set sheet simultaneousl skin slough society soil sole status step story structure substrate surface table thick tier tissue title top race rank rat rating region rete rock abstract atmosphere underneath understory material measure membrane mental mind mine /mut tart/]
*stray 06-57-48 (a.) 1. not close together in time (n.) 1. homeless cat (v.) 1. wander from a direct course or at random 2. wander from a direct or straight course 3. move about aimlessly or without any destination, often in search of food or employment 4. lose clarity or turn aside esp. from the main subject of attention or course of argument in writing, thinking, or speaking [sheer shift strain suggestion swan sweep tack touch trace tramp travel tray trip turning twist ramble rambling random range roam roll rove abandon abnormal abroad accidental adrift yaw]
*stride 05-63-78 (n.) 1. significant progress (especially in the phrase"make strides" 2. the distance covered by a step 3. a step in walking or running (v.) 1. walk with long steps 2. cover or traverse by taking long steps [set significant sit slow space stand step straddle strode ten toward track travel traverse tread tree trip raise range rapid rate reach regular ride run improve infinity development dig distance down drag droop energetic estimate extent /dirt/]
*stringency 25-46-1 (n.) 1. a state occasioned by scarcity of money and a shortage of credit 2. conscientious attention to rules and details [scarcity severity sharp shortage small stern string teeth thin tight toughness trait rarity rigid rigor roughness rugged rule inclement inflexible infrequency niggardly grim grip edge exacting exiguity careful conscientious credit]
*stringent 08-41-32 (a.) 1. demanding strict attention to rules and procedures [safety security severe sharp skill stern string tart tight tough trenchant require rigid rigorous rough rugged rule incisive inclement inflexible ironhanded great grim edge effort enforce exacting exigent expect]
*stripling 25-70-1 (n.) 1. a juvenile between the onset of puberty and maturity [schoolboy showy size slip son strip subculture tad teenager teenybopper tenderfoot trainee rocker rode rookie infant israel palestine parvenu perform puberty pubescent punk lad laddie last learner leather neighborhood neology neonate noted novice gang grow]
*strut 09-59-25 (n.) 1. a proud stiff pompous gait 2. brace consisting of a bar or rod used to resist longitudinal compression (v.) 1. to walk with a lofty proud gait, often in an attempt to impress others [sashay show slow step stiffen suggest support swagger swing tread trip trot rack resist rigid rod roll rooster ruffle rut] "He strut around like a rooster in a hen house."
*studious 13-56-10 (a.) 1. marked by care and effort 2. characterized by diligent study and fondness for reading [scholarship sedulous serious set show sophomoric studio study television tendency thorough thoughtful tireless undergraduate deep design detail determined diligent incline industrious intellectual investigate involved obsess occupy owlish] "made a studious attempt to fix the television set"
*stultify 19-56-4 (v.) 1. prove to be of unsound mind or demonstrate someone's incompetence 2. deprive of strength or efficiency; make useless or worthless 3. cause to appear foolish [seem set show silence silly strength stu stunt stupid suppress tedious throttle thwart trammel undo unintelligent unsound useless laughter

law legal lessen impair incapable inconsistent ineffectual inhibit instability interest invalidate irresponsible foolish frustrate fun /fit/] "nobody is legally allowed to stultify himself"
*stupefy 20-51-3 (v.) 1. make dull or stupid; to muddle with drunkenness or infatuation 2. be a mystery or bewildering to 3. make senseless or dizzy by or as if by a blow [sensitive set shock stagger stare stick stun stupe stupendous surprise terrorist throw thunderstruck tired torpid unable unconcerned undone unnerve unparalleled unprecedented unspeakable palsy paralyze passive perplex phenomenal pose prodigious puzzle elude enchant enthral entrance etherize exceptional extraordinary fabulous fascinate faze flabbergast flummox fox freeze fuddle /put/]
*stupendous 15-70-8 (a.) 1. so great in size or force or extent as to elicit awe [size spectacular splendid storm strange striking stunning stupe surprising temple terrific titanic towering tremendous unimaginable unique unprecedented phenomenal prodigious profound puzzling elicit enormous excellent extent extraordinary nerve noteworthy degree demand outlandish outsize overgrown /put/]
*stupor 20-51-3 (n.) 1. marginal consciousness 2. the feeling of distress and disbelief that you have when something bad happens accidentally [sedate self semiconscious shock sleep sleepy slow sluggish soporific stole stu torpor trance twitch unconsciousne paralysis passivity preoccupation oblivious obsession oscitant reverie /put/]
*stygian 25-72-1 (a.) 1. hellish 2. dark and dismal as of the rivers Acheron and Styx in Hades [shadow somber soul styx supernal swear gloomy imagine infernal acherontic across]
*stymie 11-32-15 (n.) 1. a situation in golf where an opponent's ball blocks the line between your ball and the hole 2. a thwarting and distressing situation (v.) 1. hinder or prevent the progress or accomplishment of [situation slow stalemate stall standstill stay stop sty surmount team thwart turn yourself ice immaterial impasse impede effect embarrass]
*suave 12-49-13 (a.) 1. smoothly agreeable and courteous with a degree of sophistication 2. having a sophisticated charm [seem sensitive skill smooth soft sophisticated sophistication unbroken undiplomatic uniform unrefined urbane affable affect agreeable apology ave avert error even ezra]
*subconscious 12-67-13 (a.) 1. just below the level of consciousness (n.) 1. psychic activity just below the level of awareness [seat self sensory subliminal superego suppress unconscious underlie unintentional unknown behavior below brain capacity conscious consciousness nous influence intuitive involuntary]
*subdue 06-52-45 (v.) 1. to put down by force or authority 2. put down by force or intimidation 3. hold within limits and control 4. get on top of; deal with successfully 5. make subordinate, dependent, or subservient 6. correct by punishment or discipline [sad serious silence soften soothe squelch steady stifle still stop strangle subjugate subordinate subtle suppress understated undo unenthusiastic unman unobtrusive backward balsam beat bend blank blinking blunt breakdown broken dampen defeat delicate dependent destruction discipline distant dominate down downcast due dull eggshell excellent expressionless extenuate extinguish]
*subjugate 20-54-3 (v.) 1. put down by force or intimidation 2. make subservient; force to submit [servitude slave smash subdue subject submit subordinate subservient suppress unjust unman uprise usurp bend bond break bring broken bully gate government adopt appropriate assume attempt authority terrorize eff enslave enthral /tag/]
*sublime 07-71-36 (a.) 1. worthy of adoration or reverence 2. (archaic) lifted up or set high 3. inspiring awe (v.) 1. vaporize and then condense right back again 2. change or cause to change directly from a solid into a vapor without first melting [screen separate serious splendid superb uplifting upraise upright big bright brilliant laud liberal lift lime idealistic immortalize inspire magnificent marvelous mighty mounting moving erect exalted excellent extract] "sublime iodine"
*subliminal 15-48-7 (a.) 1. below the threshold of conscious perception [subconscious unconscious unintentional below liminal imperceptible impossible message mind affect aware]
*submarine 07-46-43 (a.) 1. beneath the surface of the sea (n.) 1. a submersible warship usually armed with torpedoes 2. a large sandwich made of a long crusty roll split lengthwise and filled with meats and cheese (and tomato and onion and lettuce and condiments); different names are used in different sections of the United States (v.) 1. move forward or under in a sliding motion 2. attack by submarine 3. bring down with a blow to the legs, in sports 4. control a submarine 5. throw with an underhand motion, as of a baseball [sandwich scuba sink sky slew slip slue sub underwater bathysphere bomber boy bury marine missile athletics immerse inundate engulf] "The child was injured when he submarined under the safety belt of the car"
*submerge 10-50-18 (v.) 1. cover completely or make imperceptible 2. sink below the surface; go under or as if under water 3. fill or cover completely, usually with water 4. put under water [sag secret set settle sink sleeping slump sound speech spread steep stifle suppress surface underwater unnoticed unseen until baptize bathe below beyond breakwater brief bury macerate merge muffle mystic engulf esoteric rain reduction godown]
*submersible 22-45-2 (a.) 1. capable of being immersed in water or functioning while submerged (n.) 1. an apparatus intended for use under water 2. a warship designed to operate under water [serve setup ship

specific spherical sub supply surface underwater bathyscaphe bell boat bottom mini electric equipment exploration immerse intend level] "a submersible pump"
*submission 07-69-35 (n.) 1. the act of submitting; usually surrendering power to another 2. something (manuscripts or architectural plans and models or estimates or works of art of all genres etc.) submitted for the judgment of others (as in a competition) 3. the feeling of patient submissive humbleness 4. (law) a contention presented by a lawyer to a judge or jury as part of the case he is arguing 5. a legal document summarizing an agreement between parties in a dispute to abide by the decision of an arbiter 6. an agreement between parties in a dispute to abide by the decision of an arbiter 7. the condition of having submitted to control by someone or something else [sanction sod status submit substance suggestion summarize surrender understand union behavior bid bob body bow bring matter meek message mission model idea impose inclination invitation obedience obeisance obey offer offering okay overture nod nothing] "several of his submissions were rejected by publishers"
*subordinate 08-24-34 (a.) 1. lower in rank or importance 2. (grammar) of a clause; unable to stand alone syntactically as a complete sentence 3. inferior in rank or status 4. subject or submissive to authority or the control of another (n.) 1. someone subject to the authority or control of another 2. a word that is more specific than a given word (v.) 1. rank or order as less important or consider of less value 2. make subordinate, dependent, or subservient [screening secondary selection separate sequence size subdue subsidiary supporter underling below beneath bolt ordinary ordinate outrank range ranking rate retainer riddle degree dependent divide dominate inferior inferiority accessory aide assistant assortment taxonomy triage tributary employee enslave enthrall /rob/] "a subordinate kingdom"
*suborn 25-32-1 (v.) 1. incite to commit a crime or an evil deed 2. induce to commit perjury or give false testimony 3. procure (false testimony or perjury) [secure sensuality specify stimulate subvert bear bribe butler /rob/] "He suborned his butler to cover up the murder of his wife"
*subpoena 08-13-30 (n.) 1. a writ issued by court authority to compel the attendance of a witness at a judicial proceeding; disobedience may be punishable as a contempt of court (v.) 1. serve or summon with a subpoena [serve submit summon swear body page poe preconize process punishable officer order evoke attendance authority /neo/] "The witness and her records were subpoenaed"
*subsequent 04-59-117 (a.) 1. following in time or order [sequent sequential successive suffix ulterior ensue next] "subsequent developments"
*subservience 22-54-2 (n.) 1. the condition of being something that is useful in reaching an end or carrying out a plan 2. abject or cringing submissiveness 3. in a subservient state [secondary status submissivenes superior unhappy useful reach importance carry cheerful condition cringe] "all his actions were in subservience to the general plan"
*subservient 16-50-6 (a.) 1. compliant and obedient to authority 2. abjectly submissive; characteristic of a slave or servant [secondary serve servile shad shaw slavish status subject subordinate subs subsidiary superior underprivileged unhappy useful base behavior biddable boss bring eager employ express reach replace resigned rich rule vassal vulgar importance inferiority instrumental interest intermediary tributary truckle] "editors and journalists who express opinions in print that are opposed to the interests of the rich are dismissed and replaced by subservient ones"
*subside 09-49-25 (v.) 1. wear off or die down 2. descend into or as if into some soft substance or place 3. sink to a lower level or form a depression 4. sink down or precipitate [sag set settle shift side sink sit slip smooth soft stop undisturbed unmoved untroubled backup bate become bed bottom budge impassive incline intensity isolated decline decrease depression descend deteriorate die diminish dip dive downward drop dwindle ebb erode exhaustion] "The pain subsided"
*subsidiary 03-29-152 (a.) 1. relating to something that is added but is not essential 2. functioning in a subsidiary or supporting capacity (n.) 1. someone subject to the authority or control of another 2. a company that is completely controlled by another company [secondary serve status subordinate supplementary supportive underling unessential banana branch business immediate importance incidental institution instrumental invest diary discipline dog dot dower dowry accessory accidental add additional adjuvant aid ancillary appurtenance assist assistant authority role /raid/]
*subsist 19-44-4 (v.) 1. support oneself [set spirit stand subs support survive sustain unhurried barely bide breathe business inherent inner irresponsible tarry timeless troop]
*subsistence 16-47-6 (n.) 1. a means of surviving 2. minimal (or marginal) resources for subsisting 3. the state of existing in reality; having substance [security slight small stay subsist support survive sustenance upkeep barely bed being butter impoverish independent thin timeless endurance enough entity essence exist narrow nourishment nurture care condition continue] "social security provided only a bare subsistence"
*substantive 10-23-21 (a.) 1. being the essence or essential element of a thing 2. having substance and prompting thought 3. (law) applying to essential legal principles and rules of right (n.) 1. a noun or a pronoun that is used in place of a noun [sensible separate significant sizable solid speaker substantial underlie

utilitarian basal basic bedrock big tagmemic tangible transitive abundant adjectival amount anti apply appointment appreciable attach attributive authority autonomous native nominal impose independent individual industry intransitive value verbal vital effect elementary enforce equivalent essential]

*subsume 16-64-6 (v.) 1. contain or include 2. consider (an instance of something) as part of a general rule or principle [show subs bring embody embrace encompass /emu/] "This new system subsumes the old one"

*subterfuge 17-53-5 (n.) 1. something intended to misrepresent the true nature of an activity [shift show sick stratagem strategy blind burial bury tactic trick true entangle evasive excuse racket real refuge ruse false falsehood fraud front fuge game gimmick gloss /fret/] "he wasn't sick--it was just a subterfuge"

*subterranean 14-51-9 (a.) 1. being or operating under the surface of the earth 2. lying beneath what is revealed or avowed, especially being deliberately concealed [secret show situate surface surreptitious ulterior below beneath bertrand beyond bury terra earth engage exist reveal russell arcane avow] "subterranean passages"

*subtle 04-48-132 (a.) 1. faint and difficult to analyze 2. be difficult to detect or grasp by the mind 3. working or spreading in a hidden and usually injurious way 4. able to make fine distinctions [sensitive sharp shrewd slight sly small soul spread sub susceptible understated undeviating unerring unreal boyish tender thin thread tricky labyrinthine lacy light elegant elusive enough even experience express exquisite] "his whole attitude had undergone a subtle change"

*subversion 15-36-7 (n.) 1. destroying someone's (or some group's) honesty or loyalty; undermining moral integrity 2. the act of subverting; as overthrowing or destroying a legally constituted government [sabotage sedition somerset spill undermine upheaval upturn big bouleversement brainwash breakup version rebellion rebut refute respect ruin ruler rural indoctrinate innocence institution insurrection intend overthrow overturn]

*subvert 12-47-14 (v.) 1. cause the downfall of; of rulers 2. corrupt morally or by intemperance or sensuality 3. destroy property or hinder normal operations 4. destroy completely [sabotage school sensualize settle silence spoil strike undermine upset upturn bastardize behavior better brainwash breakup bring value vary vert vitiate evil railroad rebel reform refuse revive revolution ruin ruler ruling run teach topple track transform]

*succeed 02-48-358 (v.) 1. be the successor (of) 2. attain success or reach a goal [science score selection serial show significant stage star struggle subsequent successive supervene supplant unchallenged unsuccessful upon cadet carry cee click come coming connect conquer consequent effect effort enact engineer ensue enterprise execute expect decision deliver descend desire discharge down dramatize duty] "The enterprise succeeded"

*success 01-61-740 (n.) 1. a state of prosperity or fame 2. an attainment that is successful 3. a person with a record of successes 4. an event that accomplishes its intended purpose [satisfy score security seduction sensation sexual show sleeper smash solve soul sport star call celebrity certain cess championship color comfort complete conquest conspicuous contest ease election end enjoy entertainment exactly excellence execution eye] "let's call heads a success and tails a failure"

*successful 01-60-651 (a.) 1. having succeeded or being marked by a favorable outcome [self significant smashing succeed success surefire surgery undefeated unexpected capable celebrated coming conquer easy effective efficacious eminent extraordinary fail fame famous favorable first flourish fortune fruitful leading lot lucky lucrative] "a successful architect"

*successor 03-58-139 (n.) 1. a thing or person that immediately replaces something or someone 2. a person who follows next in order 3. a person who inherits some title or office [satellite shadow stand substitute success supporter conclusion consequence courtier effect equal occupant office offspring orphan relict remainderman replace] "he was President Lincoln's successor"

*succinct 12-50-13 (a.) 1. briefly giving the gist of something [sententious short shorten style summary clarity close compendious concise contract crisp cut inc instantaneous neat terse tight transient]

*succor 25-01-1 (n.) 1. assistance in time of difficulty (v.) 1. help in a difficult situation [save service show situation solace support unpleasant comfort console contribution cor corrective cure office rally relief rescue restore]

*succulent 12-37-13 (a.) 1. full of juice (n.) 1. a plant adapted to arid conditions and characterized by fleshy water-storing tissues that act as water reservoirs [showy soft solitary sour south spatulate spicy spike spiny stem stimulate stone store cactus capsular carp chiefly climber clump comestible condition cover creeper crystal leaf lent lentil life litho low lump luscious lush edible excite exquisite native nectar nice tantalizing tasty tender texture thick tickle tissue]

*succumb 06-67-50 (v.) 1. consent reluctantly 2. be fatally overwhelmed [sink submit surrender survive sustain swoon unable capitulate collapse come comply consent continue cum blow bodily bow breakdown buckle]

*sufferance 25-71-1 (n.) 1. patient endurance especially of pain or distress 2. a disposition to tolerate or accept people or situations [sanction situation stamina stay stoicism stress suffer fact fortitude freedom enduring reluctant acceptance acquiesce allowance authorization capacity choice connivance consent]

*suffice 10-56-19 (v.) 1. be sufficient; be adequate, either in quality or quantity [satisfy school serve stretch

suit few fice fit fulfill function capable car certain enough expectation extent]
*sufficiency 16-39-6 (n.) 1. sufficient resources to provide comfort and meet obligations 2. an adequate quantity; a quantity that is large enough to achieve a purpose 3. the quality of being sufficient for the end in view [satisfy suff sufficient suitor supply susceptibility facility fact faculty father feast fitness inadequate intelligence caliber capacity comfortable competence country efficiency enough essential young] "her father questioned the young suitor's sufficiency"
*suffocate 10-57-21 (v.) 1. deprive of oxygen and prevent from breathing 2. struggle for breath; have insufficient oxygen intake 3. feel uncomfortable for lack of fresh air 4. be asphyxiated; die from lack of oxygen 5. impair the respiration of or obstruct the air passage of 6. become stultified, suppressed, or stifled 7. suppress the development, creativity, or imagination of [sharp silence smother spark squash steam stifle stifling strong uproot flicker flush fry obstruct occlude oppressive cate close cook crackdown crowd crush abolition airless annihilation annul asphyxiate throttle toast exit expire extinguish /off taco/]
*suffrage 20-44-3 (n.) 1. a legal right guaranteed by the 15th amendment to the US constitution; guaranteed to women by the 19th amendment [say share short statutory suffragist frag franchise referendum religion representation right rule amendment association authority aye get government grant group guarantee election empower enfranchise engagement]
*suffuse 14-42-9 (v.) 1. cause to spread or flush or flood through, over, or across 2. to become overspread as with a fluid, a colour, a gleam of light [saturate saturation season sky soak spread steep undergo face fill flavor flood flow fluid flush frame fuse essence /suff/] "The sky was suffused with a warm pink color"
*suggestible 25-71-1 (a.) 1. susceptible or responsive to suggestion [suggest susceptible susceptive gullible easy impressionable influence /bit egg/] "suggestible young minds"
*suggestive 11-42-16 (a.) 1. tending to suggest or imply 2. having a covert or special meaning [sexual sexy show signify society special start statement substantial suggest sure unseemly graphic erotic evocative explicit expressive extension telling tend train transfer typical idea identify image imply improper indelicate indicative individual interpret valid vivid vulgar /egg/] "artifacts suggestive of an ancient society"
*summarily 17-44-5 (ad.) 1. without delay; in a summary manner [shortly smart spy straightaway sudden summa suspect swift manner abrupt apace aphoristic attention rapid right immediately instantly laconic /lira/] "the suspected spy was summarily executed"
*summary 05-25-61 (a.) 1. performed speedily and without formality 2. briefly giving the gist of something (n.) 1. a briefstatement that presents the main points in a concise form [sanction say score set shorten sketchy speedy stated statement style succinct sudden sum summa survey swift synopsis unofficial main meat message movie much abridgment abrupt abstract academic account alert argument attention authority rapid ready reduction resume review rush] "a summary execution"
*sumptuous 08-63-30 (a.) 1. rich and superior in quality [spectacular splendid steep stiff suggestive sum sump sun superior magnificent majestic plush poor posh premium princely proud tan top opulent /out/]
*superannuate 22-83-2 (v.) 1. retire and pension (someone) because of age or physical inability 2. become obsolete 3. declare to be obsolete 4. retire or become ineligible because of old age or infirmity [sack scrap service specify stop super supersede support suspend unchurch undergo unsaddle unseat useful pass pension perform perish petrify physical position present purge elderly emeritus equipment essence excommunicate expel reject release relinquish replace resigned retirement rid abandon abdicate adjudge age antique archaic attain nature non turnout twelve]
*superb 03-70-138 (a.) 1. of surpassing excellence 2. surpassingly good [size skillful soar solid specify splendid spry striking suitable sumptuous super surpassing unbelievable unreal performance positive prime proficient proud elaborate elegant excellent exceptional expert renowned resourceful resplendent rich rousing bad best brilliant]
*supercilious 22-59-2 (a.) 1. having or showing arrogant superiority to and disdain of those one views as unworthy 2. expressive of contempt [scornful sneer sniffy snobby snooty super superior swaggering uppity patronizing pompous pretentious pride exclusive cavalier clique condescending contemptuous insolent lofty lordly overbearing /oil/]
*superficial 08-54-30 (a.) 1. being or affecting or concerned with a surface; not deep or penetrating emotionally or intellectually 2. involving a surface only 3. relating to a surface 4. of little substance or significance [seeming shallow short show sketchy skindeep slight slow super swift pale paltry passing petty phony pointless ponderous posture prompt public effete empty expeditious external rapid rind roundabout feverish few flatness fly foreign frivolous front furious idle inconsequential indifference insincere insipid instantly carelessness casual cold cosmetic critical cursory airy amateurism apace apparent appear arid artificial leaden lifeless lightweight little low /laic/] "superficial similarities"
*superfluous 14-50-9 (a.) 1. serving no useful purpose; having no excuse for being 2. more than is needed, desired, or required [serve spare subsidiary super surplus survive unavailing unessential unneeded unused useful useless part play pointless prolix purpose

excessive excuse expletive extra redundant remanence require rib room feckless fortuitous lack leftover line lose lot lying odd ornament otiose outstanding over]
*superimpose 15-35-7 (v.) 1. place on top of [screen scum set shield simultaneousl stretch surface partial place plane pose position put eclipse element image impose incorporate mantle mask muffle obscure occult overlie overspread /mire/] "can you superimpose the two images?"
*superintendent 05-32-62 (n.) 1. a person who directs and manages an organization 2. a caretaker for an apartment house; represents the owner as janitor and rent collector [school sheriff superintend supervisor surveyor patrolman performance police policewoman prevent proctor examine reeve rent represent inspector narc taskmaster tipstaff trooper demanding demeanor deportment detective direct director]
*superlative 11-75-17 (a.) 1. highest in quality (n.) 1. an exaggerated expression (usually of praise) 2. the highest level or degree attainable 3. the superlative form of an adjective [select stage sterling stretch super supreme unbeatable unique unmatched unparalleled unrivaled untouchable peak peerless perfect pick pinnacle prime elect elevation enhance exceptional extreme rank regular level lofty absolute accomplished aspire terrific thoroughgoing top incomparable inflation intolerable /vita vital/] "the critics lavished superlatives on it"
*supernatural 11-61-16 (a.) 1. not existing in nature or subject to explanation according to natural laws; not physical or material (n.) 1. supernatural forces and events and beings collectively [salvation shadowy spiritual uncanny unearthly unnatural unusual paranormal phenomenal preternatural psychic eerie exceptional extreme rare redemptive remarkable natural abnormal agent airy arcane theosophy towering transmundane /ruta/] "supernatural forces and occurrences and beings"
*supersede 12-55-14 (v.) 1. take the place or move into the position of [school slide step subrogate substitute substitution succeed successor supplant surpass switch upon passe perse place player position efficient exchange expect extinct reject relinquish remove replacement representation resigned retired role rule dead delegation deputize desert discontinue displacement]
*supine 19-75-4 (a.) 1. lying face upward 2. offering no resistance [selfish short show situation slow spread stem unconcerned uninterested unresisting upright upward utterly palm participle passive past pine position posture prone prostrate idle inactive indifferent inert inflection neap nonchalant numb enervate erect]
*supplant 12-37-14 (v.) 1. take the place or move into the position of [school slide step substitute substitution succeed successor supersede supervene switch unseat upon usurp place plant player position left long lose agency team turnout]
*supple 11-54-17 (a.) 1. gracefully slender; moving and bending with ease 2. (used of e.g. personality traits) readily adaptable 3. (used of persons' bodies) capable of moving or bending freely (v.) 1. make pliant and flexible, as of leather and skins [sensitive sharp sinuous skin slender smooth stretch style sup svelte sylph plastic pliant politic problem last leather limber lissome literary lithe ease easy elastic excessive extend extensible] "a supple mind"
*supplementary 15-58-8 (a.) 1. functioning in a subsidiary or supporting capacity 2. added to complete or make up a deficiency [scope secondary size spare subsidiary subtract supplement ulterior unessential usual plus primary lack library excess exist extra extraneous main more new nonessential top accompany add additional amount ancillary another auxiliary read] "produced supplementary volumes"
*supplicant 22-39-2 (a.) 1. humbly entreating (n.) 1. someone who prays to God 2. one praying humbly for something [scrounge seek sincere sinner solemn solicit solicitous soul submit suitor pay petition pleadpower pray precatory imperative implore importunate cadge contribution admission adore appellant apply ask aspirant assistance trade]
*supposition 20-52-3 (n.) 1. a message expressing an opinion based on incomplete evidence 2. a hypothesis that is taken for granted 3. the cognitive process of supposing [seem sentiment speculation speculative substantiate suggest suppository surmise suspicious undertone unusual perception perhaps positive possibility precondition premise proof proposition purpose putative observation opinion oppose overtone iffy import impression incomplete infer inference insight intuitive involve tentative theory thesis thought notion nuance /itis/]
*suppress 06-49-50 (v.) 1. control and refrain from showing; of emotions 2. come down on or keep down by unjust use of one's authority 3. to put down by force or authority 4. keep under control; keep in check 5. put out of one's consciousness; in psychiatry [secret setback shrink silence sit smash smother snuff squash squelch stem stifle still stop strangle subdue subjugate ulterior underplay unman unspoken untold press prevent prohibit put putdown reduce refuse reject removed repress resist restraint restricted embargo end enigmatic enthral esoteric expression extinguish] "suppress a nascent uprising"
*suppression 13-42-11 (n.) 1. (botany) the failure to develop of some part or organ of a plant 2. (psychology) the conscious exclusion of unacceptable thoughts or desires 3. forceful prevention; putting down by power or authority 4. the act of withholding or withdrawing some book or writing from publication or circulation [security silence stop preservation pression prevention purge reduction remote restraint retirement eliminate end icy inhibition injunction interruption obstructionist

occlusion ontogeny opposition overthrow negativism nullification] "a suppression of the newspaper"
*surcharge 10-40-18 (n.) 1. an additional charge (as for items previously omitted or as a penalty for failure to exercise common caution or common skill) (v.) 1. charge an extra fee, as for a special service 2. rip off; ask an unreasonable price 3. place too much a load on 4. fill to an excessive degree 5. fill to capacity with people 6. print a new denomination on a stamp or a banknote 7. show an omission in (an account) for which credit ought to have been given [skin soak stick stuff supplement usury rack repletion rob charge clip crowd handicap holdup hook hyperemia additional gazump gorge gouge encumbrance exploitation extortion extra /crus/] "The air raids had surcharged the emergency wards"
*surety 22-51-2 (n.) 1. something clearly established 2. one who provides a warrant or guarantee to another 3. a prisoner who is held by one party to insure that another party will meet specified terms 4. a guarantee that an obligation will be met 5. property that your creditor can claim in case you default on your obligation [security service specify stated stock store sum support sure underwriter reception recognizance reluctant replevy require right enter escrow establish temporary tie transfer trust truth]
*surfeit 16-63-6 (n.) 1. the state of being more than full 2. the quality of being so overabundant that prices fall 3. eating until excessively full (v.) 1. supply or feed to surfeit 2. indulge to satiety, as of one's appetite [satiety satisfy sicken soak stall stuff superabundant supply surf surplus swollen until render repel repletion revulsion round fall feed fill flood flush food freight full furnish eat engorge enjoy excessive indulge /tie/]
*surmise 15-42-8 (n.) 1. a message expressing an opinion based on incomplete evidence (v.) 1. imagine to be the case or true or probable 2. infer from incomplete evidence [say sense shot speculation spite substantiate successful supposition suspicion understanding unusual reason reckon refute regard repute maintain message mise imagine incomplete inference insight intuitive establish esteem estimate evidence expect expression]
*surmount 15-42-7 (v.) 1. be on top of 2. get on top of; deal with successfully 3. reach the highest point of 4. be or do something to a greater degree [silence soluble subdue superable surpass upset ramp realize resolve manageable master measurable mount operable outdo outstrip overturn negotiate throw tip top traverse]
*surreptitious 14-45-9 (a.) 1. marked by quiet and caution and secrecy; taking pains to avoid being observed 2. conducted with or marked by hidden aims or methods [sale secretive shadow sharp show skulk slippery sly sneaky stealthy unconcealed underhand underhanded unobtrusive resistance enemy engage escape pain practice privy prowl prowler pussyfoot titi treacherous tricky troop try indirect insidious intelligence intrigue investigate observe openly operation overt]
*surrogate 10-29-19 (a.) 1. providing or receiving nurture or parental care though not related by blood or legal ties (n.) 1. someone who takes the place of another person 2. a person appointed to represent or act on behalf of others [settle sibling sign spare sperm standin substitute symbol unconscious understudy receive relief reliever replacement representative reserve respect ruler organization gate ghostwriter give administrative adoptive agent alternate alternative appointed artificial attorney authority token egg equal exchange /ago tag/]
*surround 02-53-400 (n.) 1. the area in which something exists or lives (v.) 1. surround so as to force to give up 2. envelop completely 3. extend on all sides of simultaneously; encircle 4. be around 5. surround with a wall in order to fortify [scene sea seal separate set shield shut side simultaneousl situation skirt smother social space specific spread stake start stated stockade suburb race rampart range region restrictive rim ring river round roundabout run one orbit organism outline outpost outskirt nearby neighboring net damage danger decorate definite demarcate destruction determined direct down driven] "Developments surround the town"
*surveyor 08-90-27 (n.) 1. an engineer who determines the boundaries and elevations of land or structures 2. someone who conducts a statistical survey [scientist sirdar solve statistics structure supervisor survey range review value verse visitor elevation engineer estimate evaluate examine occupation oceanography overseer]
*susceptibility 17-55-5 (n.) 1. the state of being susceptible; easily affected [sensitivity sentimentality sexy specific status strong suggestion supple upset capacity cast cep chemical clever cold eager easy efficiency emotion exposure pathogen penchant physics predisposition prejudice prone talent tendency touchy treatment turn twist impervious impressionable inclination intelligence bent bias brightness lean legal liability like likelihood /bit pecs/]
*susceptible 09-49-25 (a.) 1. (often followed by 'of' or 'to') yielding readily to or capable of 2. easily impressed emotionally [sensitize stimulus stir suasible suggestible sway sympathetic unprotected capable cep clever cold compliant conscious convince easy educate elastic emotional extensible perceptive permit persuasible physical plastic predispose prone proof protection teachable tempt tenderhearted touched impressionable impressive incline influence interpretation bend bright lack liable likely limber lissome lithe /bit pecs/] "susceptible to colds"
*suspense 09-34-24 (n.) 1. an uncertain cognitive state 2. apprehension about what is going to happen 3. excited anticipation of an approaching climax [stew stimulate stirring strain striking suspension unaccountable uncertainty uneasy unsettle unsure upset passivity pen pending pessimism piquant play pleasurable provoke pucker edgy electric enjoyable entropy excited exciting

exhilarate expectation nervous novel] "the matter remained in suspense for several years"
*suspension 03-42-167 (n.) 1. a mixture in which fine particles are suspended in a fluid where they are supported by buoyancy 2. temporary cessation or suspension 3. a time interval during which there is a temporary cessation of something 4. the act of suspending something (hanging it from above so it moves freely) 5. an interruption in the intensity or amount of something 6. a mechanical system of springs or shock absorbers connecting the wheels and axles to the chassis of a wheeled vehicle 7. a temporary debarment (from a privilege or position etc) [slow solution sound spell unfrock unseat pause pension period postpone preparation eliminate end nullification impeach inactivity interval obstruction orchestrate oust]
*suspicious 05-58-81 (a.) 1. (informal) not as expected 2. openly distrustful and unwilling to confide [seek shady shifty show shy sinister skeptical speak spic suggest suspect uncertain uneasy unquestionable unreliable unsure untrustworthy unwilling preposterous problematic imitate immoral implausible incline indicate insidious careful cautious chary circumstance colloquial communicate confide create criminal openly]
*sustenance 16-50-6 (n.) 1. a source of materials to nourish the body 2. the financial means whereby one lives 3. the act of sustaining [salt scoff spread uphold upkeep table treat tucker eat endowment extension nance nosh nourishment nurture nutrition aid alimentation alimony care carry cheer convenience]
*swarthy 22-76-2 (a.) 1. naturally having skin of a dark color [sable sad skin smile sober somber swart weather archaism raven tan tawny hair]
*swerve 11-70-16 (n.) 1. the act of turning aside suddenly 2. an erratic deflection from an intended course (v.) 1. turn sharply; change direction abruptly [sharp sheer shy slew slue stray sudden sway sweep swing wander warp winding worsen elbow err erratic evade excursus rambling retreat reverse revive right roving vagrant variation vary veer]
*sybarite 20-84-3 (n.) 1. a person addicted to luxury and pleasures of the senses [seek sensuality barite addicted aesthete enjoy epicurean]
*sycophant 17-73-5 (n.) 1. a person who tries to please someone in order to gain a personal advantage [satellite scandal self servile sign sincerity slave slimy smooth soap sponge suck superior cajolery compliment crawl cringe crouch obeisance obsequious oil palaver parasitic peon people personal please polish powerful praise prostrate puppet handshake hangdog helot henchman high honeyed humble abject adherent adulate advantage ant apple ass attempt thug timeserver toady tool truckle try]
*syllable 13-42-10 (n.) 1. a unit of spoken language larger than a phoneme [scale secret separate shred slight solmization sound speaker squeak statement stop strain language large last lateral letter line linguistic liquid able add alone analyze antepenultimate aspiration assimilation atom bite book breathe burden end envoi explosive expression /ally ball bally/] "the word `pocket' has two syllables"
*syllabus 17-79-5 (n.) 1. a course of academic studies [series skeleton sketch skill study survey lead lecture list literacy abridgment abstract academic admit brief bus undertake university /ally ball bally/]
*sylph 25-57-1 (n.) 1. a slender graceful young woman 2. an elemental being believed to inhabit the air [salamander slender slight slim soulless sprite young legend leprechaun peri pixie pooka hob /ply/]
*symmetrical 15-44-7 (a.) 1. exhibiting equivalence or correspondence among constituents of an entity or between different entities 2. having similarity in size, shape, and relative position of corresponding parts [shape size smooth steady sweet symmetric measured methodical equal euphonious even tripping regular routine coequal commensurate coordinate arrange]
*symmetry 13-48-11 (n.) 1. (mathematics) an attribute of a shape; exact correspondence of form on opposite sides of a dividing line or plane 2. balance among the parts of something [same science shape share show side space spatial structure sweetness system marshal math matter measured meet member mutuality energy equally equation equilibrium equivalency essential even exact tally time tranquillity regularity relation rhythm routine]
*sympathetic 05-52-77 (a.) 1. (physiology; anatomy) of or relating to the sympathetic nervous system 2. showing or motivated by sympathy and understanding 3. having similar disposition and tastes 4. expressing or feeling or resulting from sympathy or compassion or friendly fellow feelings; disposed toward 5. relating to vibrations that occur as a result of vibrations in a nearby body 6. (of characters in literature or drama) evoking empathic or sympathetic feelings [sensitive supportive susceptible magnetize melt merciful pathetic peaceful pleasant pull agree akin approve assure together touchy tug harmonious hearten humane empathetic encourage impressionable irritable itch care charitable cheer concerned considerate console /cite/] "sympathetic neurons"
*sympathize 11-01-15 (v.) 1. be understanding of 2. share the feelings of; understand the sentiments of 3. to feel or express sympathy or compassion [sensation sentiment share show sponsor stalwart suffering supporter maintain partisan path patron pity promoter admire advocate ally happen idea identify intimate emotional empathize encourage endorse experience explain exponent express]
*symphonic 12-31-12 (a.) 1. relating to or characteristic or suggestive of a symphony 2. harmonious in sound [sonata sound suggestive million musical philharmonic phonic pleasing harmonious hum orchestral insect instrumental choir classical color content] "symphonic

choir"
*symphony 04-41-96 (n.) 1. a large orchestra; can perform symphonies 2. a long and complex sonata for symphony orchestra [share solidarity sound string madrigal mambo mass metal moderato monody mutuality peace perform philharmonic phony piano player pop punk harmony hear homophony hymn oneness operetta oratorio orchestra overture] "we heard the Vienna symphony"
*syndicate 07-37-42 (n.) 1. an association of companies for some definite purpose 2. a loose affiliation of gangsters in charge of organized criminal activities 3. a news agency that sells features or articles or photographs etc. to newspapers for simultaneous publication (v.) 1. join together into a syndicate 2. organize into or form a syndicate 3. sell articles, television programs, or photos to several publications or independent broadcasting stations [solidify soviet staff syncretism syndic synthesis directory distribute inclusion incorporate industry integration coalition combine composition concern conspiracy corporation court add agency agreement ally association tribunal trust embody encompass enterprise /acid/] "The banks syndicated"
*synod 16-73-6 (n.) 1. a council convened to discuss ecclesiastical business [see sit special staff nod dance date diet discussion /don/]
*synonym 17-41-5 (n.) 1. two words that can be interchanged in a context are said to be synonymous relative to that context [say selfsame speaker specific style substitute syllable native non mean metonym monosyllable]
*synopsis 19-47-4 (n.) 1. a sketchy summary of the main points of an argument or theory [short show skeleton sketch sketchy sum survey ops outline overview pandect play plot point precis present /pony/]
*systematic 07-44-41 (a.) 1. characterized by order and planning 2. not haphazard [scientific smooth stable steady system tabular taxonomy efficient equal even exclude manner measured mechanical methodical accordance administrator alike always analytic arrange automatic immutable intermittent invariably investigate carry classification constitute continuous correspondent /met tame/] "the investigation was very systematic"

T

*tableau 12-35-14 (n.) 1. any dramatic scene 2. a group of people attractively arranged (as if in a painting) [tab table tapestry theater tormentor abstraction altarpiece arise arrange aspect attractive ballet bomb border likeness effect exhibition exposition]
*tacit 11-48-16 (a.) 1. indicated by necessary connotation though not expressed directly [agreement assume calm connotation consent custody imply indicate inexplicit infer inherent intimate /cat/]
*taciturn 16-60-6 (a.) 1. habitually reserved and uncommunicative [tacit talk terse tight trait truncate abbreviate abridge aloof concise contract crisp cut incline incommunicative introvert uncommunicative ready reserved reticent nature necessary not /cat/]
*tack 08-46-33 (n.) 1. the heading or position of a vessel relative to the trim of its sails 2. a line (rope or chain) that regulates the angle at which a sail is set in relation to the wind 3. gear for a horse 4. a short nail with a sharp point and a large head 5. sailing a zigzag course 6. (nautical) the act of changing tack (v.) 1. turn (a boat) into the wind 2. fasten with tacks 3. fix to; attach 4. make by putting pieces together 5. sew together loosely, with large stitches 6. reverse, as of direction, attitude, or course of action [tactic tie tone trend alternate append approach articulate attach clip comfit construct corner couple course create kit /cat/] "tack the notice on the board"
*tact 17-64-5 (n.) 1. consideration in dealing with others and avoiding giving offence [taste technique tender thoughtfulnes ability act acute address appropriate avoid care careful concern consideration control /cat/]
*tactician 17-60-5 (n.) 1. a person who is skilled at planning tactics [contrive negotiate]
*tactics 04-56-126 (n.) 1. the branch of military science dealing with detailed maneuvers to achieve objectives set by strategy [tactic tone achieve act air architect armed art attack attain calculator campaign conduct contrive custom idea immediate implement influence intrigue investment scheme science service set setup strategy style /cat/]
*tadpole 22-68-2 (n.) 1. a larval frog or toad [tail toad amphibian dogie duckling paddock parent pole pollywog pup puppy lambkin larval limb litter egg]
*talon 20-58-3 (n.) 1. a sharp hooked claw especially on a bird of prey [teeth toe turn administration architecture authority lock look nail nipper]
*tamp 20-14-3 (n.) 1. a tool for tamping (e.g., for tamping tobacco into a pipe bowl or a charge into a drill hole etc.) (v.) 1. press down tightly [tam tap tight tobacco tool assault miner packing pang pipe pit practice pressing prod push /mat/] "tamp the coffee grinds in the container to make espresso"
*tamper 09-36-23 (n.) 1. a tool for tamping (e.g., for tamping tobacco into a pipe bowl or a charge into a drill hole etc.) (v.) 1. fool or play around with 2. intrude in other people's affairs or business; interfere unwantedly [tamp threat tinker tobacco tool transform try affair affect alter manipulate meddle miner monkey move packing people pipe play practice ram rig /mat/] "Someone tampered with the documents on my desk"
*tangent 20-49-3 (n.) 1. a straight line or plane that touches a curve or curved surface at a point but does not intersect it at that point 2. ratio of the opposite to the adjacent side of a right-angled triangle [tan topic touch trace transversal travel trigonometric adjacent airline angle approach axis normal gent give edge equal express /gnat/]
*tangential 20-45-3 (a.) 1. of superficial relevance if any 2. of or relating to or acting along or in the direction of a tangent [tangent touching allusion almost approach asymptotic nudge glancing grazing extraneous impinge indirect irrelevant issue lateral line loose /gnat lait/]
*tangible 08-52-31 (a.) 1. possible to be treated as fact 2. perceptible by the senses especially the sense of touch

3. capable of being perceived by the senses or the mind; especially capable of being handled or touched or felt 4. having substance or material existence; perceptible to the senses 5. (of especially business assets) having physical substance and intrinsic monetary value [tactile tang touched toughness treat abstract actual anger apparent aspect asset atom noticeable give good gross imaginary immaterial impalpable incapable indisputable industrial intrinsic barely benefit bodily body brief bring business estate evaluate evident existence explicit express /big gnat/] "skin with a tangible roughness"
*tannery 25-52-1 (n.) 1. workplace where skins and hides are tanned [tanner abattoir animal armory arsenal refinery yard]
*tantalize 13-01-10 (v.) 1. harass with persistent criticism or carping [taking taste taunt teacher tease telling tempt thwart tie torment torture treat trouble twit acceptable agitate annoy anta appeal aroma arouse attractive laugh let letdown lively lovely luxurious impressive infatuate interesting intrigue inviting endear engage enrapture entice]
*tantamount 13-46-11 (a.) 1. being essentially equal to something [admission alike amount analogous answer match measure outcome unequal uniform unpleasant /mat/]
*tapestry 11-46-17 (n.) 1. something that is felt to resemble a tapestry in its complexity 2. a wall hanging of heavy handwoven fabric with pictorial designs 3. a heavy textile with a woven design; used for curtains and upholstery [tableau tap textile triptych abstraction altarpiece arras artifact pattern pest photograph picture piece place print edge embroidery engrave stencil stitch synthetic reproduction resemble rich rug /pat/] "the tapestry of European history"
*tarnish 08-55-28 (n.) 1. discoloration of metal surface caused by oxidation (v.) 1. make dirty or spotty, as by exposure to air, of metals; also used metaphorically [taint tar tarn touch affair affect appearance aspersion attaint reflection reputation revile ruin rust rusty nasty impair imperfection infect injure inky senator serious shine silver smear smoky smudge soil spoil spotted spotty stain sully surface harm hurt] "The silver was tarnished by the long exposure to the air"
*tarry 22-58-2 (a.) 1. having the characteristics of pitch or tar (v.) 1. be about 2. leave slowly and hesitantly [tar temporary temporize tend trail trifling abide adhesive aim apparent around arrival await remain repose resiny rest run]
*tassel 16-46-6 (n.) 1. adornment consisting of a bunch of cords fastened at one end [tasse thread tie top trim tuft add adorn agriculture see stamen stem sword ear edge loose /less sat/]
*taunt 08-56-32 (n.) 1. aggravation by deriding or mocking or criticizing (v.) 1. harass with persistent criticism or carping [talk tantalize task tease tie treat twit accuse affront aggravation anger annoy article aunt unfriendly upbraid]
*taut 10-50-18 (a.) 1. subjected to great tension; stretched tight 2. pulled or drawn tight [tau tension tidy tight trim anxious apprehensive uptight] "taut sails"
*tautology 25-69-1 (n.) 1. (logic) a statement that is necessarily true 2. useless repetition [talkative tedious teem tend tirade true abundant amplitude analyze unessential useless ology original ornamentation outpour overlap length linguistic logical logorrhea luxury gift gingerbread gratuitous great gushy /lot/] "the statement `he is brave or he is not brave' is a tautology"
*tawdry 15-57-8 (a.) 1. tastelessly showy 2. cheap and shoddy [tacky tasteless tatty taw tinsel trashy aesthetic appearance decency dry ring yet /wat/]
*taxation 05-28-80 (n.) 1. charge against a citizen's person or property or activity for the support of government 2. government income due to taxation 3. the imposition of taxes; the practice of the government in levying taxes on the subjects of a state [tax title toll transfer tribute additional adjust amount annual assessment attribute available imposition impost income increase inheritance insurance interest ion item organization net /tax xat/]
*taxidermy 20-53-3 (n.) 1. the art of mounting the skins of animals so that they have lifelike appearance [taxonomy tin anatomy animal anthropology appearance art artistry ichthyology irradiation dead dehydration deliver derm desiccate dry ecology embalm entomology ethology ranger refrigerate rescue malacology mammalogy marinate mounting mummify /xat/]
*technicality 13-57-10 (n.) 1. a detail that is considered insignificant [tangle technical trifle triviality type entangle complication condition consider convolution crabbed naught nihility nullity inessential insignificant interpretation intricate involve isolated item apply area arise law legal line]
*technique 03-47-234 (n.) 1. skillfulness in the command of fundamentals deriving from practice and familiarity 2. a practical method or art applied to some particular task [task tech technology texture tissue tone tooth touch treatment efficiency enamel expertise capacity cognitive command computer control course curve handy horseman image imply improve information intelligence intimacy quick]
*technology 01-42-549 (n.) 1. the discipline dealing with the art or science of applying scientific knowledge to practical problems 2. the practical application of science to commerce or industry [technique techno tool engineering equipment expertise concern craft ology]
*teem 10-52-18 (v.) 1. be teeming, be abuzz 2. move in large numbers [tautology tee theater thrive thorough throng total transfuse engender exhaustless exist expect extremely exuberant many maximal mind move much multiply /meet/]
*teetotal 17-86-5 (a.) 1. practicing complete abstinence from alcoholic beverages (v.) 1. practice teetotalism

and abstain from the consuymption of alcoholic beverages [ten total absolute abstinence affect alcoholic appetite avoid /tee tote/]
*telepathy 19-70-4 (n.) 1. apparent communication from one mind to another without using sensory perceptions [talk telekinesis telepath touch traffic transference exchange extrasensory linguistic paranormal perception psychic answer apparent automatism /ape pele tape/]
*telephony 17-86-5 (n.) 1. transmitting speech at a distance [transmit try electronicall let line phone phony hang hold open operate /pele/]
*telescope 10-41-20 (n.) 1. a magnifier of images of distant objects (v.) 1. crush together, as of cars in a collision 2. make smaller or shorter [target transit trim truncate elide epitomize laboratory light look scope squash station stunt contract cosmic crop crush cut observation observatory optical orrery planetarium pollard prune] "the novel was telescoped into a short play"
*telltale 15-43-8 (a.) 1. disclosing unintentionally (n.) 1. someone who gossips indiscreetly [tabby tale taleteller tattletale track tunnel evidence lead leak light look low across aloft apparent]
*temerity 19-73-4 (n.) 1. fearless daring [trait merit might rash reckless risk impertinent imprudent impudent indiscretion intrusive involve /met tire/]
*temperance 20-52-3 (n.) 1. the trait of avoiding excesses 2. abstaining from excess 3. the act of tempering [teetotal tempera temperate total trait tranquillity eat eschew even excesse measure mild moderation mortification pacifism personal practice prohibition prudent reasonable refrain restraint abstinence alcoholic appetite asceticism austerity avoid neutrality nonviolence calm combine compound control cool /met/]
*temperate 16-46-6 (a.) 1. (of weather or climate) free from extremes; mild; or characteristic of such weather or climate 2. not extreme 3. not extreme in behavior [tame tempera tranquil tropical eat effect equable equatorial even excessive exist extreme measure measured meteorology microbiology mild moderate modest muted pacifistic peaceful penalty physical plant pleasant prudent range rational reasonable region regulate reserved response restrained abstemious abstinence ascetic attitude austere average /met tare/] "a temperate region"
*temporal 19-48-4 (a.) 1. not eternal 2. of or relating to or limited by time 3. of or relating to the temples (the sides of the skull behind the orbit) 4. of the material world 5. of this earth or world 6. concerned with secular rather than sacred matters (n.) 1. the semantic role of the noun phrase that designating the time of the state or action denoted by the verb [tempora temporary tense terrestrial timekeeper earthly earthy entity ephemeral eternal evanescent existence expression measure moment momentary mortal mundane passing permanent physical popular possession process profane progressive orbit realize religion reprobate role abstraction art laic laity lasting lie life limited /met/] "temporal matters of but fleeting moment"
*temporary 03-42-224 (a.) 1. not permanent; not lasting 2. lacking continuity or regularity [tempora tentative terminable toil token transitory employee ephemeral episodic equivalent evanescent makeshift migrant mock momentary mortal palm parttime pass pay pinch precarious pro provisional office regularity reserve risky roustabout acting alternative arrange automatic /met/]
*tempt 05-75-83 (v.) 1. induce into action by using one's charm 2. give rise to a desire by being attractive or inviting 3. provoke someone to do something through (often false or exaggerated) promises or persuasion 4. dispose or incline or entice to 5. try presumptuously 6. try to seduce [tantalize tease temp tickle tour train transgression trap try turn twist emotion engage enlist entice entrap exaggerate excite magnetize mesmerize mistake money move peace persuade position possible power presumptuous principle promise prompt proper provoke /met/] "We were tempted by the delicious-looking food"
*tenacious 08-53-28 (a.) 1. stubbornly unyielding 2. sticking together 3. (of memory) having greater than average range [ten tend thicken tight tireless truth earnest easy enduring engrossment nervy absorbing accurate achieve adamant adhesive assiduous cling cold commit constant continue inflexible insistent insult intolerance invincible irresolute obdurate obstinate opinionated undaunted unflinching uninterrupted unwilling unyielding serious set shake sheet solid steadfast sticky stubborn /can cane/]
*tenacity 12-60-13 (n.) 1. persistent determination [achieve city insistent irresolute /can cane/]
*tenant 04-41-105 (n.) 1. someone who pays rent to use land or a building or a car that is owned by someone else 2. a holder of buildings or lands by any kind of title (as ownership or lease) 3. any occupant who dwells in a place (v.) 1. occupy as a tenant [title endorse evict nest note abide addressee agreement ant apartment arrange] "the landlord can evict a tenant who doesn't pay the rent"
*tendency 04-53-92 (n.) 1. an inclination to do something 2. a characteristic likelihood of or natural disposition toward a certain condition or character or effect 3. an attitude of mind especially one that favors one alternative over others 4. a general direction in which something tends to move [tend thing toward track type easy eccentricity effect electron equally ethos expectation natural nature navigation negative non denomination desire develop device dharma direction disapproval disfavor disposition divine drift capacity cell certain chance complex condition course current]
*tenet 10-41-18 (n.) 1. a religious doctrine that is proclaimed as true without proof [teach tene theory true

establish net norm /tene/]
*tenor 06-38-51 (a.) 1. (of a musical instrument) intermediate between alto and baritone or bass 2. of or close in range to the highest natural adult male voice (n.) 1. the pitch range of the highest male voice 2. the adult male singing voice above baritone 3. an adult male with a tenor voice 4. pervading note of an utterance [tendency theme tone track transcript turn type effect enrico essence exact extension nature navigation nor noted operatic orientation outstand overall overtone range recording register relation reply role run /one/] "a tenor sax"
*tense 05-55-69 (a.) 1. in or of a state of physical or nervous tension 2. (phonetics) pronounced with relatively tense tongue muscles (e.g., the vowel sound in 'beat') 3. taut or rigid; stretched tight (n.) 1. a grammatical category of verbs used to express distinctions of time (v.) 1. stretch or force to the limit 2. increase the tension on 3. make tense 4. become tense or tenser [talk taut tax ten tension term tight tongue transform turn twist twitchy ease edgy effect effort elongate emotional enter entire express extend nailbiting narrow nasalize natural nervy sanskrit security see slow sound space speak stiff stop straint stretch string strong strung suspensive syntactic] "tense piano strings"
*tentative 05-30-71 (a.) 1. unsettled in mind or opinion 2. under terms not final or fully worked out or agreed upon [temporary tent timid trial trying easy employee empty examine exploratory naive noncommittal acting agree alternative awkward imposing indefinite innocent inspector interim vacuous venturesome vicarious /vita/]
*tenure 05-38-73 (n.) 1. the term during which some position is held 2. the right to hold property; part of an ancient hierarchical system of holding lands (v.) 1. give life-time employment to; as of university posts [temporary tenant term time title elevate employment enfeoff engagement england enlist enure university until upgrade raise residency retirement return right /run rune/] "She was tenured after she published her book"
*tepid 12-43-12 (a.) 1. moderately warm [temperate toasty tropical enthusiasm epi equatorial perfunctory produce impart indifferent degree dim dull /dip pet/]
*tercentenary 25-62-1 (n.) 1. the 300th anniversary [tercentenary triennial exact remembrance celebrate centenary century coincide commemoration anniversary year]
*terminal 04-43-115 (a.) 1. being or situated at an end 2. occurring at or forming an end or termination 3. causing or ending in or approaching death 4. of or relating to or situated at the ends of a delivery route 5. relating to or occurring in a term or fixed period of time (n.) 1. a contact on an electrical device (such as a battery) at which electric current enters or leaves 2. station where transport vehicles load or unload passengers or goods 3. electronic equipment consisting of a device providing access to a computer; has a keyboard and display [tail tip track tube effect end railway resolution ruin maximum metro mina monitor mortal ill incorrigible incurable inevitable irrevocable nonviable anchorage apodosis lead lethal life line lose low]
*terminate 07-46-39 (v.) 1. have an end, in a temporal, spatial, or quantitative sense; either spatial or metaphorical 2. bring to an end or halt 3. be the end of; be the last of concluding part of 4. terminate the employment of [turnout end ensue expire expunge extinguish recess resign result rise mina issue negotiation notice abandon abolish adjourn adjudicate attend axe]
*termination 10-45-18 (n.) 1. a coming to an end of a contract period 2. a place where something ends or is complete 3. the end of a word (a suffix or inflectional ending or final morpheme) 4. something that results 5. the act of ending something [terminus effect end resolution result ripe maturity issue nation abandon abortion apodosis omega outcome]
*terminus 19-53-4 (n.) 1. a place where something ends or is complete 2. the ultimate goal for which something is done 3. station where transport vehicles load or unload passengers or goods 4. either end of a railroad or bus route [threshold top town track train transport traveler tube effect end endpoint equip extremity race railway reach represent resolution ripe rome route march marker mean metro minus move intend interface necessary ultimate underground unload sculpture serve side sidetrack special square statue stop storage subway supply /sun/]
*terrify 05-70-88 (v.) 1. fill with terror; frighten greatly [terrorize err intimidate fear fearful feel fill freeze frighten frozen /fir/]
*territorial 08-44-32 (a.) 1. of or relating to a territory 2. (biology) displaying territoriality; defending a territory from intruders 3. of or relating to the local vicinity (n.) 1. nonprofessional soldier member of a territorial military unit 2. a territorial military unit [train emergency enlist equip recruit regional regular reserve rial international intruder organize outside armed army assertive land limit living local /lair roti/] "the territorial government of the Virgin Islands"
*terse 12-38-14 (a.) 1. brief and to the point; effectively cut short [tart tight trim easy economically effective elegant elliptic exchange express reply reserved response retort round rude short silent simple snappy straightforward succinct]
*testament 07-62-39 (n.) 1. a legal document declaring a person's wishes regarding the disposal of their property when they die 2. a profession of belief 3. either of the two main parts of the Christian Bible 4. strong evidence for something [easy epistle evidence execute sacred scripture second serve skill soon stamen strong supplement already alter apostle authority main major /mat set/] "he stated his political testament"
*testimonial 12-62-12 (a.) 1. expressing admiration or

appreciation 2. of or relating to or constituting testimony (n.) 1. something given or done as an expression of esteem 2. something that serves as evidence 3. something that recommends (or expresses commendation) of a person or thing as worthy or desirable [test ticket tribute triumph trophy effort employer endorsement esteem evidence exaggerate expression serve show sign statement strong support indication inscription memory message monument mound obituary observance opinion ovation necrology note acknowledgment admiration admission allegation anniversary approval authority /lain omit set/] "testimonial dinner"
*theocracy 19-56-4 (n.) 1. a political unit governed by a deity (or by officials thought to be divinely guided) 2. the belief in government by divine guidance [technocracy think triumvirate tyranny heteronomous hierocracy ochlocracy official oligarchy organization orientation characterize church colonialism community racy regency religious republic rule aristocracy autarchy authority autonomy /arco/]
*theologian 12-52-13 (n.) 1. someone who is learned in theology or who speculates about theology [ian abelard]
*theological 10-40-21 (a.) 1. of or relating to or concerning theology [engage logical concerning /cig/] "theological seminar"
*theology 10-48-18 (n.) 1. the learned profession acquired by specialized courses in religion (usually taught at a college or seminary) 2. a particular system or school of religious beliefs and teachings 3. the rational and systematic study of religion and its influences and of the nature of religious truth [teach tend top torment toward traditional train truth heaven hell high hold holy homily human emanation eternity exegesis existence expiate ology originate lead learn limited liturgiology god govern grace guidance] "Jewish theology"
*theoretical 07-43-41 (a.) 1. concerned with theories rather than their practical applications 2. concerned primarily with theories or hypotheses rather than practical considerations 3. based on specialized theory [theoretic transcendental hook hypothetical empirical exist experiment observation oppose ideational ideologic imaginary impractical incline characterize closet conceptual conjecture consideration contemplate abstract abstractive academic analysis apply armchair art /cite iter roe/] "theoretical science"
*theorist 11-46-17 (n.) 1. someone who theorizes (especially in science or art) [thinker hold expound oris intellect scientific significant /roe/]
*theorize 15-01-8 (v.) 1. to believe especially on uncertain or tentative grounds 2. construct a theory about 3. form or construct theories [tentative the think hypothesize elaborate existence expect explicate rationalize reason reassemble retrace imagine infer intellectualize /roe/]
*therefore 02-63-251 (ad.) 1. (used to introduce a logical conclusion) from that fact or reason or as a result 2. as a consequence [test thence therefor thereupon thus true trust hence hold home egg empty equally ergo reason require fact fail fairly false finally follow forbidden forget formal fresh open opportunity optimistic] "therefore X must be true"
*thermal 11-61-15 (a.) 1. relating to or associated with heat 2. caused by or designed to retain heat (n.) 1. rising current of warm air [temperature tepid tropical hawk heat herma high hot effect energy equatorial retain ride rise manufacture meteorology mild molecule move aestival affect area low lukewarm] "thermal movements of molecules"
*thesis 08-49-27 (n.) 1. an unproved statement put forward as a premise in an argument 2. a treatise advancing a new point of view resulting from research; usually a requirement for an advanced academic degree [the theme theory toward treatise treatment true turn homily emphasis essay examination exposition series serve short stage statement stress study syllable idea inference ionic]
*thoroughbred 10-31-21 (a.) 1. having a list of ancestors as proof of being a purebred animal (n.) 1. a well-bred person 2. a racehorse belonging to a breed that originated from a cross between Arabian stallions and English mares 3. a pedigreed animal of unmixed lineage; used especially of horses [thorough triple hidalgo highbred horse onward organism originate race recognize refined unmixed generation genet gentleman grandee grownup bangtail baronet barton beast belonging breed bring brute earl english esquire daimio develop duke]
*thoroughfare 12-31-12 (n.) 1. a public road from one place to another [terrace thorough track traffic travel truck turnpike heavily highway open right road roadway route row freeway access alley alleyway artery avenue expressway]
*thrall 13-73-10 (n.) 1. the state of being under the control of another person 2. someone held in bondage [television turn tyranny hex high hold reality restraint absolutism age alcohol all labor land last life loan lord low]
*thrift 11-19-17 (n.) 1. any of numerous sun-loving low-growing evergreens of the genus Armeria having round heads of pink or white flowers 2. extreme care in spending money; reluctance to spend money unnecessarily [thin temperate tuft head herbaceous husbandry reluctance rift rose round family food formal frugal /fir/]
*thwart 06-49-56 (n.) 1. a crosspiece spreading the gunnels of a boat; used as a seat in a rowboat (v.) 1. hinder or prevent (the efforts, plans, or desires) of 2. hinder or prevent (the efforts, plans, or desires) of [tease transverse traverse hamper happening hinder hope wart across amazing annul arise regretful restrain rowboat rowlock ruin]

*timbre 14-36-9 (n.) 1. the distinctive property of a complex sound (a voice or noise or musical sound) [tenor throat tim tonality tone impart incorporate instrument manner meet mood mouth muffle musical bell broken range resonance resonator rich ringing roughness ear] "the timbre of her soprano was rich and lovely"
*timid 09-49-24 (a.) 1. showing fear and lack of confidence 2. lacking self-confidence 3. lacking conviction or boldness or courage 4. contemptibly timid (n.) 1. people who are fearful and cautious [temperament tentative timorous trait tremulous ignoble inarticulate incline involve manly mark mid modest mousy danger daring daunt decision demonstrate desire diffident dismay doorway /dim/] "whitewater rafting is not for the timid"
*timorous 22-62-2 (a.) 1. timid by nature or revealing timidity [timidity timor tone tremulous inarticulate intimidate mouse mousy recoil retiring reveal unman scare show shrink shy soft /omit/] "timorous little mouse"
*tincture 22-81-2 (n.) 1. a substances that colors metals 2. a quality of a given color that differs slightly from a primary color 3. (pharmacology) a medicine consisting of an extract in an alcohol solution (v.) 1. fill, as with a certain quality 2. stain or tint with a color [taste thought tinct tint tiny tone topical touch trace traffic transmit treat trial idea illuminate imbue important impregnate indication infuse ink instill intimate iodine nuance carbon cast certain charge chemical chief coloring cover criticism unicorn red reflect rose eagle effect emblazon emit enamel essence ethyl extract] "The heavy traffic tinctures the air with carbon monoxide"
*tinge 09-49-25 (n.) 1. a slight but appreciable addition 2. a pale or subdued color (v.) 1. suffuse with color 2. dye with a color [taste thought tincture tint tobacco tone touch trace idea imbue impact import indefinite influence inge inhale nuance garlic give glaze gloss grain green effect element emblazon emotion enamel]
*tipsy 19-65-4 (a.) 1. (slang) very drunk [thief tiddly tight tilt tip incline inebriate intoxicate patois pie piss pitch pixilated plastered potty slight slop slope sloshed smash smooth soak sodden souse sozzled squiffy stewed stiff stupefy substance /pit spit/]
*tirade 13-65-10 (n.) 1. a speech of violent denunciation [talkative tautology invective rade rank rant rating read abuse address angry attack debate denunciation diatribe exhortation extravagance exuberant /rit/]
*tireless 09-59-24 (a.) 1. showing sustained enthusiastic action with unflagging vitality 2. characterized by hard work and perseverance [task tenacious immune indefatigable industrious insistent invincible rapt relentless resolute right enduring energy enthusiastic equal excellence exert lasting less lethargic lively loyal show slacken spirited stable steady stop sustain /rit/]
*tiresome 12-68-13 (a.) 1. so lacking in interest as to cause mental weariness [task tease tedious train trouble trying twain insipid interest irk irksome irritate routine edmund effect exasperate excitement exhaust some soporific speaker strain stressful onerous oppressive ordinary mark mental monotonous mundane /rit/]
*titanic 10-60-21 (a.) 1. of great force or power [titan towering tremendous immense infinite abysmal astronomical average awesome colossal cosmic cyclopean]
*toady 22-63-2 (n.) 1. a person who tries to please someone in order to gain a personal advantage (v.) 1. tray to gain favor by cringing or flattering [tag timeserver toad tool trail tray truckle try obsequious abject achieve advantage ass dishonestly dupe]
*tolerable 15-50-7 (a.) 1. capable of being borne 2. neither good nor bad 3. capable of being tolerated 4. able to be tolerated or endured [tedious tidy office okay only ordinary lackluster least leastwise level livable endure enough exceptional rather reasonable relatively respectable right rule able acceptable accord actor adequate agreeable allowable average bad bear bearable /bar bare lot/] "tolerable noise levels"
*tolerance 06-54-53 (n.) 1. a disposition to allow freedom of choice and behavior 2. the act of tolerating something 3. the power or capacity of an organism to tolerate unfavorable environmental conditions 4. a permissible difference; allowing freedom to move within limits 5. willingness to recognize and respect the beliefs or practices of others [tender tole toleration open opposition overlook laxness leeway loose easy eligible embrace range reception room acceptance addiction admission attitude negligence charity coverage crash /lot/]
*tolerant 09-57-23 (a.) 1. showing or characterized by broad-mindedness 2. tolerant and forgiving under provocation 3. showing respect for the rights or opinions or practices of others 4. showing the capacity for endurance [temper tender thoughtful tolerate treatment try objective obliging open opinion opponent large lax lenient liberal libertine long love easygoing effect enduring exposure rant regardful religious respond right accept admission advance affect allow narrow neighbor newspaper /lot/]
*tolerate 05-48-66 (v.) 1. put up with something or somebody unpleasant 2. allow the presence of or allow (an activity) without opposing or prohibiting 3. Medicine: have a tolerance for a poison or strong drug or pathogen 4. recognize and respect (rights and beliefs of others) [technique toward observe oppose overlook learn let listen lot lying effect end endure existence expense expose rate recompense religion remark resistance respond right abide accept accommodate admit allow anti attempt /lot tare/]
*toleration 22-54-2 (n.) 1. a disposition to tolerate or accept people or situations 2. official recognition of the right of individuals to hold dissenting opinions

(especially in religion) [official open opinion liberality license live ration recognition religious right acceptance allowance authorization /lot tare/] "all people should practice toleration and live together in peace"
*tonic 11-65-16 (a.) 1. (physiology) of or relating to or producing normal tone or tonus in muscles or tissue 2. imparting vitality and energy 3. relating to or being the keynote of a major or minor scale 4. used of syllables 5. employing variations in pitch to distinguish meanings of otherwise similar words (n.) 1. lime- or lemon-flavored carbonated water containing quinine 2. a sweet drink containing carbonated water and flavoring 3. (music) the first note of a diatonic scale 4. a medicine that strengthens and invigorates [taut tense tensity therapy thick tissue tonality tone toni tonus treat twangy occlusive open organize oxytone narrow nasalize non normal notation note impart incorporate intonate invigorate call carbonate carry central charge cheer chinchona chord close club cold communicate contraction create] "a tonic reflex"
*topography 15-41-8 (n.) 1. the configuration of a surface and the relations among its man-made and natural features 2. precise detailed study of the surface features of a region [territorial oceanography outline parallel people place position precise projection psychometry gauger geodetic geography give globe goniometer graphy railroad region regional relation response river altimetry appraise area assessor atlas attribute hachure highway history hypsometry /pot/]
*topple 07-48-43 (v.) 1. fall down, as if collapsing 2. cause to topple or tumble by pushing [tilt tip totter trip tumble turn opp oust overthrow overturn pitch plunge position precarious precipitate pushing layout lean level list lower /pot/]
*torment 07-61-36 (n.) 1. intense feelings of suffering; acute mental or physical pain 2. extreme mental distress 3. unbearable physical pain 4. the act of harassing someone 5. a severe affliction 6. a feeling of intense annoyance caused by being tormented (v.) 1. torment emotionally or mentally 2. treat cruelly 3. subject to torture [teacher tearing tease tor torture treat trouble try twist oppress outrage overwhelm rack rag rend ride rub martyrize menace mental miserable misery molest emotional evil exasperate excruciate excruciating exercise extreme nag needle nerve nightmare nuisance] "The children tormented the stuttering teacher"
*torpid 22-53-2 (a.) 1. slow and apathetic 2. (biology) in a condition of biological rest or suspended animation [tame tor old organism remain resigned rest rigid part passive permanent persistent physical inactive indifferent indolent inert intact dead describe detached dormant dreamy dull /dip/]
*torpor 19-67-4 (n.) 1. a state of motor and mental inactivity with a partial suspension of sensibility 2. inactivity resulting from torpidity and lack of vigor or energy [tor trait oscitancy remain rest rigid partial passive passivity permanency persistence physiological] "he fell into a deep torpor"
*torque 14-79-10 (n.) 1. a twisting force [tiara tor torsion turning twist overcome resistance rhinestone ring rotation quantity earring engine exert]
*torrid 12-70-13 (a.) 1. characterized by intense emotion 2. emotionally charged and vigorously energetic 3. burning hot; extremely and unpleasantly hot [temperature toast torr tropical trumpet oratory rapid rhythm roasting impassioned inflame intensity dance describe desire dessert dry]
*tortuous 12-69-12 (a.) 1. highly involved or intricate 2. not straightforward 3. marked by repeated turns and bends [tall tangle tax tort track turn twisty orotund ostentatious overwrought reason refined repeat rhetorical road roundabout ruffle undulant scott showy sinuous sir sly sprung steer structure surprise /out trot/]
*torturous 20-48-3 (a.) 1. extremely painful [tearing torment tort torture rack rend severe sharp shoot /trot/]
*tout 07-57-43 (n.) 1. (British) someone who buys tickets to an event in order to resell them at a profit 2. one who sells advice about gambling or speculation (especially at the racetrack) 3. someone who advertises for customers in an especially brazen way (v.) 1. advertize in strongly positive terms 2. show off [television teller ticket tipster trader train triumph trumpet truth try obtain occupy odd offer out outing overstate overwrought unite] "This product was touted as a revolutionary invention"
*trait 07-54-38 (n.) 1. a distinguishing feature of your personal nature [taste temperamental think trace trick trustworthine turn rapid rash reaction recognition reliable remain representative resolve rice absence abstraction affection air ait assess attention attribute image impression inactivity index individuation inert inherit insight intellectual irresolute]
*trajectory 12-55-14 (n.) 1. the path followed by an object moving through space [thrust tory tour track trail road round route run angle aphelion apogee arc ecliptic energy equator equilibrium equinox ceiling circuit close constant course curve orbit /jar/]
*tranquil 11-55-16 (a.) 1. free from disturbance 2. characterized by absence of emotional agitation [thoughtless turbulence turmoil reflect regular relax restful resting ribbon ripple run absence acceptance agitation angry anxiety quiet quietism undisturbed unmoved unperturbed unruffled untroubled idyllic impassive inevitable isolated lagoon lake lay life]
*tranquility 22-39-2 (n.) 1. a disposition free from stress or emotion 2. a state of peace and quiet [refreshing relaxation repose absence agitation anxiety atar quietude]
*tranquilize 25-AA-1 (v.) 1. make calm or still 2. cause to be calm or quiet as by administering a sedative to [tranquil rank reassure regulate restful rock administer allay analgesic anesthetize animal anodyne appease

array assure narcotic normalize quell quieten upon incline induce layout lenify lie lineup lull ease ebb effect emotional]
*transact 22-48-2 (v.) 1. conduct business [toward trade trans render account administer amount negotiate sale service settle supply carry certain commodity complete conclude conduct] "transact with foreign governments"
*transatlantic 10-97-21 (a.) 1. crossing the Atlantic Ocean [atlantic side situate long intercontinental come crossing /alt/] "transatlantic flight"
*transcend 08-40-27 (v.) 1. go beyond 2. go beyond [top trans trump range rare rear rise rival above achievement ahead apart ascendant national soar stand standout superior surpass surpassing cap chosen eclipse eminent excel exist expectation distinguish distinguished]
*transcendent 14-32-10 (a.) 1. beyond and outside the ordinary range of human experience or understanding 2. exceeding or surpassing usual limits especially in excellence [theoretical think towering transcend range rare reality redemptive reject religion rival above absolute achievement ahead awe nebulous notion salvation state sublime supernatural supreme surpassing cap category chosen claim concern consummate eclipse entire except exist experience explicit dark defeat dim distinguished divine domination] "philosophers...often explicitly reject the notion of any transcendent reality beyond thought...and claim to be concerned only with thought itself..."
*transcontinental 20-19-3 (a.) 1. spanning or crossing or on the farther side of a continent [traveler railway america north side spaning city concerning continent continental crossing europe limited] "transcontinental railway"
*transcribe 15-35-7 (v.) 1. rewrite in a different script;"The Sanskrit text had to be transliterated" 2. write out from speech, notes, etc. 3. convert the genetic information in (a strand of DNA) into a strand of RNA, esp. messenger RNA; in biochemistry 4. make a phonetic transcription of 5. rewrite or arrange a piece of music for an instrument or medium other than that originally intended [trace transpose type record render revise adapt alphabetize amanuensis arrange nature note score scribe scrivener secretary set show calligraphy capitalize character clerk clone copier copy initial inscribe interpret edit enface engross euphony]
*transcript 08-32-29 (n.) 1. a reproduction of a written record (e.g. of a legal or school record) [tenor text trace typewritten record recording rendering reproduction retrovirus rule academic account alphabet arrangement article authority autograph nonfiction notation school score screed script scroll show speech student style carry cell cod college consider convert copy court impose infection interpretation part piece play point preserve process production program]
*transfer 02-63-401 (n.) 1. someone who transfers or is transferred from one position to another 2. the act of transfering something from one form to another 3. the act of transporting something from one location to another 4. a ticket that allows a passenger to change conveyances 5. application of a skill learned in one situation to a different but similar situation 6. transferring ownership (v.) 1. cause to change ownership 2. change from one vehicle or transportation line to another 3. send from one person or place to another 4. move from one place to another 5. transfer somebody to a different position or location of work 6. lift and reset in another soil or situation 7. move around 8. shift the position or location of, as for business, legal, educational, or military purposes 9. transfer from one place or period to another [take title track trade trans travel reach receiver recipient remove report rule announcement assign authorize negotiate next notify sell send share shift soul student feed find forward exchange expel export] "transfer the packet from his trouser pockets to a pocket in his jacket"
*transferable 15-84-8 (a.) 1. capable of being moved or conveyed from one place to another 2. legally transferable to the ownership of another [transfer transpose ready remove alienable assign negotiable suitable exchangeable bond legal /bar bare/]
*transference 25-50-1 (n.) 1. (psychoanalysis) the process whereby emotions are passed on or displaced from one person to another; during psychoanalysis the displacement of feelings toward others (usually the parents) is onto the analyst 2. the act of transfering something from one form to another 3. transferring ownership [tape technique telling therapist title toward trade transfer transmittal treat reaction real record redirect right absolute acceptable affect alienate announcement assignment noise notify sale secularize settle share sigmund suppress form freud ecclesiastical emotion enfeoff essential exchange explore carry change confer consignment convey]
*transfigure 22-46-2 (v.) 1. elevate or idealize, in allusion to Christ's transfiguration 2. change completely the nature or appearance of [transubstantiate treatment turn raise reform resurrection reverse advance allusion alter ameliorate amend appearance nature nurture socialize spiritualize story favor figure forward foster idealize great upgrade uplift educate elevate enhance enrich /rug/]
*transfusion 14-45-10 (n.) 1. the introduction of blood or blood plasma into a vein or artery 2. the action of pouring a liquid from one vessel to another [transposition travel removal replacement amount artery say serum slow spreading suffuse fusion imbue import insertion interchange introduction oppose osmosis]
*transgress 16-68-6 (v.) 1. act in disregard of laws and rules 2. commit a sin; violate a law of God or a moral law 3. spread over land, esp. along a subsiding shoreline 4. pass beyond; of limits and boundaries [temptation

thief trans trespass racketeer respect rule run across afoul astray sea serious shoreline show sin sinner spread subside gangster god goof encroach enter err exceed]
*transience 22-54-2 (n.) 1. an impermanence that suggests the inevitability of ending or dying 2. the attribute of being brief or fleeting [trans attribute short suggest impermanent indefinitely inevitable end enduring ephemeral evanescent exist chiefly continuance]
*transient 12-45-12 (a.) 1. (philosophy) of a mental act; causing effects outside the mind 2. enduring a very short time (n.) 1. one who stays for only a short time 2. (physics) a short-lived oscillation in a system caused by a sudden change of voltage or current or load [temporary tenant tourist trans transitory traveler rambling range rational regular resilient adaptable adjust alter arise astronaut attribute natural nomadic settle shift short shortlived stay succinct sudden suggest supple surface immanent impermanent impulsive indefinitely inevitable instantaneous interaction enduring ethics evanescent evaporate exist explorer] "transient laborers"
*transition 04-38-119 (n.) 1. a change from one place or state or subject or stage to another 2. an event that results in a transformation 3. the act of passing from one state or place to the next 4. a passage that connects a topic to one that follows 5. a musical passage moving from one key to another [theatrical topic transit transposition travel reduction resolve revolution abrupt accommodation active adjustment alter alternate architecture assumption atomic naturalize next nucleus scene section sentiment shift short shot speech spreading stage status stirring style swell switch idea immediate impel import improvement inflexible interrupt opinion osmosis out overt overthrow /itis/]
*transitory 19-42-4 (a.) 1. enduring a very short time [temporary traipse transit transubstantiate rambling range resilient adaptable adjust nomadic shift shortlived stray supple impermanent impetuous impulsive infatuation insubstantial /roti/]
*translate 04-43-128 (v.) 1. bring to a certain spiritual state 2. change the position of (figures or bodies) in space without rotation, in mathematics 3. make sense of a language 4. change from one form or medium into another 5. restate (words) from one language into another language 6. be equivalent in effect 7. be translatable, or be translatable in a certain way 8. express, as in simple and less technical langauge 9. genetics: determine the amino-acid sequence of a protein during its synthesis by using information on the messenger RNA 10. physics: subject to movement in which every part of the body moves parallel to and the same distance as every other point on the body [transubstantiate turn turnover reiterate relay rendering repeat rephrase rewrite alter ascertain assign say send slate spread state survey switch experiment explain export] "I have to translate when my in-laws from Austria visit the U.S."
*translator 09-46-25 (n.) 1. a person who translates written messages from one language to another 2. someone who mediates between speakers of different languages 3. a program that translates one programming language into another [tin traditional trans receive retransmit allegory alphabet alter annotate antwerp aristotle negotiate noted scholar scholiast science sequence signal skill speak symbol language lexicography linguist link omar /rota/]
*translucent 12-39-13 (a.) 1. almost transparent; allowing light to pass through diffusely [radiant allow almost amber apparent appearance see serene sheerness shin side simple skin straightforward let light lucent lucid lucidity luminous lustrous unambiguous unequivocal unmistakable clarity clear clearly cloudy come connected consistent crisp curtain explicit express] "translucent amber"
*transmissible 25-61-1 (a.) 1. (of disease) capable of being transmitted by infection 2. inherited or inheritable by established rules (usually legal rules) of descent 3. tending to occur among members of a family usually by heredity [tend tradition trait trans rule russell ancestral authority non spread member monarchy impose infectious inherit bertrand law legal lore easily estate]
*transmission 06-44-55 (n.) 1. communication by means of transmitted signals 2. the act of sending a message; causing a message to be transmitted 3. an incident is which an infectious disease is transmitted 4. the gears that transmit power from an automobile engine via the driveshaft to the live axle 5. the fraction of radiant energy that passes through a substance [telling trade travel release report reverse account announcement assignment neutral notify sale share show spreading statement medium message mission movement moving impart import information instruction optics osmosis overdrive]
*transmit 06-41-60 (v.) 1. send from one person or place to another 2. broadcast over the airwaves, as in radio or television 3. transmit or serve as the medium for transmission, as of sounds or images 4. transfer to another [television tell trade trans transpose turn radio render report rerun response route abstract across address airwave alienate allow appropriate assign negotiate newscast sell send serve set signal song sound space spill spiritual sport spread stater switch mailable makeover mean mechanism medium message metal metathesis move image impart infection instill interchange]
*transmute 20-49-3 (v.) 1. change or alter in form, appearance, or nature 2. change in outward structure or looks 3. alter in nature; of chemical elements in alchemy [trans translate turn rebuild renew revive accordance alchemy alter appearance nature nuclear salesman science sculpture shape silver stalin structure substance subversive material matter mean metamorphose modify

monster mutant ugly undergo unmitigated effect element essence eucharist experience /tum/]
*transparent 07-62-44 (a.) 1. so thin as to transmit light 2. transmitting light; able to be seen through with clarity 3. free of deceit 4. easily understood or seen through (because of a lack of subtlety) [texture thin recognize reveal round allow apparent articulate artless naive section see seethrough sheer side silk simple sky snow straight straightforward subtlety surface parent pass patent peekaboo pellucid perceive physics plain plastic pool easy evident explanation explicit express]
*transpire 11-79-16 (v.) 1. pass through the tissue or substance or its pores or interstices, as of gas 2. come about, happen, or occur 3. come to light; become known 4. exude water vapor; of plants 5. give off (water) through the skin [tissue transude turnout reek release remain residue result appear arise nature secret seep skin spire spy stomata strain stream substance surface pass percolate physiology place plant pore progress important interstice emit essence evaporate excrete exude /rip/] "It transpired that she had worked as spy in East Germany"
*transplant 06-41-54 (n.) 1. (surgery) tissue or organ transplanted from a donor to a recipient; in some cases the patient can be both donor and recipient 2. an operation moving an organ from one person (the donor) to another (the recipient) 3. the act of uprooting and moving a plant to a new location (v.) 1. lift and reset in another soil or situation 2. transfer from one place or period to another 3. be transplantable 4. in surgery [tessellation transpose turnover relay relocate remove resettle allograft amputate assign section set shift penetration plant pot process] "he had a kidney transplant"
*transposition 25-44-1 (n.) 1. any abnormal position of the organs of the body 2. an event in which one thing is substituted for another 3. (algebra) the transfer of a quantity form one side of an equation to the other along with a change of sign 4. (electricity) a rearrangement of the relative positions of power lines in order to minimize the effects of mutual capacitance and inductance 5. (genetics) a kind of mutation in which a chromosomal segment is transfered to a new position on the same or another chromosome 6. (music) playing in a different key from the key intended; moving the pitch of a piece of music upwards or downwards 7. the act of reversing the order or place of [transubstantiation travel recast reincarnation relocate retaliate revulsion abnormality alternation avatar shuffle sport spreading substitution supinate swap switch perfusion permutation position pronate osmosis import interplay inversion /itis/]
*transverse 22-27-2 (a.) 1. extending or lying across; in a crosswise direction; at right angles to the long axis [thwart trans transversal traverse rhomboid right across angle ascend athwart axis sideways slant slash slop stairway steel vibration virgule extend]
*travail 12-52-14 (n.) 1. concluding state of pregnancy; from the onset of labor to the birth of a child 2. use of physical or mental energy; hard work (v.) 1. work hard [task thining throw tighten toil toward trouble resistance rhythmic rub abnormal accouchement achieve angle application avail various violent inconvenient industry injury intense involve labour lamb least literary litter long lyingin]
*travesty 14-62-9 (n.) 1. a comedy characterized by broad satire and improbable situations 2. a composition that imitates somebody's style in a humorous way (v.) 1. make a parody of [takeoff tout trave twist replica reproduction ridicule aggrandize amplify ape art artistic version effect end enhance exaggerate expansion extreme salt satire scratch sendup serious sham situation slant spoof style]
*treacherous 10-55-19 (a.) 1. dangerously unstable and unpredictable 2. tending to betray; especially having a treacherous character as attributed to the Carthaginians by the Romans [temporary tend tentative traitorous trestle tricky true trust reach ready recreant risky road rocky roman ambidextrous artful attribute calculate carthage character confidence crooked cunning hairy harm hazardous hide hurt obligation uncertain underhand unfaithful unpredictable unreliable unsafe unsound unstable unsure sea shaky sharp shifty slippery] "treacherous winding roads"
*treachery 15-63-7 (n.) 1. betrayal of a trust 2. an act of deliberate betrayal [ticklish treason trust reach entrap ambidexterity artifice cheat cross cunning hazard honesty]
*treasonable 25-48-1 (a.) 1. constituting treason [traitorous turbulent turncoat reasonable rebellious renegade revolutionary allegiance apostate sabotage seditious subversive betray breakaway leader loyal /ban/]
*treatise 15-41-7 (n.) 1. a formal exposition [thesis tract treat require research effect essay exposition express extensive academic account advance alphabet article interest style]
*treble 08-92-31 (a.) 1. having or denoting a high range 2. having more than one decidedly dissimilar aspects or qualities 3. having three units or components or elements 4. three times as great or many (n.) 1. the pitch range of the highest female voice (v.) 1. sing treble 2. increase threefold [tenor ternary thin threefold thrice tone triplex tune twofold radio range record red refrain reproduce response role row electronicall element entity episode baritone bead beat boy bravura burden lie line low lyric]
*tremendous 04-42-120 (a.) 1. extraordinarily good; used especially as intensifiers 2. extraordinarily large in size or extent or amount or power or degree [terrific thunder titanic towering trip rare rattling redoubtable remarkable emend enormous epic exceptional experience exquisite extensive extent extremely

magnitude marvelous massive mighty monstrous noise degree dependent disconcert dismay divine dreadful ordinary outsize overgrown usual sensational shock size startling sterling successful superb sweep]
*tremor 13-49-11 (n.) 1. a small earthquake 2. an involuntary vibration (as if from illness or fear) 3. shaking or trembling (usually resulting from weakness or stress or disease) (v.) 1. shake with seismic vibrations, as of planets [temblor thrill throb tingle rem restless rictus earthquake excite main major medicine microseism minor mistake move muscular old]
*tremulous 20-53-3 (a.) 1. (of the voice) quivering as from weakness or fear [thick timid timorous twangy emulous mispronounce mousy muzzy unsteady unsure lady lisp old scary shaky show shrink shy]
*trenchant 16-61-6 (a.) 1. having keenness and forcefulness and penetration in thought, expression, or intellect 2. clearly or sharply defined to the mind 3. characterized by or full of force and vigor [tamper tart telling reason relevant rigorous robust rough edge effective effectual efficacious enchant energetic enthusiastic evidence expose expression nervous capacity caustic clearly conquest crisp criticism cut hard harsh hearty high acerbic achievement active acute aggressive argument]
*trepidation 13-61-11 (n.) 1. a feeling of alarm or dread [terror tremble trepid turbulence turmoil restless rout row ebullition excitement expectation palpitation pant perturbation inquietude involuntary dismay disorder disquiet dread agitation alarm anticipation anxiety apprehensive nervous /dip pert tad/]
*trestle 22-53-2 (n.) 1. a supporting tower used to support a bridge 2. sawhorses used in pairs to support a horizontal tabletop [tabletop timber tower track tube turnout railway reinforce rest river roadway embankment sawbuck sawhorse serve short side sidetrack slop span splay stand steel structure subway support leg line]
*triad 19-37-4 (n.) 1. the cardinal number that is the sum of one and one and one 2. a 3-note major or minor chord; a note and its third and fifth tones 3. three people considered as a unit 4. a set of three similar things considered as a unit [tercet ternion terzetto theme third threesome tierce tone tonic trey tri triangle trigon trilogy trinity trio triplet triumvirate troika responsible administration ancient arpeggio arrange atom authority degree deuce divinity dramatic /airt/]
*tribune 09-26-23 (n.) 1. the apse of a Christian church that contains the bishop's throne [terrace throne tribunal recess representative republic right rostrum institution balcony bishop building bun east elect emplacement /nub/]
*trickery 15-75-8 (n.) 1. verbal misrepresentation intended to take advantage of you in some way 2. the use of tricks to deceive someone (usually to extract money from them) [tactic trap trick tricky racket roguish ruse imposture intend intrigue cheat chicanery conspiracy coup knavery evasive expedient extract]
*trickle 08-46-31 (n.) 1. flowing in drops; the formation and falling of drops of liquid (v.) 1. run or flow slowly, or in an unsteady stream [thin trill rivulet roof run runnel ickle introduce condense continuous course crowd leach liquid empty exude /elk/]
*tricolor 20-59-3 (a.) 1. having or involving three colors (n.) 1. a flag having three colored stripes (especially the French flag) [tan three tissue rectangular red republic certain cloth coat color colored combination country crazy oriflamme large /loci/]
*tricycle 19-64-4 (n.) 1. a cycle with three wheels [ten three transport trike race rickshaw ride child container cycle young exercise]
*trident 15-63-8 (n.) 1. a spear with three prongs [teeth three trilogy trio triptych ramification rident rod instrument deltoid equivalent /dirt/]
*triennial 25-58-1 (a.) 1. occurring every third year or lasting 3 years (n.) 1. the 300th anniversary [tercentenary tertian thallophyte third three tri twelvemonth remembrance ephemeral evergreen exotic amphibian angiosperm anniversary lasting /inn lain/]
*trifling 20-66-3 (a.) 1. not worth considering (n.) 1. the deliberate act of wasting time instead of working [time tiny trivial rifle idle importance inactivity inconsequential inefficient insignificant instead fling frivolous lack later literary little live look negligible /fir/]
*trinity 06-64-53 (n.) 1. the cardinal number that is the sum of one and one and one 2. the union of the Father and Son and Holy Ghost in one Godhead 3. three people considered as a unit [tercet ternion terzetto threesome tierce trey triad triangle trilogy trio triplet troika refer responsible nature nit]
*trio 05-57-87 (n.) 1. a musical composition for three performers 2. the cardinal number that is the sum of one and one and one 3. three performers or singers who perform together 4. three people considered as a unit 5. a set of three similar things considered as a unit [teamwork tercet ternion terzetto theme threesome tierce trey tri triangle trigon trilogy trinity triplet troika reciprocity responsible instrument invention octet opus orchestrate organization origin]
*triple 04-40-132 (a.) 1. having three units or components or elements 2. three times as great or many (n.) 1. a base hit at which the batter stops safely at third base 2. a quantity that is three times as great as another (v.) 1. hit a three-base hit, in baseball 2. increase threefold [team ternary third threefold treble trinity trio trip try turn ramify reach red redouble reinforce row run runner income increase integer intensify part past player poetry product line element enhance entity exacerbate exaggerate]
*triplicate 25-56-1 (n.) 1. one of three copies; any of three things that correspond to one another exactly (v.)

1. reproduce threefold [threefold trace transcribe treble repetition replication reproduce reproduction identical increase part pastclone copy correspond counterpart augment equivalent exactly exist]
*tripod 19-44-4 (n.) 1. a three-legged rack used for support [table theodolite threelegged trip rack reflex piece pinhole pot printer projector display]
*trite 16-54-6 (a.) 1. repeated too often; overfamiliar through overuse [threadbare timeworn tired trivial recurring regular remark repeat rite routine idle inane interest empty exhaust]
*trivial 08-57-27 (a.) 1. (informal terms) small and of little importance 2. obvious and dull 3. not large enough to consider or notice 4. of little substance or significance 5. concerned with trivialities [thin tiny trashy trifling trivia regulation idle imitate important inadequate inconsiderable infraction insufficient interest vacuous vain value vapid variable airy asinine attention attitude lack law light lilliputian little low]
*troublesome 09-51-25 (a.) 1. difficult to deal with [taxing tease tough trouble try recurrent repressive require restrictive rigorous rowdy onerous opposite oppressive ugly uncooperative undisciplined unmanageable unruly uphill upset badly behave beset bothersome bug burdensome laborious easy effort endure exasperate sinister situation strangle stressful mean mental miserable] "a troublesome infection"
*truce 10-42-20 (n.) 1. a state of peace agreed to between opponents so they can discuss peace terms [treaty recess reconciliation respite rest caesura call ceasefire cessation compact /curt/]
*truculent 19-65-4 (a.) 1. defiantly aggressive 2. aggressively hostile [terrorize think refuse roughness rude ruthless uncivilized unfriendly unpleasant cavalier combative confrontation contentious cow cruelty cuss cussed lent lick enemy energetic enmity enthusiasm nasty /curt/] "as truculent as a small boy who thinks his big brother can lick anybody"
*trudge 11-60-17 (n.) 1. a long difficult walk (v.) 1. to walk or proceed draggingly, slowly 2. walk heavily and firmly, as when weary, or through mud [tentative toward trail tramp travel tread trek trip turn rack ramble relaxed reluctant roll rooftop unhurried deliberate difficult distance dogtrot drag gentle gin gradual exercise exhaust]
*truism 16-56-6 (n.) 1. an obvious truth [tag theorem trite true remark repeat rule ism say shibboleth statement maxim meaningless moral]
*truthful 12-49-14 (a.) 1. conforming to truth 2. expressing or given to expressing the truth [tell tend testimony true trustworthy reality reliable right russell ruthful undoubted unquestionable unvarnished historical honest factual faithful frank literal]
*turbulence 10-59-18 (n.) 1. unstable flow of a liquid or gas 2. instability in the atmosphere 3. a state of violent disturbance and disorder (as in politics or social conditions generally) [tide tooth trough tumult turmoil uncontrolled uneven unpredictable unrest unstable unsuitable updraft upheaval uproar upset random region revolution rip riptide river roughness row bad bluster boiling brawl lather len liquid eddy effervesce energy excitement extreme natural nervous ceiling cha chaos cloudless coaster commotion condition confusion current /brut/] "the industrial revolution was a period of great turbulence"
*turgid 19-73-4 (a.) 1. ostentatiously lofty in style 2. abnormally distended especially by fluids or gas [talk tissue tumescent tumid tumor unhealthy unwieldy rhetorical gas gassy gid give goggle good grandiloquence gross inflated inkhorn declamatory dilate distended dropsy dull /dig/]
*turmoil 05-43-69 (n.) 1. violent agitation 2. a disorderly outburst or tumult 3. disturbance usually in protest [todo trouble tumble tumult turbulence uneasy unrest untroubled upheaval uproar upset revolution riot row malaise mayhem melee mess moil motion ochlocracy outburst inquietude instability lather leader litter]
*turpitude 25-48-1 (n.) 1. a corrupt or depraved or degenerate act or practice [transgression roguish rotten pit practice principle profligate immoral improbity decadency degenerate degradation demoralize depravity duty extreme /tip/] "the various turpitudes of modern society"
*turquoise 11-57-16 (n.) 1. a blue to gray green mineral consisting of copper aluminum phosphate; blue turquoise is valued as a gemstone 2. a shade of blue tinged with green [tinge ultramarine rock royal opaque ice igneous indigo inorganic sapphire sax semiprecious shade sky slate solid steel stone substance electric]
*tutelage 16-53-6 (n.) 1. teaching pupils individually (usually by a tutor hired privately) 2. attention and management implying responsibility for safety [teach tela tuition tutor education encouragement enlightenment exercise expert legal administration advocacy attention auspice government great guardian guidance /gal gale/]
*twinge 16-62-6 (n.) 1. sudden sharp painful emotion 2. a sharp stab of pain (v.) 1. cause a stinging pain 2. squeeze tightly between the fingers 3. feel a sudden sharp, local pain [thrill tight tweak tweet twitch wince wrench writhe inge needle nip gnawing grimace grip gripe guilty emotional experience]
*typical 02-48-373 (a.) 1. of a feature that helps to distinguish a person or thing 2. exhibiting the qualities or characteristics that identify a group or kind or category 3. conforming to a type [taxonomy teenage true typal year painting particular peculiar perfect poem political predictable ical ideal identify individual interest ita cab car case category characteristic classic community conform constitute conventional curtis customary abnormal absolute accordance annoy

archetype arteritis average large level life] "a typical American girl"
*typify 12-57-14 (v.) 1. embody the essential characteristics of or be a typical example of 2. express indirectly by an image, form, or model; be a symbol [token personify pictorial portray prefigure illustrate illustrative image imitative incarnate indicate indirect instance intend ita figure finger foretoken form fugue]
*typographical 23-27-2 (a.) 1. relating to or occurring or used in typography [trade page prepare print appearance art character craft]
*typography 20-44-3 (n.) 1. art and technique of printing with movable type 2. the craft of composing type and printing from it [technique trade typeset page paper practice prepare printing printmaker process publication publishing occupation onset graphy gravure reproduction rotogravure appearance apply art]
*tyrannical 15-59-7 (a.) 1. of or relating to or associated with or resembling a dictatorship 2. characteristic of an absolute ruler or absolute rule; having absolute sovereignty 3. marked by unjust severity or arbitrary behavior [tend totalitarian tyrannic tyranny regime repressive right roughshod ruler ruling absolutism accord agreement arbitrary arrogant autarchy authoritarian authoritative autocratic ideal imperious insist irrational complete cruel last law liberty lordly /inn nary/] "tyrannical suppression of liberty"
*tyranny 10-56-21 (n.) 1. a form of government in which the ruler is an absolute dictator (not restricted by a constitution or laws or opposition etc.) 2. dominance through threat of punishment and violence [terrorism thrall threat totalitarian triumvirate regency repressive republic restricted ruler ann arbitrary ascendancy autarchy authority autocracy autonomy neocolonialism /nary/]
*tyro 19-89-4 (n.) 1. someone new to a field or activity [tenderfoot tiro trade training youth recruit rookie rudiment outdoor]

U

*ubiquitous 07-49-39 (a.) 1. being present everywhere at once [unity universal universality unlimited utter bear bizarre boundless immortal inclusive infinite intact intensive quit thematic thorough timeless totality omnipresent omniscient once one outright seeming shape spatial specify straight supreme]
*ulterior 20-46-3 (a.) 1. lying beneath what is revealed or avowed, especially being deliberately concealed 2. coming at a subsequent time or stage 3. beyond or outside an area of immediate interest; remote [unearthly unknown unspoken untold later lying thither engage enigmatic enter exist exotic expect external relationship relevant remote restricted reveal russell immediate interest intrusive obscure openly other outside overt]
*ultimate 03-57-145 (a.) 1. being the last or concluding element of a series 2. furthest or highest in degree or order; utmost or extreme 3. being the ultimate or elemental constituents of anything [ultima underlie uppermost utmost lastditch latest latter life limiting london tail terminate top truth imminent impose indirect ingredient insult intermediate introduce mandatory matter maximum mold must absolute achievement aim apotheosis approach attain eat effect elegant elemental end entertain essential eventual exist extreme /amit/] "the ultimate achievement"
*ultimatum 12-57-14 (n.) 1. a final peremptory demand [ultima urgent last lesson levy tax term threat impost indent inflict meet monition moral accompany admonition alarm /amit mut/]
*umbrage 20-58-3 (n.) 1. a feeling of anger caused by being offended [umbra mad madden miff rage real resentment adumbrate affront aggravation anger annoyance arise give glare gloom glower grievance emotion enrage exasperate exception /garb/]
*unaccountable 19-66-4 (a.) 1. not to be accounted for or explained 2. free from control or responsibility [unbelievable uncertain unexplainable unfathomable unusual account accountable alternate ambiguous answerable antic care casual cause charter consequence control odd baffle bizarre lack lawless licentious excuse exempt extraordinary /can/] "perceptible only as unaccountable influences that hinder progress"
*unaffected 11-61-17 (a.) 1. (followed by 'to' or 'by') unaware of or indifferent to 2. undergoing no change when acted upon 3. free of artificiality; sincere and genuine 4. not touched emotionally [unassuming unaware unchanged unco undergo unforced unimpressed union unman unmoved unofficial unpretentious unselfconscio native natural neat act aesthetic affected apparently artificial artistic artless authentic finished firm frank free easygoing elegant emotional excellent choice classic clear tasteful terse touched treatment trim deficient design different direct dry dull /fan/] "entirely unaffected by each other's writings"
*unanimity 15-40-7 (n.) 1. everyone being of one mind [unity accord agreement mind mity /mina/]
*unanimous 05-33-78 (a.) 1. in complete agreement 2. acting together as a single undiversified whole [understanding uniform unison unite unity unopposed nobody acclamation accordance accordant affirmative agreement ani answerable inharmony instep member merger mind share single solid symbiosis synchronous /mina/] "a unanimous decision"
*unavoidable 10-54-18 (a.) 1. impossible to avoid or evade:"inescapable conclusion" [unable uncontrollable unstoppable unyielding necessary accident avoid voidable obligatory obvious impossible incapable ineluctable inescapable inevitable inexorable definite destiny determined evade evitable /bad ova van/]
*unbearable 09-64-22 (a.) 1. impossible to bear [undeniable unendurable unequivocal unpleasant utter bearable egregious endure excruciating absolute agony arrant awful rank regular /bar/] "unbearable pain"
*unbecoming 23-38-2 (a.) 1. considered inappropriate for or unattractive on a particular person 2. not in keeping with accepted standards of what is right or proper in polite society [unattractive uncomely undue unfit unflattering unqualified unseemly unsuitable untoward unwearable becoming behavior bury cheap

chintzy clumsy conform consider curb offensive opprobrium outrageous malapropos malodorous misplace improper inappropriate incorrect indelicate inept irrelevant gauche gutter] "an unbecoming style"
*unbiased 19-51-4 (a.) 1. characterized by a lack of partiality 2. without bias [uncolored uninterested unprejudiced unselfish neutral non balance biased impartial impersonal indifferent account affiliate aloof selfless show statistics equal equitable evenhand evenhanded expect detached disinterested dispassionate]
*unbridled 15-48-8 (a.) 1. not restrained or controlled [unbridle unchecked uncontrolled ungoverned uninhibited bridle rage rampant restraint intemperate express] "unbridled rage"
*uncommon 08-38-31 (a.) 1. not common or ordinarily encountered; unusually great in amount or remarkable in character or kind 2. marked by an uncommon quality; especially superlative or extreme of its kind [unexpected unique unusual unwonted usual notable noticeable novel character common conspicuous occasional ordinary original outstanding owe mark marked marvelous money month mother] "uncommon birds"
*unconscionable 16-20-6 (a.) 1. lacking a conscience 2. greatly exceeding bounds of reason or moderation [unacceptable unbearable unequivocal unprincipled unreasonable unthinkable usury complete criminal cutting outrageous outright overweening scion severe sharp shock spend steep illogical immoral inconceivable indirect inflationary intense irrational abandon absolute acute amount appalling barbarous beyond bound boundless lack liar limit enormous entertain evil exceed exorbitant extortionate extreme /ban/]
*unconscious 07-53-38 (a.) 1. (followed by 'of') not knowing or perceiving 2. without conscious volition 3. not conscious; lacking awareness and the capacity for sensory perception as if asleep or dead (n.) 1. that part of the mind wherein psychic activity takes place of which the person is unaware [unable unaware underlie unintentional unplanned unsuspecting nap natural nod non nous calamity capacity casual catalepsy cold comatose compulsive conscious control oblivious out self sensory sleep sleeping snap stun surround idea ignorant incapable inherent injury innate innocent insentient instinct instinctive intuitive involuntary] "lay unconscious on the floor"
*uncouth 23-69-2 (a.) 1. lacking refinement or cultivation or taste [uncivil ungainly ungraceful unrefined unseemly untutored unwieldy newly clumsy coarse couth crude cultivation curious odd oddball outlandish taste tasteless troglodyte harsh hayseed hulky human]
*unctuous 20-49-3 (a.) 1. unpleasantly and excessively suave or ingratiating in manner or speech [unpleasant cajole charm complimentary convince courtly creepy tallowy texture obsequious oil oleaginous organic self sincerity sleek slick slimy slippery smarmy smooth smug soft speech suave sycophant /out/]
*underbid 23-55-2 (v.) 1. bid (a hand of cards) at less than the strength of the hand warrants 2. bid lower than a competing bidder 3. bid too low [under demand bid /bred/]
*undergarment 23-41-2 (n.) 1. a garment worn under other garments [underwear undies union upper next drawer elastic garment give article man teddy thigh tightfitting torso /rag/]
*underhanded 25-13-1 (a.) 1. marked by deception 2. (sports) with hand brought forward and up from below shoulder level [underhand unethical unobtrusive unprincipled unscrupulous dark deal deception dishonest diversion double doubtful dubious duplicity evasive exertion require rotten hand amoral artful]
*underlie 04-61-114 (v.) 1. be or form the base for 2. lie underneath [under universe uphold upkeep nature nearby necessary needful decision describe desire directly dormant down elementary elevate esoteric essential explicit express radical raise range ready reason recent reinforce right rock rudimentary latent law level lie lift locate lower lurk immediately imply important indispensable inspire]
*underling 19-48-4 (n.) 1. someone subject to the authority or control of another [under dependent dog effort employee retainer role lackey liegeman lightweight little low importance inferior]
*undermine 03-59-160 (v.) 1. destroy property or hinder normal operations 2. hollow out as if making a cave or opening [undercut unnerve upset nonplus normal damage defeat demolition demoralize denial dent deny destroy dig diminish discredit disobey earth emasculate enfeeble ermine erode eviscerate excavate exhaust explosive railroad rattle rebut refuse refute remove river ruin run malicious material memo mine mitigate impair interior]
*underrate 12-69-12 (v.) 1. make too low an estimate of [under undervalue danger decry degree devalue disparage estimate raft really renovate river assessment trip]
*undersell 25-52-1 (v.) 1. sell cheaper than one's competition [under undercut unload usual deliver denigrate dump enthusiasm equivalent exchange restrained retail sacrifice sell little]
*undersized 23-35-2 (a.) 1. smaller than normal for its kind [undersize usual normal dumpy dwarfish elfin extent rawboned rudimentary runty short size slight small stunted incipient]
*understate 07-54-38 (v.) 1. represent as less significant or important [unassuming unobtrusive unpretentious deliberate describe devalue discreet distort downplay dramatic embellish embroider emotional emphatic exaggerate excellent exhibit express really represent restraint sake seem show significant slant small state strain subdued subtle tasteful titivate travesty trivialize

true twist achieve actual aesthetic affair amount amplify artistic]
*undervalue 09-69-23 (v.) 1. assign too low a value to 2. lose in value 3. esteem lightly [under decrease decry determine devalue diminish disparage dollar esteem extent range really respect value apply assign lessen lightly little lose lower]
*underworld 10-63-18 (n.) 1. (in various religions) the world of the dead 2. the criminal class [under unlawful netherworld dead depth destiny die drink economic exist extortion region religious river want world writing obtain organize lethe limbo live]
*underwrite 07-38-43 (v.) 1. protect by insurance 2. guarantee financial support of [under unsold uphold nestle notarize damage defend designate document electronics endorse ensure exaggerate ratify register warrant wont write indemnify indorse inferiority initial insure issue tour troth]
*undue 11-48-15 (a.) 1. not appropriate or proper (or even legal) in the circumstances 2. not yet payable 3. beyond normal limits 4. lacking justification or authorization [uncalled uneven unjustified unlawful unnecessary unreasonable unsuitable unwarranted normal delinquent demand disgraceful disperse dizzy dress due elegance enormous evil excessive excite expect extreme] "an undue loan"
*undulate 13-47-11 (a.) 1. having a sinuate margin and rippled surface (v.) 1. stir up (water) so as to form ripples 2. occur in soft rounded shapes 3. increase and decrease in volume or pitch, as if in waves 4. move in a wavy pattern, as of curtains [undergo nature non dash decrease different dip down late leaf lift loop lose alternate appearance teeth toss turn edge equally essence]
*unearth 08-62-31 (v.) 1. bring to light 2. lay bare through digging [uncover unravel unveil uproot earth evolve examine excavate exhibit exhume expose extract ascertain remove reveal takeout tumble turn turnup happen hear hide] "The CIA unearthed a plot to kill the President"
*unencumbered 19-45-4 (a.) 1. free of encumbrance 2. not burdened with cares or responsibilities [unambiguous unblemished unclouded understandable unmistakable unobstructed empty encumber encumbrance evident certain clear cloudless comprehensible bright resounding rich ringing distinct /dere/] "inherited an unencumbered estate"
*unfavorable 14-AA-10 (a.) 1. not encouraging or approving or pleasing 2. not favorable 3. (of winds or weather) tending to hinder or oppose [uncomplimenta undesirable unfortunately unhappy unlikely unluckily unpropitious untoward useless negative noncooperation facilitate fateful favorable flaw foreboding fractious admonitory adverse afield alien astray attention awry obstinate ominous opposition recalcitrant refusal reproving review rigorous rival bad black boding late lower encourage enemy error evil express /bar baro ova/] "unfavorable conditions"
*ungainly 16-51-6 (a.) 1. lacking grace in movement or posture 2. difficult to handle or manage especially because of shape [uncoordinated uncouth ungraceful unhandy unmanageable unwieldy gainly gangly gauche gawky giraffe girl graceless appearance awkward inconvenient inelegant instrument lack lad leg limb load long loutish lubberly lumber] "a gawky lad with long ungainly legs"
*unguent 25-87-1 (n.) 1. semisolid preparation (usually containing a medicine) applied externally as a remedy or for soothing an irritation [unction unctuous nard non grease greasy embrocation emollient ester external extract tallowy technique therapy treat]
*unify 06-30-45 (v.) 1. to bring or combine together or with something else 2. become one 3. act in concert or unite in a common purpose or belief 4. join or combine [unite unity untie utility nation non identify immingle impartible include incorporated infusible intermix intimate introduce fall federate flux formal fuse yoke /fin/]
*unique 03-62-184 (a.) 1. (followed by 'to') applying exclusively to a given category or condition or locality 2. radically distinctive and without equal 3. the single one of its kind 4. highly unusual or rare but not the single instance [unco unexpected uniform unparalleled unsuitable unusual usual new non note novel imaginative impossible incomparable incredible inimitable instance integral irreplaceable quintessence either else entity equal exceptional exclusive exist experience extraordinary]
*unison 11-58-16 (n.) 1. corresponding exactly 2. (music) two or more sounds or tones at the same pitch or in octaves 3. occurring together or simultaneously [unanimous understanding uniformity union unity note identity incorporate inharmony intersection iso share simultaneous simultaneousl sound speak structure symphony octave oneness opinion oratorio overlap] "marching in unison"
*unitarian 16-11-7 (a.) 1. (religion) of or relating to or characterizing Unitarianism (n.) 1. adherent of Unitarianism [non adherent aria reject religious]
*unlawful 08-62-30 (a.) 1. not conforming to legality, moral law, or social convention 2. contrary to or forbidden by law 3. contrary to or prohibited by or defiant of law 4. not morally right or permissible 5. having no legally established claim [unau unconventional unethical unjust unofficial unseemly unsuitable nefarious non numerous law lawful lawless legal legitimate licit love aberrant abnormality accept accordance age allow amend anarchy appeal atrocious weapon wicked wide woman wrong fail fair felonious flaw forbidden]
*unlimited 07-47-40 (a.) 1. having no limits in range or scope 2. that cannot be entirely consumed or used up 3.

without reservation or exception [ubiquitous unconstrained universal unrestricted untrammelled utter numberless numinous lack limited limitless loving luminous immense immortal implicit indefinite infinite magnitude majestic making myriad termless theory timeless total totalitarian entirely exception express extent extreme decisive definitive despotism downright] "to start with a theory of unlimited freedom is to end up with unlimited despotism"
*unnatural 11-58-15 (a.) 1. not in accordance with or determined by nature; contrary to nature 2. speaking or behaving in an artificial way to make an impression 3. distorted and unnatural in shape or size; abnormal and hideous [ugly uncanny uncommon unconventional unexpected unusual natural nature nutty aberrant acceptable accord act affected agonistic anomalous artificial assume assumption atmosphere atypical tense theatrical tin twist restrained revolting labored law long /ruta/] "an unnatural death"
*unnecessary 05-54-88 (a.) 1. not necessary [uncalledfor unessential unjustified unwarranted necessary needless nonessential essential excessive expendable expletive extra spare supernumerary surplus absolutely avoid redundant require reserve /ass rasse/]
*unprecedented 05-67-80 (a.) 1. having no precedent; novel [unexampled unique unmatched unparalleled unspeakable noteworthy novel parallel phenomenal population precedented primary prototype rare record remarkable early enigmatic equivalent exceptional expansion extraordinary] "an unprecedented expansion in population and industry"
*unscathed 11-66-16 (a.) 1. wholly unharmed [unharmed unhurt uninjured unmarked untouched safe scathe secure harm harmless hurt damage]
*unsettle 06-57-60 (v.) 1. disturb the composure of [uncertain uncomfortable uneasy uneven unfounded unhinge unnerve upset nerve settle shake shakeup shock sick stimulate stirring strange striking ease eccentric embarrassed embroil enervate entangle establish exciting exhilarate exile tantalizing telling tense touched trouble turn loco look lose lunatic lurch]
*unsophisticated 17-48-5 (a.) 1. not wise in the ways of the world 2. awkwardly simple and provincial 3. lacking experience of life 4. lacking sophistication 5. lacking complexity [undress unguarded uniformity unity unrefined unreserved unwary unworldly naivety naked natural neat nudity sheer simplicity soft sophisticated stark straightforward oneness open outspoken persuadable plain primitive purity homogeneity inexperienced ingenuous innocent integrity trusting callow candor clarify clear crude absolute artless authentic easy exploit deceive delude direct /tacit/] "either too unsophisticated or too honest to promise more than he could deliver"
*unspeakable 14-57-10 (a.) 1. exceptionally bad or displeasing 2. defying expression or description 3. too sacred to be uttered [undesirable unnameable unprecedented untouchable unutterable unworthy utter naughty nefarious negative noteworthy sacred shameful shock speak spiritual splendor sweep painful performance phenomenal portentous prodigious profane purpose ecstasy evil exceptional expression extremely abominable allow anguish appalling atrocious awesome awful knave bad base beauty black legendary loathsome low]
*untimely 16-66-7 (a.) 1. badly timed 2. uncommonly early or before the expected time (ad.) 1. too soon; in a premature manner [uncommonly unfortunate unhappy unlucky unseasonable usual near tardy think timely ill illtimed improper inappropriate inconvenient inept inopportune intervention intrusion irrelevant malapropos manner middle misplace moment moratory early expect late latish lead /emit/]
*untoward 17-66-5 (a.) 1. not in keeping with accepted standards of what is right or proper in polite society 2. contrary to your interests or welfare [unbecoming uncomely unexpected unfavourable unfit unfortunate unhappy unpleasant unseemly unusual tactless threatening toward troublesome trying ominous opposite welfare wicked wild wrong accept adverse annoy apocalyptic approve awkward ribaldry right rigorous rough rude dark difficult dire disadvantage /draw/]
*unutterable 25-77-1 (a.) 1. too sacred to be uttered 2. defying expression or description 3. very difficult to pronounce correctly [unable unbelievable uncommunicative unimaginable unnameable unspeakable unspoken utter numinous nutter talk ecstasy emotional enigmatic esoteric expression reaction religious restricted anguish arcane awesome awful beauty latent /bar bare tun/]
*unwieldy 12-45-12 (a.) 1. difficult to use or handle or manage because of size or weight or shape 2. lacking grace in movement or posture [uncouth ungainly unmanageable weight wieldy impractical incorrect incumbent easy elephantine encumber extensive labored lack lad leaden leg long lumber difficult discommode drop] "we set about towing the unwieldy structure into the shelter"
*unwise 10-62-20 (a.) 1. showing or resulting from lack of judgment or wisdom 2. not appropriate to the purpose [unfortunate unhappy unsuitable naive wisdom wise witless wrong ignorant ill impoverish imprudent inept inexpedient injudicious investor irrational irresponsible senseless show soon stupid] "an unwise investor is soon impoverished"
*upbraid 23-48-2 (v.) 1. utter a reproach to [utter president behavior berate braid bring rate rebuke reproach revile accuse admonish impeach incriminate irresponsible]
*upheaval 08-44-33 (n.) 1. a state of violent disturbance and disorder (as in politics or social conditions generally) 2. disturbance usually in protest 3. (geology)

a rise of land to a higher elevation (as in the process of mountain building) [unrest uplift upset upthrust upward paroxysm part period politics process prostrate protest public heave height high history hoo hullabaloo hurly hurricane earth elevation escalate excitement explosion extreme abrupt accommodation adjustment agitation ascent assumption val variety violent land lift live /lava/]
*uppermost 18-57-5 (a.) 1. at or nearest to the top (ad.) 1. in or into the most prominent position, as in the mind 2. in or into the highest position [ultimate upmost upper utmost pile position premier primary prime principal prominent ranking main master mind most overrule side situate step superlative supreme top topmost toward turn] "the uppermost book in the pile"
*uproarious 20-52-3 (a.) 1. uncontrollably noisy 2. marked by or causing boisterous merriment or convulsive laughter [uncontrollabl uproar rackety rage raucous riotous riproaring rowdy obstreperous orgastic anarchic angry infuriate insensate scream sonorous sound story]
*uproot 12-49-14 (v.) 1. move (people) forcibly from their homeland into a new and foreign environment 2. destroy completely, as if down to the roots 3. pull up by or as if by the roots [undo unearth unravel unseat until people place political pull purge relocate remove replace rip root ruin overturn takeout transplant] "The war uprooted many people"
*upturn 09-69-24 (n.) 1. an upward movement or trend as in business activity [upheaval upset upside upsurge upward passive peak proliferate prosperity trend tumescent tumult turn raise recovery revival rise]
*urban 03-36-219 (a.) 1. located in or characteristic of a city or city life 2. relating to or concerned with a city or densely populated area [ban belonging borough build affair area] "urban sociology"
*urbane 13-51-11 (a.) 1. showing a high degree of refinement and the assurance that comes from wide social experience 2. marked by wide-ranging knowledge and appreciation of many parts of the world arising from urban life and wide travel 3. characterized by tact and propriety [ungracious urban refinement respectful right room balance bane becoming bland amiable appealing appreciation appropriate arise assurance attentive attitude naive ease elegant experience]
*urbanity 23-39-2 (n.) 1. polished courtesy; elegance of manner [urban refinement]
*urchin 16-51-6 (n.) 1. poor and often mischievous city child [unkempt ragamuffin ragpicker rascal rounder child chin city clothe cub hobbledehoy hobo hooligan idler imp nestle nipper]
*urgency 06-49-50 (n.) 1. pressing importance requiring speedy action 2. the state of being urgent; an earnest and insistent necessity 3. insistent solicitation and entreaty 4. an urgent situation calling for prompt action [unimportant unusual urge require resolve rush great earnest edge emergency entreaty essential exigency extremity nagging necessity need note notice calling clutch complex condition crisis critical crucial crunch] "the urgency of his need"
*usage 09-54-22 (n.) 1. accepted or habitual practice 2. the act of using [unite usance use useful utilize utterance sage sentence society specific speech steward survive abandon abuse accept acquire age americanism application area articulation automatism generally germany grammar guide employment england etiquette excessive exercise expression extent /gas/]
*usurp 12-55-14 (v.) 1. seize and take control without authority and possibly with force; take as one's right or possession 2. take possession of without permission or take with force, as after a conquest or invasion 3. take the place of [upon seize seizure stickler stock subjugation succession supervene supplant supreme sur raid requisition right rule party permission pharaoh place position possibly power preemption preoccupy prepossession pretender property]
*usury 23-43-2 (n.) 1. an exorbitant or unlawful rate of interest 2. the act of lending money at an exorbitant rate of interest [undue unlawful unreasonable unwarranted skyrocket spend steep sum sur surcharge racket rate reasonable rent return]
*utility 03-42-162 (a.) 1. used of beef; usable but inferior 2. capable of substituting in any of several positions on a team (n.) 1. the service provided by a utility company 2. the quality of being of practical use 3. a company that performs a public service; subject to government regulation 4. (economics) a measure that is to be maximized in any situation involving choice 5. a facility composed of one or more pieces of equipment connected to or part of a structure and designed to provide a service such as heat or electricity or water or sewage disposal 6. (computer science) a program designed for general support of the processes of a computer [usable use useful user task team telco telephone temporary tentative theater theory transport truck trust imitation immediate importance include increase industry inferior infielder input interpret item light lit livestock local low] "a utility infielder"
*utmost 11-63-16 (a.) 1. highest in extent or degree 2. of the greatest possible degree or extent or intensity 3. (comparatives of 'far') most remote in space or time or order (n.) 1. the greatest possible degree [ultimate ultra uppermost uttermost tip top topmost travel tree try maximum measure meridian mild most outermost outside sky space summit supreme] "he tried his utmost"

V

*vacate 09-35-24 (v.) 1. leave behind empty; move out of 2. leave voluntarily; of a job, post or position 3. annul by recalling or rescinding [vanish void voluntary abandon abdicate abolish annul cancel cate cede chairman check clear congressional countermand tonight eject embargo emperor empty evacuate] "She vacated the position when she got pregnant"
*vaccinate 08-57-29 (v.) 1. perfomr vaccinations or produce immunity in by inoculation [alleviate animal child cure immunize injection injury inoculate nurse training eat] "We vaccinate against scarlet fever"
*vacillate 18-40-5 (v.) 1. be undecided about something; waver between conflicting positions or courses of action 2. move or sway in a rising and falling or wavelike pattern [vague value vary versatile vibrate vicissitude volatile accept adrift afloat alternate alternative ambivalence capricious careen change changeful cill concerning conflicting coquette course impulsive incalculable indecisive indeterminism insecure irresolute irresponsible libration light line location low luck lurch teeter tentative think toss totter turn twice eccentric equivocate erratic /tall/]
*vacillation 25-42-1 (n.) 1. indecision in speech or action 2. changing location by moving back and forth [alternative ambivalence change concerning course indecisive irresolute location]
*vacuous 16-75-6 (a.) 1. complacently or inanely foolish 2. devoid of significance or point [vacant vacuo vain victory void airy asinine attention awkward callow calm clear comment complacent concentration content unfamiliar unfilled unintelligent unknowing unsure oblivious otiose serious show significance silly simple slight stare stupid substance]
*vacuum 06-50-48 (n.) 1. the absence of matter 2. a region empty of matter 3. an electrical home appliance that cleans by suction (v.) 1. clean with a vacuum cleaner [vac vacancy vacuous void absence achieve appliance area cant clean completely create unreality until unwanted matter]
*vagabond 20-38-3 (a.) 1. wandering aimlessly without ties to a place or community 2. continually changing especially as from one abode or occupation to another (n.) 1. anything that resembles a vagabond in having no fixed place 2. a person who has no fixed home (v.) 1. move about aimlessly or without any destination, often in search of food or employment [vag vagrant via visible abode across aimless arab arrive gabon gad gallivant gamine gypsy beach beachcomber beggar bum occupation nature next nomad derelict destination devil direct disreputable double drift /bag/] "led a vagabond life"
*vagary 13-53-11 (n.) 1. a sudden desire [aberration agar alteration /rag raga/]
*vagrant 18-41-5 (a.) 1. continually changing especially as from one abode or occupation to another (n.) 1. a wanderer who has no established residence or visible means of support [vagabond variable veer visible volatile abode adrift aimless alternate arbitrary arrive gad gamine giddy grant guilty rambling random range residence restless roam rover roving nature never nomad nomadic notional temperamental tramp travel twist]
*vale 08-92-33 (n.) 1. a long depression in the surface of the land that usually contains a river [valley vast virginia ale allegheny american angeles area asia land last loire long earth]
*valediction 25-79-1 (n.) 1. a farewell oration delivered by the most outstanding member of a graduating class 2. the act of saying farewell [address adieu audience letter long deliver depart diction instance class oration outstand /cide/]
*valedictorian 23-03-2 (n.) 1. the student with the best grades who delivers the valedictory at graduation [academic address learn long edict deliver discipline ceremony class require /cide/]
*valedictory 18-71-5 (a.) 1. of or relating to an occasion or expression of farewell 2. of a speech expressing leave-taking (n.) 1. a farewell oration delivered by the most outstanding member of a graduating class [valedictorian viaticum address adieu aloha audience last leave leavetaking long edict education eulogy exhortation expression debate deliver depart diatribe

inaugural invective class close conge course talkathon tirade occasion office oration outstand read recitation rhetorical /cide/] "a valedictory address"
*valiant 12-60-14 (a.) 1. having or showing valor [valorous ali attempt audacious lionhearted intrepid noble tiger /nail/] "a valiant attempt to prevent the hijack"
*valid 05-47-76 (a.) 1. well grounded in logic or truth or having legal force 2. still legally acceptable [value vehement verify vigorous virtue vitality absolute acceptable agreeable ali applicable argument authorize law lawful lawmaker legal legitimate license lid logical implicit indisputable inference influence intend invincible irresistible date defensible demonstrate dependable desert determined document drive] "a valid inference"
*vanquish 14-55-10 (v.) 1. come out better in a competition, race, or conflict [van victory amaze annihilate argument army astound attack quell union idea immobilize incredulous inundate scoop score screw shaft shell six smash snow spreadeagle subdue subjugate subvert superior suppress surmount surpass hero humble]
*vapid 19-60-4 (a.) 1. lacking taste or flavor or tang 2. lacking significance or liveliness or spirit or zest [vacant vacuous vain vegetable airy arid asinine pale pedestrian plain idle indifferent innocuous insipid dead diet dry dull /dip/]
*variable 07-61-41 (a.) 1. (used of a device) designed so that a property (as e.g. light) can be varied 2. marked by diversity or difference 3. liable to or capable of change (n.) 1. a quantity that can assume any of a set of values 2. something that is likely to vary; something that is subject to variation 3. a symbol (like x or y) that is used in mathematical or logical expressions to represent a variable quantity 4. a star that varies noticeably in brightness [various vary versatile volatile able adaptable adjust alternate ambiguous arrhythmia attribute ragged rambling rate resistant restless roughness impetuous impulsive inconstant instability interval irresponsible broken bump lack lurch eccentric equivocal erratic] "the weather is one variable to be considered"
*variance 16-27-7 (n.) 1. an event that departs from expectations 2. a difference between conflicting facts or claims or opinions 3. discord that splits a group 4. the quality of being subject to variation 5. the second moment around the mean; the expected value of the square of the deviations of a random variable from its mean value 6. an activity that varies from a norm or standard [value variety adjustment alienate antagonism apostasy aria rejection repugnance rift rule inconsistency inequality inharmony irreconcilable negation changeable clash conflicting]
*variant 10-60-18 (a.) 1. differing from a norm or standard (n.) 1. an event that departs from expectations 2. (biology) a group of organisms within a species that differ in trivial ways from similar groups 3. a variable quantity that is random 4. something a little different from others of the same type [value various vary version abnormal alternative animal antagonistic aria assorted assume random relation repugnant immiscible inharmonious interbreed irregular nature negative night norm taxonomy tend trivial] "a variant spelling"
*variation 04-39-93 (n.) 1. an artifact that deviates from a norm or standard 2. something a little different from others of the same type 3. a repetition of a musical theme in which it is modified or embellished 4. an activity that varies from a norm or standard 5. an instance of change; the rate or magnitude of change 6. the angle (at a particular location) between magnetic north and true north 7. (biology) an organism that has characteristics resulting from chromosomal alteration 8. (ballet) a solo dance or dance figure 9. (astronomy) any perturbation of the mean motion or orbit of a planet or satellite (especially a perturbation of the earth's moon) 10. the act of changing or altering something slightly but noticeably from the norm or standard [vacillate variegate adaptation adjustment analysis aria arrangement astronomy resolution response revolution improvement invention irregularity transition turning twist odds opposition orchestrate nocturne nonconformity novelty] "any variation in his routine was immediately reported"
*variegate 18-58-5 (v.) 1. change the appearance of, esp. by marking with different colors 2. make something more diverse and varied [various vary vein versatile add allotropy alter antigorite appearance assorted ragged rainbow relieve rough impulsive inconstant instability iris irregularity erratic gate glowing tattoo tessellate tone tortoiseshell transform tricolor /age tag/]
*variegated 19-57-4 (a.) 1. having a variety of colors [vary alter appearance rainbow different diversify]
*vassal 25-39-1 (n.) 1. a person holding a fief [villein accept ass slave society subject subordinate lackey landholder leadership liegeman lord loyalty /ass lass/]
*vaudeville 11-29-15 (n.) 1. a variety show with songs and comic acts etc. [variety vehicle antimasque artiste underplay unrelated dance devil dialogue dramaturgy duologue early ecdysiast entertain entertainer extravaganza impersonate late legitimate /live/]
*vegetarian 08-60-28 (n.) 1. eater of fruits and grains and nuts; someone who eats no meat or fish or (often) any animal products [vegan vegetative veggie eat eater egg epicure eschew exclude gastronomic gluttony gobble gourmet grain grazing taste teetotal trencherman tuberous abstinence animal appetite aria ascetic avoidance radicular refrain regimen relish rhizoid include ingest insectivore nibble nourishing nut nutritious /irate rate teg/]
*vegetation 12-48-13 (n.) 1. all the plant life in a particular region 2. an abnormal growth or excrescence

(especially a warty excrescence on the valves of the heart) 3. inactivity that is passive and monotonous, comparable to the inactivity of plant life 4. the process of growth in plants [valve verdure enlargement entropy excrescence garden general germinate geta gradual grass green group growth tangle thicket torpor tree turf abeyance abnormal accumulation animal apathy area assemblage idle implement inactivity indifference ontogeny organism outgrowth overgrow /teg/] "their holiday was spent in sleep and vegetation"
*vegetative 20-48-3 (a.) 1. of or relating to an activity that is passive and monotonous 2. composed of vegetation or plants 3. (of reproduction) characterized by asexual processes 4. (physiology) used of involuntary bodily functions [voluntary geta growth absence animal asexual autonomic inactive injury /teg vita/] "a dull vegetative lifestyle"
*vehement 09-43-24 (a.) 1. marked by extreme intensity of emotions or convictions; inclined to react violently; fervid 2. characterized by great force or energy [valid vicious vigorous violent virtue volcanic edge emotion energy enthusiasm exciting expect express extreme happy harsh hearty heated hem hot mark merciless mighty mild mordant murderous tart tear terrible tireless]
*velocity 13-41-11 (n.) 1. distance travelled per unit time [vacuum vessel escape exactly excessive expedition leaf light limp line local lockstep lurch celerity city constant impetus totter toward travel tread trot /cole/]
*velvety 14-43-9 (a.) 1. smooth and soft to sight or hearing or touch or taste 2. resembling velvet in having a smooth soft surface [varnish velutinous velvet lack lacquer taste touch]
*venal 18-57-5 (a.) 1. capable of being corrupted [value vena vice vicious voracious esurient exploitation nefarious acquisitive amoral approachable avid lack lawless limitless /lane/]
*vendor 06-34-46 (n.) 1. someone who promotes or exchanges goods or services for money [endo engage exchange dealer duffer retail /rod/]
*veneer 11-55-15 (n.) 1. coating consisting of a thin layer of superior wood glued to a base of inferior wood 2. an ornamental coating to a building (v.) 1. cover with veneer, as of furniture [varnish enamel epidermis exterior neer rasher revetment rind]
*venerable 08-42-29 (a.) 1. profoundly honored 2. impressive by reason of age [venerate elderly establish esteem extremely noble numinous reason receive religion remarkable respect royal able achievement acknowledge admire admit age ancient archdeacon attain august baby beard butler legendary live long lordly /bar bare/] "a venerable sage with white hair and beard"
*venerate 18-48-5 (v.) 1. regard with feelings of respect and reverence; consider hallowed or exalted or be in awe of [value enshrine esteem exalted rate regard respect reverence admire adore appreciate awe think /tare/]
*veneration 23-50-2 (n.) 1. a profound fear inspired by a deity 2. religious zeal; willingness to serve God [emotion esteem estimation expression ration regard religious respect reverence reverential admiration admiring adore approval awe awed theism title top idolatry idolize implore inspired observance /tare/]
*venereal 20-28-3 (a.) 1. of or relating to the external sex organs [voluptuous erogenous erotogenic external nuptial real affect amorous arouse libido literary]
*venison 14-59-9 (n.) 1. meat from a deer used as food [iso scrapple sheep /sine/]
*venom 11-71-15 (n.) 1. toxin secreted by animals (by certain snakes and poisonous insects (e.g., spiders and scorpions)) 2. feeling a need to see others suffer [vehement vicious violent virulence virus vituperation embitter evil excessive extremity neurotoxin noisome nom noxious ominous outrageous malevolent malignity mean merciless mischievous murderous /one/]
*veracity 16-57-6 (n.) 1. unwillingness to tell lies [valid verity effectual establish ethical exact express reality reliable account accuracy accurate actuality almost ascertain attest authenticity candor certify city claim conform corroborate credibility integrity tell tendency true truism truthful /care/]
*verbatim 14-67-9 (a.) 1. in precisely the same words used by a writer or speaker (ad.) 1. using exactly the same words [verb verbal verisimilar even exactly expressly realistic remark repeat rigid rigorous absolutely accordance accurate authentic identical inexact mark /tab/] "he repeated her remarks verbatim"
*verbiage 23-43-2 (n.) 1. overabundance of words 2. the manner in which something is expressed in words [verb verbosity vocabulary excessive expansive expressive redundancy repetition rhetoric idiom add appropriate gat gobbledygook grammar] "use concise military verbiage"
*verbose 20-64-3 (a.) 1. using or containing too many words [verb voluble editorial effusive embellish endless excessive expletive express expressive extended extravagance rambling redundant bedizen bigmouth bombastic boring open ornamentation overlap slush smooth sociable spare speaker style succinct /sob/]
*verdant 15-54-8 (a.) 1. green with growing things [vegetation verd verdurous vert virescent emerald experience abundant aestival naive tuft turfy]
*verification 14-29-10 (n.) 1. additional proof that something that was believed (some fact or hypothesis or theory) is correct 2. (law) an affidavit attached to a statement confirming the truth of that statement [validate ensure essay establishment ratify reinforcement fortification cation certificate check corroborate criterion ascertain assurance attest touchstone trial try ordeal /fir fire/]
*verify 07-33-37 (v.) 1. verify or regulate by conducting

a parallel experiment or comparing with another standard, of scientific experiments 2. confirm the truth of 3. to declare or affirm solemnly and formally as true 4. Law: attach or append a legal verification to (a pleading or petition) [validate veracity veritable effectual emphatic ensure essay establish evidence evince examine experiment ratify real reassert regulate reinforce research rule idea impose incontrovertible indisputable inform innocent insure investigate irrefutable fact factual firm fixed formal fortify /fir fire/] "Please verify that the doors are closed"
*verisimilitude 20-35-3 (n.) 1. the appearance of truth; the quality of seeming to be true [evidence real reliable seeming semblance similitude statement support misleading likelihood token true deliberate /sire/]
*veritable 13-51-11 (a.) 1. not counterfeit or copied 2. often used as intensifiers [verify very virtual egregious establish exhaustive exhibit radical real regular ring identify indubitable intensifier intensive table thoroughgoing total trueful absolute actual antique attest atypical authentic bear bona bull business legitimate /tire/]
*verity 18-53-5 (n.) 1. conformity to reality or actuality 2. an enduring or necessary ethical or religious or aesthetic truth [veracity veridical enduring eternal ethical exist reality religious rit threat true truism truth truthful turn /tire/]
*vermin 19-62-4 (n.) 1. an irritating or obnoxious person 2. any of various small animals or insects that are pests; e.g. cockroaches or rats [various varmint vertebrate viper voluntary extremely rat reptile rodent rubbish mammalian marsupial min mongrel mosquito move insect insectivore invertebrate irritate]
*vernacular 12-48-13 (a.) 1. being or characteristic of or appropriate to everyday language (n.) 1. a characteristic language of a particular group (as among thieves) 2. the everyday speech of the people (as distinguished from literary language) [vocabulary vulgate easy endemic everyday regional regulation rubbish natal natural niff normative accustomed applesauce argot austerity average campy capacity colloquial confined cul current uneducated universal usual language lean limited lingua /can/]
*vernal 25-29-1 (a.) 1. suggestive of youth; vigorous and fresh 2. of or characteristic of or occurring in spring [verdurous vert vigorous virginal early emerald energy equinox ern evergreen raw ripen naive nestle new aestival appear arctic autumnal leafy leave life literary living love] "the vernal equinox"
*versatile 06-51-45 (a.) 1. (used of persons) having many skills 2. (biology) able to move freely in all directions 3. changeable or inconstant 4. competent in many areas and able to turn with ease from one thing to another 5. having great diversity or variety [vacillate various vast versa volatile ease easy elastic erudition extend ragged rapid ready resourceful science show skill skillful skittish special study supple able achievement adaptable adjust allow ambidexterity antenna anther available talented task toe turn immobile impressive inconstant inequality insect instability irregularity lateral liable light living loose]
*version 02-49-497 (n.) 1. a written work (as a novel) that has been recast in a new form 2. something a little different from others of the same type 3. an interpretation of a matter from a particular viewpoint 4. a mental representation of the meaning or significance of something 5. a written communication in a second language having the same meaning as the written communication in a first language 6. manual turning of a fetus in the uterus (usually to aid delivery) [variety view edition engrossment essay report reproduction restate school side style subtitle idea imitation interpretation ion order organization original narrative nonfiction notation] "his version of the fight was different from mine"
*vertex 25-54-1 (n.) 1. the point of intersection of lines or the point opposite the base of a figure 2. the highest point (of something) [veer vert edge elbow ext extremity ridge roof tip top toward]
*vertical 07-42-42 (a.) 1. at right angles to the plane of the horizon or a base line 2. upright in position or posture (n.) 1. something that is oriented vertically 2. a vertical structural member as a post or stake [economics erectile even rampant rapid rear right ruin tail tall tical timber top topmost incline indicate camera capital chief column compass constituent consummate crossbar crown cylindrical abrupt aggression alignment amid anatomy angle apical lengthwise level line linear] "a vertical camera angle"
*vertigo 16-67-7 (n.) 1. a reeling sensation; feeling about to fall [vert vomit edema emaciate episode experience rash reel rheum tabes tachycardia tilt tumor inflammation instance itch giddy growth /git/]
*verve 11-57-16 (n.) 1. an energetic style [vehement vigour vim vitality vivid eager energy enterprise enthusiasm expression ready relish resilience]
*vestige 13-39-11 (n.) 1. a clue that something has been present [vest emboss end evidence serve shadow sign slight step suggestion table thought tincture touch trace truth important imprint indication intimate inventory glimmer /git/]
*vestment 23-46-2 (n.) 1. gown (especially ceremonial garments) worn by the clergy [veil vest vesture ecclesiastical edging embroider encircle screen shawl shelter shoulder show silk sleeve style surplice thread tog trim mantle mask mass member]
*veto 05-28-81 (n.) 1. a vote that blocks a decision 2. the power or right to prohibit or reject a proposed or intended act esp the power of a chief executive to reject a bill passed by the legislature (v.) 1. command against 2. vote against; refuse to endorse; refuse to assent [verboten vet vote embargo endorse enter exclude

executive exercise table taboo teacher thwart turndown oppose ordain order outlaw]
*vex 15-32-8 (v.) 1. cause annoyance in; disturb, esp. by minor irritations 2. change the arrangement or position of 3. be a mystery or bewildering to 4. subject to prolonged examination, discussion, or deliberation 5. disturb the peace of mind of; afflict with mental agitation or distress [vigorous ear eat elude embarrass escape examination exasperate exercise extreme]
*vicarious 16-48-6 (a.) 1. experienced at secondhand 2. (medicine) occurring in an abnormal part of the body instead of the usual site involved in that function 3. suffered or done by one person as a substitute for another [value imagine imitation immediate importance indirect instead carious climb commission conform counterfeit abnormal adopt alternative assign assume atonement authority regular relay removed reserve unexpected usual utility science secondary secondhand site spare specialty substitute suffer suitable surrogate sweat sympathy] "read about mountain climbing and felt vicarious excitement"
*viceroy 20-63-3 (n.) 1. governor of a country or province who rules as the representative of his or her king or sovereign 2. showy American butterfly resembling the monarch but smaller [vicegerent cabbage carry cero clouded collector colored comma country egypt emperor empire eparch exarch red representative roman rule orange owl yellow /yore/]
*vicissitude 18-50-5 (n.) 1. a variation in circumstances or fortune at different times in your life or in the development of something 2. mutability in life or nature (especially successive alternation from one condition to another) [vacillate variation variety version inconstant innovation instance irritation capable care change circumstance combination condition cross shift shuffling situ sport successive teeter transformation trial trouble unexpected usual development different difficulty diversity downer exploratory] "the project was subject to the usual vicissitudes of exploratory research"
*vie 07-51-40 (v.) 1. compete for something; engage in a contest; measure oneself against others [victory emulate engage equality]
*vigilance 13-49-11 (n.) 1. the process of paying close and continuous attention 2. vigilant attentiveness [vigil invigilate guardian lance lookout alert attentive aware care caution circumspect close concentration condition continuous custody eye]
*vigilant 11-54-16 (a.) 1. carefully observant or attentive; on the lookout for possible danger [vigil immunize informed groom guard lid lookout acute alert attentive avid aware toddler tow town tutelary]
*vignette 11-34-16 (n.) 1. a brief literary description 2. a photograph whose edges shade off gradually 3. a small illustrative sketch (as sometimes placed at the beginning of chapters in books) [illustrative imagery imprint itemize give gradual negative nett edge elaborate elegant engrave essay etching evocation exposure extract tendril trace transparent]
*vigorous 04-41-97 (a.) 1. strong and active physically or mentally 2. characterized by forceful and energetic action or activity [valid vigor vital vivacious vivid impressive intense irresistible glowing great gristly gutsy obstinate old operative opposition resolute robust rude rugged ruling unfalteringly unrestrained untiring shake skirt spent spirited stiff strenuous strong stubborn] "a vigorous hiker"
*vilify 12-62-13 (v.) 1. spread negative information about [vituperate vituperation inveigh language libel libelous foul]
*vindicate 09-62-24 (v.) 1. show to be right by providing justification or prove 2. clear of accusation, blame, suspicion, or doubt with supporting proof 3. maintain uphold, or defend [inculpate indicate inflict nature nonpros defend defender demand desert discharge dismiss doubt champion charge citizen claim clear clearing contend correct criminal absolve accord accusation acquit advocate affirm apologize argue assert assoil avenge exculpate excuse exonerate explain /acid/] "vindicate a claim"
*vindictive 14-59-9 (a.) 1. showing malicious ill will and a desire to hurt; motivated by spite 2. disposed to seek revenge or intended for revenge [vengeful victim ill implacable indict intend nasty nature necessary damage defendant describe desire despiteful disposed child compensate court cruel teach true educate] "more vindictive than jealous love"
*viol 25-50-1 (n.) 1. any of a family of bowed stringed instruments that preceded the violin family [vibraphone violin instrument oboe ocarina organ lute lyre]
*viola 10-35-18 (n.) 1. any of the numerous plants of the genus Viola 2. a bowed stringed instrument slightly larger than a violin, tuned a fifth lower 3. large genus of flowering herbs of temperate regions [various velvety vibraphone vibrato viol include instrument oboe ocarina octave old organ lack large last less long love low lute lyre accordion advance alto]
*violation 03-12-140 (n.) 1. a disrespectful act 2. entry to another's property without right or permission 3. an act that disregards an agreement or a right 4. a crime less serious than a felony 5. the crime of forcing a woman to submit to sexual intercourse against her will [viola violence ignore immoral incorrect infringe injury interruption intrusion oath offense onslaught outrage lawbreaker lawless loot abuse assault attack taking tort trespass naughty noncooperation] "he claimed a violation of his rights under the Fifth Amendment"
*violator 25-11-1 (n.) 1. someone who violates the law 2. someone who assaults others sexually [offend outlaw law lawbreaker legal libertine assault ravish rounder]
*virago 19-92-4 (n.) 1. a noisy or scolding or domineering woman 2. a large strong and aggressive woman [violent vixen imply incendiary insult rapist

revolutionary romp adult aggressive ago amazon androgyne goon gorilla grimalkin offensive ogress oppose /gari/]
*virile 19-59-4 (a.) 1. characteristic of a man 2. characterized by energy and vigor 3. (of a male) able to copulate [vigor voice impotent rile robust leadership energy expect] "a virile and ever stronger free society"
*virtual 05-50-65 (a.) 1. being actually such in almost every respect 2. being such in essence or effect though not in actual fact [veiled implicit impression inessential really reason respect revolution ruin technique temple unrealistic accept actually almost area aware latent lie lurk /tri/]
*virtuoso 08-38-33 (a.) 1. having or revealing supreme mastery or skill (n.) 1. someone who is dazzlingly skilled in any field 2. a musician who is a consummate master of technique and artistry [virtuoso ingenious interpreter ready remarkable require reveal ruler runner tactful talented technique senior sensation show skill skillful some sonata speaker special star supreme /out sou tri/]
*virulence 25-52-1 (n.) 1. extreme harmfulness (as the capacity of a microorganism to cause disease) 2. extreme hostility [valid venom verge violence virtue ill infectious influence inhumanity injury intensity rankle resentment rim roughness rule unfriendly unhealthy upper lethality limit lip edge energy extent extremely extremity noxious capacity cause charisma circumference clout compulsion control] "the virulence of the plague"
*virulent 13-54-11 (a.) 1. extremely poisonous or injurious; producing venom 2. harsh or corrosive in tone 3. infectious; having the ability to cause disease [vehement venomous vicious violent vitriolic vituperation incisive infective injurious insect internecine irritate remark resent rigorous rough unable unconscionable unfriendly unhealthy unpleasant lent lethal edge enemy ethics excessive extremely nasty noisome noxious talk tart tone tough toxin trenchant]
*visage 19-47-4 (n.) 1. the appearance conveyed by a person's face 2. the human face ('kisser' and 'smiler' and 'mug' are informal terms for 'face'; 'phiz' is British) [visible visual imitate interpret ireland isle sage scotland seek smile speak stance stern air appearance aspect garb good great guise ear england europe expression /gas/]
*visceral 10-50-19 (a.) 1. relating to or affecting the viscera 2. obtained through intuition rather than from reasoning or observation [viscera inn instinct internal intimate intuitive show soulful splanchnic spontaneous cardiac characterize colonic coronary correct emotion emotive enteric entrail reasoning rectal relation abdominal affecting affective anal anatomy animal lack logical] "visceral bleeding"
*viscount 13-91-11 (n.) 1. (in various countries) a son or younger brother or a count 2. a British peer who ranks below an earl and above a baron [various seignior son squire swell count country crown nobleman thoroughbred title]
*viscous 23-43-2 (a.) 1. having a relatively high resistance to flow 2. having the properties of glue [vis viscose impermeable inspissate solid sticky stiff stir substantial syrupy close concrete consistency crowded]
*vista 08-44-34 (n.) 1. the visual percept of a region [viewer vis visual image incomplete scan scenic seascape see side succession survey sweep tableau townscape tree area arise aspect]
*visual 03-48-137 (a.) 1. relating to or using sight 2. able to be seen [view viewable vis vision visional idea illustrative insight inspection instrument intend invisible scientific see sensory shakespeare showing sight sure undisguised abstract aid apparent appeal landing]
*visualize 16-02-6 (v.) 1. imagine; conceive of; see in one's mind 2. for a mental picture of something that is invisible or abstract 3. make visible 4. Medicine: view the outline of by means of an X-ray [view visible vision visual vivid ideate imagine internal science see situation specialty strategy ultrasound understand abstract alter anticipate apprehend liver envision]
*vitality 09-35-25 (n.) 1. a healthy capacity for vigorous activity 2. an energetic style 3. the property of being able to survive and grow 4. (biology) a hypothetical force (not physical or chemical) once thought by Henri Bergson to cause the evolution and development of organisms [valid verve vigour vim virtue vital vivacity imaginative immortal impatient influence inherent tenacity toughness traditional trenchant abundant accord animation anxious appetite approach authority life lifetime light live lively living]
*vitiate 25-31-1 (v.) 1. corrupt morally or by intemperance or sensuality 2. take away the legal force of or render ineffective 3. make imperfect [value violate void vulgarize idea ideology immoral impair imperfect incite infect inflict injure intercourse invalidate taint tarnish teach thwart transform twist abate abolish accuse alloy alter appearance art astray eat effective evil]
*vitriolic 18-64-5 (a.) 1. harsh or corrosive in tone 2. of a substance, especially a strong acid; capable of destroying or eating away by chemical action [vehement venomous vicious violent virulent vitriol incisive irritate talk tart tone toward trenchant rancorous remark resemble rigorous rough capable caustic chemistry clash comment conflicting constructive corrosive criticism cruel cutting]
*vivacious 16-58-6 (a.) 1. vigorous and active [vibrant vigorous vital viva vivid impatient incisive intense aggressive alert alive animation cant challenge charming cheerful chipper chirpy spiritless strong sunny]
*vivacity 23-50-2 (n.) 1. characterized by high spirits and animation [verve viable vitality vivid immortal impatient impetus activity animation anxious appetite cheerful chirp city coltish]
*vivisection 23-85-2 (n.) 1. the act of operating on

living animals (especially in scientific research) [vivisect incision instrument scientific surgical operation]
*vociferous 12-61-13 (a.) 1. conspicuously and offensively loud; given to vehement outcry [vehement vocal vociferate voluble obstreperous offensive outcry clamorous clangor conspicuous crying full enthusiastic rackety radio raucous rowdy uproar uproarious scream shout sound strident /fico/]
*vogue 07-55-36 (n.) 1. the popular taste at a given time 2. a current state of general acceptance and use [value voguish general give glory grow eclat] "leather is the latest vogue"
*volatile 05-51-88 (a.) 1. (chemistry) evaporating readily at normal temperatures and pressures 2. liable to lead to sudden change or violence 3. marked by erratic changeableness in affections or attachments 4. tending to vary often or widely (n.) 1. a volatile substance; a substance that changes readily from solid or liquid to a vapor [vapor variable vary versatile vicissitude violent occupy oil lack lead levity liable lightness likely liquid lose low lubricious adrift affection alteration alternate animation apparent apt ascent attach temperature temporary tend tender tense thin tile transitory turn impermanent impulsive inconstant indecisive instability irresponsible eccentric emotion erratic eruptive explosive] "volatile oils"
*volition 23-64-2 (n.) 1. the capability of conscious choice and decision and intention 2. the act of making a choice [velleity objective option like lust inclination inherent intention ion] "the exercise of their volition we construe as revolt"
*voluble 18-51-5 (a.) 1. marked by a ready flow of speech [verbosity vocative vociferous vol open lengthy loquacious loquacity uncommunicative babbling bigmouth blather blither bombastic easy effusive engage expansive extremely exuberant] "she is an extremely voluble young woman who engages in soliloquies not conversations"
*voluptuous 14-49-10 (a.) 1. having strong sexual appeal 2. (of a woman's body) having a large bosom and pleasing curves 3. furnishing gratification of the senses [venereal vol voluptuary oriental oversexed lavish life lovely luscious lush luxurious undersexed unsex pleasure potent prepossessing procreate provide taking tempting tend thick thrilling tight seem sensual sex sexy shapely show sonsy spent straight strong suite sybaritic /out pul/]
*voracious 12-54-12 (a.) 1. excessively greedy and grasping 2. devouring or craving food in great quantities [venal vulture omnivorous rapacious ravenous reader abstemious acquisitive appetite ardent avid consumption cormorant covet cram craving creditor idea insatiable insatiate intemperate unusual shark sordid starve stuffing]
*vortex 18-59-5 (n.) 1. the shape of something rotating rapidly 2. a powerful circular current of water (usually the resulting of conflicting tides) [volute overwhelming rapid reel roll rotate round tidal tide tornado toward turbulence turmoil turn twist twister eddy effervesce engulf exhaust]
*votive 23-28-2 (a.) 1. dedicated in fulfillment of a vow [vow oath offering] "votive prayers"
*vulgarity 15-50-8 (n.) 1. the quality of lacking taste and refinement [vile vulgar vulgarism uncouth unseemly unsophisticated unwieldy lack leaden lewd little loutish gaucherie good graceless gross rank raunch rawness refinement remark roughness rude impropriety inadequate incorrect indecent insensitive tasteless tawdry turgidity /rag/]
*vulnerable 03-55-201 (a.) 1. susceptible to attack 2. susceptible to physical or emotional injury 3. capable of being wounded or hurt 4. susceptible to criticism or persuasion or temptation [unable unprotected unready unsafe untenable lack liability liable life little living early easy emotional endanger expose exposure extremely ready refute resist risk rubber able adequate age argument assail attack body breakable bribery bridge brittle /bar bare/] "a vulnerable bridge"

W

*waft 11-60-16 (n.) 1. a long flag; often tapering (v.) 1. be driven or carried along, as by the air 2. blow gently [water wave whiffle whisk wing adrift aft airfreight airlift flag flatus float flutter fly freshen take taper tote] "Sounds wafted into the room"
*wag 10-70-19 (n.) 1. (informal) a witty amusing person who makes jokes 2. causing to move repeatedly from side to side (v.) 1. move from side to side, as of fingers and tails [wave waver way wield wiggle wisecrack wit witty write agitate amusing antic arch gag gagman gagster /gaw/] "The happy dog wagged his tail"
*waif 18-62-5 (n.) 1. a homeless child especially one forsaken or orphaned [wastrel abandon animal appearance idler item forsaken foundling fragile friendless fry]
*waistcoat 16-86-6 (n.) 1. a man's sleeveless garment worn underneath a coat [waist woman worn article impact shirt sleeveless suit tradition trouser tunic capable century clothe coat collar]
*waive 07-27-39 (v.) 1. do without or cease to hold or adhere to 2. lose or lose the right to by some error, offense, or crime [withdraw abandon abjure abolish adhere adjourn apply available idea ignore invalidate vacate void voluntary enforce error except exclude extend extra /via/]
*wane 07-48-42 (n.) 1. a gradual decline (in size or strength or power or number) (v.) 1. become smaller 2. grow smaller 3. decrease in phase [wan wasting weaken wilt woodwork worsen wrinkle abate advance age area novel ebb edge erode extent] "Interest in the project waned"
*wanton 16-53-7 (a.) 1. occurring without motivation or provocation 2. casual and unrestrained in sexual behavior (n.) 1. lewd or lascivious woman (v.) 1. waste time; spend one's time idly or inefficiently 2. become extravagant; indulge (oneself) luxuriously 3. behave extremely cruelly and brutally 4. engage in amorous play 5. indulge in a carefree or voluptuous way of life 6. spend wastefully [wander ware wasteful way weak wild willful woman worry abandon accord alternate amorous anton arbitrary attack avoid away nasty neck needless notional nymphomaniac talk tart tell toy trait tramp trifle] "wanton one's money away"
*warlike 20-55-3 (a.) 1. inclined to make war 2. suggesting war or military life [war warfare warmonger warrior aggressive antagonistic armed life like incline inimical enemy]
*warmonger 20-71-3 (n.) 1. a person who advocates war or warlike policies [war warpath advocate aggressor antagonism relation martial maturity militarist monger onward grownup eager]
*warrant 04-39-89 (n.) 1. a writ from a court commanding police to perform specified acts 2. a written assurance that some product or service will be provided or will meet certain specifications 3. formal and explicit approval 4. a type of security issued by a corporation (usually together with a bond or preferred stock) that gives the holder the right to purchase a certain amount of common stock at a stated price (v.) 1. show to be reasonable 2. stand behind [witness word worthy write accept accuracy adequate admit agreement allow amount announce aplomb appointment approve argue arrant arrest assertion assurance authorize ratify reason reasonable receive recognize refrain release right risk roman rule need nod nothing notify test think ticket tie title transfer truth try] "as a sweetener they offered warrants along with the fixed-income securities"
*wean 13-57-11 (v.) 1. gradually deprive (infants) of mother's milk 2. detach the affections of [water women early estrange evangelize ablactate accustom affection age alienate animal arouse no] "she weaned her baby when he was 3 months old and started him on powdered milk"
*wearisome 23-72-2 (a.) 1. so lacking in interest as to cause mental weariness [weary worry writing edmund effect effort exasperate excitement exhaust aggravate annoying arduous arouse attention routine interest irk irksome irritate solemn some speaker strain stressful onerous operose oppressive mark mental]
*wee 08-74-27 (a.) 1. (used informally) very small 2. very early (n.) 1. (Scottish) a short time (v.) 1. eliminate urine [water wet write early eliminate excrete expensive expression extent] "a wee tot"
*wend 18-33-5 (v.) 1. direct one's course or way [way

well world end enter expect extend necessary night noise northeastern direct /new/]
*whereabouts 10-51-21 (ad.) 1. about where or near what place (n.) 1. the general location where something is [whereabouts whither hereabout hide hole hotel emplacement extent region abode approximate area bear benchmark border brother site situation space spot stead] "I don't know whereabouts the border will be drawn"
*whereupon 16-68-7 (ad.) 1. closely following and in consequence of which 2. in consequence of which 3. upon which [whenever where wherewith hereupon export refuse rock phone point] "the Japanese refused to import U.S. made cellular phones whereupon the U.S. imposed strict tariffs on Japanese exports"
*wherever 05-59-74 (ad.) 1. in or at or to what place [where emphatic exercise /ever revere/]
*whet 14-60-9 (v.) 1. make keen or more acute 2. sharpen by rubbing, as on a whetstone [waken want weapon workup heighten het hone easy edge enhance enthusiasm excite taper tickle tool triple] "whet my appetite"
*whimsical 10-37-21 (a.) 1. determined by chance or impulse or whim rather than by necessity or reason [wander way wayward wild witty harebrained hesitate hilarious humorous ical idiosyncrasy imaginative impossible impulsive irresponsible mercurial moody mordant sharp slight smart smile strange capricious chance clever cranky creative absurd alternate amusing arbitrary laughable ludicrous /ism/]
*whine 09-48-23 (n.) 1. a complaint uttered in a plaintive whining way (v.) 1. talk in a tearful manner 2. move with a whining sound 3. complain whiningly [wail wake warble way whimper whiny whistle wind high hine hiss holler howling irritate neigh nicker engine exclaim expression]
*wholly 05-70-70 (ad.) 1. to a complete degree or to the full or entire extent [way write wrong holly only outright largely] "he was wholly convinced"
*wield 06-54-54 (v.) 1. handle effectively 2. of power or authority [wag wave weapon work immense economic effective eld employ exert dispense down] "The burglar wielded an axe"
*wile 16-58-6 (n.) 1. the use of tricks to deceive someone (usually to extract money from them) [wary wit ingenious insincere intend intrigue inventive last employ enchant entice expend extract]
*wily 12-65-14 (a.) 1. marked by skill in deception [wary wile wise indirect ingenuous intelligence inventive]
*wince 10-63-19 (n.) 1. the facial expression of sudden pain 2. a reflex response to sudden pain (v.) 1. make a face indicating disgust or dislike 2. draw back, as with fear or pain [waver withdraw writhe ince indicate involuntary non calf certain contort cower cringe embarrassment emotional evade evasion execute expression]
*winsome 16-54-7 (a.) 1. charming in a childlike or naive way [way win winning witching innocent interesting intrigue inviting naive smile some sunny sweet optimistic mesmeric mind endearing engage entrance exciting exotic eye]
*wintry 14-63-9 (a.) 1. characteristic of or occurring in winter 2. devoid of warmth and cordiality; expressive of unfriendliness or disdain [warmth weather wintery icy inclement nippy numbing try raw reception rigorous] "suffered severe wintry weather"
*wiry 15-52-8 (a.) 1. lean and sinewy [wire resistant ropy rough]
*wistful 08-48-29 (a.) 1. full of longing or unfulfilled desire 2. showing pensive sadness [wishful wist introspective sad sensitive serious show sober sorrow sorry thinking thoughtful tristful full funky unfulfilled unhappy languish little longing lose lovelorn] "those wistful little ads that the lovelorn place in the classifieds"
*witchcraft 16-63-7 (n.) 1. the art of sorcery [wizardry world incantation influence thaumaturgy theurgy charm conjure craft harness hoodoo rune alchemy alleged alluring appeal art fascination fetishism force /arch far/]
*witless 18-77-5 (a.) 1. (of especially persons) lacking sense or understanding or judgment [wacky wander wet inept insane intelligence irrational tetched thoughtless touched lack less loco loony lunatic sick silly smart soft strange stupid]
*witticism 23-62-2 (n.) 1. a message whose ingenuity or verbal skill or incongruity has the power to evoke laughter [waggery wisecrack wit witt writing imitation impersonate incongruity ingenuity insult intend irony teach text caricature catchword clever comic compliment conceit content convey crack critic sally sarcasm satirical saying scorn see serious sharp skill sport surpass swift matter maxim message moral mot motto]
*wittingly 25-54-1 (ad.) 1. with full knowledge and deliberation [intentional] "he wittingly deleted the references"
*woo 06-54-47 (v.) 1. make amorous advances towards 2. seek someone's favor [winsome witchery woman work] "China is wooing Russia"
*workmanlike 16-66-6 (a.) 1. worthy of a good workman [way wicked workman worthy okay original ready resourceful respectable magisterial masterly moderate acceptable adequate artistic neat imaginative incompetent index ingenious efficient excellent excite expert /kiln/]
*workmanship 18-47-5 (n.) 1. skill in an occupation or trade [wit wizardry wood workman writing occupation raise ready refine machine making management manufacture ability accomplishment acquisition address architecture art artistry attainment savvy shape skill stage style handiwork harvest horseman ingenuity play

preparation priest process product]
*wrangle 09-60-25 (n.) 1. an angry dispute 2. an instance of intense argument (as in bargaining) (v.) 1. to quarrel noisily, angrily or disruptively 2. herd and care for [war warfare whip word rhubarb roundup row runin aggressive agreement altercation angle angry animal apology argument negotiation noisy goad lash lengthy litigious logomachy long] "The bar keeper threw them out, but they continued to wrangle on down the street."
*wreak 10-62-19 (v.) 1. cause to happen or to occur as a consequence [work wreck rain realize relief render revenge effect effectuate emotion expect express accomplish achieve anger area]
*wrest 11-50-16 (v.) 1. obtain by seizing forcibly or violently, also metaphorically [withdraw wrench wry remove resistance rest rip ripping effort elicit eradicate evolve extract screw seize sharp snatch spring squeeze struggle takeout torsion tug twist] "wrest the knife from his hands"
*wretchedness 25-71-1 (n.) 1. a state of ill-being due to affliction or misfortune [woe extremely camp condition constant crowd happy harsh health death dejection desolate due situation slum suffering] "the misery and wretchedness of those slums is intolerable"
*writhe 14-61-10 (v.) 1. to move in a twisting or contorted motion, (esp. when struggling) [wag warp way worm wrench wrestle wriggle writ recoil rolling internal thrash tremble try tumble twist heave hurt embarrassment embrace emotion experience] "The prisoner writhed in discomfort."
*writing 02-51-428 (n.) 1. the activity of putting something in written form 2. letters or symbols written or imprinted on a surface to represent the sounds or words of a language 3. (usually plural) the collected work of an author 4. the work of a writer; anything expressed in letters of the alphabet (especially when considered from the point of view of style and effect) 5. the act of creating written works [work realize representation revision roll ruth illustration image inscription instrument tan ting title tome transcription nehemiah nonfiction notebook novel] "writing was a form of therapy for him"
*wry 07-59-42 (a.) 1. humorously sarcastic or mocking 2. disdainfully or ironically humorous; scornful and mocking 3. bent to one side [wit wound wrest wring rebellion remark ridicule]

X

*xenophobia 13-65-11 (n.) 1. an irrational fear of foreigners or strangers [eat ethnocentrism exclusive execration narrow nationalism nationalist odium outcast outsider parochialism partisan people phobia prejudice public hate hatred bigotry insulation intense irrational isolation alien apartheid aversion /one pone/]

Y

*yarn 10-61-18 (n.) 1. the act of giving an account describing incidents or a course of events 2. a fine cord of twisted fibers (of cotton or silk or wool or nylon etc.) used in sewing and weaving (v.) 1. tell or spin a yarn [account across anecdote arrange attached rap rayon recite recount relation report riot rope rug narrative nylon /ray/]

*yearling 16-57-6 (n.) 1. a young child 2. a racehorse considered one year old until the second Jan. 1 following its birth 3. an animal in its second year [yak youngster earl eutherian except age animal aurochs race racehorse lamb last leveret infant neat neonate nestle nipper nursling gosling] orbit orion diagram division drawing imaginary influence intend analyze anklet apogee apparent appear aquarius area aries aspect astrologicall cancer capricorn celestial chart cincture cingulum circle circular claim constellation cyclical /caid doz/]

Z

*zeal 09-49-22 (n.) 1. excessive fervor to do something or accomplish some end 2. a feeling of strong eagerness (usually in favor of a person or cause) [zest eager elan energetic energy enthusiasm excessive abandon absolute accomplish agreeable ahead angst ardour avid litigation lively loyalty]

*zealot 14-48-10 (n.) 1. a fervent and even militant proponent of something [zeal zealous eccentric enthusiast evangelist excessive exponent extremist addict aficionado alien ancient arbitrary arrogant obsessive oddity opinion original outsider own terrorism tie tramp trust type /tola/]

*zeitgeist 16-70-7 (n.) 1. the spirit of the time; the spirit characteristic of an age or generation [effect express idea tone geist generation situation smell spirit /tie/]

*zenith 14-44-10 (n.) 1. the point above the observer that is directly opposite the nadir on the imaginary sphere against which celestial bodies appear to be projected [edge effective elevation empyrean nit noon imaginary imperium influence tip top heaven hegemony height high horizon /tine/]

*zephyr 23-50-2 (n.) 1. a slight wind (usually refreshing) 2. (Greek mythology) the Greek god of the west wind [eiderdown pillow pressure pudding puff high hurricane refreshing rubber]

*zodiac 19-61-4 (n.) 1. a belt-shaped region in the heavens on either side to the ecliptic; divided into 12 constellations or signs for astrological purposes 2. (astrology) a circular diagram representing the 12 zodiacal constellations and showing their signs [zone

www.ingramcontent.com/pod-product-compliance
Lightning Source LLC
Chambersburg PA
CBHW080331170426
43194CB00014B/2528
9780955575150